Subject and Topic

Subject
and
Topic

Edited by
Charles N. Li
Linguistics Program
University of California, Santa Barbara
Santa Barbara, California

ACADEMIC PRESS, Inc. · New York · San Francisco · London
A Subsidiary of Harcourt Brace Jovanovich, Publishers

ACADEMIC PRESS, INC.
111 Fifth Avenue, New York, New York 10003

United Kingdom Edition published by
ACADEMIC PRESS, INC. (LONDON) LTD.
24/28 Oval Road, London NW1

Library of Congress Cataloging in Publication Data

Symposium on Subject and Topic, University of
      California, Santa Barbara, 1975.
      Subject and topic.

      Held in March, 1975.
      Bibliography: p.
      Includes index.
      1.   Grammar, Comparative and general–Topic and
comment–Congresses.   2.   Discourse analysis-
Congresses.   I.   Li, Charles N.   II.   Title.
P291.S9   1975   415   75-43861
ISBN 0–12–447350–4

Contents

List of Participants

Stephen Anderson
Department of Linguistics
Harvard-UCLA

Wallace Chafe
Department of Linguistics
UC Berkeley

Sandra Chung
Department of Linguistics
UC San Diego

Colette Craig
Department of Romance Languages
University of Oregon

Margaret Datz
Department of Linguistics
University of Colorado

Leonard Faltz
Department of Linguistics
UC Berkeley-UCLA

William Foley
Department of Linguistics
UC Berkeley

Talmy Givón
Department of Linguistics
UCLA

Jorge Hankamer
Department of Linguistics
Harvard

Robert Hetzron
Department of Eastern Languages
UC Santa Barbara

Larry M. Hyman
Department of Linguistics
U. of Southern California

Carol Justus
Linguistics Program
State U. of New York-Oswego

Edward L. Keenan
Department of Linguistics
UCLA

Robert S. Kirsner
Department of Germanic Languages
UCLA

Susumu Kuno
Department of Linguistics
Harvard

S.-Y. Kuroda
Department of Linguistics
UC San Diego

George Lakoff
Department of Linguistics
UC Berkeley

W. P. Lehmann
Department of Linguistics
University of Texas

Charles N. Li
Linguistics Program
UC Santa Barbara

Arthur Schwartz
Linguistics Program
UC Santa Barbara

Jerry Morgan
Department of Linguistics
University of Illinois

Robert Stockwell
Department of Linguistics
UCLA

Edith Moravcsik
Department of Linguistics
Stanford

Alan Timberlake
Department of Slavic Languages
UCLA

Pamela Munro
Department of Linguistics
UCLA

Sandra A. Thompson
Department of Linguistics
UCLA

Paul Schachter
Department of Linguistics
UCLA

Karl E. Zimmer
Department of Linguistics
UC Berkeley

Preface

All but three papers in this volume were presented at the Symposium on Subject and Topic at the University of California, Santa Barbara, March, 1975. The purpose of the symposium was to achieve a thorough and precise understanding of the two important grammatical notions, subject and topic, against a background of empirical evidence gathered from as many linguistic areas as possible. Thus, during the discussion of the various syntactic, semantic, and discourse characteristics of the notions of subject and topic at the symposium, data were drawn from such diverse language families as Indo-European, Malayo-Polynesian, Sino-Tibetan, Australian, Afro-Asiatic, Mayan, Niger-Congo, Finno-Ugric, Altaic, Caucasian, Iroquoian, Yuman, and Uto-Aztecan. Such data constitute the empirical foundation of the papers prepared by the participants of the symposium for this volume. The three papers not presented at the symposium are by Colette Craig, Lynn Friedman, and Elinor Keenan and Bambi Schieffelin. Aside from their theoretical contribution, these three additional articles serve to broaden further the empirical base of this book with interesting data from child language, the American Sign Language, and Jacaltec, a mixed ergative language of the Mayan family.

The basic theoretical issues with which the papers in this book are concerned may be summarized in the form of two questions: (*a*) How can "subject" and "topic" be characterized on a language independent basis? (*b*) What are the roles of "subject" and "topic" in the structure of language? An obvious conclusion one can draw from the studies here is that there is no universal definition, i.e., discovery procedure, by which one can identify either a subject or a topic in a language. The articles by Stephen Anderson, Sandra Chung, Colette Craig, Edward Keenan, and Alan Timberlake demonstrate that subjects can vary in their properties even within a specific language. The closest approximation to a universal definition of subjects is presented by E.L. Keenan in his article, "Toward a Universal Definition of 'Subject'." Here Keenan attempts to provide an exhaustive and systematized set of the properties of subjects in language. Thus a subject in any language can be understood as the combination of a subset of Keenan's subject properties. The elucidation of the properties of subjects naturally clarifies their roles in the structure of language since "subject" is basically a relational notion denoting the grammatical function performed in a sentence by a particular constituent of the sentence. Any discussion of subjects will inevitably involve the syntactic structure of sentences. This is attested by the fact that the majority of the properties of subjects listed by Keenan are syntactic in nature.

The identity of "topic" appears to be much more elusive than that of "subject." Unlike the notion of subject, the notion of topic is discourse oriented. In view of the fact that the study of discourse is still at a stage where linguists are grappling with the problem of how to analyze the data, it is to be expected that any attempt to define a discourse oriented notion such as "topic" will encounter considerable difficulties. Thus there is no exhaustive listing of the properties of topic comparable to Keenan's list of subject properties. A number of the articles in this volume are concerned with topics. They are by Wallace Chafe; Lynn Friedman; Talmy Givón; Larry Hyman and Karl Zimmer; Carol Justus; Elinor Keenan and Bambi Schieffelin; Susumu Kuno; Winfred Lehmann; Charles Li and Sandra Thompson. The most serious attempt to characterize the notion of topic is made by Li and Thompson. That characterization, however, is not absolute, in that topics are described in contrast to subjects rather than independently.

A consensus emerging from the studies in this volume is that subjects and topics may have different degrees of prominence in different languages. Consider subjects, for instance. The noun phrases serving as subjects in one language can be more systematically manifested than those in another language. In other words, for some languages the different types of noun phrases serving as subjects in different types of sentences have in common the great majority of subject properties. In other languages, separate noun phrases may each exhibit certain specific subject properties such that no common set of properties can be established for the purpose of correctly identifying a particular noun phrase in a sentence as a subject. Thus, the former type of language is more subject-prominent than the latter type. A lucid case study of languages having diffuse subjects is presented by Paul Schachter. Beyond the case of diffuse subjects, Li and Thompson point out that there are certain languages in which the basic constructions manifest a topic–common relation rather than a subject–predicate relation. Hence, they propose a typology of language based on the notions of subject–prominence and topic–prominence. An interesting diachronic implication of such a typology is that languages may drift from one type to another on the scale of subject–prominence and topic–prominence. The article by Talmy Givón suggests that subjects are in fact diachronically derived from topics, and the articles by Carol Justus and Winfred Lehmann attempt to trace the development from topic-prominence to subject-prominence in Indo-European.

As a final point, it is noteworthy that none of the articles in this volume is concerned with the formal aspects of generative mechanisms. This represents a radical departure from the syntax and semantics literature that was dominant in the 1960s. The lack of concern with formalism, however, is not to dismiss its importance to the study of language. Rather, it represents many linguists' recognition of the fact that our knowledge and understanding of the languages of the world is far from sufficient for postulating adequate generative systems or for debating the nature of generative mechanisms, or even for determining whether the generative approach to the study of language is indeed correct. At this juncture of the development of linguistic science, it appears that one of the most productive directions of research lies in the collection of valuable facts from a diverse cross-section of languages and the discovery of generalizations based on them. This volume is an example of scholarship in such a direction.

Charles N. Li

Acknowledgment

The Symposium on Subject and Topic where most of the papers in this volume were presented in their preliminary versions was funded by a grant from the National Science Foundation, Grant No. SOC75-03539. During the organization of the Symposium and the preparation of this volume, the editor was supported by a fellowship from the American Council of Learned Societies. The editor wishes to express his appreciation and gratitude to Nancy Quinn and Naomi Schwartz who helped to make the Symposium a delightful experience to all the participants, and to Kathy Barrett who typed the manuscript for this book.

ON THE NOTION OF SUBJECT IN ERGATIVE LANGUAGES*

by

Stephen R. Anderson

*This paper was prepared while the author was at Harvard University, and a consultant at Bell Laboratories, Murray Hill, New Jersey. The support of both institutions is gratefully acknowledged. I would also like to thank the participants in the UCSB conference on subject and topic for helpful comments. References for topics discussed in this paper, together with considerably more discussion, will be found in my forthcoming monograph Ergativity and Linguistic Structure.

In traditional grammar, syntactic analysis is almost exclusively based on categories revealed directly in surface structures. In particular, morphologically unified categories of constituents are often taken to be the only ones that could possibly have any importance for the description of sentence structures. If a notion like "subject of" is to have any syntactic importance, then, it must be possible to associate it with a category of the language's morphology. In most of the familiar languages of Europe which form the basis for this tradition, it is fairly easy to provide some set of morphological criteria which will (perhaps with a little fudging, such as the introduction of "notional" categories) pick out just the class of subjects which seems syntactically significant. The question of whether these properties actually have anything essential to do with "subjectness" or not, however, is seldom raised: having served their purpose, they are assumed ipso facto to be significant.

A major problem with the assumption that morphology will reveal the important categories of syntactic structure directly has long been the existence of ergative languages. In such languages, the morphological category to which the subject NP of an intransitive verb belongs is shared not with the NP we expect to be subject of a transitive verb, but rather with the NP we expect to be object of that verb. "Subjects" thus belong to different categories depending on the transitivity of the verb. This by itself would not be so important, were it not for the fact that the morphology appears to establish the existence of a category which includes subjects of some verbs, and objects, but not subjects of other verbs. This situation has engendered a vast literature, devoted to the question of whether ergative languages are or are not fundamentally different in syntactic structure from accusative languages.

The morphological identification involved may be in terms of any of the usual devices for marking grammatical function, case marking and verb agreement being by far the most general. A language in which ergativity is indicated by case marking alone is Tongan:

1 a.   na'e lea   'a etalavou
         past speak abs young man
         "the young man spoke"

   b.   na'e alu 'a tevita ki fisi
         past go abs David to Fiji
         "David went to Fiji"

3

    c.   na'e tamate'i 'a kolaiate 'e tevita
        past kill   abs Goliath erg David
        "David killed Goliath"

    d.   na'e ma'u   'e siale 'a e me'a'ofa
        past receive erg Charlie abs def gift
        "Charlie received the gift"

Case marking is combined with verb agreement to establish
the categories of ergative and absolutive in Avar:

2 a.   vas v-eker-ula
       boy m-run-pres
       "the boy runs

    b.   jas j-eker-ula
       girl f-run-pres
       "the girl runs"

    c.   vas-al r-eker-ula
       boy-pl pl-run-pres
       "the boys run"

    d.   ins:u-c:a jas j-ec:-ula
       father-erg girl f-praise-pres
       "the father praises the daughter"

    e.   vas-as: sisa   b-ek-ana
       boy-erg bottle n-break-past
       "the boy broke the bottle"

    f.   vas-as: susbi   r-ek-ana
       boy-erg bottles pl-break-past
       "the boy broke the bottles"

In some languages, case marking is absent, but the verb may
agree with a number of distinct NPs. In that case, the
agreement pattern may establish ergative and absolutive categories, as in Abaza:

3 a.   a-ph°əs   d-qa-c°'a-d
       def-woman 3-hither-sit-past(act)
       "the woman sat up"

    b.   a-ph°əs   a-qac'a   d-1-sə-d
       def-woman def-man   3-3f-kill-past(act)
       "the woman killed the man"

Distinct case marking and agreement can of course be combined
to form even more elaborate systems, such as that of Basque.
    The sort of (morphologically) ergative language we are
concerned with here should be distinguished from two other
possible systems, both of which have sometimes been brought

into the discussion of ergativity. One of these is the (rare) case where all three possible roles for NP are morphologically distinct, as in Motu:

4 a.   mero na e   gini-mu
        boy S_i 3sg stand-imperf

       "the boy is standing"

   b.   mero ese aniani e heni-gu
        boy S_t food 3sg give-me

       "the boy gave me food"

In this case, there is no morphological basis (with the possible exception of the verbal clitic) for either NP in a transitive clause being identified with the subject NP in an intransitive clause.

    Another situation distinct from that which concerns us is the existence of languages in which agent subjects are distinguished from patients, in a way which sometimes looks like the pattern of an ergative language. The most famous example of this type is Dakota; another is Wichita:

5 a.   ta-t-?i:y-s   [tac?i:ys]
        nonfut-I-see-imperf   "I saw (him)"

   b.   ta-ki-?i:y-s   [taki?i:ys]
        nonfut-me-see-imperf "(he) saw me"

   c.   ta-t-hisa   [tachish]
        nonfut-I-go   "I went"

   d.   ta-ki-hiya:s   [takihiya:s]
        nonfut-me-hungry   "I am hungry"

A similar situation apparently obtains in the Northeast Caucasian language Bats:

6 a.   as jopst' axo
        I plow land
       "I plow the land"

   b.   as wože
        I fall
       "I fell (on purpose)"

   c.   so wože
        me fall
       "I fell (e.g., by accident)"

We will have nothing further to say about either of the situations just exemplified, which we would like to distinguish from the case of ergative languages.

From the fact that the usual notion of subject cannot be given a firm morphological foundation in an ergative language, many traditional writers have drawn radical conclusions about the typological characteristics of ergative languages. In the well-known languages of accusative type, we can distinguish (at least) two fundamental grammatical relations which are basic to clause structure: subjects, and (direct) objects. Whether these are to be defined in terms of Phrase-Marker configurations (as suggested in _Aspects_), taken directly as primitives of clause structure (as proposed in Relational Grammar), or some other alternative is not relevant: the important point is that these two relations can be distinguished and are fundamental to the structure of sentences. This structure we can take as typologically characteristic of accusative languages.

One way to resolve the problem that the same notions cannot be founded morphologically in an ergative language is simply to deny that there are _any_ grammatical relations basic to clause structure in such a language. A clause contains, on this view, a verb and a collection of NP: no NP is structurally distinct from any other in a syntactic sense. There are certainly relations between these NP and the verb, but these are taken to be semantic in nature, and all of the NP involved are syntactically equivalent. This view is associated with the claim that in an ergative language, as opposed to an accusative one, the verb is "polypersonal" (i.e., relates equally to several NP at a time). Such a nihilist solution is only possible, of course, if one disregards most of what falls in the domain of syntax in contemporary views: any syntactic process which applies differentially to some but not all NP according to a specific pattern would disconfirm the notion that all are structurally parallel.

A view which is closely related to that just mentioned is found in the works of a number of writers, beginning in the early nineteenth century. This is the view that the structure of the sentence in an ergative language is not to be distinguished from that of the Noun Phrase. On this view, there is only one significant grammatical relation, common to both NP and clause: this is the relation of modifier to head. A clause is thus provided with some internal structure, of a simple hierarchical sort. This view is proposed most recently by Martinet and his student C. Tchekoff. Disconforming evidence can be provided by showing fundamental syntactic differences between NP and clause, and by showing that the syntactic function of a NP within a clause depends not only on the fact that it is a "modifier," but also on what kind of "modifier" it is. Any process which treats subjects and objects as distinct relations, that is, would be inconsistent with this view.

By far the most common view of ergative languages, however, originates at least as early as the work of Schuchardt. This is the notion that the clause in an ergative language is (if transitive) "passive" in nature. The structural positions of subject and object are distinct on this view, but in a transitive clause the NP occupying the subject position is the one corresponding to an accusative object, while the NP corresponding to a (nominative) subject is in an oblique relation of some sort. This structure is, of course, exactly that which is produced by the operation of a passive rule in languages like English: the claim here is that in an ergative language it is basic. A variant of this view, proposed by Hale, is that the rule corresponding to the English passive is obligatory in an ergative language.

This position has the merit, of course, of providing a rationalization for the morphology. The morphologically unitary category of absolutive corresponds directly to the syntactic relation of subject. Such a view has been proposed within the context of generative grammar by DeRijk, and more recently by Culicover and Wexler. If ergative languages are in fact radically distinct from accusative languages in syntactic structure, this is probably the most plausible view of the nature of that difference.

Of course, as long as we confine ourselves to the analysis of surface structures (and their morphological characterization in particular), since all of the above views are at least internally consistent any of them is possible. In contemporary syntactic theory, however, the basic features of clause structure are much more than a foundation for morphological categories. As pointed out by a number of authors (most extensively by Keenan, in his contribution to this symposium), subjecthood is related to a wide variety of other syntactic and semantic properties. The best understood of these, probably, are the roles of various grammatical relations in the structural descriptions of the major cyclic syntactic rules, such as Equi-NP Deletion, Raising, reflexive, conjunction formation, etc. The fundamental nature of grammatical relations in determining the operation of these rules (while it has been denied by some) has been argued for in a number of works.

Given the result that a rich array of syntactic processes are sensitive to the internal structure of clauses, we have a ready tool for evaluating the theories of the syntax of ergative languages discussed above. We can look beyond the morphology, to the rules of the syntax in such a language.

If we discover that NP in a particular category (e.g., absolutives) play the same role in the syntactic processes of an
ergative language that subjects do in an accusative language,
it would be appropriate to designate this category as subject, even though the subject of a sentence in an ergative
language might then not correspond to the subject in its ana-
log in an accusative language. If, however, we find that
there is no morphological category which contains all and
only subjects in this sense, but rather the NP which serve as
"subjects" for such rules as Equi-NP deletion, Reflexive,
etc. are generally those corresponding to subjects in accusative languages, it would be plausible to say that these are
indeed subjects despite the morphology. We suggest, that is,
that the syntactic concept "subject" ought to be identified
by syntactic means (in particular, the role of an NP in those
transformational processes which seem most sensitive to grammatical relations); the more straightforward the correspondence between such syntactically defined categories and those
of surface morphology the better, of course, but this is def-
initely a secondary consideration.

How, then, do subjects behave distinctively in an accusative language? English is, of course, the best investigated from this point of view, but a consideration of others
shows that it is in no important way atypical. For example,
the rule of Equi-NP deletion deletes the subject of an embedding under identity with the controlling NP in the matrix
clause. There is a certain amount of controversy over the
way in which the correct controller is to be identified, but
there is no disagreement over the fact that it is the subject
and no other NP in the lower clause which is deleted. Thus,
though 7a,b are well-formed, 7c is impossible: despite the
identity between the lower object and the controller, no deletion is possible.

7 a.   John wants to laugh
  b.   John wants to stop violence
  c.   John wants Bill to tickle *(him)

Furthermore, it is the syntactic relation of subject, rather
than an underlying (and hence possibly semantic) relation,
which is relevant here. The rule of passive changes grammatical relations, so that what was originally subject becomes
an oblique NP while the original object becomes a subject.
If passive has applied, 8a (analogous to 7c) is possible,
while 8b (well-formed if passive had not applied) becomes impossible:

8 a.   John wants to be tickled by Bill
  b.   John wants Bill to be tickled (*=by him)

Analogous remarks apply to the rule of Raising. With verbs like <u>seem</u>, subjects raise but nothing else:

9 a.   John seems to be laughing
  b.   John seems to be getting the job
  c.   *John seems for something to be bothering (him)
  d.   John seems to have been tattoed by a Dayak

It might be claimed that the existence of a rule raising objects vitiates this point, but in fact it strengthens it. With those verbs for which objects can raise, it is exactly the class of non-subjects which can undergo the rule:

10 a.   Fred is tough to catch
   b.   Harry is tough to write letters to
   c.   Bars are tough to think about metaphysics in
   d.   Metaphysics is tough to think about in bars
   e.   *John is tough to laugh
   f.   *Bill is tough to convince John
   g.   *Max is tough to be tackled by a linebacker

Thus object-raising is just as sensitive to the distinction between subjects and non-subjects as subject raising is.

Conjunction formation (whether by reduction or some other process) is another rule which is sensitive to grammatical relations. A well formed conjunction of two clauses can result when there is a shared chunk of material common to them both, but only when this material fills the same syntactic role in both:

11 a.   John and Bill are laughing
   b.   John and Bill both keep bears
   c.   John bought a banana and sold his old rutabaga
   d.   John bought the last rutabaga and gloated
   e.   Bill came in and ate John's rutabaga
   f.   *John likes but rutabagas disagree with him
   g.   *John likes rutabagas but disagree with him
   h.   *Rutabagas grow around here, but John hates

Essentially, subjects count as the same syntactic role regardless of the transitivity of their associated verbs, while no subject counts as filling the same role as an object.

Reflexive is somewhat complicated in English by conditions which are more sensitive to order than to grammatical relations; accordingly the same point cannot be illustrated for this rule without looking at other languages. A language like Danish, however, shows the cross-linguistically more natural situation. Reflexives (both the ordinary object reflexive pronoun <u>sig</u> and the possessive reflexive <u>sin</u>/<u>sit</u>) necessarily have the subject as their antecedent:

12 a.　Jørgen så sig i spejlet
　　　　(name) saw refl. in mirror-def
　　　　"Jørgen looked at himself in the mirror"

　　b.　*Sig så Jørgen i spejlet

　　c.　*Sig blev set i spejlet (af Jørgen)
　　　　　　was seen　　　　　　　by

　　d.　Rasmus leger med sin dukke
　　　　(name) plays with refl doll
　　　　"Rasmus is playing with his doll"

　　e.　Rasmus slog Sigrid med sin dukke
　　　　(name) hit　(name) with refl doll
　　　　"Rasmus hit Sigrid with his doll"
　　　　*"Rasmus hit Sigrid with her doll"

This situation is, of course, familiar from a great many
other languages.

The above remarks are, of course, perfectly familiar to
anyone with the slightest acquaintance with syntactic research. It is worth emphasizing, however, that the rules a-
bove provide a consistent and worthwhile criterion for syntactic subjecthood. This kind of fact is the basis of relational grammar, where syntactic processes are stated directly
in terms of grammatical relations (rather than in terms of
linear order and immediate constituency). It can be shown
that some such move is required since analogous facts obtain
under circumstances where order and constituent structure
give incorrect or insufficient definitions of the relevant
NP. We assume, therefore, that it is valid to base a syntactic notion of subject in an unfamiliar language on the dif-
ferential behavior of NP with respect to such rules as those
just noted. Naturally, this move is based on fairly strong
assumptions about syntactic universality, but these seem va-
lidated by the facts of a wide variety of languages, in which
these rules are remarkably stable and consistent.

When we apply the proposed test to ergative languages,
then, we might find several different situations. If we were
to find that, in such languages, NP are never subject to rules
such as those just discussed, we would be justified in saying
that no such relation as that of subject is defined in such
languages. This would be consistent with the first view
sketched above, on which there are no grammatical relations
in clause structures in such languages. If, on the other
hand, we found such rules, but found that all NP were functionally the same with regard to them, this would justify the
claim (implicit in the second view sketched above) that there
is just one structurally important grammatical relation in

10

such a language, and all NP bear this relation within the
clause. If, as a third possibility, we found that the NP
which function as syntactic subjects in this sense are those
corresponding to the subjects of intransitive verbs, but to
the objects of transitive verbs, this would justify something along the lines of the underlying or obligatory passive
theory. If, as a final possibility, we find that the same NP
function in the same ways in an ergative language as in an
accusative language, this would suggest that the notion of
subject which is syntactically relevant is the same in both
types, and the morphology is a misleading indicator of syntactic function in ergative languages.

In the overwhelming majority of ergative languages, what
actually happens is consistent only with this last possibility. Ergative languages do indeed have rules like Equi-NP
deletion, subject raising, reflexive, conjunction formation,
etc.; and furthermore the NP which function as syntactic subjects in these rules are just the same as those which serve
as subjects in the corresponding clauses and constructions in
accusative languages. For instance, in Basque there is a
process quite analogous to English Equi-NP deletion. With a
verbal expression such as <u>nahi du</u> "he wants (lit. he has
desire of it)," complements where no identity obtains appear
in a full form, with a subjunctive auxiliary agreeing (like
other Basque auxiliaries) with subject and (if present) object:

13 a.   nahi   dute   jauts   gaiten
        desire they-have-it come down we-subjective
        "they want us to come down"

   b.   nahi   dut   egin   dezan
        desire I-have-it do   he-subjunctive-it
        "I want him to do it"

Non-emphatic pronouns in Basque are generally deleted; in
14 below, there is no overt subject in the complement clause.
Nonetheless, the fact that the clause has the form with subjunctive auxiliary, as in 13, shows that the subject of the
complement cannot be identical with that of the matrix
clause:

14   nahi   du   egin   dezan
         desire he-has-it do   he-subjunctive-it
         "He$_i$ wants him$_j$ to do it"
         *"He wants to do it"

When the subject of the lower clause (in the same sense as in
an accusative language) is identical with the controller in a

higher clause, the deletion is not optional, but obligatory;
and it is accompanied by loss of the auxiliary and reduction
of the verb to the infinitive (perhaps marked with a case
ending).

15 a.   nahi   dut   joan
        desire I-have-it go-infinitive
        "I want to go"

   b.   nahi   dut   egin
        desire I-have-it do-infinitive
        "I want to do it"

When there is an overt object present in the lower clause,
and this rule of Equi-NP deletion applies, the remaining object may undergo one of two processes: either it may be converted to a genitive, as in 16a, or it may be raised into
the matrix clause as in 16b, with the result that the matrix
verb comes to agree with it.

16 a.   nahi   dut txakurraren hil
        desire I-have-it dog-def-gen kill
        "I want to kill the dog"

   b.   liburu hoik irakurtzerat noatza
        book   those read-infin-to I-go-them
        "I am going (in order) to read those books"

The operation of Equi-NP deletion does not depend on the
transitivity of the higher verb; both transitive verbs, like
'want' and intransitive ones, like 'go' can control the rule.
Notice, however, that it is always <u>subjects</u> which are deleted, in an accusative sense: identity of the higher controller with the <u>object</u> of the lower clause can never allow equi:

17 a.   dantzatzerat joan da
        dance-infin-<u>to</u> go he-is
        "he has gone to dance"

   b.   txakurraren hiltzera joan nintzen
        dog-def-gen kill-infin-<u>to</u> go I-was
        "I went to kill the dog"

   c.   ikhusterat joan   da
        see-infin-<u>to</u> go   he-is
        "He$_i$ has gone to see him$_j$."
        *"He$_i$ has gone for him$_j$ to see him$_i$."

The rule of cf Equi in Basque, then, is sensitive to the
same notion of subject as in English, and <u>not</u> sensitive to a
notion of subject that would correspond with the morphologi-

cal category of absolutives.

In Tongan, there is a rule of subject raising which applies with a very limited class of verbs to promote the lower subject into the matrix clause:

18 a.   'oku lava   ke hū   'a mele ki hono fale
          pres possible tns enter abs Mary to his house
          "It is possible for Mary to enter his house"

   b.   'oku lava   'a mele 'o hū   ki hono fale
          pres possible abs Mary tns enter to his house
          "Mary can enter his house"

In 18b, the subject 'a mele has been raised from the lower clause. The rule is also applicable to transitive embeddings:

19 a.   'oku lava   ke taa'i 'e siale 'a e fefine
          pres possible tns hit erg Charlie abs def woman
          "It is possible for Charlie to hit the woman"

   b.   'oku lava 'e siale   'o taa'i 'a e fefine
          pres possible erg Charlie tns hit abs def woman
          "Charlie can hit the woman"

The fact that the subject 'e siale originated in the embedding is shown clearly here by the fact that it is marked ergative. Subjects thus can be raised out of the complements of lava 'be possible' regardless of transitivity. Non-subjects, however, cannot be raised even if they are morphological absolutives:

20   *'oku lava   'a e fefine   'o taa'i 'e siale
          pres possible abs def woman tns hit erg Charlie
          "The woman can be hit (by Charlie)"

Tongan subject raising, then, only applies to subjects in the same sense as English subject raising. (I owe these facts to Sandra Chung.)

Conjunction formation is somewhat harder to illustrate than the other rules considered to this point. Many languages allow free conjoining, and then simply delete NP under conditions of ordinary discourse anaphora. In languages where pronominalization is by deletion, then, the process of conjunction formation is much less (if at all) sensitive to grammatical relations. One language in which grammatical relations do play a role, however, is the New Guinea language Kâte. In this language, subjects of transitive verbs are usually marked with an ergative particle -ki. A primary syntactic process in Kâte, as in other New Guinea languages, is the chaining of clauses with a common topic by means of a form of conjunction. Where several clauses are conjoined in

this way, all but the last are marked with special subordinate
verb forms which indicate the relation of this clause to the
following ones, rather than directly distinguishing the tense/
aspect combinations marked on 'main' verbs. In addition,
where two clauses have the same subject, the first takes an
inflectional form that does not indicate the person and number of the subject. 'Main' verbs and subordinate verbs whose
subjects are not identical with those of a following clause
are marked for these categories. The important point to note
is that, although the NP morphology of Kâte makes it an ergative language, the notion of subject which is relevant for
the conjoining process is the same as that in accusative languages. The ergative subject of a transitive verb counts as
subject, as does the absolutive subject of an intransitive,
while the absolutive object of a transitive does not count as
subject.

21 a. vale-la nana na-la   be? guy   fo-ve?
        come-past taro eat-past pig sleep lie-3sgpast
        "the pig came, ate taro, and lay down to sleep"

   b.   vale-la be?-ko   nana na-ve?
        come-past pig-erg taro eat-3sgPast
        "the pig came and ate taro"

   c.   mu-pe kpatala-me   hane?ke-pe
        speak-1sSPast retort-3sSPast tease-1sSPast

        kio-ve
        cry-3sPast

        "I spoke and he retorted and I teased him and he
        cried"

   d.   *go-ki (be?) hone-la (be?) gesa?ke-ve
        you-erg pig   see-past pig run-3sPast
        "You saw a pig and he ran"

In 21a,b the subjects of the conjoined clauses are all the
same, and accordingly do not appear except in the last clause.
Regardless of whether they appear as ergative or absolutive,
the inflections on the preceding clauses show no indication
of person. In 21c, the verb forms show person and number, as
well as (subordinated) tense relationship, since the subjects
of adjacent clauses are distinct. In 21d we see that person
marking cannot be omitted from the first conjunct despite the
fact that its (morphologically absolutive) object is identical with the (morphologically absolutive) subject of the
second clause.

    The behavior of reflexive with respect to case marking
is sometimes difficult to determine, since it is fairly common

for reflexive clauses to be treated as structurally intransitive. When that happens, it is impossible to determine whether reflexivization has gone "from" the ergative NP "to" the absolutive NP, or vice versa. Where we can determine a direction, however, it is generally clear that it is the (absolutive) direct object NP of a transitive clause that has undergone reflexivization. An example of this can be found in the Abkhazian languages of the Northwest Caucasian group. In the form of Abaza described by W.S. Allen, there is a verbal agreement marker /c-/ which specifically marks reflexives. This index replaces that in the first position of the verb when reflexivization takes place. The reflexive marker /c-/ is distinct from the normal verbal index (/d-/) which marks third person animate nouns in the corresponding position in non-reflexive clauses:

22 a.   c-l-ba-x-d
         refl-3sgf-see-back(iterative marker)-past
         "she saw herself (e.g., in a mirror)"

   b.   d-l-ba-x-d
         3sga-3sgf-see-back-past
         "she saw him/her (again, in return)"

Despite the fact that the Abkhazian languages (together with the other Northwest Caucasian languages) show a distinctly ergative pattern of verbal agreement, the direction of reflexivization is that which we would expect for an accusative language: it is the index corresponding to the object NP which is replaced by a reflexive form, while the index corresponding to the subject NP remains. Note in particular that it is not the case that the index corresponding to the absolutive NP serves as antecedent.

Interestingly enough, in related Abkhazian dialects there are two other reflexive constructions which differ from that in 22a, but which also show the same directionality. In a form of Abkhaz described by Lomtatidze, the reflexive NP index is replaced by the root č, together with a possessive prefix, the combination being incorporated into the verb in the position of the object prefix (a process abundantly attested elsewhere in the Northwest Caucasian verbal system):

23 a.   l-čə-l-š-wa-yt'
         3sgf-self-3sgf-kill-active-pres
         "she kills herself"

   b.   s-čə-s-š-wa-yt'
         1sg-self-1sg-kill-active-pres
         "I kill myself"

In these forms, the first index is a possessive marker, associated as a unit with c̰; the next index is that corresponding
to the subject.

Yet another construction is attested in the form of
Abkhaz described by Dumezil. Here, the reflexivized NP can
be replaced by an expression which means literally "NP's
head"; the corresponding verbal index simply becomes third
person singular inanimate, in agreement with such an expression:

24 a.   l-xe y-l-ba-yt'
        3sgf-head 3sgn-3sgf-see-pres
        "she sees herself"

   b.   s-xe y-z-ba-yt'
        lsg-head 3sgn-lsg-see-pres
        "I see myself"

   c.   s-xe   s-a-s-wa-yt'
        lsg-head lsg-3sgn-hit-active-pres
        "I hit myself"

The form in 24c involves the verb s "hit," which is from
another class than that of ba "see." While verbs like ba
take the basic transitive format, with object in first intra-
verbal position, verbs like s put their object index in
second position. As will be discussed below, these verbs are
actually to be construed not as transitives, but as intransitives taking an indirect object. The interest of 24c at
this point, however, is that it is like all of the other reflexives we have seen, in that it is the NP corresponding to
the object which is replaced by a reflexive form, while the
NP corresponding to the subject serves as the antecedent of
the reflexivization.

Rules such as those we have been considering, when investigated in virtually any ergative language, point unambiguously in the direction we have indicated. They show, that
is, that from a syntactic point of view these languages are
organized in the same way as are accusative languages, and
that the basically syntactic notion of 'subject' has essentially the same reference in both language types. The difference is simply that the correspondence between syntactic
and morphological categories is more straightforward in an
accusative language than in an ergative one: in the latter,
the transitivity of the verb, as well as the grammatical relation a NP bears to it, is relevant to the determining of
case marking and agreement patterns. The radical proposals
reviewed above for the syntax of ergativity, then, are dis-
confirmed by the syntactic facts, and this "fundamental"

typological parameter is reduced to a comparatively trivial
fact about morphology.

If one were determined to reject that conclusion, he
might argue that (for some reason not immediately evident)
the proposed notion of "subject" is not readily capable of
revealing a basic distinction between accusative and ergative
systems. It might be that the rules in question are based on
something quite different from syntactic grammatical relations, and that it is for this reason that ergative and accusative languages do not turn out to differ significantly.

This objection is shown to be false, and the notion of
ergativity is shown to be potentially more significant, by
the existence of at least a handful of exceptions to the generalization made above. For at least two languages, that is
(Dyirbal, an Australian language discussed by Dixon; and
Hurrian, a language of the ancient Near East), the test proposed above gives the opposite result. These languages have
a rule of Equi-NP deletion, but instead of deleting subjects
in the accusative sense, the rule deletes the NP which would
be subject of an intransitive verb or object of a transitive.
Dyirbal at least also has a rule of conjunction formation
which treats intransitive subjects and direct objects as
functionally the same relation, and distinguishes them from
transitive objects. Furthermore, both Dyirbal and Hurrian
have a restriction on the formation of relative clauses, that
the NP relativized must be the absolutive of the relative
clause. As Ross and, later, Keenan and Comrie have shown,
languages often have a restriction that only subjects can be
relativized. If the relativization of objects is allowed,
then subjects are relativizable too. This is exactly what
does happen in Dyirbal and Hurrian, if one takes the view
that their grammatical relations are the same as those of an
accusative language; but if one takes the position that the
NP which is (for full nouns) in the absolutive (as opposed to
the ergative) is the syntactic subject, these languages can
be brought into line with universal grammatical theory. For
these languages, then, something like the "underlying passive" theory appears to be correct (though it should be noted
that Dyirbal, at least, has a rule which has an effect on
syntactic structures entirely analogous to that of the passive in accusative languages).

We might argue that in these cases, the rules are not
really looking at syntactic structures at all, but simply at
morphological form (since for most NP, absolutives have the
same form, and this is different from that given to ergatives). This resolution will not do, however. Dyirbal has
the interesting property that while full NP are marked as

17

absolutive vs. ergative, pronouns are marked as nominative
vs. accusative. Nonetheless, the same facts obtain for pronouns as for nouns, as far as syntactic behavior is concerned:
the morphologically diverse class of (nominative) intransitive subject and (accusative) direct object, as opposed to
the morphologically uniform class of nominative subjects
functions as the class of "subjects" for the purpose of the
syntactic rules of the language. We must conclude, therefore, that Dyirbal is really ergative in a fundamentally syntactic sense, while most other morphologically ergative languages are ergative only superficially: in syntactic terms,
they are accusative.

We can conclude, therefore, that morphological patterns
are not a reliable guide to syntactic structure. A syntactic typology based on morphology cannot be adequate then. Of
course, this leaves us with the obligation to provide an alternative account of the basis of morphological categories.
If they are not based in a more or less one-to-one fashion on
syntactic categories, how are they assigned?

We might well suspect that morphological differences (at
least such distinctions as accusative vs. ergative case marking patterns) are somewhat superficial, since it is well
known that languages are often of mixed type. In some languages, for instance, transitive clauses whose verb is in a
perfect or past tense have ergative case marking, while
clauses in imperfect or non-past tenses have accusative form.
Or, as noted above, there are languages in which pronouns and
full NP follow different patterns. These differences are not
reflected by differences in the operation of syntactic rules,
and necessarily suggest that (at least) one or the other morphological pattern is syntactically misleading.

In fact, it is not hard to construct an alternative to
the traditional view that morphological categories are assigned directly on the basis of grammatical relations. Let
us first distinguish "direct-case" NP in a clause (basically,
subjects and objects) from "oblique" NP (adverbials, prepositional phrases, and other NP typically marked with oblique
cases; as well as "oblique" uses of direct case forms, such
as the accusative of duration, etc.). If we then assume that
(at least at the point at which case marking takes place) the
NP within a clause appear in some basic order (for concrete-
ness, let us assume that subject precedes object), we can
imagine two similar sorts of case marking rule that can give
quite different results. Note first that the languages with
which we are concerned have two properties, at least usually:
they allow fairly free scrambling, and insofar as a basic
order can be established, it is one with the verb in either

initial or final position. Clearly, the function of case marking in such a language is to allow the recovery of the distinction between subject and object in transitive clauses, since (a) this is not indicated by position relative to the verb; and (b) scrambling removes any other trace of the distinction, in the absence of overt morphological marks. One way to accomplish the differentiation of subject and object is to have a case-marking rule that says "put the subject in one case, the object in another." For syntactically accusative languages, this will always give accusative morphology. Another equally good way of accomplishing the function of case marking, however, would be to have a rule that says "when there are two direct-case NP in a clause, put a special mark on the one which comes first (or alternatively, on the one which comes second)." In that case, if it is the second NP which is distinctively marked, the resultant pattern is accusative; but if it is the first NP which is marked, the pattern is an ergative one (the absence of a mark constituting the "nominative" or "absolutive" form).

Such a trivial distinction between two possible case marking rules obviously has no implications for the syntactic organization of the language. If we say that morphological ergativity arises in this way, then, we have a perfect account of the fact that ergative and accusative languages have (generally) the same sort of syntactic organization. We can go further, and suggest that what has happened in Dyirbal is the following: an originally superficial ergative case marking pattern has been re-interpreted as if it were assigned by a rule which depends directly on grammatical relations. This has resulted in a wholesale re-organization of the syntactic operations of the language, so that the same rules remain, but the "subjects" to which they apply are now those NP on which absolutive case marking (for full NP) could be based.

While fundamentally syntactic in nature, the notion of "subject" is clearly related to morphological considerations in most languages. For that reason, a view such as that above, on which the notion of subject in (most) ergative languages is the same as in accusative languages, must be supplemented with an account of the basis for morphological patterns. We have sketched such an account above, and tried to make it plausible; to justify it in detail would be beyond the scope of this paper.

We can note, however, a way in which this theory of morphological marking makes different claims about language than does one in which case marking is dependent directly on grammatical relations. On this theory, that is, case-marking in transitive clauses is crucially dependent on the presence of two direct-case NP in the clause at the time case-marking applies. Suppose that, in some language, one of these NP disappears prior to the operation of case-marking. In that event, the remaining NP will no longer be eligible for assignment to the ergative (or to the accusative) case, regardless of its grammatical relation to the verb. Such an event would require, on a theory whereby case marking is based directly on grammatical relations, a separate operation to change the relational structure of the clause. In the absence of motivation for such a separate operation, such a situation would furnish strong motivation for the theory of morphology we have sketched above.

In fact, such situations are not particularly difficult to find. In ergative languages, it is often the case that rules eliminating the object of a transitive clause exist. These include reflexive, indefinite object deletion, and generic object incorporation. In most ergative languages, when one of these operations has applied, the resultant clause is case-marked as if it were intransitive (i.e., the subject fails to be assigned to the ergative case). In accusative languages, on the other hand, there are rules which eliminate the subject, such as imperative formation and the formation of impersonal infinitives. There are several languages, in fact, where the object of a verb which has undergone such a process comes to function like the subject of an intransitive, either in being assigned to the nominative or even in triggering agreement. In none of the above cases (of either type) is there any motivation (beside the morphology) for an operation which alters grammatical relations as a consequence of the removal of the subject or object from the clause. As a result, they all furnish evidence for the theory of morphological marking processes we have outlined above. Note, incidentally, that the absence of such evidence in any given language is irrelevant: we need only say that, in such a language, object deletion, imperative formation, etc. follows case marking rather than preceding it. The presence of such evidence in any language, on the other hand, is not easily explicable on the traditional grammatical-relations based view of case marking and agreement.

Having discussed the correspondence between morphology and syntax in ergative languages, there is one further proposal concerning ergativity that should be noted briefly. As we remarked above, the languages of the Northwest Caucasian group display two distinct constructions for transitive verbs:

25 a. bojetsɨ-m gamemk'e pɨjɨ-r ɨwɨk'ɨʁ
        warrior-erg dagger-instr enemy-abs killed
        "the warrior killed the enemy with his dagger"

b. bojetsɨ-r   gamemk'e   pɨjɨ-m jepidʒɨ
    warrior-abs dagger-instr enemy-obl stabbed
    "the warrior stabbed the enemy with the dagger"

These forms (from literary West Circassian, or Adyghe, cited
from Catford and in his transcription) illustrate the two possibilities: either as in 25a, where the subject appears in
the ergative and is marked by an index in the last pre-verbal
position in the verb complex, the object in the absolutive
and marked by an index in the first preverbal position; or as
in 25b, where the subject is in the absolutive, agreeing with
an index in the first position, and the object in a form homophonous with the ergative, and agreeing with an index in
second position.

According to a recent proposal of Catford's, 25a is an
ergative construction, while 25b is an accusative construction. According to the traditional analysis, 25b is actually
an intransitive construction, with the object being treated
as indirect rather than direct. Since the form of the noun
in -m serves as a general oblique case in the Circassian languages, marking indirect objects, possessors, nouns used ad-
verbially, etc., as well as ergatives (and "accusatives"),
either Catford's interpretation or the traditional one is
perfectly consistent with the morphological facts.

There are fewer verbs that appear in the construction
25b than appear in construction 25a by a significant number,
but we can get some insight into the difference between the
two constructions by examining some verbs which (in West Circassian languages) appear in both, with differences of meaning:

26 a. (erg)   č'´aaλa-m č'əg°-ər   ya-z´°a
              boy-erg field-abs 3sg(-3sg)-plows
              "the boy is plowing the field"

   b. ("acc") č'´aaλa-r č'əg°-əm   ya-z´°a
              boy-abs field-obl 3sg(3sg)-plows
              "the boy is trying to plow the field, or the
              boy is doing some plowing, in the field"

   c. (erg)   p:śaśa-m   c'əy-ər   ya-d-ə
              girl-erg cherkesska-abs 3sg(3sg)sew-pres
              "the girl is sewing the Cherkesska"

   d. ("acc") p:śaśa-r c'əy-əm   ya-d-a
              girl-abs cherkesska-obl 3sg(3sg)-sew-intrans/
                  pres
              "the girl is trying to sew the Cherkesska, or
              the girl is sewing away (on the cherkesska)"

21

e. (erg) č'ˊaaλa-m p:šaša-r šˀ°-ay-χaɣ°-ə
          boy-abs   girl-obl good-3sg(3sg)-see-
                trans/pres
          "the boy loves the girl"

f. ("acc") č'ˊaaλa-r p:šaša-m šˀ°-ay-χaɣ°-a
            boy-abs   girl-obl good-3sg(3sg)-see-
                intrans/pres
            "the boy is falling in love with the girl"

These examples (which I owe to John Colarusso) are from the
Bzhedukh dialect of West Circassian. There are numerous such
pairs, and they differ systematically in the following way:
the "accusative" form in each case indicates that the action
is carried out less completely, less successfully, less conclusively, etc., or that the object is less completely, less
directly, less permanently, etc. affected by the action.

Catford suggests that this is indeed the essence of the
ergative construction: that ergative constructions (in any
language) involve the semantic interpretation that the object
is centrally involved in the action: they present the action
from the object's point of view. Accusative constructions,
on the other hand, present the action from the subject's
point of view, and thus involve the object less centrally.
While most languages have only the one or the other, the few
languages like West Circassian that exist allow us to see
that ergative languages involve a different sort of 'topicalization' than that in accusative languages.

In fact, however, the facts cited by Catford do not support his conclusion at all. First, it is certainly not the
case that objects in sentences in accusative languages are
always presented with the sort of semantic interpretation
which we find in the accusative members of the pairs in 26.
In fact, the ergative members of these pairs (26a,c,e) seem
to present quite accurately the correspondents of ordinary
accusative sentences. In fact, the difference seen in 26 (and
other pairs, some cited by Catford) has a close parallel in
many other languages, including accusative languages like
English:

27 a. The boy plowed the field.
   b. The boy plowed (away) at the field.
   c. The girl sewed the dress.
   d. The girl sewed on the dress.
   e. The boy shot the girl.
   f. The boy shot at the girl.

Pairs like these were discussed in a paper of mine (Foundations of Language, 7:387-396) some years ago. In each case,

a semantic distinction parallel to that seen above in the
Bzhedukh examples is correlated with the difference between
a direct object and an object marked with a preposition. In
fact, this same distinction recurs in a variety of other languages, from several distinct families: Maori, Walbiri, Finnish, and many others. It appears that it is possible in
general to indicate that an object is incompletely, inconclu-
sively, etc. affected, or that an action is incompletely, in-
conclusively, etc. carried out by putting the object into an
oblique case.

Now notice that this is exactly the traditional interpretation of the Circassian data, in which 26b,d,f are intransitives, with indirect rather than direct objects. This
interpretation is supported by verbs like those in 26c-d,e-f.
For a number of Circassian verbs, we find transitive/intran-
sitive pairs differentiated by a process which was apparently
productive in the language at one time: corresponding to a
transitive verb with vocalism ə̄, we can form an intransitive
by replacing this with a vocalism a. Notice that 26d,f have
a (and are thus likely to be intransitive, while 26c,e have
ə̄, and are thus likely to be transitive. This is not a rigid
rule in modern Bzhedukh, but where paired verbs differing in
this way are found, they are almost always transitive vs. intransitive. We see, therefore, that both on internal grounds
and by comparison with the facts of other languages it is
ost likely that 26b,d,f are to be interpreted in the traditional way: as intransitives, with an indirect object. They
therefore do not present an accusative construction at all,
and so Catford's proposal about the difference between ergative and accusative constructions cannot be supported by an
appeal to such pairs as those in 26.

We have argued, then, that the notion of subject in ergative languages is, despite the morphological indications
which appear to indicate otherwise, essentially the same as
that in accusative languages. An alternative view of morphological processes, for which considerable evidence can be
adduced, shows that there is in fact no reason to expect the
notion of subject to be related in a maximally simple way to
morphological category. Dyirbal, which as noted differs fundamentally from the usual type, is in fact the exception
which proves the rule. It shows that there is a distinctively "ergative" notion of subject, which is analogous to the
usual "accusative" notion, but which is inapplicable to the
vast majority of morphologically ergative languages.

GIVENNESS, CONTRASTIVENESS, DEFINITENESS, SUBJECTS,
TOPICS, AND POINT OF VIEW

by

Wallace L. Chafe

A noun in its sentence plays many roles, or has the potential of doing so. For example, according to one traditional way of sorting out some of these roles the noun Betty in the sentence Betty peeled the onions might be said to function simultaneously as the grammatical (or superficial) subject, as the logical subject, and as the psychological subject (e.g., Hornby 1972). A typical way of demonstrating the independence of these three roles is to point out that in The onions were peeled by Betty, although Betty remains the logical subject, the other two roles are taken by the onions. In The onions, Betty peeled, furthermore, it may be said that the onions is the psychological subject, whereas Betty is the logical and grammatical one.

Like most traditional classifications, this one turns out on closer inspection to have some things wrong with it-- or at least to leave out some crucial considerations. And there are a variety of other labels that have been applied to what seem to be similar or overlapping phenomena: labels like theme, emphasis, focus, and so on, as well as those which are listed in my title. This paper is an attempt to sort out some of the considerations--particularly the cognitive considerations--involved in such matters. It is written in the spirit, not of providing any final answers, but of trying to clear the air of proliferating obfuscation as well as of providing suggestions for profitable lines of both linguistic and psychological research.

I will speak of various statuses which a noun may have. One status, for example, might be its functional role within the verbal frame: what since Fillmore (1968) has come to be called its deep case role. Such a status is not the principal concern of this paper, though it is likely to interact in various ways with the statuses to be discussed. For example, "logical subject" is another term for "agent," a fact which stems historically from the recognition that subject status and agent status interact in some way. But case statuses are primarily involved in the content of what is being said--in the "ideational function" of language as Halliday (1970) puts it. The statuses to be discussed here have more to do with how the content is transmitted than with the content itself. Specifically, they all have to do with the speaker's assessment of how the addressee is able to process what he is saying against the background of a particular context. Not only do people's minds contain a large store of knowledge, they are also at any one moment in certain temporary states with relation to that knowledge. For example, a person may be "thinking of" a certain small part of it. Language functions effectively only if the speaker takes account of such

27

states in the mind of the person he is talking to. It is only, for example, when the speaker adjusts what he says to what he assumes the addressee is thinking of at the moment that his message will be readily assimilated by the addressee. This paper, then, will be about certain ways in which a speaker accommodates his speech to temporary states of the addressee's mind, rather than to the long-term knowledge of the addressee. Nevertheless, there are important ways in which the phenomena to be discussed depend on assumptions regarding long-term knowledge as well, and one of the tasks is to identify what these interactions are. I have been using the term packaging to refer to the kind of phenomena at issue here, with the idea that they have to do primarily with how the message is sent and only secondarily with the message itself, just as the packaging of toothpaste can affect sales in partial independence of the quality of the toothpaste inside.

Our starting point, then, is that the packaging phenomena relevant to nouns include the following: (a) the noun may be either given or new; (b) it may be a focus of contrast; (c) it may be definite or indefinite; (d) it may be the subject of its sentence; (e) it may be the topic of its sentence; and (f) it may represent the individual whose point of view the speaker is taking, or with whom the speaker empathizes. I don't mean to suggest that this list is complete. However, I have excluded such statuses as generic and nonspecific (the latter being involved in the ambiguity of I want to buy a book, for example) because, while they do interact with definiteness in certain ways, they have more to do with content than packaging. And I have not included terms like theme and emphasis because I believe they are unnecessary; that is, they are at best alternative labels for the phenomena that will be discussed. The restriction of the discussion to the statuses of nouns, on the other hand, is arbitrary. Some of these statuses--quite clearly givenness and contrastiveness, for example--apply equally well to verbs, though not all of them do. The emphasis on nouns here is purely expository; the context of the paper within this volume recommends it as a unifying principle.

Strictly speaking, these are not statuses of nouns but of their referents. Philosophical obfuscation notwithstanding, I will assume that a referent is the idea a noun is used to express. Among the things we have in mind when we talk are the ideas of various particular individuals and events. We choose certain words to express these ideas. For example, we may have in mind a particular person, and we may express our idea of this person on one occasion as Bob, on another as the guy I bought the boat from, on another as he, or whatever.

It is the constant idea of the individual rather than the shifting words that may occupy one or several of the statuses listed above. If I write loosely of a noun as being in the status given, for example, what I really mean is that the idea which the noun expresses has this status.

There are two broad kinds of considerations that enter into the identification of a noun's status or statuses. It would be fashionable to call them syntactic and cognitive considerations. For example, status as grammatical subject can sometimes be established through the surface case inflection (e.g., the noun is in the nominative case) and/or the fact that this is the noun with which the verb agrees (e.g., in person, number, and/or gender). These can be called syntactic considerations. But it might also be held that the grammatical subject performs some sort of cognitive function. Perhaps it is a conditioned stimulus (Mowrer 1954), the figure of a figure-ground relation or an "interest-object" (Carroll 1958), the "conceptual focus" (Tannenbaum and Williams 1968, James 1972), the most prominent or important element in the sentence (Johnson-Laird 1968a, 1968b; Hornby, Hass, and Feldman 1970), the focus of attention (Olson and Filby 1972), and so on. Perhaps some of these characterizations are more appropriate to the psychological than the grammatical subject, and perhaps, in fact, the grammatical subject is only a syntactic phenomenon, lacking in cognitive significance altogether. This last may be the predominant view in linguistics today. The only thing that seems clear is that the syntactic considerations (or at least some of them) are easier to sort out and agree on. The cognitive considerations lead us into a morass of uncertainty from which psychological experiments have not yet, at least, succeeded in extricating us.

My principal focus here will be on these cognitive considerations, but I believe that a prerequisite to an eventual solution of these puzzles is an approach which unifies linguistic and psychological evidence into a total picture of how language functions. In what follows I will try to provide a start in that direction by suggesting various relevant hypotheses, some with empirical backing and some almost wholly speculative, and by suggesting what it would be desirable to know more about if we were to account for these phenomena in a more final way. If my assertions sound more confident than they should, my intention is only that they might help in the organization of future research in this area.

I will take up each of the six statuses listed in my title in turn. To the extent that it is appropriate, I will organize the discussion of each in the following way. First

I will speculate as to the cognitive function of the status.
I consider this first section to be the heart of the discussion in each case, the section with which I would most like
to invite agreement or disagreement. Then I will say a
little bit about how the status is expressed in English and
perhaps a few other languages. It is not my intention to
provide an extensive treatment of phenomena in particular
languages, and this section will be sketchy and uneven, with
perhaps too much attention given to the few languages I can
say something about from firsthand experience. Since most of
these statuses involve assumptions by the speaker as to temporary states of the addressee's mind, I will then give some
attention to how such assumptions are established. In some
cases (e.g., definiteness) I will have to summarize some rich
and varied criteria; in other cases I can do little more than
point out the need for further research. Then, in most cases, I will mention also the question of how long the status
is preserved within a discourse. Uusually I will have to admit that very little is known on this point. Finally, for
some of the statuses, I will cite one or more conspicuous
cases in the linguistic or psychological literature where
that status has been confused with one or more of the others.

Givenness

    What is it? The key to this distinction is the notion
of consciousness (Chafe 1974). Given (or old) information is
that knowledge which the speaker assumes to be in the consciousness of the addressee at the time of the utterance. So-
called new information is what the speaker assumes he is introducing into the addressee's consciousness by what he says.
The terminology has been and continues to be misleading to
linguists and psychologists who use it. Calling something
"old information" suggests it is "what the listener is expected to know already" and "new information" is "what the listener is not expected to know already," something that is
being introduced into the addressee's knowledge for the first
time (the quotes are from Haviland and Clark 1974). But a
speaker who says I saw your father yesterday is unlikely to
assume that the addressee had no previous knowledge of his
father, even though by the usual criteria your father would
be considered new information. The point is that the speaker
has assumed that the addressee was not thinking about his
father at the moment. Terms like "already activated" and
"newly activated" would convey this distinction more accurately, but are awkward; we will probably have to live with the
terms "given" (or "old") and "new."

The above characterization is based almost entirely on introspective evidence, which I believe must play a major role in the study of such matters as consciousness. But certainly there is a great need to look for experimentally verified connections between givenness and consciousness. The psychology of consciousness has so far concerned itself mostly with abnormal states, and not with basic manifestations like this one.

How is givenness expressed? The principal linguistic effects of the given-new distinction, in English and perhaps all languages, reduce to the fact that given information is conveyed in a weaker and more attenuated manner than new information. This attenuation is likely to be reflected in two principal ways: given information is pronounced with lower pitch and weaker stress than new, and it is subject to pronominalization. In English it seems to be the case that given information is always pronounced with low pitch and weak stress, unless it is contrastive (see below). New information, however, is not always pronounced with high pitch and strong stress. In general, in English, nouns which convey new information are more consistently given strong pronunciation than are verbs, but the distribution of "new" pitch and stress is complex. (For a preliminary attempt to unravel this problem see Chafe 1974:114-116.) As for pronominalization, it can be applied only to items that convey given information, but it tends not to be applied when the speaker is aware that ambiguity would result (when there are two or more given items competing equally for the same pronoun). Thus the speaker has to monitor his speech not only with respect to what he assumes to be in the addressee's consciousness, but also with respect to the addressee's ability to interpret the referents of pronouns correctly. Speakers frequently err in both respects. Evidently some languages also use particles to express the given-new distinction. Japanese wa (given) and ga (new) provide the best known example (e.g., Kuno 1972b).

How is givenness established? A speaker may assume that something is in the addressee's consciousness on the basis of either extralinguistic or linguistic context. Extralinguistically, the speaker may believe that both he and the addressee share the perception, and hence the consciousness of some object in the environment. If the speaker sees the addressee looking at a certain picture on his wall, for example, he might say out of the blue I bought it last week, where the idea of the picture is treated as given and hence pronounced with low pitch and weak stress, as well as being pronominalized as it. The fact that the speaker and addressee them-

selves are regularly treated as given (and pronominalized as
I and you respectively) stems from the same consideration.
The speaker is conscious of the addressee, and the addressee
is conscious of the speaker. The most common linguistic basis for the speaker's assuming something to be in the addressee's consciousness is, of course, the prior mention of a
referent: I'd like to show you a painting (new). I bought it
(given) last week. Such givenness extends not only to the
same referent, but also to any other referent that is categorized in the same way: There was a small earthquake (new)
last night. I felt one (given) last year at about this same
time. I suspect this is because one of the functions of
categorizing a particular (e.g., categorizing a particular
experience as an earthquake, or a small earthquake) is to enable it to be interpreted as equivalent to other particulars
categorized in the same way. Hence, as soon as one such particular becomes given any of the others becomes given as well.
It is also of interest that generic expressions can attain
givenness in a similar manner: I bought a painting (new) last
week. I really like paintings (generic and given). (For
further discussion see Chafe 1974:122-127.)

How long does givenness last? One indisputable property
of consciousness is that its capacity is very limited. As
new ideas come into it, old ones leave. The speaker's treatment of an item as given, therefore, should cease when he
judges that item to have left his addressee's consciousness.
Such a judgment may be difficult to make, and this is an area
in which speakers are especially prone to err, saying he, for
example, when the addressee is no longer thinking about the
referent in question. It is probably here that Halliday's
(1967) notion of "recoverability" enters the picture. That
is, even though the addressee may have stopped thinking of
the referent of he, it may still be easily accessible in
memory and retrievable into consciousness. In that case communication will not have suffered any serious setback. Nevertheless, it is important to remember that givenness is a
status decided on by the speaker, and that it is fundamentally
a matter of the speaker's belief that the item is in the addressee's consciousness, not that it is recoverable. If recovery is necessary there has been at least a slight lapse in
the communicative process.

The question of what causes the speaker to believe that
an item has left the addressee's consciousness needs systematic examination (Chafe 1974:127-132). It would not be difficult to examine tape recorded speech with this question in
mind, and to look for instances where something previously
treated as given is later treated as new. The number of in-

tervening sentences in which the item was not mentioned is one obvious variable, but more interesting would be the effect of such discourse boundaries as a change of scene, where a whole new set of items can be assumed to enter the consciousness of the addressee, presumably pushing out old ones. One could examine the effect of this kind of boundary on the speaker's assessment of what the addressee is thinking of, and hence on his treatment of referents as given or new.

Confusions. There has been a great deal of confusion of given and new status with other statuses a noun can have. A few examples will be given below when other statuses are discussed. Here I will mention only the notion of "communicative dynamism" (CD) associated with linguistic studies in Czechoslovakia. To quote Firbas (1966:270), "By the degree of CD carried by a sentence element we understand the extent to which the sentence element contributes to the development of the communication, to which it 'pushes the communication forward,' as it were." Although this characterization is somewhat vague, it appears from the examples provided by Czech linguists that CD has more in common with the given–new distinction than with the other statuses we will consider. That being the case, it is interesting that CD is said to be a matter of degree, and not a binary distinction. If we identify a low degree of CD with givenness and a high degree with newness, the question arises as to whether there are intermediate degrees of given and new. The implication would be that the speaker can assume something to be in the addressee's consciousness to a greater or lesser degree. This psychological implication would be of considerable importance if it could be established. For the moment, however, it is necessary to say that the examples cited by the Czech linguists for the scalarity of the distinction are unconvincing, and that it has not been demonstrated linguistically that given vs. new is anything more than a discrete dichotomy.

Contrastiveness

What is it? Suppose we take as an example of a contrastive sentence Rónald made the hamburgers, where the acute accent mark indicates that the highest pitch and stress are on the stressed syllable of Ronald (the remainder of the sentence being low pitched). What is conveyed by such a sentence is the speaker's knowledge that Ronald, as opposed to other possible candidates the addressee might have had in mind, is the right selection for this role. Three factors are involved here. The first is an awareness, which the speaker assumes is shared by the addressee, that someone made the hamburgers. I will call this the background knowledge.

33

Does "awareness" mean "consciousness"? In other words, does the background knowledge have to be given? One can certainly imagine the use of a contrastive sentence in a situation where there is no good reason to assume that the addressee is thinking about this matter at the time the sentence is spoken. Sherlock Holmes, for example, might have spent the whole evening in cogitation before exclaiming The butler did it to a surprised Watson whose mind was completely on the book he was reading. The two shared the knowledge that someone did it (whatever it was), but Holmes could not objectively assume that Watson had that knowledge in his consciousness at that moment. Nevertheless, Holmes evidently was treating this knowledge as if it were given--as if Watson were thinking of it even though he wasn't. A possibility, then, is that the background knowledge must be either given or "quasi-given," the latter being a pretense on the speaker's part that givenness applies.

The second factor involved in a contrastive sentence is the set of possible candidates. In saying Ronald made the hamburgers the speaker evidently assumes that the addressee was at least entertaining, and possibly believed in one or more other candidates for this role. In many contrastive sentences the speaker actually contradicts a belief of the addressee's (for example, that Sally made the hamburgers), but that is not essential. The only consistent factor seems to be that the speaker assumes that a limited number of candidates is available in the addressee's mind (whether or not the addressee could in fact list all of them). Often the number is one, often it is larger, but when it is unlimited the sentence fails to be contrastive. Bolinger once suggested (1961:87) that "in a broad sense every semantic peak is contrastive. Clearly in Let's have a picnic, coming as a suggestion out of the blue, there is no specific contrast with dinner party, but there is a contrast between picnicking and anything else the group might do. As the alternatives are narrowed down, we get closer to what we think of as contrastive accent." His suggestion was that the available alternatives may range between one and unlimited, and that we are more prone to regard the sentence as contrastive as the number gets smaller. I favor, on the contrary, the view that contrastive sentences are qualitatively different from those which simply supply new information from an unlimited set of possibilities.

The third factor involved in contrastiveness is the assertion of which candidate is the correct one, and this, of course, is the real work a contrastive sentence does. The sentence used above as an illustration says essentially, "I believe that you believe that someone made the hamburgers, that you have a limited set of candidates (perhaps one) in mind as that someone, and I am telling you that the someone is Ronald, rather than one of those others." All contrastive sentences follow this pattern, mutatic mutandis. Suppose we call the asserted alternative (in this case Ronald) the focus of contrast. As a rule of thumb for testing whether a sentence is contrastive we can ask whether the phrase "rather than (instead of, not)..." can be felicitously inserted after the focus. One question which arises is whether the focus provides new information. I would argue that it does not--or need not--in the sense of new information characterized above. The speaker may very well assume that the addressee is already thinking about Ronald, either as one of the possible candidates for this role or in some other connection. That is why pronouns can be the focus of contrast: Hé did it, Í did it. Evidently the principal condition under which given items (including those that are pronominalized) receive the intonation peak of a sentence is just when they are such a focus of contrast. One other reason for distinguishing contrastive focus from new information will be mentioned below in connection with multiple foci. The distinction between given and new which applies in noncontrastive sentences has little relevance to contrastive sentences. The background knowledge (someone made the hamburgers) perhaps has to be at least quasi-given, the set of possible candidates may include items which are either given or new, and the focus of contrast itself may be given or new. What is communicated by a contrastive sentence is that a certain focus item rather than other possible ones is correct, but that cannot be regarded as new information in the sense of a referent newly introduced into the addressee's consciousness.

It is possible for a sentence to have more than one focus of contrast: Rónald made the hámburgers. Here it is the pairing of these candidates for these roles that is being asserted. That is, if we are to take possible pairings of agents with patients of make in this particular situation, one of the correct pairings (the speaker asserts) is Ronald with the hamburgers. (Perhaps Sálly made the sálad, but Rónald made the hámburgers.) Sentences with such double contrast are common, but it is possible with some effort to set up situations where even triple contrast would be appropriate: Sálly pícked the léttuce, but Rónald bóught the méat.

How is contrastiveness expressed? The principal manifestation is the placement of higher pitch and stronger stress on the focus of contrast. Thus, it is often difficult or impossible to tell the difference between contrast and new in-

35

formation on a phonetic basis alone. Nevertheless, sentences
with multiple contrast can be used to demonstrate that contrastive intonation is sometimes phonetically different from
new information intonation, contrary to Bolinger's statement
(1961:87) that "as far as we can tell from the behavior of
pitch, nothing is uniquely contrastive" (cf. Chafe 1974:118-
119). Imagine the following sequence of question and answer:

    1. What happened at the meeting?
    2. They elected Álice président.

The entire predicate of the second sentence is presumably new
information, with the result that the nouns within it (though
not the verb) receive high pitch. But evidently the high
pitch on <u>Alice</u> here is (or may be) phonetically different
from that on the same word in:

    3. They elected Hénry tréasurer, and they elected Álice
        président.

In the latter case <u>Alice</u> and <u>president</u> are the foci of a
double contrast. (<u>Henry</u> and <u>treasurer</u> may or may not be contrastive; it is quite possible for them to be simply new information here.) A normal pronunciation for <u>Alice</u> when she
is simply new information (as in 2) is with a pitch that
falls only slightly on the second syllable. But when she is
a focus of contrast (as in 3), the pitch must fall steeply.
This difference between new and contrastive intonation evidently becomes overt only when one contrastive focus is directly followed by another, as in 3. When there is a single
focus the sentence intonation will fall in any case, obliter-
ating the distinction. That is why <u>Ronald made the hámburgers</u>
is ambiguous between the contrastive and noncontrastive (new
information) meanings. On the other hand it is also true
that the high pitch on a contrastive focus is often higher
than that on a simple new information item (and the stress
stronger). Probably this increased prominence often given to
a contrastive focus results from an increased emotional commitment that is likely to accompany contrastiveness.

    It needs to be mentioned that contrastive sentences
typically appear on the surface to be indistinguishable from
answers to so-called WH questions, in those cases where the
latter are spelled out in complete sentences. Thus <u>Rónald
made the hamburgers</u> need not be contrastive, but might be the
answer to the question <u>Who made the hámburgers?</u> But the context and intent of a contrastive sentence is different, and
the surface convergence with WH answers should not be interpreted as indicating an identity of function. In this case
too there may be an intonational difference in the situation

where two WH answers, as compared with two foci of contrast,
occur in juxtaposition. In answer to the question <u>Who did
they elect what?</u> (assuming that only one office was at issue),
the answer <u>They elected Álice président</u> need not have the
same falling intonation on both items that is obligatory in
the double contrast sentence <u>They elected Álice président</u>, as
discussed above.

An additional way in which contrastiveness may be expressed is with the use of a so-called cleft sentence, as in
<u>It was Rónald who made the hamburgers</u>. The term was used by
Jespersen, who noted (1961:147-148): "A cleaving of a sentence by means of <u>it is</u> (often followed by a relative pronoun
or connective) serves to single out one particular element of
the sentence and very often, by directing attention to it and
bringing it, as it were, into focus, to mark a contrast."
Pseudo-cleft sentences, like <u>The one who made the hamburgers
was Rónald</u>, evidently serve the same function. English thus
provides these three ways (including <u>Rónald made the hambur-
gers</u>) of expressing contrastiveness, with Ronald the focus of
contrast. (A fourth way will be mentioned in the discussion
of topics below.) The question of why a speaker chooses any
one of these three has not yet been satisfactorily answered.
I offer the following speculations. <u>Rónald made the hambur-
gers</u> is particularly appropriate when it echoes the syntax
of a preceding sentence uttered by the other party, e.g.,
<u>Sally made the hámburgers</u>. When such echoing is less impor-
tant, cleft sentences provide a way of moving the focus to
the right, so that it does not appear as the initial item in
the sentence. There may, then, be a tendency to place not
only new information, but also the focus of contrast later in
the sentence. Pseudo-cleft sentences, of course, allow this
tendency full rein.

We have seen that contrastiveness is expressed through
intonation and stress, and in a certain way through word order. In some languages, where the role of given nouns is
captured primarily through agreement in the verb, independent
pronouns appear to be used mainly to express a focus of contrast. In Seneca, for example, and in the Iroquois languages
generally, a first person referent is normally expressed only
through a verbal prefix. There is, however, a separate
Seneca pronoun <u>i?</u> "I" which appears typically in sentences
like:

4. í? ononõ?tá? kyẽthwas
    I   potatoes I-plant
    í plant potátoes.

The context might be, "Other people may plant other things,

37

but..." This is clearly a contrastive function. The independent pronouns for other persons and genders are typically used in the same way.

The sometimes confusing overlap between the expression of given vs. new and the expression of contrastiveness is evidently found in the use of the Japanese particles wa and ga as well. Besides its use to signal givenness, wa evidently appears with a focus of contrast meaning, as in Ame wa hutte imasu ga, yuki wa hutte imasen "Rain is falling, but snow is not falling" (Kuno 1972b:271). On the other hand, according to Kuno, ga may also express contrastiveness in those cases where the focus of contrast is an "exhaustive listing": John ga baka desu "(Among the people under discussion) John and only John is stupid. It is John who is stupid." This use of ga for "exhaustive focus of contrast" may be a special resource of Japanese not available in English.

How is contrastiveness established and how long does it last? It is not clear that these questions are relevant to contrastiveness in the same way they are relevant to givenness and other statuses to be discussed below. Nevertheless, the contexts in which contrastive sentences are used would surely repay further study. My chief intention here has been to point out that contrastiveness is different from other statuses, and particularly that the status focus of contrast is different from the status new.

Confusion of contrastiveness with the given-new distinction. There is an unfortunate tendency of both linguists and psychologists to pick foci of contrast as paradigm examples of new information. Thus Halliday (1970:163), as a typical example of new information, gives the sentence This gazebo can't have been built by Wren, a double contrast sentence. The point about this and can't in this sentence is, of course, that they convey foci of contrast. Whether or not they convey new information in the same sense as Harry in I just saw Harry, where I assume you were not at the moment thinking about Harry, is unclear and irrelevant to the example. Again, Clark and Haviland (in press) begin their discussion of the given-new distinction with the example It was Percival who piqued the professor. Their discussion of this sentence is essentially a discussion of contrastiveness, but they persist in using the terminology given and new throughout. These are not isolated examples; the confusion is widespread.

Definiteness

What is it? In order to understand the role of so-called definiteness in language, one must recognize that most ideas of particular objects are communicated by way of the process of categorization (see, for example, Brown 1958). Having a particular creature in mind, for example, I am perhaps most likely to categorize it in a way that leads me to call it a dog, or the dog. But there is presumably an unlimited set of objects I might categorize in the same way. It is therefore of some interest in the communicative situation whether I think you already know and can identify the particular referent I have in mind. If I think you can, I will give this item the status of definite. The assumption in this case is not just "I assume you already know this referent," but also "I assume you can pick out, from all the referents that might be categorized in this way, the one I have in mind." Thus identifiable would be a better term than definite, but again we are stuck with the traditional label.

How is definiteness expressed? In English, of course, as in a number of other languages, there is an overt surface marking of definite status, the definite article. Other languages attach less surface importance to this status, not marking it at all or marking it only in conjunction with certain other features, as with the demonstratives of Chinese or Classical Latin. Words like this or that include the status of definiteness in what they convey, but they also include an indication of why the speaker expects the addressee to be able to identify the referent: its closeness to the speaker or to this point in the discourse, its distance from the one or the other, or the like. On the other hand some languages (Modern Greek, dialectal German) extend the definite article to proper nouns as well as to common ones (as we do in the Azores and other place names). Proper nouns are in a sense definite by definition, since they are direct labels for particular referents. In Tagalog it would appear that definiteness is given a different kind of surface prominence through verbal agreement (Schachter: this volume).

How is definiteness established? There are a variety of considerations which can lead a speaker to assume that his addressee is able to identify what referent he is talking about (cf. for example Karttunen 1968, Chafe 1972). I will list briefly here the major factors I am aware of. For a few categories there is either a unique referent or a uniquely salient one, as with the earth, the moon, the sky, and so on. While other planets have moons, in most contexts a speaker can assume that the addressee will appreciate what moon he means. (On Jupiter the question Which moon? would presumably have more relevance.) Often, although there is no uniquely salient instance of the category as a whole, one instance does stand out within a particular context. In a classroom

I can talk about the blackboard, etc. with good assurance
that the referent will be identified. Sometimes the same
will hold within the confines of a particular social group,
such as a family. The stock example is Did you feed the dog?
where the people concerned have no trouble identifying what
dog is meant. Most obvious is the establishment of definiteness through prior mention in the discourse. To introduce
a new referent I will have to say something like I received
an odd letter this morning, but I will subsequently talk
about the letter, assuming that in this linguistically established context you will be able to identify it. Modifiers
often serve to produce ad hoc categories within which identifiability can be assumed, where it could not be assumed on
the basis of the head noun by itself. For example, in a context where I would not be justified in saying This morning I
ran into the mechanic, because I could not assume that you
would know what mechanic I was talking about, I might succeed
if I said This morning I ran into the mechanic with the red
beard or the mechanic who fixed our carburetor last week. Of
special interest are those cases where one particular entails
another, so that having said We looked at a new house yesterday I can go on to say The kitchen was extra large, since a
particular house can be expected to contain a particular
kitchen. Such entailments extend not only from one noun to
another, but also from verbs to nouns. Since a particular
act of selling entails some particular money, having said I
sold my bike yesterday I can continue with I wonder what I'll
do with the money.

How long does definiteness last? On page 13 of Arthur
Koestler's The case of the midwife toad there is the sentence
One of his [Paul Kammerer's] pockets contained a letter addressed 'to the person who finds my body'. The letter is not
mentioned again until page 118, where we find a sentence beginning As far as we know, he wrote four farewell letters
(apart from the note 'to the person wil will find my body')...
Thus, with the aid of the quote from the letter, the reader
is assumed to be able to identify what letter this is, and we
can say that the status of definite for this referent has
been preserved over 105 pages. It may be relevant that most
of these intervening pages contain a flashback setting forth
the events which led to Kammerer's suicide, and that it is
only at the beginning and end of the book that the reader is
led to think about the circumstances of the suicide. Thus
the scene on page 118 connects up with that on page 13. In
any case it appears that the question of how long definiteness
is preserved has a very different answer from the question of
how long givenness is preserved, and that factors analogous

to the limited capacity of consciousness do not play a role here. In fact, it would appear that context or scene is all-important, and that definiteness can be preserved indefinitely if the eventual context in which the referent is reintroduced is narrow enough to make the referent identifable. Nevertheless, there are also cases where something established earlier as definite is later reintroduced in an indefinite way: I bought a car yesterday. It's the one I told you about. Presumably the car was treated as definite during my earlier conversation with you, but in this later reference its reintroduction was again treated as indefinite. As in the case of givenness, it would be worthwhile to examine large and varied samples of natural speech to see under what circumstances a reintroduced referent preserves its definiteness and under what circumstances it does not.

Haviland and Clark (1974) report an experiment in which some of their subjects were shown the context sentence We got some beer out of the trunk, after which they saw the target sentence The beer was warm. Subjects were asked to press a button as soon as they felt they understood the target sentence. Other subjects were given the context sentence We checked the picnic supplies, followed by the same target sentence The beer was warm. Comprehension of the target sentence was slower in the latter case than in the former. Certainly givenness is involved here. In the first case, where the beer was mentioned in the context sentence, it is indeed given in the target sentence and we would expect that subjects, if they had been asked to read the target sentence out loud, would have pronounced it with low pitch. (In fact, if they had had a choice, they would most likely have preferred to pronominalize the beer as it.) In the second case, where the beer was not mentioned in the context sentence, it is not given in the target sentence and subjects, if they had read it, would have been expected to give it high pitch (and certainly they would not have pronominalized it.)

However, it is not at all clear that this was the difference that led to the longer reaction times in the second case, for the basis for the definiteness of the beer in the two target sentences is not the same. In the first case this referent was introduced explicitly in the context sentence with the words some beer, and it is for that reason that the speaker can assume that his hearer will be able to identify what beer he is talking about in the target sentence. In the second case, on the other hand, identifiability is assumed because the particular picnic supplies mentioned in the context sentence entail some particular beer (or are assumed by the speaker to do so). There is, then, reason to suppose

41

that the extra reaction time in the second case is due to the
hearer's need to find the referent of the beer by working
through the entailments of the picnic supplies, and not to
whatever time it may take to establish this referent in consciousness. And in fact Haviland and Clark's discussion of
this experiment makes it clear that they are thinking more in
terms of the establishment of definiteness than in terms of
givenness. They speak of the listener building a "bridging
structure," and in Clark and Haviland (in press) they say
that "when the listener cannot find a direct antecedent, most
commonly he will be able to form an indirect antecedent by
building an inferential bridge from something he already
knows." Certainly what they are talking about is the establishment of the definiteness of one particular by inferences
from another particular. The finding that this process takes
time is of considerable interest, but it is not the process
of accepting new information into consciousness. So far as I
know, there is no evidence now available that bears on temporal aspects of the given-new distinction.

There is, to be sure, an interaction between the status
given and the status definite. There is, for example, a
strong tendency for indefiniteness and newness to go to-
gether--for things that are not definite to be also not given,
as with the last noun phrase in I just saw a funny looking
bird. The reason is apparent. When the addressee is assumed
not to be able to identify the referent, it is hardly likely
that the referent will be something already in the addressee's
consciousness. In fact, the only likely candidates for items
that are both indefinite and given appear in contexts like
the following:

    5.   I saw an eagle this morning.
    6.   Sally saw one too.

At issue is the referent expressed as one in sentence 6. It
is clearly given, being both low pitched and pronominalized.
However, the referent of one is different from that of an
eagle in 5, and it is given only because it is a particular
which is categorized in the same way as the other (see the
discussion above of how givenness is established). Thus it
may be valid to say that indefiniteness entails newness, except in cases where the indefinite referent is different from
the referent which established the givenness.

Turning to items that are definite, on the other hand,
there is no reason why they cannot be either given or new.
Definiteness and givenness often go together, as in those
typical cases where, after having said I hired a carpenter
yesterday I may go on to call him he or the carpenter, treat-

ing him in any case as given. But certainly it is common
enough to find sentences like I talked with the carpenter yesterday, where he is both definite and new. In such cases the
definiteness is established on some other basis than immediately prior mention, which would create givenness as well.
But we have seen that many other grounds for definiteness exist. In summary, of the four possible combinations the following three are all quite common: indefinite and new, definite and new, definite and given. The fourth combination,
indefinite and given, may be found only when the referent in
question is different from the referent which established the
givenness.

Subjects

What are they? There is a view, still widely held, that
the status of a noun as surface subject of a sentence is a
strictly syntactic status, with only indirect cognitive relevance at best. I would suggest that it is a priori unlikely
that a status which is given such prominence in English and
many other languages would not do some work for the language,
and would be only arbitrary and superficial in its function.
And just as a matter of procedure it would hardly seem advis-
able to discard the possibility that subjecthood has an important cognitive role before that possibility has been thoroughly explored. On the other hand, we should not be surprised to
find that this role has been confounded, in the course of a
language's history, with other roles. It could then be the
case, and in fact in some languages does seem to be the case,
that surface subject status is not associated consistently
with a single cognitive status. In English, however, I suspect that the association is more consistent than is often
believed.

So far as I can see at present, the best way to characterize the subject function is not very different from the
ancient statement that the subject is what we are talking a-
bout (see Sandman 1954 for a comprehensive review of what
people have said about subjects). Human knowledge appears to
consist, among other things, of a large number of cognitive
units which are our knowledge of particular individuals and
events. And concerning each of these particulars we know
certain things. We might like to imagine the knowledge we
have about a particular as if it were connected by arrows to
other parts of our knowledge, or as if it were imagery that
might be activated in association with the particular, or
both. But in any case it is likely that one of the main ways
in which new knowledge is communicated--perhaps even the only

way--is by identifying some particular as a starting point
and adding to the addressee's knowledge about it. Thus, if I
tell you John broke his arm yesterday, or if I tell you John
got knocked over by a bicycle yesterday, I am in both cases
taking the particular expressed as John as a starting point,
and providing you with new knowledge about that particular.
John is the hitching post for the new knowledge. It follows
that the primary result of your hearing these sentences is
that you know something more about John. It is true that you
also know something about John's arm and about a particular
bicycle, but it may be that such additional knowledge about
these other particulars is secondarily derived from what
these sentences communicated in the first instance. These
sentences package the information in such a way that it is
communicated as knowledge about John. Once the package is
unwrapped other things may be found inside, but knowledge
directly attached to the subject may be the most immediately
accessible.

We might call this the "adding-knowledge-about" hypothesis regarding the functioning of subjects. It would seem to
have some testable consequences. For example, if knowledge
derived from hearing a sentence is checked soon afterward, we
might expect that questions about the subject would be answered more quickly than those about other particulars involved in the sentence. Knowledge about the subject is what
was gained from the sentence; knowledge about the other particulars must somehow be computed. Perfetti and Goldman
(1974) recently performed what seems to be a relevant experiment of a different kind. They constructed pairs of paragraphs, in one of which a certain referent was mentioned frequently and another referent infrequently, and in the other
of which the frequency was reversed. For example, in one
pair of paragraphs about a pseudo-historical event in Poland
in the 17th century, one of the paragraphs gave frequent mention to the serfs and infrequent mention to a certain Baron
Wozjik. The other paragraph mentioned the baron frequently
and the serfs infrequently. The final sentence in each paragraph was The serfs rebelled against the baron. Subsequently
either the serfs or the baron were tested for their effectiveness as prompts for the retrieval of this final sentence.
As might be expected, when the preceding paragraph was mainly
about the serfs, the serfs were a more effective retrieval
prompt than the baron. But of interest here are the results
when the preceding paragraph was mainly about the baron. In
that case the effectiveness of the serfs and the baron as
retrieval prompts was equal. The serfs, of course, was the
subject of the target sentence, and these results suggest

that its subject provides a particularly effective prompt for a sentence, even when the preceding context has been predominantly about something else. The fact that this sentence was about the serfs was all that was needed. Other tests of a similar sort might involve the construction of a paragraph in which the frequency of two particulars was equal, but one was always the subject and the other never the subject. By the hypothesis advocated here, knowledge about the particular presented as subject should be more readily accessible. It would seem that experimental research on the consequences of subjecthood, though already begun in a number of the studies listed as references for this paper, can easily be extended in new and interesting ways.

How is subjecthood expressed? Other papers in this volume deal extensively with the expression of subjecthood in various languages. I will add a few observations from Dakota and Seneca which are relevant to the hypothesis that all languages take account of this status in some way. One fact that emerges clearly from the various studies that have been made is that languages differ considerably in the prominence which they give to subjecthood, so far as surface manifestations of it are concerned. English and some other European languages seem to be at one extreme, where subject status plays a crucial syntactic role. At the other extreme are languages like Dakota, where such prominent surface markings as agreement within the verb are determined by case status rather than subjecthood. Thus (using examples from the Lakota or Teton dialect) the prefix wa- is used in the verb for agreement with a first person singular agent, as in walówã "I sang" and thiyópa he wapátitã "I pushed the door." The prefix mã- is used for agreement with a first person singular patient (or sometimes beneficiary), as in mãpátitã "he pushed me," mãkhúže "I'm sick," or mãhĩxpaye "I fell down." It can be seen from these examples that what is the subject (judging from the English glosses, at least) is reflected sometimes as wa-, sometimes as mã-, since it is the agent-patient distinction rather than subjecthood which is expressed in these verbal prefixes.

Nevertheless, it is probable that Dakota and other languages of this type express subjecthood in other ways. One of these ways is evidently word order, which in Dakota has the superficial appearance of being rather "free." The following two sentences provide an example:

7.   šṹka he thaló he yúte.
      dog-the meat-the ate

8. thaló he šúka he yúte.
    meat-the dog-the ate

Examination of contexts and informants' reactions suggests
that the first word in each of these sentences is the subject, in the sense that it is the particular about which
knowledge is being added. If so, the closest English translations are The dog ate the meat for 7, and The meat was
eaten by the dog for 8, even though Dakota has no passive
construction as such. To translate 8 more literally as The
meat, the dog ate is misleading, in that such a sentence can
only be contrastive in English (see below), whereas in Dakota
it need not be. Observation of sentence prosody in Dakota
tends to support the conclusion that the first major item has
special (presumably subject) status, in that this item is
often followed by a special pausal and intonational boundary.

One other piece of evidence for the existence of subjects in Dakota is provided by the conjunction yũkhã, which
appears to be the equivalent of the English conjunction and
just in case the second of the coordinate clauses has a different subject from the first:

9. inãwapha   yũkhã wičháša wã thãkál nãžĩ.
    I-went-out and   man-a   outside was-standing
    I went out and a man was standing outside.

An interesting example in this conjunction is one given by
Boas and Deloria (1939:144):

10. thaté hiyú yũkhã čhaxóta woblú iyéye?.
     wind came and   ashes blew-away

The verb in the second clause is transitive, so that the
clause does not mean the ashes blew away, but rather it (the
wind) blew away the ashes, except that the latter translation
suggests that the subject of the second clause is the same as
that of the first. That would conflict with what is otherwise known about the function of yũkhã. Evidently čhaxóta
"ashes" is the subject of the second clause, since the wind
cannot be. The closest English translation must then be The
wind came up and the ashes were blown away, again using a
passive where Dakota expresses the subject status by placing
the word first in its clause and (in this case) using the
conjunction yũkhã.

Iroquois languages like Seneca seem to represent a transitional stage between languages like Dakota, which express
case status with verb agreement, and the European languages
which use verb agreement to express subject status. Thus,
Seneca is like Dakota in showing verb agreement with agent
and patient, rather than subject, in examples like:

11. oʔkatě̃no•tě̃ʔ
    "I sang"

12. ǒkǎhtaʔt (from *waʔwakahtaʔt)
    "I got full"

The -k- in 11 is a first person agent prefix, while the underlying or reconstructed *-wak- in 12 is a first person
patient prefix. However, Iroquois verbs are not as consistent as Dakota verbs in this respect. In particular, with a
number of intransitive Iroquois verbs there appears to be an
agent prefix agreeing with a patient noun. Such is the case
with the first person agent prefix -k- in oʔkǎʔsě̃ʔt "I fell"
or oʔka•tsě̃t "I got tired." What seems to be happening is
that agenthood and subjecthood have become partially confused, presumably because these two statuses more often than
not coincide. Thus, what was originally an agent prefix has
with some verbs become a subject prefix instead. I take this
Seneca evidence to provide an argument in favor of the functional or cognitive status of subjecthood. For it is hard to
see why agreement should be moving in the direction of marking subjects unless the status of being a subject has a value
worth marking.

How is subject status established and how long does it
last? These are questions without good answers at the present time. Certainly it is not overly difficult to "change
the subject" from one sentence or clause to another. On the
other hand there is surely some tendency for the same subject to be preserved from one sentence to another. In the
sequence of sentences Ted saw Harry yesterday. He told him
about the meeting. there is not much of a problem in interpreting the referents of he and him in the second sentence,
presumably at least in part because there is an expectation
that subject status will be preserved across sentences, all
other things being equal. As with the other phenomena that
have been discussed, there is need for examination of real
speech samples to see if anything can be said about the conditions under which subjects are established, preserved, and
changed.

Confusion of subject with given. Hornby (1971:1976)
characterizes the notion "topic" in the following ways: "The
part of the sentence which constitutes what the speaker is
talking about is being called the topic of the sentence in
the present work. The rest of the sentence, the comment,
provides new information about the topic." Assuming for the
moment that what Hornby is calling topic is more or less
equivalent to what I am calling subject, we might raise a
question about the appropriateness of saying that the rest of

the sentence provides "new information." Of course this is
at least as much a problem of the terminology given and new
as it is of the nature of subjecthood or topichood. But I
will use Hornby's statement as an excuse for pointing out
that there is no necessary correlation of subject status with
givenness, or for that matter of nonsubject status with newness. In the first case, we might imagine a situation in
which I heard a crash from the next room and shouted to the
person in there What happened? The answer might be The dog
knocked over the lamp, where the speaker's knowledge is communicated as new information about the dog, to be sure, but
where the dog is also new information in the sense of being
newly introduced into my consciousness. And of course there
are countless examples of something which is not the subject
being treated as given, as with the it in What happened to
the lamp? The dog knocked it over. In brief, although there
is some tendency for subjects to be given, that may be about
all that can be said about interactions between subject status and the given-new distinction.

In another study Hornby (1972) presents results which
need to be sorted out not only with respect to subject and
given status, but also with respect to contrastiveness. The
aim of the study was to investigate the "psychological subject," as opposed to the "logical" or "grammatical." The
subjects (of the experiment) were shown two pictures at a
time, and asked which of the pictures a certain sentence was
about. One sentence, for example, was The Indian is building
the igloo. Neither of the pictures, however, showed an
Indian building an igloo. One showed an Indian building a
tepee, and the other an Eskimo building an igloo. The subjects knew that neither sentence would be "exactly correct,"
but they were instructed to say "which picture the sentence
is about" even so. With active and passive sentences there
was a strong tendency to choose the picture containing the
thing referred to by the subject, in confirmation I believe
of the hypothesis that a subject is what a sentence is about.
But Hornby also used a variety of contrastive sentences: The
Indian is building the igloo, It is the Indian who is building the igloo, The one who is building the igloo is the
Indian, etc. In these the tendency was always to choose the
picture containing the item that was not the focus of contrast: in the examples just given, the igloo. The igloo is
not the subject in these sentences, and while it is given,
there is no reason to suppose that the Indian is not given
too. These results show that with contrastive sentences
there is a tendency to believe that the background of the
contrast, rather than the focus, is "what the sentence is

about." But again it is not clear that there is any good way to generalize from contrastive sentences to sentences of other kinds.

Topics, English Style

It is often said that in sentences like:

13. The pláy, John saw yésterday.

the referent expressed as the play is the topic (or "theme," as in Halliday 1967), or that the effect of placing this item at the beginning of the sentence is to "topicalize" it. But certainly these sentences, as well as similar ones like:

14. As for the pláy, John saw it yésterday.

are contrastive sentences. The so-called topic is simply a focus of contrast that has for some reason been placed in an unusual position at the beginning of the sentence. That appears to be true in general of English examples cited to illustrate topics or topicalization.

In the two examples just given each sentence has two foci of contrast. Sentence 13 can be imagined uttered in a context where the addressee is assumed to have had in mind certain possible pairings of theatrical events (a play, a movie, an opera) with certain times that John might be attending or have attended them. The speaker is providing the information that one correct pairing is of the play with yesterday. Sentence 14 is not very different, but appears to make it more explicit that the play is one item from a list of things that are being paired. As for why the play should be placed at the beginning of such contrastive sentences, it is evidently a given item from a list which is being run through (explicitly or implicitly), whereas yesterday is being brought in as new information to be paired with it. The opposite arrangement, Yésterday, John saw the pláy, evidently belongs in a context where the speaker (again either explicitly or implicitly) is running through a list of given times, and pairing with them various items that John saw at those times.

Not all examples of so-called topicalization in English contain a double contrast, however. A sentence like Jóhn I saw can be added to the list of possible ways of presenting John as a single focus of contrast, in addition to I saw Jóhn, It was Jóhn I saw, and The one I saw was Jóhn. Putting John first seems to tie him more closely to the immediately preceding context in some sense, but the subtle differences between these four ways of presenting a contrastive focus call for further study.

49

That a contrastive focus can be placed at the beginning of a sentence, out of its normal word order in English, is obviously a commonly observable phenomenon. The only question is whether it is a good idea to speak of such items as topics, with the implication that they are to be identified with topics in Chinese and other "topic-prominent" languages. Since in those languages there is no requirement that the topic be contrastive, and since in fact the role of what we might call "real topics" is quite a different one, I suggest that it would be a step forward to stop using the term for these English cases of contrastiveness.

Topics, Chinese Style

Having no direct knowledge of "topic-prominent" languages, I will restrict myself here to a few general and possibly misguided observations. The following are typical Mandarin sentences with topics, provided by Li and Thompson:

15. nèi-xie shùmu shù-shēn dà.
    those tree tree-trunk big

16. nèi-ge rén yáng míng George Zhang.
    that person foreign name George Zhang

To begin with, it is misleading to use, as some authors do, the standard English translations As for those trees, the trunks are big or As for that person, his foreign name is George Zhang if, as I understand to be the case, no contrastiveness need be involved in the Chinese sentences. In fact Chinese seems to express the information in these cases in a way that does not coincide with anything available in English. In other words there is no packaging device in English that corresponds to the Chinese topic device, and hence no fully adequate translation.

But what is such a topic? The examples I have seen do not fit precisely the characterization that a topic is "what the sentence is about," which I think applies better to English subjects and perhaps to Chinese subjects like shù-shēn and yáng míng in the above sentences. If one considers, for example, what bigness is predicated of in the first sentence, it is not "those trees," but rather their trunks. What the topics appear to do is to limit the applicability of the main predication to a certain restricted domain. The bigness of trunks applies within the domain of those trees. George Zhang being his foreign name applies within the domain of that person. Typically, it would seem, the topic sets a spatial, temporal, or individual framework within which the main predication holds. In English we can do something similar with certain temporal adverbs: <u>Tuesday I went to the</u> <u>dentist</u>. In Chinese apparently this device is generally available, whereas in English in most cases we must use pre- positions or other such devices: <u>In Dwinelle Hall people are</u> <u>always getting lost</u>. Chinese would not require the <u>in</u>. In brief, "real" topics (in topic-prominent languages) are not so much "what the sentence is about" as "the frame within which the sentence holds." In English we accomplish some- thing similar with adverbial phrases, or with a substantial reorganization: <u>The trunks of those trees are big</u>, or <u>Those</u> <u>trees have big trunks</u>. In the latter translation the Chinese topic has become the English subject, but the packaging is not really the same.

Topics as Premature Subjects

Still another candidate for the term topic stems from what may be considered a slight aberration in the timing of choices that must be made by a speaker as he puts what he has in mind into words (cf. Chafe: in press). A speaker must, for one thing, choose how to organize a chunk of knowledge at a certain level into a sentence. Having broken down the to- tal content of what he has in mind into more or less sentence- sized chunks, he has to make a variety of specific choices relative to the construction of the sentence itself. At the moment we are interested specifically in two of these: the choice of a case frame for the sentence, and the choice of one noun included in the case frame as the subject of the sentence.

It may be that normally these two choices are made more or less simultaneously. Even though they are partially inde- pendent, there is a necessary interaction between them. The choice of a case frame provides candidates for subject sta- tus, while conversely the choice of a subject constrains the possible case frames. That is, the case frame must include the noun which is to be the subject. I would suppose that, because of this mutual interdependence, a speaker is able to think simultaneously of the most effective framework of cases to express what he has in mind and the most effective way to package it in terms of subject. It is not unusual, however, for speakers to depart from this simultaneity by choosing-- and in fact uttering--the subject before the case frame has been chosen. I will illustrate this phenomenon with several examples extracted from tape recorded stories and conversa- tions in Caddo, an American Indian language presently spoken in Oklahoma:

17. k'án?. kámbah?wá•wa? háwwi dúhya?...
    ducks   they-said   OK   now

The first word was given the intonation of a complete sentence, although it is nothing but a single noun in isolation.
The speaker evidently decided that she wanted to talk about
the ducks before she decided precisely how they would be integrated into the case frame of a full sentence. Thus she
uttered the word for ducks as if it were a sentence in itself,
before she began the full sentence in which they were assigned
an agent role. Another possibility is that a hesitation particle of some sort will be inserted between the prematurely
uttered subject and the rest of the sentence, the particle
allowing the speaker a brief time in which to decide on how
to integrate this noun into the sentence. In Caddo story-
telling a ubiquitous particle is one that means something
like "it is said":

18. sa ?u?ǔs bah?na   sinátti? tucát?i•hahwah.
    Ms. Owl it-is-said then   she-spilled-it

Evidently the speaker decided Ms. Owl would be the subject
before she decided exactly what role Ms. Owl would play. Besides the use of the hesitation particle, an additional piece
of evidence for the prematurity of subject selection here is
the position of the word for "then," which normally appears
at the beginning of its clause, just as in English. Thus the
effect would be quite similar if an English speaker said
Ms. Owl...then she spilled it. Still another possibility is
that the prematurely uttered subject will ultimately not be
integrated at all into the case frame of the sentence that
follows, since the speaker has decided in the interim to
frame things in such a way that the original subject is excluded:

19. kisí? kahutáncǔnna?ah...na• sinátti? háh?i?ǔsnisa?.
    corn cobs   that then   she-smokes-it

The speaker is talking here about smoking leather. She evidently began with the idea of saying something like She uses
corn cobs (as fuel to produce the smoke), but hesitated,
changed her mind, and eventually uttered a sentence in which
corn cobs did not play an overt role.

One might think of calling such prematurely chosen subjects topics, or even speculating that the origin of topics
as distinct from subjects lies in this kind of aberration in
the timing of the processes of sentence construction. In
short, a topic would be--or might have originated as--a subject which is chosen too soon and not as smoothly integrated

into the following sentence. Some languages seem to allow
their speakers to do quite easily what was illustrated for
Caddo above. Caddo speakers seem to put sentences together
in this fashion quite frequently, and not to be disconcerted
by it. On this basis Caddo might be regarded as at least
one kind of "topic-prominent" language, but in quite a different sense from Chinese.

Antitopics

Having collected text materials in both languages, I
have been struck by what appears to be a significant difference between Caddo and Seneca speakers in respect to the timing of the two kinds of choices just discussed: of a subject
and of a case frame. Whereas Caddo speakers are prone to
decide on a subject before they have chosen a case frame,
Seneca speakers seem often to choose a case frame before they
have decided on a subject. This sequencing is possible because of the fact that verbs in Seneca, as noted above, do
not typically express agreement with the subject, but rather
with case roles. Thus it is possible for a Seneca speaker to
utter a sentence--or partial sentence--in which a commitment
as to case roles has been made, but in which there has not
yet been a commitment as to subject. The subject is then
added, after a hesitation:

20. káeoʔtaʔ næ·   hayǽ· ʔthak...   nĕ·kĕ· ne ʔŏ·kweh.
     gun   indeed he-used-to-use this   person

Here, as is most often the case, it is the agent which is
treated as subject, but there is nothing in the initial part
of the sentence--in the expression of the case frame--that
identifies the person as the subject as opposed to the gun.
If, after the hesitation, the speaker had said big gun or the
like, the gun would be what the sentence is about. In the
following there is a sentence-final intonation after the case
frame has been presented, but the speaker then goes on and
amplifies considerably the referent he is treating as subject:

21. ta ne? wai   næ·   hotíhsaʔŏh.   nĕ·kĕ·
     and   in-fact indeed they-used-it-up those

     n'a·tikĕhtsíshŏʔŏh. nĕ·kĕ· ʔŏkwahsoshæshŏʔkĕ́·ŏʔ...
     old-ones   those   our-ancestors

     ʔŏnĕhtsi thĕnŏ́henyŏk.
     long-ago they-used-to-live

Normal word order in Seneca is to place the subject first.
But as these examples illustrate a Seneca speaker may attach

53

less importance to stating the subject at the outset; there is an inclination to uttering it as an afterthought or "anti-topic" after the case frame has already been set forth. In this respect, then, Seneca appears to have a tendency which is a mirror-image of the tendency of Caddo speakers.

Point of View or Empathy

Kuno has pointed out (this volume) that in saying John hit his wife the speaker is describing the event "from John's side" (though not necessarily siding with John), whereas in saying Mary's husband hit her the event is described "from Mary's side." Kuno speaks of "empathy" with John or Mary, and notes further that a single sentence cannot contain more than one focus of empathy; that is why *Mary's husband hit his wife is a strange thing to say. Kuno and Kaburaki (in preparation) provide many further examples of how empathy is expressed in both English and Japanese. They also provide evidence of various kinds of interaction between the focus of empathy and other statuses which referents may have. For example, if the speaker himself plays a role in the sentence, he can be expected to empathize with himself, and empathy with the addressee takes precedence over empathy with a third party. Human referents are most likely to be empathized with. Status as the focus of empathy is likely to coincide with subject status, and perhaps with definiteness.

These and other considerations suggest that empathy or point of view is one more packaging phenomenon that can be added to our list. Its cognitive basis appears to lie in the fact that people are able to imagine themselves seeing the world through the eyes of others as well as from their own point of view, and that this ability has an effect on the use of language. I will not try here to go beyond the provocative introduction to this area that Kuno and Kaburaki provide.

Conclusion

In summary, I have suggested that a particular noun in a sentence—or more properly the idea expressed by that noun—in addition to occupying some "case" status, may occupy various "packaging" statuses selected by the speaker on the basis of his assessment of what the addressee's mind is capable of at the time. Six such statuses were discussed. The item in question will be either given or new, depending on the speaker's assessment of whether it is or is not in the addressee's consciousness at the time the sentence is spoken. It may on the other hand be a focus of contrast: selected by the speaker from a limited set of possible candidates as the correct choice for the role in question. It may be definite, depending on whether the speaker assumes that the addressee is able to identify the referent. It may be the subject, if the speaker treats it as the item about which knowledge is being added. It may be the topic, but just what that means seems to differ from language to language. In English topic status has to do with the sentence-initial position of certain contrastive items. In Chinese it may have to do with the establishment of a spatial, temporal, or personal frame or domain for an assertion which follows. And in Caddo it may be a matter of uttering a subject prematurely. Finally, the referent of a noun may be the individual with whom the speaker is empathizing. This is, of course, not necessarily a complete list of packaging phenomena, nor is it likely to stand as an adequate characterization of them all. It may, however, be of some use in sorting out the several factors which a speaker must manipulate as he speaks, so as to be able to get his message across with due consideration to the current state of his listener's mind.

ON THE SUBJECT OF TWO PASSIVES IN INDONESIAN*

by

Sandra Chung

* I am grateful to Arief Budiman, Ann Soeleiman, Wendarto
Atmadja, Johnny Basuki, and Ibrahim Hasan for providing native
speakers judgements on the Indonesian sentences. An earlier
version of this paper was read at UCSD, and I have incorporated some of the comments and suggestions of the audience. This
work was supported in part by the Department of Linguistics,
Harvard University.
    In order to agree with the secondary sources, I have written
the examples in the orthography used prior to the spelling re-
form of 1972. In this orthography, j = [y], tj = [č], dj =
[ǰ], nj = [ñ], sj = [š], and reduplication is indicated by the
number 2. My orthography differs from the standard orthography in that prepositions are separate words rather than clitics.

0. Bach (1971) has proposed that linguistic theory includes a set of universal rules which contain all of the
major syntactic transformations allowed in natural language.
Since his proposal, a number of linguists have attempted to
formulate specific universal rules and to constrain them in
substantive ways. In this paper I examine the formulation of
one universal rule--Passive--in light of some facts from
Bahasa Indonesia, a Western Austronesian language. I will
show that there are strong reasons for believing that Bahasa
Indonesia has two passives: a canonical passive, and a passive which has the surface form of an object topicalization.
Further, I will show that there are differences between the
two passives which cannot be handled easily by the substantive definitions of Passive which have recently been proposed.
Finally, I will point out some of the larger implications of
the two passives for universal grammar.

1. Bahasa Indonesia is an SVO language in which functional distinctions between NPs are indicated by prepositions. Some examples of ordinary transitive sentences are
given in 1:

1 a. Ali mem-batja buku itu.
        A. Trans-read book the
        "Ali read the book."

   b. Orang itu me-mukul Ali.
        man the Trans-hit A.
        "The man hit Ali."

As is usual in Indonesian, the subject and direct object NPs
are not marked with prepositions. The verb takes the transitive prefix _meng-_, which is optional and occurs only in active transitive sentences.

Corresponding to the active sentences of 1 are two constructions which are identified as "passive" by the secondary
sources (e.g., MacDonald and Dardjowidjojo 1967; Kwee 1965).
The first construction is:

2 a. Buku itu di-batja (oleh) Ali.
        book the Pass-read   by   A.
        "The book was read by Ali."

   b. Ali di-pukul (oleh) orang itu.
        A. Pass-hit   by   man the
        "Ali was hit by the man."

In the examples in 2, the underlying direct object has been
turned into a subject, and the underlying subject has been
removed to a prepositional phrase (with _oleh_ "by"). (The
preposition _oleh_ is optional if the underlying subject imme-

diately follows the verb; we will not be concerned with this optionality here.) In addition, the verb is marked with the passive prefix di-, which replaces the active transitive prefix meng-. I will refer to this construction as the canonical Passive.

The second construction is:

3 a. Buku itu saja batja.
       book the I read
       "I read the book." or "The book, I read."

   b. Ali saja pukul.
       A. I   hit
       "I hit Ali." or "Ali, I hit."

   c. Orang lelaki itu saja akan bunuh.
       man   male the I Fut kill
       "I'm going to kill that man." or "That man, I'm going to kill."

In the examples in 3, the underlying direct object has been moved to the beginning of its clause, and the underlying subject optionally cliticizes to the main verb. This optional cliticization is illustrated in 4, where the verb is preceded by an auxiliary:

4   Mobil itu dapat kita perbaiki.
       car the can we repair
       "We can repair the car." or "The car, we can repair."

And in 5, where the underlying subject occurs in a special proclitic form:

5   Buku itu ku-beli.
       book the I-buy
       "I bought the book." or "The book, I bought."
                          (MacDonald and Dardjowidjojo 1964:238)

In addition, the verb is not marked with the transitive prefix, but appears in its stem form. In what follows I will refer to this construction as Object Preposing.

Several secondary sources (e.g., Dyen 1964; Kwee 1965) suggest that the distribution of 2 and 3 is governed by the person of the underlying subject. Object Preposing is supposed to be used when the underlying subject is first or second person; the canonical Passive is supposed to be used in all other cases. Although this may have been the historical situation, it does not accurately reflect the use of 2 and 3 in the contemporary language. In contemporary Indonesian, the canonical Passive, 2, is not restricted to third persons, but is allowed for all types of underlying subjects

60

(MacDonald and Dardjowidjojo 1967:235). Thus in 6, the underlying subject is first person:

6 a. Mobil itu dapat di-perbaiki (oleh) kita.
        car the can Pass-repair   by   us
        "The car can be repaired by us."

   b. Buku itu di-batja (oleh) saja.
        book the Pass-read by   me
        "The book was read by me."

For many speakers, Object Preposing, 3, is not restricted to
first and second persons, but is allowed whenever the under-.
lying subject is a pronoun (Danoesoegondo 1971; MacDonald and
Dardjowidjojo 1967). Thus in 7, the underlying subject is
third person:

7 a. Buku itu dia batja.
        book the he read
        "He read the book." or "The book, he read."

   b. Ali mereka pukul.
        A. they hit
        "They hit Ali." or "Ali, they hit."

Compare 8a, where the underlying subject is a full noun, and
8b, where it is a proper name:

8 a. *Buku itu perempuan ini batja.
         book the   girl   this read
         (The book, this girl read.)

   b. *Buku itu Ali batja.
         book the A. read
         (The book, Ali read.)

If we disregard the traditional labels for 2-3, we are
left with the impression that Object Preposing and the canonical Passive are produced by completely different types of
syntactic operations. The canonical Passive has all the ear-
marks of a typical passive rule: the underlying direct object
looks like a subject, the underlying subject appears in a
prepositional phrase, and there is a special marking on the
verb. On the other hand, Object Preposing does not involve
any special passive morphology, and its underlying subject
does not seem to be displaced to an oblique case. Its surface form suggests that it is produced by some kind of object
topicalization.

This impression of the two rules is strengthened by
several other facts. The canonical Passive has the meaning
of a typical passive: it is semantically stative, and is
identified by native speakers as the equivalent of the English

passive. But Object Preposing has the meaning of a topicalization: it is semantically active, and is usually identified by native speakers as the equivalent of an active sentence or object topicalization in English.

Further, the canonical Passive places no restrictions on the definiteness of its derived subject (= underlying direct object) NP. In this respect, the derived subject resembles most subjects in Bahasa Indonesia, which can be definite or indefinite:

9 a. Medja di-pegang oleh anak perempuan.
        table Pass-touch by child female
        "A table was touched by the girl."

   b. Sekerandjang makanan di-bawa-kan untuk anak2.
        a-basket   food Pass-bring-Ben for children
        "A basket of food was brought for some children."

   c. Sepuluh dolar sudah di-bajar kepada tukang
        ten   dollar Perf Pass-pay   to   worker
        "Ten dollars was already paid to the

        rumput oleh saja.
        grass by   me
        gardener by me."

   d. Dokter itu di-periksa oleh saja.
        doctor the Pass-examine by me
        "The doctor was examined by me."

But Object Preposing requires that the preposed direct object be anaphoric or generic (in the sense of Kuno 1973). This requirement is crosslinguistically quite common for the topic, rather than the subject, of a sentence: (1)

10 a. *Medja saja pegang.
        table I   touch
        (A table, I touched.)

   b. *Seorang laki2 saja akan bunuh.
         a   man   I   Fut kill
        (A man, I'm going to kill.)

   c. *Sepuluh dolar saja bajar kepada anak perempuan.
          ten dollar I pay   to   child female
        (Ten dollars, I paid to the girl.)

   d. Dokter itu saja periksa.
        doctor the I examine
        "The doctor, I examined."

e. Ikan saja makan.
fish I eat
"Fish, I eat (generally)." (but * in the meaning:
A fish, I ate.)

And it is the same requirement as is found for a copying rule in Indonesian which is clearly a topicalization (Soemarmo 1970:92):

11 a. *Anak, dia mem-beli sepatu.
child he Trans-buy shoe
(A child, he bought shoes.)

b. Anak itu, dia mem-beli sepatu.
child the he Trans-buy shoe
"The child, he bought shoes."

Facts like these, when combined with the morphology, would seem to indicate that Object Preposing should be identified as a topicalization rather than a passive. In what follows, though, I will argue that this identification cannot be correct. I will do this by examining the status of Object Preposing with respect to six syntactic properties which are characteristic of passives but not of topicalizations. The behavior of Object Preposing with respect to all of these properties argues that it, like the canonical Passive, must be identified as a passive rule.

2. A typical syntactic characteristic of passives is that they are <u>subject-creating</u> (2): they turn a nonsubject into the subject of its clause. In contrast, topicalization rules are typically not subject-creating.

In this section, I will show that Object Preposing is subject-creating by examining its interaction with three syntactic rules. These rules—Subject-to-Object Raising, Equi, and Derived Subject Raising—apply to subjects, but they do not apply to any other types of NPs. They therefore provide a clear set of tests for determining whether or not Object Preposing turns its direct object into a subject NP.

2.1. To begin with, let us consider Subject-to-Object Raising. Sentential objects in Bahasa Indonesia are usually introduced by the complementizer <u>bahwa</u> "that":

12 a. Ali anggap bahwa soal itu beres.
A. believe that prob. the settled
"Ali believes that the problem is settled."

b. Mereka kira bahwa saja mem-batja buku itu.
they think that I Trans-read book the
"They think that I read that book."

This complementizer is optional:

    13 a.   Ali anggap soal itu beres.
            A. believe prob. the settled
            "Ali believes the problem is settled."

       b.   Mereka kira saja sudah mem-batja buku itu.
            they think I Perf Trans-read book the
            "They think I already read the book."

When the complementizer has been omitted, as in 13, the subject of the embedded clause can sometimes be raised to become
the direct object of the higher clause. The rule which ac-
complishes this raising is optional, and its application is
governed by the higher verb, which must be kira "think,"
sangka "believe," anggap "believe, consider," etc. Once Subject-to-Object Raising has applied, the raised NP can undergo
Passive in the higher clause (3):

    14 a.   Soal itu di-anggap beres.
            prob. the Pass-believe settled
            "The problem is believed to be settled."

       b.   Perempuan itu di-kira ((oleh) mereka) sudah
            woman   the Pass-think by   them   Perf
            "The woman was thought (by them) to have

                mem-batja buku itu.
                Trans-read book the
                read the book."

It is also available for other rules, such as Reflexive and
Heavy NP Shift, which apply to direct objects but not to subject NPs.

    Crucially, Subject-to-Object Raising can only operate on
NPs which are the syntactic subjects of their clause. The
rule applies to subjects of active sentences, as in 14. It
also applies to derived subjects of Passive sentences, as in
16, where buku ini "this book" has undergone Raising and then
Passive:

    15   Mereka anggap (bahwa) buku ini sudah di-batja
            they believe   that book this Perf Pass-read
            "They believe (that) this book has been read

                (oleh) perempuan itu.
                 by   woman   the
                by the woman."

    16   Buku ini di-anggap (oleh) mereka sudah
            book this Pass-believe by   them Perf
            "This book is believed by them to have

16, cont'd
    di-batja (oleh) perempuan itu.
    Pass-read by   woman   the
    been read by the woman."

However, the rule does not apply to direct objects, indirect
objects, or oblique NPs. In 17, for instance, buku ini is
the direct object of the embedded clause. Attempting to
raise and then passivize this NP produces the ungrammatical
18:

17   Mereka anggap (bahwa) perempuan itu sudah
        they believe that   woman   the Perf
        "They believe (that) the woman has

            mem-batja buku ini.
            Trans-read book this
            read this book."

18   *Buku ini di-anggap (oleh) mereka perempuan
        book this Pass-believe by   them   woman
        (This book is believed by them for the woman

            itu sudah (mem)-batja.
            the Perf Trans-read
            to have read.)

        What we are interested in is the effect of Subject-to-
Object Raising on embedded clauses which have undergone
Object Preposing:

19   Mereka anggap (bahwa) buku ini sudah saja batja.
        they believe   that   book this Perf I   read
        "They believe (that) this book, I have read."

Since Subject-to-Object Raising is limited to subjects,
whichever NP in 19 undergoes the rule can be identified as
the syntactic subject of the embedded clause. Significantly,
it is the underlying direct object of 19--not the underlying
subject--which is able to undergo the rule. Applying Raising
and then Passive to buku ini in 19 gives:

20   Buku ini di-anggap (oleh) mereka sudah saja
        book this Pass-believe by   them Perf   I
        "This book is believed by them to have been

            batja.
            read
            read by me."

But applying these rules to saja "I" produces an ungrammatical sentence:

65

21 *Saja di-anggap (oleh) mereka buku ini sudah batja.
    I Pass-believe by   them book this Perf read
    (I was believed by them this book to have read.)

Notice that 20 is ungrammatical if the underlying subject is not a pronoun, or if the verb does not occur in its
stem form. These facts establish that the embedded clause in
20 has in fact undergone Object Preposing. Further, 20 is
ungrammatical if the verb of the higher clause (here di-
anggap "he believed") does not allow Subject-to-Object Raising. This fact establishes that buku ini in 20 must have
undergone Subject-to-Object Raising and Passive, and not some
other combination of rules.

The fact that the underlying direct object in 20 undergoes a rule which is otherwise limited to subjects shows that
it is the syntactic subject of the Object Preposing construction. That is, Object Preposing, like the canonical Passive,
turns its underlying direct object into a subject NP.

2.2 Further evidence that Object Preposing creates subjects is provided by one version of Equi. This Equi applies
to adverbial complements of purpose, which are typically introduced by the complementizers supaja or sehingga "so that":

22 a. Dia datang sehingga dia dapat ber-tjakap2 dengan Ali.
       he   come   Comp   he can Intr-talk   with A.
       "He came so that he could talk with Ali."

   b. Dia meng-endarai mobil itu supaja dia dapat
       he Trans-drive car the Comp he can
       "He drove the car so that he could

           men-tjoba-nja.
           Trans-try-it
           test it."

When the subject of such a complement is coreferential with
some NP in the higher clause, it can optionally be deleted.
As a result of this deletion, the complementizer is replaced
by the preposition untuk "for":

23 a. Dia datang untuk ber-tjakap2 dengan Ali.
       he   come   for Intr-talk   with A.
       "He came to talk with Ali."

   b. Dia meng-endarai mobil itu untuk men-tjoba-nja.
       he Trans-drive car the for Trans-try-it
       "He drove the car to test it."

NPs which are deleted by Equi must be syntactic subjects
at the time when the rule applies. Thus Equi can delete subjects of active sentences, as in 23. It can also delete the

derived subject of a canonical Passive:

24   Saja mem-bawa surat itu supaja surat itu dapat
         I Trans-bring letter the Comp letter the can
      "I brought the letter so that the letter could

               di-batja (oleh) perempuan itu.
               Pass-read by   woman   the
               be read by the woman."

After Equi:

25   Saja mem-bawa surat itu untuk (dapat)
         I Trans-bring letter the for   can
      "I brought the letter to be

               di-batja (oleh) perempuan itu.
               Pass-read by   woman   the
               read by the woman."

In 26, on the other hand, the potential target for deletion is the direct object of an active sentence. That deletion of this NP is ungrammatical is shown in 27.

26   Saja mem-bawa surat itu supaja perempuan itu
         I Trans-bring letter the Comp   woman   the
      "I brought the letter so that the woman

               dapat mem-batja-nja.
               can Trans-read-it
               could read it."

27   *Saja mem-bawa surat itu untuk perempuan itu
         I Trans-bring letter the for   woman   the
      (I brought the letter for the woman

               dapat (mem)-batja.
               can Trans-read
               to read.)

Now when the complement has undergone Object Preposing, it is the underlying direct object rather than the underlying subject which serves as the target for deletion. Thus from 28:

28 a. Mereka mem-beli ikan itu supaja ikan itu dapat
         they Trans-buy fish the Comp fish the can
      "They bought the fish so that the fish,

               saja masak.
               I   cook
               I could cook."

b. Kami mem-bawa mobil itu supaja mobil itu
   we Trans-bring car the   Comp car   the
   "We brought the car so that the car,

       mereka perbaiki.
       they   repair
       they would repair."

Equi deletes the underlying direct object to give:

29 a. Mereka mem-beli ikan itu untuk (dapat) saja masak.
      they Trans-buy fish the for   can   I   cook
      "They bought the fish to be cooked by me."

   b. Kami mem-bawa mobil itu untuk mereka perbaiki.
      we Trans-bring car   the for   they   repair
      "We brought the car to be repaired by them."

But from a sentence like 30:

30 Saja pergi supaja mobil itu dapat kau perbaiki.
    I   go   Comp   car   the can   you repair
    "I went so that the car, you could repair."

deletion of the underlying subject is not allowed:

31 *Saja pergi untuk mobil itu (dapat) perbaiki.
    I   go   for   car   the can   repair
    (I went for the car to repair.)

Notice that 29 is ungrammatical if the underlying subject is
not a pronoun, or if the verb does not occur in its stem
form. As before, these facts establish that Object Preposing
must have applied in the embedded clause.

    Since Equi can only delete syntactic subjects, sentences
28-31 argue that Object Preposing turns the underlying direct
object into the subject of its clause. In this respect, the
interaction of Object Preposing with Equi is exactly like its
interaction with Subject-to-Object Raising.

    2.3 A third argument that Object Preposing creates sub-
jects is provided by a process which I refer to as Derived
Subject Raising. This rule operates on complex sentences of
the type:

32 a. Sulit bagi kami untuk mem-perbaiki mobil ini.
      hard for us   for   Trans-repair car   this
      "It's hard for us to repair this car."

   b. Sangat menjenangkan bagi anak2 untuk
      very   nice   for children for
      "It's very nice for the children to

32b, cont'd

        mem-batja buku ini.
        Trans-read book this
        read this book."

c. Mudah buat dia untuk men-dapat-kan langganan.
     easy for him for Trans-find-Ben customer
    "It's easy for him to find customers."

In 32, the predicate adjectives <u>sulit</u> "hard," <u>menjenangkan</u> "nice," and <u>mudah</u> "easy" are modified by an embedded clause. The subject of the embedded clause occurs in an upstairs prepositional phrase (4), and the rest of the embedding is introduced by the preposition <u>untuk</u> (5).

Under certain conditions, an NP from the embedded clause can be raised to become the subject of the adjective. These conditions are rather restrictive; as 33 shows, subjects of active sentences cannot undergo the rule:

33 a. *Kami sulit untuk mem-perbaiki mobil ini.
      we hard for Trans-repair   car   this
     (We are hard to repair this car.)

    b. *Anak2 sangat menjenangkan untuk mem-batja buku ini.
       children very   nice   for Trans-read book this
      (The children are very nice to read this book.)

And, as 34 shows, direct objects, indirect objects, and oblique NPs cannot undergo the rule either:

34 a. *Mobil ini sulit (bagi kami) untuk (mem)-perbaiki.
       car this hard for   us   for Trans-repair
     (This car is hard (for us) to repair.)

    b. *Hasan mudah untuk mem-beli hadiah (untuk).
       H. easy   for Trans-buy present   for
     (Hasan is easy to buy presents for.)

    c. *Danau ini menjenangkan untuk ber-enang (di).
       lake this   nice   for Intr-swim   in
     (This lake is nice to swim in.)

If the embedded clause has undergone the canonical Passive, however, the derived subject can be raised to become the subject of the adjective. Thus from 32, it is possible to derive (6):

35 a. Mobil ini sulit untuk di-perbaiki (oleh) kami.
      car this hard   for Pass-repair   by   us
    "This car is hard to be repaired by us."

b. Buku ini sangat menjenangkan bagi anak2 untuk
   book this very   nice   for children for
   "This book is very nice for the children to

   di-batja.
   Pass-read
   to read.

c. Langganan mudah untuk di-dapat-kan-nja.
   customer   easy   for Pass-find-Ben-(by) him
   "Customers are easy to be found by him."

Sentences like these suggest that it is derived subjects--
and only derived subjects--which are allowed to undergo
Derived Subject Raising.

Consider now the interaction of Derived Subject Raising
with the Object Preposing of 3. When Object Preposing has
applied to the embedded clauses in 32, the underlying direct
object can be raised to become the subject of the adjective:

36 a. Mobil ini sulit untuk kami perbaiki.
      car this hard for us   repair
      "This car is hard to be repaired by us."

   b. Langganan mudah untuk dia dapat-kan.
      customer   easy   for he find-Ben
      "Customers are easy to be found by him."

But the underlying subject is not allowed to undergo this
rule:

37 a. *Kami sulit untuk mobil ini perbaiki.
       we   hard for   car this repair
      (We are hard for this car to repair.)

   b. *Dia mudah untuk langganan dapat-kan.
       he   easy for   customer find-Ben
      (He is easy for customers to find.)

Notice that 36 is ungrammatical if the underlying subject is
not a pronoun, or if the verb does not occur in its stem
form. These facts show that the embedded clause in 36 has in
fact undergone Object Preposing.

Sentences 34-37 show that the underlying direct object
of Object Preposing functions exactly like the derived subject of a canonical Passive; for these two NPs are the only
types of NPs for which Derived Subject Raising is allowed.
Sentences 34-37, then, provide a particularly satisfying argument that Object Preposing turns its direct object into a
(derived) subject NP.

3. Another syntactic characteristic which differentiates passives from topicalizations is cyclicity: passives are
typically cyclic, but topicalizations are not. In this section, I show that Object Preposing is cyclic on the basis of
its interaction with Subject-to-Object Raising, Equi, and
Derived Subject Raising.

In order to show that Object Preposing is cyclic, it is
first necessary to establish the cyclicity of the other
rules. I will begin with Subject-to-Object Raising.
Consider the following sentences:

38   Mereka anggap buku itu sudah di-batja oleh Ali.
       they believe book the Perf Pass-read by A.
       "They believe this book to have been read by Ali."

39   Perempuan itu di-anggap (oleh mereka) sudah
       woman   the Pass-believe by them   Perf
       "The woman is believed (by them) to have

          mem-batja buku itu.
          Trans-read book the
          read the book."

40   Buku itu di-anggap (oleh mereka) sudah di-batja
       book the Pass-believe by   them   Perf Pass-read
       "The book is believed (by them) to have been read

          oleh Ali.
          by   A.
          by Ali."

Sentences 38-40 give examples of different derivations involving Subject-to-Object Raising and Passive. In 38, Passive
applies before Subject-to-Object Raising; in 39, it applies
after Subject-to-Object Raising; in 40, the rules apply in
the order Passive-Subject-to-Object-Raising-Passive. In
principle, there is no limit to the number of times that one
of these rules can apply to the output of the other. So we
have sentences like:

41   Koran itu di-kira (oleh) Ani di-anggap
       newsp. the Pass-think by   A. Pass-believe
       "The newspaper is thought by Ani to be believed

          (oleh) mereka sedang di-batja (oleh) Ali.
          by   them Prog Pass-read by   A.
          by them to be being read by Ali."

Sentences 38-40, and particularly 41, show that the interaction of Passive and Subject-to-Object Raising cannot be
accounted for if these syntactic rules are arranged in a
single linear list.

Sentences 38-41 leave open the possibility that the rules could be completely unordered with respect to each other. In this case, Subject-to-Object Raising and Passive would be able to apply freely to each other's outputs, and all of 38-41 would be produced. However, an argument against this alternative is provided by the interaction of Subject-to-Object Raising and Reflexive:

42   Saja me-lihat diri saja di dalam air.
       I Trans-see self my in-side water
       "I saw myself in the water."

As 42 shows, reflexive direct objects in Indonesian consist of diri "self" plus an optional possessive pronoun. The rule which produces these reflexives is obligatory:

43   *Saja me-lihat saja di dalam air.
       I Trans-see me in-side water
       (I saw me in the water.)

Further, it only applies when antecedent and anaphor are within the same clause:

44 a.   *Saja anggap (bahwa) Ali me-lihat diri saja
         I believe that   A. Trans-see self my
         (I believe (that) Ali saw myself

             di dalam air.
             in-side water
             in the water.)

   b.   *Dia meng-atakan bahwa diri-nja men-tjuri
         he Trans-say   that self-his Trans-steal
         (He said that himself stole

             uang itu.
             money the
             the money.)

45 a.   Saja anggap (bahwa) Ali me-lihat saja di dalam air.
         I believe that   A. Trans-see me in-side water
         "I believe (that) Ali saw me in the water."

   b.   Dia meng-atakan bahwa dia men-tjuri uang itu.
         he Trans-say   that he Trans-steal money the
         "He$_i$ says that he$_i$ stole the money."

Compare 44 with 46, where antecedent and anaphor have been turned into clausemates by Subject-to-Object Raising, and Reflexive is allowed:

46   Perlu orang2-nja me-rasa diri ber-satu.
        nec.   men-Spec Trans-feel self Intr-one
        "The people must feel themselves united."
                    (MacDonald and Dardjowidjojo 1967:233)

Consider now the interaction of Reflexive and Subject-to-Object Raising in a sentence like:

47   *Mereka anggap bahwa dia$_i$ telah bunuh dia$_i$.
        they believe that he Perf kill him
        (They believe that he$_i$ has killed him$_i$.)

If the rules are completely unordered with respect to each other, then there should be derivations in which Subject-to-Object Raising and Passive apply before Reflexive in 47. Then, the environment for Reflexive would be destroyed before the rule has had a chance to apply. Sentence 48 shows, though, that this sort of derivation is not allowed:

48   *Dia$_i$ di-anggap telah bunuh dia$_i$.
        he Pass-believe Perf kill him
        (He$_i$ is believed to have killed him$_i$.)

49   Dia$_i$ di-anggap telah bunuh diri$_i$.
        he Pass-believe Perf kill self
        "He$_i$ is believed to have killed himself$_i$."

The contrast of 48 and 49 shows that Subject-to-Object Raising must be prevented from applying on a higher clause before Reflexive has had a chance to apply on a lower clause. It follows from this that the rules cannot be completely unordered with respect to each other. Further, since the behavior of Reflexive and Subject-to-Object Raising cannot be explained by extrinsic ordering (cf. 46), sentences 48-49 argue that these rules must be applied cyclically. That is, Subject-to-Subject Raising is a cyclic rule.

Once the cyclicity of Subject-to-Object Raising has been established, it is fairly easy to show that Equi and Derived Subject Raising are also cyclic rules. Sentence 50, for instance, is a sentence in which Equi applies before Subject-to-Object Raising:

50   Orang itu di-anggap pergi untuk ber-bitjara
        man the Pass-believe go   for Intr-talk
        "The man is believed to have gone to talk

        dengan Ani.
        with A.
        with Ani."

Sentence 51 is one in which Derived Subject Raising applies before Subject-to-Object Raising:

51   Mobil ini di-anggap sulit untuk di-perbaiki.
        car this Pass-believe hard for Pass-repair
        "This car is believed to be hard to be repaired."

Since there are derivations in which these rules feed Subject-to-Object Raising, and Subject-to-Object Raising is cyclic, Equi and Derived Subject Raising must also be cyclic.

The cyclicity of Object Preposing follows automatically from the cyclicity of these other rules. As we have seen, Object Preposing must precede Subject-to-Object Raising, Equi, and Derived Subject Raising in order to produce sentences like 20, 29, and 36. Since all of these rules have been shown to be cyclic, and Object Preposing precedes them, Object Preposing must also be a cyclic rule. In this respect it resembles a passive, not a topicalization.

4. A third syntactic characteristic of passives is that they are typically clause-bounded. In contrast, topicalizations are typically unbounded.

Sentences 52-53 show that Object Preposing, like other passives, is clause-bounded:

52 a.   Saja men-tjoba (untuk) mem-bunuh orang itu.
        I Trans-try for Trans-kill man the
        "I tried to kill that man."

   b.   Saja ingin (supaja) laki2 itu men-emui orang itu.
        I want Comp man the Trans-meet pers. the
        "I want that the man meet that person."

   c.   Saja tanja mereka apakah kita harus mem-perbaiki
        I ask them Q we must Trans-repair
        "I asked them if we should repair

                lontjeng ini.
                clock   this
                repair this clock."

After Object Preposing:

53 a.   *Orang itu saja tjoba (untuk) (mem)-bunuh.
        man the I try for Trans-kill
        (That man, I tried to kill.)

   b.   *Orang itu saja ingin (supaja) laki2 itu temui.
        pers. the I want Comp man the meet
        (That person, I wanted the man to meet.)

   c.   *Lontjeng ini saja tanja mereka apakah harus
        clock this I ask them Q must
        (This clock, I asked them if we

kita perbaiki.
we   repair
should repair.)

5. A fourth syntactic characteristic of passives is
that they are typically nonroot transformations, in the sense
of Emonds (1970), as refined by Hooper and Thompson (1973).
Topicalizations, on the other hand, are typically root transformations.

As pointed out by Green (1974) and Aissen (1975), it is
difficult to characterize exactly where root transformations
do and do not apply. In general, though, it seems to be true
that root transformations do not occur in complements of factive verbs like <u>regret, be surprised</u>, <u>be strange</u> (Hooper and
Thompson 1973:479). Further, root transformations which involve leftward movement of an NP (such as topicalization or
left dislocation) typically do not occur in restrictive relatives, or indirect questions (cf. Aissen 1975); nor can an NP
moved by such a rule be raised, deleted, or relativized.

Significantly, Object Preposing is subject to none of
these restrictions. In 54, Object Preposing applies in the
complement of a factive verb:

54 a. Mereka ter-kedjut bahwa anak itu saja pukul.
         they Accid-surp. that child the I   hit
       "They were surprised that the child, I hit."

   b. Mereka menj-esali bahwa kesalahan ini saja temukan.
         they Trans-sorry that error this I   find
       "They regret that this error, I found."

In 55, it applies in a restrictive relative:

55 a. Ini-lah rumah di mana buku tersebut saja
       this-Emp house in which? book aforem. I
       "This is the house in which that book, I

            tinggal-kan.
            leave-Caus
            left."

   b. Tidak seorang pun suka kepada wanita kepada siapa
       not   someone even like to   woman   to   who?
       "No one likes the woman to whom

            bunga itu saja beri-kan.
            flower the I   give-Ben
            whom the flowers, I gave."

In 56, it applies in an indirect question:

56 a.   Dia tidak tahu apa sepeda motor itu sudah saja
     he   not know Q bicycle motor the Perf I
     "He doesn't know if the motorcycle, I've

        djual, atau tidak.
        sell   or   not
        sold, or not."

  b.   Saja tanja mereka apakah lontjeng ini harus kita
     I   ask   them   Q   clock this must we
     "I asked them if this clock, we should

        perbaiki.
        repair
        repair."

Further, once Object Preposing has applied, the preposed
direct object can be raised (sentence 36) and deleted by Equi
(sentence 29). It can also be relativized (7):

57   Mobil jang akan saja perbaiki adalah Mercedes.
     car Comp Fut I   repair   be   M.
     "The car that I'm going to repair is a Mercedes."

The ability of Object Preposing to occur in 54-57 places it
in sharp contrast with most root transformations, which do
not occur freely in embedded clauses. Sentences 54-57, then,
argue that Object Preposing--like most passives--is a nonroot
transformation.

    6. A fifth syntactic characteristic which differenti-
ates passives from topicalizations is government: passives
are typically governed rules, but topicalizations are typically not governed.

    Governed rules have been characterized as rules with
lexical exceptions (Lakoff 1965), or rules whose application
is determined by semantic as well as syntactic categories
(Green 1971). Under either of these definitions, sentence
59 shows that the canonical Passive is governed:

58 a.   Saja ingin buku ini.
     I   want book this
     "I want this book."

  b.   Kamu mirip ibu-mu.
     you resemble mother-your
     "You resemble your mother."

  c.   Mereka mem-punjai mobil ini.
     they Trans-own   car this
     "They own this car."

59 a. *Buku ini di-ingin (oleh) saja.
     book this Pass-want by   me
     (This book is wanted by me.)

    b. *Ibu-mu   di-mirip (oleh) kamu.
     mother-your Pass-res. by you
     (Your mother is resembled by you.)

    c. *Mobil ini di-punjai (oleh) mereka.
     car this Pass-own   by   them
     (This car is owned by them.)

Although the sentences in 58 meet the structural description of Passive, the rule fails to apply. Further, there is some ill defined sense (which I will not discuss here) in which we would expect Passive not to apply to these verbs.

    Like the canonical Passive, Object Preposing is also a governed rule:

60 a. *Buku ini saja ingin.
     book this I want
     (This book, I want.)

    b. *Ibu-mu   kamu mirip.
     mother-your you resemble
     (Your mother, you resemble.)

    c. *Mobile ini mereka punjai.
     car   this they   own
     (This car, they own.)

    Significantly, although the canonical Passive and Object Preposing are both governed, the classes of verbs which govern them appear to be distinct. Many verbs of emotion, realization, and knowledge allow Object Preposing, but are marginal or ungrammatical in the canonical Passive. Thus from sentences like:

61 a. Saja suka anak lelaki itu.
     I   like child male the
     "I like that boy."

    b. Saja pertjaja surat kabar itu.
     I   trust   letter news the
     "I trust the newspapers."

    c. Mereka tahu semua restoran ini.
     they know all   restaurant this
     "They are acquainted with all these restaurants."

    d. Saja lupa pajung kami.
     I forget umbrella out
     "I forgot our umbrella."

it is possible to derive:

62 a. Anak lelaki itu saja suka.
    child male the I   like
    "That boy, I like."

   b. Surat kabar itu saja pertjaja.
    letter news the I   trust
    "The newspapers, I trust."

   c. Semua restoran ini mereka tahu.
    all restaurant this they know
    "All these restaurants, they're acquainted with."

   d. Pajung kami saja lupa.
    umbrella our I forget
    "Our umbrella, I forgot."

but not (8):

63 a. *Anak lelaki itu di-suka (oleh) saja.
    child male the Pass-like by   me
    (The boy is liked by me.)

   b. ??Surat kabar itu di-pertjaja (oleh) saja.
    letter news the Pass-trust   by   me
    (The newspapers are trusted by me.)

   c. *Semua restoran ini di-tahu (oleh) mereka.
    all restaurant this Pass-know by   them
    (All these restaurants are known by them.)

   d. *Pajung kami di-lupa (oleh) saja/John.
    umbrella our Pass-forget by   me/John
    (Our umbrella was forgotten by me/John.)

Sentences like 62–63 suggest that one factor in the government of the two rules may be whether or not the direct object is directly affected by the action. Passive seems to be limited to verbs whose direct objects are directly affected by the action; Object Preposing does not seem to have this requirement.

    A few verbs allow the canonical Passive, but do not allow Object Preposing. The verbs of this type which I have found do not form a semantically coherent class, and the reasons why they fail to undergo Object Preposing are obscure (9):

64 a. Saja tidak mem-pertjajai tetangga kami.
    I   not Trans-trust   neighbor our
    "I don't trust our neighbors."

b. Kita rusak mobil itu.
   we wreck car the
   "We wrecked the car (on purpose)."

After Passive:

65 a. Tetangga kami tidak di-pertjajai (oleh) saja.
      neighbor our not Pass-trust by me
      "Our neighbors are not trusted by me."

b. Mobil itu di-rusak (oleh) kita.
   car the Pass-wreck by us
   "The car was wrecked by us (on purpose)."

After Object Preposing:

66 a. *Tetangga kami saja tidak pertjajai.
      neighbor our I not trust
      (Our neighbors, I don't trust.)

b. *Mobil itu kita rusak.
   car the we wreck
   (The car, we wrecked (on purpose).)

It seems, then, that Object Preposing and the canonical Passive are governed by distinct classes of verbs, although these classes intersect to a large extent. This point will be useful in Section 8. For the moment, we are only interested in the fact that Object Preposing is a governed rule; in this respect it behaves like a passive, not like a topicalization.

7. Finally, passives can be distinguished from topicalizations by their interaction with discourse phenomena. It has been observed that sentences generally do not undergo more than one discourse-related operation at a time (10). For instance, once one constituent of a sentence has been topicalized, it is generally impossible to topicalize or focus another:

67 a. *Harriet, bagels she likes. (Topicalization and Left Dislocation)

b. *Rosie, what she was doing was amusing herself. (Left Dislocation and Wh-Clefting)

c. *Marie, easy though he is to get along with, Joe refuses to speak to.

d. *Easy though he is to get along with, Marie Joe refuses to speak to. (Attribute Preposing and Topicalization)

79

Presumably, some functional explanation can be found for the ungrammaticality of sentences like 67.

It remains to be seen whether all discourse-conditioned rules obey the constraint illustrated by 67. Something like it, though, seems to be responsible for the interaction of topicalization and focus processes in Indonesian. In Indonesian, subjects and direct objects can be topicalized by a process resembling Left Dislocation in English. The topicalized NP is copied, moved to the left, and separated from the rest of the sentence by an intonation break (11):

68 a.   Anak itu, dia akan datang besok.
        child the   he Fut   come tomorrow
        "The child, he's coming tomorrow."

   b.   Dokter itu, saja periksa dia.
        doctor the   I   examine him
        "The doctor, I examined him."

Subjects and direct objects can be focused by a rule which moves them to the left and separates them from the rest of the sentence with **jang**. This process is available for ordinary nouns and Wh-words:

69 a.   Kamu jang men-ulis buku itu.
        you Comp Trans-write book the
        "It's you who wrote the book."

   b.   Apa jang kamu beli untuk anak2?
        what? Comp you buy for children
        "What was it that you bought for the children?"

Finally, prepositional phrases can be focused by a rule which moves them to the left, gives them emphatic stress, and separates them from the rest of the sentence by an intonation break. This process is also available for Wh-words:

70 a.   Di dalam kerandjang, kita taroh sajur2an.
        in-side   basket   we   put   vegetables
        "Inside the basket, we put the vegetables."

   b.   Kapada siapa, kamu beri-kan kembang2 itu?
        to   who? you give-Ben flowers   the
        "To whom did you give those flowers?"

Now when a subject or direct object has been topicalized or focused, it is impossible to focus on any other constituent in the sentence. Thus in sentences like:

71 a.   Surat ini jang akan kami kirim kepada John.
        letter this Comp Fut we   send   to   J.
        "It's this letter that we're going to send to John."

b. Sajur2an jang kita taroh di dalam kerandjang.
   vegetables Comp we put in-side   basket
   "It's the vegetables that we put inside the basket."

c. Permen itu jang dia ambil dari anak2.
   candy the Comp he take from children
   "It's that candy that he took away from the children."

the prepositional phrase cannot be focused to give (12):

72 a. *Kepada John, surat ini jang akan kami kirim.
       to   J.   letter this Comp Fut we send
       (To John, it's this letter that we're going to send.)

   b. *Di dalam kerandjang, sajur2an jang kita taroh.
       in-side   basket   vegetables Comp we put
       (Inside the basket, it's the vegetables that we put.)

   c. *Dari anak2, permen itu jang dia ambil.
       from children candy the Comp he take
       (From the children, it's that candy that he took
       away.)

And in sentences like:

73 a. Si Hasan, dia tidur di mana?
      pers. H. he sleep at where?
      "Hasan, where's he sleeping?"

   b. Anak itu, kamu pukul dia di mana?
      child the you hit him at where?
      "The child, where did you hit him?"

   c. Anak itu, dia mem-beli sepatu untuk Ali.
      child the he Trans-buy shoe for   A.
      "The child, he bought shoes for Ali."

focusing the prepositional phrase is not allowed:

74 a. *Di mana si Hasan, dia tidur?
       at where? pers. H. he sleep
       (Where Hasan, is he sleeping?)

   b. *Di mana anak itu, kamu pukul dia?
       at where? child the you hit him
       (Where the child, did you hit him?)

   c. *Untuk Ali, anak itu, dia mem-beli sepatu.
       for   A. child the he Trans-buy shoe
       (For Ali, the child, he bought shoes.)

The constraint which prevents 72 and 74 applies to topicalization and focus processes, but it does not extend to all
leftward movement rules. Passive, for instance, involves

leftward movement, but it can cooccur with a focused prepositional phrase:

75 a. Kepada siapa, bunga itu di-beri-kan?
       to   who? flower the Pass-give-Ben
       "To whom were those flowers given?"

   b. Di mana sajur2an itu di-letakkan?
       at where? veg.   the Pass-put
       "Where were the vegetables put?"

   c. Kepada John, pajung itu di-pindjam-kan.
       to   J.   umbrella the Pass-lend-Ben
       "To John, the umbrella was lent."

Since topicalizations and focus rules are discourse-conditioned, but Passive is not, it seems that the contrast of 72,
74 and 75 is due to some constraint on the applicability of
discourse operations. This constraint may or may not be the
same as the one which excludes sentences like 67, or the
English translations of 72 and 74.

The contrast of 72, 74, and 75 provides a sixth test for
determining the syntactic character of Object Preposing. If
Object Preposing is a topicalization, then it can be expected
to obey the same constraint as the rules in 72 and 74; if not,
it can be expected to disregard the constraint, like Passive.
In fact, Object Preposing can cooccur with a focused prepositional phrase:

76 a. Kepada siapa, bunga itu kau beri-kan?
       to   who? flower the you give-Ben
       "To whom those flowers, did you give?"

   b. Di dalam kerandjang, sajur2an itu kita taroh.
       in-side   basket   vegetables the we put
       "Inside the basket, we put the vegetables."

   c. Dari anak2, permen itu kita ambil.
       from children candy the we take
       "From the children, the candy we took."

In this respect it behaves like a passive, not like a topicalization.

8. The evidence of the preceding sections establishes
that Object Preposing behaves syntactically like a passive,
not like a topicalization. Like other passives, Object Preposing creates derived subjects which can undergo Subject-to-
Object Raising, Equi, and Derived Subject Raising. Like
other passives, it is a cyclic, clause-bounded, governed rule
which applies freely in matrix and embedded clauses. Finally,
like passives but unlike topic or focus rules, it fails to

obey the constraint on discourse operations discussed in Section 7.

These facts would be difficult to account for if Object Preposing were identified as a topicalization. However, if Object Preposing is identified as a passive, they can be explained in a natural and unified way. The syntactic evidence therefore argues that—despite its morphology and active meaning—Object Preposing must be recognized as a type of passive rule.

Conceivably, it might be proposed that Object Preposing is not a separate rule, but is simply the canonical Passive plus some minor, housekeeping rule (13). Such a proposal would claim that Object Preposing behaves like a passive because it has undergone the same syntactic operations as the canonical Passive of sentence 2. However, we have seen that Object Preposing and the canonical Passive differ in several important respects: they differ in meaning (active vs. stative), they have different definiteness requirements for their direct objects, and they are governed by distinct, though intersecting, classes of verbs. In order to describe these differences, a proposal which claimed that the two rules were versions of one passive would have to resort to numerous ad hoc complications.

We can conclude, then, that Object Preposing and the canonical Passive must be identified as separate syntactic rules. Indonesian therefore has two passives: a canonical Passive, and a passive with the surface form of an object topicalization.

It follows from this that any universal characterization of Passive must be able to account for the syntactic properties of Object Preposing. It must also be able to account for the presence of two separate passives in a single language. Below, I will try to show that these requirements are problematic for the substantive definitions of Passive which have recently been proposed. I will consider two definitions in particular: Langacker and Munro's (ms.) characterization of Passive as a cluster of syntactic/semantic properties, and Perlmutter and Postal's (forthcoming) characterization of Passive as a universal rule.

9. In a recent paper (ms.), Langacker and Munro propose that Passive is a (universal) cluster of syntactic/semantic properties. These are:

77 Langacker and Munro's Definition of Passive:

    i.   embedding to a higher stative-existential predicate BE

   ii. unspecified underlying subject

iii. topicalization of underlying direct object

Langacker and Munro state that there "is no necessary relation among these properties," so that a construction may exhibit some of the properties but not others. They identify
constructions with all three properties as prototypical passives, and constructions with two of the three as semipassives.
    This formulation makes several interesting claims about
the derivation of passive sentences; in particular, it claims
that passives are not derived by rule, but are a separate
underlying structure, and that promotion of the direct object
to subject is not an absolute requirement. These claims allow Langacker and Munro to include in the class of passives
some previously recalcitrant constructions (notably impersonal
passives). Although these claims merit serious consideration,
I will not deal with them here. Instead, I will concentrate
on the question of whether the two passives of Indonesian
satisfy a weaker version of Langacker and Munro's proposal.
In this version, "embedding to a stative-existential predicate BE" corresponds to stative meaning, and "unspecified
underlying subject" corresponds to the possibility of unspecified agent deletion. The resulting cluster of properties:

78 Langacker and Munro's Definition of Passive (revised):

    i.   stative meaning
    ii. possibility of unspecified agent deletion
    iii. topicalization of underlying direct object

is similar to some traditional definitions of Passive (e.g.,
Lyons 1971:376) (14).
    There is no question that the canonical Passive of 2
qualifies as a passive under this definition. The canonical
Passive is semantically stative; it topicalizes the underlying direct object by promoting it to subject; and it allows
unspecified agent deletion:

79 a. Orang itu di-pukul.
        man the Pass-hit
        "The man was hit."

    b. Semua surat2 di-letakkan di atas medja.
        all   letters Pass-put   on top table
        "All the letters were put on the table."

However, the status of Object Preposing under this definition
is less clear.
    To begin with, sentences which have undergone Object
Preposing are semantically active rather than stative (cf.
Section 1). Such sentences are usually identified by native
speakers as versions of active sentences, and they are trans-

84

lated as active sentences or object topicalizations in English (15). In addition, there is no syntactic evidence which suggests that Object Preposing involves embedding to a higher predicate BE. These two facts show that Object Preposing does not exhibit property i.

Further, Object Preposing does not allow unspecified agent deletion. While the underlying subject of a canonical Passive can be the generic, unspecified agent, the underlying subject of Object Preposing cannot:

80 a. *Orang itu pukul.
     man   the hit
     (The man was hit.)

   b. *Mobil ini akan perbaiki.
     car this Fut repair
     (This car is going to be repaired.)

The ungrammaticality of 80 seems related to the fact that, once Object Preposing has applied, the underlying subject cannot be moved or deleted by any later rule. For instance, the underlying subject cannot be focused or relativized (16):

81 a. *Saja jang mobil itu perbaiki.
     I   Comp car   the repair
     (It's me that the car repaired.)

   b. *orang itu jang isteri-nja tjari
     man   the Comp   wife-his look
     (the man who's looking for his wife)

Compare 82, which shows that these operations are allowed if Object Preposing has not applied:

82 a. Saja jang mem-perbaiki mobil itu.
     I   Comp Trans-repair car   the
     "It's me that repaired the car."

   b. orang itu jang men-tjari isteri-nja
     man   the Comp Trans-look wife-his
     "the man who's looking for his wife"

Sentences 80-82 show that the underlying subject of Object Preposing must appear as an overt constituent in surface structure; it cannot be semantically empty, and it cannot be moved or deleted by a later syntactic rule. It seems, then, that Object Preposing does not exhibit property ii.

In short, the only criterion for Passive which Object Preposing does satisfy is topicalization of the underlying direct object iii. This topicalization is realized by promoting the direct object to subject, as with the canonical Passive. But in order to qualify as a passive under the definition in 78, a construction must exhibit two or all of the properties i-iii. It follows from this that Object Preposing is not identified as a passive by 78, although we have seen strong reasons for believing that it is one. Object Preposing therefore causes problems for any universal characterization of Passive as a cluster of properties (17).

10. Perlmutter and Postal (forthcoming) propose their version of Passive as part of a larger theory of relational grammar. Relational grammar is intended to be a substantive theory of grammar, and it consists of a set of universal rules and the principles which govern their form and application. In this theory, grammatical relations--such as subject, direct object, indirect object (terms)--are taken to be central to the operation of a small number of universal rules which alter the grammatical relations of a sentence. The relation-changing, or universal, part of Passive is referred to as its core:

83 Perlmutter and Postal's Definition of Passive:

Core: Direct Object → Subject

Once the direct object has been promoted to subject by 83, the grammatical relation of the original subject is changed in accordance with the Relational Annihilation Law:

83 Relational Annihilation Law: When an NP_i assumes the term of a grammatical relation previously borne by NP_j, NP_j ceases to bear any term grammatical relation; it becomes a chômeur.

Other characteristics which we normally associate with passives--such as passive morphology, and appearance of the agent in a particular oblique case--are stated as language-specific side effects of the rule. That is, promotion of the direct object (and subsequent demotion of the underlying subject) is the only aspect of Passive which is universal.

One result of defining Passive in this way is that it is relatively easy to describe Object Preposing as a type of Passive. Because Object Preposing promotes direct objects to subjects, it automatically falls within the definition of 83. However, the Indonesian facts cause some larger problems for Perlmutter and Postal's definition. We can see this by examining some of the assumptions which lie behind stating Passive as a universal syntactic rule.

According to Bach (1971), one of the purposes of including universal rules in linguistic theory is to narrowly delimit the range of possible human languages. If it can be shown that all languages pick their major transformations

from the same set of universal rules, then the number of possible grammars of human language will be constrained in a
strong and interesting way. That is, universal rules will
restrict the range of options available to a child learning
language. This possibility is attractive, and has led to
several attempts to characterize the class of universal rules
more precisely. For instance, Bach (1974) has proposed that
all universal rules are arranged in a list which indicates
their (universal) ordering as well as their form; particular
languages are checked for having or not having a given universal rule. Perlmutter and Postal (forthcoming) have proposed that all rules which create terms of grammatical relations are cyclic.

The question of how these universal rules are related to
the transformations of particular languages has not been discussed much in the literature (but see Andrews 1973). It
seems clear, though, that the strongest claim worth considering would be that a language can have only one instance of a
given universal rule. This claim would maximize the restrictive power of universal rules, by requiring all languages to
have the same grammar (or parts of the same grammar) for the
major transformations. It would also account for the fact
that most languages seem to have only one instance of certain
types of syntactic rules (essentially, the cyclic and global
rules). Thus, most languages seem to have only one rule of
Subject-to-Subject Raising; most languages seem to have only
one rule of Subject-Verb Agreement; etc. Attributing this to
some general principle would help to constrain the range of
possible languages in a substantive way.

I think there is no question that the sort of claim outlined above would be desirable in universal grammar. However, no such claim can be maintained in view of the existence of two separate passives in Indonesian. As shown above,
both Object Preposing and the canonical Passive are instances
of the universal Passive rule in 83. This suggests that there
can be no one-to-one correlation between universal rules and
their realizations in particular languages.

Adopting this conclusion has several important consequences for the view of universal grammar sketched above. First,
it means that there is no nonarbitrary way of limiting the
number of language-specific instances of a given universal
rule. As a result, there is no nonarbitrary way of limiting
the number of possible grammars of human language (19).
Second, it suggests that universal rules like the one in 83
cannot constitute an adequate universal grammar by themselves.
Rather, linguistic theory must include mechanisms to explain
why a (particular) language would choose to have more than

one version of Passive. Such mechanisms would be of a very different kind than the substantive universals which have been proposed so far.

Both of these consequences reflect the more general fact that universal rules like 83 cannot restrict the range of possible languages as much as we would like. This suggests that, in order to impose the proper restrictions, universal grammar must consist of something more than a set of universal rules and the principles which govern their form and application. It is in this sense that the two passives of Indonesian are problematic for Perlmutter and Postal's definition.

11. Given the results of the preceding section, it is not entirely clear how the two passives of Indonesian should be accounted for in universal grammar.

One possible approach to the problem would be simply to claim that Object Preposing and the canonical Passive are instances of different universal rules. The canonical Passive could be taken to be an instance of 83; Object Preposing could be taken to be an instance of some other universal rule. This approach is objectionable for several reasons. First, there are processes in other languages which have the status of a "second passive" but bear no resemblance to Object Preposing. These include reflexive passives, as in Spanish, and impersonal passives, as in German. Claiming that all of these processes were instances of different universal rules would result in an endless proliferation of such rules. It would vitiate the claim that universal rules can substantively constrain the range of possible languages. Second, this approach claims that transformations like Object Preposing should be no less frequent or surprising in natural language than transformations like the canonical Passive. As far as I know, this claim is false. Transformations like the canonical Passive are commonplace, but transformations with the properties of Object Preposing seem relatively rare.

A second approach would be to claim that Object Preposing and the canonical Passive are both instances of the universal rule in 83. In this case, it would be necessary to find some principled differences between the two which could explain why they coexist in a single language. I will not attempt this investigation here; however, it is possible to suggest one direction which it might take.

Apparently, there are systematic differences between the side effects associated with the canonical Passive and the side effects associated with Object Preposing. Sentence 85 lists the principal side effects which have been discussed so far:

85 Side Effects associated with canonical Passive:

    chômeur appears in PP with <u>oleh</u>
    verb is stative
    verb is prefixed with <u>di-</u>

  Side Effects associated with Object Preposing:

    chômeur optionally cliticizes to verb

Notice that the verb remains active in Object Preposing, but not in the canonical Passive; the underlying subject keeps its preverbal position in Object Preposing, but not in the canonical Passive. The underlying subject must also be overt and definite in Object Preposing, although it can be the generic, unspecified agent in the canonical Passive. Roughly, it seems that Object Preposing involves less change in the character of the sentence than does the canonical Passive. Following the morphology, we can guess that this is due to the fact that the chômeur of the canonical Passive is an explicitly oblique constituent, but the chômeur of Object Preposing is not.

    This conjecture is supported to some extent by the syntactic properties of the two types of chômeurs. Consider, for instance, control of Equi. There is evidence in Indonesian that controllers of Equi must be subjects or direct objects in underlying structure, and subjects or direct objects at the end of the cycle on that clause (Chung 1976). Thus, the active subject in 86 can control Equi:

86 a. Mereka meng-antjam Ahmad untuk men-akuti-nja.
        they Trans-threaten A.   for Trans-scare-him
      "They threatened Ahmad in order to frighten him."

   b. Kita mem-buka sendjata itu untuk mem-perbaiki-nja.
        we Trans-open weapon the for Trans-repair-it
      "We opened the gun to repair it."

But the Passive chômeur in 87 cannot:

87 a. ??Ahmad di-antjam (oleh) mereka untuk
         A. Pass-threaten by   them   for
     (Ahmad was threatened by them to

           men-akuti-nja.
           Trans-scare-him
           frighten him.)

   b. ??Sendjata itu di-buka (oleh) Ali untuk
        weapon   the Pass-open by   A. for
     (The gun was opened by Ali to

```
mem-perbaiki-nja.
Trans-repair-it
repair it.)
```

Significantly, although sentences like 87 are unacceptable, sentences in which the chômeur of Object Preposing controls Equi are much better. Such sentences are considered marginal by some speakers, and grammatical by others:

88 a. (?) Ahmad mereka antjam untuk men-akuti-nja.
      A.   they threaten for Trans-scare-him
"Ahmad, they threatened to frighten him."

b. (?) Sendjata itu kita buka untuk mem-perbaiki-nja.
    weapon the we open for Trans-repair-it
"The gun, we opened to repair it."

c. Kertas jang bagaimana saudara pakai untuk bungkus
    paper Comp which?   you   use for wrap
"What kind of paper did you use to wrap

    barang2 tadi?
    things before
    things in before?"

(Dyen 1964:19b.15)

With respect to control of Equi, that is, the Passive chômeur acts as an oblique constituent, but the chômeur of Object Preposing does not.

Similarly, there is some evidence in Indonesian that sentences with second person underlying subjects passivize less easily than sentences with other types of subjects. This shows up most clearly in questions:

89 a. Apakah kamu makan makanan itu?
    Q   you   eat   food the
"Did you eat the food?"

b. Kepada siapa, kamu kirim-kan surat itu?
    to   who? you send-Ben letter the
"To whom did you send the letter?"

Compare the Passive sentences:

90 a. ??Apakah makanan itu di-makan (oleh) kamu?
    Q   food   the Pass-eat   by you
(Was the food eaten by you?)

b. ?*Kepada siapa, surat itu di-kirim-kan (oleh) kamu?
    to who? letter the Pass-send-Ben by you
(To whom was the letter sent by you?)

The explanation for this seems to lie in some observations of

90

Kuno (1974:38) about empathy and the surface syntactic position of particular NPs. Kuno proposes that "it is easier for
the speaker to empathize with the referent of the subject than
with the referent of any other constituent in a given sentence." In Indonesia, it seems that second persons are high
on the empathy hierarchy, while Passive agents are extremely
low (20).

Significantly, although questions with second person underlying subjects cannot undergo Passive, they can undergo
Object Preposing:

91 a. Apakah makanan itu kamu makan?
     Q   food   the you   eat
    "Did you eat the food?"

   b. Kepada siapa, surat itu kamu kirim-kan?
      to   who? letter the you send-Ben
    "To whom did you send the letter?"

The contrast of 90 and 91 suggests that underlying subjects
of Object Preposing have a higher empathy rating than Passive
agents; that is, they are closer than Passive agents to em-
pathy-focus (or subject) position. This amounts to saying
that the Passive chômeur acts as an oblique constituent with
respect to empathy, but the chômeur of Object Preposing does
not.

It is important to note that there are many syntactic
processes for which the chômeurs of both rules act as oblique
NPs. Both chômeurs fail to undergo Subject-to-Object Raising
and Derived Subject Raising; both fail to serve as targets
for Equi; and both fail to undergo the major strategies for
focus and relativization. But in contrast to these characteristics, which are predicted by the Relational Annihilation
Law, the control properties and empathy rating of the chômeurs
are not predicted by any universal principle. These characteristics will therefore have to be listed among the side effects of 85. Like the other side effects, they reflect a
difference in the obliqueness of the two types of chômeurs.

I propose, then, that the side effects associated with
Object Preposing and the canonical Passive differ in a principled way. These differences follow from the fact that the
Passive chômeur is an explicitly oblique constituent, but the
chômeur of Object Preposing is not. If this proposal is correct, it suggests that all possible types of passive transformations could be accounted for by systematic differences
in the side effects of Passive. Passive in universal grammar
would then consist of a universal rule (or core) plus a range
of possible types of side effects. Conceivably, a precise

characterization of the possible types of side effects would explain why a language like Indonesian would choose to have two passives. I suggest that such a characterization is crucial to any adequate definition of Passive.

Notes

1. The different definiteness requirements of Object
Preposing and the canonical Passive are noted briefly by Dyen
(1964:13a.9).
An apparent counterexample to the claim that Object Preposing requires an anaphoric/generic direct object is provided by examples like:

> (i) Apa-kah   kamu beli untuk anak2 saja?
> what?-Q you buy for children my
> "What did you buy for my children?"

> (ii) Apa akan kita kerdjakan sekarang?
> what? Fut we   do   now
> "What shall we do now?"
>
> (Dyen 1964:19b.4)

The preposed direct objects in (i-ii) are Wh-words, and are
neither anaphoric nor generic in the sense of Kuno (1973).
The appearance of Wh-words in (i-ii) is surprising, since the
NPs which undergo Object Preposing otherwise meet the criteria
indicated in the text. I have no explanation for the ability
of Wh-words to undergo Object Preposing.
2. Cf. Jesperson (1969); Perlmutter and Postal (forthcoming).
3. It is possible to show that the derivation of 14
must involve a rule of Subject-to-Object Raising, by demonstrating that the canonical Passive only operates on direct
object NPs. For instance, the canonical Passive does not
apply to locatives or other objects of prepositions:

> (i) *Danau itu di-renang (di) (oleh) mereka.
> lake the Pass-swim in   by   them
> (The lake was swum in by them.)

And it does not apply to the underlying direct object in a
Dative construction:

> (ii) *Surat itu di-kirim-i Ali oleh mereka.
> letter the Pass-send-Ben A. by   them
> (The letter was sent Ali by them.)

Further, the canonical Passive must be stated so that it refers to direct objects rather than to the NP immediately following the verb. See Chung (1976).
4. Berman (1974) argues that the for-phrase in the English analogue of 32 originates in the matrix clause. In
Indonesian, the major evidence for this analysis is that the
PP can be preposed in the matrix clause:

> (i) Bagi kami, sulit untuk mem-perbaiki mobil ini.
>   for   us   hard for Trans-repair car this
>   "For us, it's hard to repair this car."

5. The preposition <u>untuk</u> does not appear if the embedded clause is in subject position:

> (i) Mem-perbaiki mobil ini sulit bagi kami.
>   Trans-repair car this hard for   us
>   "Repairing this car is hard for us."

In all other cases, <u>untuk</u> seems to be optional, and its presence or absence is determined by obscure stylistic considerations which vary from speaker to speaker. I have used <u>untuk</u> in all the examples in this section because, without it, some of the sentences have a second reading where the adjective functions as the adverb of a simple sentence:

> (ii) Kami sulit mem-perbaiki mobil ini.
>   we   hard Trans-repair car this
>   "We are repairing this car with difficulty."

> (iii) Langganan mudah di-dapat-kan.
>   customer   easy Pass-find-Ben
>   "Customers are easily found."

This reading is possible for many adjectives which allow Derived Subject Raising (including <u>mudah</u> "easy" and <u>sulit</u> "hard"), but not for all:

> (iv) *Anak2 sangat menjenangkan mem-batja buku ini.
>   children very   nice   Trans-read book this
>   (The children are reading this book very nicely.)

> (v) Buku ini sangat menjenangkan di-batja.
>   book this very   nice   Pass-read
>   "This book is very nice to read." (* in the
>   meaning: This book was read very nicely.)

6. Notice that the underlying subject of the embedded clause can occur as a downstairs prepositional agent (sentence 35a), or as an upstairs <u>for</u>-phrase (sentence 35b). The derivation of sentences like 35b raises interesting syntactic questions which cannot be gone into here.

7. Notice the absence of the transitive prefix and the cliticization of the underlying subject, which show that Object Preposing has actually applied in the relative clause of 57.

8. The direct objects of some of the verbs in 61 can optionally be preceded by the preposition <u>pada</u> "at." This does not affect the argument.

Although the verbs in 61 do not undergo Passive, many of

them have derivatives which are able to undergo both Passive
and Object Preposing. These derivatives are formed with
several affixes, principally -i, which elsewhere has a locative meaning. The process which forms these derivatives appears to be lexical rather than syntactic, since it is non-
productive; cp. pertjaja "think, trust," pertjajai "trust
(in)" but lupa "forget," *lupai in the speech of some of my
informants. It also alters the meaning of the verb stem in
unpredictable ways; cf. suka "like, be fond of," sukai "love,"
and tahu "know," ketahui "know, find out."
  9. Pertjajai "trust (in)" is derived from pertjaja
"think, trust" by the process described in fn. 8. Rusak
"wreck (trans.)" is derived from the homophonous stative adjective rusak "wrecked." Given the homophony of the two
rusaks, it might be proposed that 66b is ungrammatical because
of the possibility of misinterpreting the second two constituents as "we were wrecked." But it is hard to see how such
a proposal could account for the fact that 64b, which allows
for the same ambiguity, is grammatical.
  10. Kuno and Robinson (1972:477), for instance, propose
that there is "a general constraint that prohibits dislocation of more than one constituent from its original location."
Their proposal is intended to account for contrasts like:

    (i) This book, I gave to Mary.
    (ii) *Mary, this book, I gave to.

As stated above, Kuno and Robisnon's proposal could conceivably account for the examples in this section. However,
their constraint is usually interpreted as a general constraint against application of two syntactic rules which
would leave a "hole" (e.g., chopping or deletion rules). As
such, it cannot account for examples like 67 or 74, in which
one of the NPs is displaced by a copying rule.
  11. For many speakers, this topicalization is allowed
for subject but not for direct object NPs. This additional
restriction does not affect the argument.
  12. There are several exceptions to the generalization
that prepositional phrases cannot be focused out of focus
constructions.
  First, it appears that a prepositional phrase can be
focused alongside a focused Wh-word, given the appropriate
context:

    (i) Untuk anak2, barang apa jang kamu beli?
        for children thing what? Comp you buy
        "For the children, which things did you buy?"

Sentence (i) is only grammatical if the focused NPs are inter-

SANDRA CHUNG

preted as paired; e.g., in a discussion of which things were
bought for which people.

Second, it appears that prepositional phrases can be focused alongside a focused NP if they were directly dominated
by S, rather than VP, in underlying structure. Compare 72,
where the PPs were originally dominated by VP, with (ii),
where the PP was originally dominated by S:

> (ii) Di Indonesia, permainan sepak bola jang paling
>   in   I.   game   soccer Comp most
> "In Indonesia, it's the game of soccer that's
>
>   di-gemari orang.
>   Pass-enjoy man
>   most enjoyed by people." (Dyen 1964:22b.3)

The original position of the PPs in 72 and (ii) is correlated
with other syntactic characteristics. For instance, the PPs
in 72 occur in the subcategorization of the verb; the PP in
(ii) does not.

It seems clear that the ability of the PPs in (i-ii) to
be focused is related to their "scope." I will not explore
the implications of this here. For the moment, what is important is that sentences like 72, which do obey the constraint,
provide a frame for determining whether a particular syntactic rule is a focus operation.

13. John Lawler makes such a proposal for the Achenese
analogue of 3, in a paper which I have not seen. From what
I understand of the situation, the properties of 3 in Achenese
are rather different from its properties in Indonesian. These
properties make it appropriate to analyze the Achenese version
of 3 as a variant of the canonical Passive, but the Indonesian
3 as a separate passive rule.

14. The definition in 78 is weaker than Langacker and
Munro's original definition in that it does not claim that
stative meaning is equivalent to "embedding to a stative-
existential predicate BE," or that the possibility of unspecified agent deletion is equivalent to "unspecified underlying subject."

15. Unfortunately, I have not been able to find any
clear syntactic tests for the active/stative distinction in
Indonesian. Polite imperatives (including negative imperatives) can occur in the canonical Passive or Object Preposing;
hence they do not provide a test for stativity. Simple imperatives occur in the active, but not the canonical Passive:

> (i)   Makan makanan itu!
>   eat   food   the
>   "Eat the food!"

> (ii)   *Makanan itu di-makan!
>   food   the Pass-eat
>   (Eat the food)

Despite the contrast of (i-ii), however, simple imperatives cannot be used to test for the stativity of Object Preposing. This is because the underlying subject of Object Preposing must always be overt in surface structure, but the underlying subject of a simple imperative must always be deleted:

> (iii)   *Kamu makan makanan itu!
>   you   eat   food   the
>   (You eat the food!)

Given this conflict, a sentence like (iv) reveals nothing about whether or not Object Preposing is stative:

> (iv)   *Makanan itu (kamu) makan!
>   food   the you   eat
>   (Eat the food!)

16. Sentence 81 illustrates the strategies for focus and relativization of subject or direct object NPs. Bahasa Indonesia also has strategies for focus and relativization of oblique NPs; these do not apply to the underlying subject of Object Preposing.

17. Conceivably, one could include Object Preposing in the class of passives defined by 77 by changing property (ii) to include less-than-fully specified subjects. Assuming that pronouns are in some sense less fully specified than nouns, Object Preposing might be able to satisfy (ii) as well as (iii). (This was suggested to me by Ron Langacker and Allen Munro.) I have little to say about this proposal, except that it leaves a number of properties of Object Preposing unexplained; for instance, it fails to explain why the underlying subjects in 3 do not act as subjects for the purpose of most syntactic rules. In addition, it allows for the disturbing possibility that English topicalizations like "Bagels, she likes" (with pronominal subject) will also be identified as passives by 77.

18. According to Perlmutter and Postal, all rules which create terms of grammatical relations are cyclic.

19. This was pointed out to me by Avery Andrews.

20. Kuno (1974) presents the following empathy hierarchy:

> (i)   Speaker $\geq$ Subject $\geq$ Object $\geq$ ... $\geq$ Passive Agent

The existence of a hierarchy like (ii) may seem surprising, so it is important to note that there are other syntactic characteristics of Bahasa Indonesia which are oriented towards the hearer rather than the speaker. Soemarmo (1970), for instance, shows that definiteness/specificity in Indonesian is assigned according to whether the speaker assumes that the hearer knows the referent of a given noun. This contrasts with English, where definiteness/specificity is assigned according to whether the speaker himself knows the referent.

PROPERTIES OF BASIC AND DERIVED SUBJECTS IN JACALTEC*

by

Colette G. Craig

*The data were gathered during field sessions in 1972-73-74 in the town of Jacaltenango, Department of Huehuetenango, Guatemala. Jacaltec is a language of the Kanjobalean branch of the Mayan family of languages.

54757

0. Introduction. This paper is a case study of subjects in Jacaltec, a Mayan language spoken in Guatemala, and my purpose is to show how the data support the Promotion Hierarchy postulated by Keenan.

Keenan (Definition of Subject, this volume) divides the characteristics of subjects into three types: coding properties, behavior properties, and semantic properties. He further postulates that certain subject properties are harder for derived subjects to acquire than others and hypothesizes a Promotion Hierarchy, claiming that coding properties are the most easily transferred, while the semantic ones are the most difficult to acquire.

I will first present the properties of Jacaltec's basic subjects and then analyze the inherited properties of its derived subjects. These derived subjects will be shown to lie on a scale of subjecthood from the most subject-like one which acquires all three types of properties to the least subject-like one which violates semantic properties and even lacks clear coding properties.

While most contemporary discussion on subjects and their properties centers around basic and cyclically derived subjects, this case study of Jacaltec will introduce three subjects which are post-cyclically derived.

PROPERTIES OF BASIC SUBJECTS

1   Coding Properties

1.1 Position. Jacaltec has a VSO word order. In the absence of a VP node, no criteria of immediate dominance may be used to define subjects:

1   xil ix   naj
     saw she him
     V   S   O
     "she saw him"

2   xil naj ix
     saw he   her
     V   S   O
     "he saw her"

1.2 Case Marking and verb agreement. Jacaltec is known as an ergative language. Both subjects and objects are marked for one of two cases, ergative (E) or absolutive (A). The case markers appear as agreement features on the predicate, and two sets of rules--Case Marking rules and placement rules--account for the phenomenon of case agreement.

Jacaltec is a mixed ergative language with two patterns of Case Marking. In main and finite clauses, Case Marking

101

operates on an ergative pattern illustrated in 3:

```
3   V   S   O           V   S
    E   A               A
```

In aspectless clauses, Case Marking operates on an accusative pattern shown in 4:

```
4   V   S   O           V   S
    E   A               E
```

Case Marking precedes deletion rules such as Relative Deletion. The reverse ordering--Relative Deletion preceding Case Marking--would yield the wrong case marking of a subject NP remaining after the deletion of a relativized object. It would assign it an absolutive case marker instead of the correct ergative one. The later rules of Case Placement which inflect the case markers on the verb are formulated in terms of case rather than function. Ergative case markers are placed first and are always prefixed while absolutive case markers take one of several positions. Several rules which need not concern us here account for the placement of absolutive case markers (1). Sentences 5-8 are given as examples of case agreement:

```
5   xc-ach    w-ila
    asp.-A2   E1-see
    "I saw you"

6   sicinaj   hach
    tired     A2
    "you are tired"

7   xc-oŋ to      hach cu-col-o'
    asp.-A1pl. go A2 E1pl.-help-suff.
    "we went to help you"

8   xc-oŋ to      cu-sajch-oj
    asp.-A1pl. go E1pl.-play-suff.
    "we went to play"
```

Jacaltec constitutes another example of a language in which the phenomenon of ergativity is not a very deep one (see Anderson, this volume). The only process to refer to specific cases is the set of very late rules which place case markers as verbal agreement features. There is otherwise no need to refer to a specific case in the structural description of a syntactic rule, the notion of subject being the significant one as will be seen in the presentation of behavior properties.

1.3 Disambiguation. All operations involving the deletion or movement of the subject of a transitive verb are marked by the simultaneous deletion of the ergative case marker of that subject and suffixation of -n(i) on the verb. This double process may be considered as a "decoding" mechanism used to identify the function of NPs.

I have argued elsewhere (Craig, forthcoming) that this double process corresponds to a disambiguation mechanism, the purpose of which is to identify the missing NP as the subject. The reason ambiguity would arise is that the language has a VSO word order. In addition it does not mark case on the NPs themselves, so that the deletion or movement of one of the two NPs would erase the only indication of function-- the relative position of one NP to the other (2).

The disambiguation mechanism is used with the two movement rules of Question (Q) and Clefting (C), and the deletion rule of Relativization (R). Example 9 represents a basic transitive sentence. The sentences of 10 show how disambiguation marks all operations on subjects:

9 xil   naj   ix
   saw   cl./he   cl./her
   "he saw her"

10 Q mac   x'il-ni   ix
      who   see-suff.   cl./her
      "who saw her?"

   C ha'   naj   x'il-ni   ix
      cleft cl./he   see-suff.   cl./her
      "it is he who saw her"

   R wohtaj   naj   x'il-ni   ix
      I know   cl./he see-suff.   cl./her
      "I know the man who saw her"

Because of the interaction of several morphophonemic rules in the verb form, the presence or absence of the ergative case marker is not directly observable, but it is signalled by the presence or absence of the initial glottal stop of the verb stem. Compare 10 with 11, which shows operations on objects:

11 Q mac   xil   naj
      who   saw   cl./he
      "who did he see?"

   C ha'   ix   xil   naj
      cleft cl./her   saw   cl./he
      "it is her that he saw"

```
R  wohtaj  ix      xil  naj
I know  cl./her  saw  cl./he
"I know the woman that he saw"
```

Notice the contrasting verb forms <u>xil</u> and <u>x'ilni</u>.

2   Behavior Properties

2.1 Behavior properties of NPs. Among the general behavior properties that subjects share with other NPs are the
rules of Relativization, Clefting and Question. In addition,
Jacaltec has a language specific rule of Noun Classifier
Deletion by which a controller noun classifier deletes any
number of subsequent coreferential noun classifiers within a
sentence:

12   a. *x-$\emptyset$-to   naj   boj y-uxtaj   naj$_i$ y-atut
         asp.-A3-go cl./he with E3-brother cl.   E3-house

             s-mam   naj$_i$
             E3-father cl.

         "he$_i$ went with his$_i$ brother to his$_i$ father's house"

     b. x-$\emptyset$-to naj boj y-uxtaj [____]   y-atut
                                          N Cl. Del.

             s-mam [____]
                    N Cl. Del.

         "he$_i$ went with his$_i$ brother to his$_i$ father's house"

The targets of the deletion are the noun classifiers functioning as pronouns only. The deletion may also affect a
subject NP, as shown in 13:

13   a. *y-atut   s-mam   naj$_i$ hat   x-$\emptyset$-to
         E3-house E3-father cl.   there asp.-A3-go

             naj$_i$
             cl./he

         "to his$_i$ father's house, that is where he$_i$ went"

     b. y-atut s-mam naj hat x-$\emptyset$-toyi [____]
                                           N Cl. Del.

         "to his$_i$ father's house, that is where he went"

The deletion of the subject noun classifier in 13b leaves the
verb in sentence final position, a position in which it must
take a stem final suffix <u>-(y)i</u>.

2.1 Reflexivization. Subjects of transitive verbs
control the reflexivization of coreferential objects. The
reflexive object has the shape of a possessed NP, E-ba "pos-
sessive-self":

14 x-∅-w-il   hin-ba
    asp.-A3-E1-see   E1-self
    "I saw myself"

In example 14 the subject inflects as an ergative first person before being deleted by the rule of Pronoun Drop, while
the reflexive object inflects as an absolutive third person.
    When the coreferential NPs are third person, only one
NP--the reflexive object--appears after the verb in surface
structure:

15 x-∅-y-il   s-ba   naj
    asp.-A3-E3-see   E3-self   cl.
    "he saw himself"

If the third person were present, the sentence would be as
*16 in which Noun Classifier Deletion has applied to the pos-
sessor of the reflexive object:

16 *x-∅-y-il   naj   s-ba   ☐
     asp.-A3-E3-see   cl./he   E3-self   N Cl. Del.
    "he saw himself"

2.2 Equi-NP Deletion. Jacaltec has three instances of
Equi-NP Deletion rules. All three have in common that they
delete subjects, with the restriction that it be the subject
of an intransitive verb. After the deletion of the subject,
the intransitive embedded verb takes on an infinitival form.
Each rule of Equi has to be specified as to whether it is
subject or object triggered, whether it operates forward or
backward, and whether it is obligatory or optional.
    With verbs of motion and desire, Equi is subject trig-
gered. It operates forward and is obligatory:

17 xc-ach to   sajchoh
    asp.-A2 go   to play
    "you went to play"

18 xc-ach to   hin-aw-ila'
    asp.-A2 go   A1 E2-see
    "you went to see me"

As shown in 18 no Equi applies to subjects of transitive
clauses which appear as aspectless embedded clauses fully inflected for both subject and object.
    With certain verbs of motion the rule operates backward
to delete the subject of the intransitive main verb. The

105

motion verb then takes on the appearance of an impersonal
auxiliary verb. The deletion may be triggered only by the
coreferential subject of a transitive verb and is optional:

19 a. xc-<u>in</u> to   hach-w-ila'
      asp.-A1 go A2-E1-see
      "I went to see you"

   b. x-∅-to   hach-w-ila'
      asp.-?-go A2-E1-see
      "I went to see you"
      (lit.: it went I see you)

With an embedded intransitive clause forward Equi is obligatory, and no backward Equi ever applies:

20 a. xc-in to   <u>sajchoh</u>
      asp.-A1 go to play
      "I went to play"

   b. *xc-<u>in</u> to   hin-sajchi
      asp.-A1 go E1-play

   c. *x-∅-to   hin-sajchi
      asp.-?-go E1-play

The last instance of Equi occurs with verbs of command
and causation which take an aspectless complement sentence.
The deletion is triggered by a higher object. It operates
forward but is optional in this case:

21 a. xc-ach y-iptze   naj   ha-munlayi
      asp.-A2-E3-force cl./he E2 work
      "he forced you to work"

   b. xc-ach y-iptze   naj   munlahoj
      asp.-A3-E3-force cl./he to work
      "he forced you to work"

There is no possible Equi of the subject of a transitive:

22 a. xc-ach y-iptze   naj   hin-ha-colo'
      asp.-A2 E3-force cl./he A1-E2-help
      "he forced you to help me"

   b. *xc-ach y-iptze   naj   hin colo'
      asp.-A2 E3-force cl./he A1 help
      "he forced you to help me"

The lack of Equi in *22b corresponds to a general constraint
on all movement or deletion operations in transitive aspectless clauses (3).

2.3 Causative collapsing. In the collapsing operation
of a causative construction the subject of the embedded clause
is reassigned a new function. Once the complex structure is
collapsed the sentence acquires the characteristics of a basic
simplex sentence (see Aissen 1974 and Craig 1975).

The characteristic of importance here is the uniqueness
of the subject. If the collapsed sentence is to have the
structure of a simplex sentence, it needs to eliminate one of
the two old subjects. In order to eliminate this doubling of
function, the second subject--the old embedded subject--is
reassigned a new function. The choice of that function depends on the next function available in the hierarchy of NP--
subject > object > indirect object. The subject of an intransitive embedded verb is reassigned the function of object,
while the subject of an embedded transitive verb is assigned
the function of indirect object in order to avoid further
doubling of object function. This reassignment of function
is diagrammed in 23 and 24.

23 V   S   V   *S →

    V   S   V   <u>O</u>

24 V   S   V   *S   O →

    V   S   V   O   <u>IO</u>

Once the old subject has been assigned a new function, it
also moves to the appropriate place assigned to that function
by the word order of the language (4). Sentence 25 shows the
embedded old subject of an intransitive appearing as object
of the main causative verb:

25 ch-oŋ y-a'   naj   munlahoj
    asp.-Alpl, E3-make   cl./he   to work
    "he makes <u>us</u> work"

Sentence 26 shows the old embedded subject of a transitive
appearing as indirect object (dative) of the main causative
verb, following the old embedded object which is now object
of the main verb:

26 x-Ø-w-a'   coc'tze' w-ixim   <u>t-aw-et</u>
    asp.-A3-El-make   grind   El-corn   <u>augt.-E2-to</u>
    "I make you grind my corn"
    (lit.: I make grind my corn <u>to you</u>)

2.4 Promotion. The optional rule of Promotion consists of providing an impersonal aspectual main verb with a
copy of the subject of its embedded clause:

27 a. x ∅-'ichi   ha-munlayi
       asp.-A3-begin E2-work
       "you began to work"
       (lit.: it began you work)

   b. xc-ach 'ichi   ha-munlayi
       asp.-A2 begin E2-work
       "you began to work"

For all speakers Promotion is restricted to animate subjects:

28 a. x-∅-'ichi   s-taj   te' hubal
       asp.-A3-begin E3-dry cl. beans
       "the beans have begun to dry"

   b. *x-∅-'ichi   te' hubal s-taji ☐
        asp.-A3-begin cl. bean   E3-dry N Cl. Del.
       "the beans have begun to dry"

Some speakers have the additional restriction that the subject be subject of an intransitive verb.

   2.5 Conclusion. The behavior properties specific to
subjects are: control of the reflexivization of a coreferential object, Equi-Np Deletion, Causative collapsing reassignment of function, and the language specific rule of Promotion
with impersonal aspectuals (5).

   There is no raising rule and no reduction of coordinate
structures in Jacaltec. No rule was found to operate on
objects either. The importance of the notion of subject in
the syntactic operations of Jacaltec underlines the super-
ficiality of the phenomenon of ergativity which is never
referred to in the structural description of a rule.

3   Semantic Properties

   3.1 Selectional rules. Subjects of intransitive verbs
may be animate as well as inanimate. Subjects of transitives, on the other hand, are restricted to animate agents.
Notice the ungrammaticality of the inanimate subject of *30:

29 speba naj   te' pulta
   close cl./he   cl. door
   "he closed the door"

30 *speba cake   te' pulta
    close wind   cl. door
   "the wind closed the door"

Inanimate agents like cake "wind" are expressed in agentive
prepositional phrases, as shown in 31:

```
31  xpehi    te'  pulta  yu  cake
    closed   cl.  door   by  wind
    "the wind closed the door"
    (lit.:  the door closed by the wind)
```

The same preposition E-u introduces indirect causative agents
and instrumentals:

```
32  Xtzah  hin-c'ul    haw-u
    burn   my-stomach  you-by
    "you make me angry"
    (lit.: my stomach burns because of you)
```

```
33  xintzoc'ic'oj  te'  te'   yu    ch'en  machit   an
    I cut          cl.  tree  with  cl.    machete  1p. part.
    "I cut the tree with a machete"
```

In addition, E-u marks passive agents. This results in ambiguous passive sentences in which the third person agentive
phrase may express either a direct or an indirect agent:

```
34  xmakot    ix        yu              naj
    was hit   cl./she   by/because of   cl./him
    "she was hit by/because of him"
```

The only difference between the two types of agents is that a
direct agent of passive is restricted to the third person
while an indirect agent, which may be used in active sentences as well as passive sentences, appears in any of the three
persons:

```
35  xmakot    ix       haw-u
    was hit   cl./she  you-because of/*by
    "she was hit because of you"
    (she was hit by you)
```

The selectional rules of transitive verbs which restrict subjects of transitives to animate direct agents will often be
violated by derived subjects, as will be seen in later sections.
    3.2 Impersonal transitive constructions. The only in-
stance of a transitive verb with no expressed animate agent
is found with the verb a'a' "to give, to cause" used in constructions expressing weather conditions:

```
36  cha'  cake
    give  wind
    "it is windy, the wind is blowing"
```

```
37  laŋan  Ø-y-a'-ni          ha'  nab
    prog   A3-E3-give-suff.   cl.  rain
    "it is raining"
```

The transitivity of the verb can be clearly seen in the complex sentence structure of the progressive form of 37 in which it is signalled by the undeleted ergative marker and the -ni suffix of aspectless embedded transitive verbs. As expected, objects of such impersonal transitive constructions do not undergo passive transformation:

38 *ch'alax   ha'   ŋab
    was given   cl.   rain
    (it was rained)

3.3 Surface structure pronouns. Many Jacaltec sentences do not have overt subject or object NPs. This is due to two facts. First, non-emphatic personal pronouns in the first and second person are deleted by a rule of Pronoun Drop:

39 a.   *ch-in ha-mak   hach   hayin
         asp.-A1 E2-hit   you   me
         "you hit me"

    b.   ch-in ha-mak-a   □   □
         asp.-A2 E2-hit-suff. Pr. Drop   Pr. Drop
         "you hit me"

Second, some lexical nouns do not have corresponding pronominal forms and remain unexpressed in surface structure.

Third person pronouns in Jacaltec are usually the noun classifiers. There are 19 noun classifiers in the language. They order nouns in concrete categories such as male or female humans, animals, water, plant, objects made of wood, dirt, thread, etc... In the presence of other determiners of the noun they optionally drop in full NPs, but they become the only pronominal form after the rule of Pronominalization has deleted all coreferential determiners and lexical nouns.

40 xul   naj   pel   yaj mach xcan   naj
    came   cl.(man)   Peter but not   stayed   cl.(man)/he
    "Peter came but he did not stay"

41 xawil   no'   txitam bakich tu'   la   -
    you see   cl.(animal)   pig   fat   that part.

         w-et   no'   an
         me-to   cl.(animal)it   1p. part.

    "do you see that fat pig there? it is mine"

A certain number of nouns are not assigned a noun classifier. They include abstract nouns (happiness, work), isolated words (star, air, path), and more recent borrowings from Spanish (plastic objects in particular). These words

110

consequently lack any pronominal form:

42 ilc'anab   txumel   tu'   la   - chawila ⬚
    look   star   that   part.   you see   (it)
    "look at that star! do you see it?"

43 sab   ichi   caŋal   yaj   maʼto   ʼtaŋiloj ⬚
    early   start   dance   but   not yet ended   (it)
    "the dance started early but it has not ended yet"

Jacaltec does not have a sentential pro form either:

44 chach munla   yiŋ   naj   pel   - chawoche ⬚
    you work   for   cl.   Peter   you like   (it)
    "you work for Peter! do you like it?"

In sum, Jacaltec does not exhibit any constraint on the presence of an overt subject or object in the surface structure
of every sentence. It has no dummy subjects for agentless
weather constructions; it drops non-emphatic first and second
personal pronouns and has no substitute pronominal form in
the absence of noun classifiers.

4   Summary of Properties of Basic Subjects

The formal coding properties of subjects are their
position immediately following the verb and their case agreement on the verb. In addition, a decoding mechanism marks
all operations on subjects of transitives. This disambiguation process consists of the deletion of the ergative case
marker and the suffixation of the verb.

Subjects share with other NPs the general behavioral
properties of undergoing Relativization, Clefting, Question,
and the language specific rule of Noun Classifier Deletion.
As is characteristic of their function, subjects control
Reflexivization, undergo Equi-NP Deletion and function reassignment in collapsed causative constructions. In addition,
Jacaltec subjects may be copied by a language specific rule
of Promotion.

Besides the general semantic properties of indispensability and uniqueness, Jacaltec subjects obey verbal selectional restrictions. While subjects of transitive verbs are
restricted to animate direct agents, instrumentals and indirect agents appear as oblique NPs in basic sentences. There
are no substitute pronoun forms for nouns lacking noun clari-
fiers and no dummy subjects.

PROPERTIES OF DERIVED SUBJECTS

1 Passive Subjects

1.1 Passive in Jacaltec. Jacaltec has four different
forms of passive which all share the structural characteristics of the advancement of the object to subject function,
the demotion of the old subject, and the concurrent marking
of the verb with a passive intransitivizing suffix. The
various passives differ in their suffixation-- -lax, -ot, -lo,
and -cha --and in the semantic properties of the agent--
whether it is present or not, expresses a predictable or unpredictable, specific or non-specific agent. Of interest
here is only the nature and status of the derived passive
subject. An example of a passive construction is given in 46:

```
46  xc-ach mak-laxi   (y-u  naj)
    asp.-A2 hit-PASS   (E3-by cl./him)
    "you were hit (by him)"
```

1.2 Properties of passive subjects. Passive subjects
inherit all of the coding properties of basic intransitive
subjects. They are assigned an absolutive in main and finite
clauses and an ergative in aspectless embedded clauses:

```
47  xc-ach 'il-laxi
    asp.-A2 see-PASS
    "you were seen"
```

```
48  x-Ø-tuci      ha-tohla-laxi
    asp.-A3-stop  E2-pay-PASS
    "you stopped being paid"
    (lit.: it stopped you were paid)
```

Passive subjects feed into syntactic processes such as
Relativization, Clefting, Question, and Noun Classifier Deletion. An example of how Noun Classifier Deletion may affect
passive subjects is given in 49:

```
49  y-u         s-mul     ix   x-Ø-mak-laxi       ☐
    E3-because  E3-fault  cl.  asp.-A3-hit-PASS   N Cl. Del.
    "it is because of her own fault that she was hit"
```

However, in the speech of most speakers, passive subjects do
not acquire all of the behavior properties specific to subjects. Although Equi-NP Deletion may still apply to derived
passive subjects with verbs of causation:

```
50  xc-ach w-iptze     aŋte-laxoj
    asp.-A2-E1-force   cure-PASS
    "I forced you to be cured"
```

it does not freely apply to passive subjects embedded under verbs of motion or desire:

51 a. mach x-∅-w-oche   <u>hin-mak-laxi</u>
        not   asp.-A3-E1-like E1-hit-PASS
        "I do not like to be hit"

    b. *mach x-∅-w-oche   mak-laxoj
        neg   asp.-A3-E1-like hit-PASS
        "I do not like to be hit"

Similarly, passive subjects are not promoted with impersonal aspectual verbs:

52 a. x-∅-'ichi   ha-mak-laxi
        asp.-A3-begin E2-hit-PASS
        "you began to be hit"
        (lit.: it began you be hit)

    b. *xc-ach   'ichi ha-mak-laxi
        asp.-A2 begin E2-hit-PASS
        "you began to be hit"

Passive subjects, therefore, function almost like basic subjects but are partially restricted with respect to behavior properties. They conform to all of the semantic properties of subjects.

2   Promoted Subjects

    2.1 The Promotion operation. This operation has already been introduced as one of the behavior properties specific to subjects. It is a copying rule rather than a raising rule, and is restricted to animate subjects. It is of interest in this section because it also produces a surface structure subject.
    2.2 Properties of promoted subjects. They acquire all of the coding properties of basic intransitive subjects: they follow the verb and are marked absolutive (6). Their behavior properties are difficult to assess but appear to be very restricted. Surface sentences give no indication of whether promoted subjects may undergo Relativization or Question because of the action of the very late rule of Noun Classifier Deletion. Promoted subjects themselves may become controllers of the deletion:

53 x-∅-'ichi   naj   s-munlayi □
    asp.-A3-begin cl./he E3-work   N Cl. Del.
    "he began to work"

They do not undergo Equi-NP Deletion, but this limitation is not specific to derived subjects. Equi-NP Deletion never applies to the subject of a clause if another clause is embedded under it.

Considering the copying nature of the rule, it may be said that promoted NPs violate the general semantic property of independent reference specific to subjects. The presence of a promoted animate NP as subject of the impersonal aspectual verb also represents a clear violation of verbal subcategorization rules. Intransitive aspectuals may only take inanimate subjects in basic sentences as shown by the ungrammaticality of *54b:

54 a. x'ichi caŋal
           began   dance
           "the dance began"

     b. *x'ichi naj
           began   cl./he
           "he began"

Only the transitive form of the aspectual verb may take an animate subject:

55 xiche naj   munil
     began cl./he   work
     "he began the work"

The ungrammatical intransitive imperative reflects the restriction on the animacy of the subject. Compare it to the grammatical transitive form:

56 a. *ich-aŋ
          begin-IMP (Intr.)
          "begin!"

     b. iche-∅
          begin-IMP (tr.)
          "begin!"

Unlike passive subjects, promoted subjects inherit few of the properties of subjects. While they clearly acquire their coding properties they are characterized by multiple violations of the semantic properties.

3   Instrumental Subjects

3.1 Subjectivization of instrumentals. As mentioned earlier, the function of a subject of a transitive verb is restricted to animate agents and instrumentals appear only in oblique NPs in basic sentences:

57 x-∅-in-tzoc'i-c'oj   te' te' y-u   <u>ch'en</u>
     asp.-A3-E1-cut-dir. cl. tree E3-with cl.

      <u>machit</u>   an
      machete 1p. part.

"I cut the tree with the machete"

However, when an operation applies to an instrumental, the instrumental advances to subject function while the animate old subject becomes an oblique NP:

58 Q   tzet x-☐-tzoc'-ni-c'oj   te' te'   haw-u --
         what asp.-☐-cut-suff.-dir. cl. tree E2-by

           ch'en machit
           cl.   machete

       "what did you cut the tree with? the machete"
       (lit.: what cut the tree by you? the machete)

    C   ha'   ch'en machit ti' x-☐-tzoc'-ni-c'oj
         cleft cl.   machete this asp.-☐-cut-suff.-dir.

           te' te'   w-u
           cl. tree E1-by

       "it is with this machete that I cut the tree"
       (lit.: it is this machete that cut the tree by me)

    R   al   ch'en machit x-☐-tzoc'-ni-c'oj
         heavy cl.   machete asp.-☐-cut-suff.-dir.

           te' te'   w-u
           cl. tree E1-by

       "the machete that I cut the tree with is heavy"
       (lit.: the machete that cut the tree by me is heavy)

The advancement rule feeds obligatorily into a syntactical operation and there is no declarative simplex sentence with an instrumental subject:

59 *x-∅-tzoc'i-c'oj   ch'en machit   te' te'
     asp.-A3-cut-dir. cl.   machete cl. tree
     (the machete cut the tree)

The close relationship of instrumentals to the subject function was expressed in Fillmore's case grammar by a rule which made an instrumental the subject of a sentence only in the absence of an agent (Fillmore, 1968). The subjectivization of instrumentals in Jacaltec seems to be another manifestation of the affinity of instrumentals for the subject function, although in this particular case, the choice of the instrumental cannot be said to depend on the absence of an

agent. Rather, agents and instrumentals co-occur and exchange the functions of subject and object of preposition
whenever instrumentals become the target of an operation.

Unlike the advancement rule of Passive, the advancement
of instrumentals is not accompanied by a change of voice.
There is no instrumental voice marker parallel to the passive
voice marker.

3.2 Properties of instrumental subjects. The instrumental NP is not directly identifiable by position or case
marking as the subject of the sentence. It inherits only the
"decoding" property of the disambiguation mechanism which
signals operations on subjects of transitives--deletion of
the ergative case marker and suffixation of -n(i) on the verb.

Compare the identical verb forms of 60 and 61:

60 mac x-[____]-peba-n   te' pulta y-u
    who asp.-[____]-close-suff. cl. door   E3-with

    te' ẍila
    cl. chair

    "who closed the door with the chair?"

61 tzet x-[____]-peba-n   te' pulta y-u   naj
    what asp.-[____]-close-suff. cl. door   E3-by cl./him
    "what did he close the door with?"
    (lit.: what closed the door by him?)

In 60 the questioned NP is the subject agent. By comparison,
the identical marking on the verb in 61 indicates that a
questioned instrumental functions as subject also while the
two other NPs are identifiable as non-subjects. The old object is still in object function, and the old subject is
clearly demoted to an agentive phrase.

As already mentioned, oblique instrumentals advance to
subject function only to undergo post-cyclic operations.
These derived subjects therefore occur only as questioned,
relativized or clefted NPs.

An instrumental does not advance to subject function to
be further demoted by a Passive transformation. Only the
basic agent subjects are demoted by the application of Passive, and they are then assigned the same oblique function
of object of the preposition -u as that of instrumentals.
This preposition -u marks all non-subject agents and instrumentals in Jacaltec; it marks direct inanimate agents and
indirect animate agents in active sentences, direct agents in
passive sentences, and instrumentals in both. However, a
sentence may contain only one such -u phrase and a passive
sentence may have in surface structure only a direct agent
or an instrumental, but never both:

```
62   x-Ø-mak-lax          me   tx'i'    y-u      naj   Xuwan
     asp.-A3-hit-PASS      cl.  dog      E3-by    cl.   John
     "the dog was hit by John"

63   x-Ø-mak-lax          me   tx'i'    y-u      hune'  c'ojwal
     asp.A3-hit-PASS       cl.  dog      E3-with  a      stone
     "the dog was hit with a stone"

64  *x-Ø-mak-lax          me   tx'i'    y-u      naj   Xuwan
     asp.-A3-hit-PASS      cl.  dog      E3-by    cl.   John

        y-u       hune'   c'ojwal
        E3-with   a       stone
```

"the dog was hit by John with a stone"

In 63 the -u phrase is an instrumental phrase and the direct
agent is understood, although it is not expressed.

A significant characteristic of the derived instrumental subjects is their violation of semantic properties. They
violate the selectional restrictions of transitive verbs
which take only animate agents for subjects. This violation
is particularly striking in the presence of an agent NP and
in the lack of modification of the transitive verb.

4   Indirect Causative Agents

4.1 Causative agents. Jacaltec distinguishes between
direct and indirect causative agents. Both are found in a
causative construction with the causative verb a'a' "to make,
to cause." The direct causative agent behaves as a usual
subject of a transitive:

```
65   xc-ach y-a'          naj   munlahoj
     asp.-A2 E3-make      he    to work
     "he made you work"
```

The indirect agent of causative constructions, on the
other hand, appears in an obligatory clefted position at the
head of the sentence:

```
66  a.   hin-mam      x-Ø-☐─┤☐├─'a'-ni
         E1-father    asp.-A3-☐├─make-suff.

             Ø-w-a'acan-n-oj           hin-munil
             A3-E1-leave-suff.-suff.   E1-work
```

"my father made me leave my work, i.e.,
before of my father I had to leave my work"

```
    b.  *x-Ø-y-a'          hin-mam     ...
         asp.-A3-E3-make   E1-father   ...
```

Although the indirect agent is in clefted position, it does not carry the usual emphasis attributed to clefted elements.

The indirect agent is derived by an advancement rule parallel to the advancement rule of the instrumentals. In basic simplex sentences, the indirect agent may only function as object of the preposition -u, as shown in 67:

```
67  ch-in oki      y-u              hin-mi'
    asp.-A1 cry   E3-because of   E1-mother
    "I cry because of my mother"
```

In complex causative constructions the indirect agent advances to subject function and undergoes obligatory clefting. Unlike the advancement rule of instrumentals, the advancement of an indirect agent is not accompanied by the demotion of an old subject. In the absence of any other NP which could fulfill the function of subject, the indirect agent qualifies as a "subject by default" produced by a rule of unmarked subject choice.

4.2 Properties of indirect causative agents. Since these indirect agents are clefted, they lack any positive subject coding as was just noted in the case of instrumentals. They, too, seem to inherit the "decoding" subject property of the disambiguation mechanism. However, indirect agents do not behave exactly like first and second person clefted subjects. Usually, when a basic first or second person subject is clefted, the verb remains fully inflected; there is no deletion of ergative marker and no suffixation:

```
68  a.  hach   x-∅-a-watx'e       hun tu'
        you    asp.-A3-E2-make   one that
        "it is you who made that"

    b.  *hach  x-∅-[    ]-watx'e-n      hun tu'
        you    asp.-A3-[    ]-make-suff.  one that
        "it is you who made that"
```

In contrast, when the indirect causative agent is first or second person, the deletion of ergative and suffixation of -n(i) occur, as it does with third person:

```
69  a.  *hach  x-∅-aw-a'          ∅-hin-cuy-ni        abxubal
        you    asp.-A3-E2-make   A3-E1-learn-suff.   Jacaltec
        "you made me learn Jacaltec, i.e., because of you
         I had to learn Jacaltec"

    b.  hach   x-∅-[    ]-'a'-ni        ∅-hin-cuy-ni
        you    asp.-A3-[    ]-make-suff.   A3-E1-learn-suff.

           abxubal
           Jacaltec
```

69b (cont'd)

"you made me learn Jacaltec, i.e., because of you
I had to learn Jacaltec"

It seems, therefore, that the indirect causative agent does
not inherit all of the "decoding" properties of clefted subjects. Since instrumentals are by nature third person NPs,
it was not possible to test whether they also acquired
limited decoding properties.

Like instrumentals, indirect agents advance to subject
function only to undergo obligatory post-cyclic operations.
When they are not clefted as in 66, they appear questioned or
relativized, as in 70 and 71:

70 mac   x-[   ]-'a'-ni   Ø-ha-cuy-ni   abxubal
    who   asp.-[   ]-make-suff.   A3-E2-learn-suff.   Jacaltec
    "because of whom did you learn Jacaltec?"

71 caw   icham-xa   ya'   cumi'   x-[   ]-'a'-ni
    very   old-already   cl.   lady   asp.-[   ]-make-suff.

    Ø-hin-cuy-ni   abxubal
    A3-El-learn-suff.   Jacaltec

    "the lady because of whom I learned Jacaltec is very
    old already"

Examples 70 and 71 also represent question and relativization
of a direct agent.

Causative constructions with indirect agents differ
from causative constructions with direct agents in their
limited collapsing operation. Although subjects of intransitive verbs undergo reassignment of function as new objects
of the main causative verb, their absolutive case marker is
commonly not placed in the usual absolutive slot in the verb
form:

72 skani   x-[   ]-'a'-ni   hin   eloj-tij   yiŋtaj
    noise   asp.-[   ]-make suff.   Al   out-come   inside
    "the noise made me come out (from inside)"

If there were no collapsing, the embedded subject of 72 would
be marked ergative, El: w- .

Collapsing does not occur when the embedded clause is
transitive; the embedded subject is not assigned the new
function of indirect object as it was in 66 and 69b above.
It was argued earlier that in causative sentences the reassignment of function is motivated by the doubling of the subject
function in the collapsed construction. The very limited
process of reassignment of function considered here may
therefore be another indication that the level of subjecthood

119

of the indirect causative is so low as to create no clear
clash of subject function.

With respect to semantic properties, indirect causative
agents violate the selectional restrictions of transitive
verbs. In basic sentences subjects of transitives are restricted to direct agents, while indirect agents, as well as
inanimate direct agents, are objects of the preposition -u,
as shown in 67 and 73:

73 a. x-Ø-taj   xil kape   y-u   cake'
       asp.-A3-dry cl. clothes E3-by wind
       "the wind dired the clothes"
       (lit.: the clothes dried by the wind)

    b. *x-Ø-s-taj-ņe   cake' xil kape
       asp.-A3-E3-dry-tr. suff. wind cl. wind
       "the wind dried the clothes"

Thus, all indirect causative agents violate the restrictions
that subjects of transitive verbs be direct agents and inanimate causative agents further violate the restriction on the
animacy of the subject, as instrumental subjects did too:

74 cake' x-[   ]-'a'-ni   tajoj xil kape
    wind asp.-[   ]-make-suff. dry   cl. clothes
    "the clothes dried because of the wind; the wind
    dried the clothes"

75 tzalalal   ch-[   ]-'a'-ni   hin okoj
    happiness asp.-[   ]-make-suff. Al   cry
    "I cry because of happiness; happiness makes me cry"

5   Summary of Properties of Derived Subjects

No derived subject matches all of the properties of a
basic subject. The passive subjects are the closest to it.
They inherit the coding properties of intransitive subjects
and are the only derived subjects to feed into syntactic
operations. They undergo all of the operations shared by all
NPs, such as Relativization, Clefting, Questions, and Noun
Classifier Deletion. With respect to semantic properties,
passive subjects are also the only derived subjects to conform to selectional and subcategorization rules of Jacaltec
verbs. Nevertheless, their subject specific behavior properties are somewhat restricted. For most speakers, passive
subjects may not undergo Equi-NP Deletion nor Promotion with
aspectual verbs.

The promoted subjects inherit only coding properties.
Their behavior properties are not directly observable due to
the operation of the rule of Noun Classifier Deletion and to

independent constraints on the application of the rule of Equi-NP Deletion. The presence of the promoted NP is in clear violation of the semantic properties of basic subjects of aspectual verbs. No semantic relationship holds between the impersonal aspectual verb and the promoted animate subject. The instrumental subjects are the result of an advancement rule which obligatorily feeds into post-cyclic operations. They inherit only limited coding properties since they are found in positions which exclude case marking of the subject. The occurrence of the "decoding" disambiguation mechanism is their only inherited coding property. Since they surface only as the result of post-cyclic operations, they inherit no behavior property specific to subjects. Furthermore, these derived subjects constitute a violation of the selectional restrictions of Jacaltec transitive verbs which are marked to take only animate agents for basic subjects. The advancement of the inanimate instrumentals to subject function is accompanied by the demotion of the animate subject agents to an oblique NP with no mark of voice change on the verb.

The last derived subjects are the indirect causative agents. Like instrumentals, they are derived from an oblique function by an advancement rule which obligatorily feeds into post-cyclic operations. They inherit only the "decoding" property but do not even follow the pattern of disambiguation of subjects in first and second person. They acquire no behavior property specific to subjects; in particular they do not control the same reassignment of function which occurs in the collapsing operation of causative constructions with direct agents. They, too, violate the selectional restrictions of transitive verbs. In view of the scarcity of their positive subject properties, they are best qualified as "subjects by default" in sentences which contain no other candidate NP for the subject function.

CONCLUSIONS

In this paper I have systematically reviewed the properties of the basic and derived subjects of a particular language.

In the course of the discussion on case marking and behavior properties, I claimed that Jacaltec is a language which is only superficially ergative, first because it has a mixed ergative and accusative set of case marking rules, and second because no rule ever needs to refer to a specific case. The lack of syntactic operations applying specifically to objects was said to also contribute to the importance of the notion of subject in the language.

The survey of the four types of derived subjects established that none of them acquired all of the properties of basic subjects. Furthermore, the study of the particular types of properties that they inherited provided support to Keenan's claim that certain properties are easier for derived subjects to inherit than others.

As postulated by the Promotion Hierarchy, coding properties were the easiest transferred. Passive and promoted subjects exhibited the positive coding properties of position and case marking. Instrumental and indirect causative agent subjects inherited only the indirect "decoding" mechanism of disambiguation. With indirect causative agents it was even a limited form of "decoding" property which was inherited.

Limited behavior properties were acquired by the derived subjects. General behavior properties of NPs such as the ability to undergo Question, Clefting, and Relativization were acquired by passive subjects. Advanced subjects—instrumentals and indirect causative agents—were in fact the obligatory target of one of these post-cyclic operations. Very restricted behavior properties specific to subjects were inherited by the derived subjects. Passive subjects could undergo one form of Equi and indirect causative agents controlled limited reassignment of function in embedded clauses. The promoted subjects, which were copied by a very late rule, were syntactically non-productive.

With the exception of passive subjects, the derived subjects were characterized by clear violations of the semantic properties of basic subjects. They violated either the general subject property of independent reference, or the general selectional restrictions of transitive verbs, or verb specific subcategorization rules. Such violations supported the claim that the hardest properties for derived subjects to acquire are the semantic ones.

Notes

1. Absolutive case markers are either postposed to an aspectless predicate, or cliticized to an aspect marker, or made to precede an ergative case marker within an aspectless predicative constituent following an A > E Ordering Constraint.

2. The arguments given for the disambiguation analysis were that, whenever the operation on a transitive subject were not marked, they corresponded to sentences in which ambiguity was not likely to arise, as for example in transitive reflexive sentences.

3. The rule of Equi-NP deletion is to be distinguished from that of Noun Classifier Deletion; the former deletes the whole NP including the case marker on the verb while the latter deletes specifically a noun classifier in pronominal form leaving the case agreement on the verb.

a) x-∅-aw-iptze   naj   s-munlayi   ☐
    asp.-A3-E2-force   cl./him E3-work   N Cl. Del.
    "you forced him to work"

a') x-∅-aw-iptze   naj   munlahoj ☐
    asp.-A3-E2-force   cl./him to work   Equi
    "you forced him to work"

The presence of the two coreferential NPs in complex sentences with verbs of causation indicates that there is not raising of the embedded subject.

4. A parallel reassignment of function occurs with the doubling of the predicate function, and the second verb becomes an infinitive.

5. All of these rules are treated in different chapters of Craig (1975).

6. The promoted subject acquires the case of the displaced sentential subject as predicted by the Functional Succession Law of Relational Grammar.

THE MANIFESTATION OF SUBJECT, OBJECT, AND TOPIC
IN THE AMERICAN SIGN LANGUAGE (1)

by

Lynn A. Friedman

Introduction

In order to understand the nature of topic in the American Sign Language (ASL), it is important to describe various aspects of the discourse situation. Essential to this discussion are: word order (or lack thereof), the formal elements available for marking the relation of argument to verb, the use of space, the use of pro-forms versus true nominals, analysis of text versus that of isolated sentences. This paper attempts to (a) refute previous claims in regard to word order in ASL, (b) accurately describe the discourse situation and its relation to the question of word order, and (c) relate this description to the nature of topic in ASL.

I will dispense with the now familiar preliminaries about the nature and the history of ASL (i.e., that it has a unique phonological, syntactic, semantic structure, that it is not a derivative of oral language, etc.). Such information may be found in almost all sources cited herein. Those properties of ASL which are crucial to this discussion will be mentioned in context.

Fischer (1975) makes various claims regarding word order and word order change in ASL. She states that:

"The basic word order in ASL is Subject-Verb-Object (SVO). This is the order one finds in a sentence with reversible subject and object which are full noun phrases and not 'appositivized' with pronouns... Any other order will have intonation breaks." (p. 5)

"The American Sign Language...has a basic word order of SVO. Other orders are allowed under the circumstances that (a) something is topicalized, (b) the subject and object are non-reversible, and/or (c) the signer uses space to indicate grammatical mechanisms." (p. 21)
There are serious problems with these claims, when viewed in the light of the discourse situation.

Sociolinguistic situation

In analyzing various videotaped portions of text (discourse) and series of isolated sentences translated from English cue sentences, I have found a striking difference between the two types of elicitation, in regard to grammar. These findings are not surprising when viewed in terms of the Sign Language Continuum. In addition to ASL, there is another variety of Sign Language which is a pidgin of ASL and English (i.e., Signed English), composed of signs from ASL, words from English (articulated by means of the manual alphabet), and has primarily English syntax (2).

"The literate signer, therefore, controls several
visual 'languages,' ranging from American Sign Language
to any one of a variety of visual codes for English...
It is apparent that there is a continuum of visual language, and that point on the continuum chosen by the
signer is determined by the sociological and sociolinguistic circumstances of the discourse situation (3).

In the light of the continuum, it is easy to see why
signers, when asked to translate written English sentences,
might tend to produce signed strings which look remarkably
like English (even with repeated instructions to the informant not to translate literally). In the data I have examined (4), elicitations of isolated sentences show a marked
resemblance to English. Textual data, however, bears no resemblance to English, and it is the grammar of these texts
that I describe herein. As will become clear, the discourse
situation in ASL is such that it is imperative, when analyzing the grammar of the language, to rely solely on continuous
textual material.

Verb Classes in ASL

There are several classificatory distinctions of verbs
in ASL that we may use to elucidate the discourse situation.
Important to this discussion are the phonological and semantic characteristics and the characteristic syntactic behavior
of each class.

Like all other signs, all verbs are either articulated
in contact with or in close proximity to the body, that is to
say anchored to the body, or made in the signing space in
front of the body (i.e., neutral space). The four articula-
tory parameters of Sign are: hand shape, place of articulation (one possible place is neutral space), orientation of
hands in relation to the body, and type of movement.

There is a class of verbs, called <u>multi-directional</u>
verbs, which have a core hand configuration and place of articulation, but whose movements and orientations are determined by the location, real or grammatically established, of
the source and the goal of the action. For example, the
signs GIVE, GO/COME, SEE, TELL, BORROW/LEND, and BRING/TAKE
always entail movement from source to goal. That is, the
Sign sentences which may be glossed as "You tell me" and "I
tell you" differ only in direction of movement. In "you tell
me" the sign TELL (an extended index finger brushing past the
chin), the palm is facing the signer and the hand moves from
neutral space directly in front of the signer (representing
the location of the addressee) inward toward the signer's

chest (representing first person); for "I tell you," the hand
moves outward from the signer to neutral space (5). A very
small number of multi-directional signs have been analyzed as
moving from goal to source. For example, the sign INVITE
entails a movement of a slightly cupped hand, palm upward
from the invitee toward the inviter. However, we might also
interpret the movement in INVITE as a representation of direction of movement of the invitee rather than a representation
of the direction of the invitation. All multi-directional
verbs are articulated in neutral space. The movements of
these verbs always unamibugously indicate agent/experiencer/
source and patient/beneficiary/goal with or without overt
"pronominal" markers.

All "pronominal" reference (and most locative reference)
in ASL is achieved by the use of indexing, which entails establishing a point in space (or pointing to a previously established place) for referring to a person, object or location, either real world or hypothetical. The language has
general conventions for establishing the location of particular referents (6).

There is a second class of pro-forms, which we may call
markers (7). These markers are established in much the same
way as indices--that is, a nominal sign is made and then the
marker is articulated, replacing, as it were, the nominal
sign. These markers may then move around to indicate action
of the referents. Thus we may say that the sign MEET (two
hands, facing each other with extended index fingers, make
contact in neutral space) is actually an analogic representation of two people (marked by the two hands with extended index fingers) coming in contact, i.e., meeting. Signs like
MEET and FOLLOW (two fists, one behind the other, moving outward, in citation form) can be viewed as analogic representations of real world or hypothetical actions of nominal referents (8).

What I would point out about these pro-forms is that
their use in discourse is much more widespread than has been
previously indicated. Fischer (1975) states that the multi-
directional verb

"does not have this flexibility [of indicating source
and goal] unless locations have been established...
Verbs incorporate the location only of pronouns, or...
cliticize only pronouns." (p. 17)

However, it is the case that in discourse the locations of
referents are almost always established prior to the occurrence of the verb, and that the multi-directional verbs always indicate direction of movement. The use of indexic pro-
forms and markers in discourse is much more widespread than

the use of true nominals. The vast majority of nominal ref-
erence--in discourse--is made with indexic pro-forms or markers, movement of verbs between locations in space (without
overt pronominal markers), or with body movement (discussed
below).

The majority of verbs in ASL are multi-directional, made
in neutral space (and therefore not anchored to the body).
With the use of these verbs, the signer may unambiguously indicate subject and object without any overt nominal sign per
se. But what of verb signs which are not multi-directional,
which cannot move off the body from source to goal, from subject to object, but which are semantically transitive? Verbs
of this type include the signs ANGRY, LIKE, LOVE, SURPRISE(D),
SCARE(D) (9). (Not surprisingly, all of these verbs are stative, psych verbs. Active verb signs all entail a movement
in space--and thus in some way metaphorically iconically represent the action.)

There is a third class of verbs, whose phonological realization entails a combination of characteristics of multi-
directional and non-multi-directional anchored verbs. These
verbs, which include HATE, PITY, BOTHER, TEASE are articulated in neutral space and thus are not anchored to the body.
However, their core phonological shapes always include a
movement. (Compare with multi-directional verbs, whose core
structures do not have a movement component.) The movements
of these verbs do not represent the direction of movement of
the action as do the movements of the multi-directional verbs.
However, with this class of verbs, the orientation of the
hand(s) is variable, and always represents the location of
the agent/experiencer and the patient/beneficiary. For example, the sign HATE is a one-handed sign made by sharply
flicking the middle finger outward from its starting position
in contact with the thumb; PITY is articulated by a slightly
circular up and down movement of the open hand with the middle finger bent inward toward the palm. In the articulation
of both of these signs, the direction that the palm faces indicates the beneficiary; the back of the hand is toward the
experiencer. Thus for "I pity you" the palm faces the addressee; for "You pity me" the palm is toward the signer. The
sign BOTHER is odd (for this class) in that it is made in the
direction of the experiencer from the location of the agent.

All verbs of this class are non-action verbs. We will
find that their surface realization is similar to that of the
anchored verbs. For this reason, I will group these two classes together for the purposes of this discussion under the
classification non-multi-directional verbs.

It would seem that the different verb classes although

seemingly phonologically determined, are in fact semantically determined, in that a distinction is made between action and non-action verbs and that this difference is reflected in the phonological design. One aspect of ASL that is overwhelmingly evident is that it chooses, whenever possible, to maximize the use of visual iconicity. This is reflected in the use of the movement of verb signs to represent actual movement. It is also evident in the form of those verb signs which are anchored to the body. Signs in this class are all iconic representations of the states they designate. For example, SURPRISE is a two-handed sign made with a sharp flicking movement of the forefingers from contact with the thumbs at the cheeks, accompanied by a rapid (closing and) wide opening of the eyes.

It would appear that verbs are multi-directional if their meaning entails an action or a definite direction of movement from source to goal. Whether non-multi-directional or non-action verbs are free (articulated in neutral space) or anchored (to the body) is semantically determined.

Edge and Hermann (1975) investigate the use of eleven non-multi-directional verbs both in isolated sentences and in discourse. They find that when instructed to use only the desired verb sign and two name signs (to describe non-verbal skits), the informant invariably gave sentences in SVO order, for example

LEORA BOTHER VICKI

As they point out, it is unclear whether these data support Fischer's claim about SVO order or whether they are a reflection of the fact that the informant knows English. They report also that the informant claims to prefer

"not to use non-multi-directional verbs to describe an interaction between two people when either of them could be S or O. This indicates that either the SVO order is an artifact or at least a seldom used way of differentiating S from O for these verbs. (p. 5)

When they revised their elicitation procedure in that the skits were lengthened--to induce continuous discourse-- and that the only instructions given were to use the desired verb, the results were of a very different nature. They found that through various strategies, the informant

"could basically eliminate the object from his 'sentences' with non-multi-directional reversible verbs [reversible S and O]. (p. 8)

I would point out here that the signer has an alternative way of indicating third person referents: he can, by

moving or orienting his body or merely his head in a particular direction, or different directions, "take on" one or more
third person "roles" (10). That is, he may move his body (or
head) and without additional overt pronominal reference, convey third person reference.

It is with the use of just this type of third person
reference that signers may avoid possibly ambiguous transitive constructions. An illustration of the means of this
type of construction follows in an example of discourse cul-
minating in "Sam bothers Hilda."

1. Give the nominal (name) signs and establish body orientations for each, or
        Give the nominal signs and establish markers for
each, or
        Give the nominal signs and establish body orienta-
tions with the first verb sign.

2. If markers are established, move them into location,
for example producing the sign MEET.

3. In the body position for SAM (e.g., facing leftward)
articulate the sign FLIRT.

4. In the body position for HILDA (e.g., facing rightward) and in the direction of SAM (i.e., to the right) make
the sign HATE.

5. In the SAM position, and in the direction of HILDA
(i.e., leftward), sign BOTHER.

Thus we might transcribe this sequence:

    body facing forward
                    HILDA MARKER (11)   SAM MARKER MEET

    body left   body right   body left
        FLIRT   HATE   BOTHER

    "Hilda and Sam meet. He flirts with her. She hates
    him. He bothers her."

[Instructions for reading text examples: Sign glosses
appear in upper case print. Simultaneous articulations of
two signs (when occurring) are indicated by two coordinated
lines of glosses--the top line for the dominant (usually
right) hand, the bottom line for the non-dominant (left) hand.
Lower case print above the gloss line (and below in later examples) indicates body positions or orientations (as they
occur) and direction of indices and verbs (following the index or the verb gloss). For ease of interpretation, all
transcriptions are simplified to indicate only relevant information.]

Thus the surface construction, after an establishment of
the nominal referents, completely avoids ambiguity by the use

of body orientations, indices and markers and thereby unambiguously indicates who's the subject and who's the object.
There is no need in this type of construction for any overt
lexicalization of either argument. This example represents
by far the most common type of construction in which non-
multi-directional verbs occur.

A variation of the strategy described above for avoiding
surface transitive constructions entails using the name signs
for each third person referent after each body turn. For example, consider

⎡body leftward, head down   body rightward, head
⎣   LYNN   SIT   READ   up

⎡   (marker moves from far left toward body)
⎣TOM   MARKER   COME

⎡body right, head down   (toward LYNN)
⎣   TELL   WRONG ANGRY

⎡body left, head up
⎣   LYNN SURPRISE(D)   SCARE(D)

"Lynn was sitting, reading. Tom comes along and tells
her she's wrong. He's angry at her. Lynn is surprised,
and she's scared."

It is important to point out here that subject nominals
and pro-forms are deletable. Once a subject is established,
it is assumed to be the subject until a new one is mentioned
(or established by body direction). It would appear that the
use or deletion of subject nominal signs and pro-forms are in
free variation--with the exception that they seem to always
be used for the purpose of contrast. Use of verb signs without overt subject (at the beginning of a discourse) always
indicates unmarked first person reference.

Although constructions entailing the use of body movement are the most common with these non-action (non-multi-
directional) verbs, other grammatical mechanisms are available to indicate agent/experiencer. One common alternative
construction has subject (agent/experiencer) designated by an
index to a previously established location for the nominal
referent. Consider, for example

⎡   to right   to left
⎣LYNN   INDEX   ASA   INDEX   /   LYNN   BOOK

⎡   right to left   to left   from left in to-
⎣LEND   / HE(INDEX)   LEND   ward signer

⎡   to left   to right
⎣/   HE(INDEX)   NERVOUS   /   I   GIVE   /

```
⎡               to left
⎣ HE(INDEX)                CALM  /
```

"...Lynn lent a book to Asa. He lent it to me. He was
nervous (so) I gave (the book) back to Lynn. He calmed
down."

If the object of a transitive verb does occur on the
surface, it usually appears as a "pronominal" index to the
pre-established location of the object referent. If the pro-
form appears, the verb and the index most commonly are articulated simultaneously. An example of this type of construction is:

```
⎡ ...YOU (INDEX to addressee)   KNOW?
⎣                               HER (INDEX to right, pre-
                                    established location of
                                    object referent)
```

"Do you know her?"

Another example appears in the text given below.
Similarly, the subject may be indicated by an indexic
gesture simultaneous to the verb phrase. In this type of
construction, the word order of the verb phrase may be OV or
VO or more commonly, merely V. For example

```
⎡ ...GIRL   HER (INDEX to established location)   NOT-KNOW?
⎣                                                 YOU (INDEX to
                                                      addressee)
```

or

```
⎡ ...NOT-KNOW?    HER (INDEX)
⎣    YOU (INDEX)
```

"You don't know her (the girl)?"

There is another class of verbs in ASL which may be said
to incorporate object (12). Each verb sign of this class has
a core hand configuration and movement, but the location
(place of articulation) and orientation of the sign is dependent on the location of the incorporated object. For example
consider the sign CHOP (an open flat palm hand, with a sharp
up and down, side to side, or to and fro movement--an iconic
representation of chopping). For the construction "chop meat"
the sign is made by first articulating MEAT and then making
the sign CHOP at the same place of articulation (the fleshy
part between the thumb and index finger of the non-dominant
hand); for "chop a tree," the signer forms the sign TREE with
his non-dominant hand, while CHOP is made with the dominant
hand at the location representing the trunk of the tree.

For verbs of this class, either the object and the verb signs are articulated simultaneously (remember there are two available articulators), or the object is signed first and then the verb sign is made at the same location. I believe that the choice of whether to articulate the object sign before or simultaneous with the verb sign is dependent on the phonological structure of the object sign. That is, for example, that it is possible to sign TREE and CHOP simultaneously (13), whereas it is phonologically impossible to sign MEAT--which is a necessarily two-handed sign--and CHOP at the same time. Thus, for verbs of this class, either the word order is OV or the object and verb are articulated simultaneously, an option only available to a manual/visual language.

Word order in ASL

The vast majority of propositions in ASL discourse appear on the surface as either a verb alone, subject verb (SV) or conjoined subject plus verb (SSV, SSSV). Constructions like SVVV are common and can be analyzed as subject + verb, deleted subject + verb, etc. I stated above that the subject may be deleted. As mentioned there, if the verb appears alone, i.e., without a subject, the subject is assumed to be the last one mentioned, unless the first verb in the discourse has a deleted subject, in which case there is always first person reference. (That is, first person reference may be completely unmarked.)

Although the majority of constructions are SV (or permutations thereof), we do find SVO order, but relatively infrequently. However, we also find SOV and OSV order. (And I would add that, contrary to Fischer's claim, in the texts I have analyzed, the OSV constructions do not have intonation breaks between object and subject--indicating that there is no topicalization in these constructions, or at least none marked by intonation breaks.)

Interestingly, there are also a significant number of OV constructions. For example, consider the sentence

GIRL DROP-OFF

in which GIRL is clearly the patient (in context). We could analyze this patient-verb type of construction as SV. But the construction is unmarked, and we might expect a grammatically marked construction where patient-verb is understood as subject-verb (i.e., as in English passive constructions). However, ASL has no grammatical inflections for verbs (14), so we can't expect to find this kind of markedness. A more satisfactory analysis, though, of these patient-verb constructions is that they are in fact OV and that the subject has been deleted from an (underlying) SOV construction. As I have stated, the subject is quite deletable in discourse. So, if this analysis is valid, we find evidence, not for SVO, but for SOV.

Another common construction--much more frequent than SVOV--is SVOV, with no pauses (where the verbs are identical). For example, consider these constructions taken from recorded discourse:

...I PACK (PUT-IN) CLOTHES PACK FINISH...

"I packed my clothes." (FINISH is a positive perfective
marker.)

...(I) MEET DEAF MEET...

"I met some deaf people."

Again, there are several ways to analyze these strings. One might say that they represented SVO plus (SO)V (with a dele- ted subject and object), or SVO + (S)V, or SV (agent verb) plus SV (patient verb) as above, or SV (agent verb) plus OV (patient verb), or, and I prefer this analysis for the rea- sons given above, SV + (S)OV with a deleted subject. In any case, that this type of construction is far more prevalent than SVO strikes me as significant.

For these data, then, the only thing we can say in re- gard to fixed word order when a transitive verb and two argu- ments appear on the surface, is that the preference seems to be for verb-last constructions. We will see the significance of this below in regard to topic and comment.

What is striking, though, is that the language tends not to have constructions with (semantically) transitive verbs and two lexical arguments appearing on the surface. We have seen that different strategies are available for the various classes of verbs for avoiding overt lexical mention of the object. For multi-directional verbs, often neither the sub- ject nor the object overtly surface in lexicalized form. The direction of movement from source location to goal location indicates who's who. (It seems obvious that what's happening is that the movement of the verb represents the direction of movement of the action.) If the subject or object does sur- face, the form is most commonly that of pro-forms--indices to the locations of source and goal. These may be articulated before, after, or simultaneous to the verb. Occasionally lexical items, such as name signs (signs for names of people), appear before the verb, usually for clarification (i.e., who is that person you're indexing?).

For non-multi-directional verbs, those which are physi- cally anchored to the body, body positions are established

for referents in the discourse and the verbs are signed in
the position of agent or experiencer (subject) in the direction of patient or beneficiary (object), so that there's
never any ambiguity as to who's the subject and who's the
object.

    I should mention that the body position strategy is of-
ten used with multi-directional verbs in conjunction with the
movement of the verb from source to goal locations.

    I offer as an example of discourse in ASL, the following
text.

```
[                                    to the left
[ ONE TIME /(15) I WALK / MEET               / ASA
                                 HE (INDEX)
                                                           to the left
[     to left        to left        to left                   to right
[ MEET          TALK           TALK            / I         SEE
                                           HE(MARKER)-------------
                                                       (maintained)
                                                       on far left
[                       on right            (marker moves) toward
[ LYNN SHE (INDEX→MARKER)          MOVE-ALONG              signer  /
[ ------------------------------------------------------------------
[     to left     head left                          head left
[ I ASK      /            ASA KNOW?      / LYNN /
                      HER(INDEX)---------
                                        to right
[           to right        head left              from right to
[ HER(INDEX)          NOT-KNOW /           INTRODUCE?          left
[          to left                       to left
[ / HE(INDEX)        ASA SCARE(D) HE(INDEX)       SCARE(D)  /
[                         body leftward (LYNN's position)
[ I  gesture-of-annoyance  /
[       to left (to signer's original position)          to left
[ BOTHER                                          / HE(INDEX)
[                            to right
[ gesture-of-annoyance /  I WAVE          / LYNN
[          from right to left (toward signer)
[ COME(MARKER)                                   / I
[          right hand from right leftward to meet left hand
[ INTRODUCE                                      on left  /
```

137

```
           body rightward (ASA's position)
⎡ ASA
⎣ HE(INDEX)
           to left
⎡ LYNN                / TALK / BOTH LIKE LAUGH TALK / I TIME /
⎣ SHE(INDEX)
                 to right
⎡              side to side
⎣ I LEAVE / 2(MARKER)             / I LEAVE / 2(MARKER) TALK
⎡            straight out from signer
⎣ GO-OFF-TOGETHER                       / BOTH
⎡              outward
⎣ GO-OFF-TOGETHER             / WOW / PAST WORK / WOW /
⎡    outward                    to right
⎣ WATCH          / WOW / I  GO              /
```

"One time, I was walking and met Asa. I met him (we
met), and we talked and talked. I saw Lynn (to my right)
coming along. I asked, do you know her, Asa? (or I
asked Asa if he knew her.) That's Lynn. He didn't know
her. Should I introduce her to you (or do you want me
to introduce her to you)? Asa was scared. He was
scared. I (thought) eh! I waved to her. Lynn came
over. I introduced them (her to him). Asa and Lynn
talked. I (saw the) time. I left. The two of them
(stood there). I left. The two talked and went off together. Both (of them) went off together. Wow. That
was fast work. Wow. I watched them. Wow. I went."

Analysis of the text is as follows:

```
⎡                          in the direction of referent₁ /
⎣ time-adverbial / S  V  /  V
⎡              toward R₁   toward R₁   toward R₁ /
⎢ 0₁            V          V          V
⎣ placement of R₁
⎡                      toward R₂
⎢ S                  V            0₂ and S (+ placement of R₂)
⎣ R₂ (and placement of R₂)
⎡             toward R₁      head to R₁
⎣ V / S  V          /              S  V?                /
                                   0₂ (pro-form)
```

$$
\left[\begin{array}{l} \text{predicate} \end{array}\right. /\ \begin{array}{c} \text{head to } R_1 \\ O_2 \ V \end{array} /\ \begin{array}{c} \text{head to } R_1 \quad \text{from } R_2 \text{ to } R_1 \\ V \end{array} /
$$

$$
\left[\begin{array}{l} \text{S(pro-form)} \end{array}\right. \begin{array}{c} \text{to } R_1 \\ \end{array} S\ V\ S(\text{pro-form}) \begin{array}{c} \text{to } R_1 \\ \end{array} V\ /\ S\ V
$$

$$
\left[\begin{array}{l} \text{body in } R_2 \text{ position} \qquad \text{toward signer position} \\ V \end{array}\right. /\ O_1(\text{pro-form})
$$

$$
\left[\begin{array}{l} V\ /\ S \end{array}\right. \begin{array}{c} \text{to } R_2 \\ V \end{array} /\ S \begin{array}{c} \text{from } R_2 \text{ position toward signer} \\ V \end{array} /
$$

$$
\left[\begin{array}{l} S \end{array}\right. \begin{array}{c} \text{from } R_2 \text{ to } R_1 \\ V \end{array} /\ S \begin{array}{c} \text{body in } R_1 \text{ position} \\ R_1 \text{ placement} \end{array}
$$

$$
\left[\begin{array}{l} S \\ R_2 \text{ placement} \end{array}\right. /\ V\ /\ S\ V\ V\ V\ /\ S\ V\ /\ S\ V\ /\ S\ /
$$

$$
[S\ V\ /\ S\ V\ V\ /\ S\ V\ /\ \text{interjection}\ /\ \text{predicate}\ /
$$

$$
\left[\begin{array}{l} \text{interjection} \end{array}\right. /\ \begin{array}{c} \text{toward } R_1 R_2 \\ V \end{array} /\ \text{interjection}\ /\ S\ V\ /
$$

Summary: distinguishing subject and object in ASL

In all languages, there have to be ways of distinguishing subject and object in constructions with transitive verbs and reversible subject and object. Oral languages have two means of doing this. One is to have fixed word order and the other is to have case markings on the nouns which indicate their relation to the verb. Many languages use a combination of these two strategies. However, ASL (and I suspect all sign languages) does not avail itself of these options. How does a language without fixed word order or case markings allow speakers to identify subject and object (and other arguments)?

1. With intransitive verbs there is clearly no problem. There is only one (main) argument.

2. In constructions with transitive verbs and non-reversible subject and object, again no difficulty arises. Differentiation by any means is unnecessary, as by the semantic nature of the arguments, only one could be the subject and one the object. (Of course in a language such as ASL, it might be difficult to "create worlds" in which one could say "The zucchini ate the man" but I don't believe that it's impossible.)

3. For constructions with (semantically) transitive verbs and reversible subject and object, the language has the following strategies available:

139

(a) Use of the signing space to establish locations of referents and to move verbs between (among) those locations (especially with multi-directional verbs--action verbs).

(b) Use of the body and the body-space to indicate different third person referents without overt lexical items for those referents. (With multi-directional and non-multi-directional verbs, especially non-action verbs.)

(c) Avoidance of ambiguous transitive constructions by, for example, choosing (surface) one-place verb constructions in those cases in which many oral languages have a choice between one-place and two-place constructions. For example, English has the intransitive verbs "angry," "bothered," "scared," "frightened," "pleased," "surprised," " in love," and the corresponding transitive verbs "anger" (or "make angry"), "bother," "scare," "frighten," "please," "surprise," "love." ASL allows for only the (surface) one-place constructions with this class of verbs. (I am purposely avoiding the use of the term intransitive to describe these ASL verbs.)

It would appear then that for the class of psych verbs, ASL has signs which designate only either the reaction of the experiencer or only the action of the agent but which do not lexicalize or "package" the whole "scene."

(d) Heavy reliance on context. If a language has a grammatical system which entails establishing locations in space and body positions for referents in order to distinguish subject from object (and agent from patient, etc.)--as ASL does--then there must be, by necessity, great reliance on the context of that pre-establishment of referents. In establishing location and/or body positions for referents prior to comment, expectations are set up by the text. Consider, for example, a text which begins by establishing markers for two people (2 extended index fingers pointing upward), say Judy and Fred. The Judy marker moves upward and goes past the Fred marker. Then the Fred marker moves up behind the Judy marker. If the next sign is TAP-ON-THE-SHOULDERS, it is reasonable for the signer to assume that his addressee will understand that Fred and only Fred could be the agent of TAP. Of course, I don't intend to imply that oral language systems, which have grammatical systems entailing case markings or fixed word order, or both, do not depend on context for establishing the identity of referents.

ASL has a tendency to avoid adding (or having appear on the surface) the grammatical "trappings" that regularly occur in oral languages (16)--which could be called leaving out anything you don't absolutely need. (e.g., no tense or case markings, aspectual markings by phonological alternation, avoidance of surface object, deletion of identical subjects, "incorporation" of object, number, manner adverbials (by phonological alternation), etc.) We have seen examples of this tendency in the text given above. There are two possible explanations of this phenomenon--both relating to the modality of communication.

It has been demonstrated (17) that, although the rate of transmission of proposition per minute is the same or similar for ASL and for English, the rate of words or signs (i.e., lexical items) per minute in ASL is about one-half that of English. This difference can be accounted for in that ASL does avoid grammatical "trappings" so that it takes far fewer signs to say the same proposition in ASL than it takes words in English. An explanation of this fact lies in the use of the manual/visual modality. The articulation space used in a manual/visual language is far larger than that of a language in the oral/auditory mode. Thus articulations are grosser and take more time to perform. It is not difficult to see why a language so constructed (constrained?) would tend to avoid syntactic redundancy and to incorporate a lot of information into a single sign. It is also possible that due to the very (necessary) slowness of articulation, the kind of syntactic redundancy we find in all oral languages is unnecessary in manual/visual languages.

Another possible explanation of this phenomenon lies in the nature of visual perception. (I think that the real explanation is probably a combination of both of these factors.) It has been shown (18) that short term iconic memory is considerably shorter than short term auditory memory. It may be that the brevity of short term iconic memory imposes just those conditions on a visual language which would force it to reduce strings to the least complex (or least time consuming) constructions, thus the tendency for reduction (or lack) of grammatical redundancy.

Discourse situation

To summarize the general discourse situation in ASL:

1. Nominal signs are articulated and established in space, either by indexic or marker reference or by body position.

2. Verb signs are then (a) manipulated between or among these previously established locations for nominal referents or (b) articulated on the body which is in the appropriate pre-established position for agent or experiencer.

3. If the first verb in a discourse appears without a subject, first person reference is assumed. After the first

instance of a new subject, subsequent identical subject may
be deleted, with apparently no change in meaning. The subject is assumed to be the same as the last one given, until a
new subject is mentioned (19).

4. Word order is relatively free, with the exception of
the tendency for the verb to be last. The vast majority of
strings have merely SV constructions (or variations of SV
like SSV (conjoined subject + verb), or just V with the subject deleted). Various strategies are available for avoiding
overt two-place verb constructions (i.e., for not having the
object appear on the surface).

5. Nominal lexical items may appear on the surface after their spatial establishment seemingly wherever they
please. Their appearance would seem to be in free variation
with their non-appearance--possibly a nominal sign is added
for the purposes of clarification, emphasis or contrast.

6. Up to four or five (20) different referents or locations may be established in space and maintained (remembered)
within a given discourse. The signer then may index the
space corresponding to the location of the referent (real or
grammatically established) and simultaneously articulate the
comment.

Topic, comment, and topicalization in ASL

Given the discourse situation in ASL, the nature of topic is relatively straightforward. For the purposes of this
discussion I would define topic as that or those nominals
which are established first--thus creating a scene (21)--and
as such become definite.

In ASL discourse then, the topic(s) is (are) mentioned
first, and then subsequent comment is made. Given this definition of topic, any nominal (or several), whether appearing
later as agent or patient (or whatever) of a particular verb,
may be the topic of any given sentence or discourse. Given
the discourse situation--the establishment of nominal referents first and only then the articulation of verb signs in
most constructions--it seems clear that this is the case (or
at least a viable analysis).

But consider the case where the nominals are indefinite.
Generally, indefinite nominals also occur before the verb.
Are these then topics as well, and is the definition incorrect, or are they not? I feel that we can safely call these
indefinite nominals topics, in that, as we have seen, they
are established in discourse in much the same way that definite nominals are. First, the nominal lexical items are articulated, either with nominal or question intonation (22),
or when questioned, preceded by the phrase YOU KNOW _____?

Immediately following, location or body position for these
referents may be established. Then comment may be made as if
they had been definite (because they are definite in a sense,
at this point in the discourse).

We find discourse beginning as follows, for example:

```
⌈                                               to right
⌊YOU  KNOW  LYNN?   INDEX   (establishment of location)           /

⌈                          to left
⌊ALICE?  INDEX   (establishment)          /

⌈          right marker moves left          markers make  contact
│MOVE-ALONG                               MEET
│MOVE-ALONG
⌊          left marker moves right

⌈     alternate right and left
⌊TALK                            ...
```

For the sake of simplicity, we might <u>translate</u> ASL constructions of this kind as follows (23):

You know X? You know Y? Well...

ASL appears with or without the "You know," of course. Thus,
a good translation of the text above may be:

"You know Lynn? How about Alice? Well, they were coming along and then they met and started talking..."

If the referents are completely unknown to the addressee
--that is if the signer isn't merely bringing them to the consciousness of (reminding) the addressee--then a description
or explanation of the referents will occur subsequent to or
prior to the establishment of location.

I would point out that oral languages, as well as sign
languages, have this type of option available in discourse.
English has, mainly for the purposes of clarification of
nominal referents, constructions like the following:

You know Sam? (pause) You know his sister? (pause)
You know her husband, Burt? Well Burt's mother...

Sequences like the one above are much more likely in English
discourse than complex nested constructions like

Sam's sister's husband's mother...

(and of course, are easier to process) (24).

Some interesting evidence for this analysis of topic in
ASL comes from attempts at elicitation of sentences (from
written English cue sentences) like

LYNN A. FRIEDMAN

I want to meet someone.
He wants to marry the girl next door.

in which the object of the English sentence has either an
opaque or a transparent meaning (i.e., He wants to marry a
girl who is the "girl next door" type or the girl who actually does live next door). The more common reading in English is the opaque one (25).

When asked to give ASL counterparts of sentences of this
type, the informant consistently gave the transparent reading
of the object, and claimed not to be able to give the opaque
meaning in his ASL sentence. (This informant's knowledge of
English is excellent.) Thus, he would establish a hypothetical definite reference for example GIRL, and establish the
referent's location in space. Then the previously (or newly) established subject is indicated and the verb formed in
the direction of the object--as we have seen with definite
object constructions. Thus the string would appear as, for
example:

```
         to right              to left
GIRL  INDEX          /  HE(INDEX)         WANT
```

```
    marker for HE makes contact with GIRL marker at right
MEET                                         location    /
```

These data suggest that it is impossible (or at least
difficult) to have an indefinite object as such in ASL (that
is to distinguish an indefinite from a definite). Further
study is needed to confirm or disprove this hypothesis.

These data also clearly support the claim that topic--in
the sense of definite nominals--must be established before
discourse can proceed.

To indicate the role that the establishment of topic--or
what some may call topicalization--plays in ASL discourse, I
offer the following short text.

```
YOU KNOW-THAT  /  TRAIN  /
```

```
       marker for train--fist--moves side to side be-
       tween right and left end points
GO-BETWEEN
```

```
at left end point        at right end point
              s-j  /                    s-f  /
```

"There's a train that runs between San Jose and San
Francisco."

This string resulted from an elicitation asking for a
translation of the above English sentence. TRAIN is established, movement of the verb made between two locations and

144

then the locations are named. I asked the informant what he would have been talking about before that string could be uttered. Without hesitation, he answered, "trains." I then asked whether the following construction was viable:

$$
\begin{bmatrix} \text{at the left} & \text{at the right} \\ \quad \text{s-j} \; / & \quad \text{s-f} \; / \quad \text{TRAIN} \; / \end{bmatrix}
$$

$$
\begin{bmatrix} & \text{marker for train moves between right and left} \\ \text{GO-BETWEEN} & \text{locations} \; / \end{bmatrix}
$$

His answer was that it was not <u>unless</u> I had been discussing cities or San Jose and San Francisco before the string was uttered!

In this example, I think we find clear-cut evidence for the type of topic-establishment--or topicalization, if you will--that I have discussed above.

Conclusion

Of course, the discourse situation in ASL is much more complex than I have indicated here. Far more detailed study must be made to give a completely accurate picture. I have tried to give a basic account of various aspects of the discourse situation, including the different classes of verbs in ASL and the mechanisms (depending on the type of verb) by which the language avoids surface objects. These mechanisms have either been developed because of or have resulted in a lack of fixed word order in the language. I have analyzed these facts about ASL discourse in regard to the notion and the nature of topic.

I do not deny the possibility of influence of English grammar on ASL because of the unique linguistic situation in which ASL (or any sign language) exists. However, I believe that the effect of English on ASL has been minimal and would expect it to remain so (despite social pressure to make ASL conform to English). The grammatical mechanisms and the way in which grammatical relations are indicated in ASL are unique to visual language and more importantly are a highly efficient means of utilizing the modality of communication. Language in the oral/auditory modality must rely on case markings and/or linearly fixed word order to mark grammatical relations because it does not have the options of spatial relations and expression that manual/visual language has. There is no need for fixed word order in a language that has a more efficient means (within the modality) for expressing the relations between argument and verb, so we would expect such a language neither to develop nor to adopt such a system.

Hopefully, we can gain insight into the workings of oral

language and language in general, by first looking in a "non-oral-language-centric" way at visual language and then returning with our findings for another fresh look at oral language.

Notes

1. I am grateful to Charles J. Fillmore, John H. Cro-
thers, and Wallace L. Chafe for their comments and suggestions, to the members of my class on the structure of ASL for
their enthusiasm, creativity, questions, criticisms, and answers, and to Hedy Udkovich, Mary-Ellen Lentz, Lisa Jacobs,
and especially Tommie Radford, informants par excellence.

2. There are also several manual/visual codes for English, used primarily for pedagogical purposes.

3. Friedman (1973), p. 3.

4. These data have been accumulated over a three-year
period from five informants of both sexes and of various
ages.

5. For further discussion of multi-directional verbs
see Friedman (1973).

6. Friedman (1973) presents a more complete discussion of
"pronominalization" in ASL.

7. The distinction between indices and markers was
pointed out and discussed in detail by Mandel (1975).

8. These observations were made by both Mandel (1975)
and De Matteo (1975).

9. Given here are standard glosses of signs. The reader should not infer anything about the semantic or syntactic
nature of the Sign verbs by comparing the glosses to their
English counterparts.

10. See Friedman (1973) for detail.

11. Here an extended index finger pointing upward.

12. See Friedman (1973) for further discussion. Mark
Mandel has pointed out to me that to view these verbs as incorporating object is very oral-language-centric. He discusses these verbs and similar phenomena at some length in
Mandel (1975).

13. I'm not at all sure we should be analyzing signs
like CHOP-TREE as two signs. I feel more comfortable thinking of these as single signs. Mandel (1975) discusses this
point. However, I will consider it two signs for the purposes of this paper, in which I am particularly examining the
placement of the object in relation to the verb.

14. ASL does have aspect markers which change the phonological shape of the verb.

15. The slashes indicate actual pauses.

16. Bellugi and Fischer (1972) describe this aspect of
the grammar of ASL.

17. Bellugi and Fischer (1972).

18. Boyes (1972).

19. The same holds true for locative and temporal ref-

erence. See Friedman (1973) for details.

20. Different informants report (and display) different capacities.

21. The term "scene" is borrowed from Fillmore (1975).

22. Question intonation on a given lexical item entails raising the eyebrows, furrowing the brow, and holding the questioned sign for an extra beat. For detail see Friedman (1974a, 1974b, 1975).

23. This translation of ASL strings was suggested to me by Leonard Talmy.

24. C.J. Fillmore has pointed out to me that Japanese has two particles attached to nominals which serve to inform the addressee of topic. "Wa" is a standard topic or topicalization marker (the analysis of "wa" varies depending on the analyst). "Ne" following a nominal means something like "you know?" or "do you follow?" and requires an acknowledgement (of understanding) from the addressee. It seems to me that the type of constructions I have described in ASL serve the function of either "wa" or "ne" or both, depending on the discourse situation. My informants seem to use YOU KNOW X? constructions (rather than just X plus establishment without question intonation) far more frequently when addressing non-native or non-fluent signers like me than when signing to other deaf people or hearing people with native knowledge of ASL.

25. This elicitation, its results and the ensuing analysis and other implication to ASL grammar are discussed in Thompson (1975).

TOPIC, PRONOUN AND GRAMMATICAL AGREEMENT

by

Talmy Givón

1.   Introduction (1)

In this paper I would like to lay to rest two myths about grammatical agreement. The first identifies grammatical agreement with subject-verb agreement. I will suggest below that this is an unfortunate view of the phenomenon, and that the underlying reality upon which grammatical agreement rises is that of topic-verb agreement. The second is the tacit assumption that agreement and pronominalization are two distinct processes. I will suggest below that they are fundamentally one and the same phenomenon, and that neither diachronically nor, most often, synchronically could one draw a demarcating line on any principled grounds. In diachronic terms first, I will show that agreement arises via topic-shifting constructions in which the topicalized NP is coreferential to one argument of the verb. As a result, in languages in which pronouns--rather than zeroes--are used in anaphora, the coreferent noun within the sentence itself is replaced by an anaphoric pronoun. This pronoun should be viewed as topic agreement. I will also show that when a language reanalyzes the topic constituent as the normal subject or object of the neutral, non-topicalized sentence pattern, it perforce also has reanalyzed subject-topic agreement as subject agreement and object-topic agreement as object agreement. One can then make the prediction that languages which use zero anaphoric pronouns and in particular do not use anaphoric pronouns in topic-shift constructions, will not develop subject-verb or object-verb agreement (2). In synchronic terms, when erstwhile pronouns get re-analyzed as agreement morphemes, they most commonly continue to perform their anaphoric function. Thus, it is well known that languages with a viable paradigm of subject-verb agreement may anaphorically delete the subject NP without replacing it with an independent pronoun. Numerous examples throughout this paper will point out to this anaphoric use of both subject and object agreement. Further, many examples of object agreement will also illustrate the lingering role of grammatical agreement in signaling relative topicality of various NPs (3). In addition I will also illustrate a variety of other functions which grammatical agreement may assume once it had "matured."

2.   The Implicational Hierarchy

In a recent paper Moravcsik (1974) has pointed out that a certain implicational relation holds in languages between the existence of subject agreement, definite object agreement and (unrestricted) object agreement with the verb. She observes that among all logically possible types, the following seem to be most prevalent in languages:

1   Subject agreement only
     Subject and definite-object agreement
     Subject, definite-object and indefinite-object
          agreement

These observations may be summed up in the following implicational schema:

2   INDEF.OBJ. ⊃ DEF.OBJ. ⊃ SUBJ.

where the implicational sign "⊃" is a one-way conditional. Moravcsik has further suggested that another link in this implicational hierarchy may be human-object, so that 2 above may be recast as:

3   INDEF.OBJ. ⊃ HUMAN OBJ. ⊃ DEF.OBJ. ⊃ SUBJ.

In this paper I would like to show how this implicational hierarchy of the likelihood of verb agreement is governed by the universal hierarchy of topicality, i.e., the likelihood of various NP arguments being the topic of sentences, and more particularly the topic in topic-shift constructions. Although the hierarchy discussed above may be expressed as one linear expression, I think it is nevertheless the result of a number of binary hierarchic relations which may be given as:

4   a.   HUMAN > NON-HUMAN
     b.   DEFINITE > INDEFINITE
     c.   MORE INVOLVED PARTICIPANT > LESS INVOLVED PARTICIPANT
     d.   1ST PERSON > 2ND PERSON > 3RD PERSON

Of these, 4a reflects the tendency for humans to speak more about humans than non-humans, i.e., the ego/anthropocentric nature of discourse. 4b is merely a reflection of old information being the topic and new information being the assertion. 4c would predict the following case hierarchy with respect to topicality:

5   AGENT > DATIVE > ACCUSATIVE

It is born out by the consistent and highly universal pairing of the discourse function "topic" and the semantic function "agent" into one highly universal agregate function "subject" (4). It is also supported by the overwhelmingly human composition of agents and datives in discourse (5). It is further supported by the correlation between more vs. less involvement in the action in the pairing of dative vs. accusative (6). The case hierarchy in 5 also correlates with the high frequency of definiteness of the normally human arguments "agent" and "dative" as compared with "accusative" (7). Finally, 4d expresses the ego-centric character of discourse, where the speaker tends to be the universal point of reference and the most highly presupposed argument. This is reflected in speech acts, dexis, the government of coreference relations (8), as well as the choice of dative over accusative (9). What I will show further below is that the hierarchy in 4d may have some correlates in grammatical agreement. To summarize at this point, while the four hierarchies in 4 above exhibit a number of inter-dependencies (or "redundancies"), I will claim that their combined weight produces the seemingly stable overall case hierarchies in 3 and 5.

3.   Anaphoric Pronouns and Topic-Shift in Discourse

In this section I will outline the difference between two discourse devices, both used in contexts when the topic of discussion has been mentioned in the preceding discourse and is thus presupposed by the speaker to be known to the hearer. The first device is anaphoric pronominalization (AP), the second topic-shift (TS). I will contrast the felicity of their use following two discourse contexts, one in which the topic has been mentioned directly before and no ambiguity of reference is to be expected, the other where an intervening gap between the first and subsequent mention of the topic occurs, and in addition other topics, some pertaining to the same pronominal gender, have been discussed during that intervening gap.

6   Context: Once there was a wizard.
        AP: He lived in Africa.
        TS: ?Now the wizard, he lived in Africa.

7   Context: Once there was a wizard. He was very wise,
                   rich, and was married to a beautiful witch.
                   They had two sons. The first was tall and
                   brooding, he spent his days in the forest
                   hunting snails, and his mother was afraid
                   of him. The second was short and viva-
                   cious, a bit crazy but always game.
        AP: ?He lived in Africa.
        TS: Now the wizard, he lived in Africa.

The oddity of the TS strategy in context 6 derives from the fact that it is unnecessary, it is an over-use of a powerful or more-marked discourse device in a less-marked context. The oddity of the AP strategy in 7, conversely, derives from its insufficiency, it is not a powerful enough tool in the more marked context of 7, where the most natural coreferent for "he" is the last mentioned second son. When a discourse device is said to be "infelicitous" for being either too powerful or too weak in a given context, this is not to suggest that it may not be used, but only that it may be either wasteful or insufficient. And while the latter will always create ambiguity and confusion, the wasteful over-use of discourse machinery, via "unnecessary" repetition, may actually have a useful function: When the channel of communication is noisy, or when the communicative system is relatively frail, over-use may be just the right strategy to insure that the hearer knows what the speaker is talking about (10).

One more discourse device must at this point be introduced, labeled after-thought topic-shift (AT). This device represents a hedge between the two strategies outlined above, so that the speaker starts out by assuming that the weaker, AP strategy will do, then changes his/her mind and--just to be safe--repeats the topic again:

8   Context: Once there was a wizard.
     AT: He lived in Africa, the wizard did.

In some sense, then, the AT strategy represents a certain amount of wastefulness, and is in this sense akin to the over-use of the TS strategy as discussed above. In the next two sections I will try to show why the two over-use strategies, of topic-shift and afterthought-topic, underlie the diachronic development of subject and object agreement from topic agreement.

4.   The Rise of Subject Agreement

One universal restriction on TS constructions, both left-dislocated (TS) and right-dislocated (AT), is that the topic constituent may be either definite or generic, but never referential-indefinite (11). The subject in many languages, such as Mandarin, KinyaRwanda or Malagasi, also show this restriction. Thus subjects tend to be overwhelmingly definite and referential even in languages which tolerate, at the "competence" level, indefinite subjects (12). Seeing that in "subject-prominent" languages the subject NP holds most of the topic functions, it is of course not altogether an accident that subjects are highest of all case-arguments on the topicality hierarchy. And thus it is not an accident that they are the first and most frequent of all cases to develop grammatical agreement. The process by which this is done may be called de-marking: A subject topic-shift construction is over-used in a weaker context. Speakers eventually recognize the context as being much too weak to justify a marked status for the TS construction. Thus they re-analyze it as the neutral syntax. The erstwhile topic-subject gets re-analyzed as "mere" subject, while the topic-agreement anaphoric pronoun gets re-analyzed as subject-agreement:

9
TS ("MARKED")	NEUTRAL (RE-ANALYZED)
The man, he came ==>	The man he-came
TOP PRO	SUBJ AG

The morphological binding of the pronoun to the verb is an inevitable natural phenomenon, cliticization, having to do with the unstressed status of pronouns, their decreased information load and the subsequent loss of resistance to phonological attrition (13).

The re-analysis process schematized in 9 above is widely attested in non-standard dialects of English (14) and French, where the subject pronouns are in the process of becoming obligatory subject-agreement markers. It is also widely attested in Pidgins and Creoles derived from either English or French vocabulary. Thus, in the Tok-Pisin English-based pidgin of the New Guinea Highlands one finds the third person singular masculine pronoun "he" as the invariant subject-agreement marker (15):

10   ol i sindaun
        all he sit-down
        "They sat down"

        em i paitim
        him he fight-him
        "He beat him"

        mipela i go go go
        me-fellow he go go go
        "I went for a long journey"

Similarly, in a French based Creole (16):

11   lé dié i sont malin
        le Dieu il sont malin
        "God is clever"

        lé démon i pensé
        lé démon il pensée
        "The devil thought"

Occasionally, where the accusative pronoun ("him") spreads into the subject-topic position, as is very common in non-standard French and English, it is this pronoun that is used for subject agreement, rather than the nominative, as may be seen in the following example from Hawaiian English Pidgin (17):

155

12   Mai brada <u>him</u> no skeed
       my brother <u>him</u> not scared
       "My brother is not scared"

The naturalness of this process in child language was
first suggested in Gruber (1967), where the possibility is
raised that in early child-language, <u>over-topicalization</u>
strategies are much more pronounced than in subsequent adult
speech. Similar suggestions concerning the role of repetition in establishing the topic in child language have recently been made by Keenan (1974). Further, Limber (1973) has
noted the strong role which discourse-pragmatic strategies
play in early acquisition of syntax, as well as the fact that
at some early stage "subject" NPs are very seldom lexical
nouns, but only pronouns or names. Both child language and
Pidgins/Creoles share one condition in common: They develop
under a heavy <u>communicative stress.</u> If under these conditions
over-elaboration and over-topicalization are used with higher
frequency, as is only natural, then the development of subject
agreement from topic agreement is even better motivated: In
this context, one may choose to view the seeming abundance of
subject agreement in non-standard dialects (of English or
French) as a reflection of this highly natural process. While
the school system weeds this "incorrect" feature out of the
grammar of the educated minority, the natural tendency sur-
vives longest in the language of the less educated or illiter-
ate.

5.   The Rise of Object Agreement

In this section I will disregard the problem of <u>dative</u>
objects, to which I will return in the following section. In
contrast with subjects, accusative objects tend to show a
large percentage of <u>indefinites</u>, and the slot is in fact a
major one in which new arguments are presented in discourse
(18). This is also a case slot where <u>non-humans</u> abound. Given
the topicality hierarchies discussed above, it is thus likely
that their frequency as discourse topics will be much lower
than that of subjects. If this will also reflect in a lower
frequency of topic-shifted objects, as is only reasonable to
assume, then the lower frequency of object agreement vs. subject agreement finds a natural explanation. What I'd like to
suggest here is that the development of object-verb agreement
follows roughly the same process of demarking an over-used
topic-shift construction. Except that in this case, at least
for SVO languages, I suspect the afterthought-topic construction (AT) may play an important role as an intermediate, being
that it does stand in some type of intermediate position

between topic-shifting and "mere" anaphoric pronominalization
(19). Schematically, then:

13

TS ("marked")	AT ("semi-marked")	NEUTRAL ("demarked")
the man, I saw him =>	I saw him, the man =>	I saw-him the man

In the remainder of this section I will illustrate the feasi-
bility of this model by tracing the development of object
agreement in Bantu languages, showing how it follows closely
the implicational hierarchy given in 3 above, with the order of development being: SUBJECT > DEF. OBJECT > HUMAN OBJECT
> OBJECT.

All Bantu languages have obligatory subject-verb agreement, where the pronominal origin of the agreement morpheme is
established beyond a shred of doubt. Subject agreement morphemes still retain their older function as anaphoric pronouns. Thus, in Swahili:

14 mtoto   a-li-kuja   "The child came"
            a-li-kuja   "He came" (the child)
    watoto wa-li-kuja   "The children came"
            wa-li-kuja   "They came" (the children)
    kikopo ki-li-vunjika   "The cup broke"
            ki-li-vunjika   "It broke" (the cup)
    vikopo vi-li-vunjika   "The cups broke"
            vi-li-vunjika   "They broke" (the cups)

Object anaphoric pronominalization is also universal in Bantu,
as in Swahili (20):

15 ni-li-vunja kikopo   "I broke a cup"
    ni-li-ki-vunja   "I broke it"
    ni-li-vunja vikopo   "I broke some cups"
    ni-li-vi-junja   "I broke them"

Further, the marked preposed-topic pattern is attested,
to my knowledge, in all Bantu languages. The topicalized object is obligatorily definite (unless it is generic), and the
anaphoric object pronoun appears obligatorily, as in Swahili:

16 mtoto, ni-li-mw-ona   "The child, I saw him"
    watoto, ni-li-wa-ona   "The children, I saw them"
    kikopo, ni-li-ki-vunja "The cup, I broke it"
    vikopo, ni-li-vi-vunja "The cups, I broke them"

Initially, Bantu languages had no definite article per
se. They all have spatial demonstratives, and in many languages one of those, normally the distal one, got de-marked
into a discourse-reference device, i.e., a definitizer. Such

157

an innovation is attested in Swahili, as in:

17   mtoto <u>yule</u>   "That child" (away from speaker &
                                hearer)
      <u>yule</u> mtoto   "the child" (mentioned in previous
                                discourse)

In many Bantu languages, e.g., Rwanda, Bemba and others, this
development may be superfluous for subject NPs, since it is
very hard to get anything except a <u>definite</u> interpretation on
subject nouns to begin with. Further, in a number of languages, e.g., Dzamba (21), the pre-prefix (initial) vowel,
historically a <u>referentiality</u> marker, has extended its func-
tion--at least in some environments--to become a ·definitizer.
In most Bantu languages, however, unmarked object nominals
may be interpreted as either definite or indefinite (disre-
garding their discourse frame), as in Bemba:

18   naa-mweene umuana   "I saw the/a child"

In a number of languages such as Luganda, Rwanda-Rundi and, I
suspect, others, one may observe the beginning of using the
object pronoun as a definitizer for object nouns--i.e., as a
<u>definite object agreement</u> marker. This is clearly done via
the marked topic construction 12b. In Luganda this also involves a contrast between the presence and absence of the pre-
prefix vowel, and is further confined to negative environments (22). Thus:

19 a. ya-laba <u>omu</u>-sajja   "He saw <u>a/the</u> man"
   b. ta-ya-laba <u>mu</u>-sajja   "He didn't see <u>any</u> man"
   c. *ta-ya-laba <u>omu</u>-sajja
   d. <u>omu</u>-sajja, ta-ya-<u>mu</u>-laba {"He didn't see <u>the</u> man" }
                                  {"The man, he didn't see <u>him</u>"}
   e. *<u>omu</u>-sajja, ta-ya-laba

Thus, the only way in Luganda of expressing a referential (and
thus <u>definite</u>) object of a negative verb is via the marked-
topic construction with obligatory pronominalization. This
creates an obligatory co-occurrence, albeit in a restricted
environment, between definite object and the anaphoric object
pronoun.

    The next step toward generalizing this incipient definite-
object agreement may be observed in Rwanda, a Lake-Bantu language closely related to Luganda. In this language (i) the
co-occurrence of anaphoric object pronouns with definite objects is extended to non-negative environments, (ii) the last
vestige of the function of the pre-prefix vowel is lost, and
(iii) the definite object NP does not need to be preposed anymore, but rather it may occur in its neutral post-verbal

position, not only as a <u>marked</u> "afterthought topic," but virtually as an unmarked pattern of object definitization. Thus (23):

20 a. ya-bonye umunhu   "He saw <u>a</u> man"
   b. nhi-ya-bonye umunhu   "He didn't see <u>any</u> man"
   c. umuhnu, nhi-ya-<u>mu</u>-bonye   "The man, he didn't see <u>him</u>"
   d. *nhi-ya-<u>mu</u>-bonye umunhu
   e. ya-<u>mu</u>-bonye umunhu   { "He saw <u>him</u>, the man" }
                                      { "He saw <u>the</u> man" }

Thus, while in the negative the older situation (cf. Luganda) still prevails, i.e., topic-fronting of the definite object is obligatory, in the affirmative further development has already occurred, yielding 20e where the anaphoric object pronoun functions as a definitizer, i.e., has become a <u>definite object agreement</u> marker.

The next step in this development may be observed in Swahili, but not in many other languages. Constructions such as 20e above are the most typical way of definitizing inanimate (non-human) objects in Swahili, as in:

21   ni-li-soma kitabu   "I read <u>a</u> book"
       ni-li-<u>ki</u>-soma kitabu   "I read <u>the</u> book"

Swahili has thus complete the first step in the implicational hierarchy of accusative-object agreement, much like Rwanda: The development of definite-accusative agreement. It is also one of the very few Bantu languages which have gone one step further, extending accusative-object agreement to <u>indefinite humans</u>. In other words, it has developed a human object agreement, as in (24):

22 a. *ni-li-ona mtu
   b. *ni-li-ona yule mtu
       I-past-see the person
   c. ni-li-<u>mw</u>-ona yula mtu   "I saw <u>the</u> person"
                                        (definite)
   d. ni-li-<u>mw</u>-one mto mmoja   "I saw <u>one</u> person"
                                        (indefinite)
   e. si-<u>mw</u>-oni mtu yeyote   "I didn't see any person"
                                        (non-referential)

One may interpret the Swahili development as comprising of two steps:
    (a) <u>De-marking</u>: Definite object agreement probably began as <u>definite-human</u> object agreement, and then generalized by dropping the restrictive feature [human];
    (b) <u>Re-interpretation</u>: Since human objects are much more likely to be topics and thus are mostly <u>definite</u> in

discourse, speakers could quite easily re-interpret
definite-object agreement as human-object agreement
with relatively little loss in the predictability of
the model, given the high co-occurrence of these two
features.

One would expect now, in a language which has developed human-
object agreement, that the next step would again be that of
de-marking, by which the restrictive feature [human] would be
removed and human-indef.-object agreement would be re-interpreted as indef.-object agreement. This step is not yet attested in Swahili.

6.   Dative vs. Accusative Object Agreement

There are grounds for believing that with respect to the
topicality hierarchy, datives stand above accusatives. This
is reflected in the higher percent of definites and humans
for datives as compared to accusatives (25). It is also reflected in the degree of contribution of participants in
events, where dative object seem to be ranked higher than
accusatives (26). Recently Hawkinson and Hyman (1974) have
noted that in four syntactic processes in Shona (Bantu) that
are broadly linked to topicality--passivization, pronominalization, dative-shift and topic-shift, the dative takes primacy over the accusative, and that the overall topicality
ranking for the various cases was:

24   AGENT > BENEFACTIVE > DATIVE > ACCUSATIVE

There are a number of phenomena, in addition to agreement,
which seem to spread down the hierarchy in this order, probably hitting human-accusative or definite-accusative first.
The Romance locative-dative (directional) case marker à has
spread in Spanish from datives to human accusatives, and is
now spreading further to definite (non-human) accusatives. In
Gascogne this preposition is obligatory in the dative for
both NPs and pronouns, but has spread into the accusative
only for pronouns (27). In a number of Philipino languages
the erstwhile locative-dative preposition sa- has become a
definite-accusative marker. In both Ge'ez and Neo-Aramaic,
the Semitic locative-dative preposition 1- has spread to the
definite-accusative (see discussion further below). In this
section I will first show a number of languages in which
(a) dative object agreement takes precedence over accusative
agreement, and (b) where object agreement is sensitive to the
relative topicality of the dative and accusative. I will then
consider a number of cases which are counter examples to my
claims, where definite-accusative agreement takes precedence

over dative agreement. I will then show that the interven-
tion of another factor, namely the case-marking differentiation of dative vs. accusative objects, intervenes to explain
these counter examples.

Let us consider first object agreement in Spanish. For
the neutral pattern with a verb taking both a dative and accusative object, such as "give," dative agreement is obligatory and accusative agreement unacceptable (28):

24   <u>le</u> di el libro a Juan   "I gave the book to John"
       *di el libro a Juan
       *<u>lo</u> di el libro a Juan

When the accusative is <u>topic-shifted</u>, accusative object
agreement is added on top of the dative agreement for some
speakers, while for others accusative agreement is added and
dative agreement is dropped:

25   ⌈el libro <u>se lo</u> di a Juan⌉ "The book, I gave it to
       ⌊el libro <u>lo</u> di a Juan ⌋   John"
       *el libro <u>le</u> di a Juan

What is clear is that dative agreement <u>alone</u> cannot be maintained when the accusative object is topic-shifted. Finally,
when the dative object is topic-shifted, again only dative
agreement is permitted--and is again obligatory:

26   Juan, <u>le</u> di el libro   "John, I gave him the book"
       *Juan, <u>lo</u> di el libro
       *Juan, <u>se lo</u> di el libro

Since dative agreement is obligatory in the neutral pattern,
it is not surprising that it is also obligatory in <u>contras-
tive</u> topic-shifting, a pattern normally closer to the neutral
one (29):

27   a Juan <u>le</u> di el libro   "To John I gave the book"
                                        (in contrast to someone
                                        else to whom I gave some-
                                        thing else)

       *a Juan <u>lo</u> di el libro
       *a Juan di el libro

The next case is that of Amharic, a Semitic language. In
this language, object agreement may first mark the definite--
as against the non-agreeing indefinite--accusative (30):

28   Kassa borsa-<u>w-i</u>n wässädä-<u>w</u>
       K.   wallet-<u>the</u>-OBJ took-he-<u>it</u>
       "Kassa took <u>the</u> wallet"

       *Kassa borsa-<u>w-i</u>n wässädä

Kassa borsa wässädä
K.   wallet took
"Kassa took a wallet"

When both an accusative and dative-benefactive are present in
the neutral word order, dative agreement takes precedence
over accusative:

29   Kassa lä-Mulu däbtarocc-u-n sät't-at
      K.   to-M. notebooks-the-OBJ gave-her
      "Kassa gave Mulu the notebooks"

      *Kassa lä-Mulu dabrarocc-u-n sät'ta

      *Kassa lä-Mulu däbtarocc-u-n sat't-accäw
                                  gave-them

Finally, topicalization-shifting of any object argument may
change the agreement in favor of the topicalized constituent.
Thus, Haile (1970) shows that in some constructions in the
neutral order there is no object agreement:

30   Almaz betun bä-mäträgiya-w   tärrägä-cc
      Almaz house-the-OBJ with-broom-the swept-she
      "Almaz swept the house with the broom"

      *Almaz betun bämäträgiyaw tärrägä-cc-iw
                                swept-she-it

      *Almaz betun bämäträgiyaw tärrägä-cc-ibb-at
                                swept-she-with-it

When the accusative is topic-shifted, accusative object agreement is obligatory (31):

31   betun Almaz bämäträgiyaw   tärrägä-cc-iw
      house-the-OBJ Almaz with-broom-the swept-she-it
      "The house Almaz swept (it) with the broom"

      *betun Almaz bämäträgiyaw tärrägä-cc

      *betun Almaz bämäträgiyaw tärrägä-cc-ibb-at
                                swept-she-with-it

When the instrumental is topic shifted, it controls obligatory object agreement (31):

32   bämäträgiyaw Almaz betun tärrägä-cc-ibb-at
      with-broom-the Almaz house-the-OBJ swept-she-with-it
      "With the broom Almaz swept the house"

      *bämäträgiyaw Almaz betun tärrägä-cc

      *bämäträgiyaw Almaz betun tärrägä-cc-iw
                                swept-she-it

Finally, the precedence of dative over accusative object agreement is discernible in many Bantu languages, in particular those such as Shona, Swahili or Zulu where no prepositional marking is used to mark dative-benefactive objects. Rather, they are marked positionally (closer to the verb than the dative) or via object agreement. Thus in Swahili:

33   ali-m-pa   mkewe   watoto
      he-past-her-give wife-his children
      "He gave the children to his wife"

      *ali-wa-pa   mkewe   watoto
      he-past-them-give wife-his children

And in Zulu (see Kunene, 1975):

34   u-yi-nige   soona intoombi
      he-her-gave it   girl
      "He gave it to the girl"

      *u-si-nige soona intoombi
      he-it-gave it   girl

      u-yi-nige   intoombi isiinkwa
      he-her-gave   girl   bread
      "He gave the girl the bread"

      *u-si-niga intcombi isiinkwa
      he-it-gave girl   bread

Similar agreement primacy of dative over accusative objects may be seen in Micronesian (Sohn, 1973), Mesquital-Otomi (Oto-Manguean, Hess 1968), Mojave (Yuman-Hokan, Munro 1974), Tzeltal (Mayan; E.L. Keenan, in private communication).

The classical counter example normally cited is Hungarian, where definite-accusative agreement exists but no dative agreement. The agreement particle is probably of pronominal origin, and is still used in anaphoric pronominalization (32):

35   látok   "I see"
      láto-m   "I see it"
      latok egy hazat   "I see a house"
      lato-m a hazat   "I see the house"

36   A fiúnak ádok egy könyvet
      the boy-to I-am-giving one book
      "I am giving a book to the boy"

      A fiúnak ádo-m a könyvet
      the boy-to I-am-giving-it the book
      "I am giving the book to the boy"

In Ge'ez, a Semitic language used in the Ethiopian liturgy, one finds obligatory definite-object agreement for accusatives but not for datives (33):

37   rɨʔɨy-o   lä-bɨʔɨse
       he-saw-him DEF-man
       "(he) saw the man"

       rɨʔɨyä bɨʔɨse
       he-saw man
       "(he) saw a man"

       nägärä   lä-bɨʔɨse
       he-talked DEF-man
       "He talked (to) the man"

       *nägär-o lä-bɨʔɨse

However, here the erstwhile dative preposition l- has spread to the definite-accusative, so that it may very well be that object agreement has actually started as dative agreement, then when the case marking of dative and definite-accusative fell together, the definite-accusative agreement remained as the signal differentiating these two cases.

The next case is somewhat reminiscent of Ge'ez, involving the Zakho dialect of Eastern Neo-Aramaic (34). In this language the dative preposition l- has spread into the pronominal agreement of all objects, dative and accusative alike. In addition it has also spread into the subject agreement paradigm, probably via a stative-participial form of the verb (see discussion further below). Further, dative objects are marked, as full NPs, with a new preposition, ta-, while accusatives are not case marked. In this language in neutral patterns, definite accusative objects require agreement while dative objects do not:

38 a. baxta xze-la   xa gora
      woman seen-her one man
      "The woman saw a man"

    b. baxta qam xazy-a-le aw gora
      woman past saw-she-him that man
      "The woman saw the man"

    c. baxta qam xazy-a-le xa gora
      { *"The woman saw a man"
      { "The woman found one man for him" }

    d. baxta qam yaw-a-le aw hammash ta dan gure
      woman past gave-she-it that book to those men
      "The woman gave the book to the men"

e. *baxta qam yaw-a-lu aw hammash ta dan gure
        gave-she-them

The primacy of accusative over dative agreement is maintained
when the (definite) accusative object is topic-shifted, as
in:

39   aw hammash, baxta qam yaw-a-le ta dan gure
        that book, woman past gave-she-it to those men
        "The book, the woman gave it to the men"

        *aw hammash, baxta qam yaw-a-lu ta dan gure
                                gave-she-them

However, when the dative object is topic-shifted, dative
agreement over-rules accusative agreement, as in:

40   an gure, baxta qam yaw-a-lu aw hammash
        these men, woman past gave-she-them that book
        "The men, the woman gave them the book"

        *an gure, baxta qam yaw-a-le aw hammash
                              gave-she-it

And this tendency is so strong that even the participial past,
which normally doesn't take any object agreement, takes topic-
object agreement in this construction:

41   an gure, baxta hul-la-lu aw hammash
        those men, woman given-her-them that book
        "The men, the woman gave them the book"

There are several ways in which one may choose to account
for these counter examples. First, notice that they are all
cases where definite accusative agreement over-rules dative
agreement. So that one may argue that given the two separate
hierarchic pairs in 4--human > non-human and definite > indefinite, the topicality of "definite" takes precedence over
that of "human." One may also point out that at least in
Ge'ez and Aramaic the spreading of the dative preposition to
the accusative (or rather to the definite accusative) may suggest that the agreement situation could have been re-analyzed,
so that first the dative had primacy over the accusative,
then with the change in case marking the situation reversed
itself. To my mind, however, the most plausible explanation
is one suggested to me by Bernard Comrie (in private communication). This involves the seeming fact that in all languages
in which the accusative and dative objects are equally case-
marked (or un-marked), dative agreement takes precedence over
accusative agreement. While in languages in which the dative
is case-marked but the accusative is not, accusative (rather,
definite accusative) agreement prevails over dative agreement.

165

Thus, the agreement system penetrates the case-marking system (see discussion further below). When all other things are equal, the topic hierarchy consideration of DATIVE > ACCUSATIVE takes precedence. Above and beyond this, if it is true that in languages where seemingly the hierarchy of topicality is reversed in agreement it is definite accusatives that always take precedence over datives, then one could plausibly argue that this doesn't represent any counter examples to the claims advanced in this paper. Since datives are normally definite and accusatives much more frequently indefinite, the definitization of an accusative object increases its topicality way above the normal pattern, so that now it competes with the dative successfully for topicality--and agreement.

7.   Personal Pronouns and the Topic Hierarchy

In the hierarchic schemata of 4 above I have suggested that in terms of topicality speaker over-rules hearer and hearer over-rules third persons. In this section I will suggest, albeit briefly and with only scanty evidence, that this may reflect in facts of grammatical agreement. In terms of the distinction HUMAN/NON-HUMAN first, the first and second persons stand out as against third persons, the latter not being obligatorily human. In terms of degree of participation, next, the speaker is involved in discourse as both a speech producer and comprehender, the hearer as a comprehender, while third persons as none of the above. Further, while in discourse initial situations third person pronouns are odd, second--and in particularly first--person pronouns in discourse initial contexts are felicitous, and in fact are one of the major devices used to hinge a story into an acceptable context, i.e., present it as relevant. This is so because the identity of the speaker and hearer is taken for granted as a background assumption for any discourse. It may also be so because people obviously talk about what concerns them, so that the universe of the speaker/hearer is in some sense more strongly presupposed as the background upon which discourse is carried out (35).

As a first example, consider the case of many Bantu languages, where the first and second personal pronoun--together with a copula that seems to be obligatory for them only--must appear in predicate expressions, but not the third person pronouns, which are "mere" zeros. Thus from Bemba:

42	n-di múu-suma	"I am good"
	u-li múu-suma	"You are good"
	múu-suma	"He/she is good"

<u>tu</u>-li báa-suma	"We are good"
<u>mu</u>-li báa-suma	"Y'all are good"
báa-suma	"They are good"

To put the contrast on more equal terms, since one may argue
that the over-marking of first and second pronouns here is
done to avoid ambiguity, whereas third persons can be linked
to their coreferents in discourse context, consider the topic-
shifted paradigm:

43	ine, <u>n</u>-di múu-suma	"As to me, I am good"
	iwe, <u>u</u>-li múu-suma	"As to you, you are good"
	ulya, múu-soma	"As to him/her, he/she is good"

A further fact about Bantu languages is that while the non-
agreeing copula <u>ni</u> apparently was used only for third persons,
the other copula -<u>li</u> --which requires subject agreement--was
the obligatory suppletive form for first and second person
subjects (36).

Next, Munro (1974) has shown that while subject agreement
for the first and second persons is obligatory in Mojave, the
normal situation for third person is zero agreement. Katalin
Radics (in private communication) suggests that this is fairly typical for many American Indian languages. Finally, it
has been universally observed that the <u>least marked verb form</u>
in conjugations tends to be the <u>third person</u> singular. I
believe this is a faithful reflection of the fact that the
third person tends more often to not show subject agreement,
as compared with the first and second persons.

8.   The Function of Grammatical Agreement

There is a certain tradition in linguistics of viewing
grammatical agreement of various nominal arguments with the
verb as a redundant, predictable, automatic feature of language and therefore one lacking in functional load. A detailed study of both subject and object agreement in language
will show that this view is both unjustified and unfortunate.
Even if one accepts the diachronic explanation to the rise of
agreement as a predictable offshoot of the pronominal reference system of language, it would be unlikely that such a
universal, well motivated process would fail to exhibit some
rather specific functional properties. In this section I
will survey some of the more common functions of agreement
and comment, whenever appropriate, on their more interesting
implications.

167

8.1 Reference-topic related functions

In many languages both the subject and object agreement still retain their original <u>anaphoric-pronoun</u> function (cf. Bantu, Spanish, Semitic). It is thus universally observed that languages with viable subject-verb agreement allow "subjectless sentences" in anaphoric contexts more readily.

The use of object agreement/pronouns as <u>definitizers,</u> as described above for Swahili, Aramaic, Amharic, Ge'ez (and to some extent Hungarian), should be considered a natural extension of the anaphoric-pronominal function. Since both definites and pronouns are topics, i.e., appear in context where the noun is presupposed to be known to the hearer, this type of extension is to be predicted.

In the same vein, the use of object agreement to signal variation in the <u>relative topicality</u> of the various object NPs in the sentence, as shown above for Spanish, Amharic and Aramaic, again falls in the same general cluster of topic-reference related functions.

8.2 Marking the verb-type

If a language develops a "complete" subject, accusative and dative agreement on the verb, one may consider the possibility that the agreement system can then become, for the speaker, a way of signaling the syntactic type ("transitivity") of verbs. That is, verbs with only one affix will automatically be considered intransitives (having only a subject), verbs with two agreement affixes will be considered transitives, etc. In fact, a development of this type is attested in New Guinea Highlands Pidgin, where the accusative pronoun "him" of English has become the obligatory marker for <u>transitive verbs</u>. Thus (37):

44   em <u>i</u>-go
        him <u>he</u>-go
        "He went"

        em <u>i</u>-har-<u>im</u> John
        him <u>he</u>-hear-<u>him</u> John
        "He heard John"

Thus, the lexical citation form of transitive verbs includes the -<u>im</u> suffix (37):

45   har-im "hear"
        pait-im "beat, fight"
        pam-im "pump"
        bruk-im "break"
        tan-im "turn (tr.)"

harharim "listen intently"
paitpaitim "beat very hard"
pampamim "pump real hard"
brukbrukim "smash"
tantanim "turn violently, abruptly (tr.)"

Finally, for some dialects of the same Pidgin intensification
as in 45 may be achieved, for some lexically complex transitive verbs, by reduplicating the -im transitivity suffix, as
in (37):

46   lipt-ap-im "raise"
      lift-up-him

       bagarap-im "ruin"
      bugger-up-him

      siker-ap-im "scratch"
     scratch-up-him

      lipt-im-ap-im "raise forcefully"

      bagar-im-ap-im "ruin completely"

      siker-im-ap-im "scratch intensely"

There are some indications (see discussion of Kimbundu
and Indonesian further below), that subject agreement markers
could also become the morphological signal for de-transitivized
verb forms, probably via topic shifting.

8.3 Case marking

As I have suggested in Section 6 above, when the dative
and accusative are similarly marked or unmarked, the agreement
primacy of one (mostly the dative) over the other becomes
effectively the signal differentiating the two object cases
from each other. This is indeed the situation in many Bantu
languages (Swahili, Zulu, Shona, Rwanda), in Amharic and in
Spanish. In Amharic the definite object case suffix -n
doesn't differentiate between accusative and dative objects,
and the benefactive/adversive prepositions ll-/bb- are restricted to datives which carry in addition a benefactive/
adversive import. In Spanish the erstwhile dative preposition à has spread to the human accusative, and is further
spreading to definite non-human accusatives, at least in
topicalized positions.

In languages such as Hungarian, Ge'ez and Aramaic, where
the dative is case-marked but the accusative is not, the primacy of accusative object agreement over that of dative may
also be viewed as a device for supplying case marking for the
accusative object.

A more subtle variation related to case marking is that
of marking the type of verb via case-differentiation between
dative and accusative. Thus, in Spanish the dative/accusa-
tive distinction may lexically differentiate the same verb as
to the degree of involvement of the object NP, with the dative
marking a higher degree of personal involvement, as in (38):

47   lo vi en la calle
      ACC
      "I saw him in the street" (he was a patient, not a
          participant)

      le vi en su oficina
      DAT
      "I met him in his office" (he was a participant, not
          a patient)

      la guerra le sorprendió mucho
             DAT
      "He was very surprised that the war happened" (he
          was cognitively affected)

      la guerra lo sorprendió en Paris
             ACC
      "The war caught him by surprise in Paris" (he was a
          patient)

8.4 Differentiation between main and subordinate clause

Dillard (1972) and Tyson (1974) claim that in Black English, where subject agreement with he-, she- or they- is a
widespread feature, this development has occurred only in
main clauses but not in relative clauses. This is of course
not surprising, since main clauses (and in particular declar-
ative-affirmative ones) are the most progressive, innovative
environment in language, where innovations are first introduced and from where they spread later on into other environments (39). At any rate, Tyson (1974) argues that because in
Black English (and in fact in most non-standard American English dialects) there is a tendency to drop the subject relative pronoun, the subject-agreement in main clauses has become a marker differentiating main from relative clauses.
That is:

48   the man he-came to dinner
      "The man came to dinner" (main)

      the man came to dinner
      "The man who came to dinner" (relative)

While the extent to which this distinction is made systematically remains to be seen, it nevertheless indicates another potential function of grammatical agreement.

8.5 Selectional restrictions and the hierarchy of semantic features

What I'll suggest here pertains to both agreement and pronouns. In all languages, pronouns carry a smaller phonological weight than nouns. This is probably due to the fact that they undergo phonological attrition much faster. And this is in turn understandable, given what we know of the resistance of languages to assimilatory reduction which creates irrecoverable loss (40): Since pronouns are used in contexts where their antecedents have already been mentioned (or are assumed by the speaker to be known to the hearer), their message value is therefore recoverable from that context.

Further, notice that pronominal systems represent not only a phonological reduction of the nominal system, but also a parallel semantic reduction or "bleaching." That is, of all the semantic features that characterize the noun universe in the lexicon, only a small sub-set appear--rather universally--as pronominal features. The most common of those are: Plurality, mass/count, human, animate, sex-gender (plus, in most languages, the [speaker/hearer] features underlying the personal pronoun sub-system). Specific languages, given their particular cultural context, may add other features. But in general, it is easy to see that the pronominal agreement features represent only the top of the hierarchy of semantic features that underlie the noun universe. That is, they are the more general features. The reason why this arrangement is both possible and natural is again not difficult to discern: Given the discourse context in which coreferent nouns have been mentioned, the more specific semantic characterization of the coreferent nouns is easily recoverable.

Now, given the function of pronouns in singling out a unique referent out of a potential group mentioned in previous discourse, why is it that the more generic properties/features of the referent noun are used, rather than the more specific ones? On the face of it, this is a more circuitous route, compared with a "safer" strategy of identifying more specific features of the coreferent. The strategy of pronominal reference, however, is that of economy. That is, since the referent has already been mentioned in previous discourse, the more specific safety-first strategy would have been rather wasteful, since in fact one could just as well differentiate between potential referents by their more

171

generic properties. Thus, while the specific/safe strategy
would create a great proliferation of pronominal/agreement
classes--to the point where the saving engendered by using
pronouns rather than nouns would begin to melt away, the
generic/economy strategy creates only few pronominal/agree-
ment classes but with a much more general applicability. In
fact, there are a number of indications that in the construction of definite description in language, a strategy of from-
the-general-to-the-specific is preferred. To begin with,
Gruber (1967b) has suggested that the rigidity of the order
of modifying adjectives in English is motivated by the tendency to have the more generic properties closer to the head
nouns--i.e., the ones who restrict the scope of the referent
first. The more specific properties, in turn, are used to
further restrict the domain of the referent, in case the more
generic ones have failed. Similar phenomena crop up in
Rwanda (41), where adjectives--which represent inherent (permanent) properties of nouns, must appear closer to the noun
in a chain of restrictive modifiers, while relative clauses--
which represent mostly temporary and incidental events true
of the noun under specific time-place circumstances, must
appear second. A similar situation shows up in Bikol, a
Philipino language, and I suspect that in one guise or another all languages reflect this strategy.

Where does it all tie in to agreement? The very same
features at the top of the semantic hierarchy of nouns also
turn out to categorize the verb with respect to its selectional restrictions. These features obviously represent a
more gross portion of the overall classification of verbs as
to the types of case-arguments which they can take (concrete,
animate, human, agentive, compact/scattered, etc.). Now, in
Section 8.2 above I have suggested that the presence of
agreement morphemes on the verb could become a way of marking
the verb's "syntactic" type. Given that pronominal-agreement
features represent the more general semantic features of the
noun universe, their presence on the verb could also mark the
general semantic-selectional typology of verbs.

9. Diachronic Change in Grammatical Agreement

Agreement systems meet their predictable demise via phonological attrition much like other bound affixes. This
attrition is due largely to assimilatory, reductive processes
within the verbal word. It results in the eventual disappear-
ance of old generations of pronominal/agreement morphemes and
the recurrent re-generation of new pronominal series, which
in turn again become bound affixes and eventually disappear.
This process may be hastened when a language has changed its

syntactic order, so that the bound pronouns/agreement are syntactically in conflict with the position of the full NPs. Thus languages seem to strive to bring the pronominal order in line with the nominal one, rather than vice versa. And this motivates, in part, the rise of new series of pronouns (42). In this section, I would like to discuss a number of systematic diachronic changes which may have some universal implications towards our understanding of the rise and fall-- and evolution--of pronominal agreement systems.

9.1 Existential expressions

Existential constructions are one of the main devices in language for introducing new arguments into discourse. In fact, many languages can introduce indefinite non-generic nouns as subjects only in existential constructions. The number of verbs that may be used in these constructions is very small, mostly "verb of emergence" which show the following hierarchy:

49   "be"   > "live" > "come"
        "exist"   "stand"
                             "remain"

Other, mostly locational or motion verbs, may be used in a more restricted way but only if they may pragmatically help to introduce the new argument into the physical scene or stage of the recounted action (43).

Formally speaking, the new argument is introduced via this device as the subject of the existential verb. However, existential constructions tend to be marked in two ways, as compared to the neutral declarative sentence in which the subject is the presupposed information ("topic"). To begin with, there is a strong tendency to move the existential verb to the beginning of the sentence, or use a verb-first syntax. This may be viewed in the context of a universal tendency to present old information--or sentential subjects--first in the sentence (44).

In addition, there is an equally strong tendency in language to remove the control of grammatical agreement of the existential/emergence verbs from the logical subject, and either neutralize it altogether or, quite commonly, change it into a locative/existential agreement. Let me cite a few examples from Bantu languages to illustrate this. In Rwanda, non-generic subjects of neutral declarative sentences could only be definite, and they control the verb agreement (45):

50   umugabo ya-riho ku-nzu
       man   he-was in-house
       "The man was in the house"

51   abagabo ba-riho ku-nzu
       men   they-were in-house
       "The men were in the house"

In discourse initial formulae, however, where an existential
construction introduces an argument for the first time, the
verb agreement turns locative:

52   kyeera ha-riho   umugabo a-ka-kira abaana batatu
       long-ago there-was man   he-CONS-had children three
       "Long ago there was a man (and) he had three chil-
          dren"

Thus the locative agreement-gender ha- controls the subject
agreement, and one may perhaps argue that the directionality
of the expression has shifted from the "grammatically underlying" 53a below to the re-analyzed 53b:

53 a. "A man was at the place"
   b. "The place had a man"

In other words, since "man" is less topic than "place," this
is reflected in the re-analyzed subject agreement. This may
be further suggested by the more conservative version of the
same construction in Swahili:

54   Definite subject: mtoto a-li-kuwa nyumba-ni
                          child he-past-be house-in
                          "The child was in the house"

55   Existential: nyumba-ni pa-li-kuwa na mtoto
                          house-in there-past-be with child
                        { "In the house there was a child" }
                          "There was a child in the house"

When the verb is "be," one may indeed argue that both 52 and
55 are well represented by 53b. However, consider the dis-
course-medial context below, again from Rwanda, in which the
physical scene has already been described, say a village,
part of the story has already been told, and now a new actor
is introduced into the scene by an "emergence" verb that is
much more specific, in terms of its semantic and selectional
restrictions, than "be" or "exist":

56 ....buceeye ha-a-za umugabo...
       next-day there-past-come man
       "Next day there came a man..."

57 ....haafi y-umugezi <u>ha</u>-a-rgyamye umugabo...
    near of-river <u>there</u>-past-lie man
"...Near the river there lay {<u>the</u> / *<u>a</u>} man..."

The verb "come" could not possibly take "place" as its subject. So that an "underlying" structure such as 53b won't
work here. Further, while "be" and "come" may introduce a
new argument, "lie down" may only <u>re-introduce</u> a previously-
mentioned topic/argument, presumably across a certain gap in
discourse. And in order to use "lie down" as a presentative
verb for an entirely new argument, one must use the auxiliary
"be," as in:

58 ....haafi y-umugezi <u>ha</u>-a-ri <u>ha</u>-rgyamye umugabo...
    near of-river <u>there</u>-past-be <u>there</u>-lay man
"...Near the river there lay <u>a</u> man..."

In functional terms, one may say that the locative agreement
serves, together with the variant word order, to <u>mark</u> the
existential construction, and thus distinguish it from the
neutral declarative sentence type in which the subject controls agreement. In the light of the tendency in language to
<u>disallow locative subjects</u> in normal declarative construc-
tions, the perceptual efficiency of the locative agreement
strategy in existentials is all the more striking. The fact
that it is <u>locative</u>--rather than any other possible oblique
case--that is chosen here, may be explained as follows: In
discourse initial constructions, such as existentials, <u>the</u>
<u>stage</u> is set before the human actors are introduced. That is,
the time and place are mentioned first, and in this sense
they are then the <u>highest</u> in topicality--before the real actors are introduced. It may thus not be an accident that the
locative/temporal agreement genders <u>there/then</u> are most commonly used to neutralize subject agreement in existential
constructions (46).

9.2 Possession

Languages seem to have three strategies for lexicalizing
expressions of possession. The first involves an overt lexical verb "have" as in English, whose subject is the possessor
and object the possessed. In many languages which have this
verb it is possible to show that it is etymologically derived
from "hold," "seize" or "grab," i.e., physical holding acts
which <u>entail</u> possession.
    Other languages, such as Swahili and Bantu in general,
still maintain the possessor as subject, but lexicalize "have"
as "be with," as in:

59 mtoto a-li-kuwa na kitabu
   child he-past-be with book
   "The child had a book"

In languages of this type there is often a tendency to dispense with the overt "be" in the present tense and re-analyze "with" as "have":

60 mtoto a-na kitabu
   child he-with book
   "The child has a book"

  Finally, in another type of language where no lexical verb "have" exists, the subject-object directionality in possession is reversed, so that the possessed becomes the subject of the expression, while the possessor is a dative object. Thus, in Israeli Hebrew:

61 haya l-o sefer
   it-was to-him book
   "He had a book"

62 hayu l-o sfarim
   they-were to-him books
   "He had books"

These expressions of possession tend to share two characteristics of the existential constructions. First, the grammatical verb "be" is attracted to a sentence-initial position, while the logical subject of "be" is consistently placed after the possessor-dative. And second, the verb agreement on "be" tends to neutralize. This neutralization is more evident in the present tense in Hebrew, where a neutral particle meaning roughly "there is"--and the same one used in existentials--replaces the normal "be":

63 yesh l-o sefer
   there to-him book
   "He has a book"

   yesh l-o sfarim
   there to-him books
   "He has books"

   yesh l-o et ha-sefer she-ratsita
   there to-him ACC the-book that-you-wanted
   "He's got the book you wanted"

But in spoken Israeli Hebrew this is spreading to the past paradigm, where the third-person-singular-masculine gender haya is becoming the neutral gender, as in:

176

64   haya lo sefer exad...   "He had one book..." (sg., count)

       haya lo harbe zman   "He had lots of time" (sg., mass)

       haya lo harbe sfarim   "He had many books" (pl.)

It seems to me that both tendencies reflect the same underlying fact: The possessor--or the <u>whole</u> in cases of whole/part relationships--is normally <u>more topical</u>. It is more commonly the human argument and more commonly the more <u>agentive</u> one. The reordering as seen in these possessive expressions reflects this, since the more topical--and most commonly <u>definite</u>--possessor is moved ahead of the possessed. And the grammatical agreement reflects this again, since while the "grammatical subject" agreement on "be" is neutralized, as in 63 and 64, the dative argreement controlled by the possessor --the real <u>topic</u>--is alive and well, as in:

64a   yesh l-<u>o</u> sefer   "He's got a book"
       yesh l-<u>a</u> sefer   "<u>She</u>'s got a book"
       yesh l-<u>ahem</u> sefer "<u>They</u>'ve got a book"

And also one suggests that the peculiar properties of <u>yesh</u> per se control this behavior, notice how <u>yesh</u> acquires subject agreement when the subject of "be" is the real topic:

65   Yo?av yesh-<u>no</u> kan   "Yo?av is here" (sg. ms. agreement)

       hu? yesh-<u>no</u> kan   "He is here" (sg. ms. agreement)

       Rina yesh-<u>na</u> kan   "Rina is here" (sg. fem. agreement)

       hi yesh-<u>na</u> kan   "She is here") (sg. fem. agreement)

       Ham yesh-<u>nam</u> kan   "They are here" (pl. agreement)

Thus, the "semantic" rather than "grammatical" topic is the one that controls verb agreement in these constructions, regardless of whether it was originally a dative object (as in 54-58) or another prepositional <u>object</u> case, as in 59 above.

    A rather confusing situation, admittedly an intermediate that is likely to be eventually zeroed out of the grammar, arises when the agreement on "be" is not neutralized, as in the past tense, but the possessed NP is definite and thus requires the accusative preposition <u>et</u>, as in:

66   lo hay<u>a</u> <u>li</u> et hasfer haze etmol
      neg was-<u>it</u> <u>to-me</u> ACC the-book the-this yesterday
      "I didn't have this book yesterday"

lo hay<u>u</u> <u>li</u> et hasfarim babayit
neg was-<u>they</u> <u>to-me</u> ACC the-books at-home
"I didn't have the books at home"

lo hay<u>ta</u> <u>li</u> et habrera hazot
neg was-<u>she</u> <u>to-me</u> ACC the-option the-this
"I didn't have that option"

Formally speaking, this is a case where an accusative object controls the subject agreement of "be," an obvious potential confusion that is only likely to hasten the neutralization of the agreement on "be" in the past tense toward the invariant third person singular masculine <u>haya</u>.

9.3 Subject agreement/pronouns as passive markers

Indonesian, according to Chung (this volume), has two passivization patterns. One of them has a "more active" sense (somewhat reminiscent of the "get" passive of English), is restricted to first and second person underlying agents--which then appear at the normal pre-verbal clitic position characteristic of subject pronouns, as in:

67   buku itu <u>saja</u>-batja
        book that <u>I</u>-read
        {"The book, I read (it)"}
        {"The book was read by me"}

Chung (this volume) notes that this pattern is probably derived from topic-shifting, which in Indonesian is done, for object nouns, without the use of an anaphoric object pronoun. This pattern still preserves the characteristic restriction of topic-shifting, i.e., that the topic constituent cannot be referential-indefinite, but only definite or generic.

The second, clearly older passivization pattern, is not restricted to any particular underlying agent, its subject can be referential-indefinite, its agent-of-passive appears after the verb as an oblique object NP, and the passive verb is marked by the prefix <u>di-</u>, as in:

68   buku itu <u>di</u>-batja (oleh) saja
        book that <u>pass</u>-read (by) I
        "The book was read by me"

However, etymologically the passive prefix <u>di-</u> goes back to the third person singular (subject) pronoun (47). In other words, the old subject-agreement pronoun has become the current passive marker. With this in mind, and given the topicality hierarchy of [Speaker] > [Hearer] > [third person] discussed above, one could reconstruct the sequence of events which led to the development of the two passives in Indonesian as such: (i) First a topic-shifting process developed, but it was confined only to active sentences with third person subjects. In other words, the higher topicality of first and second person agents <u>resisted</u> the topic-shifting of objects over them. (ii) The first topic-shift construction slowly began to be re-analyzed as "true" passivization, still maintaining the constraint against first and second person agents. (iii) Eventually a second topic-shift process developed, this time confined to actives with first and second person agents, i.e., those which so far had no promotion-to-subject device. (iv) Eventually the first topic-shift process became completely generalized, the erstwhile subject pronoun lost its old significance and became the morphological marker of the passive verb. (v) Clearly, according to Chung (this volume), the second, more restricted topic-shift construction has been also moving toward being re-analyzed as a passive construction.

There are certain parallels in another, totally unrelated language, which suggests that this interpretation is plausible. In Maasai, a Nilo-Hamitic language, the underlying order is VSO and the subject and object NPs are differentiated tonally. In passivization, the agent and patient reverse their order but retain their underlying tones. Now, if the underlying agent was a third person, the new subject-of-passive (underlying patient) controls subject agreement. However, if the patient is <u>third</u> person and the underlying agent <u>first</u> or <u>second singular</u>, the underlying agent retains control of the prefixal verb agreement (48). This is a clear parallel to the Indonesian case, where first and second person agents seem to resist more strenuously the transfer of subject properties--such as verb agreement--to the new topic, the erstwhile patient.

A clear case of re-analysis of a topic-shift construction as passivization is also seen in Kimbundu (a Bantu language). In this language the old Bantu passive suffix -<u>wa</u> has been absorbed into the lexicon to the point where it is not anymore functional. The language then innovated two new passivization patterns, one of which is restricted to human-subjects of the passive. This pattern is derived from the normal Bantu <u>marked-topicalization</u> construction, see Section 5 above, which is still viable in Kimbundu, as in (49):

67   aana <u>a</u>-mono Nzua
       children <u>they</u>-saw John
      "The children saw John"

68   mwana u-mono Nzua
        child he-saw John
        "The child saw John"

69   Nzua, aana a-mu-mono
        John, children they-him-saw
        "John, the children saw him"

In the new passivization pattern, the third-person-plural
subject agreement "they" has become petrified as an invariant
marker, as in:

70   Nzua a-mu-mono kwa meme
        John they-him-saw by me
        "John was seen by me"

        Nzua a-mu-mono kwa mwana
        John they-him-saw by child
        "John was seen by the child"

        meme a-ngi-mono kwa Nzua
        I they-me-saw by John
        "I was seen by John"

        aana a-a-mono kwa meme
        children they-them-saw by me
        "The children were seen by me"

Thus, the new topic--subject of "passive"--has gained control
of verb agreement. And the new "subject agreement" of the
passive is the old object pronoun/agreement, which together
with the petrified plural-human agreement now marks the passive form of the verb.

9.4 Syntactic change and verb agreement

One overriding theme--and claim--of this paper is that
verb agreement paradigms always arise from anaphoric pronoun
paradigms. One may argue that there are a number of traditional counter examples to this generalization, and one most
often cited is the suffixal verb conjugation of Indo-European.
There are two ways in which this is an apparent counter example to my central thesis. First, the suffixal conjugation of
IE does not seem to relate etymologically, in any hard-and-
fast way, to the reconstructed anaphoric subject pronouns of
IE. Second, while IE is reconstructed as an SOV language,
for which one would expect the development of bound subject
pronouns/agreement prefixed on the verb, the IE agreement conjugation is verb-suffixal. In this section I will show that
it is possible to explain all these phenomena within the context of this paper without doing violence to any universal

principles concerning diachronic change, and with a number of
examples from other language groups which help to make the
explanation plausible.

9.4.1 Agreement change in Aramaic

In the Zakho dialect of Eastern Neo-Aramaic (see details
in Section 6 above), a certain development has occurred in
one paradigm of past tense, the one derived from a stative-
participial form of the verb. The subject agreement pronouns
are etymologically dative-object pronouns. Thus, to contrast
with the suffixal subject-agreement conjugation in the other
past form (etymologically related to the Semitic perfect conjugation):

71 a. baxta xze-<u>la</u> xa gora
       woman seen-<u>her</u> one man
       "The woman saw a man" (PARTICIPIAL)

  b.   baxta qam xazy-<u>a</u> xa gora
       woman past saw-<u>she</u> one man
       "The woman saw a man" (PERFECT)

Another difference between the two conjugations is that while
the older, active (PERFECT) past readily takes object pro-
nouns/agreement, the participial past takes them only under
topic-shift of the object:

72 a. *baxta xze-<u>la</u>-<u>le</u> wa gora
       woman seen-<u>her</u>-<u>him</u> that man

  b.   wa gora, baxta xze-<u>la</u>-<u>le</u>
       "The man, the woman saw him"

  c.   baxta qam xazy-<u>a</u>-<u>le</u> aw gora
       woman past saw-<u>she</u>-<u>him</u> that man
       "The woman saw the man"

  d.   aw gora, baxta qam xazy-<u>a</u>-<u>le</u>
       "The man, the woman saw him"

The origin of the participial construction as an active past
tense is fairly clear: It was a stative-passive construction
in which the underlying agent was <u>demoted</u> to a dative-object
case, and the nominalized verb basically lost subject agreement altogether. That stative-passive construction was later
re-analyzed again as active, with the oblique-case agreement
of the agent becoming the new <u>subject</u> agreement. The gist of
it is that a situation was created in which the current subject agreement conjugation in the paradigm doesn't conform to
the <u>subject</u> anaphoric pronoun series, but rather to the <u>ob-
ject</u> pronouns.

A similar re-analysis of a stative-passive back into active is reported for some North-Russian dialect by Timberlake (this volume). Comrie (1975) reports similar processes in Finnish and Polish, where erstwhile detransitivized reflexive constructions became re-analyzed as active. One can also show that the Spanish "impersonal-reflexive" is another clear case in which a de-transitivized passive-stative construction got re-analyzed partially as an active construction. This shows in a number of ways.

First, while in the reflexive or stative use, the reflexive-agent or stative-patient controls the subject agreement on the verb, the subject agreement in the impersonal reverts to neutral third person singular (50):

73 a. se-cur<u>aron</u> los brujos a s<u>í</u> mismos
   ref-cured-<u>they</u> the sorcerers upon themselves
   "The sorcerers cured themselves" (REFLEXIVE)

 b. se-cur<u>aron</u> los brujos
   ref-cure-<u>they</u> the sorcerers
   "The sorcerers were cured" (STATIVE)

 c. se-cur<u>ó</u> <u>a</u> los brujos (*a si mismos)
   ref-cure-<u>3s</u> <u>OBJ</u> the sorcerers
   "Someone cured the sorcerers" (IMPERSONAL ACTIVE)

Another clear indication of the re-analysis is that "los brujos," as a human accusative, must take the object preposition <u>a</u>. The difference further shows in the use of subject-motivated reason clauses:

74   se-curaron las brujas a s<u>í</u> mismos <u>por sus razones</u>
     <u>propias</u> (REFLEXIVE)
   "The sorcerers cured themselves <u>for their own</u>
     <u>reasons</u>"
   *se-cur<u>ó</u> a las brujas por sus razones propias
     (IMPERSONAL)

It also shows up in topicalization movement and subject fronting:

75 a. las brujas se-curaron a s<u>í</u> mismas
   "The sorcerers cured themselves"

 b. *a las brujas se-cur<u>ó</u>

 c. las brujas, se-<u>las</u>-cur<u>ó</u>
   "The sorcerers, someone cured them" (topic shift)

 d. a las brujas se-<u>las</u>-cur<u>ó</u>
   "The sorcerers someone cured" (contrastive)

To sum up then, re-analysis of stative-passive constructions as active is not uncommon, and therefore agreement re-analyses such as the one seen in Aramaic are natural phenomena in language change.

9.4.2 The Semitic perfect conjugation

There are a number of discrepancies between the pronominal and nominal syntax of the Semitic verb conjugation which are, on the surface, rather baffling. Traditional Semiticists reconstruct Proto-Semitic as a VSO dialect. But if that is so, the prefixal subject-agreement/pronouns of the imperfect conjugation is inexplicable, since it suggests an earlier subject-first syntax. Further, that conjugation is already attested in Akkadian, basically an SOV language (though with modifiers following the head noun in the NP). On the other hand, the subject agreement conjugation in the perfect is suffixal, suggesting an earlier VS syntax. However, that conjugation developed first in Akkadian, as a participial-nominal conjugation, and was only later generalized to the entire active-verb paradigm (51). And Akkadian was an SOV language, i.e., a subject-first language. Traditional Semiticists have been assuming that the SOV syntax of Akkadian is a substratum influence from Sumerian. However, in Northern Akkadian dialects, which were quite remote from any Sumerian contact, the same SOV syntax is observed (52). One last fact concerning the perfect and imperfect conjugations of Semitic should be noted: While the imperfect prefixal agreement bears regular etymological relationship to the anaphoric pronoun series of Semitic, the suffixal conjugation of the perfect, while bearing some unmistakable relationship to some pronominal series, does not bear that relation to the same pronominal series as the imperfect. Hetzron (in personal communication) suggests that the pronominal suffixes of the perfect conjugation are reconstructible to the subject of "be" series. With all this in mind, I believe I could suggest the following hypothesis that would explain all these facts in a reasonable, natural way.

(i) Proto-Semitic was an SOV language, like Akkadian. The suffixal case systems of Akkadian, Classical Arabic and Pre-Hebrew cannot be explained any other way (53).

(ii) The Akkadian-Semitic perfect conjugation indeed arose as a participial-stative construction, with the verb "be" being the main/higher verb. The subject-agreement in this construction was therefore with "be," while the complement verb was in a participial-nominal form, without any subject agreement (i.e., in a non-finite form, as seen for Aramaic, above). In an SOV language, this would mean a configuration such as:

76

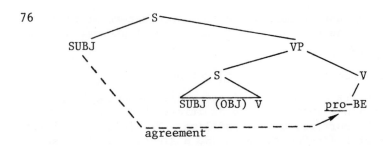

(iii)   When the auxiliary "be" became cliticized as a verb suffix, the erstwhile subject agreement of "be" got sandwiched between the new main verb and the auxiliary "be," and this is the source of the considerable morphophonemic variation so characteristic of this conjugation, as contrasted with the more regular prefixal imperfect conjugation.

(iv)   The classical Semitic languages changed to VSO later on, with the result that when object pronouns were cliticized, their position was solidified as post-verbal.

9.4.3   The Indo-European suffixal conjugation

It seems to me that the Indo-European suffixal agreement paradigm represent a complete parallel to the hypothesis outlined above for Semitic.   It is known that Indo-European was an SOV dialect.   The suffixal conjugation of verb agreement in IE shows precisely the type of heavy morpho-phonemic variation one would expect of "sandwich" situations outlined in 76 above.   The change from a participial-perfective-stative conjugation to past-tense conjugation is widely attested as a highly natural diachronic development.   While it cannot be at this point pointed out what was the identity of the auxiliary verb which participated in such a construction as the main verb bearing subject agreement, it could have very easily been "be" or "have," the two most universal auxiliaries used in participial/nominal/resultative verb conjugations.   Since in all other respects, such as the nature of its underlying semantic features (persons, gender, number) and its use in anaphoric context subject pronouns (attested as early as Vedic and Hittite), the IE suffixal conjugation functions much like pronominal subject agreement (to this very day in some IE dialects), it would be rather strange to assume that it arose from any other source except the classical, natural one from which all verb-agreement systems rise, namely from anaphoric pronouns.

10. Conclusion

I think I have shown that grammatical agreement is fundamentally a topic related phenomenon, arising from anaphoric pronominalization in topical discourse contexts. The diachronic rise of grammatical agreement from pronouns, as well as many synchronic functions universally characteristic of grammatical agreement, cannot be explained otherwise. This is not to say that a system, once established, cannot change independently of its point of origin. Indeed, I have shown a wide range of instances in which agreement has assumed predictable and less predictable added functions. Our fundamental understanding of the synchronic phenomenon, however, could not be separated from our understanding of its natural diachronic origins. For in a number of subtle ways, those origins persist in haunting a phenomenon and shaping its destinies long after the current observer has ceased to recognize their hand. This may be because of some mysterious Sapirean "drift," or it may be because linguistic change is motivated by natural universal principles which transcend the artificial boundary of synchrony and diachrony.

Notes

1. I have benefited from many comments and suggestions made to me by Ed Keenan, Edith Moravcsik, Robert Hetzron, Robert Kirsner, Benji Wald, Katalin Radics, Bernard Comrie, David Zubin, Erica Garcia and Carlos Otero.

2. Languages of this type are Mandarin, Japanese or Lisu, which Li and Thompson (1974d) call "Topic prominent languages." While one may choose not to go along with their classification, it is nevertheless clear that languages which do not use anaphoric pronouns in topic-shifting do not develop grammatical agreement.

3. By "relative topicality" I here mean the relative degree to which one NP is considered "more old information," "more presupposed," "less focused" or "less foregrounded" than another.

4. See E.L. Keenan (Definition of Subject, this volume).

5. See Kirsner (1973).

6. See Zubin (1972), where the term "degree of contribution of the participant" is used.

7. See text counts in Givón (1975a).

8. See Kuno (1972a).

9. See Zubin (1972).

10. For a reflection of this in child language, where a system is only being acquired and thus "relatively frail," see E. Keenan (1974).

11. See discussion in Li and Thompson (1974d), Kuno (1974), Givón (1975b).

12. For data and discussion see Kirsner (1973), E.L. Keenan (Definition of Subject, this volume), and Givón (1975a).

13. For details and discussion see Givón (1971), as well as further below.

14. See Tyson (1974), Dillard (1972).

15. See Mülhausler (1973).

16. See Valdman (1975).

17. From Peet (1975).

18. See discussion in Givón (1975a), Kirsner (1973), E.L. Keenan (Definition of Subject, this volume).

19. For some diachronic considerations concerning "after-thought-topic," see Hyman (1974), Vennemann (1974). For interesting synchronic details in two Bantu languages, see Kimenyi (1975), Kunene (1975).

20. The pre-verbal position of object clitic pronouns in Bantu is a relic of earlier SOV syntax, as in Romance languages (see Givón, 1971, 1974a).

21. For details see Bokamba (1971), Givón (1974b).

22. For discussion of the naturalness of this particular

constraint, see Givón (1974b). Negative-verb environments pioneer this development probably because in these environments referential nouns must obligatorily be definite. This is a highly universal phenomenon arising from the more marked presuppositional status of negatives, see discussion in Givón (1975b).

23. For the Rwanda data I am indebted to Alexandre Kimenyi.

24. For some of the Swahili data below, as well as enlightening discussion, I am indebted to Benji Wald and Tom Hinnebusch.

25. See Givón (1975a).

26. See Zubin (1972, 1974).

27. Robert Hetzron (in private communication).

28. For the Spanish data I am indebted to Carlos Otero (in private communication).

29. For a discussion of contrastive vs. "recall" topic shifting, see Givón (1975b).

30. For the data and further discussion see Haile (1970), Fulas (1974).

31. While Haile (1970) does not make the distinction, the existence of the case markings in the topic-shifted constructions above suggest strongly that this is a contrastive topic pattern.

32. For the data I am indebted to Robert Hetzron (in private communication). For the etymology of the agreement morpheme, see Hetzron (1973).

33. For the data I am indebted to Robert Hetzron (in private communication).

34. For the data I am indebted to Yona Sabar (in private communication).

35. For similar insights, see Kuno (this volume).

36. For further details see Givón (1974b).

37. See Mülhausler (1973).

38. For the data I am indebted to Carlos Otero (in private communication).

39. For details and examples, see Givón (1975a).

40. See discussion in King (1967), Kiparsky (1969) and Vennemann (1968).

41. See Kimenyi and Wilkins (1974).

42. In Spanish, for example, the emphatic use of the dative object pronouns a el, a ella, is currently being demarked in many dialects. A similar situation may be observed in Zulu, where the "absolute" (or emphatic) CV-na pronominal series may be used emphatically following the verb, while the old object anaphoric pronouns are still bound pre-verbally, reflecting the earlier SOV syntax of Niger-Congo.

43. See details in Hetzron (1971).

44. See E.L. Keenan (Definition of Subject, this volume). For details of this subject-first strategy in existential constructions, see Hetzron (1971), Kirsner (1973), Li and Thompson (1975).

45. For the data I am indebted to Alexandre Kimenyi.

46. As to the underlying relationship between time and place features in language, see Traugott (1974). One may further suggest that if indeed time and place are the most presupposed/mentioned-first arguments in discourse, then they certainly are an apparent counter example to my suggested topic hierarchy. An obvious explanation as to why this is so is the fact that time/place are never the actual topic of the conversation, but only the stage. In other words, their topicality is the most unmarked one. This may also explain the seeming paradox that while the percent of definites is much higher for locative than accusative objects (Givón, 1975a), in the development of grammatical agreement--presumably via topic-shift constructions, accusative objects clearly have primacy over locatives.

47. Bill Foley (in private communication).

48. For details see E.L. Keenan (Definition of Subject, this volume).

49. For the data I was initially indebted to Charles Uwimana, but see also Chatelain (1888).

50. For a number of details, see Otero (1970, 1969, 1974).

51. For a detailed discussion and survey of the literature on the historical origin of the Akkadian/Semitic perfect conjugation, see Hudson (1974). See also Haupt (1878).

52. Carol Justus, in personal communication.

53. For a discussion of the possible diachronic origins of case markers, see Givón (1974a).

EMBEDDED TOPIC IN FRENCH

by

Larry M. Hyman
Karl E. Zimmer

0   Introduction

In Hawkinson and Hyman (1974) four general strategies
were illustrated which are used in the encoding and decoding
of topical information: 1) word order (topical information
usually comes early in the sentence); 2) case (topical information is usually associated with the more animate cases);
3) person (first and second persons are more topical or
"topicworthy" than third person human, which is more topicworthy than third person non-human); and 4) definiteness
(topical information is more likely to be definite rather than
indefinite). Of course, these are only general tendencies,
and it should not be surprising to find counterexamples to one
or more of the above.

In this paper we will discuss the use of strategies 1),
3) and 4) in French (1). As in the Hawkinson and Hyman paper,
the notion of "natural topic" is intended to reflect universal
tendencies in what speakers are likely to talk about (2).
Thus, statistically, speakers talk about people-topics, and
these topics, as in the above strategies, are generally found
early in the sentence, in animate cases, and with a definite
interpretation. Our paper will add a further dimension in
that all of our examples will involve natural topics which
are embedded one level down. In particular, we shall take our
examples mostly from the causative construction, which is
especially revealing in this regard.

1   Topic and Word Order

In Hyman and Zimmer (1974) a number of conflicting strategies (both syntactic and semantic) were presented which,
when taken together, account for many of the complexities of
the French causative construction. One of the most striking
aspects of this construction is the fact that "grammaticality"
judgments vary widely from speaker to speaker. (We put the
word "grammaticality" in quotation marks since, as we shall
see, many of the judgments are based rather on the likelihood
that a given set of circumstances will be met--or on the person's ability to imagine that set of circumstances.) The
framework presented in our earlier paper was designed to
account for this variation. Our basic premise was that the
(on-going) grammaticalization of the lexical verb _faire_ "to
make" leads to syntactic and semantic complications in the
grammar. As _faire_ becomes more and more of a grammatical
morpheme (i.e., a causative marker), it will tend to attach
itself to the following infinitive (henceforth the "embedded
verb") and disallow any intervening elements. Already, the
historical structure in 1,

1   *j'ai fait Maurice partir   (cf. Gougenheim 1929:357-8)
     I   made   Morris leave

must be realized as in 2:

2   j'ai fait partir Maurice
     I   made   leave Morris

In this latter construction, one might argue that Maurice has
become the direct object of the single verbal complex faire
partir "to make leave."

One of the syntactic complications which arises is
created by a historical structure such as that in 3:

3   *j'ai fait Maurice préparer la mayonnaise
     I   made   Morris prepare the mayonnaise

This sentence differs from 1 in that the embedded verb préparer has an object of its own. However, if the embedded
subject Maurice were to move out historically, as was the
case in obtaining 2 from 1, the following ungrammatical sentences in 4 would result:

4   *j'ai fait préparer Maurice la mayonnaise
    *j'ai fait préparer la mayonnaise Maurice

Since French does not allow two surface direct objects in a
row, the embedded subject is realized as an indirect object
(a process called "case demotion" by Comrie 1974):

5   j'ai fait préparer la mayonnaise à Maurice
     I   made   prepare the mayonnaise to Morris

Sentence 5 represents the modern French reflex of the historical word order in 3. Fuller (1971) points out that the demotion of Maurice to an indirect object is not unlike what
happens elsewhere in the grammar, as seen in 6, 7 and 8:

6   j'ai payé Maurice
     I   paid   Morris

7   j'ai payé le journal
     I   paid   the newspaper

8   j'ai payé le journal à Maurice
     I   paid   the newspaper to Morris
    "I paid Maurice for the newspaper"

In 6 we see that the verb payer "to pay" can take a direct
object which is the logical dative. In 7 we see that the
direct object can also be what in Fillmore's (1968) system
would be the objective case. In 8, however, where we attempt
to combine the two kinds of surface direct objects in the
same sentence, we observe that the underlying dative object

must be realized as a surface indirect object. The generalization which Fuller notes is that no French verb can take two surface direct objects. Thus, the change from hypothetical (sentence 4) to the correct structure in 5 is exactly parallel to the sentence in 8. Faire préparer "to make prepare" has become a single verb, in a sense, just as the verb payer is a single verb. Neither can allow two direct objects.

The tendency for the two verbs to come together and be treated as one (complex) verb can be said to be motivated by the semantic shift of faire from meaning "to make" (direct causation) to "to have, get" (indirect causation). It should follow, then, that in cases where faire keeps its meaning of "force" or "pressure" exerted on the embedded agent, the syntactic reinterpretation as a single verbal complex should be retarded. In fact, as we pointed out in our earlier paper, such examples do exist (at least for some speakers) and therefore provide evidence for our position. Thus, consider the examples in 9 and 10:

9 je l' ai fait préparer la mayonnaise
    I him/ made   prepare the mayonnaise
      her

10 je lui   ai fait préparer la mayonnaise
     I to him/ made   prepare the mayonnaise
       her

Sentence 9 represents the historical structure, with the pronominal subject of préparer realized as the superficial direct object l' "him/her" of faire. Unlike the historical structures we have cited thus far, sentence 9 is acceptable to some speakers of French. However, many speakers prefer the structure in 10, where the embedded agent is realized as an indirect object pronoun lui "to him/her" (exactly parallel to the indirect object noun à Maurice seen in 5 above).

It should be noted that a difference between 9 and 10 will be possible only when the pronoun in question is third person, since first and second person pronouns are not morphologically distinguished for case. Where the possibility of having both 9 and 10 is recognized in recent treatments of French causatives, it is usually assumed that they are synonymous. However, 9 differs, at least potentially, in a very important way from 10; namely, in 9 the causation is more direct, or may involve force or pressure. As such, it is adequately translated as "I made him prepare the mayonnaise." In 10, on the other hand, the causation is indirect, and the translation "I had him prepare the mayonnaise" is more accurate. Perhaps this difference is more obvious in 11 and 12:

11 je l' ai fait manger des épinards
    I him made eat   spinach

12 je lui ai fait manger des épinards
    I to him made   eat   spinach

Sentence 11 is translated "I made him eat spinach" and suggests a child who is being forced to eat the spinach against
his will. (Alternatively, as pointed out to us by Martine
Mazaudon, this may mean that I developed the taste of spinach
in him, i.e., made him acquire a permanent characteristic.)
Sentence 12, on the other hand, is translated "I had him eat
spinch," and might be conceived as a hungry person being
offered the only thing I had in the house to eat. What is
crucial is that where the verb faire retains its original
meaning of "make," faire préparer and faire manger, etc.,
resist reinterpretation as a single verbal complex. As a result, there are two surface direct objects in 9 and 11, one
the object of faire, the other the object of the embedded
verb.

        While this semantic "weakening" of faire is important
in explaining the subsequent syntactic changes which have
taken place in French (and other Romance languages), we would
like to suggest in this paper that this does not represent
the whole picture. In particular, one thing which did not
receive attention in Hyman and Zimmer (1974) was the role of
topic considerations in the causative construction. Changes
of word order frequently reflect a different topic status of
the various sentential elements. This is not surprising,
since we have already said that word order is a frequent
strategy in the encoding and decoding of topical information.
Very generally, topical (old) information will tend to come
early in a sentence, while focus (new) information will tend
to come later.

        In order to see how this might have worked in the early
days of French causativization, it is necessary to turn to
other constructions which have not evolved as quickly. Two
good candidates are the verb laisser "to let" and perception
verbs such as voir "to see," entendre "to hear," etc. Consider first the sentences in 13 and 14:

13 j'ai entendu l'enfant pleurer
    I heard   the child cry

14 j'ai entendu pleurer l'enfant
    I heard   cry   the child

The historical sentence is that in 13, which is still acceptable, although many French speakers prefer the sentence in
14. It is clear that we are not dealing with some grammati-

calized sense of <u>voir</u> in the second sentence. Rather, a
subtle difference is sometimes distinguished between 13 and
14, which we can assume to have been more evident at an
earlier stage of the language. In 13, the "new information"
of the sentence can be <u>l'enfant pleurer</u>, just as the new
information of 14 can be <u>pleurer l'enfant</u>. If this is the
case, the two sentences are synonymous. However, there is a
potential <u>difference</u> in the break between old and new information in these sentences (Benoit de Cornulier, personal communication). In 13 the new information can consist solely of
<u>pleurer</u> (in which case we assume <u>l'enfant</u> as part of the
topical information), and in 14 the new information can be
limited to <u>l'enfant</u> (in which case we assume <u>pleurer</u> as part
of the topical information).

Because this potential difference is pragmatic in nature, and not semantic, it cannot be fully appreciated when
these sentences are considered in isolation. This difference
can be perceived, however, in the following sentences:

15 a. j'ai entendu l'enfant <u>pleurer</u>, pas rire
        I   heard   the child crý   not laugh

    b. ?j'ai entendu <u>pleurer</u> l'enfant, pas rire
        I   heard   crý the child not laugh

16 a. j'ai entendu pleurer <u>l'enfant</u>, pas l'adulte
        I   heard   cry   the child   not the adult

    b. ?j'ai entendu <u>l'enfant</u> pleurer, pas l'adulte
        I   heard   the child   cry   not the adult

Because it is <u>new</u> information which is contrasted, the a sentences are more natural than the b sentences. Of the four,
15b is the least natural, while 16b can be rendered acceptable
with heavy stress on <u>l'enfant</u> (3). What this establishes is
that the new information may be limited to the last element
of the sentence (although it may in other cases encompass
several of the latter elements together). Put in other terms,
<u>l'enfant</u> in 13 and <u>pleurer</u> in 14 are capable of being part of
the topical information of their respective sentence. As
further evidence of this, consider the following sentences:

17 a. après l' avoir couché, j'ai entendu l'enfant
        after him putting to   I   heard   the child
              bed

        pleurer
        cry

b. après l' avoir couché, j'ai entendu pleurer
    after him putting to   I   heard   cry
        bed

    l'enfant
    the child

Both of these sentences are translated as "after putting him
to bed, I heard the child cry" in English. The interesting
fact about French, however, is that l'enfant can be coreferential with l' "him" in 17a, but it cannot be coreferential
in 17b. In other words, l'enfant is necessarily new information in 17b. It can, of course, be either new (and therefore
non-coreferential) or old (and therefore probably coreferential) in 17a (4).

We would like to suggest at this point that such potential differences may have been involved in the history of the
faire construction. Thus, in 1 it is more likely that
Maurice is topical than in 2; similarly, 5 places à Maurice
in a new information position, as opposed to its original
position in 3, where Maurice can potentially be topical.
Thus, the word order strategy for topicalization is probably
an important factor in explaining these developments (see
also below).

If we turn to the verb laisser "to let," we now observe
that the definiteness strategy plays a role in embedded topics. Consider the following sentences:

18 j'ai laissé l'enfant manger un gâteau
    I   let   the child eat   a   cake

19 j'ai laissé l'enfant manger le gâteau
    I   let   the child eat   the cake

In 18 the old-new relationship is clear, since enfant (old)
is preceded by a definite article, and gâteau (new) is preceded by an indefinite article. In 19 it is likely that both
the child and the cake have been mentioned before; compare
also 20,

20 j'ai laissé un enfant manger un gâteau
    I   let   a child eat   a   cake

where both enfant and gâteau are probably new information. In
both 19 and 20 the two noun phrases are of equal definiteness/
indefiniteness, and (at least as far as concerns that strategy) of equal old/new information. A potential problem arises
in 21,

21 j'ai laissé un enfant manger le gâteau
    I   let   a child eat   the cake

where <u>enfant</u> is in an old information position, but is indefinite; and where <u>gâteau</u> is in a new information position, but is definite. As is not surprising, some French speakers are not entirely comfortable with this sentence. Perhaps as a result, the sentence in 22 is possible for some speakers (5).

22 j'ai laissé manger le gâteau à un enfant
    I   let   eat the cake to a child

Sentence 22, which means the same thing as 21, should be of course compared to 5. In 5 it was seen that the embedded noun agent must be moved out to the right in <u>faire</u> constructions. In 21 we saw that <u>laisser</u> is more permissive, since a noun can occur between it and the following infinitive.

What 21 and 22 indicate is that topic considerations are important in determining when one rather than the other construction is likely to be used. It all depends on the extent to which the resulting action represented by the embedded verb is topical. That is, if the speaker is talking more about this action than about the agent of the action (i.e., the subject of the embedded verb), we expect the two verbs to come together. This hypothesis is supported in another way by the French data. We can assume that the resulting action will be more topical with <u>faire</u> than with <u>laisser</u>, since the speaker will naturally be more interested in something that has been <u>caused</u>, rather than simply <u>permitted</u>. That is, since causation represents a more active interest in the resulting action than does permission (which can simply represent passive acquiescence), we can explain why <u>faire</u> comes to be in proximity with the following infinitive earlier than does <u>laisser</u> (which still permits a noun between it and the following verb). Similarly, we can now predict that <u>laisser</u>, which at least represents an attitude towards the resulting action, will combine with the following infinitive more readily than <u>entendre</u> "to hear," <u>voir</u> "to see" and other verbs of perception. Although the two possibilities in 23 are encountered,

23 a. j'ai vu un enfant manger le gâteau
       I saw a child   eat   the cake

    b. ?j'ai vu manger le gâteau à un enfant
        I saw   eat   the cake to a child

some speakers who accept 22 do not readily accept 23b. Also, it should be noted that 23a does not cause the same "discomfort" that is caused by the corresponding <u>laisser</u> sentence in 21. We therefore conclude that there is a scale of the form <u>faire</u> > <u>laisser</u> > <u>voir</u>, which combine into verbal complexes in this order.

It still remains, however, that <u>faire</u> (and also <u>laisser</u>) do undergo some semantic "weakening." In the first case we have said that <u>faire</u> changes to mean "indirect causation." This is particularly clear when there is no expressed agent, as in 24,

24 j'ai fait préparer la mayonnaise
    I made prepare the mayonnaise

Sentence 24 is translated as "I had the mayonnaise prepared." As seen in 25 and 26,

25 I made Morris prepare the mayonnaise

26 *I made prepare the mayonnaise

the more direct causative verb "make" can be used in English only if there is an overt agent. We would like to suggest, however, that if 26 were ever to become (by indefinite agent deletion) an English sentence, it would necessarily signal indirect causation; i.e., it would mean "I had the mayonnaise prepared." In order to indicate direct causation, we must have an agent, as in 27:

27 I made someone prepare the mayonnaise

The ungrammaticality of 26 shows that the semantics of the verb "to make" requires an orientation towards the embedded agent--and therefore that the embedded agent would not be moved out to the right, or deleted, without a semantic change. The verb <u>laisser</u> originally meant "to loosen, to set free" and later developed into "to leave, to let" (and even "to permit"). However, in conjunction with a following infinitive, it is best interpreted as "fail to obstruct." Thus, in 28,

28 j'ai laissé Maurice tomber dans l'eau
    I let Morris fall in the water

it is most likely perceived that Morris was going to fall in the water (or I suspected that he would), and I either did nothing to stop it, or I tried to stop it, but I failed.

There is thus a curious interplay between topic/focus and the semantics of <u>faire</u> and <u>laisser</u>. When the topic/focus relations are changed in these constructions, the semantics of the head verb is also somewhat modified. In each case the semantic change can be seen as a "weakening," since the idea "have" is included in "make" and "fail to stop" is included in "leave" or "permit." The reverse is of course not true, since I can have someone do something without making him do it; and I can let someone do something without physically leaving him, or without giving my permission.

2 Topic and Passive

Many of the above sentences involving <u>faire</u>, <u>laisser</u>
and <u>voir</u> can alternatively appear with the agent marked by
<u>par</u> "by" (6):

29 j'ai fait préparer la mayonnaise par Maurice
    I made   prepare the mayonnaise by Morris
    "I had the mayonnaise prepared by Morris"

30 j'ai laissé préparer la mayonnaise par Maurice
    I let   prepare the mayonnaise by Morris
    "I let the mayonnaise be prepared by Morris"

31 ?j'ai vu préparer la mayonnaise par Maurice
    I saw prepare the mayonnaise by Morris
    "I saw the mayonnaise be prepared by Morris"

Kayne (1969), Fuller (1971), Comrie (1974) and Pinkham (1974)
all agree that <u>par</u> constructions involve passivization. They
also either implicitly or explicitly assume that sentences
with <u>par NP</u> are synonymous with sentences with <u>à NP</u>. However, this is not the case, as can be seen in the following
examples, which we owe to Martine Mazaudon (personal communication):

32 j'ai fait nettoyer les toilettes au général
    I made   clean   the toilets to the general
    "I made the general clean the toilets"

33 j'ai fait nettoyer les toilettes par le général
    I made   clean   the toilets by the general
    "I had the toilets cleaned by the general"

As can be seen in the two glosses, there is an important
difference between these sentences. In 32, it is the case
that I did something to the general, e.g., because I didn't
like him, I made him do an undesirable task. In 33, the
general is more incidental to the task. I wanted to get the
toilets cleaned and it happened to be the general that I got
to do it. In other words, in 32 it is important that the
general do the toilet-cleaning, whereas in 33 it is important
that the toilet-cleaning be done (by someone). While this
difference does not always come out as clearly as in these
examples, it is apparently always possible to assign such
interpretations to <u>à NP</u> and <u>par NP</u>.

Syntactically, 32 and 33 differ in that the embedded
sentence in the former is active, while the embedded sentence
in the latter is passive, as seen in 34 and 35:

34 j'ai fait

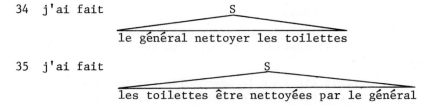

le général nettoyer les toilettes

35 j'ai fait

les toilettes être nettoyées par le général

(The verb être "to be" does not show up on the surface in
embedded passives.) Thus, since the topicalizing function of
passivization has long been known, it is not surprising to
find le général in a topic position in 34, but les toilettes
in a topic position after passivization in 35. At this point,
of course, we need a further strategy for the realization of
topic, since in the faire construction, a noun cannot appear
before the infinitive. Thus, le général goes down the Comrie
hierarchy and becomes a dative in 32 (recall the high topic
position of datives in the Hawkinson-Hyman hierarchy), while
par le général is realized in 33 in what is a very low position on the topic hierarchy. (In fact, par phrases can be
seen as functioning to remove the highly topical agent material from topic position; evidence for this is the fact that
they are optionally deleted when indefinite, e.g., j'ai fait
nettoyer les toilettes (par quelqu'un) "I had the toilets
cleaned (by someone).")
    What we would like to discuss in the remainder of this
paper is when passivization under faire must occur, is likely
to occur, or cannot occur. We have already seen that topic
plays a role in laisser and voir/entendre constructions, and
we have suggested that at an earlier stage of the language,
similar phenomena were associated with faire. What we would
like to demonstrate now is that topic plays an even greater
role in the faire construction as evolved in present day
French.
    Consider the following sentences:

36 a. j'ai fait battre un oeuf à Maurice
        I made   beat an egg to Morris
        "I made Morris beat an egg"

    b. j'ai fait battre un oeuf par Maurice
        I made   beat an egg by Morris
        "I had an egg beaten by Morris"

37 a. j'ai fait battre l'oeuf à Maurice
        I made   beat the egg to Morris
        "I made Morris beat the egg"

b. j'ai fait battre l'oeuf par Maurice
   I made   beat the egg by Morris
   "I had the egg beaten by Morris"

As discussed earlier, the a sentences differ slightly in
meaning from the b sentences, which involve passivization.
What is important is that in varying un oeuf/l'oeuf and
à Maurice/par Maurice, four acceptable sentences are obtained.
Now consider the following sentences:

38 a. ?j'ai fait battre un flic à Maurice
       I made   beat a cop to Morris
       "I made Morris beat a cop"

    b. j'ai fait battre un flic par Maurice
       I made   beat a cop by Morris
       "I had a cop beaten by Morris"

39 a. ??j'ai fait battre le flic à Maurice
        I made   beat the cop to Morris
        "I made Morris beat the cop"

    b. j'ai fait battre le flic par Maurice
       I made   beat the cop by Morris
       "I had the cop beaten by Morris"

In 38 and 39 it is observed that by varying un flic/le flic
and à Maurice/par Maurice, only two of the four possibilities
are fully acceptable. Sentence 38a causes some discomfort,
while 39a is even less acceptable.

In comparing the sentences in 36 and 37 with those in
38 and 39, it is clear that the only difference is that flic
"cop" is human, while oeuf "egg" is nonhuman. It thus appears
that when the direct object of the embedded verb is human,
passivization is almost certain to occur. Thus, 38b and 39b
are more natural-sounding at first glance than 38a and 39a.
As already guessed, the unnaturalness of these latter sentences is due to the inherent topicworthiness of the human noun
in focus (i.e., direct object) position. Consider, first,
38a. While many French speakers abruptly reject such sentences upon first hearing them, this probably is due to the
relatively unexpected circumstances which most hold in order
for this sentence to make sense. Thus, 38a is well-formed
if we assume that I am focusing more on my effect on Morris
(e.g., my responsibility for his actions), rather than on the
beating of a cop. Recall that sentence structures such as
38a have an embedded active sentence, and as a result, à
Maurice is topical. The problem which arises is that flic
"cop" is topicworthy by virtue of its humanness. In order
for 38a to make sense, à Maurice must be clearly established

as more topical than <u>un flic</u>. Thus, if after speaking to
Morris about the need to beat cops, he goes out and does it,
I may say <u>j'ai fait battre un flic à Maurice</u>, emphasizing the
effect I had on him. If, on the other hand, I am really talking about beating a cop, Morris will be more incidental to the
event, and I will be more likely to passivize <u>un flic</u> into
topic position, yielding a construction with <u>par Maurice</u>.
What makes 38b more natural than 38a is that this second situation is more likely, since <u>beating a cop</u> is <u>inherently</u> more
topicworthy than <u>beating an egg</u>. This has to do with the
fact that statistically people talk more about people than
about things (Givón, this volume).

Turning to 39a, it is somewhat more difficult to find
the circumstances to fit this construction. The fact that <u>le
flic</u> is definite makes it even more topicworthy than <u>un flic</u>.
It is therefore harder to imagine that the beating of <u>the</u> cop
would not be topical. As a result, <u>le flic</u> triggers passivization and we obtain <u>par Maurice</u>. In order for 39a to make
sense, we have to imagine that I spoke to Morris about beating a specific cop, and then he went out and did it. If
Morris winds up in jail, I may lament what I have done to him,
and attempt to say 39a. While this works for 38a, many French
speakers balk at 39a. Nevertheless, it may still be grammatical and only harder to imagine the appropriate situation.

We can therefore establish that <u>le flic</u> is more topicworthy than <u>un flic</u>, which is more topicworthy than either
<u>l'oeuf</u> or <u>un oeuf</u> (we have not presented evidence that <u>l'oeuf</u>
is more topicworthy than <u>un oeuf</u>, although we suspect that
this is the case). Where a highly topicworthy item falls in
a focus position (here, the direct object of the embedded
verb), passivization is likely to convert it to being the
subject of the passivized embedded verb, and the underlying
agent is therefore likely to be realized in a <u>par</u> phrase, as
we have seen.

The hierarchy of topicworthiness (or "natural topic")
does not stop here, however. Consider the following sentences:

40 a. ?*il m'a fait battre à Maurice
         he me made   beat to Morris
        "he made Morris beat me"

    b. il m'a fait battre par Maurice
         he me made   beat by Morris
        "he had me beaten by Morris"

41 a. ?*il te fera battre à Maurice
         he you will-make beat to Morris
        "he will make Morris beat you"

b. il te fera battre par Maurice
he you will-make beat by Morris
"he will have you beaten by Morris"

In 40a and 41a we observe that à Maurice is possibly ungrammatical (see below) when the direct object of the embedded
verb is me "me" or te "you." Passivization must occur as in
40b and 41b. The reason why the a sentences are odd is that
the speaker and hearer are likely to be topical in any discourse, i.e., it is likely that they will talk about themselves and about each other. Since 40a and 41a start with an
embedded active sentence, me and te will be in the position
of new, rather than old (topical) information. There is a
conflict, however, because my or your getting beaten is more
topicworthy, i.e., more likely to be in the minds of the
speakers, than is the fact that Morris did the beating. If
either the identity of Morris or the fact that coercion was
involved is important, French speakers will use a different
construction (e.g., with forcer "to force"). What is interesting is that topic-motivated passivization will be likely
with un flic, almost certain with le flic, and virtually required with me or te. This is not to say that the agentive
à NP is impossible with me and te. Both Gilles Fauconnier
and Martine Mazaudon have tried to imagine plausible situations where such a construction would be likely (e.g., ils
m'ont fait élever à ma pauvre grand'mère "they made my poor
grandmother raise me," where emphasis is on the effect of
raising me on my grandmother, rather than on the effect on
me) (7). Thus, to speak of degrees of grammaticality may be
incorrect. Rather, the likelihood of a situation occurring
can be hierarchized, and this hierarchy can then be syntac-
ticized into a language, i.e., we reach a point where French
speakers are no longer free to imagine the appropriate situation, but rather are constrained by the syntax of their language. That is, the syntax has become rigid.

We recognize, then, the following personal hierarchy:

42 3rd   3rd person   3rd person   1st, 2nd
    person   human   human   person;
    nonhuman   indefinite   definite   reflexive

---→

    1   2   3   4

NATURAL TOPIC SCALE

The highest position in the natural topic scale includes
first person, second person and reflexive pronouns, i.e., me,
te, se, nous, vous in French. The addition of nous "us" and
vous "you (pl.)" is straightforward, since persons closely

associated with the discourse will be highly topical. A few
words are necessary concerning the third person reflexive
pronoun se which is illustrated in the following sentences:

43 a. *il s' est fait battre à Maurice
he self made beat to Morris
"he$_1$ made Morris beat him$_1$"

b. il s' est fait battre par Maurice
he self made beat by Morris
"he had himself beaten by Morris"

(An alternative reading of 43b is "he got himself beaten by
Morris," where getting beaten was unintentional.) The reason
why reflexives are highly topicworthy is not necessarily because they tend to have human definite referents (though this
is probably an important fact), but rather that they almost
always represent old information, defined by discourse. (The
most common exception is when there is contrast on the reflexive, e.g., he kicked himsélf, not Morris, although such
situations do not arise that often). Of course, the common
language-specific constraint that a reflexive pronoun must be
preceded by its referent noun will mean that by the time the
reflexive pronoun is met by the hearer, its referent will be
old (given) information. This constraint is responsible for
the uneasiness which French speakers experience when exposed
to sentences such as 44 and 45:

44 ?j'ai fait se laver Maurice
I made self wash Morris
"I made Morris wash himself"

45 ?j'ai fait se laver la figure à Maurice
I made to-self wash the face to Morris
"I made Morris wash his (own) face"

In both cases se precedes its referent, and as a result grammaticality judgments vary. Sentence 44 is somewhat worse
than 45, since the embedded verb laver appears to have two
direct objects, se "self" and Maurice. When Maurice is pronominalized, both sentences become grammatical, e.g.,

46 je l' ai fait se laver
I him made self wash
"I made him wash himself"

47 je lui ai fait se laver la figure
I to him made self wash the face
"I made him wash his (own) face"

since l', the referent of se, precedes.

The hierarchy established in 42 is remarkably similar
to that presented for Shona by Hawkinson and Hyman (1974)
(cf. also Kuno, this volume; Kirsner 1973; Givón, this volume,
and works cited therein). In Shona, however, it was possible
to recognize 3rd person animal as being intermediate between
3rd person human and 3rd person inanimate on the natural
topic scale (Shona does not overtly distinguish definite and
indefinite nouns). A final piece of evidence for this hierarchy in French is seen in the following examples involving a
third person definite pronoun:

48 a. je l' ai fait battre à Maurice
        I it   made   beat to Morris
        "I made Maurice beat it" (?*him/her)

    b. je   l'   ai fait battre par Maurice
        I him/her/it made   beat by Morris
        "I had him/her/it beaten by Morris"

The pronouns le "him/it" and la "her/it," when elided before
a vowel, become l', which then is potentially three-ways
ambiguous between "him," "her" and "it," as seen in 48b.
However, in 48a, only one reading is possible. Because passivization has not occurred, it is naturally assumed that l'
is inanimate, e.g., the egg. Otherwise the pronoun would
have been more topicworthy (i.e., if it were human) and passivization would have occurred to produce the sentence in 48b.
Since 48b is ambiguous, but 48a is not, we have good evidence
for the view being presented here.

3   Topic and Experiential Verbs

In several of the above examples it was seen that given
certain circumstances, passivization must occur. We shall
now treat a class of verbs which in most cases require that
passivization not occur. These "experiential" verbs include
a number of stative verbs (e.g., connaître "to know," voir
"to see," aimer "to love," etc.), as well as certain nonsta-
tive sensory verbs (e.g., regarder "to look at," écouter "to
listen," etc.). A perceptive treatment of these verbs can be
found in Pinkham (1974). Consider, then, the following sentences:

49 a. j'ai fait voir le film à Maurice
        I made   see the film to Morris
        "I had Morris see the film"

    b. ?j'ai fait voir le film par Maurice
        I made   see the film by Morris
        "I had the film seen by Morris"

With the verb <u>voir</u>, passivization cannot occur--or at least
the resulting sentences are somewhat odd (these sentences
will all be glossed with "have" rather than with "make" because of the semantics of the experiential verbs). Pinkham's
generalization is that passivization cannot occur with this
class of verbs because the object of the embedded verb is not
affected by the action of the verb, e.g., when a film is
seen, it is not affected (whereas it <u>is</u> affected if it is
censored, for instance).

To her arguments we add the following data:

50 a. j'ai fait lire la lettre à Maurice
     I   made   read the letter to Morris
     "I had Morris read the letter" (to himself)

    b. j'ai fait lire la lettre par Maurice
     I   made   read the letter by Morris
     "I had the letter read by Morris" (to others)

(Sentence 50a is ambiguous, and can also mean "I had the letter read to Morris," although we shall ignore this possibility.) In 50a Morris is assumed to have read the letter to
himself, while in 50b (which was first brought to our attention via Italian by Francesco Antinucci, personal communication), it is necessarily the case that the letter was read
aloud, i.e., to someone else. One might argue that the letter was not "affected" in 50a, but it was in 50b. In this
case the same generalization could be extended to the reaction of a few speakers for whom 49b can be interpreted as "I
got the film seen (to others) by (means of) Morris," i.e.,
Morris showed the film to others. Similarly, a distinction
is made by such people between <u>j'ai fait écouter la musique</u>
<u>à Maurice</u> "I had Maurice listen to the music" and <u>j'ai fait</u>
<u>écouter la musique par Maurice</u> "I got the music listened to
by Morris," i.e., Morris is the intermediary.

A slightly different way of looking at the same facts
would be to say that such stative and sensory verbs are
naturally oriented (or focused) towards their subject. That
is, in talking about film-seeing, letter-reading, music-
listening, etc., we are more interested in the reactions of
the experiencer, than in the goal of the action. Thus, in
50a I was interested in what Morris' personal reactions to
the letter would be, while in 50b I was more interested in
getting the letter read (to someone) (8). In other words,
in this reformulation, the subject of the experiential verb
is highly <u>topical</u>, and as a result, resists passivization
(which would assign it to a lower status on the topic case
hierarchy). Where the subject of the embedded verb is less
topical, as in 50b, passivization can occur. This is not to

suggest that we bypass what all of these verbs have in common. To the contrary, it is their semantic content which determines that the expected topic will be the experiencer, rather than the goal.

This approach also explains another fact, seen in 51:

51 a. j'ai fait voir Alain à Maurice
      I   made   see Alan to Morris
      "I had Morris see Alan"

   b. ?j'ai fait voir Alain par Maurice
      I   made   see Alan by Morris
      "I had Alan seen by Morris"

Sentence 51a is acceptable, although it places a human definite noun in the direct object position (cf. the questionable sentence ?j'ai fait battre Alain à Maurice). In 51b we see that where there is a conflict between the topic hierarchy and experiential verbs, the latter win out (9). Because these verbs are oriented away from the direct object, a highly topicworthy noun such as Alain is no threat to an à NP realization of the underlying agent/experiencer. As a final example, consider the sentences in 52:

52 a. j'ai fait connaître Alain à Maurice
      I   made   known   Alan to Morris
      "I introduced Alan to Morris"
      (lit. I had Morris know Alan)

   b. j'ai fait connaître Alain par Maurice
      I   made   know   Alan by Morris
      "I had Alan known by Morris"

The verbal complex faire connaitre is commonly used as in 51a, as pointed out to us by Gilles Fauconnier (personal communication), even though it breaks the topic hierarchy. The verb connaître "to know" is obviously an experiential verb; but in addition, the verbal complex has gone a long way to becoming lexicalized, and in fact is synonymous in most respects with the verb présenter "to introduce." Another candidate for lexicalization is faire voir "to make see," which is becoming synonymous with montrer "to show." Both of these verbs take an à NP agent. This is not surprising. As faire and a following infinitive become reanalyzed as a single verbal complex, we should expect this complex to freely take any direct object and indirect object independent of the topic hierarchy. Thus, just as we can say j'ai présenté Marie à Maurice "I introduced Mary to Morris," we should expect to be able to say j'ai fait connaître Marie à Maurice (lit. I made known Mary to Morris) "I introduced Mary to Morris."

The interesting thing about the role of topic in all of the above examples is that it is more evident in <u>embedded</u> sentences than in independent sentences. Thus, we can say <u>Alain était vu par Maurice</u> "Alan was seen by Morris," although when this sentence is embedded in 50b, the resulting sentence is not entirely satisfactory. What we hope we have shown is that considerations of natural topic provide "intrinsic" variations in discourse which can be rigidified into syntactic rules. It would be interesting to know if other languages syntacticize topic relations first in embedded sentences as in French.

Notes

1. We would like to thank the following people for helping us analyze this aspect of French syntax: Jean-Pierre Beland, Richard Bonte, Benoit de Cornulier, Francine Desmarais, Gilles Fauconnier, Jean-Marie Hombert, Martine Mazaudon, Michelle Mieusset, Marie-Claude Paris, and Jacqueline Warnier. Their conflicting judgments are directly responsible for our interest in this topic. Needless to say, none of the above is responsible for any sentences they disagree with.

The first author was supported by a Postdoctoral Fellowship from the Miller Institute for Basic Research in Science, University of California, Berkeley, during all phases of research on this paper.

2. This notion should be contrasted with that of "actual topic," i.e., what a speaker may be talking about at any given moment. While natural topic, or "topicworthiness" as we shall refer to it, in part determines what will be an actual topic, items low on the natural topic hierarchy may be topical in any given discourse.

3. While all of the French speakers we have interrogated agree with these judgments concerning 15a and 15b, there is at least some confusion concerning 16a and 16b. However, Francesco Antinucci and Alessandro Duranti have informed us that the equivalent of 16b is clearly less acceptable in Italian than the equivalent of 16a. This is particularly interesting, since we would like to claim that Italian has gone further in the evolution of these structures, as we shall have occasion to point out again (see note 5). In both Italian and French it would appear to be the case that the b sentences can be rendered somewhat more acceptable by taking a pause where the comma is indicated. Our interpretation of this is that the whole of the information after the verb "hear" is new, but that a contrastive afterthought is then appended. That is, if the speaker had planned a contrastive sentence from the beginning, he would have uttered one of the a sentences instead.

4. Dick Oerle has pointed out to us a parallel distinction concerning particle movement in English. Thus, in the following sentences

a) after weighing it, John brought the package in

b) after weighing it, John brought in the package

a coreferential reading is possible only in a) and not in b). Again we would claim that the new information in a) can consist either of brought the package in (non-coreferential and therefore with some stress on package) or of brought in (or

209

even just <u>in</u>), in which case <u>the package</u> is new and therefore
cannot be coreferential with <u>it</u>. In both the French and English examples, speakers may fail to recognize these differences in new vs. old information when the simple sentences
are presented in isolation. Other more discerning speakers
may recognize, though not be able to verbalize the slight
difference, since this difference is not attributable to the
meaning of these sentences, but rather is derived from the
way in which the elements of each sentence relates to a particular discourse.

     5. One problem which needs to be dealt with in this
regard is the fact that in "substandard" French NP à NP is a
substitute for a possessive NP de NP construction. Thus,
many French speakers say <u>le livre à Jean</u>, rather than <u>le liv-</u>
<u>re de Jean</u> "John's book." While this may appear to be only
a side issue, we have discovered that some speakers of French
reject some sentences involving surface NP à NP, presumably
as a "hypercorrection." This applies, for instance, to 22,
where one is tempted to interpret <u>le gâteau à un enfant</u> as "a
child's cake." Just to what extent the judgments we have
obtained can be attributed to this particular problem is not
clear. It is interesting to note that in Italian, where we
do not have a possessive NP à NP construction, sentence b) is
clearly preferable to sentence a) (Francesco Antinucci, personal communication):

  a) ho lasciato un bambino mangiare il dolce
      I   let   a   child   eat   the   cake

  b) ho lasciato mangiare il dolce a un bambino
      I   let   eat   the   cake to a   child

Of course this may be another indication that Italian has
evolved further than French in these constructions.

     6. A continuum is observed in these examples, since 29
is more acceptable than 30, which in turn is more acceptable
than 31. This follows from our observation that the action
of preparing the mayonnaise will be more topicworthy with
<u>faire</u> than with <u>laisser</u> than with <u>voir</u>. Thus, by default,
one might say, the agent <u>Maurice</u> will be more topicworthy
with <u>voir</u> than with <u>laisser</u> than with <u>faire</u>. Since we accept
the argument that passivization is involved in these senten-
ces, and since we follow Kirsner in viewing passivization as
a strategy which knocks an agent "out of focus," the relative
expectancy of <u>par</u> phrases in these examples is explained: the
more <u>préparer la mayonnaise</u> is "in focus" the more <u>par Maurice</u>
is out of focus.

     7. Perhaps we should not overemphasize this point,
since most of the French speakers we interrogated would not

accept sentences such as <u>ils m'ont fait élever à ma pauvre</u> <u>grand'mère</u> under any circumstances. Since we believe that speakers generally underestimate rather than overestimate what they actually can or do say, we tentatively conclude that some speakers of French actually do say such sentences. The uneasiness which accompanies these sentences is attributable to any existent conflict within the strategies utilized for the realization of topicworthy material.

    8. These sentences should thus be compared to those in 32 and 33 where <u>au général</u> focuses on the effect of toilet-washing on the general, while <u>par le général</u> focuses on getting toilet-washing done.

    9. Sentence 51b is acceptable, however, if <u>Maurice</u> is a doctor whom <u>Alain</u> is seeing (Marie-Claude Paris, personal communication).

RELATIVIZATION AND TOPICALIZATION IN HITTITE (1)

by

Carol Justus

1.0   Li and Thompson (1974d) have proposed that languages are to be typologically differentiated on the basis of
topic prominence as opposed to subject prominence. E.L.
Keenan (Definition of Subject, this volume) and others have
argued on the basis of subject properties which appear to be
language universal that subject-predicate is a universal organizational principle in language rather than a typological
criterion. Givón (this volume) has further suggested that
topic is language universal rather than typological. It is
the purpose of this paper to present data from a synchronic
analysis of Old Hittite in support of a classificational dichotomy in language based on topic prominence as opposed to
subject prominence. The argument presented here assumes with
Li and Thompson (1974d) that topic prominence is a semantically based organizational principle as opposed to the syntactically based subject-predicate organizational principle,
and that, while both topic and subject may be expressed, one
principle of organization systematically dominates the grammatical patterns of a particular language. It is the purpose
of this paper to show that, although Hittite codifies the
subject-verb relationship very often, the semantic organizational principle based on topic prominence is primary in a
way that it is not in subject prominent languages like English and other modern Indo-European languages.
    1.1   The material presented here attempts to fill a gap in
the synchronic description of Hittite syntax by adding data
concerning the treatment of semantic discourse constituents,
topic and comment, theme and focus. Although Friedrich
(1960:115-169) has provided an unusually thorough description
of the constituent structure of Hittite, he has not included
data as to how or whether Hittite differentiates topic from
subject. In looking for basic structural delimitations of
topic and subject, I have investigated the nature of topic as
it relates to Hittite syntactic units, basic discourse strategies, behavioral processes and codification patterns. In
addition to what Hittite scholars have known for a long time,
I have found one particularly striking syntactic correlation
between topic and the relative construction. I find that the
topic status of the head noun determines the morphemic marking of two different types of construction. Relative clauses
modifying the primary topic in a construction have no morphe-
mid marker, but those modifying a focus which becomes a subsequent theme locally use ku- to mark the initial occurrence of the
shared noun phrase. I conclude from the ku-patterns, related
discourse strategies and behavioral processes that Hittite
differs from English, for example, in that the underlying
principle of syntactic organization is topic-comment rather

subject-predicate.

1.2   This study consists of three parts. First I consider previous scholarship. I state the Hittite problem and
its relationship to work on subject and topic, then sketch
the nature of the Indo-European syntactic and morphological
controversy which topic prominence clarifies, and define
topic and its subdivisions in terms of previous work which I
find particularly relevant to a presentation of the data under discussion. Second, I present basic Hittite syntactic
data together with facts pertinent to its interpretation.
Finally, I analyze more complex examples, including those
with relative constructions, and show how topic prominence as
a typological classification clarifies the synchronic analysis of Hittite relative constructions.

2.0   The Li and Thompson identification of topic prominence as a typological principle clarifies a fundamental
difference which Indo-Europeanists have long recognized as
obtaining between early Indo-European complex constructions
as opposed to those of the later language. Delbrück (1900:
415f. and others), on the basis of clause sequences without
subordinating conjunctions in early texts, concluded that at
some stage of the proto-language there were only paratactic
constructions. As the language developed, then, it became a
language with subordinate constructions. Löfstedt (1970
[1911]:81ff.) compares the paratactic type to constructions
typical of Vulgar Latin and concludes that this type of organization is a characteristic by which less sophisticated
speech and thought patterns can be differentiated from the
developed subordination of the classical language.

2.0.1 Hittite, the oldest attested Indo-European language (2), has as its relative construction, a clause sequence usually marked by an inflected ku-marker and consistent noun deletion patterns, a construction which has been
analyzed first as a paratactic sequence characteristic of an
older stage of language which had not yet developed a formal
means of syntactic subordination (Sturtevant 1930; Hahn 1946,
1949), and more recently, as a type of relative construction
consistent with syntactic processes for expressing both subordination and noun modification in languages which are verb
final (Raman 1972) (3). When one recognizes that the syntactic organization of a normal Hittite construction is based on
the principle of topic as primary rather than subject-predicate or even subordinate-coordinate oppositions, a natural
explanation for the morphological problem of the derivation
of the Hittite base ku- primarily as a topic marker, and
secondarily as an indefinite and relative marker suggests itself. Further investigation shows, in fact, that relative

constructions without a relative marker, as one expects in
an OV language, occur, and that these relative constructions
without ku- are in complementary distribution with those
marked by ku-. The basis of the distribution, further, is
the topic status of the shared noun phrase in the syntactic
construction as a whole.

2.1   For Indo-Europeanists, the derivation of the
relative pronoun constitutes a morphological problem, first
because two separate bases, *jo- and *kʷo-, function as relative markers in the older languages (in no one language do
both bases function as relative), and second because one base,
the base *kʷo-, has alternative functions as indefinite and
interrogative (4). Scholars have proposed various morphological and syntactic solutions to this problem. Some have reconstructed the Proto-Indo-European bases *jo- and *kʷo- as
relative pronouns differing from one another as regards definiteness (Sturtevant 1930; Szemerenyi 1970:191ff. for the
literature on this problem). Others have proposed *jo- as
the original relative base (Schwyzer 1968 [1938]:614f. and
others) and explained the appearance of *kʷo- in both Latin
and Hittite, for example, as an independent development from
indefinite (Hahn 1946) or interrogative (Hoffmann and Szantyr
1965:555) paratactic constructions, while yet another view
reconstructs the Proto-Indo-European relative pronoun as *kʷo-
and explains *jo- as an independent innovation (Szemerenyi
1970:194).

2.1.1   In addition to the morphological problem, archaic
syntactic constructions such as the Hittite relative construction have led scholars to suppose that the proto-language con-
stituted at some stage a language without subordinate structures. The variant Indo-European relative construction, for
example, which classicists call attractio inversa and which
Hittite grammatical studies agree is the standard form for
the relative construction in Hittite (Goetze 1925:86; Sturtevant 1930; Hahn 1946; Held 1957; Raman 1972, 1973), differs
radically from the standard Greek and Latin type (Schwyzer
1966 [1949]:641; Löfstedt 1970 [1911]:222ff.). The construction "I gave to the temple the booty (which) I took" has the
attractio inversa form "What booty I took, (it) I to the temple gave." Scholars traditionally explained this variant as
a syntactic archaism which gave evidence for a stage at which
Indo-European did not yet have fully subordinated relative
constructions (Delbrück 1900:415f.; Hahn 1946 and others).
Combining the morphological and syntactic problems, Hahn
(1949) proposed to derive the relative construction from an
earlier paratactic indefinite construction. Such an analysis
assumes that the preposing of the relative clause in Hittite

at one time marked the construction as coordinate and that
the ku-marker signalled indefinite. At some stage, then,
one must suppose that the same signals acquired functions
subordinate and definite. Subsequent synchronic studies of
the Hittite relative construction suggest that the syntactic
type attractio inversa represents a variant relative construction in OV type languages (Raman 1972; 1973:7ff.).

2.1.2   Although the syntactic analysis of attractio inversa as a variant OV construction explains the word order
peculiarities of this subordinate type, it poses again the
problem of the origin of the ku-marker. Typical OV relative
constructions are preposed to the left of the head noun with
no relative marker or pronoun. Position and deletion of the
shared noun phrase mark the modifier clause. The construction "What booty I took, (it) I to the temple gave" would
have the standard OV order "I the I took booty to the temple
gave." This lack of relative marker in consistent OV languages suggests that neither *k^{w}o- nor *jo- had original
functions as relative markers, and poses again the question
as to why *k^{w}o- may have developed its relative function. In
this study, I propose that *k^{w}o- originated as a topic marker, and that it had indefinite and relative functions which
were redundant features of its particular type of topic-
marking function.

2.2   In distinguishing properties which separate topic
from subject, Li and Thompson (1974d) have used topic to
mean "center of attention" or a definite NP with either anaphoric or generic reference. A subject, then, is not necessarily a definite NP. E.L. Keenan (Definition of Subject,
this volume) has noted that it is a property of the subject
to be more accessible to relativization. Kuno (this volume)
has brought evidence from English that subjects as theme, nor
as focus, relativize. Hittite data suggest that two sorts of
topics relativize, but that the hierarchic relationship between these topics determines the form of the relative marker
(5). In order to be more precise about the relationship between these two topics or "centers of attention," I have
subdivided the term topic using the Prague School designa-
tions "theme" and "focus."

2.2.1   Throughout this study I use "topic" as a general
term to subsume the more specific "theme" and "focus" as defined by Halliday (1967:199-244) and further clarified by
Chafe (1974) in relation to the speaker's assumptions about
his addressee's consciousness. By topic organization and
topic hierarchy, I mean the specific way in which Hittite constructions and clauses use "theme" as the point of departure and
"focus" to push the message further in conveying information (5).

218

2.2.2   With Firbas (1966a:245ff.), Halliday (1967:212f.) and Chafe (1974:119ff., 123ff.), I define "theme" as the point of departure for the message, as given or old information in the sense that it is something assumed by the speaker to be present in the addressee's consciousness at the time he is speaking. While Halliday assigns theme specifically to the clausal unit, Chafe has pointed out that as the discourse progresses the "given" status of what is in the addressee's consciousness (theme) may be acquired or lost (123ff.). In the Hittite construction larger than the clause, "theme" is the meaningful constituent, and appears to dominate for the duration of the constructional unit, although a new focus is added with each new clause.

2.2.3   While theme is the given point of departure, focus is new information in the sense that it is textually and situationally nonderivable, nonanaphoric, although not necessarily factually new information (Halliday 1967:204ff.). Focused information occurs noninitially in the discourse as part of the rheme (6). Its newness as information consists in its being asserted by the speaker as part of the proposition, that part of the information which the speaker assumes he is conveying to the addressee as unknown to him (Chafe 1974:119). It is assumed not to be momentarily in the addressee's consciousness or part of his present memory.

2.2.4   In order to avoid the ambiguity inherent in the term "topic," which Halliday points out (1967:200) designates aspects of both "theme" and "rheme," then, I use "topic" as a cover term for "theme" and "focus." As subdivisions of the more general "topic," one might view "theme," the primary point of departure or center of attention in the clause or construction, as a primary topic, and focus, whose function is to introduce a new element to move the discourse further, as a secondary topic when it is anaphorically referred to in a subsequent clause as given. Both the theme and a focus which continues as focus over more than one clausal period thus constitute high points of attention in the constructional unit. In Hittite, the construction begins with a theme and may introduce one or more noun focuses without having to reestablish the theme as a given in the addressee's consciousness. For this reason, I say that the theme dominates the construction.

2.3   Li and Thompson (1974d) have differentiated topics from subjects on the basis of discourse strategy, noun-verb relations and transformational properties. The Hittite data show that topics have a characteristic role in discourse syntax which subjects do not have, unless they are also topics. Basic discourse strategies based on the initially positioned topic and subsequent deletion, pronominalization and repetition patterns are conditioned by both subjects and topics. While noun-verb relations seem to define subjects, codification of the relationship subject-verb cannot be unequivocally shown to be the primary relationship which is marked. Schachter (this volume) has shown that both topics and agents condition a marking on the verb in Tagalog, and only when topicality and agency co-occur can the category subject be identified. Subsequent studies in Hittite will need to further investigate subject properties such as agency and topic status criteria for noun-verb agreement (see below).

    2.3.1   In examining coding properties such as position and affix agreement, behavioral processes and pragmatic or semantic properties (E.L. Keenen, Definition of Subject, this volume) of subjects and topics, however, I find that coding evidence for topics occurs (position and the ku-marker) and that behavioral processes which one identifies with subjects in other languages are either lacking (passive) or are not subject conditions in the same way that they are in subject-predicate languages (reflexive and deletion). Discourse strategy, noun-verb relations and transformational properties, thus, indicate that Hittite is a language of a fundamentally different type. The dominance of topic suggests that the difference in type is to be identified in terms of topic as opposed to subject prominence.

    3.0   Anyone examining the syntax of Hittite immediately notices two mechanisms which divide phrasal and constructional units, mechanisms which function at least as efficiently for Hittite as modern punctuation does for English. One is morphological and syntactic, the other scribal. Noninitial clauses begin, either with a sentence connecting particle such as nu, ta or su (Friedrich 1960:155ff.), or with enclitic affixes on the clause initial word (Friedrich 1960:63f.; 147ff.). Sentence connecting particles are often followed by enclitic particles to form sequences such as nu-us (nu plus -us, which signals anaphoric reference to a common gender plural noun here used as an accusative object) or n-as (nu plus -as, anaphoric reference to a common gender singular noun, here functioning as subject), or nu-mu-kan (nu plus -mu "me" and -kan, a directional particle with the following verb). Some clauses, particularly in the older language, have no initial marker, but in normal word order, the verb marks the end of the clause. Sentence initial particles and verbs at the end of the clause, then, are the morphological and syntactic markers of clausal units. Examples are:

1. Otten and Souček 1969:24 line 17

   LUGALuš- mu   DUMU.É.GAL   pai
   king–nom–me   nobleman   gives–3s
   "the king gives me a nobleman..." (7)

The first constituent, LUGALuš "the king," is marked as the
first constituent by the enclitic particle -mu "me," and the
end of the clause is marked by the verb pai "gives." This
particular clause, although noninitial in the construction,
varies somewhat from the usual noninitial clause in that it
introduces two noun phrases at once (see below).

2. Friedrich 1959:20 line 52

   nu- ši   12 GÍN   KUBABBAR pai
   ptc–to him 12 shekel(s) silver   gives–3s
   "...he gives him 12 shekels of silver..."

Example 2 likewise illustrates the final position of the
verb and the sentence connective nu. Here nu plus the dative
enclitic -ši mark the beginning of a noninitial clause.
3.0.1 Another Old Hittite text, however, illustrates
asyndeton, or the omission of any connective, which is characteristic of the older language (Friedrich 1960:161):

3. Neu 1970:18 lines 16ff.

   UGULA   lu.mešMUHALDIM   uzuNÍG.GIG   udai
   chief   men   cook (s)   meat liver   brings–3s

   kuttaš   piran   katta   dai
   wall–gen before   down   places–3s

   hašši   dai
   hearth–dat/loc places–3s

   kuršaš   piran   dai
   shield–gen   before places–3s

   halmašuitti   lutti-   ja   dai
   throne–dat/loc window–dat/loc–and   places–3s

   hattaluwaš GISi   dai
   bolt–gen   wood–dat/loc   places–3s

   namma hašši   dai
   again hearth–dat/loc places

   "The chief of the cooks brings the liver, places
   (it) before the wall, on the hearth, before the
   shield, on the throne and window, and on the wood
   of the bolt, then back on the hearth."

Here, the only connecting type of word is <u>namma</u> "again, further" in the final clause. The final position of the verb and the characteristic deletion pattern leaving a basic two constituent dichotomy in subsequent clauses clearly marks out clausal boundaries, even without the sentence connectives or enclitic particles.

3.0.2   In addition to phrasal divisions marked by morphological and syntactic devices, the scribe usually drew a ruled line across the tablet at intervals after as few as one or two and as many as twenty or more lines of cuneiform script. These ruled lines usually agree when there are duplicate copies of the same text and seem to segment semantic units. Occasionally one version will omit a line, but this type of variance seems to be of the same nature as other scribal errors (8). With these linguistic and textual devices, it is usually clear what constitutes a clausal unit and the much larger unit which I will call construction. The construction may correspond to the sentence unit, but it usually comprises more than what is normally considered a sentence in English, and is characteristically a complex structure. That is, it is typically composed of at least an initial clause and a matrix.

3.1   There are certain difficulties in using E.L. Keenan's (<u>Definition of Subject</u>, this volume) definition of basic sentence to identify a single type as basic in Hittite (9). Keenan includes in his definition of basic sentence clauses to which some other sentence constitutes some modification, and those which have the greatest morphological and syntactic potential, the greatest freedom of occurrence and undergo more syntactic transformations. In Hittite, clauses which are first in a construction tend to include more full noun phrases and should have more freedom of occurrence because they make statements which do not depend upon anaphoric reference or noun deletion from an equivalency elsewhere. Construction initial clauses, however, usually serve to introduce information which is to be understood as a function of a subsequent clause in the construction. Noninitial clauses in the construction often have sentence connecting particles, but characteristically some function in the noninitial clause is performed by a constituent from a preceding clause. Construction final clauses have the least freedom of occurrence and the greatest number of constituents which may be understood to be modified or expanded by another, preceding clause. Final clauses are matrix sentences in which noun phrases with selectional restrictions to its verb have been deleted on the basis of identity with a preceding noun phrase constituent. Because of this difficulty in defining basic

sentences in Hittite, I will first consider typical clausal types.
3.1.1 Typical construction initial clauses are:

4.   UGULA ^{lú.meš}MUHALDIM   ^{uzu}NÍG.GIG udai
     chief   men   cook(s)   meat liver brings-3s
     "The chief of the cooks brings liver..."
     (example 3 above)

5.   É   ^dHalmašuittaš ... É   ^dSiunašummiš ABNI
     house god-Halm.-gen ... house god-Siun.-gen I-built
     "I built the temples of Halmasuitta (of ... and)
     of Siunasummi..." (example 34 below)

6.   takku ^{gud}AB arnuwandan   kuiški   walahzi
     if   cow   pregnant-acc someone-nom strikes-3s
     "If someone strikes a pregnant cow..."
     (example 19 below)

7.   takku LÚaš   GUD-ŠU ÍDan   zinuškizzi
     if   man-nom ox-his river-acc cross-caus-iter-3s
     "If a man usually has his ox cross a river..."

The theme occurs in initial position and may coincide with the
subject or some other argument of the verb. If the theme and the
subject are the same, the basic constituent order is subject,
(dative), object, verb (10). In examples 4 and 7 the theme
and subject are the same, while in 5 and 6 the object is the
theme (11). In all of these examples (4-7) several noun
phrase constituents are introduced into the discourse at once,
but the theme takes the prominent initial position (10).
3.1.2 Typical noninitial clauses are:

8.   hašši   dāi
     hearth-dat/loc places-3s
     "(he) places (it) on the hearth..."
     (example 3 above)

9.   tamaiš-   an   šuwaizzi
     another-nom-him shoves-3s
     "another shoves him"
     (example 38 below)

10. ta   ÍDan   zāi
     ptc river-acc crosses-3s
     (example 38 below)

11. nu   ^{uru}Zippaššanan   harninkun
     ptc city-Zippassa-acc destroyed-I
     "I destroyed the city Zipassana..."
     (Laroche 1976: CTH4: KBo X 2 III 3)

12. DINGIR^{mes}-ma- ssi sara   dahhun
    gods-   ptc-from it preverb took-I
    "I took from it (its) gods..." (ibid. III 4)

13. nu   sarhuwanda pessijazi
    ptc embryo   throws-3s (variant for example 19
                                                below)
    "(it) throws (its) embryo..."

The typical noninitial clause in a construction has two basic
parts which correspond to the topic-comment dichotomy. The
first part characteristically introduces a new noun phrase,
while the second part is the verb marked for agreement with a
noun constituent, very often the theme from a preceding
clause (12). Connecting particles and enclitics at the beginning of the clause relate it to previous parts of the discourse. In 12 the preverb sara is part of the verbal half of
the clause (13). Certainly pronominal enclitics, and probably sentence connectives, relate to previously given information (14).

   3.1.3   Final matrix clauses very often have two full
constituents much like noninitial clauses:

14. [...] apedanda   halissijanun
          with that   inlaid-I
    "(those) I inlaid with that." (example 34 below)

15. nu-za apun-   pat   danzi
    ptc   that one-acc-ptc seize-3p
    "...they seize that one." (example 39 below)

16. 2 GIN   KUBABBAR pai
    2 shekel(s) silver   gives-3s
    "(he) gives 2 shekels of silver (for it)." (example 19)

Again the clause has two clear constituent units, although
final matrix clauses very often use pronominal enclitics or
deletion for the arguments of the matrix verb, if they are
already mentioned in a prior clause of the construction. In
16 the unit "2 shekels of silver" introduces a new noun concept, but very often, as in 14 and 15, the noun constituent
has reference to the previously stated theme or focus, so
that the verb introduces the new information (15). Since
noninitial and final matrix clauses occur most often in the
discourse, on the basis of frequency of occurrence and freedom of occurrence, one might consider the topic-comment dichotomy which is characteristic of these clauses to represent
a more basic or unmarked structure. Construction initial
clauses are marked by restrictions on their freedom of occurrence, although they also represent a basic type, one which

is more likely to be "internally reorderable and embeddable" (E.L. Keenan, Definition of Subject, this volume). On the basis of freedom of occurrence, though, the unmarked clause structure in Hittite is the one that is based on the semantic dichotomy topic-comment.

3.2 On the construction level, as well as at the clause level, Hittite syntax reflects the semantic organizational principle based on topic-comment as primary. I show first how word and clause order mark the theme in the construction, then how the function of the morpheme <u>ku-</u> is primarily related to the topic-comment structure of the larger syntactic unit and only secondarily a marker of subordination and indefiniteness.

3.2.1 Two passages, one from an Old Hittite oracle and one from a ritual, illustrate simple theme constructions and have the characteristic asyndesis of the old language (Friedrich 1960:157). The first introduces the theme in the initial clause, also as agent-subject of the verb. Succeeding clauses introduce new noun phrases (one each) in the typical topic-comment structure of noninitial clauses:

17. (Unal and Kammenhuber 1974:174 paragraph 3)

| hurlaš | araiš | "The Hurrian (who) |
| Hurrian-nom | stood up-3s | arose, |

| nakki- | šet taš | took his diffi- |
| difficulties-his | took-3s | culties, |

| harkan taš | | took his defeat, |
| defeat | took-3s | |

| ulhalis-šet taš | | took his <u>ulhali</u> |
| ulhali-his | took-3s | |

DINGIR^{meš}	para pitaš	(all of which) he
gods	preverb brought-3s	brought to the
		gods."

Structurally and semantically <u>huriaš</u> "the Hurrian" is the theme of this construction, and is so marked by its initial position. The final position of para pitaš "he brought (to)," however, marks it as the matrix verb to which all preceding actions are prior and subordinate. "The Hurrian" functions as agent to each verb. In its initial occurrence it is the sole argument of an intransitive verb. The subsequent transitive <u>taš</u> "he took" adds further objective arguments, while the matrix <u>para pitaš</u> "he brought (to)" adds a dative argument without letting either the agentive or objective arguments from preceding clauses be lost from the speaker-hearer's consciousness. To render the unity and thematic structure of such a construction into English, one might resort to relative pronouns.

3.2.2 A similar construction occurs in the Old Hittite storm ritual (Neu 1970:18; cf. example 3 above):

18.   UGULA   lú.meš MUHALDIM   uzuNIG.GIG   udai
      chief men   cook(s)   meat liver   brings-3s

      kuttaš   piran   katta dai
      wall-gen before down places-3s

      hašši   dai
      hearth-dat/loc places-3s

      kuršaš   piran dai
      shield-gen before places-3s

      haimašuitti   lutti-   ja dai
      throne-dat/loc window-dat/loc-and places-3s

      hattaluwaš GIŠi   dai
      bolt-gen   wood-dat/loc places-3s

      namma hašši   dai
      again hearth-dat/loc places-3s

      "The chief of the cooks brings the liver, places (it) before the wall, on the hearth, before the shield, on the throne and on the window, on the wood of the bolt, then back on the hearth."

Here the initial clause states both the agent and object arguments of the verb udai "brings." Subsequent clauses focus on new places where the same agent places (dai) the same object before finally replacing (namma ...dai) it on the hearth (hašši). Syntactically, initial statement of the theme with subsequent deletions and appropriate lexical choices inserted into topic-comment positions marks the semantic cohesion of the construction.

3.3   Further examination of such processes as noun-verb coding, position, deletion, reflexivization and the passive show that the topic-comment, not the subject-predicate relation is dominant. Li and Thompson (1974d) have pointed out that topics differ from subjects with regard to the selectional relationship obtaining between noun and verb. Topics are independent of verbal selection, while subjects are dependent upon their relationship to the verb. While in Hittite subject has identifiable and often codified relationships to a verb, the status as theme is independent of any particular verbal relationship but also codified by position, deletion and the distribution of the morpheme ku-.

3.3.1   Although Hittite subjects show case inflection, the coding of noun-verb relationships within the clausal unit is at best illusory support for subject-predicate organization in Hittite. Common gender nouns mark the subject case (nominative). Neuter or inanimate nouns, however, case-mark subjects and objects alike, so that subjects are marked only for animate nouns. Friedrich (1960:115ff.) has pointed out that Hittite very often makes use of constructions according to the sense, moreover, rather than observing strict grammatical subject-predicate agreement. Nominal sentences (verbless sentences, 117f.) perhaps represent more clearly the two-constituent dichotomy, and further attest to the loose syntactic connection between the clausal constituents. Although Hittite normally marks noun agreement for case, number and gender, Friedrich (1960:118) notes examples of nonagreeing predicates in nominal sentences. Very often scribal practice omits the case marking on the noun when writing logographically, so that the subject-predicate must be inferred from other syntactic or semantic factors implicit in the context. For example (Freidrich 1959:42; Laws I 77a, lines 78f. and notes 15 and 16 for Text A which I cite):

19. takku ᵍᵘᵈÁB   arnuwandan   kuiški   walahzi
     if   cow   pregnant-acc someone-nom strikes-3s

     ŠA LIBBI- ŠA pešsizzi   2 GÍN   KUBABBAR pai
     ptc embryo- her throws-3s 2 shekel(s) silver gives-
                                                        3s

     "If someone strikes a pregnant cow (which) (then) miscarries, (he) gives 2 shekels of silver (for it)."

Here the theme, ᵍᵘᵈÁB arnuwandan "the pregnant cow," is in construction initial position and also case marked as object of the verb walahzi "strikes," while kuiški "someone" is preverbal and case marked as subject (nominative case). But both focus noun phrases in subsequent clauses, LIBBA-ŠA "her embryo" and 2 GÍN KUBABBAR "two shekels of silver," are implicit from the context as regards noun-verb relation. The semantic arrangement, not the syntactic marker, makes it implicit.

3.3.1.1   Likewise, in example 18 above the logographic noun sequence, UGULAlú.mešMUHALDIM "chief of the cooks" and uzuNÍG.GIG "liver," is understood from the context to represent subject and object, respectively, of the verb udai "brings," so that noun marking and verbal agreement have, very often, a redundant role as syntactic signals in Hittite.

Some combination of the semantic factors of topic hierarchy,
and feature hierarchy as regards human, animate and inanimate, and transitivity instead signal these relationships (16).

3.3.2 Closely related to the question of case marking
and verbal agreement is the passive. Hittite does not have a
true passive, but often expresses transitivity by means of
lexical selection. An animate being might be agent of the
transitive verbs kuen- "kill," dai- "place," ija- "make, do,"
for example, or of the intransitive verbs ek-/ak- "die," ki-
"lie, be placed," kiš- "become, be made" (Friedrich 1960:136).
Although Hittite attests a verbal inflection for voice, the
medio-passive, studies of the problem of voice in Indo-European
agree that there was no formal passive in either Hittite (Neu
1968:109ff; Kammenhuber 1969a:204,215) or in Indo-European
(Kammenhuber 1969a:215,255ff; Brugmann 1916:700f). It remains
now to thoroughly investigate Hittite to see whether instances
of lack of subject-verb agreement might not in fact be theme-
verb agreement. Clear evidence exists that, at least for verbs
like "kill," "make" and "place," the noun argument determines
the lexical selection of the verb allowing the noun to function as the focused argument to dominate the syntax (Kammenhuber 1969a:255; Friedrich 1960:136). I suggest that lexical
selection of the verb in agreement with the focus is a consequence of topic-comment structure (17). Just as topic-comment
organization is a semantic device and subject-predicate syntactic, passivization is syntactic and lexical selection semantic. Passivization is a transformational subject property
for which there is no formal inflection or syntactic devide in
Hittite, and thus constitutes a negative argument against
subject-predicate organization.

3.3.3 Another process, reflexivization, appears to
correlate with agency plus topic, but not with agency minus
topic. Although more study will clarify in greater detail
the syntactic constructional restrictions on the use of the
particle -za, it is clear from these examples that its use,
while very often translatable in terms of the subject's involvement in the action of the verb (Friedrich 1960:132f.),
also marks the subject of a nominal sentence as first or
second person (Hoffner 1969), and is determined by syntactic
constraints from the constructional unit (examples follow).

3.3.3.1 The Laws I 20, 21 and 23 furnish two sets of
minimal pairs which illustrate how the occurrence of -za differs from the occurrence of -šši, another enclitic with anaphoric third person reference. In examples 20-23 -za correlates with continuance of the focus from a previous clause
agent while -šši signals that the noun phrase now has a dative function with regard to the verb:

228

20. Laws I 23 Friedrich 1959:22 lines 59-60 with notes 6
and 7

takku îRas̆   h̄uwai
if   slave-nom runs away-3s

n- as̆ ANA KUR ^{uru}Luwija paizzi
ptc- he into land city-Luwians goes-3s

kuis̆- an āppa uwatezzi
ptc-nom- him back brings-3s

nu- s̆s̆e 6 GÎN   KUBABBAR pāi
ptc-him 6 shekel(s) silver   gives-3s

"If a slave (who) runs away goes into the city of
the Luwians, they give 6 shekels of silver to the
one who brings him back."

21. Laws I 23 Friedrich 1959:22 lines 60-62

takku îRas̆   h̄uwai   n- as̆ kururi
if   slave-nom runs away-3s ptc-ptc enemy-dat/loc

    KURe   paizzi
    land-d/1 goes-3s

kuis̆- an āppa- ma uwatezzi
ptc-nom-him back-ptc brings-3s

n- an- za- an apās̆- pat dāi
ptc-him-ptc- him dem-nom-ptc takes-3s

"If a slave runs away, and goes into an enemy land,
the one who brings him back shall take him (the
slave) as his" (or, "if a slave (who) runs away
goes into an enemy land, he shall be taken by the
one who brings him back": see below concerning the
passive)

In both examples, the runaway slave (îRas̆ or îRis̆) is theme
theme and an unnamed focused person who brings him back is
introduced by ku-. The two laws differ from each other primarily as to the agent-dative relation with the final verb of
the focused person kuis̆. As dative of the verb, kuis̆ is
referred to in the matrix clause by the argument dative particle matrix, -s̆s̆e, the noun phrase introduced by kuis̆ in the
previous clause as agent of the matrix, by -za (and apās̆).
This usage of -za contrasts elsewhere with deletion of previous nouns (see above, for example).
except that the other focused person is specified as ishas-
sis "his owner," and a third unspecified party steals the
slave, rather than the slave's running away of his own voli-
tion.

22. Friedrich 1959:20 lines 53-55

takku ÍR ... kuiški taízzi
if   slave   someone-nom steals-3s

n- an ANA KUR ^{uru}Hatti uwatezzi
ptc-him into land city-Hatti brings-3s

išhaš- šiš- an ganešzi   nu- za
owner-nom-his-him recognizes-3s ptc-ptc

 ÍR- ZU- pat daí
 slave-his-ptc takes-3s

"If his owner recognizes (his) slave (whom) someone
stole and took into the Hatti land, he (the owner)
shall take his slave as his own."

23. Friedrich 1959:20 lines 50-52

takku IR ... kuiški taízzi
if   slave ... someone-nom steals-3s

n- an ANA KUR ^{uru}Hatti uwatezzi
ptc-him into land city-H. brings-3s

išhaš- šiš- an ganešzi   nu-šši
owner-nom-his-him recognizes-3s ptc-ptc

 12 GÍN   KUBABBAR paí
 12 shekel(s) silver   gives-3s

"If his owner recognizes his slave (whom) someone
stole and took into the Hatti land, 12 shekels of
silver shall be given to him."

These sets of pairs differ from each other only in that the
agent of the verb paí "gives" was unspecified in 20-21, while
in 22-23 the agent must be the deleted kuiški. Both enclitic
dative -šši and enclitic -za (with -ZU) refer to the second
topic, that is the focus of a noninitial clause. Although
these examples clearly illustrate a function which -za performs in signalling the transitivity relation of topic-agent,
it is questionable as to whether -za constitutes a subject
transformation, like the reflexive. Rather, it appears to be
part of the constructional set of deletion, pronominalization
and repetition pattern determined, at least in part, by topic
arrangement (17a).
  3.3.3.3 One further example illustrates another topic-
related role of -za. In Laws I 30 (Friedrich 1959:36 lines
14-15), instead of the usual preverbal kuiški "someone" in
the topic clause after a theme noun, the topic clause uses

the form LÚš (LÚaš or LÚiš) "a man" in initial position followed by the object DUMU.SAL "a/the girl" in preverbal position. Although "someone" and "a/the man" are semantically an
unidentified person, LÚaš in initial position functions as
theme in the construction, while preverbal kuiški is never
theme (18). Here LÚaš conditions the occurrence of -za in
the succeeding clause:

24.　takku LÚš-a　　　　DUMU.SAL nawi　　dāi
　　　if　　man-nom-ptc girl　　　not yet takes-3s

　　　n-　an- za　mimai　　kušata-　　　　　　ma
　　　ptc- her-ptc　refuses　brideprice-nom/acc-ptc

　　　　　kuit　　　　　piddāit
　　　　　ptc-nom/acc brought-ws

　　　n-　aš- kan　šamenzi
　　　ptc-he-ptc　　relinquishes-3s

　　　"And if a man (who) has not yet taken a girl
　　　refuses her, he shall relinquish the bridepiece
　　　which he brought."

The verb in the second clause, mimai "refuses," could have
had either human noun, LÚaš "man" or DUMU.SAL "girl" from the
topic clause, as agent (the enclitic -an "her/him" refers
only to an animate, or genus communus noun, cf. Friedrich
1960:42f.). Here -za marks continuance of LÚaš "man" as a-
gent also in the -za clause.
　　　3.3.4　Although both forms LÚaš "a/the man" and kuiški
"someone" are casemarked as nominative, their distribution in
the clause, their morphemic shape and their discourse functions are clearly different. Semantically, LÚaš "man" is
generic or anaphoric while kuiški is indefinite. When kuiški
continues as agent in succeeding clauses, which it very often
does, the normal pattern in subsequent clauses is noun phrase
deletion or pronominalization using the demonstrative base
apa. Examples 20-24, thus, illustrate sufficient facts about
the use of -za to state that one of its primary functions is
to signal agent continuance of a topic, either of a theme or
a focus. A thorough study of Hittite -za is needed to supplement morphological investigations of its function within the
clausal unit (Goetze 1933; Friedrich 1960:63,132f.; Hoffner
1969; Carruba 1964:430ff; Josephson 1972:1) before the Hittite
reflexive particle can do more than indicate possible problems
for a subject relating analysis of the reflexive.
　　　4.0　Indo-Europeanists and Hittitologists have traditionally identified Hittite relative clauses by the occurrence

of noun-inflected forms of the base ku-, forms which can
easily be shown to be cognate with relative pronouns in
other Indo-European languages. If one finds with Lehmann
(1972; 1972a; 1973; 1974a) that Greenberg's implicational
universals (1966) lay the basis for a word order typology
which can be used to reconstruct earlier syntactic stages of
a language, and analyzes the peculiar Hittite type as a variant OV construction in a language in the state of transition
from OV to VO (Raman 1972), one would expect to find traces
at least of clauses more like a consistent OV relative construction. One would expect relative constructions without
relative markers to occur, at least marginally.

4.1   Since Hittite relative constructions have traditionally been identified on the basis of the equivalency of
the ku- forms with corresponding Indo-European relative pronouns, in order to proceed further one needs universal syntactic criteria for the identification of a relative construction. Cross linguistic surface phenomena for marking a
relative construction vary from position of the dependent
sentence with regard to the head noun and noun deletion in
the subordinate clause to use of a relative pronoun or particle and subordinate verbal inflection (Hermann 1893-94:
488ff.; Reiner 1951; Raman 1973:9ff.). Although surface
phenomena tend to cluster within a limited range of possibilities (special particles or pronouns, position of the modifier with regard to the head noun, deletion and pronominalization processes, and verbal inflection, for example), no one
marker defines the relative construction universally. Semantically, however, all relative constructions function as a
sentential unit to further define the head noun of the matrix
(Bach 1974:266f.). Formally, the construction consists of a
matrix in which the head noun has one noun function and a
sentential modifier which contains another noun function for
the same noun phrase. The head noun in the matrix and the
relative noun in the modifier constituent thus constitute two
separate functions for a single noun concept (Chomsky 1965:
137f.; 144f.; Klima 1969 [1964]:233 ff.; Bach 1974:102; 257f.;
269).

4.2   Using both semantic and formal criteria in examining the Hittite data, one finds in fact that sentential nominal modifiers with characteristic Hittite position and deletion processes occur with and without the ku- marker. In
this section I first gave data to illustrate the uses of ku-
in relative constructions. The data show that, even in ku-
constructions, ku- is not a typical relative marker. The inflected ku-marker introduces the first occurrence of the
shared noun as the relative noun in the subordinate clause.

The head noun in the matrix, then, is deleted, pronominalized or, in later texts, repeated. Examples 25-27 illustrate the introduction of the relative noun with ku- and matrix deletion, pronominalization and repetition:

25. Otten and Souček 1969:36 line 9

kuiš   šagaiš   kišari   ta
ptc-nom sign-nom appears-3s-mid ptc

LUGALi   ... tarueni
king-dat/loc ... report-we

"We report to the king the sign which appears."

26. Neu 1974:14 line 58 with note 18

KASKALaz   kuit   assu   utahhun
campaign-abl   ptc-nom/acc   goods-nom/acc   brought-I

[ptc ?] apedanda   halissijanun
         dem-instr inlaid-caus-I

"I had (the temples) inlaid with the goods which I brought back from the campaign."

27. Goetze and Pedersen 1934:6 lines 18-19

gud ‑
   puhugarin   ma   kuedani   UDti
ox-substitute-acc-   ptc   ptc-dat/loc   day-dat/loc

unueir
decorated-they

nu- za ᵈUTUŠI   apedani   UDti
ptc-ptc my sungod dem-dat/loc   day-Dat/loc

warapta
bathed-3s

"The roi soleil ('sungod' refers to the king) bathed on the day on which they adorned the substitute ox."

4.2.1   The same deletion patterns occur with pronominal ku- usages when the shared noun phrase is unspecified:

28. Friedrich 1959:80 Laws II 71, line 15

2 GUD. GAL   UZU- ŠUNU   kuiš   wasi   1
2 ox(en)-large meat-their ptc-nom buys-3s one

UDU   pai
sheep gives-3s

"Whoever buys the meat of two large oxen gives one sheep."

29. Friedrich 1959:22 Laws I 23, lines 59-60

kuiš-   an   appa uwatezzi   nu- šše 6 GÍN
ptc-nom-him back brings-3s   ptc-him 6 shekel(s)

KUBABBAR pai
silver   gives-3s

"They give 6 shekels of silver to the one who
brings him back."

30. Friedrich 1959:22 Laws I 23, lines 61-62 with notes 9
                                              and 10

kuiš-   an   appa-ma   uwatezzi   n- an- za
ptc-nom-him back-ptc brings-3s   ptc-him-ptc

apaš-   pat dai
dem-nom-ptc takes-3s

"The one who brings him back takes him as hiw own."

4.2.2 The same semantic relationships and deletion
patterns occur in constructions without the ku- marker. The
structural differences between examples 31-33 and examples
25-30 above are that the theme introduces the modifying
clause, and the theme is not accompanied by ku-.

31. CTH 414 (see note above on data: KUB XXIX 1
     III 3-4)

DINGIR^mes humanteš HUR.SAGi   taruppanteš
gods   all-nom   mountain-dat/loc assembled-nom

nu- za-   kan LUGALun   duškeškanzi
ptc-ptc-   ptc king-acc   welcome-they

"All the gods (who are) assembled on the mountain
welcome the king."

32. Otten 1973:12 line 9

^mTamnaššun-a hušwantan IṢBATU   š- an
Tamnassu-acc   alive-acc they seized ptc-him

^uruHattuša uwatet
city-H.-dir brought-3s

"Tamnaššu (whom) they seized, he brought to
Hattuša."

33. Friedrich 1959:32 Laws I 48, lines 49-50

lúhipparaš   luzzi   karpizzi
man-hippar-nom fief duty performs-3s

nu ^{lú}hippari　　　　　　happar　　　　le
ptc man-hippar-dat/loc business-acc not-imper

kuiški izzi
someone does-3s

"Let no one do business with a hippar man (who)
performs fief duty."

4.2.3　In examples 25-30 the ku-introduced relative
noun is new information in the construction and pushes the
message further as part of the constructional rheme. In its
clause, ku- singles out a noun as a center of attention
which will have a role in subsequent part(s) of the construction. Examples 31-33, however, begin with information which
is either anaphoric or generic, that is, in some way presupposed already as a part of the addressee's consciousness. As
such, the relative nouns in the modifying clauses are sufficiently introduced by initial thematic position. In introducing new, focused information into the discourse, ku- functions primarily as a topic-marking, or more exactly, as a
focus-marking particle.

4.2.4　To illustrate the topic-marking function of ku,
I have chosen examples of whole constructions in which relativization on the theme contrasts with relativization on a
focus noun introduced by ku-:

34.　Neu 1974:14 lines 57-58 with note 18

É　^dHalmašuittaš É　^dIŠKURnaš　BELI-JA
house god-H.-gen　house god-I.-gen　lord-my

Ù　É　　^dŠiunašummiš ABNI
and house god-S.-gen　I-built

KASKALaz　　kuit　　　aššu　　　　utahhun
campaign-abl ptc-nom/acc goods-nom/acc brought-I

[ptc ?] apēdanda　halissijanun
(them)　　dem-instr　inlaid-I
(?)

"The temples of Halmašuitta, of the Stormgod my
lord, and of Šiunašummi (which) I built I inlaid
with the goods which I brought back from the campaign."

The translation of this passage assumes that the first clause
and the second are independently embedded in a matrix:

35. *É   (...)   assuit   halissijanun
    house(-acc)   goods-instr   inlaid-caus-I
    "I had the house(s ...) inlaid with goods." (19)

The analysis of 34 as two modifying clauses embedded in the
final matrix finds further support from an examination of
the noun-verb selectional restrictions determined by the semantics of the verb halissija- "inlay." An examination of
other attestations of the verb (Raman 1973:130-33) has indicated that an accusative object is obligatory with halissija-,
and that the instrumental is also usual, so that a topic
clause with halissija- would look like this:

    SOMEONE-nom SOMETHING-acc SOMETHING-instr halissija-.

In his translation of this passage, "Welches Gut ich aus dem
Kampagne gebracht hatte, mit jenem schmückte ich (sie, d. h.
die Zeile 57 genannten Tempel)," Carruba (1969:233) has im-
plied the same analysis without being explicit about it.

    4.2.4.1   Another type containing a modified theme and
focus is:

36. Otten and Soucek 1969:20 lines 32-34

    ERÍN^{mes}n- an kuis anda petai
    troop-acc-ptc ptc-nom preverb brings-3s

    DUMU.É.GALs- a peras- set ^{gis}zupari harzi
    nobleman-nom-ptc before-him torch   holds-3s

    ERÍN^{mes}n- an appan anda petai
    troop-acc-ptc preverb preverb brings-3s

    "The troop (which) is brought in by someone before
    whom a nobleman holds a torch is brought in after-
    wards."

Initial theme in the same clause as the ku- introduction of
the focus constitutes a variant use of kuis best rendered by
the English passive. Otten and Soucek have indicated by
stylistic use of dashes that this translates awkwardly into a
subject-predicate language: "Wer die Truppe hineinbringt --
und der Hofjunker hält eine Fackel vor ihm -- dahinter
schafft er die Truppe herbei" (1969:21). ERÍN^{mes}n "the
"the troop" occurs in initial position as topic (theme) relative noun and is repeated as head noun in the matrix:

37. *ERÍN^{mes}n- an LÚas appan anda petai (20)
    troop-acc-ptc man-nom afterwards brings-3s
    "a man brings (is to bring) the troop in afterwards"

236

One expects kuiš to fall in the second clause, although similar conflation of topics in one clause occurs sporadically in
the later language (for example, the copy of an old text, CTH
414, which has a number of other syntactic variants). Raman
(1973:133-4; 136ff.) gives a more detailed explanation of the
difficulties of translating Hittite topic-marking into idiomatic English together with other Hittite examples. Two of
the principal problems involve the differences between Hittite and English as regards passivization and the fronting
rule which moves the relative noun to the head of the embedded sentence in English relativization. Hittite uses topic
organization and lexical selection instead of the passive
(see above) and either initial position or the ku- marker to
correlate topicality with the relative noun, whereas English
tends toward the use to both position and a wh- word (21).

   4.2.4.2   The final passage is attested in an old original copy and several later copies (22). The interesting
thing about these two versions is that the later copy inserts
a ku- clause to refer to the second actor in the context,
while the older version uses topic organization, preposing of
clauses, deletion and pronominalization without a ku- to mark
modification of both theme and focus. If one is to find re-
lics in the attested language of an earlier stage with no
marker at all in the relative construction, it is in passages
like this one (cf. also Friedrich 1959:24 lines 9-10 and note
29 for another). Example 38, then, gives evidence for a
stage at which even the ku- marker for focused relative nouns
was not obligatory, as well as evidence for the function as
focus for ku-. The younger copy inserts kuiš very clearly to
refer to the important focused actor, not the theme:

38.   Friedrich 1959:30 Laws I 43 lines 52-53 and notes 18-23

   Text A:

   takku LÚaš   GUD-ŠU   ÍDan   zīnuškizzi
   if   man-nom   ox-his   river-acc   cross-caus-iter-3s

      tamaiš-an   šuwaizzi
      another-nom-him   shoves-3s

      nu   GUDaš   KUNan   epzi
      ptc   ox-gen   tail-acc   seizes-3s

      ta   ÍDan   zai
      ptc   river-acc   crosses-3s

      U   BĒL   GUD   ÍDaš   pedai
      and   owner ox   river-nom   carries-3s

      nu-   zza   apun-   pat   danzi
      ptc- ptc   dem-acc-   ptc   take-they

"If a man (who) usually brings his ox across a river, another (who) shoves him, seizes the tail of (his) ox, (and) crosses the river, (so that) the owner of the ox, the river carries away (is carried away by the river), that one (the other) they (the relatives of the owner) seize" (23).

39. Text C:

nu B̄ĒL   GUD ĪDaš̌   pēdāi
ptc owner   ox river-nom brings-3s

š̌uwajazi- ma- an kuiš̌
shoves-3s-ptc-him ptc-nom

nu- za   apun-   pat dāi
ptc-ptc   dem-acc-ptc takes-3s
"...the owner of the ox (whom) the river carries away, shoves him, the one who did, that one shall be taken (lit.: 'he', i.e. the family of the ox's owner (?), shall take that one)

The matrix, before deletion and pronominalization, would read:

40. *LŪaš̌ (or his relatives) tamain   dāi/ danzi
    man-nom   another-acc takes/take
    "the man takes (possession of, calls to account)
    the other"

Prior clauses define more narrowly the arguments of the matrix verb. As elsewhere, both theme and focus are deleted in subsequent clauses in which they function as verbal arguments, although the demonstrative base apa- (apun "that one") here, as very often, expresses anaphoric reference to the focus ku- (Raman 1973:142ff.).

4.3 Because the relative pronoun/adjective and the indefinite pronoun use the same base and share the semantic quality of introducing unspecified information (information which is not "given" in the context at the time of the use of the ku- base), Hahn (1949) proposed to derive the Hittite relative construction from the indefinite. In fact, focus, as new information, is nonanaphoric and unspecified in contrast with theme, which is either anaphoric or generic (Halliday 1967; Chafe 1974; Li and Thompson 1974d). The semantic feature definite, therefore, tends to correlate with theme, indefinite with focus. By showing that the relative ku- introduces the relative noun as new information before its status is changed in the subsequent matrix to given, I suggest that the indefinite, unspecified or non-anaphoric character of the relative ku- results from its function as focus marker.

4.3.1 The analysis of the base ku- as focus marker can

be further corroborated by usages of the indefinite ku-
(kuiški "someone" and its other inflectional forms). As
already noted, kuiški, although subject, regularly occupies the rhematic preverbal position, while the theme occupies initial position. The indefinite kuiški thus marks the
agent as secondary to a more primary noun constituent, and as
not being assumed to be in the addressee's consciousness, but
part of the rhematic information. Having isolated topic as
the "center of attention," and having further defined topic
as theme and focus with correlations to the topic-comment
halves of the discourse unit, it is possible to delimit the
topicality nature of the ku- marked noun phrase as focus.
The ku- base introduces information which is nonanaphoric,.
new information, which serves as a focus at some point in the
construction, but which is secondary in thematic importance
to the construction (24). Thus the topic-marking function
common to both the indefinite and the relative constitutes
the basic function of ku-. The features indefinite and relative are consequences of introducing new information. As
such they do not constitute primary functions. While the
position of kuiški and its distribution in the basic dichotomy
of the clause corroborate its topic-marking capacity, it is
the distribution of the relative marker ku- to introduce
focus-topics, but not theme-topics as relative nouns that
identifies the primary focus-marking function of ku-.

    5.0 The organization of Hittite syntax based on fun-
damental dichotomies between the semantically identifiable
constituents topic and comment rather than subject and predicate offers data in support of a typology based on topic prominence as opposed to subject prominence. In the constructional unit the theme from the initial clause dominates the
unit in such a way as to constitute an argument of the verb
in the construction-final matrix, and often in medial clauses
as well. Each clause is organized on the basis of topic-
comment as a fundamental dichotomy with topic (theme or focus) initial, although the noun-verb relation is also usually
marked. The topic-comment dichotomy of the clause is particularly clear in noninitial clauses where deletion processes
have removed all but two main constituents.

    5.1 While many codification features need further
study, sufficient evidence exists to raise doubts as to the
consistency with which noun-verb agreement is subject-verb
agreement rather than agent-verb or topic-verb. Certainly
the transformational process associated with the subject, the
passive, does not exist in Hittite. Instead, lexical selection expresses transitivity relations very often without disturbing the basic theme dominance in a construction. Clear

evidence does exist, however, for the codification of theme and focus distinctions in the relative construction. Semantic analysis of clausal relationships, together with an observation of typical noun deletion processes, shows that relative constructions without a relative marker occur systematically marked by the topicality of the shared noun, and that their distribution complements those marked by ku-. The theme-focus dichotomy constitutes the principle of this distribution.

5.2   Hittite, thus, furnishes evidence from discourse strategy, codification and behavioral processes in support of topic prominence. The organization of this evidence in support of topic prominence has the further advantage of clarifying syntactic and morphological problems in Hittite and Indo-European concerning the development of subordination and the origin of the relative and indefinite marker *k^wo- (*k^we-). Instead of having to choose between a derivation of one function from the other, neither of which was satisfactory, this analysis shows how both functions are natural consequences of the primary function focus marker. The analysis also suggests how *k^wo- could come to be a relative marker when subjects became prominent as the language shifted in the direction of a VO structure.

Notes

1. This paper constitutes a revision of the paper presented at the Conference on Subject and Topic at the University of California at Santa Barbara, organized by Charles Li. I have benefited from comments and discussions which arose in the course of the conference, as well as from individual papers. I am grateful to all of the participants collectively for the atmosphere which allowed some of my own ideas to formulate themselves, and particularly to specific comments by Talmy Givón, Robert Kirsner, Wallace Chafe, Robert Stockwell, Arthur Schwartz, Sandra Thompson, and Charles Li, especially to Talmy Givón for his patience with and interest in the complex data of earlier versions. I am also grateful to W.P. Lehmann and Calvert Watkins for comments on a revised written version. The point of view maintained here, and its possible fallacies, however, are my own.

2. The earliest date for the attestation of Hittite varies according to one's adherence to High, Middle, or Low chronology (Goetze 1957:84f.; 1964:23ff.; Otten 1964:18; Cornelius 1973:353ff.). Kammenhuber (1969:258 with references) gives the date circa 1650-1500 B.C. (middle chronology) or 1590-1440 B.C. (low chronology) for Old Hittite. For the later period, synchronisms with Egypt establish the chronology at the end of the Empire ca. 1200 B.C. (cf. general destruction layers in the eastern Mediterranean at the period).

Evidence for the Hittite language has been preserved in cuneiform written on clay tablets, most of which have been excavated from a site in modern Turkey, Boghazköy, 100 miles from Ankara. Over sixty-five volumes of cuneiform texts in hand copy have now been published. The two major German publications, Keilschriftexte aus Boghazköi (Wissenschaftliche Veröffentlichungen der deutschen Orient-gesellschaft. Leipzig and Berlin, 1921--) and Keilschrifturkenden aus Boghazköi (edited by the Staatlichen Museen, Vorderasiatische Abteilung. Berlin, 1921--; later edited by the Deutsche Akademie der Wissenschaft) are still in progress. See Laroche (1971) for other publications of texts. In addition to older text editions, two current series are now being published by Harrassowitz (Otten 1965--) and Winter (Kammenhuber 1971--). A catalogue of all published texts has been revised (Laroche 1971), and a new dictionary is being prepared in Munich by Annelies Kammenhuber (Friedrich and Kammenhuber 1973--) updating the files accumulated by Friedrich in the preparation of the standard grammatical and lexical works now in use (Friedrich 1960; 1952-66).

Transcriptions of the cuneiform script as used for

Hittite poses some problems, as the script is a combination of syllabic and logographic symbols (Friedrich 1960a). Logograms represent lexical items from both Sumerian and Akkadian in italic capitals, while regular lower case letters represent the syllabically written Hittite lexical items and phonetic complements to logograms. Because Hittite scribes also made use of pre- and post-word determinatives, some symbols have had to be raised above the line to mark these usages of Sumerograms (Gelb 1963:105f. for terminology).

The Hittite texts which form the basis of this study belong to the Old Hittite period. Laroche (1971) has assembled a catalogue of all Hittite texts and organized them according to subject. CTH numbers refer to this indispensable tool:

CTH Number	Text Edition and Translation	Content of Text
CTH 1	Neu 1974	Anittaš Proclamation
CTH 3	Otten 1973	Concerning the city of Zalpa
CTH 4	Imparati & Saporeti 1965	Deeds of Hattušilis I
CTH 5	no edition	Edict of Hattušilis I
CTH 8	no edition	Palace Chronicle
CTH 19	Hardy 1941:190ff.	Telipinuš Family History
CTH 291	Friedrich 1959	Personal law (Laws I)
CTH 292	Friedrich 1959	Property damage (Laws II)
CTH 414	Schwartz 1947 and later translation, Goetze 1955:357f.	Ritual for the Building of a new Palace
CTH 416	Otten & Souček 1969	Ritual for the King and Queen
CTH 631	Neu 1970	Storm Ritual
no number	Ünal & Kammenhuber 1974	Oracle

3. Concerning an interpretation of these constructions as a colloquial variant (Löfstedt 1970 [1911]:222ff), Hittite texts usually represent codified versions of standard documents, including such variant genres as laws, historical recitation, proclamation, rituals and literary texts (Laroche 1971), which are typified by "paratactic" constructions. I conclude, therefore, that the Hittite data represent the sophisticated idiom. I have not, however, investigated possible similarities with creole types.

4. Pokorny (1959:644) differentiates the relative as unstressed (unbetont) and the interrogative as stressed (betont).

5. This use of topic hierarchy varies somewhat from Hawkinson's and Hyman's (1974) notion of "natural topic" hierarchy in that it is conditioned by the discourse structure, not universal semantic hierarchy (see note below).

6. This distinction between theme and focus is striking-
ly similar to Li and Thompson's (1974d) dichotomy between
topic and subject. In Hittite, at least, focus need not be
either subject or agent; however, I have not further explored
how subject-predicate languages syntacticize focus nor how
Prague School studies would treat this.

7. In citing examples from Hittite texts in this paper,
I use only examples for whose reconstruction there is little
doubt, and refer to appropriate text editions. I do not mark
orthographic syllable divisions of the text either, but segment words by spaces and enclitic morphemes by hyphens. For
the use of capital letters see note 2. References are to the
text edition page and line number, but the translation is my
own interpretation of the syntax in instances of disagreement.
Very often translators make separate sentences of each clause
or join them by "and."

8. Scribal error is not as frequent in Hittite as one
might expect, but there is well attested evidence for it.
For example Ünal and Kammenhuber (1974:172) note that line 2
and 5 (should read 7) refer obviously to the same person, but
in line 2 the syllable -il- is omitted. Similarly, in the
Laws, for example, different versions of the same material
occasionally leave out or add the divisional ruled line across
the tablet: cf. Friedrich 1959:24 note 28, for example.

9. Near the conclusion of this study I discovered that
Cashinawa, a Peruvian language, raises the same basic problem. In his descriptive grammar of Cashinawa, Cromack (1968:
142ff.) noted the difficulties of identifying independent or
free (as opposed to bound) clauses which might constitute a
basic or simple sentence. Concerning linear structuring in
Cashinawa, he says (135) "the overriding principle for understanding linear structure discourse is that it is semeni-
cally dominated but grammatically articulated." He further
defines semenic spans as (1) discourse spans, (2) paragraph
spans, and (3) clause spans. He does define a sentence, but
in terms of its having at least one clause with an enclitic
"realizing a primary semenic modal, such as ..."declarative,"
... interrogative, or ... imperative" (145f.).

10. Delbrück (1900:80ff.) found the order Subject, Dative, Object, Verb to be the unmarked order in Indo-European.
From a frequency count based on the Hittite Laws, Raman
(1973:39f.) found this to be true also for Old Hittite. As
regards initial position in Hittite, Held (1957:11) has defined it as absolutely initial or first after sentence connectives or conjunctions. Watkins (1963:28ff.) gives further
examples as regards the position of particles and preverbs in
relation to the verb in Hittite.

11. I have confined myself in this study to a consideration of third person topics. Hawkinson and Hyman (1974: 16f.) have noted in relation to data in Shona that the first and second person constitute a separate relation to the discourse and as such occupy the highest rung of the hierarchy as regards "natural topic." Within the total thematic organization Hittite data appears to show the same order. This study, however, has focused on contexts in which third person topics are more usual, and examined third person behavior also where first and second persons occur. Cromack (1968: 138ff.) has noted in Cashinawa, a Peruvian language whose phrase, clause and discourse structures show very striking similarities to those in Hittite, that topic marking (among other things) varies according to discourse type. While one expects third person topics to dominate in a monologue, or narrative structure, first and second persons will play a role in dialogue. The patterns which I describe in Hittite are those which are typical of the monologue-type discourse as opposed to the dialogue type.

12. Subject-verb agreement is usually assumed in Hittite, as in the other Indo-European languages. See below for discussion of Hittite peculiarities.

13. Watkins (1964:1035ff.), in discussing the Indo-European position of the constitutents sentence connective, enclitic pronominal element, preverb, and the finite verb form, concluded that preverb and verb, whether separated by other sentence constituents or not, form constituents of a single semantic "word" (1037). Watkins (1963:13ff.) in describing the patterns of sentence connectives and enclitics in Hittite and Old Irish, draws nice parallels with particle usages in the other Indo-European languages.

14. Friedrich (1960:161) takes connectives to mark coordination; Watkins (1963:13) takes nu as "purely a formal connective"..."devoid of the lexical content 'and'." For suggestions as to the function of nu cf. Raman (1973:126ff.) or Güterbock's (1974:325) translation of line 16, for clausal relationships, also with nu.

15. Variant orders also occur in which the verb, referring to a previously discussed and topical action, is initial. For verb-initial clauses of this sort, see Laws I, 25 (the pair, paprizzi kuis "who (ever) defiles" and kuis paprizzi "who defines" according to Held (1957:11), might fit better taken as a minimal pair in which the verb is comment or topic); Laws I, 28c Text C (Friedrich 1959:24 note 29); Laws I, 43 Text C (Friedrich 1959:30 note 21); and Imparati and Saporeti 1965: lines I 13 and 39, for example.

16. Givón (this volume) has shown that perceptual stra-

tegies in interpreting pronominal reference depend upon a natural hierarchy which obtains among semantic features. From a cursory check of Hittite pronominal enclitics and deletions, the principle appears to hold true. A thorough study of deletion, pronominalization, and repetition processes, however, needs to be done to work out the precise rules governing these processes.

17. Cromack (1968:77) finds that Cashinawa, a language based on a similar topic organizational principle (see note above), likewise has no passive. From numerous examples (1968:89 and 176, for example), one concludes that Cashinawa is predominantly SOV in type.

17a. Friedrich (1960:132 and others) have noted that da- "take" with -za means "take for oneself, as one's own." I do not find this meaning to be inconsistent with the syntactic function I note here for -za.

18. See below for discussion of kuiški and the semantic feature "indefinite." See also Li and Thompson's (this volume) discussion of the position of indefinite pronominals and topicalization.

19. The king very often carried off gold and silver as "goods" taken in a raid against enemy territory.

20. I reconstruct Lûas instead of kuiški because the matrix occurrence is already specified rather than nonanaphoric and unspecified.

21. I use the word "tends" to allow for contexts in which English deletes wh- or extraposes.

22. An old original is a tablet which is written in the typical Old Hittite duktus (Otten and Souček 1969:42ff; Kammenhuber 1969:257ff., for example). Further texts which are written in Old Hittite are often later copies of the old original texts and as such, may have incorporated usages of the later language.

23. Probably to replace the ox's owner as a member of the work force or to make reparations for the drowning (?). Cf. Friedrich (1959:98 and note 2) concerning the interpretation, and Raman (1973:148-150) on the structural signals consistent with the interpretation. Clearly, the ox's owner constitutes the theme of the construction and dominates the agency of the matrix verb danzi, while the introduced focus tamais "another" constitutes a secondary topic.

24. The anaphoric use of kuiš in Text C of example 39, which inserts the ku- clause to explain the earlier unspecified tamais "another" contradicts the normal indefinite, unanaphoric use of ku- as noted by Hahn (1946) and others, an inconsistency one might expect to result from a later interpolation.

REMARKABLE SUBJECTS IN MALAGASY*

by

Edward L. Keenan

* I wish to acknowledge the National Science Foundation (post-doctoral Fellowship) and the Wenner-Gren Foundation (grant 2384) for supporting my original field work on Malagasy.
   In addition, much of the work reported here was supported by a Wenner-Gren grant (2994) for work on subject-final languages.

The primary purpose of this paper is to exhibit a language, Malagasy (a Malayo-Polynesian language, spoken by c. 7 million people in various dialects throughout Madagascar) which is highly subject prominent in the sense that very many of the syntactic processes of the language distinguish subject from non-subject NPs.

Having established this in Section I, we show in Section II that Malagasy is distinct in its subject orientation from the Philippine languages (e.g., Tagalog, Cebuano, etc.) with which it is nonetheless closely related genetically and typologically. Indeed Schachter (this volume) argues that the notion of subject is not very useful in the description of the Philippine languages in that no consistently identifiable NP possesses those properties usually characteristic of subjects (see K.L. Keenan, Definition of Subject, this volume). We will show that with one partial exception the evidence adduced by Schachter does not obtain in the case of Malagasy.

Finally we will show in Section III that the NP we call subject in Malagasy has several of the critical properties which distinguish subjects from "mere" topics. Thus Malagasy will not be a "mere" topic prominent language in the sense of Li and Thompson (this volume). Malagasy subjects, however, will be shown to have certain characteristic topic properties, which makes Malagasy more topic prominent than, for example, English.

Finally, one general conclusion we wish to draw from this work is that the Malagasy data we present provide substantive support for a theory of universal grammar in which generalizations are stated in terms of notions like "subject of," "direct object of," etc. Specifically, the Accessibility Hierarchy (Keenan and Comrie, 1972) is supported by Malagasy; so is the Relational Succession Law (Perlmutter and Postal, 1974), and many (but not all!) of the word order universals in Greenberg (1966).

I.   Grammatical Properties of Subjects in Malagasy

We shall consider first a variety of surface properties of subjects of "simple" sentences, and then the behavior of subjects under five major types of transformations: Advancements (e.g., Passive), Movement Rules, Topicalizations, Coreferential Deletions, and Raisings.

1.   Surface syntactic properties of subjects

1.1   Position

In simple sentences the verb occurs first and the subject occurs in sentence final position.

1   Nividy mofo ho'an'ny ankizy   aho
     bought bread for   the children I
     "I bought some bread for the children"

Word order after the verb is generally rigid as concerns the
relative position of the direct object, the subject, and the
major obliques (in contrast, e.g., to Tagalog).

2   *Nividy aho mofo ho an'ny ankizy
     bought I   bread for   the children

     *Nividy ho an'ny ankizy   aho mofo
     bought for   the children I bread

If, however, a simple sentence presents several oblique NPs,
Place and Time NPs having adverbial function (that is, ones
which do not represent essential logical arguments of the
predicate) may occur to the right of the subject.

3   Nividy mofo ho an'ny ankizy   aho tamin'ny assabotsy
     bought bread for   the children I on   the saturday
     "I bought bread for the children on Saturday"

Even here, however, it is also natural to put <u>tamin'ny asa-
botsy</u> "on Saturday" immediately to the left of the subject
<u>aho</u> "I." Further, an SVO order is sometimes encountered, but
normally has a contrastive, emphatic, or subordinating effect. See Section 2.2.6 for discussion of this possibility.
In isolation, then, a sentence like 4 would not be judged
acceptable.

4   *Aho nividy mofo ho an'ny ankizy
     I   bought bread for   the children

1.2   Verb agreement

Predicates, whether verbal, adjectival, or nominal, do
not vary in form with the person, number, or noun class of
their subjects or objects.

5   a.   Nividy mofo ianao
          bought bread you (sg)
          "You bought bread"

     b.   Nividy mofo ianareo
          bought bread you (pl)
          "You bought bread"

     c.   Nividy mofo izahay
          bought bread we (excl)
          "We bought bread"

     d.   Nividy mofo izy
          bought bread he/they
          "He/they bought bread"

1.3 Case marking

The pronominal system distinguishes three cases: a nominative, used primarily to replace subject NPs; an accusative, which replaces direct objects and sometimes indirect objects (example 7); and a possessor form which occurs clitically to NPs or verbs, according as it expresses possessors or non-subject agents (see 2.1, Advancement Rules, for examples of the latter usage). We give the singular forms here for later reference.

	Nominative	Accusative	Possessor
1sg	aho	aho	-ko
2sg	ianao	anao	-nao
3sg/pl	izy	azy	-ny

Promonimal objects of prepositions in Malagasy are most commonly taken from the possessor series, and most prepositions can be seen historically as derived from a primitive preposition plus noun, to which the object is attached as a possessor. E.g., anilako "beside me" = an "at" + ila "side" + -ko "my." So "beside me" is literally "at my side." Some prepositions, however, take accusative objects. A few of these, like lavitra "far from," appear to be primitive prepositions, and the others appear to be verb derived, e.g., momba "to follow, accompany" as a verb, and "about, concerning" as a preposition. Two prepositions, afa-tsy "except" and noho "against, in comparison with," take their objects in the nominative.

As regards full NPs rather than pronouns, subjects are unmarked. Direct objects are often unmarked, but sometimes occur with a marker an- (1).

```
6   Nahita an-dRabe  Rakoto
    saw    acc-Rabe  Takoto
    "Rakoto saw Rabe"
```

Notional indirect objects are sometimes introduced by the generalized preposition amina (past tense: tamina) but are often also presented as accusatives:

```
7   a. Nanome vola  an-dRabe  aho
       gave   money acc-Rabe  I
       "I gave money to Rabe"

    b. Nanome azy       an-dRabe  aho
       gave   it (acc)  acc-Rabe  I
       "I gave it to Rabe"

    c. Nanome vola  azy        aho
       gave   money him (acc)  I
       "I gave money to him"
```

(But note that due to a like-form constraint, 7d is not grammatical):

    d. *Nanome azy azy aho
          gave   it   him I
          "I gave it to him"

1.4 Particle placements

A variety of sentence types in Malagasy separate the subject NP from the rest of the sentence by a grammatical particle. This suggests that in surface Malagasy simplex Ss have a Predicate Phrase which contains the objects and oblique NPs but not the subject. We give three independent examples: Questions, Exclamations, and "no-longer" Negations.

1.4.1 Sentential question formation (one version): Insert the particle _ve_ just before the subject NP.

8   Nanome vola an-dRabe ve ianao?
     gave   money acc-Rabe ? you
     "Did you give money to Rabe?

1.4.2 Exclamation formation: Insert the particle <u>anie</u> before the subject NP and optionally put ế after the subject NP.

9   a. manasa lamba   Rasoa
          washes clothes Rasoa
          "Rasoa is washing clothes"

      b. manasa lamba anie Rasoa (ế)
          washes clothes ! Rasoa
          "Boy, is Rasoa ever washing clothes!"

1.4.3 No-longer negation: Put the negative particle _tay_ in front of the predicate and the particle <u>intsony</u> before the subject NP.

10   Tsy manasa lamba   intsony Rasoa
     not wash   clothes longer Rasoa
     "Rasoa is no longer washing clothes"

1.5 Surface semantically based properties of subjects

1.5.1 Definiteness: Surface subjects of Malagasy simplex Ss are necessarily definite. Semantically this means there are always objects which the subject phrase refers to, and further this referentiality is not lost when the sentence is negated or questioned. Thus 11a-11c all imply that there exists at least one student.

11   a. lasa ny mpianatra
         gone the student(s)
         "The student(s) left"

(Note that plurality is not marked on lexical NPs. In fact
it is marked only in the pronoun system and in the demonstrative adjectives and pronouns. In translating common nouns,
then, we shall henceforth pick singular or plural translations as seem appropriate, without noting the alternate possible translations.)

      Lasa ve ny mpianatra
      gone ? the students
      "Have the students left?"

11 b. Tsy lasa ny mpianatra
      not gone the student(s)
      "The students haven't left"

Syntactically speaking, the definiteness requirement on
lexical NP subjects requires that they either be proper
names, definite pronouns, or common nouns with demonstrative
adjectives or definite articles. The normal way of making
indefinite reference is to use a common noun without any determiners. Such NPs may occur as objects, but never as subjects.

12 *lasa mpianatra
    gone students
    "Some students left"

13 Nahita mpianatra Rabe
    saw students Rabe
    "Rabe saw some students"

The only way to express the indefinite specific reading of
sentences like 12 in Malagasy is to use an Existential construction, which is usually complex and arguably subjectless
(see 2.2.3).

We will assume for purposes of exposition in this paper
that the definiteness requirement on subjects is a surface
structure constraint. The main justification is that there
appear to be cases where we need indefinite subjects in underlying structure, but where these cannot surface in subject
position. The principal case is in the formation of existential sentences (ESs) of the sort "There are women who wash
clothes" (see 2.2.3 for examples). The existential NP in
such Ss, namely "women" above, must be understood as the subject of the verb "wash." Thus we cannot say "There are
clothes that women wash" where the existential NP would be an
object of the verb "wash" (but we can, of course, say "There
are clothes that are washed by women"). But existential NPs
are indefinite par excellence. So it appears that we must
allow indefinite NPs as subjects in early stages of derivations but not allow them to surface in subject position.

1.5.2 Relative scope: Subjects generally have wider
scope than objects in the paradigm case of indefinite objects
and universally quantified subjects. Thus 14 is possibly
true in a situation in which the students saw different birds.

14 Nahita vorona ny mpianatra rehetra
    saw   bird(s) the students   all
    "All the students saw some birds"

1.5.3 Dummies: Subjects are in general absolutely referential in Malagasy, so there are no dummy NPs. Weather
expressions, the paradigm case of dummies in many languages,
normally take the lexical NP ny andro "the day" as subject,
and either verbal or adjectival predicates:

15 mafana ny andro
    hot   the day
    "It's hot"

16 man-drivotra ny andro
    vb prefix-wind the day
    "It is windy" (lit: the day winds)

Occasionally other NP subjects are used:

17 avy   ny orana
    comes the rain
    "The rain is coming"

The other major case where dummies occur across languages is in replacing what would otherwise be sentential subjects. But in Malagasy sentential subjects naturally occur
after the other major constituents of the sentence and so do
not present the perceptual problem which presumably accounts
for their extraposition in languages in which subjects are
usually initial.

18 mazava fa   efa   lasa ny mpianatra
    clear that already gone the students
    "That the students have already left is clear"

As long as the fa- clause in sentences like 18 is considered the subject (but for one objection to this analysis
see 2.5.2), most sentence types in Malagasy have "full" sub-
jects--either lexical NPs or nominalized Ss. In any case, it
is clear that Malagasy possesses no dummy subjects.

The properties discussed in 1.1-1.5 are ones which distinguish surface subject NPs from others in simple sentences.
They can thus be easily used as criteria for subjecthood in
complex sentences.

2.   Transformational properties of subjects

2.1   Advancement transformations

Malagasy verbs exhibit four distinct voices: <u>active</u>, <u>circumstantial</u>, <u>goal</u>, and <u>intermediary</u>. We shall consider first the formation of sentences whose main verbs present each of these voices and justify calling the last two voices considered collectively a <u>passive</u> voice. Then, despite the prominence of the Malagasy passive (compared with, e.g., European passives), we argue that sentences whose main verbs are active are the most basic sentence types in the language. Sentences in non-active voices then are to be derived by promoting to subject various non-subject constituents of active sentences (or of structures more directly underlying active sentences than non-active ones).

2.1.1 The four voices: The <u>active</u> voice is formed by prefixing verb roots in any of several ways. Most commonly a prefix <u>mi-</u> or <u>man-</u> is used. If a given root accepts both prefixes, then <u>mi-</u> forms intransitive verbs and <u>man-</u> forms transitive verbs. For example, from <u>sasa</u> "wash" we have <u>misasa</u> "to wash (oneself)" and <u>manasa</u> "to wash (someone/something)" (2). The initial <u>m-</u> of the prefixes indicates present tense (and is the form used normally in infinitival nominalizations; see 2.1.3). Replacing the <u>m-</u> by <u>n-</u> yields a past tense meaning; replacement by <u>h-</u> yields a future tense meaning.

19    $\begin{Bmatrix} \text{Manasa} \\ \text{Nanasa} \\ \text{Hanasa} \end{Bmatrix}$ lamba   Rasoa

$\begin{Bmatrix} \text{is washing} \\ \text{washed} \\ \text{will wash} \end{Bmatrix}$ clothes Rasoa

Normally in active sentences, the semantic agent (if there is one) is the surface object, as illustrated in 19.

The <u>circumstantial</u> voice is formed from the active form by deleting the initial <u>m-</u> (for present tense forms) and adding a suffix <u>(a)na</u>, shifting the stress (phonemic in Malagasy) one syllable to the right. (The morphophonemics of this suffixation is again complex and will be ignored here.) The NP which has the surface properties of subjects, as presented in Sections 1-1.5, is an NP which would have an oblique case function in an active sentence. E.g.:

20   a.   manasa lamba   amin'ity   savony ity   Rasoa
            +act
            wash   clothes with this soap   this Rasoa
            "Rasoa is washing clothes with this soap"

   b. anasan-dRasoa lamba   ity savony ity
       +circ
       wash-by-Rasoa clothes this soap   this
       "This soap is being washed clothes with by Rasoa"

21 a. mividy mofo ho'an ny ankizy aho
        +act
        buy   bread for   the child I
        "I am buying bread for the child"

    b. ividiana-ko   mofo ny ankizy
        +circ
        bought for by-me bread the child
        "The child is bought bread for by me"

22 a. mitoetra amin'ity trano ity izahay
        +act
        live   in   this house this we (excl)
        "We live in this house"

    b. itoerana + nay (= itoeranay) ity trano ity
        +circ
        live by   us   this house this
        "This house is lived in by us"

In general, subjects of circumstantial sentences can express
the instrument, benefactee, location, time, purpose, manner,
...of the action. (For discussion of 13 semantically distinct types of circumstantials which this voice subjectivizes, together with some discussion of certain restrictions on
this process, see Rajemisa-Raolison (1966:111-118).)

   We note further that the NP we are calling the subject
of the circumstantial sentence does in fact possess the properties of subjects given in 1-1.5. Specifically: 1) It
occurs in sentence final position. 2) It is constructed
without a preposition and is replaced by nominative pronominal forms. (Thus 23 is the pronominal form of 21b above.)

  23 ividiana-ko   mofo izy
      + circ
      bought for by-me bread he (nom)
      "He was brought bread for by me"

3) Particles are placed between it and the rest of the sentence:

  24 a. anasan-dRasoa lamba   ve ity savony ity
          +circ
          wash-by-Rasoa clothes ? this soap   this
          "Is this soap being washing clothes with by Rasoa?"

    b. anasan-dRasoa lamba   anie ity savony ity
       +circ
      wash-by-Rasoa clothes ! this soap   this
      "Is this soap ever being washed clothes with by
      Rasoa!"

4) It is always definite. And 5), it has wider scope than
objects. Thus 20b can easily be true if each child is having
different clothes washed for him.

    The goal voice is formed by directly suffixing the root
form of the verb with -ana/-ina. (For a few verbs an infix
form putting -in- after the initial consonant of the verb
root is possible as well. E.g., from vaki "broken" we have
either vakina "broken (by)" or vinaki "broken (by)," Semantically speaking, the subject NP of goal voice sentences
(that is, that NP which presents in surface the properties
1-1.5) is best considered to be a kind of "endpoint" of the
action. Thus it will be an (underlying) indirect object if
the main verb normally takes one (but see the next section on
the intermediary voice), but a patient NP if the verb does
not normally take an indirect object. As an example of the
latter case, consider:

24 a. manasa ny lamba   Rasoa
       +act
      wash   the clothes Rasoa

    b. sasan-dRasoa   ny lamba
       +goal
      washed-by-Rasoa the clothes
      "The clothes are washed by Rasoa"

    Finally, what I shall call the intermediary voice is
formed by prefixing a- to the verb root. Subject NPs of
intermediatary voice sentences generally express intermediaries of actions. Thus they include patient NPs in sentences
which have indirect objects, and often include certain types
of "weak" instrumentals as well. Example 25 below illustrates how the goal and intermediary voice differ in a simple
case. (The affixes indicating voice are underlined.)

25 a. manolotra ny vary ny vahiny aho
       +act
      offer   the rice the guests I
      "I offer the rice to the guests"

    b. atolo-ko   ny vahiny ny   vary
       +intermediary
      offered-by-me the guests the rice
      "The rice is offered by me to the guests"

c. tolor<u>ana</u> + ko (= tolorako) ny vary ny vahiny
    +goal
    offered-by-me   the rice the guests
    "The guests are offered the rice by me"

Thus in the act of offering, the person receiving the thing
offered is the endpoint of the action, and is present as a
subject in the goal voice form of the verb. The thing offered is considered an intermediary of the action and is thus
present as a subject of an intermediary voice verb.

2.1.2 The concept of passive in Malagasy: We shall refer to the goal and intermediary voices collectively as <u>Pas-</u>
<u>ive</u>. This is largely a matter of shorthand, as the English
translations of these voices are usually passives, and for
most of our purposes we do not care which particular voice
was used to subjectivize a given "object." However, the justification for this term does run deeper.

First, several very common verbs which take notional
direct and indirect objects and would thus be expected to
have both goal and intermediary voices have in fact only one
or the other, and that form is used to present as surface
subject either the direct or indirect object. Thus <u>manome</u>
"to give" in practice has only the suffix "passive" (= goal
voice), as illustrated in 26.

26 a. manome ny vola an-dRakoto aho
         +act
         give   the money acc-Rakoto I
         "I am giving the money to Rakoto"

(Note that both the direct and indirect objects here are surface accusatives, either being replacable by the accusative
form of the pronoun <u>azy</u>, and either being passivized by the
suffix passive.)

    b. omena + ko (= omeko) ny vola Rakoto
        +goal
        given-by-me   the money Rakoto
        "Rakoto was given the money by me"

    c. omena + ko (= omeko) an-dRakoto ny vola
        +goal
        given-by-me   acc-Rakoto the money
        "The money was given by me to Rakoto"

Second, it appears that at least for some speakers, the
use of the intermediary voice is being usurped by the circumstantial. Thus, while Rajemisa-Raolison (1966) cites the
form in 28a as "passive" of 27, many informants simply use in
its stead the circumstantial form, 28b.

27 manosotra menaka (amin') ny   kanakana aho
    +act
    rub   grease   on   the duck   I
    "I am rubbing grease on the duck"

28 a. ahosotra + ko (= ahosotro) amin' ny kanakana ny
        +intermediary
        rubbed-by-me   on   the duck   the

        menaka
        grease
        "The grease is rubbed on the duck by me"

    b. anosorana + ko (= anosorako) ny   menaka ny   kanakana
        +circumstantial
        rubbed-on-by-me   the grease the duck
        "The duck had grease rubbed on it by me"

There may, then, be a growing tendency for verbs to take only
one of the "passive" forms, using it to subjectivize either
goal or intermediary NPs. We shall henceforth refer to these
NPs simply as "objects" and any voice which subjectivizes
them as a "passive" voice.

2.1.3 The active voice is grammatically the most basic:
It is not obvious that passive and circumstantial sentences
in Malagasy should be considered derived from active ones, or
from structures more closely resembling the active forms than
any others. In later sections we will present several cases
where non-active forms of sentences are grammatically required. In addition, as with many Malayo-Polynesian languages, we find many grammatically neutral situations in which
speakers show a marked preference for passive over active
forms (a point discussed at length in E.O. Keenan, 1974). One
such case is in imperatives. All four voices have distinct
imperative forms.

Active imperatives are formed by shifting the stress in
the active declarative form one syllable to the right. Thus,
corresponding to the active 29a we have the imperative 29b
(where ´ marks stress).

29 a. manása lamba   ianao
        wash   clothes you

    b. manasá lamba
        wash   clothes!

Such imperatives, however, are sociologically marked and tend
to be used when the orderer is confronting the person ordered. By far the more normal way to order someone to wash
clothes is to use the passive form 30b, which corresponds to
the declarative 30a.

EDWARD L. KEENAN

30 a. sasana + nao ny lamba
washed-by-you the clothes
"The clothes are being washed by you"

b. sasao ny lamba
wash the clothes

Note that the subject of the imperative is <u>ny lamba</u> "the clothes." The addressee phrase is presented as a passive agent if present. We note as well that passive imperatives are the normally elicited translations of English transitive imperatives. On the other hand, if one wants to emphasize some circumstance of the act of washing, it is most natural to use the imperative form 31b of the circumstantial sentence 31a.

31 a. anasana + nao (= anasanao) lamba ity savony ity
+circ
wash-by-you clothes this soap this
"This soap is washed clothes with by you"

b. anasao lamba ity savony ity
wash clothes this soap this
"Use this soap to wash clothes"

Despite the prevalence of non-active voices in Malagasy discourse, we still argue that, grammatically speaking, the active voice is the most basic of the voices, and that non-active sentences then should be derived from more active like underlying structures by any of a family of Advancement Transformations which create subjects from non-subjects and demote the original subject. The following criteria support the grammatical primacy of the active voice:

1) Morphological considerations. The active form of the verb is morphologically more primitive than the circumstantial form, as the latter is derived from the former; it uses the active prefix, omitting the initial <u>m-</u> in the present, and adds a suffix to the active form. As there are several active prefixes, those verbs which admit of more than one also have more than one circumstantial form. Thus from the root <u>sasa</u> "wash" we can form two actives: <u>manasa</u> "to wash (something)," and <u>miasa</u> "to wash (oneself)," and both active forms determine circumstantial forms: <u>anasana</u> and <u>isasana</u>. (Both these circumstantial forms have their own imperative forms as well.)

On the other hand, by and large the two passive forms are morphologically as primitive as the active, as all are formed by directly affixing the verb root (which may or may not occur independently as a word in the language. If it does, it is usually a stative adjective, a noun, or sometimes

260

an active intransitive verb).

However, there are a few cases where the passive form does retain the active prefix less the initial m-. Thus from the root halatra "stolen goods" we form the active mangalatra "to steal" and the passive angalarina. (The circumstantial is angalarana.) Further cases are cited in Rajemisa-Raolison (1966:102). Yet there are no cases where actives are formed from passives, so even here actives seem very slightly more basic than passives.

2) Distribution. Active based forms are more widespread than passive forms, since only verbs subcategorized for "goals" or "intermediaries" have passives, and while this class is much much larger than the class of natural passives in, for example, English, it is still smaller than the active based class. There are practically no verbs that have only a passive form, although there are a very few where the morphological active, in practice, only shows up in derived nominalizations. In main clauses the active and passive form are identical.

3) Nominalizations. The major nominalizations of the language are limited to active and circumstantial (= active based).

a) Agent nominals. Restricted to actives. To form, replace the initial m- of the active form by mp-. For example, mividy "to buy" → mpividy "buyers"; mangalatra "to steal" → mpangalatra "thief."

b) "Infinitival" nominals. Restricted to actives and circumstantials. To form, simply add the definite article ny to the active based form. Thus from, for example, mitondra "carry, drive, wear" we have ny mitondra "the driving, carrying, wearing" as in:

32　Sarotra　ny　mitondra taxi
　　difficult the driving　taxi
　　"It is difficult to drive a taxi"/"driving taxis is difficult"

When applied to circumstantial forms, this nominalization yields factive nominals, as in:

33　mahagaga　ahy ny　anasan-dRasoa　lamba
　　　　　　　　　　+circ
　　surprises me　the washing-by-Rasoa clothes
　　"The fact that Rasoa is washing clothes surprises me"

Note that both active and circumstantial forms of this nominalization are still inflected for tense. E.g.,

34 Nahagaga ahy ny nanasan-dRasoa lamba
   surprised me the washed-by Rasoa clothes
   "The fact that Rasoa washed clothes surprised me"

   c) f-nominalizations. Restricted to active and circumstantial forms. To form, replace the initial m- of active
present tense form by f-, or simply add f- to present tense
circumstantial forms. The meanings of these nominals is
quite diverse. They often refer to some object normally associated with the action (usually the instrument if the underlying verb is active, often the location as well if the
underlying verb is circumstantial), never the agent. They
also often refer to the manner of the action, or some abstract quality associated with the action, especially if the
verb is circumstantial. Thus from mamaky "to cut (active" we
have famaky "hatchet"; from manjaitra "to sew (active)" we
have fanjaitra "needle." From itiavana "to love (circ)" we
have fitiavana "love," and from ifidianana "to elect (circ)"
we have fifidianana "elections." Note the manner usages of
the nominalized circumstantial verb in 35 as contrasted with
the factive use in 33.

35 mahagaga ahy ny fanasan-dRasoa lamba
                      +circ
    surprises me the wash-by-Rasoa clothes
    "The way Rasoa is washing clothes surprises me"

We should note that all three nominalizations referred to
above apply to verb phrases, but never include the surface
subject. They do, of course, include various objects, as in
34 and 35, and may include adverbial elements as well. E.g.,

36 mahamenatra ny tsy fitiavan-dRakoto an-dRasoa
   shameful   the not love-by-Rakoto acc-Rasoa
   "Rakoto's not loving Rasoa is shameful"

37 sosotra ny mpividy omby t-any   Betafo
   angry the buyers cows past-there Betafo
   "The buyers of cows in Betafo were angry"

Nominalizations, then, provide further evidence for the existence of a VP in Malagasy. Further, subjects are distinguished as being the only major NP that cannot survive under
these nominalizations. And, of course, passives are distinguished as not undergoing any of these nominalizations (3).
   4) Causatives. Causatives are formed by prefixing the
active verb with mampa- or mampi-. Only active verbs undergo
this prefixation.

38 a.   mampa + manasa (= mampanasa) lamba   an-dRasoa aho
              +act
         cause + wash   clothes acc-Rasoa I
         "I make Rasoa wash clothes"

    b.   *mampa + sasana (= ?mampasasana) ny lamba   aho
              +pass
         cause + wash   the clothes   I
         "I made the clothes washed"

5) Reflexivization. Control of reflexivization is largely limited to active subjects. Passive subjects never control reflexives.

39 a.   namono tena Rabe
         +act
         killed body Rabe
         "Rabe killed himself"

    b.   *novonoin'(ny)   tena-(ny) Rabe
          +pass
         killed-by-(the)-body-(his) Rabe
         "Rabe was killed by himself"

Note as well that despite the VOS active word order, direct
objects of active sentences cannot control the reflexivization of an active subject:

40 *namono an-dRabe ny tena-ny
     +act
     killed acc-Rabe the body-his
     "He-self was killed by Rabe"

We should note that the use of <u>tena</u> "body, trunk (of person
or tree)" as a reflexive pronoun is probably an innovation,
and its priviledges of occurrence are largely restricted to
direct objects, and even there many uses of English reflexives do not translate directly into Malagasy. A preferred
alternative, where it exists, is to use an appropriate intransitive form of the verb. Thus where we might expect
<u>manasa tena</u> "wash self" we only get the intransitive form
<u>misasa</u> "wash (oneself)."

     2.1.4 Formulating the advancement transformations: On
the basis of 1)-5) above, we take the active form of a sentence as closer to the basic form from which the non-active
forms are to be transformationally derived. It might seem
natural to posit then three advancement transformations: Goal,
Intermediary, and Circumstantial. However, we prefer a more
general formulation in which there is but a single advancement to subject transformation. It can subjectivize different constituent NPs, and the derived verb morphology is a

263

function of which NP has been subjectivized. A rough structural characterization of this transformation is given in 41.

41 Advancement-to-Subject (A-to-S)

$$\underset{+act}{V} + X + (Prep) + \underset{+\alpha}{NP_1} + Y + \underset{+nom}{NP_2}$$

$$\underset{+\alpha}{V} + \underset{+poss}{(NP_2)} + X + Y + \underset{+nom}{NP_1}$$

Conditions:

1. V, NP_1, and NP_2 are clausemates

2. α = intermediary, endpoint, locative, instrumental,...

Basically, 41 says that a non-subject NP gets moved to clause final position, losing its preposition if it had one and taking on the nominative case. The old subject, NP_2, is either eliminated or else attached to the end of the verb as a possessor NP. A morphological rule will later yield the correct shape of the derived verb. Note as well that 41 assumes the surface structure constraint requiring subjects to be definite. As formulated, then, 41 will generate Ss with indefinite subjects. An analogous, though less well motivated, approach could have been taken with regard to case assignment. As the later discussion of NP-Questions and Clefts shows, there is some motivation for allowing intermediate stages of derivations in which subjects carry prepositions. But such subjects cannot surface as such; rather, they must be moved out (e.g., by clefting or questioning). In a more detailed treatment, then, case reassignment would be an operation that would operate after A-to-S. But justification of this point goes beyond the concerns of this paper.

Our purpose in expressing A-to-S in structural terms is merely to express the generalization that all non-active forms behave the same with respect to the positioning and case marking of the major NPs. All that differentiates the non-active voices is the shape of the verb, and that can be given as a function of which NP has been advanced to subject. We are explicitly ignoring many problems in the formulation of this transformation: e.g., how to identify whether an NP is endpoint, locative, etc., whether the NPs in the input to A-to-S should be unordered, whether a relational formulation (Perlmutter and Postal, 1974) is more general (4), and the exact relation of A-to-S and whatever transformations are needed to derive simple active sentences.

2.2 Major movement transformations

Malagasy has a large number of complex constructions
which may informally be thought of as being generated by
moving an NP from a simpler construction. Movement is always
leftward across the verb end, with a few partial exceptions
discussed below, NPs which can move are restricted to subjects.

2.2.1 Relative clauses (RCs): RCs can be formed by
moving an NP to the left of the verb and optionally inserting
a morphologically invariable particle _izay_. Only subjects
can be relativized. Thus from 42 we can form 43 but not 44.

42 manasa ny lamba   ny zazavavy
    +act
    wash   the clothes the girl
    "The girl is washing the clothes"

43 ny zazavavy (izay) manasa ny lamba
    the girl   (that) wash   the clothes

44 *ny lamba   (izay) manasa ny zazavavy
    the clothes (that) wash   the girl

(44 could only mean here that the clothes are washing the
girl.) To talk about the clothes that the girl is washing,
we must first present "clothes" as a subject, which we can do
by passivizing, and then relativize it. Thus from 45a we
easily form 45b.

45 a. sasan'ny zazavavy ny lamba
        +pass
        wash   the girl   the clothes
        "The clothes are washed by the girl"

    b. ny lamba   (izay) sasan'ny zazavavy
        the clothes (that) wash   the girl
        "the clothes that are washed by the girl"

And, in general, to relativize any NP it must first be promoted to subject using the elaborate voicing system and then
relativized. Perceptually speaking, this means that it is
the verb form that codes the underlying role of the head NP
in the relative clause. That is, if the verb of the RC is,
for example, in the goal voice, then the head of the RC is an
underlying goal of the subordinate verb—for the goal voice
had to be used to make it a subject. Note then that RCs
whose subordinate verbs are in the circumstantial voice are
potentially ambiguous, since the head NP could be an underlying instrumental, locative, benefactee, etc. In fact, this
potential is not often realized, since NPs which reference,

EDWARD L. KEENAN

for example, locations are not also likely to reference instruments or benefactees. Still some such ambiguities can be constructed, as in 46, which has either the locative or instrumental reading.

46 ny vato izay anasan-dRasoa lamba
+circ

the stone { where / with which } wash-by-Rasoa clothes

"the stone where with which clothes are washed by Rasoa"

For more details on RCF in Malagasy, see Keenan (1972a).

2.2.2 Whatever-clauses (WCs): These can be formed by moving the NP to the left of the verb, inserting izay to the left of it, and then optionally deleting the moved NP. These clauses are the only means of expressing embedded (indirect) Wh-questions in Malagasy. They also cover the meaning of Whever clauses like "Whatever you do, do it well," or "whoever comes, tell them to wait." These clauses occur in normal NP positions in Malagasy.

47 a. izay manasa lamba
+act
whoever washes clothes

b. izay zazavavy manasa lamba
whatever girl washes clothes

48 tsy fanta-dRakoto izay nanasa lamba omaly
not known-by-Rakoto who washed clothes yesterday
"Rakoto doesn't know who washed clothes yesterday"

The restrictions on which NPs can be moved to form WCs are exactly the same as on RCs: namely, only subjects.

49 a. izay lamba manasa Rasoa
whatever clothes wash Rasoa
"whatever clothes Rasoa is washing"

b. izay lamba sasan-dRasoa
whatever clothes are washed by Rasoa

Note that WCs differ from RCs in that izay occurs to the left of the moved NP, not to the right as in the case of RCs. Further, the presence of izay is obligatory in WCs but only optional in RCs.

2.2.3 Existential sentences (ESs): To form, move the subject NP (and only the subject NP) to the left of the verb, insert misy "exist" to its left, and optionally delete the moved NP if it is animate. For example, from 50 we can form either 51a or 51b.

50 mitomany ny zaza
    cries   the child

51 a. misy zaza mitomany
       exist child cry
       "Some child is crying"

    b. misy mitomany
       exist cry
       "Someone is crying"

We note that <u>misy</u> is a full verb, taking normal voice and
tense inflections. This suggests that sentences like 51a are
merely ones whose subject is an RC in which the optional <u>izay</u>
is deleted. Indeed, 52 is well formed.

52 misy zaza izay mitomany
    exist child who cry
    "There exist children who cry"

But 52 differs in meaning from 51a in that it refers most
naturally to a general state of affairs, not a specific instance of crying. Thus 53a is quite unnatural, while 53b and
53c are fine.

53 a. ??omaly   hariva dia   nisy   zaza izay
       yesterday evening topic existed child who

           nitomany tao   an-trano-ko
           cried   there at-house-my

       "Yesterday evening there existed children who cried
       at my house"

    b. omaly   hariva dia   nisy   zaza nitomany tao
       yesterday evening topic existed child cried   there

           an-trano-ko
           at-house-my

       "Yesterday evening there was a child crying at my
       house"

    c. omaly   hariva dia   nisy   nitomany tao
       yesterday evening topic existed cried   there

           an-trano-ko
           at-house-my

       "Yesterday evening someone cried at my house"

We note that since subjects are obligatorily definite, the
only way to express a sentence with all indefinite NPs is
with the existential construction.

2.2.4 Cleft Sentences (CSs): To form a CS, move the NP
to the left of the verb and insert the invariable particle <u>no</u>
between the moved NP and the verb. So from 54a we can form
54b.

54 a. manasa ny lamba   amin'ity savony ity Rasoa
        +act
        wash   the clothes with this soap   this Rasoa
        "Rasoa is washing the clothes with this soap"

    b. Rasoa no   manasa ny lamba   amin'ity savony ity
        Rasoa cleft wash   the clothes with this soap   this
        "It's Rasoa who is washing clothes with this soap"

As with the other movement rules, direct objects cannot be
directly moved. So to say "It was the clothes that Rasoa
washed" we must passivize the underlying verb.

55 a. *ny lamba   no   manasa amin'ity savony ity
        the clothes cleft wash   with this soap   this

                Rasoa
                Rasoa

    b. ny lamba   no   sasan-dRasoa   amin'ity savony
        the clothes cleft washed-by-Rasoa with this soap

                ity
                this

        "It was the clothes that Rasoa washed with this
        soap"

As regards oblique case NPs, however, Cleft is more complex
than the other movement transformations so far considered (5).
As predicted, many types of obliques, e.g., benefactives,
cannot cleft unless they are subjectivized by the circumstantial voice.

56 a. mividy mofo ho an'ny ankizy aho
        +act
        buy   bread for the child I
        "I am buying bread for the child"

    b. *ho an'ny ankizy no   mividy mofo aho
                               +act
        for   the child cleft buy   bread I
        "It's for the child that I am buying bread"

    c. ny ankizy no   ividiana-ko mofo
                         +circ
        the child cleft bought   me bread
        "It is the child that is being bought bread for by me"

However, some oblique NPs can directly cleft, even though they are not subjects. This is so in general for instrumentals, locatives, and temporals. Thus from 54a above, we can form 57.

57 amin'ity   savony ity   no   manasa lamba   Rasoa
                                    +act
   with this soap   this cleft wash   clothes Rasoa
   "It is with this soap that Rasoa is washing clothes"

Note that the verb remains active, and the preposition obligatorily remains on the circumstantial NP. However, 57 admits of an interesting and commonly occurring variant, 58.

58 amin'ity   savony ity   Rasoa no   manasa lamba
                                         +act
   with this soap   this Rasoa cleft wash   clothes

Example 58 has the same meaning as 57, and differs in form only in that the real subject has been moved along with the oblique NP, for protection so to speak. We shall refer to this phenomenon as the Bodyguard Condition. Whenever a non-subject is moved, it may always be optionally accompanied by the real subject. Some informants, however, but not all, prefer to restrict the Bodyguard Condition to active subjects.

59 a. amin'ity   savony ity   no   sasan-dRasoa   ny   lamba
                                        +pass
       with this soap   this cleft wash-by-Rasoa the clothes
       "It was with this soap that the clothes were washed
       by Rasoa"

   b. (?)amin'ity   savony ity   ny   lamba   no
       with this soap   this the clothes cleft

       sasan-dRasoa
       wash-by-Rasoa

       "It was with this soap that the clothes were washed
       by Rasoa"

2.2.5 NP-questions (NP-Q): The NP to be questioned is replaced by an appropriate interrogative word and then generally moved to the front of the sentence followed by the particle no. The conditions on movement are exactly the same as for Clefts, including the Bodyguard Condition, and so will not be discussed in detail. The only variant is that if the NP to be questioned is an oblique case NP, then the movement is optional. Thus from 54a we can form all of the following synonymous questions:

60 a. manasa lamba   amin'inona Rasoa?
        +act
        wash   clothes with what   Rasoa?

    b. amin'inona no   manasa lamba   Rasoa?
        with what   cleft wash   clothes Rasoa?

    c. amin'inona Rasoa no   manasa lamba   ?
        with what   Rasoa cleft wash   clothes

    d. inona no   anasan-dRasoa lamba?
                      +circ
        what   cleft wash-by-Rasoa clothes
        "With what were clothes washed by Rasoa?

2.2.6 Subordinate fronting: In certain types of subordinate clauses, particularly of an adverbial sort, the subject, preferably an active subject, may move to the left of
its verb with no intervening particle. The result is a
stylistic variant of the first, so this transformation is the
only movement process we have considered which is, at least
nearly, paraphrastic.

61 a. tsy miasa androany Rabe satria marary ny vadi-ny
        not work today   Rabe because sick   the wife-his
        "Rabe isn't working today because his wife is sick"

    b. tsy miasa androany Rabe satria ny vadi-ny marary
        not work today   Rabe because the wife-his sick
        "Rabe isn't working today because his wife is sick"

It is also possible for certain locative and temporal NPs to
front in this way even though they are not subjects. In
these cases the movement accepts the Bodyguard Condition.

      The full range of contexts in which Sub-Fronting applies
has not been determined. In texts the use of this transformation is not very apparent. It appears more natural in adverbial clauses than in complements, and will not survive at
all under any of the nominalizations discussed in 2.1.3. It
is not clear, however, whether the domain of Sub-Fronting
should include the contrastive fronting illustrated in 62b
considered as an answer to 62a. Here it appears that a main
clause subject has been fronted. However, on hearing the
fronted subject, a hearer expects some sort of contrastive
clause to follow, so perhaps these types of clause pairs, constructed without overt conjunction in distinction to the normal Malagasy manner of joining clauses of any sort, are best
considered a particular type of subordinate construction.

62 a. Inona no   ataon'ny   ankizy?
        What   cleft done-by-the children
        "What are the children doing?"

b. ny   zazalahy miasa, ny   zazavavy matory
   the boys   work   the girls   sleep
   "The boys are working, the girls are sleeping"

Finally, to conclude this section, we observe that
structures generated by movement transformations, as we have
been using that term, are islands with respect to other movement transformations. This almost follows from the fact that
by and large, only subjects move and the plausible assumption
that a given constituent can't move twice. Nonetheless, even
in cases where a non-subject is moved, we cannot afterwards
apply a movement transformation to the real subject (with the
exception of the Bodyguard Condition, if that is formulated
as a separate transformation). Thus from 63a we cannot form
63b.

63 a. amin'ity savony ity no   manasa lamba   ny
                                    +act
        with this soap   this cleft wash   clothes the

        vehivavy
        woman

        "It is with this soap that the woman is washing
        clothes"

    b. *ny vehivavy izay amin'ity savony ity no
         the woman   that with this soap   this cleft

         mansas lamba
         wash   clothes

         "The woman who it is with this soap that washes
         clothes"

2.3   Topicalization transformations

In addition to the topicalization inherent in the voicing system, Malagasy possesses two ways of more overtly topicalizing a constituent.

2.3.1 Strong topicalization (S-Top): S-Top copies an
NP to the front of the sentence, obligatorily preceeding it
with raha "when, if" and following it with the invariable
particle dia. In addition, the occurrence of raha may optionally be followed by either ny momba "the (things) concerning"
or ny amina "the with." Further, the occurrence of dia may
optionally (and in some cases obligatorily) be preceeded by
adverbs of emphasis. The original position topicalized obligatorily retains a pronoun if that position was not the subject. If it was the subject, then sometimes no pronoun is
retained (there appears to be significant "stylistic" variation across speakers concerning the preference for retaining

EDWARD L. KEENAN

subject pronouns here). It is only in this optional deletion
that S-Top distinguishes subjects from non-subjects.

64 a. raha ny momban-dRasoa aloha dia mbola manasa
if the around Rasoa ahead top still washes

lamba izy/?∅
clothes she/ ∅

"If it's a question of Rasoa, well she's still
washing clothes"

b. raha io lamba io (aloha) dia mbola manasa
if that clothes that ahead top still wash

azy /*∅ Rasoa
it ∅ Rasoa

"As for those clothes, well Rasoa is still washing
them"

2.3.2 Weak topicalization (W-Top): W-Top merely copies
an NP to the front of the S, obligatorily inserting dia between it and the main verb. As with S-Top if the NP copied
was not a subject a pronominal copy is left behind. If the
copied NP is subject normally no pronoun is left, although
informants will generally accept sentences with the pronoun
present.

65 Rasoa dia manasa lamba (∅ / ?izy)
Rasoa top wash clothes ∅ / she
"Rasoa, she's washing clothes"

It is not impossible that W-Top should be considered
some sort of reduced form of S-Top. However, there are some
differences, both syntactically and semantically. As regards
the former, we have already noted the preference for deleting
subject pronouns under W-Top and the reluctance to do so under S-Top. On the other hand, the positions that can be topicalized by either transformation are the same, and the priviledges of occurrence of the resulting sentences are also
identical.

Semantically, however, the differences are greater.
S-Top seems really to define a topic of importance for the
current conversation. We expect a sentence which follows a
strong topic to really be about that topic. Weak topics, on
the other hand, are rather items which have some momentary
importance in the conversation, but are not perhaps true topics of conversation. Thus W-Top is very frequently used to
highlight certain place and time adverbials. For example,

272

66 a.   Ho   any   Antsirabe rehampitso izahay
         fut there Antsirabe tomorrow   we (excl)
         "We will go to Antsirabe tomorrow"

    b.   rahampitso izahay dia ho   any   Antsirabe
         tomorrow   we   top fut there Antsirabe
         "Tomorrow, we'll go to Antsirabe"

Note that W-Top, as well as S-Top, accepts the Bodyguard Condition.

Using Top as a cover term for either form of topicalization, note that despite some formal similarities between them and Cleft, the differences are considerable. Thus it is not possible to embed topicalized sentences under certain sentence operators (which are constructed without a complementizer) whereas Clefts accept such embedding freely.

67 a.   tsy Rasoa no   manasa lamba
         not Rasoa cleft wash   clothes
         "It's not Rasoa who is washing clothes"
         (it's someone else)

    b.   *tsy Rasoa dia manasa lamba
          not Rasoa top wash   clothes

68 a.   toa   Rasoa no   manasa lamba
         seem Rasoa cleft wash   clothes
         "It seems that it is Rasoa who is washing clothes"

    b.   *toa Rasoa dia manasa lamba
          seem Rasoa top wash   clothes

On the other hand, Top being primarily a copying rule, it is not subject to the islandhood of structures generated by movement transformations.

69 ity radary ity dia ny Rosiana no   nanao azy
    this radar this top the Russians cleft did   it
    "As for this radar, it was the Russians who built it"

In general, then, Top is more rootish than Cleft. However, it can be embedded in adverbial clauses of various sorts as well as in sentence complements, in contrast to "as for" type topicalizations in English.

70 a.   manantena Rabe fa   Rasoa dia efa   nanasa lamba
         hopes   Rabe that Rasoa top already washed clothes

    b.   faly be   Rabe satria Rasoa dia efa   nanasa
         happy great Rabe because Rasoa top already washed

              lamba
              clothes

2.4   Coreferential deletions

We consider here three types of coreferential deletion:
NP Drop, Conjunction Reduction, and several types of Equi-NP
deletion.   The last two processes are sensitive to the subjecthood of the NPs involved.   NP Drop is discussed because it
provides information that may influence our understanding of
these processes.

2.4.1 NP Drop: It is common in Malagasy discourse to
omit NPs whose referents have been established earlier in the
discourse.   Subject NPs are particularly prone to be omitted,
but the process is not limited to subjects.

71   tonga nitady   an-dRasoa Rabe fa   tsy nahita
     came   looked-for acc-Rasoa Rabe but not saw
     "Rabe came looking for Rasoa but (he) didn't see (her)"

We note that _fa_ above is a very general sentential connective
in Malagasy.   It is often used with contrastive effect, like
but in English, but also serves to introduce sentential complements of verbs of thinking, saying, etc., and as well
serves as a largely contentless discourse connective.   Speakers may often finish a clause with _fa_, drawing out the intonation, thereby indicating that something more is coming but
without making explicit its semantic relation to the preceeding clause.   The possibility of dropping NPs as in 71 is
largely limited by pragmatic factors--the plausibility that
the addressees can reconstruct the referent.   A more complete
analysis of NP Drop is not available at the moment.   However,
on further analysis, it is possible that certain coreferential deletions, noted below, could be analyzed as due to NP
Drop.

2.4.2 Conjunction Reduction (CR):   In one type of CR,
hereafter CR-1, the subject NP of the first conjunct of a
sentence of the form "S_1 and S_2" deletes, and the resulting
conjunction is expressed with the phrasal conjunction _sy_,
which is never used to conjoin full Ss, rather than the sentential conjunction _ary_.

72   a.   misotro taoka Rabe ary mihinam-bary Rabe
          drinks   booze Rabe and eats   rice Rabe

     b.   [misotro taoka sy   mihinam-bary] $_{VP}$ Rabe
          drinks   booze and eats   rice   Rabe
          "Rabe is drinking booze and eating rice"

Note that CR-1 cannot function to delete objects.

73   a.   Nividy ny omby Rabe ary namono ny   omby Rakoto
          bought the cow Rabe and killed the cow Rakoto

b. *nividy Rabe sy/ary namono ny omby Rakoto
   bought Rabe and killed the cow Rakoto
   "Rabe bought and Rakoto killed the cow"

CR-1, however, is fed by the Advancement-to-Subject (A-to-S)
rule, and the semantic effect of 73b can be expressed by 74b.

74 a. novidin-dRabe ny omby ary novonoin-dRakoto ny
    +pass   +pass
    bought by-Rabe the cow and killed by-Rakoto the

    omby
    cow

b. [novidin-dRabe sy novonoin-dRakoto] $_{VP}$ ny omby
   bought by-Rabe and killed by-Rakoto the cow
   "The cow was bought by Rabe and killed by Rakoto"

Furthermore, CR-1 feeds the other cyclic rules which are sensitive to subjects. That is, the subject NP remaining in S_2 after the deletion of the subject of S_1 comes to function as the subject of the derived S. Thus it can relativize, cleft, question, etc., and it is this that justifies introducing a derived VP node in 72 and 74 and entails the right node raising of the original subject of S_2. For justification of this note that 75 is the well formed result of applying Cleft to 72b, and 76 the well formed result of relativizing the derived subject in 74b.

75 Rabe no misotro taoka sy mihinam-bary
   Rabe cleft drinks booze and eats rice
   "It's Rabe who is drinking booze and eating rice"

76 ny omby iazay novidin-dRabe sy novonoin-dRakoto
   the cow that bought by-Rabe and killed by-Rakoto
   "the cow that was bought by Rabe and killed by Rakoto"

(We note in passing that CR-1 does not feed the A-to-S rule. Thus no NP in the derived VP of 72b or 74b can be advanced to subject. But this problem is probably universal, and will not be discussed further here.)

Malagasy may have a second type of CR, CR-2, in which the subject of the second sentential conjunct deletes and the sentential conjunction does not become phrasal. Thus from 72a, repeated as 77a below, we can form 77b.

77 a. misotro taoka Rabe ary mihinam-bary Rabe
    drinks booze Rabe and eats rice Rabe

b. misotro taoka Rabe ary mihinam-bary
   drinks booze Rabe and eats rice
   "Rabe is drinking booze and (he) is eating rice"

Rather than posit a second type of CR, however, it is possible
that Ss like 77b are the result of NP Drop (assuming the conditions on that discourse operation could ever be formally
stated). This would justify the intuition of some speakers
at least that 77b represents a kind of after-thought deletion.
Note further that CR-2, if it exists, does not feed any other
of the major transformations we have discussed. In particular, it is not possible to cleft, question, or relativize it.

78 *Rabe no   misotro taoka ary mihinam-bary
     Rabe cleft drinks booze and eats   rice
    "It is Rabe who is drinking booze and eating rice"

(Note that the only difference between 78 and the well formed
75 is that in the former we use a sentential conjunction ary
whereas in the latter we have the phrasal conjunction sy.)

2.4.3 Equi NP Deletion: The variety of surface paradigms plausibly involving some type of Equi are enormously
varied in Malagasy. A full analysis would be of dissertation
proportions, so we shall here mention only a few of the types
which are clearly sensitive to subjecthood in one way or
another.

2.4.3.1 Equi-1. In Equi-1 the subject NP of verbs of
thinking and saying controls the deletion of a coreferential
NP in the complement S, as illustrated in 79.

79 a. mihevitra Rabe$_i$ fa   handeha ho any   Antsirabe
        +act
        thinks   Rabe$_i$ that will-go fut there Antsirabe

        rahampitso Rabe$_i$ $\Rightarrow$
        tomorrow   Rabe$_i$

    b. mihevitra Rabe$_i$ fa   handeha ho any   Antsirabe
        thinks   Rabe$_i$ that will-go fut there Antsirabe

        rehampitso $\emptyset_i$
        tomorrow

        "Rabe thinks that (he) will go to Antsirabe
        tomorrow"

Note first that the surface order of Ss with sentential objects is VSO. VOS order is generally unacceptable here.

80 a. *mihevitra fa   mitady   ny zaza Rasoa Rabe
         thinks   that looks-for the child Rasoa Rabe
        "Rabe thinks that Rasoa is looking for the child"

    b. mihevitra Rabe fa   mitady   ny zaza Rasoa
        thinks   Rabe that looks-for the child Rasoa
        "Rabe thinks that Rasoa is looking for the child"

We would posit nonetheless an underlying VOS order for three
reasons: 1) Informants understand such VOS sentences easily,
but simply say that it is too heavy to have a sentential object preceeding the subject. 2) If VOS is taken as the underlying order, then the A-to-S transformation works as usual,
yielding, for example, 81 from 80.

81 heverin-dRabe   fa   mitady   ny   zaza   Rasoa
    +pass
    thought by-Rabe that looks-for the child Rasoa
    "It is thought by Rabe that Rasoa is looking for the
    child"

The use of such passives is extremely common. And 3), all
matrix verbs of thinking, saying, etc., allow the embedded
subject to be raised to the object position of the matrix
verb (see 2.5), in which case the underlying subject remains
in sentence final position. If VSO order were adopted as
underlying, then an otherwise unmotivated transformation
would be needed to move the subject to the otherwise "normal"
position in this case.

The major properties of Equi-1 are the following:
1) Only subjects of active verbs can trigger the deletion.
Thus corresponding to 79 we do not have:

82 *heverin-dRabe   fa   handeha ho any   Antsirabe
    +pass
    thought by-Rabe that will-go fut there Antsirabe

    rehampitso
    tomorrow

    "It is thought by Rabe that he will go to Antsirabe
    tomorrow"

2) The complementizer fa "that" cannot be deleted, and the
complement S remains tensed. In simple cases at least only
subjects can undergo the deletion; objects and non-subject
agents cannot.

83 mihevitra Rabe$_i$ fa   mitady   azy$_i$ /*$\emptyset_i$ Rasoa
    thinks   Rabe$_i$ that looks-for him$_i$ $\emptyset_i$ Rasoa
    "Rabe thinks that Rasoa is looking for him"

84 milaza Rabe$_i$ fa   ho-tadiavi-ny$_i$ / *ho-tadiavina-$\emptyset_i$
    +act   +pass   +pass
    says   Rabe   that fut-look for by-him$_i$ / fut-look for by
    "Rabe says that Rasoa will be looked for by him"

3) The A-to-S rules feed Equi-1. Thus the sense of 83 can be
expressed by 85.

85 mihevitra Rabe$_i$ fa   tadiavin-dRasoa $\emptyset_i$
    thinks   Rabe$_i$ that looked for by-Rasoa

"Rabe$_i$ thinks that (he$_i$) is being looked for by Rasoa"

4) It is not fully clear whether Equi-1 is obligatory. Certainly a pronoun can appear in the embedded subject position, but in such cases informants prefer a reading on which it is not coreferential with the matrix subject. For some informants this preference is absolute, but others are more hesitant.

86 ??mihevitra Rabe$_i$ fa tadiavin-dRasoa izy$_i$

"Rabe$_i$ thinks that he$_i$ is being looked for by Rasoa"

This hesitancy on the judgment of coreference suggests that Equi-1 might be considered a special case of NP Drop, although the use of A-to-S to feed the deletion, thus making the pattern of coreference clear, argues against this.

2.4.3.2 Equi-2. Equi-2 is distinguished from Equi-1 in that no complementizer can be present and the subject of the derived S normally occurs in sentence final position (though some matrix predicates also admit that the subject can occur immediately following the matrix predicate).

87 a. manaiky [manasa ny   zaza Rasoa]$_s$ Rasoa
         +act   ==>
         agree   wash   the child Rasoa   Rasoa

    b. manaiky manasa ny   zaza Rasoa
        agree   wash   the child Rasoa
        "Rasoa agrees to wash the child"

As with Equi-1 only subjects can trigger this deletion, passive agents cannot (although the matrix verbs generally have commonly used passive forms); only subjects undergo the deletion (but see below), objects never. Moreover, the deletion is obligatory and is fed by the A-to-S rule.

88 a. manaiky [sasan-dRasoa   ny   zaza]$_s$ ny zaza
         +pass   ==>
         agree   wash by-Rasoa the child   the child

    b. manaiky sasan-dRasoa   ny   zaza
        agree   wash by Rasoa the child
        "The child agrees to be washed by Rasoa"

Further, the originally embedded verb can in surface still be inflected for tense, although the semantically permissible possibilities are much more restricted here than for Equi-1. Example 89 illustrates a future tense lower verb and contrasts in meaning with the otherwise identical 87 in which the

initial m- marks the lower verb for present tense. Example
89 might easily be used if, for example, Rasoa was making a
contract to wash the children over a future period.

89 manaiky h-   anasa ny zaza Rasoa
    agrees fut- wash the child Rasoa
    "Rasoa agrees to wash the child (in the future)"

Note finally that the controller of Equi-2 is clearly the
subject of the derived S. It has the coding properties, e.g.,
sentence final position, nominative case, definiteness, takes
particles immediately before it, etc.

90 hanaiky   hanasa   ny zaza ve Rasoa
    fut-agree fut-wash   the child ? Rasoa
    "Will Rasoa agree to wash the child (in the future)?"

These facts argue that Ss derived from Equi-2 have the surface
structure VP-NP, where NP is the subject and VP is the derived
predicate, e.g., "agrees to wash the child." Note further
that the derived subject has the transformational properties
of subjects so far discussed. Thus it relativizes, clefts
(example 91), and may itself undergo Equi-2 (example 92).

91 Rasoa no   manaiky manasa ny zaza
    Rasoa cleft agrees washes the child
    "It is Rasoa who agrees to wash the child"

92 a. [tia [hanaiky [hanasa ny zaza Rasoa] Rasoa]
       want fut-agree fut-wash the child Rasoa Rasoa

       Rasoa] fa tsy afaka
       Rasoa but not able

   b. [tia [hanaiky   hanasa ny zaza Ø   Rasoa]

       Rasoa] fa tsy afaka

   c. [tia hanaiky   hanasa ny zaza Ø   Ø

       Rasoa] fa tsy afaka

   = te-hanaiky hanasa ny zaza Rasoa fa tsy afaka
      want agree wash   the child Rasoa but not free (to
      do so)
      "Rasoa wants to agree to wash the child but (she)
      isn't free (to do so)"

Note that the higher verb tia cliticizes to the lower verb
hanasa giving further (weak) support for the existence of a
surface VP in this case.
    Of the verbs which govern Equi-2 there is an interesting
subclass which behaves in one respect differently from our
example manaiky "agree to." This class includes mikasa

"intend," $\underline{tia}$ "want," and $\underline{mahazo}$ "can, be able to" (6). Example 93 below illustrates a straightforward application of Equi-2 with $\underline{mikasa}$ "intend." Example 94 shows that passive may apply in the lower S, feeding Equi-2 with this verb. Example 95 shows that passive cannot apply unilaterally on the matrix verb. In all these respects $\underline{mikasa}$ behaves like the paradigm case $\underline{manaiky}$. However, 96 shows that in distinction to $\underline{manaiky}$, $\underline{mikasa}$ can passivize in the higher class if (and only if) the lower clause is passive and the agents of the matrix and embedded verbs are identical.

93 mikasa hanasa ny zaza Rasoa
    +act   +act
    intend fut-wash the child Rasoa
    "Rasoa intends to wash the child"

94 a. mikasa [$_s$ho- sasan- dRasoa ny zaza] ny zaza
        +act   +pass
        intend   fut-wash by-Rasoa the child the child

    b. [mikasa ho-sasan-dRasoa]$_{VP}$ ny zaza
        intend will-be washed by Rasoa the child
        "The child intends to be washed by Rasoa"

95 *kasain-dRasoa   hanasa   ny   zaza
    +pass   +act
    intend by-Rasoa fut-wash the child
    "It was intended by Rasoa to wash the child"

96 a. kasain-dRasoa$_i$ sasana- $\emptyset_i$ ny lamba
        +pass   +pass
        intended by-Rasoa$_i$ washed by -(her$_i$) the clothes

        "It was intended by Rasoa that the clothes be washed by her"

    b. *eken-dRasoa$_i$ sasana- $\emptyset_i$ ny lamba
        +pass
        agreed by-Rasoa$_i$ washed by (her$_i$) the clothes

        "It was agreed by Rasoa that the clothes would be washed by her"

Note that 96a clearly means that Rasoa intended to wash the clothes herself, not merely that the clothes get washed.

Generating sentences like 96a poses several difficult problems if A-to-S and Equi-2 are cyclic in the ordinary sense. Using 97 as a rough representation of the underlying structure for 96, consider:

97   [$_S$ mikasa [$_S$ hanasa   ny   lamba   Rasoa]$_S$ Rasoa]$_S$
          $_1$ +act $_0$ +act $_0$ $_1$
         intend   fut-wash the clothes Rasoa   Rasoa

If Passive applies first on the S_0 cycle, then Equi on S_1
must delete a non-subject agent phrase--something which would
make Malagasy resemble Philippine languages (Schachter, this
volume) but which otherwise appears unmotivated in Malagasy.
Further, if Passive applies on the higher cycle before Equi,
then we have a case where non-subject agents control Equi--
again a similarity with Philippine languages but not something that is terribly well motivated in Malagasy (but recall
that an exhaustive study of a large class of Equi-predicates
with respect to all voicing possibilities remains to be done).
And even if Passive applies after Equi on the higher cycle,
its application would have to be made contingent on the prior
application of Passive on the lower cycle in order not to
generate, for example, 95. And a condition of that sort is
unusual and in need of explanation to be justified. Furthermore, application of Passive on the higher clause would have
to be made obligatory if Passive had applied on the lower
clause, and Equi had deleted the passive agent, since 98 is
clearly ungrammatical.

98 *mikasa sasana ny   lamba   Rasoa
      +act   +pass
      "Rasoa intends the clothes to be washed by her"

In no other case could Passive apply in the higher S.

An alternative analysis we propose is as follows: Passive does not apply on the lower cycle at all; Equi applies
on the higher cycle and then a derived VP is created as argued
above. We suggest that this process should be formulated so
that the lower verb forms a kind of compound verb with the
higher verb, and the lower direct object, if present, is understood as the direct object of the derived verb. Thus 97
after Equi and "VP creation" would have the following form:

99

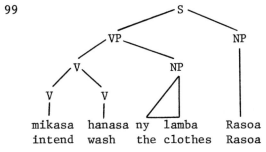

        mikasa hanasa ny   lamba   Rasoa
        intend   wash   the clothes Rasoa

Now A-to-S can apply, promoting <u>ny lamba</u> "the clothes" to

subject and demoting the old subject <u>Rasoa</u>. A-to-S would
have to be extended so that when the underlying verb was
compound the voice affixes attach to both parts of the derived
verb, but the demoted subject still attaches to only the first
part of the derived verb. This last fact is unpleasant, in
this approach, but certainly do-able.

One very important advantage of our proposal is that it
automatically accounts for why <u>ny lamba</u> "the clothes" in 96,
repeated as 100 below, behaves like a subject, e.g., it takes
question particles, relativizes, etc.

100 kasain-dRasoa$_i$ sasana- $\emptyset_i$ ny lamba
   +pass   +pass
   intended by-Rasoa$_i$ washed by-(her$_i$) the clothes

   "It was intended by Rasoa that the clothes be washed
   by her"

101 kasain-dRasoa   sasana ve ny lamba
   intend by Rasoa washed ?   the clothes
   "Was it intended by Rasoa that the clothes be washed
   by her?"

102 ny lamba   izay kasain-dRasoa   sasana
   the clothes that intended by-Rasoa washed
   "the clothes that were intended by Rasoa to be washed
   by her"

(NB: The more natural translations of these sentences in English would, of course, be active.)

If, on the other hand, Passive were to apply first on
the lower cycle and then Equi delete a passive agent on the
higher cycle, there is no reason to believe that the original
direct object of the lower S has been raised to subject status of the derived VP, and hence the original direct object
should not be subject to those transformations which are
sensitive only to subjects.

A final piece of support for our analysis, which does
not, however, distinguish it from the alternative proposed, is
that if the direct object of the compound verb is indefinite,
as illustrated in 103a, then we cannot put the compound verb
in the passive, 103b. This result is accounted for on our
approach since 103b would be derived by passivizing 103a,
thereby creating an indefinite subject, and subjects must, of
course, be definite.

103 a. [$_{VP}$[$_V$mikasa hanasa] lamba]   Rasoa
       intend wash   clothes   Rasoa

b. *kasain-dRasoa   ho   sasana lamba
    +pass   +pass
    intended by-Rasoa fut washed clothes
    "It was intended by Rasoa that clothes be washed
    by her"

2.5 Raising

In general, Malagasy is rich in Raising processes.
Raising to Object (R-O) is very productive, applying in a uniform way to a large class of predicates and satisfying the
Relational Succession Law (RSL) discussed below. Raising to
Subject (R-S) is more restricted in application, although two
and possibly three sub-types must be distinguished. R-S also
generally satisfies the RSL. And third, a restricted type of
raising applies to possessor NPs (Poss-R). Poss-R appears to
violate the RSL. Both R-O and R-S apply only to subjects,
and Poss-R applies only to possessors of subjects.

2.5.1 Raising to Object (R-O): From an underlying
structure like 104a, R-O may derive 104b.

104 a. nanantena [$_S$fa nanasa ny   zaza Rasoa] Rabe
        +act
        past-hope   that washed the child Rasoa   Rabe

b. nanantena an-dRasoa ho   nanasa ny   zaza Rabe
    hoped   acc-Rasoa comp washed the child Rabe
    "Rabe hoped that Rasoa washed the child"

R-O has a great many structurally interesting properties:
1) The underlying subject is clearly the surface subject. Thus in 104b "Rabe" satisfies the subject properties
discussed so far:

105 nanantena an-dRasoa ho   nanasa ny   zaza ve Rabe
    hoped   acc-Rasoa comp washed the child ? Rabe
    "Did Rabe hope that Rasoa washed the child?"

106 Rabe no   nanantena an-dRasoa ho   nanasa ny   zaza
    Rabe cleft hoped   acc-Rasoa comp washed the child
    "It was Rabe who hoped that Rasoa washed the child"

2) Clearly, only subjects undergo R-O. Thus 107 could
only mean that Rabe hoped that the child washed Rasoa, and
even there "Rasoa" should be preceeded by the object particle
an- (though some speakers accept omitting it).

107 *nanantena ny   zaza ho   nanasa Rasoa Rabe
    hoped   the child comp washed Rasoa Rabe
    "Rabe hoped that Rasoa washed the child"

3) A-to-S feeds R-O. Thus the effect of 107 is obtained

by first passivizing the embedded S in 104, shown in 108a below, and then applying R-O, as in 108b.

108 a.   [nanantena [fa   sasan-dRasoa   ny   zaza] Rabe]
            hoped   that washed by-Rasoa the child Rabe

     b.   nanantena ny zaza ho   sasan-dRasoa   Rabe
            hoped   the child comp washed by-Rasoa Rabe
            "Rabe hoped that the child was washed by Rasoa"

4) R-O feeds A-to-S. Thus in 108b, "Rabe" is the subject and "ny zaza" is the direct object. That Passives applies to such Ss is illustrated in 109.

109 nantenain-dRabe ho   sasan-dRasoa   ny zaza
    +pass
    hoped by-Rabe   comp washed by-Rasoa the child
    "It was hoped by Rabe that the child was washed by
    Rasoa"

And by the tests established earlier "ny zaza" is clearly the
subject of 109. It takes question particles (example 110)
and relativizes (example 111). And for some speakers, but not
all, it even re-raises to object (example 112b) (7).

110 nantenain-dRabe ho   sasan-dRasoa   ve ny zaza
    hoped by-Rabe   comp washed by-Rasoa ? the child
    "Was it hoped by Rabe that the child was washed by
    Rasoa"

111 ny zaza izay nantenain-dRabe ho   sasan-dRasoa
    the child that hoped by-Rabe   comp washed by-Rasoa
    "the child that was hoped by Rabe to have been washed
    by Rasoa"

112 a.   [Nilaza [$_S$fa   nantenain-dRabe ho   sasan-dRasoa
            +act
            said   that hoped by-Rabe   comp washed by-Rasoa

            ilay zaza] Rakoto]
            that child Rakoto

     b.   ??Nilaza an'ilay zaza ho   nantenain-dRabe ho
            said   acc-that child comp hoped by-Rabe   comp

            sasan-dRasoa   Rakoto
            washed by-Rasoa Rakoto

            "Rakoto said that that (aforementioned) child was
            hoped by Rabe to have been washed by Rasoa"

The facts in 108 and 109 present the classical sandwich type
arguments showing that A-to-S is cyclic. Those in 112 that
R-O is cyclic.

284

5) In partial distinction to English, however, R-O does not feed Reflexivization. Thus 113b is not well formed. The way to express that idea is to apply Equi-1 first, as in 114.

113 a. $\{\begin{array}{l}\text{[manantena}\\\text{[milaza}\end{array}\}$ [fa   hanasa   lamba   Rabe]   Rabe

   $\{\begin{array}{l}\text{hopes}\\\text{says}\end{array}\}$ that fut-wash clothes Rabe   Rabe

b. $\{\begin{array}{l}\text{*manantena}\\\text{*milaza}\end{array}\}$ tena hanasa   lamba   Rabe

   $\{\begin{array}{l}\text{hopes}\\\text{says}\end{array}\}$ self fut-wash clothes Rabe

"Rabe hopes/says himself to wash clothes"
= "Rabe hopes/says that he will wash clothes"

114 $\{\begin{array}{l}\text{manantena}\\\text{milaza}\end{array}\}$ Rabe fa   hanasa   lamba

   $\{\begin{array}{l}\text{hopes}\\\text{says}\end{array}\}$ Rabe that fut-wash clothes

"Rabe$_i$ hopes/says that (he$_i$) will wash clothes"

6) Note finally that R-O in Malagasy clearly supports the Relational Succession Law (RSL) which states that a raised NP takes over the function (subject of, object of, etc.) relative to the matrix predicate that the clause out of which it was raised originally had. Thus NPs raised by R-O are raised only from object clauses and are presented as sur-face objects (taking the object marker an, being replaced by accusative pro-forms, and undergoing A-to-S via Passive).

2.5.2 Raising to Subject (R-S): There appear to be three sub-types of R-S in Malagasy. The most productive is illustrated by 115b.

115 a.   nantenain-dRabe [$_{NP}$fa   nanasa lamba   Rasoa]
      +pass   +act
      hoped by-Rabe   that washed clothes Rasoa
      "It was hoped by Rabe that Rasoa washed clothes"

b.   [$_{VP}$nantenain-dRabe fa   nanasa lamba] Rasoa
      hoped by-Rabe   that washed clothes Rasoa
      "Rasoa was hoped by Rabe to have washed clothes"

This type of R-S requires some justification, particu-larly since it does not introduce any new grammatical mater-ial, delete, or reorder any part of the structures it applies to. It merely reorganizes the constituent structure. So to justify the transformational status of R-S in this case, we note:

First, the clause marked NP in 115a does appear to
satisfy the relevant requirement to be a subject. It occurs
in sentence final position, it can be questioned (example
116a), whereas the active counterpart of 115a cannot have its
object clause questioned (example 116b), and it undergoes
What-Cl formation (example 117).

116 a. Inona no   nantenain-dRabe?
       What cleft hoped by-Rabe
       "What was hoped by Rabe?"

    b. *Inona no   nanantena Rabe
                      +act
        what cleft hoped   Rabe
        "What did Rabe hope?"

117 izay nantenain-dRabe
    what hoped by-Rabe
    "whatever is hoped by Rabe"

We note, however, that many of the subject tests either do
not apply when the subject is sentential or else they give
new results. Thus sentential subjects simply cannot be relativized or cleft. And the pro-forms for sentential subjects
(izany "that") are not marked for case and occur equally well
as subjects or objects. And sentential subjects do not Raise
to Object.

And second, if the structure in 115b is correct, then
"Rasoa" should behave as a derived subject, and it does. It
can, for example, be cleft (example 118), takes question particles, etc., and can even raise to object (example 119).

118 Rasoa no   nantenain-dRabe fa   nanasa lamba
    Rasoa cleft hoped by-Rabe   that washed clothes
    "It was Rasoa that was hoped by Rabe to have washed
    clothes"

119 a. [Nilaza [fa   nantenain-dRabe fa   nanasa lamba
          +act
        said   that hoped by-Rabe   that washed clothes

        Rasoa] Rakoto]
        Rasoa   Rakoto

    b. ?Nilaza an-dRasoa ho   nantenain-dRabe fa   nanasa
        said   acc-Rasoa comp hoped by-Rabe   that washed

        lamba   Rakoto
        clothes Rakoto
        "Rakoto said Rasoa was hoped by Rabe to have washed
        clothes"

(Note that 119b, like 112b, is complicated and rejected by some informants. On reflection, however, some of those informants accept them (and some don't), so we consider their difficulties to reflect performance and allow them marginal grammatical status.)

Note that if we do not posit a R-S to relate 115a and 115b, then the definition of those transformations which are sensitive to subjecthood will have to be modified to apply to subjects or to subjects of sentential subjects...ad infinitum. This is in fact the alternative taken in Keenan (1972).

Regardless of which of these approaches is taken, however, one troublesome fact would have to be accounted for. Namely, sentential subjects introduced by the fa complementizer admit of R-S only if they are derived subjects, as in 115a. If they are underlying subjects, however, as in 120, then most speakers reject R-S.

120 a. tsara fa   efa   lasa ny mpianatra
        good that already left the students
        "It's good that the students have already gone"

   b. *ny mpianatra izay tsara fa   efa   lasa
        the students that good that already gone
        "The students that it's good have already left"

The fact that we cannot relativize (or cleft, or question, or raise to object, etc.) ny mpianatra "the students" in 120a indicates that the subject of the embedded S cannot be treated as a subject of the entire S. The only explanation of this fact we can think of is that the embedded S in 120a is in fact a subordinate clause introduced by fa in its meaning of "for, because (Fr. car)." Quite generally, NPs cannot be raised out of subordinate clauses:

121 a. faly Rabe fa / satria efa   lasa ny mpianatra
        happy Rabe for/ because already gone the students
        "Rabe is happy because the students have already gone"

   b. *ny mpianatra izay faly Rabe fa / satria efa
        the students that happy Rabe for/ because already

        lasa
        gone

        "the students that Rabe is happy that've already gone"

There is, however, another, restricted, class of predicates which might be thought to take sentential subjects and which do admit of R-S. This class includes toa "seem," tsy "not," and tsy <u>maintsy</u> "it is necessary that" (lit: "not able to"). Thus from 122a we can form 122b.

122 a. toa   manasa lamba   Rasoa
        seem wash   clothes Rasoa
        "Rasoa seems to be washing clothes"

    b. Rasoa no   toa   manasa lamba
        Rasoa cleft seem wash   clothes
        "It's Rasoa who seems to be washing clothes"

This class, however, is quite small compared to those constructed with <u>fa</u> complements (8). (In addition to <u>tsara</u> "good," that class includes emotive predicates generally, e.g., <u>ratsy</u> "bad" and several "cognitive" predicates like <u>marina</u> "true," <u>mazava</u> "clear" and <u>azo antoko</u> "is certain.") Note that if the complements of these predicates are interpreted as subordinate clauses of a <u>because</u> sort, then the sentences they form, like 120a, will have no subjects and the subject-sensitive transformations we have discussed will be, correctly, predicted not to apply to them. This would, however, give us one class of primitively subjectless Ss in Malagasy. (Note that Existential Sentences (Section 2.2.3) are also subjectless by our criteria.)

Note finally that, as we have given it, R-S clearly applies only to subjects of sentential subjects. Thus any attempt to raise <u>lamba</u> "clothes" (even making it definite) from 115 or 122 yields clearly ungrammatical sentences, 123 and 124 respectively.

123 *nantenain–dRabe fa   nanasa Rasoa ny   lamba
     hoped by-Rabe   that washed Rasoa the clothes

124 *toa   manasa Rasoa ny   lamba
     seems wash   Rasoa the clothes

Finally, there appears to be a third class of predicates, very restricted indeed, which govern a slightly different kind of R-S. Thus from the hypothetical underlying source 125a we can form either 125b directly or 125c by first passivizing and then raising.

125 a. sarotra [mamaky ity boky ity Δ]
        difficult cut   this book this Δ

    b. sarotra   ny mamaky ity boky ity
                   +pres+act
        difficult the cut   this book this
        "It is difficult to read this book"

   c.   sarotra   vakina ity boky ity
                  +pass
      difficult cut   this book this
      "This book is hard to read"

In 125b the underlying clause minus its subject takes a definite article in surface and clearly seems to function as the
subject of the entire S. It can, for example, be cleft and
questioned.

  126 ny mamaky ity boky ity no   tena sarotra   mihitsy
      the read   this book this cleft very difficult indeed
      "To read this book is very difficult indeed"

Example 125c, on the other hand, illustrates that the derived
subject of the embedded clause has been raised to subject.
Thus "this book" is clearly the subject of 125c, as it can
cleft (example 127), relativize, take question particles, etc.

  127 ity boky ity no   sarotra   vakina
                          +pass
      this book this cleft difficult read
      "It is this book which is difficultly read"

At the moment, however, it seems that the class of verbs
which accept this raising is quite small. It includes <u>saro-
tra</u> "difficult" and <u>mora</u> "easy," but to our (current) knowledge has no further members. Further, if R-S does apply in
these cases, it would have to be made obligatory, since the
passive clause out of which raising occurs does not itself
appear to have much independent subject status. Thus it will
not cleft (example 128a) or take question particles (example
128b). On the other hand, the raising, if it exists, does
satisfy the RSL, since direct objects cannot be so raised
(example 129). Clearly, more work needs to be done here before the status of R-S is clear in these cases.

  128 a. *vakina ity boky ity no   sarotra
         +pass
        read   this book this cleft difficult
        "It's this book's being read that is difficult"

      b. *sarotra   ve vakina ity boky ity
        difficult ? read   this book this
        "Is it difficult for this book to be read?"

  129 *ity boky ity no   mamaky sarotra
      this book this cleft cut   difficult
      "It is this book which is difficult to read"

    2.5.3 Possessor Raising (Poss-R): Example 130 below
illustrates a much more unusual type of raising--one in which

the possessor NP of a subject raises and in fact incorporates
into the surface VP.

130 a. marary ny zanan- dRabe
        sick the child of Rabe
        "The child of Rabe is sick"

    b. marary zanaka Rabe
        sick   child Rabe
        "Rabe has a sick child"

In 130a it is clearly ny zanan-dRabe "the child of Rabe"
which is the subject: It relativizes, takes question particles, etc. In 130b, on the other hand, it is clearly Rabe
which is subject:

131 marary zanaka ve Rabe
    sick   child ? Rabe
    "Does Rabe have a sick child?"

132 Rabe no   marary zanaka
    Rabe cleft sick   child
    "It is Rabe who has a sick child"

This type of raising exhibits several interesting properties.
First, the raised NP satisfies most of the criteria for incorporation (see Mardirussian, 1975 for justification). Thus
the raised NP is not referential: It cannot take definite
determiners (example 133a), nor can it be a definite pronoun
(example 133b).

133 a. *marary ny zanaka Rabe
         sick the child Rabe

    b. *marary azy Rabe
         sick   him Rabe

Further Ss generated by Poss-R sometimes have an idiomatic
flavor.

134 a. lava ny tongon-dRabe
        long the foot of Rabe
        "Rabe's feet are long"

    b. lava tongotra Rabe
        long foot   Rabe
        "Rabe walks a lot"

Second, the raised NP apparently does not have to be in
an inalienable possession relation to its head, although most
of the natural examples found are of that sort.

135 a. nianjera ny tranon-dRabe
        fell   the house of-Rabe
        "Rabe's house fell down"

    b. nianjera trano Rabe
       fell   house Rabe
       "Rabe had his house fall"

It may be the case, however, that the derived subject must be
in some kind of "affective" relation to the predicate, somewhat as in the case of affective passives in, for example,
Japanese (McCawley, N. 1972). Thus, although a detailed investigation of a large class of examples would be needed to
substantiate this claim, 136b, in which the subject <u>Rabe</u>
bears no obvious affective relation to the predicate, is
rejected by informants even though it appears to be formed
from 136a just as 135b was formed from 135a.

136 a. mihira ny zanan-dRabe
       sings the child of-Rabe
       "Rabe's child is singing"

    b. *mihira zanaka Rabe
       sings   child   Rabe

Third, only possessors of subjects undergo Poss-R.

137 a. manadino ny anaran' ny   mpianatra aho
       forget   the names of the students I
       "I forget the names of the students"

    b. *manadino anarana mpianatra aho
       forget   name   student   I

Fourth, the VP into which the raised NP is incorporated
must be intransitive.

138 a. manadino boky ny zanan-dRabe
       forget   books the child of Rabe
       "Rabe's child forgets books"

    b. *manadino boky zanaka Rabe
       forget   books child   Rabe

    c. *manadino zanaka boky Rabe
       forget   child   books Rabe

Fifth, the VP may, however, be a derived intransitive.
Thus the semantic effect of 137b above is obtained by first
passivizing, as in 139a, and then raising, 139b.

139 a. hadino-ko   ny anaran' ny mpianatra
        +pass
        forgotten by-me the names of the students
        "The names of the students are forgetten by me"

   b. hadino-ko   anarana ny mpianatra
        forgotten by-me name   the students
        "The students had their names forgotten by me"

These data suggest, then, that the NPs which undergo Poss-R
must not only be possessors of surface subjects, but that
those subjects must be underlyingly absolutive, that either
subjects of intransitive predicates or direct objects of transitive predicates. This claim receives support from the fact
that underlying possessors of instrumentals (example 140a),
even when advanced to subject of an intransitive verb (example 140b), still cannot undergo Poss-R (example 140c).

140 a. misasa   amin'ny savonin-dRabe aho
        +act
        +intrans
        wash   with the soap of- Rabe I
        "I wash with Rabe's soap"

   b. isasa-ko   ny savonin-dRabe
        +circ
        +intrans
        wash by-me the soap of- Rabe

   c. *isasa-ko   savony Rabe
        +circ
        +intrans
        wash by-me soap   Rabe

Again, a larger range of circumstantial constituents would
have to be tested with circumstantial verbs to fully substantiate that only underlying possessors of absolutives undergo
Poss-R, but at least it is clear that underlying possessors
of instrumentals cannot undergo Poss-R, and instrumentals are
among the prime NPs which can be advanced to subject by the
circumstantial voice.

Finally, as regards the Relational Succession Law, it
appears that Poss-R violates it since an NP is raised from
subject but does not itself become a subject. Note, however,
that despite its position, the raised possessor does not become an object. It cannot, for example, be advanced to subject (example 141b). Rather, it simply incorporates into the
VP, which remains intransitive.

141 a. nianjera trano Rabe
        fell   house Rabe
        "Rabe had his house fall"

    b. nianjeranan-dRabe trano
        fell by-Rabe   house

There are perhaps two ways the RSL might be modified to account for Poss-R. On the one hand, as suggested by Perlmutter and Postal, "partitive" raisings may simply have to be distinguished from non-partitive raisings. This seems to me reasonable in that generally the most productive raisings are from clauses. Raisings from NPs with lexical heads is very likely an ontologically different being. On the other hand, perhaps operations in which a raised NP does not take on any grammatical relation to the verb, as is the case in Poss-R in Malagasy, should be distinguished from raisings which do feed the system of grammatical relations. Thus, perhaps, the RSL could simply be weakened to read "A raised NP takes on the grammatical relation borne by the NP out of which it is raised, if it takes on any grammatical relation at all."

II. Malagasy Compared with Philippine Languages

Philippine languages (Tagalog, Cebuano, Kalagan, etc.) are genetically related to Malagasy and their surface syntactic organization appears similar to that of Malagasy. In particular, they are verb initial, and verbs are marked according to which of the underlying NPs is "in focus." E.g., from Tagalog we have:

142 a. sumampal ng babae ang lalake
        +actor
        strike   obj woman   man
        "The man struck a woman"

    b. sinampal ng lalake ang babae
        +object
        strike   by man   woman
        "The woman was struck by a/the man"

The NP which is in focus according to the form of the verb is marked by ang. And as ang-NPs have many properties which subjects usually have, it is tempting to consider the ang-NP as a basic subject in 142a and a derived subject in 142b. The object focus form of the verb in 142b would then be a passive form. However, Schachter (this volume) has argued that ang-NPs cannot be consistently identified as subjects. Rather, the properties usually characteristic of subjects are divided fairly evenly between surface ang-NPs on the one hand and non-focus actors (e.g., "man" in 142b) on the other. Here we shall summarize Schachter's evidence for his claim and then show that by and large this division of properties does not occur in Malagasy. As the relevant examples from Philippine languages are given in Schachter (this volume), we will not repeat them here.

First, ang-NPs are like subjects in that 1) they are always definite; 2) they are the most necessary (very few sentence types occur without any ang-NP); 3) they are the only relativizable NP in a S, and 4) only ang-NPs launch floating quantifiers. Further, ang-NPs may control Equi-NP deletion and may in certain cases control reflexivization, and may in those languages where relevant (Kampampangan) control verb agreement.

On the other hand, non-focus agents (hereafter simply "agents") are like subjects in that 1) they express the addressee phrase of imperatives, regardless of the focus form of the verb; 2) they may control Equi-NP deletion (9); 3) they are the preferred controllers of reflexivization (for many Philippine languages, in simple cases of reflexivization like "The man struck himself" surface control of the reflexive pronoun is restricted to non-focus actors and the reflexive pronoun itself takes the ang marker); 4) they may undergo Equi-NP deletion; 5) they have a fixed position in the sentence in those Philippine languages with fairly fixed word order (Cebuano, Kalagan, but not Tagalog), again regardless of the focus of the verb (thus word order is expressed as V + Actor + Other); 6) they also trigger verb agreement (in Kampampangan) (see E.L. Keenan, 1975 for example). Finally, Schachter notes that certain simplex sentences occur only in non-actor focus forms, making the actor focus form appear less basic than Ss with actor subjects in Malagasy.

In Malagasy we find, however, that the NP we have been calling the subject possesses the subject-like properties of ang-NPs in Philippine languages, but the non-subject agents in Malagasy by and large do not have the subject-like properties of agents in Philippine languages. Thus, on the one hand, subjects in Malagasy are always definite, they are the most necessary (with the possible exception of the sentences cited in Sections 2.2.3 and 2.5.2, all Ss in Malagasy have surface subjects), and they are the only relativizable NPs. Quantifier placement in Malagasy is a complex phenomenon, but quantifiers do not appear to "float" in any simple way in Malagasy, so that possible point of similarity between Malagasy subjects and ang-NPs does not apply.

On the other hand, non-subject agents in Malagasy do not control Equi-NP deletion. Nor do they undergo Equi.

Further, they generally do not control reflexives, and subjects never get reflexivized in Malagasy. Agents do not have
a fixed position in that the position varies according to
whether the actor is subject or not. Subjects, of course, do
have a fixed position. There is, of course, no verb agreement (which is the norm as well for Philippine languages),
and as we have argued, the sentence form with actor subjects
is the most basic. There are basically no verbs which only
exist only in non-agent "focus" forms (though there are a very
few in which the root form of the verb functions as both the
active and passive form, e.g., tia "to love," but in which
the "real" active form shows up in certain nominalizations,
e.g., fitiaviana "love."

There is one point, however, where underlying agents in
Malagasy resemble underlying agents in Philippine languages.
Namely the underlying agent expresses the addressee of imperatives, regardless of the voice of the imperative verb (see
Section 2.1.3). Despite this fact, however, it is clear that
the NP we have been calling subject in Malagasy possesses an
overwhelming abundance of properties characteristic of subjects generally, so the division of subject properties in the
Philippine languages is overall not present in Malagasy.

III.   Subject Prominence vs. Topic Prominence in Malagasy

Li and Thompson (this volume and 1974) have attempted to
characterize certain languages as topic prominent in opposition (at least partial opposition) to languages which are subject prominent. We have already shown that Malagasy is subject prominent in any intuitive understanding of that term.
However, many of the properties which positively characterize
topics are also characteristic of Malagasy subjects. Hence,
it might be the case that Malagasy is, in addition, a topic
prominent language.

We shall group the large number of criteria used by Li
and Thompson to determine their typology in two groups: General properties and Specific properties. General properties
are those which concern the overall syntactic organization of
a language, and specific properties are those which characterize the specific relation the topic NP of a sentence bears
to the rest of the sentence. Needless to say, the division
between the two categories is somewhat arbitrary, and we
adopt it largely for purposes of exposition.

1.   General properties of topic prominent languages

Following Li and Thompson we list seven general properties of topic prominent languages (TPL). Of these, Malagasy

does not possess the first five. The sixth is not very criterial since many non-TPL also possess it. But Malagasy does possess the seventh.

1) TPLs do not have passives, or if they do, they are restricted in usage. Malagasy clearly has very productive passives.

2) In TPLs Topicalization is not a marked process, if indeed it is a "process" at all. In Malagasy, however, there are at least two topicalization processes, S-Top and W-Top (Sections 2.3.1 and 2.3.2, respectively). Further, the A-to-S rule is a topicalizing process to some extent, and it is clearly marked on the verb.

3) In TPLs, the topic does not play a major role in cyclic transformations. But in Malagasy, the most topic-like NP in most sentences, namely the subject, does play a critical role in the cyclic processes, as we have shown. It is the case, of course, that NPs topicalized by S-Top and W-Top do not play any serious role in cyclic transformations.

4) In TPLs the topic NP is not overtly coded as such in surface. It may have a characteristic position, but does not have a characteristic case marking or verb agreement paradigm. But in Malagasy, subjects do have a characteristic position and to a lesser extent case marking. They do not, however, trigger verb agreement, as there is none. Topics generated by S-Top or W-Top are, furthermore, overtly marked.

5) TPLs often have the so-called "double subject" construction. Malagasy does not.

6) TPLs do not have dummy subjects. This is also the case in Malagasy. But it is also the case in many rather subject prominent languages, as indeed relatively few languages have dummy subjects.

7) TPLs exhibit common discourse deletion of topic NPs when the referent is clear from context. As for our discussion of NP-Drop in Malagasy, Malagasy seems to have this property to some extent, though it appears not to be limited to deletion of topics.

As regards these general properties, then, Malagasy does not appear to be very topic prominent, although it is perhaps somewhat more topic prominent than, for example, English.

2.   Specific properties of topic NPs

Of the properties specific to topic NPs, we distinguish two "positive" properties and three "negative" ones.

2.1 Positive properties

1) The topic is old information, and so obligatorily definite.

2) The topic is in some sense the center of attention.

The subject NP in Malagasy appears to have both these properties in main clauses. The restriction that many major syntactic processes apply only to subjects, however, does mean that the choice of subject is governed by additional principles other than merely being the center of attention. Thus, while we may raise an embedded subject to object, the principle center of attention may still be the subject of the matrix verb. Nonetheless, restricted to main clauses, Malagasy subjects are topics.

2.2 Negative properties

1) Topics do not trigger verb agreement. And Malagasy subjects do not, as noted above.

2) Topics do not necessarily bear selectional restrictions to the verb. Since locatives, instrumentals, benefactives, and temporals, etc., can be advanced to subject in Malagasy, it is clear that surface subjects do not necessarily bear any selectional restriction to the verb.

3) The "role" of the topic NP cannot be predicted by the verb form. By and large, not so in Malagasy. The verb form does tell us whether the subject NP is an underlying actor, goal, intermediary, or "circumstantial" complement. Thus, up to a tolerable level of ambiguity, the verb form does allow us to predict the underlying role of the derived subject.

With regard to the specific properties of topics, then, it appears that Malagasy subjects are rather topic like, though clearly less so than in the paradigm cases (e.g., Lisu) cited by Li and Thompson. We conclude, somewhat weakly, then, that while Malagasy is clearly less topic prominent than, for example, Lisu, it is probably more topic prominent than in languages like English.

Notes

1. For many informants, an- is obligatory before proper name direct objects. It also usually occurs with objects beginning with /i/. (/i/ itself functions in a few cases as a proper name marker, namely for those which are not constructed with Ra-. The use of Ra- may be largely restricted to the major dialect, merina, from which all the data in this paper are drawn.

Interestingly, an- also functions as a locative marker meaning "at" and occurs very frequently in place names. Thus Antsirabe is morphemically an- "at" + sira "salt" + be "big" = "at the place of great salt" (there are many mineral springs in Antsirabe, which was used as a spa by the French).

an- also functions as the predicate of possession, as in (i).

(i)   an-dRabe io
        at   Rabe that
        "That is Rabe's"

2. We will ignore in this paper the considerable morphophonemic complexity involved in adding the man- prefix. For a thorough discussion of Malagasy morphology, see Rajemisa-Raolison (1966).

3. We can, however, correctly form an NP by adding a definite article ny "the" to a passive VP. But the result is semantically a relative clause, not a nominalized VP.

(i)   ny angalarina
             +pass
        the stolen
        "the stolen ones/things"

This type of NP formation can occur with any intransitive stative predicate.

(ii)   ny eto
        the here
        "the ones (who are) here"

(iii)   ny mena
        the red
        "the red ones"

4. The formulation of Passive as Direct Object ==> Subject (Perlmutter and Postal, 1974) is obviously not general enough. It would require at least another transformation "Circumstantial ==> Subject" which would replicate most of Passive. Further, it is not easy to see how the "endpoint" vs. "intermediary" distinction would be made.

A more general formulation would be to specify a universal hierarchy of accessibility to advancement to subject, advancement to object, etc. Universal constraints on the interaction of these advancement possibilities would have to be given. (For one such suggestion, see Trithart 1975.) Then there would be only one advancement rule, "Advance(X)." Which positions X were advancable would vary with the language, though where they would advance to would be predictable, or at least constrained, by universal principles. And the language specific features of an advancement would (hopefully) be predictable from the role that the advancee, X, played. At the moment, however, these universal formulations remain to be worked out.

    5. The cleft construction in Malagasy presents an additional complication pointed out in Gross (nd). It is possible for a cleft subject to be apparently indefinite, or at least to occur without a definite determiner. Thus from (i) we can apparently form (ii) (but not (ii).

(i)   manasa lamba   Rasoa
        +act
        wash   clothes Rasoa
        "Rasoa is washing clothes"

(ii)   lamba   no   sasan–dRasoa
        clothes cleft wa

(ii)   lamba   no   sasan–dRasoa
                      +pass
        clothes cleft wash by–Rasoa

(iii)   *lamba   no   manasa Rasoa
                      +act
        clothes cleft wash   Rasoa

"clothes are being washed by Rasoa/clothes are what Rasoa is washing/clothes are what Rasoa is washing"

Thus the underlying object lamba "clothes" must be a subject when cleft, but it seems to violate the general requirement that subjects are definite. The meaning of (ii), however, is somehow generic. That is, "clothes" does not have the specific indefinite reading. Rather it answers a question like "What sort of thing is Rasoa washing?" The most natural pronominal form of (ii) would be (iv), which uses the "impersonal" pronoun izany "that" rather than the definite pronoun izy "it," or izy-io "it-inanimate"

(iv)   izany no   sasan–dRasoa
        that   cleft wash by–Rasoa
        "That is what Rasoa is washing"

This fact is further support for the claim that the requirement that subjects be definite is a surface constraint. See Existential Sentences, Section 2.2.3, for additional support for this claim.

6. One informant in fact included <u>manaiky</u> itself in this sub-class. Clearly the limits of the sub-class must be further researched, but its existence is not in doubt. All that is in doubt is whether the sub-class is coextensive with the entire class or not.

7. We cannot tell to what extent the difficulty with 113b is one of "mere" performance or not. Clearly R-O should be cyclic, as it feeds other cyclic transformations, e.g., Passive. But note that 113b does contain two <u>ho</u>- phrases. Now the <u>ho</u>- complementizer is clearly homophonous with the benefactive marker (as well as the future tense marker-- indicating not yet realized action?). It may be the case, then, that the remainder of the clause from which the NP was raised is itself being assimilated to an NP position in the sentence. (Note that such clauses in English are preceeded by an item homophonous to the indirect object marker, e.g., "John believes Fred <u>to</u> have signed the petition.") But in Malagasy a sentence cannot contain two benefactives.

(i)   *manasa lamba   ho an'i Bosy ho   an-dRabe aho
        wash   clothes for   Bosy for   Rabe I
        "I am washing clothes for Bosy for Rabe"

Thus, according to informants, (i) cannot be forced to mean "At Rabe's request, I washed clothes for Bosy (who was sick)."

8. Furthermore, the putative underlying sentential subject of 123a does not in any way behave like a subject, even by the limited tests that usually apply to sentential subjects. Thus it cannot take question particles (i), it cannot be questioned (ii), and it cannot form What-Cls (iii).

(i)   *toa ve manasa lamba   Rasoa
        seem ? wash   clothes Rasoa
        "Does it seem that Rasoa is washing clothes?"

(ii)   *Inona no   toa
        what cleft seems
        "What seems?"

(iii)   *izay toa
        what seems
        "whatever seems"

R-S on this formulation would appear to be obligatory, to say the least. But this rather looks like a rationalization for a bad analysis to begin with. A preferable analysis, in our

opinion, would be one in which the small class of words including toa, etc., are not underlyingly verbs with sentential
subjects (note that as verbs they would be highly anamolous--
taking no tense marking, no voicing distinctions, no imperatives, etc.) but rather are some kind of adverb or verb
operator. Thus the underlying structure would be [$_{VP}$toa
manasa lamba] Rasoa, and so Rasoa would be an underlying subject and have the subject properties as predicted.

    9. As examples of agent control of Equi in Philippine
languages are not given in Schachter (this volume), we illustrate this point here (examples from Schachter, personal communication).

(i)   binalak   ng   babae-ng   mamalengke
        +goal focus   +actor focus
        planned   agent woman-linker go-marketing
        "A/the woman planned to go marketing"

The corresponding sentence in which an ang-NP controls Equi
is:

(ii)   nagbalak   ang babae-ng   mamalengke
        +actor focus   +actor focus
        planned   foc woman-linker go-marketing
        "The woman planned to go marketing"

TOWARDS A UNIVERSAL DEFINITION OF "SUBJECT"*

by

Edward L. Keenan

*Research for this paper was supported by a grant (#2994) from the Wenner-Gren Foundation and a grant from the Social Science Research Council in Britain.

I   The Problem

In this paper I will attempt to provide a definition of
the notion "subject of" which will enable us to identify the
subject phrase(s), if any, of any sentence in any language.
Such a definition is needed in universal grammar in
order for the many universal generalizations which use this
notion to be well defined. For example:

1   Accessibility Hierarchy (Keenan and Comrie, 1972): NPs
     on the upper end of the AH, given below, are univer-
     sally easier to relativize than those on the lower end.
     Thus some languages (Ls) have relative clause forming
     strategies which apply only to subjects; other Ls have
     strategies which apply only to subjects and direct
     objects, others have ones which apply only to the top
     three positions on the AH, etc.

     Subj > Dir Obj > Ind Obj > Obl > Gen > Obj of Comp

2   Functional Succession Principle (Perlmutter and Postal,
     1974): If one NP can be raised out of another then it
     assumes the grammatical relation (subject of, direct
     object of, etc.) previously borne by the other.

3   Advancement Continuity Principle (Johnson, 1974c;
     Trithart, 1975; Keenan, 1975a): If a L can advance
     (e.g., via operations like Passive) NPs low on the AH
     to subject then it can advance all intermediate posi-
     tions to subject. Thus if a L has a locative voice
     (e.g., the school was seen Mary at by John) then it
     necessarily has a direct object (= Passive) voice.

Clearly generalizations like 1-3 determine constraints
on the form, and substance, of possible human languages. But
to verify them and determine their universality it is necessary to be able to identify subjects, direct objects, etc., in
a principled way across Ls. If we use different criteria to
identify subjects in different Ls then "subject" is simply not
a universal category and apparently universal generalizations
stated in terms of that notion are not generalizations at all.
In addition, absence of identifying criteria for subjects,
etc. makes verification of putative universals like 1-3
difficult. Counter examples can be rationalized away by
merely saying that an offending NP is not "really" a subject,
etc. Finally the claim that we have primitive intuitions
concerning which NPs are subjects founders, like all arguments from intuition, when the intuitions of different individuals do not agree. For example, it would appear that
George (1974) and Kennan and Comrie (to appear) have differ-

ent intuitions concerning which NPs are subjects of simple
transitive sentences in Dyirbal (Dixon, 1972).

II.0 Defining "Subject of"

We are not free to define a notion like "subject" in
any way that suits our purposes. There is a large body of
lore concerning the notion, and any proposed definition must
at least largely agree with the traditional, and to some
extent, pretheoretical usage of the term. Our approach then
will be to collect a large and diverse set of cases from
different Ls in which our pretheoretical judgments of subjecthood are clear. Then we shall attempt to abstract from
this set a set of properties which are characteristic of subject NPs and then try to determine some combination of the
characteristic properties which will be jointly necessary and
sufficient to pick out the subject of an arbitrary sentence
in an arbitrary L in a way that is in conformity, of course,
with our pretheoretical intuitions in the clear cases.

However, even a cursory examination of subjects across
Ls reveals that in many Ls subject NPs are characterized by
properties which are not only <u>not</u> universally valid, they
are peculiar to the particular L in question. For example,
in Latin, subject NPs carry a characteristic case marking
(the nominative). But that particular ending probably occurs
as a nominative marker in no other L; there is no universal
nominative case marker. And in Malagasy (Malayo-Polynesian;
Madagascar) subjects characteristically occur clause finally,
whereas in most Ls subject NPs precede the other major NPs
within clauses. Nonetheless, we do want to say that the
prima facie evidence that an NP is the subject of some sentence in Latin is that it is nominative, and in Malagasy that
it is clause final. Consequently we want to phrase a universal definition of "subject" in such a way as to allow that
different Ls may use language specific means to mark subject
NPs. This we shall do in the following way:

First, universal means of distinguishing a privileged
subset of sentences in any L will be given. These sentences
will be called the <u>semantically basic sentences</u> (henceforth
b-sentences) and their subjects will be called <u>basic subjects</u>
(henceforth <u>b-subjects</u>). Then we shall attempt to provide
universally valid criteria for identifying subjects of b-
sentences in any L. Once the b-subjects have been identified
in any particular L then the full set of properties characteristic of b-subjects in that L can be determined. So in
some Ls b-subjects may have a certain case marker, or position, or they may exhibit a very specific type of transforma-

tional behavior, or even have semantically specific properties. Finally, once the full complement of b-subject properties has been determined for a given L, subjects of non-basic
sentences will be defined to be those NPs, if any, which present a clear preponderance of the properties characteristic
of b-subjects. Thus in any given L, subjects of non-basic
sentences may present very few of the universal properties of
subjects, but still be clearly identifiable as subjects in
that L since they possess very many of the language specific
properties of b-subjects in that L.

Note further, that on this type of definition, subjects
of certain sentences, and more generally of certain sentence
types, will be more subject-like than the subjects of others.
The reason is that they will exhibit more of the complement
of properties which characterize b-subjects in general. Thus
the subjecthood of an NP (in a sentence) is a matter of
degree.

In addition, it seems to me that subjects in some Ls
will be more subject-like than those of other Ls in the sense
that they will in general, present a fuller complement of the
properties which universally characterize b-subjects. Very
possibly, for example, European Ls are more subject oriented
than those Sino-Tibetan Ls discussed by Li and Thompson (this
volume).

II.1 The Definition of Basic-Sentence in a Language

4 For any Language L,

   a. a syntactic structure x is <u>semantically more basic</u>
   <u>than</u> a syntactic structure y if, and only if, the
   meaning of y depends on that of x. That is, to
   understand the meaning of y it is necessary to
   understand the meaning of x.

   b. a sentence in L is a basic sentence (in L) if, and
   only if, no (other) complete sentence in L is more
   basic than it.

Concerning 4a, there is no simple way of determining
whether some sentence e.g. is more basic than another since
such a determination requires that we understand the meaning
of the two sentences. So some cases will surely be problematic. But many cases we feel are quite clear. E.g., <u>John is</u>
<u>a linguist</u> is clearly semantically more basic than <u>Fred</u>
<u>thinks that John is a linguist</u> since we cannot understand the
meaning of the latter without understanding that of the former. If we didn't know what <u>John is a linguist</u> meant, we
wouldn't know what Fred is thinking. Further, each of the

following structures is semantically more basic than all of
those which follow it: John sang, John sang off-key, John
didn't sing off-key, the fact that John didn't sing off-key,
some newspaper reported the fact that John didn't sing off-
key, some newspaper which reported the fact that John didn't
sing off-key, etc. The relation more basic than (henceforth
MBT is transitive. If x MBT y, and y MBT z, then x MBT z.
For if we need to know the meaning of x in order to know that
of y, and that of y is required in order to know that of z,
then clearly we can't understand the meaning of z without
understanding that of x. Note however that the meanings of
two different structures may simply be independent, so neither
need be more basic than the other (1). E.g., the meaning of
John's leaving surprised everyone neither depends on nor is
dependent upon the meaning of if anyone screams Mary will
faint.

Concerning 4b, the b-sentences in any L are defined to
be the maximally basic structures having the category "sentence," although we do require that a sentence be in the set
of b-sentences if the only other sentences more basic than it
are "too context dependent" for their meaning (that is, they
do not express a "complete thought"). The intent here is to
rule out cases where the only NPs occurring in b-sentences
would be pronouns. Thus in many Ls, if not in English, it is
arguably the case (Keenan, 1972a) that pronominal sentences
like he hit him are more basic than ones like John hit Bill.
Compare e.g. 5a and 5b from Swahili.

5   a.   a-   li-   m-   piga
         3sg   past-3sg   hit
         human   human
         subj   obj
         "he hit him"

    b.   Juma a- li- m- piga Faru
         Juma he-past-him-hit   Faru
         "Juma hit Faru"

Sentence 5b differs in meaning from 5a solely in that the
reference of the pronominal elements in 5a is made more specific. To determine e.g. the truth of 5b we must first
determine the reference of the pronominal elements as Juma
and Faru, and then determine that 5a is true. So we can't
really understand the meaning of 5b without being able to
understand that of 5a, so 5a is plausibly more basic than 5b.
Nonetheless 5a is "imcomplete" in that it does not really
tell us who is being talked about. Plausibly then no complete
sentence in Swahili is more basic than 5b, or 5a, so both of
these are among the b-sentences in Swahili (although the

basicness of the tense marking in the example would have to be further considered).

II.2 Some General Properties of Basic Sentences

While there is no mechanical procedure for identifying the set of b-sentences in a L, the set will generally have several characteristic properties which makes the identification of a fairly large set of relatively basic sentences reasonably easy.

Thus, in general, if the meaning of one structure depends on that of another, then the form of that structure also depends on the form of the other. In general then we expect that b-sentences will exhibit the greatest morphological and syntactic potential of the sentences in a L. Thus they will present the greatest range of tense, mood, aspect, mode, and voice distinctions. They will have the greatest privileges of occurrence: they will accept the greatest range of verbal and sentential modifiers; they will be the easiest to embed and adjoin to other sentences, the easiest to nominalize and internally reorder, the easiest to relativize, question and topicalize out of, the easiest to pronominalize and delete into, etc. In other words, the b-sentences are roughly the "simplest" sentences syntactically. For example, 6a below is clearly more basic than 6b.

6 a. Mary doesn't like John anymore

   b. As for John, Mary doesn't like him anymore

For clearly, to understand 6b we need to know what <u>Mary doesn't like him anymore</u> means, where <u>him</u> is understood to refer to John. But this is exactly what we need to know to understand 6a. The syntactic test for b-sentencehood then predicts that 6a has more potential than 6b, which is clearly correct. E.g., we can nominalize 6a, <u>Mary's not liking John anymore</u>, but not 6b, we can cleft on <u>Mary</u> in 6a, <u>It is Mary who doesn't like John anymore</u>, but not in 6b, etc.

Semantically speaking as well, b-sentences can be expected to have certain characteristic properties. They will e.g. generally be structurally unambiguous. The reason is that in general the operations which form less basic structures from more basic ones affect only part of the meaning of the less basic one. And since b-sentences in general have fewer "parts" than non-basic ones they present fewer possibilities for the interpretation of which parts are understood to be affected by the operation.

Consider for example passives in English. Although the case is less clear than the ones considered earlier, we consider passives to be, in general, less basic than the corresponding actives. For what we must understand about the relations between the participants and the action in a passive sentence is basically the same as that of the active. But in addition, in the passive we require that the referent of the object NP be identifiable independently of that of the agent (see 3.0 in Section II.3 for more discussion), that is, loosely, the patient is more of a topic in the passive than the active sentence. Assuming then that actives are more basic than passives then we would expect from our argument above that at least some ways of forming complex structures from simpler ones would engender more ambiguities when applied to passives than to actives. And this seems to be the case. Consider e.g. the addition of adverbials like <u>willingly</u> in 7. (See Lasnik and Fiengo, 1974, for some discussion.)

7 a. The police arrested John willingly

   b. John was arrested by the police willingly

In 7a no indication that John was a willing participant in the act is given. But 7b is ambiguous according as it was John or the police who acted willingly. A further instance, more problematic in some respects, concerns pairs like

8 a. Every boy kissed a girl

   b. A girl was kissed by every boy

Sentence 8b seems to me more clearly ambiguous according as it was necessarily the same girl or not. But 8a seems to me to have only the reading on which it is not necessarily the same girl (though it might be). Not everyone agrees with these judgments, however, and in the (remarkable) absence of a clear pretheoretical intuition concerning what it means to say that a structure is ambiguous the case is hard to argue.

    In addition to the general absence of structural ambiguity b-sentences may be expected to have other semantic properties which more directly depend on the fact that they are the semantically primitive sentences. Thus they will in general be declarative and affirmative. Further in many cases non-basic sentences seem semantically richer than the more basic ones whose meaning they depend on. It is tempting to think that the b-sentences of a L will always be among the least informative sentences of the L (Talmy Givón, personal communication). But while this is often so, I think it not always the case. Thus there is a class of non-basic sentence forming operators whose semantic effect is precisely to attenuate to some degree the more specific meaning of the more basic sentences. Thus I would want to say that <u>John left</u> is

more basic than John didn't leave, John might have left, and
It is possible that John left. Yet all the latter sentences,
in some intuitive sense, tell us less about how the world is
than does the more basic John left.

Another measure of the semantic "simplicity" of b-
sentences concerns their relative freedom from presupposition.
Thus many of the clear examples of presuppositional structures
(see e.g. Keenan, 1970) involve embedded sentences (e.g. relative clauses, factive complements of verbs like realize,
surprise, etc.). And generally if a sentence contains an
embedded sentence then its meaning depends on that of the
embedded one and so it is not basic. Unfortunately, however,
b-sentences are not presupposition-free. The use of proper
names and demonstrative NPs in b-sentences normally carries
the presupposition that the NP has a referent. It seems to
me likely however that aside from lexically specific presuppositions of basic predicates the presuppositions of b-
sentences can be limited to existence claims.

A final characteristic of b-sentences: It is not necessarily the case that a b-sentence of one L will translate as
a b-sentence of another L. The basic predicates of different
Ls codify somewhat different concepts. So e.g. the president
resigned receives no b-sentence translation in Ls spoken only
by peoples which do not have the sort of political institutions referenced by terms like president and resign. A more
interesting question perhaps is whether the syntactic types
of b-sentences are the same across Ls. The question is an
empirical one and the answer is not obvious. E.g. while passive sentences may be non-basic in English they are at least
much more basic (see Note 1 for this more generalized use of
"basic") in many Malayo-Polynesian Ls such as Maori, Tagalog,
Malagasy. In particular the privileges of occurrence of passives in those Ls are much greater than in English. Further,
syntactic properties which are obligatory in some Ls may only
be optional in others, and possibly then not present in the
b-sentences of those Ls. E.g. in English all sentences, and
therefore the b-sentences, are marked for tense/aspect. But
in Indonesian such marking is optional. Sentences lacking
such marking occur frequently in discourse (and in isolation,
in translation). Plausibly then the b-sentences in Indonesian express "naked propositions" whose meaning is made more
specific by the addition of tense/aspect adverbs in non b-
sentences.

II.3 Characteristic Properties of Basic Subjects

Below we present a list of 30 odd properties which subjects characteristically possess (if any NP in the L does).

The properties may be pragmatic, semantic, or syntactic. And of the syntactic ones, some concern properties internal to a single sentence and others concern the relation between a b-sentence and some modification of it. The properties are organized into groups and sub-groups according to their relationships. Plausibly in many cases properties in the same sub-group are not independent (although they can be verified independently) but we cannot at the moment show this, in general.

Furthermore, we have not been able to isolate any combination of the b-subject properties which is both necessary and sufficient for an NP in any sentence in any L to be the subject of that sentence. Certainly no one of the properties both necessary and sufficient, and in our statement we point out counter examples both ways for properties which might have been thought fully general.

Consequently we must have recourse to a somewhat weaker notion of definition. We shall say that an NP in a b-sentence (in any L) is a subject of that sentence to the extent that it has the properties in the properties list below. If one NP in the sentence has a clear preponderance of the subject properties then it will be called the subject of the sentence. On this type of definition then subjects of some b-sentences can be more subject-like than the subjects of others in the sense that they present a fuller complement of the subject properties.

Note further that on this type of definition "subject" does not represent a single dimension of linguistic reality. It is rather a cluster concept, or as we shall say, a multi-factor concept. Many basic concepts in social science are multi-factor concepts. Thus one's intelligence is a combination of abilities (Thurstone, 1956): verbal comprehension, immediate recall, numerical manipulation, visualizing flat objects in three dimensions, and deductive reasoning. So one can be intelligent in different ways and to different degrees. And being a subject is, we claim, more like being intelligent than, for instance, like being a prime number. The factors which compose the concept of subject might coincide with our groupings of properties, though in the worst of cases each of the 30 odd properties would be an independent factor.

II.3.1 The Subject Properties List (SPL)

We present four major categories of b-subject properties. The first, Autonomy Properties, is by far the largest.

A.   Autonomy Properties

    1. Independent Existence. The entity that a b-subject

refers to (if any) exists independently of the action or property expressed by the predicate. This is less true for non-subjects. Thus in a student wrote a poem the existence of the poem is not independent of the act of writing, whereas the existence of the student is. Other examples: someone committed a booboo, defined a term, proved a theorem, etc.

2. Indispensability. A non-subject may often simply be eliminated from a sentence with the result still being a complete sentence. But this is usually not true of b-subjects. E.g. John hunts lions (for a living), John hunts (for a living), *hunts lions (for a living).

Several ergative Ls however do appear to permit unspecified subject deletion. Notably Tongan, Eskimo, and Tibetan.

Tongan (Churchward, 1953)

9 a. Na'e tamate'i 'e   Tevita 'a Koliate
        killed   subj David obj Goliath
        "David killed Goliath"

    b. Na'e tamate'i 'a Koliate
        killed   obj Goliath
        "Goliath was killed"

(NB: 'a marks both transitive objects and intransitive subjects.)

3. Autonomous Reference. The reference of a b-subject must be determinable by the addressee at the moment of utterance. It cannot be made to depend on the reference of other NPs which follow it. Thus if two NPs in a b-sentence are to be stipulated as being the same in reference it will either be the non-subject which gets marked (perhaps deleted) or the rightmost NP. Thus in English we could never say He-self admires John$_i$ for John$_i$ admires himself, for in the first sentence the reference of the subject cannot be determined independently of that of a following NP, so the subject would not be autonomous in reference. Note however that in Ls in which b-subjects can follow other NPs it is sometimes (but not always) possible for a leftmost NP to control the reference of the subject. The subject's reference is still determinable at the moment of utterance since it is stipulated as being coreferential to an NP whose reference has already been established.

Tagalog

10 a. sinampal ng lalake ang   babae
        +pass
        hit-by Agt man   subj   woman
        "the woman was hit by a/the man"

   b. sinampal ng lalake ang kaniyang sarili
      hit-by Agt man   subj his   self
      "the man hit himself"

Here subject NPs i.e. ang phrases (see Schachter, this volume,
for some problems with the notion of "subject" in Philippine
languages) normally may preceed or follow objects, as long as
both follow the verb. But when objects are definite (as they
are if specified as being coreferential to a definite sub-
ject--and subjects are always definite in Tagalog) they must
be presented as surface subjects. And in this case, contrary
to the usual pattern, the subject must follow the agent
phrase. Thus its reference is determinable at the moment of
utterance.

Samoan (ex. from Chapin, 1970)

11 a. sa   sogi e   ioane ia lava
       past cut Agt John he emph
       "John cut himself"

     b. sa   sogi ioane ie ia lava
        past cut John Agt he emph
        "John cut himself"

Here again the NP whose reference is dependent on that
of another occurs second. In 11a that NP is plausibly a subject if that sentence is passive. If Samoan is ergative in
this case then John is the subject and it is the object that
is pronominalized. But then in 11b it would be the ergative
subject whose reference was not independent. But on either
analysis the reference of the b-subject is always determinable at the moment of utterance. In fact, we know of no
clear counter examples to this property. So autonomous reference is plausibly a universal necessary condition on b-
subjecthood.

    But this property does seem to understate the facts a
bit. Thus in many Ls in which the subject may follow the
objects, such as Malagasy, Gilbertese, and Tzeltal (see
Keenan 1974), the reference of the subject cannot be made to
depend on that of the object, even though the object precedes
and so the property of autonomous reference would not be
violated. E.g.

Malagasy

12 a.   manaja   tena Rabe
         respect self Rabe
         "Rabe respects himself"

b. *manaja   an-dRabe   tena/ ny   tena-ny
   respect acc-Rabe   self   the self-his
   "He-self respects Rabe"

There are several other properties of subjects that plausibly are related, more or less closely, to the property of autonomous reference.

3.1 b-subjects are always (in general, not necessarily in every sentence) among the possible controllers of stipulated coreference, either positive or negative (see Keenan, 1975a for discussion). Thus,

3.1.1 b-subjects in general can control reflexive pronouns. And in some Ls control of reflexives within clauses is largely restricted to b-subjects. E.g. in Malagasy, Japanese, and German.

3.1.2 b-subjects are among the possible controllers of coreferential deletions and pronominalizations. Note:

13 a. John$_i$ talked to Bill$_j$ for awhile and then he$_{i,j}$ left
   b. John$_i$ talked to Bill$_j$ for awhile and then $\emptyset_{i,*j}$ left

3.1.3 The possible controllers of backwards pronominalization and deletions include b-subjects. E.g.

14 a. When he$_{i,?j}$ got home, John$_i$ talked to Bill$_j$
   b. On $\emptyset_{i,*j}$ arriving home, John$_i$ talked with Bill$_j$

3.2 The NPs which control "switch reference" indicators include b-subjects. Thus in the Eastern Highlands Ls of New Guinea as well as among many groups of American Indian Ls, subordinate verbs will carry either one of two affixes according as their subject is coreferential or <u>not</u> coreferential with the <u>subject</u> of some other clause. E.g.

Hopi (ex. from Pam Munro, personal communication)

15 pam navoti:ta pam mo:titani$\{$ $^{-q}_{-qa?e}$

   he   thinks   he   win $\{$ $^{-diff. subj.}_{-same subj.}$

   "He thinks that he will win"

Thus if the suffix -q is chosen on the subordinate verb the person who is being thought about is necessarily different from the one doing the thinking, whereas they are the same if the suffix qa?e is chosen. For further discussion see Keenan, 1975a; Jacobsen, 1967, Munro, 1974a. Our point here is only that control of switch reference is largely limited to subjects. We note however that switch location markers rather than switch subject markers are reported for Angaataha (Huisman, 1973) in New Guinea.

3.3 The NPs which control verb agreement, if any, include b-subjects. (For an argument that verb agreement is, at least historically, pronominalization, see Givón, this volume). We further note that verb agreement across clauses appears restricted to subjects, though this is only attested to our knowledge for the Ls of the E. New Guinea Highlands. See Keenan, 1975a for examples.

Since verb agreement is one of the properties which people have considered definitional of subjects, it is worth noting that it fails to be a necessary condition on b-subjecthood since in very many Ls verbs agree with no NP. E.g. Swedish, Sinhalese, Afrikaans, Thai, Vietnamese, Chinese, Japanese, Maori, Malagasy, etc. Similarly verb agreement fails to be a sufficient condition on b-subjecthood since in many Ls verbs agree with NPs in addition to subjects, e.g. Basque, Chinook, Arosi (Melanesian), Jacaltec (Mayan), Kapampangan (Philippine), Hungarian, Georgian, Blackfoot, Machiguenga (Arawak; Peru), etc. Note further that in a very few cases verbs may agree with objects but not with subjects. E.g. Avar (Caucasian), Mabuiag (Australia), and, very partially, Hindi.

3.4 b-subjects are the easiest NPs to stipulate the coreference of across clause boundaries.

3.4.1 If reflexive (i.e. essentially anaphoric) pronouns in sentence complements of verbs of thinking can be bound by NPs in the matrix clause then these pronouns can always occur in subject position in the complement clause.

Yoruba

15 Ojo$_i$ ro   po   on$_i$ / ò$_j$ mu sasa

Ojo$_i$ thinks that he$_i$ / he$_j$ is clever

"Ojo thinks that he is clever"

3.4.2 NPs which can be coreferentially deleted in sentence complements when coreferential with matrix NPs always include subjects.

Malagasy

16 Nihevitra Rabe$_i$ fa   notadiavin-   dRasoa $\emptyset_i$ / izy$_j$

thought   Rabe$_i$ that was looked-for-by Rasoa $\emptyset_i$ / he$_j$

"Rabe thought that (he) was being looked for by Rasoa"

Similarly the most likely NPs to under Equi-NP deletion include b-subjects.

17 a. John$_i$ wants $\emptyset_i$ to help Fred

    b. *John$_i$ wants Fred$_j$ to help $\emptyset_i$

3.4.3 The NPs which can be coreferentially deleted across coordinate conjunctions include b-subjects.

18 a. John$_i$ went up to Fred$_j$ and $\emptyset_i$ insulted him$_j$

    b. *John$_i$ went up to Fred$_j$ and he$_j$ insulted $\emptyset_i$

    c. *John$_i$ went up to Fred$_j$ and he$_i$ insulted $\emptyset_j$

3.4.4 The NPs which can be coreferentially deleted under verb serialization generally include b-subjects.

<u>Akan</u> (ex. from Schachter, 1974a)

19 Kofi de   aburew$_i$ $\emptyset_i$ gu   nsum

    Kofi takes corn   flows water-in

    "Kofe pours corn into the water"

3.5 Absolute Reference. In the overwhelming majority of cases, if a b-sentence is true then we understand that there is an entity (concrete or abstract) which is referred to, or has the property expressed by, the b-subject. Thus John worships the Sun Goddess, if true, requires that there be someone referenced by "John" but does not require that there exist a Sun Goddess, in distinction to The Sun Goddess worships John, where Sun Goddess is a subject. Other examples of this sort: John bought a present for the prime minister, cursed Santa Claus, is talking about the perfect woman, etc.

Even if the subject of a basic (or at least fairly basic) sentence is "indefinite" we still normally understand that there must be an object with that property, whereas this is often not the case for indefinite object phrases. Thus a student owes John a report, if true, does imply the existence of a student but not of a report. Other examples of not necessarily referential objects: John ordered a beer, painted a pony, resembles an elephant, imitates alchemists, etc.

However if weather expressions are basic, and they appear to be, then absolute reference is not a necessary condition on b-subjecthood, since weather expressions may have "dummy" i.e. non-referential subjects. E.g. it is raining, etc. Most b-sentences distinguish between an object spoken about and some property it has or some activity it is involved in. But in simple statements about the weather there appears to be little distinction between the activity (the raining) and the object involved (the rain). So in general, if a weather sentence a subject-predicate form (they may consist of just a single verb) then either the subject will be semantically weak or the predicate will (e.g. Russian <u>rain goes</u>).

3.6 Presupposed Reference. Certain operations like negation, questioning, and conditionalization (below) have the effect of suspending the reference of normally referential NPs. The reference of a b-subject however is harder to suspend under these operations. Thus (from Donellan, 1966) <u>De Gaulle was the king of France</u> implies the existence of a king, but <u>De Gaulle wasn't the king of France</u> need not have this implication. It can be used simply to deny that De Gaulle had a certain title or office. On the other hand, <u>The king of France wasn't de Gaulle</u>, where <u>the king of France</u> is subject, still does imply the existence of a king. Analogous claims hold for the pair <u>Was de Gaulle the king of France?</u> and <u>Was the king of France de Gaulle?</u>. Conditionalization of the following sort (Larry Horn, personal communication) seems to work the same way. Thus <u>if the coup had succeeded de Gaulle would have been the king of France</u> does not imply the existence of a king of France, whereas <u>if the coup had succeeded the king of France would have been de Gaulle</u> does, and the difference between the two sentences is merely that in one <u>the king of France</u> is a subject and in the other it isn't.

Note of course that if b-sentences may have indefinite subjects, e.g. <u>a student attacked John</u>, then under the most natural form of denial, <u>no student attacked John</u>, the existence implication of the subject is not preserved. It is not clear to me at the moment whether we want to consider such sentences as basic in English or not (see 3.8). Arguably understanding such a sentence requires that we understand <u>there exists a student</u>, or perhaps <u>students exist</u>, and so sentences with indefinite subjects are perhaps not basic.

3.7 Metaphoric Idioms. These often suspend the reference or existence implication of NPs. And again, b-subjects are the most reluctant of the major NPs to abandon their reference. Thus in <u>the man took the bull by the horns, let the cat out of the bag, has an ace up his sleeve, is looking for a needle in a haystack</u>, etc. only <u>man</u> has its literal referent. Normally if the reference of a b-subject is suspended in an idiom then so also is the reference of the other major NPs. E.g. <u>the fat's in the fire</u>, <u>the early bird gets the worm</u>, etc.

3.8 Topic. b-subjects are normally the topic of the b-sentence, i.e. they identify what the speaker is talking about. The object they refer to is normally known to both

speaker and addressee, and so is, in that sense, old information. If a L has special topic or old information markers
(Japanese, Korean) they will most naturally be used on subjects.

3.9 "Highly Referential" Nps, e.g. personal pronouns,
proper nouns, and demonstratives can always occur as subjects.
In some Ls, e.g. Malagasy, Tagalog and Philippine Ls generally, Kinyarwanda (by and large) and probably much of Bantu
generally, subjects of b-sentences must be definite. And in
Tagalog, direct objects must be indefinite. So if an NP
position cannot be filled by definites that is evidence that
it is not a subject, and if it cannot be filled by indefinites
that is evidence that it is a subject.

3.10 Subjects are the most natural targets of "advancement" (Perlmutter and Postal, 1974) transformations. That is,
roughly, if a L can assign to one NP in a clause the position,
case marking and verb agreements appropriate to another NP in
the clause then it can assign the position, case marking, and
verb agreements of subject NPs to non-subjects (and we say
that that NP has been advanced to subject). E.g. Passive in
English advances direct object to subject. Many Ls, e.g.
Bantu generally (see Keenan 1975a), can advance NPs to object.
But all such Ls can also advance NPs to subject, whereas the
converse fails. So subjects are the most accessible targets
of advancement processes. (See Johnson, 1974c for discussion.)

3.11 Basic, or relatively basic, subjects have wider
scope, logically speaking, than non-subjects. (See Keenan,
1974 for justification of why this is related to the autonomous reference property of subjects.) Thus suppose we are
given a sentence in some L containing the main verb kiss and
two quantified NPs, every man and a woman. If the truth of
the sentence most naturally allows that the choice of woman
can vary with the choice of man, as in every man kissed a
woman, then that is evidence that every man occurs as a subject. But if, on preference, the choice of woman must be
made independently of that of the man, as in a woman was
kissed by every man, then that is evidence that a woman is
subject.

3.12 b-subjects are normally the leftmost occurring
NP in b-sentences. Note, however, that in a few cases Ls
have fairly fixed word order in which the subject follows one
or more objects. E.g. Malagasy, Tzeltal (Mayan), Mezquital
Otomi (Oto-Manguean; Hess, 1968), Gilbertese (Micronesian).
Note also Ls like Walbiri (Hale, 1967) in which basic word

order appears totally free, and Ls like Tagalog in which NPs in b-sentences occur in any order as long as they are all after the verb.

3.13 The NPs which can be relativized, questioned, and cleft include b-subjects. In some Ls, e.g. Malagasy, only subjects can be relativized.

3.14 The NPs whose possessors can be relativized, questioned, and cleft include b-subjects. E.g. in Tagalog, it appears, possessors of objects cannot be questioned, but possessors of subjects can.

3.15 A personal pronoun is rarely present in a position relativized if that position is a b-subject one. So even if a L, like Arabic, Fijian, or Welsh, normally presents such pronouns, as in <u>the girl that John gave the book to her</u> it will not normally say <u>the girl that she gave the book to John</u> but only <u>the girl that gave the book to John</u>.

3.16 b-subjects are always among the NPs in a L which can undergo raising. E.g.,

20 a. John believed Fred to have struck the gatekeeper

  b. *John believed the gatekeeper Fred to have struck

3.17 Subjects can always be expressed by morphologically independent, possibly emphatic, pronouns. These pronouns can be conjoined with full NPs.

3.18 NPs which "launch" floating quantifiers (e.g. <u>all the boys left</u>/<u>the boys all left</u>) include subjects (Perlmutter and Postal, 1974).

B. Case Marking Properties

1. b-subjects of intransitive sentences are usually not case marked if any of the NPs in the L are not case marked (Greenberg, 1966). Exceptions: in Motu (Malayo-Polynesian, New Guinea; Capell, 1969) both transitive and intransitive subjects are marked (different markers) but transitive objects are not marked. Similarly in several Yuman Ls, e.g. Mojave (Munro, 1974) direct objects are unmarked but transitive and intransitive subjects are marked (some marker).

2. The NPs which change their case marking under causativization include b-subjects.

Malagasy

21 a. manasa lamba Rasoa
            +acc +nom
        wash clothes Rasoa
        "Rasoa is washing clothes"

   b. mampa-nasa lamba   an-dRasia Rabe
          +acc   +acc   +nom
       cause-wash clothes Rasoa   Rabe
       "Rabe is making Rasoa wash clothes"

3. The NPs which change their case marking action nominalizations include b-subjects. Usually a b-subject changes
to a possessor case or the non-subject agent case. E.g.,

22 a. John swept the floor

    b. John's sweeping (of) the floor

    c. the sweeping (of) the floor by John

C. Semantic Role

   1. The semantic role (Agent, Experiencer, etc.) of the
referent of a b-subject is predictable from the form of the
main verb (Li and Thompson, this volume). Some semantic
category information, e.g. animacy, is uaually also predictable, but semantic restrictions on objects are usually more
specific than those on subjects (Edith Moravscik, personal
communication).

   2.1 b-subjects normally express the agent of the action, if there is one. Note that this property cannot be
used to identify subjects of sentences in which there is no
agent, and sentences of that sort will be numerous among the
b-sentences in a L. E.g. <u>John is tall</u>, <u>is in Chicago</u>, <u>is a
plumber</u>, etc. Note further that in Dyirbal (Australia;
Dixon, 1972) the NP in b-sentences which has most of the Reference properties cited in B.3 above does not express the
agent. See Keenan and Comrie (1972) for justification of
this point. Thus expressing the agent, if there is one, does
not seem even a sufficient condition on b-subjecthood.

   2.2 Subjects normally express the addressee phrase of
imperatives. But note that in many Malayo-Polynesian Ls,
e.g. Maori and Malagasy, imperatives are frequently in non-
active forms, and the addressee phrase, if present, appears
as a passive (or other type of non-active) agent phrase. E.g.,

<u>Maori</u> (ex. from Hale, 1968)
23 tua- ina   te raakau raa   (ke   te   toki)
    fell-passive the tree   yonder (with this ax)
    "be chopped down (by you) the tree there (with this ax)"
    ="chop down the tree there (with this ax)"

   2.3 b-subjects normally exhibit the same position,
case marking, and verb agreements as does the causer NP in
the most basic type of causative sentence. Again we note

however that Maori and Malagasy causatives are very easily
passivized, so the agent there is not a surface subject.

Malagasy
24 a. mampianatra angilisy an-dRabe aho
        cause-learn English acc-Rabe I
        "I am teaching Rabe English"

    b. ampianara-ko   angilisy Rabe
        cause-learn-by me English Rabe
        "Rabe is taught English by me"

D.   Immediate Dominance

The b-subject is immediately dominated by the root node
S. This is the type of definition given in Aspects (Chomsky,
1965) and may represent a necessary condition on b-subjecthood. It is difficult to tell, since, as far as I know,
there is no simple test to determine whether or not a subpart
of a sentence is a constituent.

For example, in many Ls person/number particles or
tense/aspect particles form a higher level constituent with
the main verb. By parity of reasoning then they should form
higher level constituents with the subject in those Ls in
which they are bound to the subject. If so, then the subject
would not be immediately dominated by the root node S. Thus
in Fred's the one, or Fred'll go, only Fred is the subject,
not Fred'll or Fred's. In the English cases, however, such
sentences are arguably not basic. But in Luiseño (Uto-
Aztecan) or Walbiri they arguably are.

Luiseño (ex. from Hyde, 1971)
25 Xwaan-po   wiiwish   naachaxan-an
    Juan -2 or 3 sg acorn mush eat   +future
         +future
    "Juan will eat acorn mush"

Further, it is quite clear that being immediately dominated by the root S is not a sufficient condition for b-
subjecthood. We note three categories of cases where more
than one NP is arguably immediately dominated by the root S.

1. Ls whose unmarked word order is VSO. While these
are a minority type across Ls, they probably constitute between 5 to 10 percent of the worlds Ls. Thus, Malayo-Polynesian: Maori, Samoan, Tongan. Semitic: Classical Arabic.
Celtic: Welsh, Breton, Scots Gaelic. Nilo Saharan: Maasai.
American Indian: Chinook (Penutian), Jacaltec, (Mayan),
Zapotec (Oto-Manguean).

2. In some Ls the relative position of subject and object is completely free. E.g. Walbiri (Australia), Tagalog (Philippines).

3. In many Ls cited as SOV there is little evidence for a VP constituent. E.g. in Turkish, Hindi, and Persian wh-interrogative words are naturally placed in the object slot, even if they question the subject NP. In Tibetan this placement seems obligatory. For arguments that Japanese lacks a VP constituent see Hinds (1974). For arguments that VP constituency is limited to SVO Ls see Schwartz (1972).

III.0 The Utility of a Multi-Factor Concept of "Subject"

Using the Subjects Properties List (SPL) one can, we claim, identify the b-subjects in any L. Then the full set of properties characteristic of b-subjects in any given L can be determined, and then subject NPs of non basic sentences can be identified. While complex, this means of identifying subjects does permit us to verify the universal generalizations stated in terms of "subject" at the beginning of this paper.

This concept of subject has, however, another use: It suggests that we look for cross-L generalizations which express relations between the properties in the SPL. One such generalization, which seems to us to be valid is the following: In general, non-basic subjects are never more subject-like than basic subjects. In other words, in any given L, subjects of non-basic sentences frequently do not have quite as full a complement of the subject properties as do subjects of b-sentences. One reason for this is that syntactically derived subjects are, by our tests, usually somewhat less subject-like than b-subjects. To consider just the case of passive sentences in English, note that the subject does not express the agent, need not have the property of autonomous existence (e.g. a beer was ordered by John does not imply the existence of a beer), and controls reflexives less easily than b-subjects (*?John was insulted by himself). This suggests that operations which create derived subjects may do so to a greater or lesser extent.

Thus perhaps some properties of subjects are harder to pass on to underlying non-subjects than are others, and conversely some properties will be harder for NPs which have lost their subject status to lose. If the subject properties can be ordered in terms of how hard they are to pass on to other NPs then we would have another universal generalization. Namely, if an operation which derives a complex sentence from a simpler one passes on one of the subject properties to another NP in the derived sentence then it necessarily passes on all the properties higher on the ordering than the given property. Further, if certain transformations were actually defined as subject creating ones (e.g. Perlmutter and Postal, 1974 would define Passive as an operation which converts an object to a subject) then each such transformation could simply be marked according to how far down the ordering of subject properties it could extend in assigning subject properties to another NP. So some operations would be more subjectivizing than others.

An attempt to empirically support any particular ordering of the 30 odd subject properties, however, would go beyond the bounds of this paper. So we shall here simply suggest a hypothesis concerning a partial ordering of the properties, and then present some evidence in support of that hypothesis, acknowledging that more evidence would be needed for our conclusions to be definitive.

III.1   The Promotion to Subject Hierarchy (PSH)

Coding Properties	>	Behavior and Control Properties	>	Semantic Properties
position > case marking > verb agreement		deletion, movement, case changing properties, control of cross-reference properties, etc.		Agency, autonomous existence, selectional restrictions, etc.

The claim made by the PSH is that if an NP in a derived sentence is assigned any of the three categories of subject properties then it is assigned all the higher categories. And within the category of coding properties, if an NP acquires the verb agreements characteristic of subjects then it must also acquire the case marking and position; and if it acquires the case marking then it must acquire the position. So the characteristic position of subjects is the easiest property to assign to a derived subject. Further, the PSH also claims that the subject properties assigned to a derived subject may be any initial sequence of those on the PSH. So a derived subject may e.g. present the coding and behavioral properties of b-subjects but not the semantic properties (which is very frequently the case. We know of no clear cases in which derived subjects become e.g. agents. However, the direct and inverse theme markers in Algonkian need to be further investigated in this regard. See Frantz, 1971 for some discussion.) Or a derived subject may present only the coding properties of b-subjects. Thus derived subjects may look like subjects without behaving like them, but if they behave like subjects then they look like subjects.

We should stress here that the relation we postulate between coding and behavioral properties represents merely a hypothesis. It states that while a derived subject may have the position and morphological characteristics of b-subjects, it is possible that they do not raise, or delete, or relativize, or control co-reference, etc. in the way characteristic of b-subjects. E.g. Maori has a transformation which moves certain types of possessives, namely pronouns, preverbally. But it applies only to active subjects, not to subjects of passive sentences. In Jacaltec (Craig, 1975) certain types of Equi apply only to active (i.e. basic) subjects, and do not apply to subjects of passive sentences. And so on. But our evidence in support of the hypothesis is only impressionistic, and not systematic. (See Timberlake, this volume, for more systematic support for this claim from N. Russian.)

We have, however, more evidence in support of the ordering of the coding properties, which we shall refer to as the Coding Hierarchy (CH).

III.2 The Coding Hierarchy

The first prediction made by the CH is that some derived "subjects" in some Ls would take on the characteristic position of b-subjects in those Ls but not acquire the characteristic case marking and verb agreements.

Some support for this claim comes from Biblical Hebrew in which subjects characteristically occur after the verb, are not case marked, and trigger verb agreement. In passive sentences, however, two major patterns appear (Richard Steiner, personal communication). Either the derived subject has the full complement of coding properties, as in 26a, or it has only the position, retaining its former case marking, and the verb going into a 3rd sg, masc. form, so not agreeing with anything, as illustrated in 26b.

26 a. lɔ-'ellɛ teḥɔleq   hɔ- 'ɔrɛṣ   (Numbers 26:53)
        to-these shall-be-divided the-land
              fem. 3sg, pass. fem, 3sg.

    b. bĕ-ɣorɔl   yeḥɔleq   'ɛθ hɔ- 'ɔrɛṣ
        by-lottery shall-be-divided acc the-land
              masc. 3sg pass.   fem. 3sg.
                                    (Numbers 26:55)

A second piece of supporting evidence comes from Kimbundu (Bantu, spoken in Angola. Data from Talmy Givón. See also

Chatelain, 1888). The basic word order in Kimbundu is SVO.
NP subjects and objects are not case marked, and verbs agree
with subjects only. In the passive, however, the derived
subject moves to subject position, but does not trigger the
expected subject agreement. Rather that is filled by the 3pl
human prefix (regardless of the person and number of the
derived subject). The verb does, however, take the direct
object pronoun which does agree with the derived subject. The
clear inference here is that this type of passive developed
from an "impersonal" active of the sort they saw John, then a
topicalization of the object yielding, John, they saw him,
and finally the possibility of reintroducing the agent, John
they saw him by me. Sentences 27a-27d illustrate the relevant data.

27 a. nga-mono Nzua
        I -saw John

    b. nga-mu- mono
        I -him-saw
        "I saw him"

    c. Peter na Dick a-   mono Nzua
        Peter and Dick they-saw John
        "Peter and Dick saw John"

    d. Nzua a-   mu- mono kwa meme
        John they-him-saw by me
        "John was seen by me"

This type of passive may be characteristic of a group of West
Bantu Ls (it occurs as well in Luvale; see Horton, 1949) and
is distinct from the suffixal passive characteristic of
Swahili, Shona, Luganda, etc.
    A third piece of very interesting support for the pre-
diction comes from Maasai (Nilo-Saharan. All data from
Tucker and Mpaayei, 1955). The basic word order is VSO, and
in passives the old object occurs in the immediate postverbal
position, as predicted.

28 e-nyer Tinkoi nkishu
    3-love Tinkoi cattle
    "Tinkoi loves cattle"

29 e-rik-i   nkishu aainei lmurran
    3-led-pass cattle by   young-men
    "my cows will be led by the young men"

Further, full NPs are case marked, by tone!

30 a. e-dol embártá
        3-see horse (acc)
        "he sees the horse"

    b. e-dol embartá
        3-see horse (nom)
        "the horse sees him"

And in passive sentences the derived subject retains the accusative tone. (We mark tone only where it is relevant to our discussion.)

31 e-isis- i   Sirónkà
    3-praise-pass Sironka (acc)
    "Sironka is praised"

Compare:

32 a- dol Sirónkà
    1sg-see Sironka
    "I see Sironka"

Note as well that passive sentences in Maasai are intransitive in that no NP other than the derived subject is needed for the sentence to be complete.

As regards agreement, verbs normally only agree with subjects. (Note that the prefixal e- indicates either 3sg or 3pl subject agreement.) However, when the direct object is first or second person singular, the agreement prefix changes. Compare:

33 a. áa-   dol (nánú)
        3sg subj   (acc) 1sg
        1sg obj
        "he sees me"

    b. á-   dol (nanú)
        1sg subj see (1sg, nom)
        "I see him"

Thus we can tell by the verb marking whether a first or second person singular functions as a subject or an object. And in passives, when the derived subject is first or second person singular, it triggers the verb prefix appropriate to 3 person subject and 1sg or 2sg object!

34 áa-   rik-   i
    3sg subj nauseate-pass
    1sg obj
    "I am nauseated"

Thus it appears that in Maasai the passive verb always has a 3 person subject agreement marker, reminiscent of the Kimbundu

passive in this respect, and that where the passive verb
agrees with the derived subject, namely when it is 1sg or 2sg,
it agrees with it as though it were an object. Thus the
derived subject retains its object case marking and verb
agreements, acquiring only the position of subject.

Final, but in some ways less convincing, evidence for
our claim comes from Ls like Latin and German. Here when
Passive advances accusative direct objects to subjects they
acquire the full complement of coding properties. However, a
few verbs in both Ls take their direct objects in the dative
case. And in these cases one could argue that when the verbs
are passivized the dative NP takes on the subject position
but retains its dative case marker and does not trigger verb
agreement, the verb reverting to a 3sg form. (Exs. from
Gildersleeve and Lodge, 1913.)

35 mihi invidetur (ab aliquo)
    1sg envied   (by someone)
    dat +pass
    "I am envied"

The problem with this data for our analysis, as Paul Postal,
(personal communication) pointed out, is whether there is any
real sense in which the underlying object has acquired the
subject position (it very clearly has not taken subject case
or subject verb agreement). This is perhaps better analyzed
as an impersonal passive in which the old subject gets demoted
to oblique status and the verb becomes passive, but nothing
gets promoted to subject position, the other NPs merely remaining where they were. (See Keenan, 1975b for some discussion of impersonal passives.)

The PSH might also be interpreted to mean that we could
expect to find Ls in which subjects demoted by operations
like Passive lost only their characteristic position but not
their case marking or verb agreements. That is the subjects
properties that are the hardest to acquire are also the hardest to give up. At the moment we have relatively little
evidence for this, although the Maasai data, if further analyzed, might support it. Further, the following example from
Luiseño (Munro, 1974a) is suggestive.

36 ?ivi no-naawu-ki   no-yo   po-lo?xa
    this my-dress-poss my-mother her-make
    "this dress was made by my mother"

Now Luiseño is dominantly SOV, with objects case marked, usually. Subjects trigger a kind of agreement which may tack
onto the end of the first word in the sentence or, in more
complex sentence types, show up as a possessive-type affix on

the verb. Now, as the passive above illustrates, the demoted
subject loses its sentence initial position, but remains
nominative and appears to trigger a kind of possessive agreement on the verb. Historically speaking this is natural,
since it would appear that passives in Luiseño, at least this
type, are similar to those in Chemehuevi (Munro, 1974b),
which look like <u>this dress is what my mother made</u>, where
<u>mother</u> would be expected to remain nominative and trigger
verb agreement.

III.3 A second prediction made by the Coding Hierarchy is
that derived subjects in some Ls would acquire the position
and case of b-subjects, but not trigger the verb agreements
characteristic of b-subjects. We have less evidence for this,
but some nonetheless which is suggestive.

    Thus in Welsh, active (=basic) sentences present VSO
order. Verbs agree only in person with subjects (although
they also agree in number with pronominal subjects). Neither
full NP subject nor object are case marked but pronominal
constructions for subjects and objects are different. In
passives, the old object now occurs in the expected subject
position, and uses the nominative pronominal construction,
and so to that extent, acquires the case of b-subjects. But
the derived subject does not trigger verb agreement. The
verb becomes morphologically invariable. (Examples below
from Bowen and Jones, 1960).

37 a. gwelir fi
          is-seen I
          "I am seen"

      b. gwelir di
          is-seen you
          "you are seen"

      c. dysgir   Cymraeg gan yr athro
          is-taught Welsh by the teacher
          "Welsh is taught by the teacher"

    A second example which supports this point in the CH
concerns cases where a demoted subject loses its position and
case marking, but does not lose its ability to trigger verb
agreement. Kapampangan (Philippines; all data from Mirikitani, 1972) is illustrative here. Kapampangan is verb initial in basic word order and seems to permit a fair degree of
freedom of word order of full NPs after the verb, although
this cannot be judged with certainty on the basis of the
data in Mirikitani, op. cit. Surface subjects take the preposition <u>ing</u> and other NPs have other prepositions. Verbs

agree with subjects in b-sentence types.

38 sumulat ya ng poesia ing lalaki
    write   he obj poetry subj boy
    "the boy will write a poem"

In passive sentences the former object gets assigned the subject pre-position and appears to take the subject position
(but position may not really be criterial of subjects), and
it acquires the capacity to trigger verb agreement. The old
subject, while losing its position and most importantly its
pre-position, still retains the possibility of triggering
verb agreement. Thus the derived verb now agrees with two
NPs, the derived subject and the former subject.

39 isulat   na ya (=ne) ning lalaki ing poesia
    be-written it he   agent boy   subj poem
    "the poem was written by the boy"

Another example of a L in which demoted subjects still trigger
verb agreement is Achenese (Lawler, 1975).

III.4 Some Possible Counter Examples

     One interesting class of possible counter example to
the claims in the CH is presented by the possibility of promoting to subject various types of locatives in Bantu Ls.
Consider 40a and 40b from Chicewa. (See Trithart, 1975 for
discussion.)

40 a. John a- nathamang-ir- a   ku sukulu
        John he- ran   dir-indic to school
        "John ran to school"

    b. ku sukulu ku- nathamang-idw- ir- a-   ko
        to school loc- ran   -pass-dir-indic loc

            ndi John
            by John

        "School was run to by John"

It appears in 40b that the derived subject triggers verb
agreement and acquires the subject position but retains its
locative case marking. If so, this clearly violates the
claim of the CH. Note, however, that the subject agreement
it triggers is not one of the normal noun class markers, as
is the case for b-subjects. Rather, it is the locative marker
itself. This suggests that the original locative phrase ku
sukulu "to school" has been reanalyzed as a mere NP, the old
locative ku now being interpreted as the noun class marker.
Then the verb agreement is regular, and the subject no longer

carries an oblique case marker, and the CH is not violated. Further work is needed to determine whether this analysis receives any independent motivation.

A second counter example comes from Biblical Hebrew (again supplied by Richard Steiner, personal communication). While the general pattern for passives is as cited in Section 3.1 above (either the derived subject takes the position, case, and agreements of b-subjects, or else it only takes the position, retaining its case and the verb becoming 3sg), there are a very few cases in which a derived subject remains accusative but does trigger verb agreement.

41 wĕ- 'εθ ho- 'ɔh   lĕfɔnɔw   mĕvoʼɔrεθ
    and-acc the-brazier in front of him was-kindled
         fem 3sg   fem 3sg pass

It would appear then that Hebrew, at this stage, was in the midst of analyzing subjects of passive sentences as real objects. Sometimes all the surface, i.e. coding, properties are assigned to subjects, and sometimes not. In a large majority of cases where not all the coding properties are assigned to derived subjects the properties that are assigned are in accordance with the CH, but in a few cases this is not so. (Note incidentally, that the accusative NP which triggers verb agreement in 41 also occurs clause initially, plausibly not the subject position in Biblical Hebrew.)

This type of historical shift may also serve to rationalize a final counter example to the CH pointed out by Butler (personal communication) in which the evolution of impersonal constructions in Old and Middle English is discussed. Such constructions had a major NP which was dative/accusative and did not trigger verb agreement--the verb being fixed as 3sg. Such constructions survive in frozen expressions until somewhat later, e.g. me-thinks, if you please, etc. Now one of the ways the impersonal constructions were lost is that the surface dative/accusative was reanalyzed as a subject, becomes nominative and triggers verb agreement. Butler points out, however, that during the reanalysis "Constructions like the following occasionally turn up with think, seem, and ail: Me-seem my head doth swim. (1571. Damon and Pythias. 79.) ..." It appears then that during an historical transition in the reanalysis of a subject NP we can have NPs with subject position and verb agreements but which do not have subject case marking. Judging from Butler's use of "occasionally," however, we may infer that, like Hebrew, this violation of the CH was not the norm, but merely the reflection of an instability a surface pattern. Nonetheless the instability does lead to "occasional" violations of the CH and cannot be dismissed.

331

IV.0   Conclusion

We have attempted to provide a definition of the notion "subject of" which would be universally valid in the sense that it would allow us to identify subjects of arbitrary sentences from arbitrary languages. The definition we proposed, while cumbersome, does nonetheless allow us to verify many universal generalizations stated in terms of that notion. And in addition it has suggested further generalizations concerning universal properties of subjectivizing transformations.

Postscript: The information on the evolution of impersonal constructions in Old and Middle English communicated to me by Butler, cited on p. 331, is contained in an unpublished paper by Milton C. Butler, titled, "The re-analysis of impersonal constructions in Middle English."

Note

1. We might note, however, that in general the meaning of a non-basic structure will depend on the meaning of only finitely many other structures. We might take this number to determine the degree of basicness of the structure. Then any two structures can be compared with regard to basicness using the normal "greater than or equal to" relation. Thus the basicness of a structure x would be greater than or equal to that of y if and only if the degree of basicness of x is greater than or equal to that of y. In this way the relation more basic than can be extended to apply to all the structures in a L.

TOPIC AS A DISCOURSE NOTION: A STUDY OF TOPIC IN THE
CONVERSATIONS OF CHILDREN AND ADULTS* (1)

by

Elinor Ochs Keenan
Bambi B. Schieffelin

*We would like to thank the following kind people for their
assistance in and patience throughout the formulation of this
paper: Edward L. Keenan, Edward L. Schieffelin, Rich Frankel,
Gillian Michell, Martha Platt, Sharon Sabsay, Jim Heringer,
and Emanuel Schegloff.

I. Orientation and Goals

Topic has been described as a discourse notion (see, for example, Chafe 1972; Li and Thompson, this volume). However, there has been no systematic study in linguistics of the way in which topics are initiated, sustained, and/or dropped in naturally-occurring discourse. This paper addresses itself to this concern. It draws from notions developed by sociologists engaged in conversational analysis and integrates them with our own observations of the conversations of children and adults. Our observations include non-verbal as well as verbal contexts in which topics are entertained by interlocutors. On the basis of this record, the prerequisite steps for getting a topic into the discourse are characterized and a notion of discourse topic is defined.

In everyday conversations much of the talk that occurs concerns propositions about persons, objects or ideas. Moreover, when individuals, objects, etc., are not known to the hearer, the hearer initiates a series of fairly predictable exchanges directed at clarifying and locating the referent about which some claim is being made.

Consider, for example, the following exchange in which the speakers are eating dinner:

1   a. Bambi: It's coming out fast. (shaking salt on food)
    b. Elinor: What's coming out fast?
    c. Bambi: The salt.

In this exchange, Bambi assumes that Elinor is attending to her actions and is able to locate in the environment the referent of "it." Elinor, however, has not been attending to Bambi's action and cannot identify that referent. Further, Elinor had no clues from prior discourse; Bambi did not precede the utterance with talk about salt, e.g., "Pass me the salt." In other words, Elinor had no source for identifying the referent, and consequently, she did not understand what Bambi was talking about.

Clark (1973) has pointed out that when speaker-hearers engage in talk, they abide by a "Given-New contract," that is, the speaker is responsible for marking syntactically as "Given" that information that he thinks the listener already knows, and marks as "New" what he thinks the listener does not know. For example, it is appropriate for the speaker to use syntactic devices such as definite articles, pseudo-cleft constructions, and anaphoric pronouns when he thinks the listener knows the referent. Indefinite articles and cleft constructions appropriately mark the information that is New to the listener. The appropriate marking of Given and New is critical to the listener's comprehension of particular utter-

ances. Information marked as Given leads the listener to
search for its "unique antecedent" in memory or in the ongoing
situation. The listener "then integrates the New information
into memory at that point." (Haviland and Clark, 1974:513)

Analyses of spontaneous conversations show that listeners demand that the Given-New contract be adhered to. That
is, listeners will not accept as Given referents that they
cannot identify in terms of general knowledge, prior discourse
or present context. Speakers make an effort as well to insure that listeners can identify what or whom they are talking about. One device employed by the speaker (in English)
is to describe an object or individual using rising intonation. Sacks and Schegloff (1974) call such a construction a
"try-marker." The speaker leaves a short pause following
this construction in which the listener can evidence his recognition or non-recognition of the referent. Absence of a
positive listener response (uh huh, head nod, etc.) in this
pause indicates non-recognition. This in turn leads the
speaker to offer further try-markers in an attempt to elicit
a positive listener response.

2 a. A: ...well I was the only one other than than the
        uhm tch <u>Fords</u>?, Uh Mrs. Holmes Ford? You know
        uh//the the cellist?
   b. B: Oh yes. She's she's the cellist.
   c. A: Yes
   d. B: <u>Ye//s</u>
   e. A: Well she and her husband were there....
       (Sacks and Schegloff 1974:6)

Another such device is to overtly introduce a referent
into discourse such as "Do you remember Tom?" or "Do you remember the guy we met in Paris?" "You know those boots we
tried on yesterday with the fur lining?" or "Do you see that
chair over there?" and so on.

The point to emphasize here is that speakers are reluctant to make claims involving individuals or objects that
have not been or cannot easily be identified or recognized by
the hearer. That is, they are reluctant to add New information to the discourse if the objects or individuals to which
they are referring cannot be established as Given.

The phenomenon that we have been describing--establishing
referents--is a prerequisite for successful collaboration on
a DISCOURSE TOPIC. We take the term discourse topic to refer
to the PROPOSITION (or set of propositions) about which the
speaker is either providing or requesting new information.
E.g.,

3   Allison III, 20.3$\frac{1}{2}$ months

   a. Mother: (trying to put too large diaper on doll,
       holding diaper on) Well we can't hold it on like
       that. What do we need? Hmm? What do we need for
       the diaper?
   b. Allison: pin/

In 3 the mother is requesting New information about the proposition 'we need something for the diaper.' The proposition
thus constitutes a discourse topic. When Allison says "pin/",
she is providing the New information requested. The proposition attended to in both the question and the answer is the
same; thus the discourse consisting of that Question-Answer
pair has a single discourse topic.

When speaker and hearer are directing their utterances
to a particular proposition of this type, they are collaborating on a discourse topic. To collaborate on a discourse
topic, the hearer must know what proposition the speaker is
adding new information to or requesting new information a-
bout. If the speaker wants collaboration, he must select a
discourse topic that takes account of the listener's knowledge. That is, he must insure that the proposition that constitutes the discourse topic is known to or knowable by the
listener. There are several things the speaker can do to
this end: He can draw on general background knowledge he
shares with the listener; or he can draw on information available in the interactional setting; or he can draw on prior
discourse in the conversation at hand. (Garfinkel 1967)

In practice we find that much conversational space is
taken up by exchange in which speaker and hearer attempt to
establish a discourse topic. In these exchanges, the speaker
tries to make the discourse topic known to the hearer.

We propose here a dynamic model of the way in which
speakers establish a discourse topic. The model represents
the initial work involved in making a discourse topic known.
We suggest that getting a discourse topic established may involve such basic work as securing the attention of the listener and identifying for the listener objects, individuals,
ideas, etc. (Atkinson 1974) contained in the discourse topic.

The model is based on child-adult and child-child conversations. However, the application of the model is not
limited to these interactions. The model can be applied to
adult-adult discourse as well. Child language simply offers
abundant and salient instances of this behavior.

II. Data Base

The data used in this study are drawn from three major

sources. The first source consists of six 30-minute video tapes of a mother and her child (16.3 months-34 months). The first four of these tapes have been analyzed by Lois Bloom in One Word at a Time (1973). The second major source consists of 25 hours of audio- and video-taped interactions of twin boys with one another and with adults. The tapes were made over a period of a year, from 33 months to 45 months. (See Keenan, E.O. 1974, 1975a, 1975b; Keenan, E.O. and Klein 1975 for other analyses of this material.) Transcriptions of the videotaped data included extensive nonverbal information. The contextual information forms an integral part of our analysis. The third major source consists of transcriptions of audio-taped conversations between five adolescents and a therapist in five Group Therapy Sessions (GTS). These tapes were transcribed by Gail Jefferson.

In addition, we wish to acknowledge several other sources: L. Tweed has provided transcriptions of audio-tapes of monolingual and bilingual children interacting with adults (Infant Development Study UCLA). E. Schegloff and members of his graduate seminar on conversational analysis have provided illustrations from adult-adult discourse.

III. Defining Discourse Structure

Before defining discourse topic more formally, let us describe in brief the context in which discourse topics emerge, i.e., the discourse itself. For the purpose of this analysis, we take a discourse to be any sequence of two or more utterances produced by a single speaker or by two or more speakers who are interacting with one another (at some point in time and space). Discourses may evolve or develop in several ways.

For example, a stretch of discourse may contain a series of linked discourse topics. The discourse topics are linked in the sense that the propositional content of each is drawn from one or more of the utterances already produced in the discourse. These utterances, unless otherwise challenged (Givón 1975), form a "presupposition pool" (Venneman, in press) out of which discourse topics are selected.

The discourse topics may be linked in at least two ways:
1. Two or more utterances may share the same discourse topic. This is the case in question-answer pairs, for example (see 3), and in some repetitions; e.g.,

4 Allison IV, 22 months

    a. Allison: (looks in box, finding calf) cow/
    b. Mother: A cow!
    c. Allison: (holding calf) moo/↑ (2)

    d. Mother: Moo, cow says moo.↓

In this example the same discourse topic is sustained from speaker to speaker in lines 4.2 and 4.b. Both utterances provide new information relevant to an object Allison is attending to, the new information being that the object that Allison has noticed is "a cow." Likewise, utterances in 4.c and 4.d appear to address the same discourse topic, i.e., 'The cow (Allison is holding) makes some sound.' Allison provides the information that the cow makes the sound "moo" and her mother confirms this claim in her subsequent utterance.

    We refer to a topic that matches exactly that of the immediately preceding utterance as a COLLABORATING DISCOURSE TOPIC. Sequences in which a discourse topic is sustained over two or more utterances are TOPIC COLLABORATING sequences. (For other examples of topic collaborating sequences see examples 3 and 5.)

    2. Discourse topics may take some presupposition of the immediately preceding discourse topic and/or the new information provided relevant to the discourse topic preceding (all part of the presupposition pool) and use it in a new discourse topic. For instance, the dialogue between Allison and her mother in example 3 continues as follows: (We repeat the initial turns for convenience)

3 (continued)
    a. Mother: Well, we can't hold it on like that. What do we need? Hmm? What do we need for the diaper?
    b. Allison: pin/
    c. Mother: pin. Where are the pins?
    d. Allison: home/

Here, the discourse topic is established at 3.a ('we need something for the diaper') and is collaborated on in 3.b. In 3.c Allison's mother poses a different but related question (of immediate concern). It is related in the sense that the proposition about which information is being elicited, "the pins are somewhere," presupposes that 'there exists pins,' a presupposition that is assumed as well in Allison's preceding claim, "pins/ (are needed for the diaper)." This new discourse topic becomes collaborated on in 3.d by Allison's providing the new information requested.

    We refer to a topic that uses the preceding utterance in this way as an INCORPORATING DISCOURSE TOPIC. Sequences in which a discourse topic integrates a claim and/or presupposition of an immediately prior utterance are TOPIC-INCORPORATING sequences (3).

We refer to stretches of discourse linked by topic collaboration and/or topic incorporation as CONTINUOUS DISCOURSE.

Continuous Discourse	
Collaborating Discourse Topic	Incorporating Discourse Topic

On the other hand, we may find discourse in which the discourse topics of each utterance are not linked in any obvious
way, i.e., where the discourse of one utterance does not draw
on a claim and/or presupposition of the preceding utterance.
In these discourses a speaker disengages himself from a set
of concerns addressed in the immediately preceding utterance
and turns to an unrelated set of concerns. (See examples 8,
9, 14) We refer to such stretches of discourse as DISCONTIN-
UOUS DISCOURSE. (Keenan and Schieffelin, ms 1975)

Discontinuous discourse may have two types of discourse
topic. The first type reintroduces a claim and/or a discourse
topic (or part thereof) that has appeared in the discourse
history at some point prior to the immediately preceding utterance. (It could draw from the discourse topic and/or claim
of the last utterance but one.) We call such discourse topics
RE-INTRODUCING TOPICS. Constructions such as "concerning...",
"as for...", "as far as...is concerned (goes)", may mark this
sort of discourse for adult English speakers, along with remarks such as "getting back to...", "like you said before..."

A second type of discontinuous discourse topic introduces a discourse topic that is in no way related to the preceding utterance, and does not draw on utterances produced
elsehwere in the discourse. We refer to such topics as INTRO-
DUCING DISCOURSE TOPICS.

Discourse			
Continuous		Discontinuous	
Collaborating Discourse Topic	Incorporating Discourse Topic	Re-introducing Discourse Topic	Introducing Discourse Topic

IV.A Defining Discourse Topic

We turn our attention now to a more detailed definition
of discourse topic. As noted previously, a discourse topic

is a proposition (or set of propositions) expressing a concern (or set of concerns) the speaker is addressing. It should be stressed that each declarative or interrogative utterance in a discourse has a specific discourse topic. It may be the case that the same discourse topic is sustained over a sequence of two or more utterances. We have described these as topic collaborating sequences (see section III). On the other hand, the discourse topic may change from utterance to utterance, sometimes drawing on the previous utterance (incorporating topic) and sometimes not (introducing topic, re-introducing topic).

In determining the discourse topic of an utterance, it is useful to determine the purpose or reason behind each utterance. Why did the speaker say what he did? Although we may never have access to the more remote or global motivations underlying a particular utterance, we can make some headway by determining what low-level, immediate considerations the speaker may be attending to.

These low-level considerations are found in the utterance context (verbal and non-verbal). For example, an utterance may be produced in response to something heard (prior utterance) or in response to something witnessed or noticed. We may think of some utterances as providing an answer to some specific question related to something in the utterance context. For example, if a speaker hears a crashing noise, he may respond "An accident." This utterance may answer the implicit question, 'What was that noise?' Similarly, when in 4 Allison notices an object and says "cos/", she may be answering the question, 'What is this object?'

The listener "constructs" questions of this sort in interpreting utterances addressed to him: The listener takes the utterance and relates it to some aspect of the utterance context. For example, in 4 Allison's mother takes Allison's utterance "cow/" and relates it to the non-verbal context, in particular, to what Allison is noticing. The listener then must ask how the utterance is related to that feature of the context, that is, the listener asks, 'What is the speaker informing me of? Is the speaker providing me with an explanation of some phenomena? An evaluation of some phenomena? A description of some phenomena? An identification of some phenomena? Or what?'

Another way of putting this is to say that the listener tries to determine what question the speaker may be answering. For example, in interpreting Allison's utterance "cow/," Allison's mother tries to construct a plausible question Allison may be providing the answer to. In this case, the mother interprets Allison's utterance, "cow/" as possibly an

343

answer to the question, 'What is this object?'

Of course what the listener considers to be the question the speaker is answering may not always correspond to the question the speaker believes he is answering. In conversations between adults and children, it is often the case that an adult will not be able to determine exactly what question the child is addressing. (See section V.B-E) Or, a child may not understand the point, i.e., the question behind an adult's utterance, and so cannot respond relevantly. Adults often have to make their questions explicit. We treat this behavior in fact as a defining characteristic of speech directed to small children. (Section IV.E considers this and related behaviors.)

We will refer to the question (or set of questions) an utterance is a response to as the QUESTION OF IMMEDIATE CONCERN.

In many cases the question of immediate concern is explicit, i.e., a question actually appearing in the discourse. The question can be produced by one conversational partner and answered by the same speaker. For example,

5 Allison V, 28 months
     a. Allison: (looking into box) What's in here?/
     b. Allison: (reaching into toy box) It's a pig!/

On a more abstract level, the question of immediate concern can be treated as a theoretical construct. The linguist may use it to explain more precisely what a discourse topic is: The discourse topic is based on the question of immediate concern. It is the proposition or set of propositions that the question of immediate concern presupposes. It has been shown (Keenan and Hull 1973) that such a set of propositions can always be represented by a single one, one that implies all the others. Let us call this presupposition the PRIMARY PRESUPPOSITION. Hence, in example 3 line a, the discourse topic is derived from the question of immediate concern, 'what do we need for the diaper?' The discourse topic is the primary presupposition of this question, namely, 'we do need something for the diaper.' And in example 4 line a, the discourse topic is the primary presupposition of 'what's in here?', namely, that 'something is in here.'

Questions of immediate concern themselves request specific information about the primary presupposition (the discourse topic). Informative responses to these questions presuppose the primary presupposition (the discourse topic), and provide new information relevant to the question posed. For example, in 3 Allison's response (3.b) presupposes the primary presupposition ('we need something for the diaper') of

the question, and adds the new information, "pin/". In 5,
Allison's response (5.b) presupposes the primary presupposition 'something is in here' of the question asked and adds
the new information that something 'is a pig.' The discourse
topics for these responses are the primary presuppositions of
the questions of immediate concern.

$$\begin{array}{ll} \text{Declarative} \\ \text{(Response)} \end{array} = \begin{array}{l} \text{New Information} \\ \text{relevant to Q of} \\ \text{immediate concern} \end{array} + \begin{array}{l} \text{Primary Presupposition of Q} \\ \text{of immediate concern} \\ \text{(Discourse Topic)} \end{array}$$

IV.B Determining the Question of Immediate Concern

Of course, not all questions of immediate concern appear
overtly in a discourse. A declarative utterance may address
itself to some _implicit_ question of immediate concern. In
this case, the linguist may not have access to the information needed to determine the question. In many instances the
question of immediate concern may be understood by speaker
and hearer because it arises from their shared background
knowledge. Where a declarative utterance initiates a social
interaction, the linguist may have no clue whatsoever as to
what the discourse topic is. If A says to B: "Tom called today," the question of immediate concern may be 'What happened
today?' or 'Who called today?' or 'What did Tom do today?' or
'What's the good news?' or some other question relevant to
speaker and/or hearer.

The more information about the speaker's and hearer's
shared knowledge the observer has access to, the easier it
will be for him to determine the question of immediate concern and the discourse topic. Given that questions of immediate concern may be drawn from both verbal and non-verbal
dimensions of the immediate situation, it is to the advantage
of the observer to have available the most complete record of
the situation.

IV.B.1 Non-verbal Context

For example, interlocutors often make reference to some
non-verbal action or event that they are observing or experi-
encing, or that they have just observed or experienced.
Speakers assume that listeners perceive these occurrences.
They treat these occurrences as old or given information for
the listener, and base questions of immediate concern on them.
If the listener has not in fact perceived the event or activity in question, he will not be able to determine the discourse topic. For instance, in 1 above, Bambi incorrectly
assumed that Elinor was aware that Bambi was putting salt on
her food (with a saltshaker). Bambi's discourse topic was

something like, 'it (the salt) comes out (in some manner).'
The question of immediate concern was, 'In what manner does
it (the salt) come out?'. However, Elinor could not reconstruct the discourse topic because she had not noticed, i.e.,
identified, the referent of "it" and so did not understand
exactly what claim is made by the primary presupposition 'it
(the salt) comes out (in some manner.'

Just as interlocutors may fail to determine the discourse topic, because they have not attended to a relevant
phenomenon, so the linguist may repeat this experience if he
does not have access to a visual record. The need for a
visual record is, in fact, critical for understanding children's utterances in these terms. In interpreting the communicative intentions of young children, others (adults and
other children) make full use of ongoing context. What constitutes the discourse topic may only be reconstructable on
the basis of observing what the child is doing, where the
child is looking, and so on.

6   Allison IV, 22 months
    (Mother and Allison are sitting on a big chair)
    a. Allison: (pointing at TV monitor, seeing herself)
        Baby Allison/
    b. Mother: Do you see Baby Allison?

For instance, in 6, it is critical to take into account
Allison's pointing at the monitor, seeing herself, in interpreting her utterance, "Baby Allison/". Among other things,
her pointing indicates she is aware of something being at a
designated location. Allison's utterance provides the information that that something is "Baby Allison/" (4). We can
think of "Baby Allison/" as new information being added to the
discourse topic 'something is there (where I am pointing).'
If we or her mother did not know that Allison was pointing,
we would not be able to reconstruct the discourse in this way.
The discourse topic could be different if Allison were patting
herself, playing with her doll or reaching for a cookie as
she produced her utterance.

IV.B.2   The Verbal Context

Another resource available to speakers for determining
discourse topic is the ongoing discourse itself. That is,
speakers often draw discourse topics from the dialogue as it
proceeds. They base their discourse topic on some proposition (or set of propositions) that has been produced in the
course of the conversation. In so doing, they may employ
either a topic-collaborating or a topic-incorporating strategy.

7   Adolescents GTS 4 (p. 31)
    (pause)
    a. Ther: There are such things as con-artists.
    b. Jim: I'm one.
    c. Ther: Are you?

For example, in 7, Jim employs a topic-incorporating strategy.
He uses the immediately prior proposition "There are such
things as con-artists" as a discourse topic. He adds the new
information that he is one of these "things" called con-
artists. (The proposition at 7.a represents New information
with respect to a prior discourse topic.)

This process of formulating discourse topics from prior
propositions is part of what it means for a speaker to make
his conversational contribution <u>relevant</u> to the current state
of talk (Grice 1975). Grice states that interlocutors usually expect one another to make their utterances relevant.
Interlocutors use the history of the discourse in making sense
of a particular conversational contribution. From our point
of view, interlocutors make use of the discourse history in
reconstructing one another's discourse topics. At least, a
listener assumes that a discourse topic is some proposition
relevant to the ongoing talk, because the listener assumes
the speaker is following the conversational norm of relevance.
For example, in 7, Ther assumes that Jim's discourse topic is
drawn from his own (Ther's) prior proposition because he
assumes Jim is responding relevantly to his utterance.

The constraints on when a relevant response is to be provided will vary across cultures and across situations. For
example, Philips (1974) notes that Wasco Chinook Indians in
speaking English, do not necessarily expect each turn in a
conversation to be relevant to an immediately prior turn.
Speakers often provide a relevant response to some proposition
long after the proposition first appeared in the discourse
(and after numerous intervening turns) without marking it in
any overt way (5).

IV.B.3   'Breaking and Entering'

If a speaker is conforming to the convention of making
his utterance relevant to those that precede his, then he
normally assumes that the listener can compute his discourse
topic. That is, he can assume that the listener knows to
turn to the discourse history to locate the discourse topic.
The speaker does not have to mark the discourse topic explicitly.

When a speaker produces a conversational contribution
that he realizes is not relevant to the discourse history

(i.e., an introducing discourse topic) or may not seem relevant (from the listener's point of view), then he is under some constraint to make the discourse topic known to the listener. Typically, the speaker marks a break in the continuous discourse, alerting the listener to the fact that the discourse topic may not follow from previous discourse. Speakers often announce a break with some metalinguistic remark such as "I am sorry to change the subject but..." or "Not to change the subject but..." and so on. These remarks are often accompanied by attention getting devices, e.g., hey!, listen!, look!, wait! (see sections V.B and V.D) along with hesitations and word searches (Sacks, 1968 ms).

8   Adolescents GTS 3 (p. 25)
    (pause)
    a. Ken: E-excuse me changin' the subject but didju hear
        anything about what happened Monday night?
        (pause)
    b. Dan: no, w-weren'tchu uh--
    c. Louise: What happened Monday night? (pause)
    d. Ken: Oh I came in here y'know, Mom and Dad decided
        I should...

Other remarks of this ilk are, "Before I forget, I have to tell you something" or "Hey, I heard a good joke."

9   Adolescents GTS
    (pause)
    a. Ken: hey,
            wait.
            I've gotta- I've gotta
            joke. (pause)
            What's black 'n white 'n
            hides in caves (pause)
    b. Roger: a' right I give up, what's black 'n white//
        'n hides in--
    c. Al: a newspaper.
    d. Roger: hhhh.
    e. Ken: no, (pause) pregnant nun.

In addition, discourse topics may be explicitly introduced into the discourse by the speaker. The speaker may, for example, pose a question that has as its primary presupposition the intended discourse topic.

10 Allison IV, 22 months
    (Allison had been wiping a chair, is now sitting with
    fingers in mouth, staring at the camera)
    a. Mother: What were we gonna do?
    b. Allison: eat/↑cookies/

In 10 Mother initiates a "new discourse topic" ('we were going to do something') by proposing a question of immediate concern that is not contingent on prior discourse.

In example 8, Ken introduces the discourse topic 'something happened Monday night' as a SECONDARY PRESUPPOSITION of the question, "Did you hear anything about what happened Monday night?" (the primary presupposition is that 'you (the addressee) either did, or did not, hear something about what happened Monday night') This strategy is a common one for speakers of English. Speakers often introduce discourse topics as secondary presuppositions of yes-no questions such as "Do you know what happened today?" "Did you see in the paper where Tom Dixon resigned?" and the like. Used in this way, these questions function primarily to direct the listener to attend to a "new" proposition.

The main point to be made here is that the speaker, in order to communicate felicitously, should make sure that the listener has sufficient resources to reconstruct the discourse topic. One body of resources is the discourse history itself. The speaker may assume that the listener knows this history as a co-creator of it (or witness to it). As long as the speaker bases his discourse topic on the preceding talk, he may assume his discourse is reconstructable. If the speaker wishes to focus on a concern that is not part of the discourse history, he may not be certain that the listener will realize what this concern is. In this case, it may be necessary for the speaker to 1) alert the listener that the speaker is turning to a different set of concerns, 2) introduce this set of concerns explicitly as a presupposition of a new question of immediate concern.

V. The Model

V.A Prerequisites for Establishing a Discourse Topic

The model we present here represents the interactional work involved in getting a discourse topic known to a listener. We claim that in order to determine a particular discourse topic the hearer minimally must:

1. Be attending to the speaker's utterance.
2. Decipher the speaker's utterance.
3. Identify those objects, individuals, ideas, events, etc., that play a role in the discourse topic.
4. Identify the semantic relations obtaining between referents in the discourse topic.

We may rewrite these prerequisites for topic establishment from the perspective of the speaker in the form of steps the speaker must take to make a discourse topic known to the

listener:
Step 1: The speaker must secure the attention of the listener.
Step 2: The speaker must articulate his utterance clearly.
Step 3: The speaker must provide sufficient information for the listener to identify objects, etc., included in the discourse topic.
Step 4: The speaker must provide sufficient information for the listener to reconstruct the semantic relations obtaining between referents in the discourse topic.

Steps 1 and 2 are general requirements on any successful communication. Steps 3 and 4 are more specifically prerequisites on topic establishment and might be restated as Felicity Conditions on the successful establishment of a discourse topic.

The steps described here may correspond to actual moves taken by speakers. These moves may take up varying amounts of conversational space. For example, if the attention of the interlocutor has already been secured prior to the utterance, if the utterance is comprehensible, and if relevant objects, persons, ideas, etc., and their semantic roles are known to the hearer, then all four steps may be completed in a space of a single utterance:

11 Adolescents GTS
(in context of a discussion on the merits and dismerits of smoking cigarettes)
a. Roger: Cigarettes aren' (very) healthy.
(pause)
b. Roger: You shouldn't be smokin' Ken.
(short pause)
c. Ken: So the coaches tell me.

For example, in 11.b, Roger has addressed Ken specifically; therefore Ken at 11.c can assume that Roger will be attending to his response. Hence step 1 is taken care of for Ken. Second, because the interlocutors are engaged in face to face verbal interaction, with no concurrent distracting activity, they can assume that their utterances will be heard and decoded without interference; that is, they can operate on the assumption that the noise to signal ratio is low. Hence, step 2 is satisfied for Ken. Third, Ken's discourse topic at 11.c 'that Ken should not be smoking,' is drawn from Roger's assertion (11.b, topic-incorporating). Ken can assume that Roger knows the referents specified in the discourse topic on this basis. In fact, Ken can assume that Roger knows the

discourse topic itself. Hence, steps 3 and 4 are accomp-
lished. However, it is often the case that several utterances or even several conversational turns will be needed to
take care of these steps.

12 Adolescents GTS 4 (p. 15)
    a.   Ken: Uh Pat McGee. I don't know if you know him,
        he- he lives in// Palisades
    b.   Jim: I know him real well as a matter of fa(hh)
        (he's) one of my best friends.
    c.   Ken: He- he used to go to the same military school
        I did.

For example in 12, two turns, 12.a and 12.b, are taken up
with insuring that a referent (critical to the topic) is
known to the listener.

It sometimes happens that one or another step is never
completed and the discourse topic is dropped by the speaker:

13 Toby and David at 36 months, in the bedroom. (calling
    out to mother who is not present)
    a.   David: Honey!/ calling honey!/ honey!/ we lost our
        blankets/
    b.   David & Toby: honey!/ honey!/ honey!/
    c.   David: honey!/
    d.   Toby: honey!/ honey!/
    e.   David: honey!/ (4 sec. pause) where are ya/
    f.   Toby: no/ mummy/ (gloss: no, she's not called Honey,
        she's called Mummy)
    g.   David: no/ honey/ honey/ honey/

In 13, step 1 is never satisfied as the intended addressee
(the mother) never responds to either the vocative (13.a-
13.e) or the question (13.e) directed to her. It is difficult to assess exactly what constitutes the discourse topic
for the utterance "we lost my blankets/", as the utterance
attempts to initiate the interaction with the mother. There
is no preceding context from which a discourse topic can be
determined (by an outsider). We suggest that the discourse
topic associated with such discourse-initial assertions (i.e.,
an Introducing Topic) is of the general form 'something happened.' This discourse topic is dropped, as step 1 is unsuccessful. Having failed to secure the attention of the mother,
the children redirect their utterances to one another, and
engage in a different discourse topic, roughly 'what name to
use in calling mother.' By 13.g this new topic becomes collaborated on, as Toby has secured David's attention, David
has indicated that he has understood (13.f) and has accepted
it as discourse topic by adding new information to the dis-

course topic proposed by Toby.

14 Allison III, 20.3$\frac{1}{2}$ months

> (prior context: Mother had brought out glass of juice
> set into a stack of paper cups. Allison had commented
> "glass/" since she had previously been served juice in
> either a paper cup or a can)
> (Allison eats cookie, looking at cookie)
>
> a. Allison: (putting cookie in her cup like the way the
> glass of juice was in the cup) glass/↑↓
> b. Mother: Well, what did you do?
> c. Allison: glass/
> d. Mother: What did you do? Where's the cookie?
> e. Allison: cup/
> f. Mother: in the cup.

In this example, Allison makes eye contact with her mother, helping her to secure the attention of the mother,
(step 1 is taken care of), and mother does not question
Allison's articulation (step 2 is taken care of). However,
step 3 is unsuccessful for a number of reasons. The mother
cannot identify the specific object referred to by Allison's
utterance "glass/". From Allison's point of view, "glass/"
is part of a comment on her non-verbal activity, i.e., that
the cookie in the cup is like the glass in the cup witnessed
earlier. But because the specific referent of "glass/" never
becomes known to mother, neither "glass/" or the event that
it relates to, becomes part of an established discourse topic.

Our model for proceeding through conversational space is
basically an interactional one. The amount of conversational
space taken up with completing these steps is related to the
kind of response the speaker receives from the hearer. If
the speaker receives a positive response from the listener,
then he can assume that the steps for topic establishment
have been satisfied. On the other hand, if at any point the
speaker gets negative feedback, then he will have to do more
interactional work, take up more conversational space, to
complete steps. For example, the listener often will question
some assumption of the speaker: if the speaker believes that
he has secured the attention of the listener but in fact has
failed to do so, then the listener may respond "Who me?" or
"Are you talking to me?", etc. If the attention of the listener has been secured, but he has not heard all or part of
the speaker's utterance, he may request a second hearing, or
he may state "I didn't hear you," "I didn't quite catch that,"
and the like. If the speaker believes that the identity of
the referents of the discourse topic are known to the hearer,
but in fact, their identity is not known, then the hearer may

challenge the speaker's belief, and/or request further information concerning these referents.

The dynamic model for establishing a discourse topic can be represented as follows:

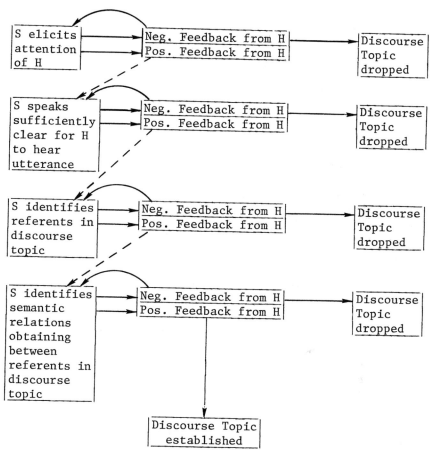

The interactional work described here is similar to material described by sociologists involved in conversational analysis. In particular, the work of correcting misunderstandings and mishearings is tied to the notion of REPAIR in conversation (E. Schegloff, pers. comm.). The work of RE-PAIRING some communication involves minimally a REPAIRABLE, the item or set of items that need to be corrected, and a REPAIR RESPONSE, in which the source of misunderstanding or mishearing is attended to. The repair response may or may not actually repair the misunderstanding or mishearing. If it does not, it may in turn be treated as a repairable, requiring some further repair response.

Two major types of repair are relevant to establishing discourse topic. First, there are cases in which the speaker who produces the repairable perceives the repairable and repairs it. These are SELF-INITIATED REPAIRS, and they normally occur within the space of a single conversational turn.

15 Adolescents GTS 3
    a. Louise: Doc-Mister Cheibe- when 're ya gonna be a doctor?

16 Toby, 45 months
    a. Toby: (looking at his mother)↑ daddy/ uh mommy/
    b. Mother: yeah?
    c. Toby: Are we gonna go↓ now?/

Examples 15 and 16 illustrate self-initiated repairs on the vocatives used to elicit the attention of the addressee.

In addition, we find many examples in our data of OTHER-INITIATED REPAIRS. In this type of repair, someone other than the speaker who produces the repairable indicates that some repair is necessary. This type of repair may take up several turns. For example, one interlocutor may produce a repairable in one turn, a second interlocutor evidence his misunderstanding or mishearing in the next turn, and in a third turn, the first interlocutor may produce a repair response. Example 17 illustrates such an exchange:

17 Toby, David, 35 months, bedroom
    a. David: (drawing on misty window) (?) moon/ I make moon/
    b. Toby: (pointing to window) there?/
    c. David: there/

In this exchange, Toby indicates that he needs further information about David's utterance; he needs to know which of David's drawings is the moon. David repairs Toby's misunderstanding by indicating the location of the moon drawn. Example 1 also illustrates this type of repair. In 1 Elinor indicates her lack of understanding, and Bambi repairs this misunderstanding by providing a more explicit referent for "it" ("the salt").

It is not always the case that other-initiated repairs are repaired by the speaker producing the repairable. The "other" can repair the repairable of a conversational partner directly in the next turn:

18 Allison IV, 22 months
    (Allison starting to eat cookie)
    a. Allison: ↑chocolate↓chip↑cookie/

b. Mother: Chocolate chip cookie? I think that's just a chocolate cookie.

In 18, Allison's mother points out an error in Allison's identification of the cookie (18.b) and then repairs the error in her subsequent utterance. Schegloff (pers. comm.) has pointed out that repairs of this sort frequently appear in adult-child discourse. Adults feel they have a responsibility (or right) to correct judgements of a child. In talking with one another, however, adults show a preference for giving the individual who produced the repairable an opportunity to correct himself. These latter alternates are face-preserving (Goffman 1963) and hence more polite than direct repair of another's error.

Integrating the notion of repair into our model, we can say that repair procedures tend to be inserted into conversational space when one or more of the four steps have not been satisfied by a speaker. For example, in 15 and 16, the speakers introduce repair machinery to secure the attention of the intended addressee (step 1). In 1, the speaker repairs her utterance so that the addressee can identify an important referent in the discourse topic (step 3).

On a more general level, repair machinery tends to be introduced when an interlocutor has misjudged the communicative needs of a conversational partner. Sacks and Schegloff (1974) refer to the shaping of utterances to meet these needs as "recipient design," the "recipient" being the intended conversational partner. When some utterance fails to meet the needs of a partner, then that utterance has poor recipient design.

The notion of recipient design is useful to the analysis at hand. From our point of view, collaboration on a discourse topic demands good recipient design on a number of levels. Utterances must be designed so that the recipient knows he/she is being addressed and so that the recipient can hear the utterance. Good recipient design is also needed to insure that the recipient can identify who or what is being talked about (Sacks and Schegloff 1974). In the discussion to follow, we consider recipient design in developmental terms. The bulk of our data shows that young children experience communicative difficulties because their utterances have poor recipient design.

V.B How to Secure the Attention of the Hearer

Atkinson (1974) explores the use of attention drawing devices used by small children (look! see! - pointing) which demonstrate to the listener which persons, objects, or events

the child wishes the listener to focus on. If both participants focus on the selected object, it can be presumed that
the speaker has obtained the attention of the hearer, as well
as directing him to a specific object. Here we discuss only
the first of these procedures: attention-getting.

Before any communication can take place, the speaker
must secure the attention of the hearer. This is done in a
variety of ways and is one of the earliest acts a child must
learn. Crying and other distressful sounds usually bring attention to the infant, indicating the "something is the matter." Gazing at the other is also one of the earliest ways
to secure his/her attention (Stern 1974). These acts may not
be intentional at the age of three months, but by one year of
age, the child starts using these as conscious devices
(Schieffelin 1975a) (6). Smiling plus gazing, as well as
laughing while gazing at the other often elicits not only the
attention of the hearer, but a query from the hearer, e.g.,
"What happened?" or "What's so funny?". They elicit attention to self even if that is not what is always intended.

Smiling and laughing are thought of as social phenomena.
People feel that they can ask another individual why he/she
is laughing--especially if the context does not provide an
explicit explanation or source. Presumably one is laughing
about something--laughing being a comment or new information
about a proposition.

Other non-verbal means of getting a listener to attend
to the speaker are touching the listener, tugging, poking,
turning towards the listener, getting closer. These behaviors as well typically elicit such queries such as "What do
you want?", etc.

In addition to several non-verbal means of securing the
attention of a specific individual, the child develops verbal
ways of performing the same act. While crying and other distressful sounds do not specify who should attend, the use of
vocatives, i.e., "Mama" and "Papa," etc., do. The number of
times a name will be called out repeatedly, the pitch and
loudness of the calls depend on the utterance context and the
desires of the individual. For instance in example 13 the
mother does not respond to her childrens' calls since she
doesn't hear them, and subsequently she is not involved in
the interaction. By way of comparison:

19 Maria, 24 months, Spanish-speaking
   (in same room with mother)
   a. Maria: mommy/
   b. Mother: ¿Qué ? ¿Qué quieres? Huh?

Maria succeeds in calling attention to herself in one turn,

and her mother indicates that she is attending to the proposition that 'Maria wants something' with her response.

In the next example, Maria has assumed that the attention of the listener has been secured, when in fact it has not.

20 (several people present in the room)
   a. Maria: sientate aca/ sientate aca/ sientate aca/
   b. friend (2 1/2 yrs. old): ¿mi?/
   c. Maria: sientate aca/

(transcribed by L. Tweed)

Not only must children learn to secure the attention of the listener, but when several potential respondents are available, they must select explicitly. For example:

21 (dinner table, 3 adults, 3 children (aged 4 yrs.), noisy)
   a. Zachary: You know what I saw today?
   b. David: What?/
   c. Zachary: ↑Not you, I'm talking to my mom↓/ ↑Mommy?/
   d. Mother: ↑yeah?

These problems also face adults in conversation with each other. Using vocatives also serves as a check on the other's attention, during conversation, and is one of several devices available to maintain the attention of the listener, e.g., "George, George, are you there?" used when one suspects that the listener has not been completely attending. Other devices used are expressions like, "hey!" or "wait!" plus eye contact and touching the individual. Both children and adults use as well expressions such as "You know what?" or "Guess what" to shift attention to themselves. (See Section IV.B.3) Another way to call attention to oneself (used by both adults and children) is to use one of the many expressive particles such as "uh oh," "oh dear," "ouch," "woopsey," "wow," etc. Placed in the beginning of an event, the listener hearing such an exclamation will usually look to the speaker and inquire, "What happened" or "What's wrong?", in an attempt to find out what has caused such an outburst. The occurrence of one of these expressions during an ongoing interaction usually draws the focus away from what is happening and causes a shift in attention to occur. These particles can simultaneously draw attention to the speaker and the event that he is commenting on. Schegloff (pers. comm.) treats these expressions as a "pre" to a "noticing" by a copresent individual or individuals. That is, they are expressions that elicit a "noticing."

357

V.C On Articulating Utterances for the Listener

To collaborate on a discourse topic, a listener must
have received a minimally comprehensible message from a speaker. Adults in talking with one another may miss part or all
of an utterance if it was delivered too quickly or too softly
or if noise from the context interfered with the signal. The
problem of poor articulation is even more apparent in interactions involving children as interlocutors.

For example, young children often distort the phonological shape of their utterances to the extent that conversational partners cannot interpret them as meaningful strings
in the language. It is often necessary for young children to
repeat their utterances several times to get them understood
at this basic level. In many cases, the utterance is not deciphered and the topic is dropped:

22 Toby, David, 33 months
   (eating midday meal, facing caretaker, Jill)
   (Jill has just asked if Toby and David would like a
   banana in jelly (British term for jello))
   a. Toby: no no jelly/[tɨnkɛl]/
   b. Jill: You eat your dinner then.
   c. Toby: [tɨnkɛl]/
   d. Jill: What?
   e. Toby: [tɨnkɛl]/
   f. Jill: tinkle?
   g. David: yeah
   h. Toby: no tinkle/[tɨnkɛl] (repeats)/
   i. Jill: You're a prack.

In this example, Toby repeats his utterance but with little
success. He never gets his message across. It is possible
that "[tɨnkɛl]/" is intended as "tin of jello" (unclear), but
in any case Jill interprets the utterance as a distortion of
"tinkle," a lexical item which makes little sense in this
context. This example illustrates as well the use of repair
machinery to achieve comprehensibility. Jill initiates repair procedures twice (22.d and 22.f) to this end.

At the one word stage, children experience even greater
problems in articulating their utterances with sufficient
clarity. Scollon (1973) has documented the way in which many
of these early utterances are lost on co-present adults:

> For example, one day, this little child (20 mos.), whose
> name is Brenda, said to me, [kʰa] [kʰa] [kʰa]. I didn't
> understand and said "What?". She then said [gɔo] [go].
> The next thing I said cannot be heard clearly enough on
> the tape to transcribe, but Brenda then said [bəis],

nine times. I still didn't understand what she was
saying and said "What? Oh, bicycle? Is that what you
said?" Her answer was [na']. I said, "No?". She,
[na']. I, "No-- I got it wrong."

When Scollon listened to his recording of this conversation,
he heard the sound of a car passing just before Brenda started to speak. On this second hearing, he realized that [k^{h}a]
was Brenda's equivalent of "car," [gɔo] corresponds to "go"
and [bəis] corresponded to "bus." Scollon's analysis illustrates the point that caretakers and others rely heavily on
utterance context in interpreting phonologically ill-formed
utterances of children. Where no salient referent in the
immediate environment can be isolated, adults find it difficult to understand what a child is saying (7).

We can well imagine that these early attempts to communicate are laced with repair machinery. In fact, Scollon
reports that the one-word peried is "cluttered" with self-
repetitions on the part of the child and attempts at clarification by a co-present adult. The child repeats a lexical
item over and over until he/she receives some sort of assurance from the adult that the utterance has been deciphered.

Scollon observes that the child may repeat an utterance
with or without a verbal prompt from the adult. From our
point of view, even when there is no verbal repair-initiator
such as "What?", "Hm?" or trial repetition of the child's
utterance, absence of a verbal response from the adults may
count as a negative response for the child. That is, silence
on the part of a conversational partner may initiate a repair
from the child. When the child does not get an immediate
verbal confirmation, the child attempts to clarify the utterance (repair) through repetition.

Aside from problems of phonological distortion, the com-
munications of young children may suffer because the child's
voice is too soft or too low:

23 Allison VI, 34 months
   (Allison climbs up on a big chair, trying to move bars
   into their holes)
   a. Allison: I'm-I'm put-putting these bars in there/
   b. Mother: I can't hear you.
   c. Allison: (pointing to holes) in these holes/
   d. Mother: What honey?
   e. Allison: (moving hand up and down bars) ə these
      bars/
   f. Mother: What about these bars?
   g. Allison: (trying to move bars) I'm trying to put
      them in these hole - mommy?/ I can't get it in

these holes/

In many instances, the child may not in fact be directing utterances to others present. The child may be speaking
softly because he is engaged in some activity and talking to
himself. Others overhearing such talk may try to re-direct
it so that it includes themselves. In these cases, the child
is not "guilty" of poor recipient design. Rather it is the
co-present other who demands to be recognized as the recipient.

It is important to note that adults regularly apply repair machinery to these communication roadblocks and that
very young children respond appropriately to this machinery.
That is not to say that young children respond exactly as an
adult would respond. Adults tend to treat a mishearing as a
misunderstanding and offer an alternate phrasing of their
original utterance (Schegloff, pers. comm.). Children up to
about 2 1/2 years of age tend to repeat what they uttered
previously. However, they do recognize that a re-delivery is
appropriate when a repair initiation is addressed to them.

In many cases, children do provide a clearer articulation of the utterance in the repair response. In her study
of peer interaction, Garvey (1975) found that children 34-67
months regularly altered such "repeated" utterances. In contrast to the original formulation (i.e., the repairable),
these utterances (i.e., the repair responses) were marked by:

a. reduction in tempo, e.g., clear separation of
   syllables
b. increase in precision of articulation, e.g., release
   of final consonants
c. increase in volume
d. use of contrastive stress on portion of the queried
   segment
   (Garvey 1975:28)

Before the age of 3 years, then, a child evidences some sensitivity to, and use of, "recipient design."

V.D On Identifying Referents in the Discourse Topic

The given-new contrast (Clark 1974) requires that speakers refer to individuals, objects, events, etc., in such a
way that the listener can mentally identify the referent.
Applied to discourse topic, this means that the speaker
should take into account the listener's knowledge or awareness of a particular object in making reference to that object within a discourse topic.

The speaker can misjudge the listener's knowledge/awareness in two ways. It is possible that the speaker may under-estimate the listener's knowledge. He may, for example, des-cribe an individual without naming him with the mistaken be-lief that the listener does not know that individual or at least does not know the name of that individual. In these instances, the listener may indicate his knowledge of the referent's name, e.g., through comments such as "You mean John?", "Oh yeah, John," "Are you talking about John," etc.

In many cases, such errors on the part of the speaker are taken as "talking down" and insulting by the listener. In "talking down" the speaker believes that the listener is not informed about some individual, event, process, etc., to the extent that the speaker is. For example, a speaker might say, "Do you know what John Kennedy, a famous president who was assassinated, once said? 'Ask not what your country can do for you, but what you can do for your country.'" The dis-course topic, 'You (the addressee) do or do not know what John Kennedy, a famous president, who was assassinated, once said,' makes explicit that John Kennedy was a famous presi-dent who was assassinated. In cases where the listener al-ready knows this information, the listener may feel that the speaker has underestimated the state of his general knowledge. In other words, the speaker should have presupposed more.

Far more often are cases in which the speaker overesti-mates the speaker's knowledge or awareness of a referent. We have discussed this behavior with respect to example 1. In cases such as this, the listener will not be able to under-stand what claim is being made or elicited. And, in our society at least, such overestimations of the listener's knowledge provoke some sort of clarification request (repair initiator) from the listener, e.g., "Who?", "What?", "What comes out fast?", etc.

The speaker, then, must take steps to aid the listener in identifying particular referents within the discourse topic. This is part of good recipient design (Sacks & Schegloff 1974). In identifying requests, speakers appeal to two major sources. First, there are appeals to the physical setting in which the communication is conveyed. Second, there are appeals to the listener's background knowledge. In the first case, the speaker directs the listener to locate the referent in physical space. In the second case, the speaker directs the listener to locate the referent in memory space.

Let us consider the way in which young children aid the listener in locating particular referents within discourse topic.

V.D.1 How to Locate a Referent in Physical Space

Overwhelmingly, the conversations of young children are about objects, people, or events that are present in the utterance context. Further, from a very early point in their development, children employ a variety of devices to direct the listener's attention to these entities. These devices include both verbal and non-verbal behaviors.

Non-verbal means for locating a referent (X) include:

a) Looking at (X)   COMMENTARY

   24 Allison II
   (Allison had been pointing
   to mike on her mother)
     a. (Allison looks at   ← referent = object
        hanging mike)   looked at
     b. Mother: That's another   ← referent identified
        microphone.   by listener

b) Holding (X)

   25 Toby & David, 35 months
     a. David: oh dear/X/*
        (sitting up, looking   ← referent = object
        at his blanket)   looked at
        (picking up blanket,
        facing Toby) that
        messing up/ this/X/X/
        don't mess it up/ you
        mess it up/ like this/
     b. Toby: mummy did/   ← referent identified
        mummy did/   by listener
     c. David: yes/
   (see also examples 30, 32)   * /X/ = repetition of
                          prior utterance

c) Reaching for (X)

   26 Allison III
   (Allison and mother had
   been talking about
   putting a diaper on the
   baby doll)
     a. Allison: (reaching   ← referent = object
        for doll) baby doll/   reached for
     b. Mother: Oh, there   ← referent identified
        she is!   by listener

d) Offering (X)

   27 a. (Allison offering   ← referent = object
        cookie to mommy) ↑mommy/   offered

b. Mother: Oh, thank   ← referent identified
   you.   by listener

e) Pointing at (X)

   28 Allison II
      a. Allison: (crawling
         into mother's lap
         and pointing to   ← referent = object
         microphone) man/   pointed at
      b. Mother: The man put   ← referent identified
         the microphone on.   by listener
   (see also example 6)

f) Touching (X)

   29 Allison III
      a. Allison: (touching   ← referent = object
         overhead mike) mike/   touched
      b. Mother: That's the   ← referent identified
         microphone.   by listener
      c. Allison: (turns to
         mother, touching   ← referent = object
         her mike)   touched
      d. Mother: Mommy has a   ← referent identified
         microphone.   by listener

From the single word stage on, the child does not rely
on non-verbal means alone to locate referents for the listener (Schieffelin 1975b). As Atkinson (1974) points out, non-
verbal means are efficient only when the listener is already
visually attending to the speaker.

In the data at hand we find that gestures such as reaching, pointing, and the like are accompanied by verbal means
of expression; or verbal means can be used to direct the
listener to the relevant referent.

The child can locate a referent verbally (with or without accompanying non-verbal devices) by using:

a) Notice verbs: (look, see, etc.)   COMMENTARY
   (Atkinson 1974, Keenan and
   Klein 1975)

   30 David & Toby, 35 months, in
      bedroom
      a. David: (standing, facing
         Toby, David holding up
         a battery)
         a battery/ this is   ← referent = object
         battery/X/   held & identified
         look I find battery/

    b. Toby: I see: that   ← referent identified
        Jiji's/   by listener

b)   Expressive particles: (see
      Section V.B)

    31 Allison III, 20 mos., 3 1/3 wks
      a. Allison: (noticing that
          mother's juice has   ← referent = object/
          spilled) uh oh!/   event noticed
      b. Mother: uh oh.   ← referent (implicit-
                                  ly) identified by
                                  listener

      c. Allison: (smiling,
          looking at juice
          spilled on floor)
          mommy/
      d. Mother: What did mommy
          do?
      e. Allison: ↑spill/↓   ← referent identified
                                  explicitly

c)   Deictic particles

   1) Declarative

    32 Allison V, 28 months
      a. Allison: (holding truck) ← referent = object
          This is a dump truck/   being held
      b. Mother: This is a dump   ← referent identified
          truck. Yeh.   by listener

    33 David & Toby, 35 months
      a. David: (pointing out   ← referent = object
          moth in room) [i] moth/X/X/* pointed at
      b. Toby: I see/ (put out   ← referent identified
          window)/   by listener
      c. David: yes/
   *[i] = general deictic particle for "there" "it" "this",
      etc.

   2) Interrogative

    34 David & Toby, 34 months
      eating dinner
      a. David: (looking at his   ← referent = object
          bowl of food) what's zis?/ looked at
      b. Toby: kamoniz/   ← referent identified
                              by listener

      c. David: no macaroniz/
          sketiz/

d) Descriptive or identifying NP

In many cases, the child identifies a referent for a
listener (or himself) by "naming it." This is the case
in 29, 30, 32, 33, etc. In some instances the child is
not secure about the appropriateness of his identification, and waits for a confirmation of the identification from the listener. In other cases, as Atkinson
(1974) points out, the child may be secure about his
identification, but may not be sure that the listener
has identified the item. Often the child may refer to
the item but wait for evidence that the adult has identified the object, action, etc., before going on to
supply new information about it. Atkinson calls this
behavior PRIMING. Priming gets the listener to focus on
what the speaker wants to talk about.

As is evident in these examples, several means may be
employed by the child to locate a referent in physical space.
(Of course adults use these same devices when interacting
with children as well as when interacting with each other.)
A child may first try to locate the referent with an identifying NP, then follow this NP with a string of notice verbs,
pointing, showing, etc.

We do not want to imply that every time a child touches,
holds, points, or names some entity that he is trying to locate a referent for the listener. Indeed, at the one word
stage, children often employ these behaviors in the course of
their own exploration of the environment. The adult may simply be an observer of this process. And if the adult wishes
to enter into the interaction with the child, he may use one
or another of these behaviors to locate exactly what the
child is talking about.

In many cases, however, the child wants a listener to
attend and acknowledge the claim he is making about some discourse topic. In these cases, the child employs means such
as those described above.

The variety of means and the frequency with which they
are employed suggest that young children are often sensitive
to the fact that listeners must be able to identify specific
entities addressed in a discourse topic proposition. This
sensitivity is evidenced as well by the number of tries the
child will produce to get the referent located. In many
cases the child will repeat a try 9 or 10 times, stopping
only when the listener evidences verbally that he is attending to the child's focus of attention.

35 David & Toby, 35 months   COMMENTARY
   (David holding a truck,
   picks up rabbit. Toby
   whistling on pretend
   flute continuously,
   while facing David)
   a. David: rabbit/X/   ← referent = object
       I find truck/   being held
       rabbit/ (?) as
       like rabbit/ truck/
       rabbit/X/X/ truck
       truck rabbit/
       truck/ rabbit
       (showing truck
       and rabbit to Toby)
       truck/ rabbit/X/X/
   b. Toby: truck/ rabbit/   ← referent identified
       (continues whistling)   by listener
   c. David: let me blow?/
   (for other examples, see E.O. Keenan 1974)

The listener indicates that he has identified the referent in question by repeating the identification of the referent, examples 4, 14, 32, 35, by offering an alternate identification of the referent, examples 18, 34, by explicitly
stating that he "sees" the object, etc., examples 30, 33, or
by providing some other comment concerning the referent,
example 25. These responses are characteristic of both the
child-adult and child-child discourse under study.

On the other hand, there is a way of evidencing awareness of the referent in question that is characteristic of
adult behavior only. An adult may state explicitly the question of immediate concern, addressed by the child, and in so
doing specify the object, event, process, etc., pointed out
earlier by the child. For example, in 31 Allison notices
that her mother did something and directs her mother to notice this action (specifically the result of this action).
Allison's mother shows that she has noticed in two ways:
First, she repeats Allison's comment, "uh oh!/", and second,
she formulates a possible question of immediate concern,
"What did mommy do?" This question has as its discourse topic 'mommy did something,' a proposition that expresses what
Allison noticed.

Although in the discourse described above, the child is
relatively successful in calling attention to a referent,
there are cases in which the child does not provide adequate
cues. In these cases, the referent is located only after one
or more repair initiators by the listener; or the referent is

never located at all, and the communication fails. In our
data, the listener's difficulties in locating referents in
the discourse topic derive from at least two major sources:
1. First, the child may confuse the listener by providing <u>conflicting non-verbal cues</u>. For example,

36 Allison II, 19.2 months	<u>COMMENTARY</u>
(sitting on mother's lap)	
a. Allison: (pointing toward photographer, touching her mouth) man/	← referent = object pointed at
b. Mother: mouth?	← repair initiator on identify of refer-ent
c. Allison: (pointing to her tongue) ↑(?)/↓(whimpers) down/	
	(referent not iden-tified by listener)

In 36, line a, Allison incidently touches her mouth as she is
pointing out the photographer. At 36.b, Allison's mother is
misled by Allison's touching her mouth, and tentatively interprets her utterance as "mouth," not "man." The utterance
"mouth?" requests clarification (initiates a repair) but
Allison interprets her mother's utterance as a question about
her mouth, e.g., 'where is your mouth?'. Step 3 of the prerequisites for establishing a discourse topic is, then, not
successful, and the discourse topic is dropped.
   In other interactions of this sort, the child may be
looking at one thing, and holding up another, and commenting
on just one of these things.

37 Allison IV, 22 months	<u>COMMENTARY</u>
(Allison has taken a calf then a cow out of a box. She has called the calf "cow/" and the cow "big cow/") she then,	
a. Allison: (looks at calf, holding up cow) tiny ku/↑↓	← referent = object looked at
b. Mother: what?	← repair initiator on step 2
c. Allison: (looking at cow) tiny cow/	← repair response on step 2

d. Mother: Where's   ← repair initiator on
   the tiny cow?   identity of referent
e. Allison: (showing
   mother calf, holding
   it next to cow, then
   lifting it up)
   right here/   ← repair response
f. Mother: Right,↑↓
   that's the tiny cow.   ← referent identified
                                         by listener

In 37, the adult is using the child's gaze direction as a cue
in helping to locate what the child is referring to. At
37.d, the adult initiates a repair to establish the unique
referent of "tiny cow." (The adult knows which object is the
tiny cow; she does not know which object the child is calling
a tiny cow.) At 37.e Allison is able to repair this misunderstanding through non-verbal and verbal means.

   2. A second source of confusion for the listener stems
from the child's failure to specify the referent in a precise
enough manner. Again, in many of these cases, the communication was never intended as social and so not oriented to listener needs. In other cases, however, the child does want to
convey the discourse topic and locating a key referent for
the listener is a means to this end.

   In the data at hand, vagueness is a result of a failure
to provide sufficient non-verbal cues, and/or sufficient verbal cues. For example, we find that a child will often look
at an object or an event, or hold an object and refer to it
as if it were already identified by the listener. In many
cases, the child looks at or touches something present in the
environment, and refers to it by some deictic term, such as
"this," [i], "it." This is illustrated in a different "spill"
sequence from that in example 31.

38 Allison V, 28 months   COMMENTARY
   (Allison had been eating
   a cookie, drinking juice,
   she spills some juice
   from her mouth)
   a. uh/ (looks at her
      dress, purposely
      pours juice onto it)
   b. Mother: Oh, what
      happened? What did
      you do? What did
      you do?

368

c. Allison: (touching her knee, looking at original spill) spill something/

d. Mother: What did you do?

e. Allison: (holding up cookie, scraping it with her finger) it came down from əↆcookie/   ← referent = objects being scraped (cookies)

f. Mother: What?   ← repair initiator on step 2

g. Allison: (rubbing her dress) it came ↓ on my dress/   ← repair response

h. Mother: It came on your dress. It didn't come on the cookie. ↓Oh means we better wipe you off.

(referent not identified by listener)

In 38.d Allison's mother is eliciting information about the spilling of the juice by Allison. Allison, however, turned her attention to something else that fell on her dress along with the juice, that is, cookie crumbs. Her utterance at 38.e is a claim that the crumbs ("it") 'came down from a cookie.' The discourse topic is something to the effect, 'the crumbs came from somewhere.' But, because Allison did not clarify sufficiently the referent of "it," Allison's mother takes the term to refer to the juice, rather than the crumbs. This is evident at 38.f when Allison's mother comments, "it came on your dress. It didn't came on the cookie."

Underspecification may also result from a child's deletion of a lexical item, or items within an utterance. Greenfield and Smith (1975) have observed that children in the one word stage delete certain 'presupposed' information and make explicit what they consider to be important or noteworthy, i.e., 'informative.' Often the information deleted concerns an individual(s) or an event(s) about which the child's utterance provides a 'comment.' We find that deletion of taken-for-granted material continues, but to a lesser extent, throughout our child data sample. (In fact, adult discourse is laced with these deletions as well.) In some contexts, the deleted referent (or set of referents) is not altogether obvious to the listener, and the listener initiates a repair on this referent.

	COMMENTARY
39 Allison IV, 22 months	
(Allison seeing herself on the TV monitor)	
a. Allison: (putting hand to her head) comb hair/	← referent = agent
b. Mother: Comb hair?	← repair initiator on step 2
c. Allison: Baby Allison comb hair/	← repair response
d. Mother: Baby Allison comb hair?	← repair initiator on steps 2 and 3
e. Allison: yeah/	← repair response
	(referent identified by listener)

Notice that the child is able to repair the unclarity and successfully locate a critical referent. We find that children at the single word stage can repair misunderstandings related to referents located in the present physical space. However, the same cannot be said for their ability to initiate repairs on locating referents in the utterances of other children or adults. We found no instances of such repair initiators in the Allison Bloom sample, ranging from age 16 months to 28 months. Repair initiation of this sort starts at 35 months in the Toby and David sample, see example 17. However, it is a rare occurrence (Keenan, Schieffelin and Platt, work in progress). Much more frequent in the Toby and David sample is repair initiation on step 2, articulation. (See Garvey 1975 for a careful discussion of this phenomenon.)

We have seen, then, two striking differences between adult-child and child-child discourse. The first is that the adult often explicitly reconstructs a question of immediate concern on the basis of a referring expression by the child. The second is that the adult initiates a repair from the child if a referent is insufficiently located. These observations need to be confirmed by looking at a wider sample of children's discourse.

V.D.2 How to Locate a Referent in Memory

We have stated that most of the claims made or elicited by young children concern entities that exist in the physical environment of the verbal interaction. However, even very young children sometimes refer to events or individuals that

are not present in the ongoing setting. Some of these references are ficticious events or individuals (fantasy) and some
are actual individuals or events known to the child from some
prior experience. We find child-child discourse up to 37
months to include primarily the first of this type of "non-
situated reference" (fantasy), whereas child-adult discourse
contains primarily the second type of these references.

Both types of reference are usually provoked by some object or event, or individual that is situated in the ongoing
physical context. In the case of fantasy, something noticed
in the setting is associated with some imaginary entity.
For example, a battery picked up from the floor by David at
35 months of age is identified first as a battery, and then
as a steam roller. Subsequent stretches of discourse use
steam roller in various roles within a discourse topic. In
the case of "real world" non-situated reference, some event,
etc., triggers off a remembering by the child of a similar
entity in the past.

We find that before the age of three, children experience enormous difficulty in getting "real world" non-situated
events, individuals, etc., established as a discourse topic.
Typically, the transition from the here and now to past experience, is not clearly communicated by the child. In
adult-child interaction, the transition often takes the adult
by surprise, and the referent in question cannot be determined. Example 14 illustrates this type of communication
road block. Here the particular "glass" being referred to by
Allison cannot be identified by the listener, and so "glass"
is not included in subsequent discourse topics.

There are numerous reasons, why these referents are often
not identified by the listener. To sort out these reasons,
it is useful to compare means available to the child for locating referents in physical space with those available for
memory searches:

1. Salient from the video record is the fact that
children rely heavily on non-verbal cues to locate what they
are talking about. This is true both in initial identifica-
tions of referents, and in responses to repair initiators.
These cues are appropriate to the here and now context, but
ineffective in locating objects in the listener's memory.
Thus, one important class of 'locators' play no role in helping the listener to retrieve the referent from memory space.

2. Second, although the children in this study use
"notice verbs" such as "look" and "see" to direct the listener to an object in physical space, they do not use these notice verbs to locate referents in memory. Adults, on contrast, often direct the listener's attention to some indivi-

dual or event not present through such utterances as "Look at what happened to Joe...he got a very raw deal from that company." In certain Scots dialects the verb see is used in this way. Atkinson (1974) quotes Macrae as saying that sentences of the form, "See Jimmy? See chips? He likes 'em" are perfectly appropriate even when "Jimmy" and "chips" are not present in the speaker's or hearer's environment.

Additionally, adults have several other notice verbs that are used to focus attention on a referent in memory (Atkinson 1974). As discussed in part 1, adults often explicitly request the listener to search in memory for some particular referent. They ask the listener if he "remembers" or "knows" or "recalls" a particular individual, object or incident before going on to say anything about it (e.g., example 2). The use of these verbs is not evident in the childrens' discourse under study.

3. A further impedance to locating referents in the listener's memory is the late development of old information markers in the speech of young children. The use of anaphoric pronouns, for example, is not part of the child's competence until his average utterance length is at least 2.5 morphemes (Bloom, Lightbown and Hood 1975). (The child is regularly producing three word utterances.) Before this point, a child may use pronominal forms, but they are used deictically, i.e., to point out things present in the environment, rather anaphorically. The same can be said of definite articles. Their use in referring to entities not present is not part of the child's competence before 32 months (Maratsos 1974). Relative clauses as well do not appear anywhere in our corpus of children's utterances.

Thus it is difficult for the young child to mark specifically that he/she is talking about something that he/she has already experienced. Allison at 20 months, 3 1/2 weeks has no way of marking that the glass she is referring to (example 14) is that or the glass that was set in the cups.

4. It is also important to note that the transition from present to prior experience is confounded by the child's non-existent (or later) inconsistent use of tense marking.

In general, referring to objects, persons, etc., not contextually situated puts a greater burden on the child's verbal resources. The child must rely exclusively on verbal means to locate the referent in question. In many cases, the listener can simply not determine this referent, as adequate syntactic and semantic marking has not yet emerged in the child's speech. Adults often treat these references of the child as coming "out of the blue" or irrelevant. They may initiate repairs on the referent, e.g., "where is the X?" or

372

shift the discourse to a discourse topic that can be determined by both conversational partners (8).

V.D.3 Identifying Referents and Old Information

Our observations of adult-adult, adult-child, and child-
child conversations indicate overwhelmingly that objects,
events, and persons, etc., that play a role in a discourse
topic are known to or knowable by the listener as well as the
speaker. This is evidenced in two ways:

First, in adult-child discourse, if a child refers to
some entity that cannot be located by the adult in physical or
memory space, the adult listener usually initiates a repair in
an effort to elicit information that will facilitate an identification.

Second, both adult and child speakers are reluctant to
use a referent in a discourse topic without confirmation that
the referent is known to, or knowable by the listener. (See
also Sankoff and Brown 1975 for a discussion of this phenomenon in Tok Pisin.) We have provided numerous examples in
which young children wait for confirmation from the listener
that the relevant referent is identified. And, while adults
in talking to one another elicit such confirmation less often, at times they spend considerable efforts in insuring
that the entity that they are referring to is a piece of
"shared knowledge." The following conversation illustrates
the amount of conversational space that a speaker can take up
with this endeavor.

```
40 (2 women in a dress shop)
   Marie tapes (transcribed
   by Francoise Brun-Cottian)
   (pause)
   a. Marie: Hah-Hah-Ha
            Remember that red
            blazer you got on
            the other-you had
            on the other day?
            (pause 3 sec.)
   b. Dottie: Me?
   c. ┌Marie: Yah that r//ed
   d. └Dottie: Sweater?
   e. Marie: Ya That red-
            (.6sec) thing that
            uh (1sec) that uh
            keeps the cold out
            (but) (2sec)
            The red one
```

373

```
    (it's-) (2sec)
    thin thin thin
    (7sec)
f.  Dottie: You mean with
    the roun' neck?
    (2sec) (what cha)
    talking about (.4sec)
Marie turns to third woman
and discusses a dress for
several turns. She then
returns to her conversation
with Dottie.
g.  Marie: (finds object
    in shop, shows to
    Dottie)                          COMMENTARY
    This. (1.2sec)
h. ┌Dottie: Oh the red one    ← referent identified
   │I had on// ya:h              by listener
i. └Marie: Yeah uh-
    somebody wanted one,
    who wanted it
```

V.E Identifying the Discourse Topic Proposition

When adults talk to one another, they may not always be certain of the discourse topic addressed by a speaker. That is, the speaker may not always state the discourse proposition as part of an explicit question of immediate concern. On the basis of the utterance itself, prior utterances exchanged and other shared background knowledge, however, the listener may reconstruct a plausible discourse topic addressed by the speaker. On the basis of this reconstruction, the listener then provides (what he perceives to be) a relevant or appropriate response.

There are a number of reasons why this reconstruction process for the listener is easier in adult-adult conversations than in adult-child or child-child conversations.

As noted earlier, adults usually conform to the conversational convention of making their utterances relevant to the current discourse (unless otherwise marked). If an adult (in this society) is attending to a discourse topic that is not tied to the prior discourse topic and/or claim (introducing topic, re-introducing topic) then he is expected to mark this break in some overt manner, e.g., through expressive particles ("Hey," "Oh no," "I forgot," etc.), explicit topic-switching expressions, or explicit questions of immediate concern. (See Sections III and IV.B.3)

This convention is not well-established for young children, particularly those at the one- and two-word stages. There are several reasons for this:

    a. First, children at this point in their development have a more limited attention span than do older children and adults. This limitation makes it difficult for them to collaborate on or incorporate discourse topics for an extended period of time. At a point of topic exhaustion (Keenan and Klein 1975) the child may suddenly turn to a radically different focus of attention.

    b. Second, the child is easily distracted by some new thing he/she has noticed in the physical environment. In producing an utterance, the child may be focussing on a novel entity rather than on a discourse topic or claim in some last utterance.

    c. Third, the child may not provide a relevant next utterance because he does not understand the point (the discourse topic) of the preceding utterance. This is particularly the case where the preceeding utterance is a declarative produced by another speaker. In declarative utterances, the question of immediate concern is implicit. In contrast to explicit questions of immediate concern, the child must construct for himself the concern underlying a declarative. This process may often be too difficult for the child, leading him to produce an irrelevant next utterance.

    d. Fourth, the child may not respond relevantly to a preceding utterance because he had not attended to it in the first place. The child may, for example, be absorbed in his own description of some activity and not attend to utterances directed to him from a conversational partner. This behavior is characteristic of egocentric speech, what Piaget (1926) calls "collective monologues." Thus, if an adult directs a question to a young child, the subsequent utterance by the child may not be a response to that question but a comment relative to the child's previous discourse.

In many cases, the conversational partner realizes that the child has not attended to the immediately preceding utterance but to some other concern. In other cases, however, the child does not provide sufficient cues that his/her attention is directed to some utterance other than the preceding one. For example, attention to a novel object in the environment may be marked only by a shift in gaze direction. The listener is often not aware of this non-verbal behavior. Thus he is not aware of the concern the child's utterance addresses.

In some cases, the child provides no salient cues whatsoever that his attention has shifted, e.g., where the child is referring to some past experience. For example,

41 Jason, 24 months
  a. (Jason falls on floor)
      Mother: What happened? (2X)
      (long pause)
  b. Jason: book/
  c. Mother: Is that a book?
  d. Jason: me/
  e. Mother: This isn't your book. Where's your book?
  f. Jason: me/
  g. Mother: Where's your chicken book?
  h. (Jason picks up book)
      Mother: No, that's Gramma's book.
  i. Jason: me/
  j. Mother: You can't read Gramma's book.
  k. Jason: yeah/
  l. Mother: No. Where's your book?
  m. Jason: me/
  n. Mother: Where's Jason's book?
  o. (Jason looks at book)
      Mother: Gramma's book.
  p. Jason: me/
  q. Mother: Oh, what did you hurt?
  r. Jason: nose/
  s. Mother: Oh, you hurt your nose.
  t. Jason: bleed/
  u. Mother: Oh, does your nose bleed?
  v. Jason: yeah/ nose

                    (transcribed by L. Tweed)

In 41, Jason falls down but does not respond immediately to his mother's query about the fall. He turns his attention to a book in the room. This shift is perceived by the mother, and she directs a number of utterances to Jason concerning the book. However, by 41.d, Jason shifts the focus of attention back to himself. The mother, however, continues to interpret Jason's utterance, "me/," in terms of the immediately preceding focus of interest, identification of the book. For example, Jason's utterance at 41.d is treated as a response to 41.c, and it is corrected by the mother at 41.e. For the bulk of the discourse, two distinct concerns are being handled by child and mother. In addition to the mother's (and occasionally Jason's) concern with the book, Jason is apparently saying something about his fall in uttering "me/" (41.d). He is not replying to his mother's question. This becomes clearer when Jason stops repeating "me/" and answers his mother's question at 41.q. This question articulates

Jason's concern (his discourse topic), i.e., 'Jason hurt something (some part of himself).' He collaborates on this discourse topic at 41.r and from this point on in the discourse, matters relating to this proposition are addressed.

The misunderstanding in 41 prevails for an extraordinary number of turns (9). We find nothing of this length in the Allison tapes, for example. The length of this confusion was probably affected by Jason's occasional verbal and non-verbal collaboration on/incorporation of his mother's discourse topic and claim (41.h, 41.k, 41.o).

A second problem in determining the discourse topic proposition of a child's utterance is linked to the child's limited syntactic/semantic competence. It is usually much more difficult for a listener to determine the discourse topic for utterances that express only part of a claim than for utterances that express a claim explicitly. For example,

42 Allison II, 19 months, 2 weeks
   a. Allison: (crawling into her mother's lap and pointing to microphone) man/
   b. Mother: The man put the microphone on. Right.

In 42, it is more difficult to reconstruct the discourse topic for Allison's utterance (42.a) "man/" than it would be if the utterance were syntactically and semantically more complete. At 42.a, the child conveys only that "man/" is somehow related to the object she is pointing to (the microphone). If the utterance were more complex, then the listener would have a clearer idea of the claim being made by the child and would be better equipped to determine the question of immediate concern being addressed (10).

Faced with utterances such as these, the listener has to bring in a great deal of contextual knowledge to reconstruct the question of immediate concern. (See Section IV.A) The listener considers plausible questions that the communicative act (pointing at one object and uttering "man/") could be a response to: Is the child telling me (the listener) 'what a man did' (discourse topic: 'the man did something'); or 'who did something to the microphone' (discourse topic: 'someone did something to the microphone'); or what? When Allison's mother EXPANDS (interprets) Allison's utterance as "The man put the microphone on," she creates a range of possible questions of immediate concern that Allison's utterance might be a response to; e.g., 'What did the man do?' 'Who put the microphone on?'

EXPANSIONS can be seen as one of several means of delimiting possible discourse topics addressed in a child's communicative act. An expanded interpretation can be expressed

377

as an assertion or, more tentatively, as a clarification request (repair initiator). The first alternative assumes that unless otherwise challenged, the expansion (interpretation) is plausible. The second alternative requests an explicit confirmation check (repair response) from the child.

As noted previously, an additional means for arriving at the intended discourse topic of the child is to propose it as a primary presupposition of an explicit question of immediate concern. This response is illustrated in examples 31 and 38. This alternative differs from expansions in that the speaker commits himself to a specific discourse topic. In expansions, the speaker merely reduces the number of possible questions the utterance is relevant to. On the other hand, questions of immediate concern share certain characteristics of expansions used as repair initiators. They both generate a topic-collaborating sequence of utterances. In both cases, the listener is eliciting information about a particular proposition, and the child (speaker) is providing information relevant to that same proposition.

VI. Implications for the Notion of Competence in Child Language

The four steps described here for establishing a discourse topic are fundamental to successful communication. Children must develop means to accomplish each of these steps, if they are both to contribute to, and sustain, a coherent discourse. We propose that the extent to which a child is capable of completing these steps is an important measure of the child's developing communicative competence. We say communicative, rather than strictly linguistic, because the child relies on both verbal and non-verbal means for accomplishing these steps.

We need to examine the visual and verbal records of children's speech to determine

1. which steps are taken by the child:

For example, the first analysis of children's speech at the one- and two-word stage shows that steps 1, 2, and 3 are taken by the child. Children at this point in their development can point out referents that are relevant to a discourse topic proposition, but they do not specify the semantic roles of such referents in the discourse topic (step 4). As we have seen, the listener is left to reconstruct the proposition on the basis of the referent located, and shared background knowledge.

2. how much conversational space (number of utterances, number of turns) is taken up with satisfying each step:

One of the most important things to consider here is the

context in which the interaction is occurring. The amount of conversational space taken up depends on the number of individuals present, the extent to which they are attending to the child, and the extent to which they are familiar with the child and his experiences. In addition, it is important to consider whether the intended listener is an adult, an older child, or a peer. The same string of sounds could be successfully interpreted in one context, yet not understood at all in another context. Those who are intimate with a child may compensate for poor articulation, idiosyncratic expressions, and "out of the blue" references.

Contexts in which the listener is not intimate with the child reveal more clearly the child's competence. In these contexts, the child must work harder to accomplish these steps. Further, these contexts generate repair procedures. These procedures make explicit what information the child can and cannot provide at each step.

It would be useful to examine adult speech to children to see the extent to which adults initiate repairs on each of these steps. It may be the case that adults only request repairs on those steps the child is capable of carrying out. In this case, we would see a shift in the nature of the repair initiator over time. (This shift would also be affected by what needs to be repaired, e.g., as the child articulates his message more clearly, there should be fewer repair initiators on step 2.)

3. <u>the means employed by the child for implementing each step</u>:

Although speakers never stop relying on non-verbal means in conveying messages, the extent of their reliance varies developmentally. That is, children come to rely more and more on verbal means to convey their messages, and this in turn provides more explicit cues as to what discourse topic is being addressed. This process has often been noted, but only recently has documentation of this process begun (Greenfield and Smith, in press).

Looking to verbal means, we need to examine developmental changes in the child's ability to refer to entities in both physical and memory space. And we need to document when and how a child makes it explicit (verbally) that he is introducing a novel topic, or reintroducing a topic addressed earlier.

VI.B Comprehension

A further dimension in the development of competence concerns the extent to which a child is able to determine the discourse topic of a conversational partner. As has often been noted, the relationship between comprehension and production at any one point in time is difficult to determine. However, we can get some indication of what the child is understanding from observing two kinds of responses:

1. When an adult does not understand an utterance, he has the option of initiating a repair on that utterance. It would seem reasonable to look at the child language data for these responses. We find, however, that children initially do not evidence their misunderstanding in this form. As noted, we find no such verbal repair initiators in our data until the child is almost 3 years of age. Once they have emerged in the child's speech, it is important to document the changing character of the repair-initiators, that is, the order in which repairs on each step emerge.

2. The second response that may be said to indicate comprehension on the part of the child (listener) is topic collaboration. This is clearest in question-answer topic-collaborating sequences. To answer a question, the child must locate the discourse topic of the question (i.e., the proposition about which information is requested) and use this discourse topic in his/her answer (see examples 3, 10, 13, 14, 34).

It is necessary to examine the child's ability to both collaborate on "old" topics and initiate "new" topics into the discourse. We find in our data that asking questions is a speech behavior more characteristic of adults speaking to children than children speaking to adults, or to each other. A consequence of this is that children often collaborate on a discourse topic proposed by an adult. We expect to find variation in the extent to which one child can introduce a discourse topic rather than collaborate on a discourse topic. In many of the interactions between adults and children, for example, the adult controls the direction of the conversation by repeatedly initiating discourse topics which the child is then expected to respond to (Corsaro 1974). This is particularly characteristic of experimental situations, where a question-answer tactic is employed. In these situations, only the child's ability to determine the discourse topic proposition is evident. The child's ability to establish new discourse topics cannot be observed.

VIII Why Discourse Topic?

Our treatment of topic as a discourse notion should be considered as distinct from other descriptions of topic in the linguistic literature. From our point of view, topic is not a simple NP but a proposition (about which some claim is made or elicited). In the linguistic literature, left –

dislocation of an NP (e.g., 'This paper, it's almost done.') has been treated as a topicalization device (Gruber 1967, Gundel 1975). From our point of view, these left-dislocated NPs vary in the roles they play with respect to discourse and discourse topic.

For example, unstressed left-dislocated NPs preceded by As for or Concerning typically retrieve earlier discourse material. In our framework, these constructions mark re-introducing topics. The construction brings a prior proposition or a referent within a prior proposition back into focus. This function might explain why the NPs appearing after As for or Concerning are not drawn from an immediately preceding utterance. For example, a sequence such as "Where is John?" "As for John, he's at home" seems inappropriate. It is in-appropriate, because there is no need to retrieve or fore-ground the referent. This function explains as well why As for constructions followed by stressed NPs are used to con-trast or emphasize referents or propositions, e.g., "Mary said she wouldn't help, but as for me, I'm willing."

Left-dislocated NPs not preceded by As for or Concerning are considerably less restricted in discourse. We find that these constructions may both introduce novel referents and propositions or reintroduce previously mentioned referents and propositions. We find that in many cases the left-dislo-cated NP may be part of the new information or comment on a discourse topic, e.g., "What's the matter?" "My father, he's bugging me again." Here the left-dislocated NP is part of the new information provided about the discourse topic propo-sition, 'something is the matter.' The NP 'my father' is the 'center of attention' (Li and Thompson, this volume) of the sentence in which it is couched. It is not the 'center of attention' of the discourse in which the sentence is couched (11).

It would be valuable to have some understanding of dis-course dynamics in topic-prominent languages (Li and Thomp-son, this volume). In languages where topic-comment con-structions alternate with subject-predicate constructions, e.g., Chinese, the use of topic constructions may be contex-tually constrained. It would be useful to examine spontan-eous conversational discourse in these languages to determine the functions of the topic construction in the discourse con-text. Can these constructions re-introduce, introduce, col-laborate, incorporate discourse material? Or is their use restricted to some of these functions only? Where topic-constructions are always the norm, we would like to determine as well 1) if all these functions are handled; and 2) if the language differentiates these functions morphologically or syntactically. In general, we want to establish a frame-work for comparing topic constructions in their discourse contexts across languages.

We offer here a baseline description of topic in dis-course. We refer to this notion as discourse topic, because it is usually discourse-generated (relevant) and often dis-course-generating.

Notes

1. This research was supported by a grant from Social Science Research Council grant #HR/2941/1.

2. For the Allison data, only gaze directed to the mother is marked. ↑ = child makes eye contact with mother. ↓ = child terminates eye contact with mother.

3. This notion is very close to that of topic-shading as discussed by Schegloff and Sacks (1973:305): "One procedure whereby talk moves off a topic might be called 'topic shading' in that it involves no specific attention to ending a topic at all, but rather the fitting of differently focussed but related talk to some last utterance in a topic's development." We do not employ the same term, as the co-creators of it may not agree with the notion of discourse topic developed in this paper.

4. Greenfield and Smith (in press) have discussed the notion of informativeness for children at the one word stage. In their framework, the child tends to encode that aspect of a situation that the child considers to be the least certain. For example, in volitional acts (requests, demands), "when the object is securely in the child's possession..., it becomes relatively certain and the child will first encode Action/State...When the object is not in the child's possession, it becomes more uncertain, and his first utterance will express the object" (ms. p. 20 chap. 4).

5. Anglo speakers of English, of course, also 're-introduce' concerns discussed at some prior time. The difference between the two cultures is that Anglo speakers of English mark these re-introducing topics in formal social contexts with constructions such as "As for...", "Concerning...", etc., whereas Indian speakers do not. In less formal contexts, Anglo speakers too are under less constraint to mark overtly that they are addressing their utterance to a prior concern (not addressed in the immediately preceding utterance).

6. For children of 13+ months the establishment of eye contact is one of the most reliable measures of having secured the attention of the listener (Huttenlocher 1974).

7. These utterances are typically omitted in developmental psycholinguistic literature. They are characterized as unintelligible. From our point of view, they are often unreconstructable, from the hearer's point of view.

8. Frequently the adult can reconstruct what the child is talking about despite the child's inability to provide adequate information. The amount of shared experience is critical in this reconstruction process. Someone who spends

many hours a day knowing what the child has been doing can
often understand an "out of context" utterance to a much
greater extent than an investigator making infrequent visits.

    9. It is difficult to say to what extent the child has
designed his communication to meet the recipient's needs without access to a video record of the event. The child might
have been giving additional cues that the mother didn't
attend to.

    10. There is adequate evidence prior to this utterance
that Allison knows the appropriate label for "man" and for
"microphone." Her utterance combined with the pointing can
be assumed to be an intentional linking of man and microphone.

    11. We wish to point out that a left-dislocated simple
NP may be either an explicit 'representation' of an implicit
proposition or a referring expression only: "Champagne, that's
a fantastic idea" vs. "Champagne, it makes me feel fine."

ON THE SUBJECTLESS "PSEUDO-PASSIVE" IN STANDARD DUTCH
AND THE SEMANTICS OF BACKGROUND AGENTS

by

Robert S. Kirsner

1. Introduction (1)

In a typical Dutch sentence such as 1, the so-called
"agent of the action" is referred to with a definite noun-
phrase which traditionally is both "grammatical subject"
(with which the verb "agrees in person and number") and
"topic"--i.e., old information, hence unstressed and in initial position:

   1. De jongens fluiten
       the boys   whistle
       "The boys whistle/are whistling."

This typical situation may be deviated from in at least two
ways. First, the "agent" can remain grammatical subject but
need not be topic. This occurs in so-called "presentative"
sentences (2), where indefinite subjects are introduced with
weak deictic er "there."

   2. Er fluiten jongens
       there whistle boys
       "Boys are whistling (there)/There are boys
            whistling there."

In Kirsner (1972 and 1973), sentences such as 2 are discussed in detail. It is demonstrated that, with active finite verbs, whose morphology assigns no constant semantic
role to the subject, use of er to "detopicalize" that subject subtly decreases the possibility of interpreting it as
fully agentive. In other words, since agentive entities are,
in some sense, "natural topics," an indeterminate noun-
phrase which is not topic is less likely to be taken as an
"agent" (3).
    The second deviation from the state of affairs in 1 is
when the "agent" is not grammatical subject at all. This
occurs in so-called "pseudo-passive" sentences illustrated
in 3:

   3.a. Er wordt gefloten
        there becomes whistled
        "There is whistling/People whistle/Someone
            whistles."

     b. Er wordt door de jongens gefloten
        there becomes by the boys whistled
        "There is whistling by the boys."

     c. Door de jongens wordt gefloten
        by   the boys   becomes whistled
        "By the boys (there) is whistling."

387

In 3 there is no grammatical subject and no "verb agreement."
Furthermore, it would appear that neither in 3a or 3b could
the prepositional phrase door de jongens be profitably considered "topic" (4).

The present paper will be concerned with the semantics
of the so-called "pseudo-passive" in sentences such as 3.
Specifically, it will

    i. argue that, like the "true" Dutch passive (not
        shown above), the "pseudo-passive" explicitly as-
        serts that the "agent" is non-focussed or back-
        grounded,

and, as a means of validating i., it will

    ii. explore the many semantic, pragmatic, and stylistic
        consequences of this backgrounding.

2.   "True" Passive and "Pseudo-Passive"

If one is to explain the particular properties of the
Dutch pseudo-passive (why it is used in the ways it is), one
must first discover what it itself contributes to the messages that it helps to communicate. This necessarily raises
an important analytical issue, for alongside the subjectless
pseudo-passive in Dutch there is also a subjectful "true"
passive. Since both contain the same passive morphology
(the auxiliary verb worden "become" plus a past participle),
the question naturally arises of their "relationship." More
precisely, are the "two passives" a single linguistic entity, a single linguistic unit, or are they not? Although we
will be unable to answer this question within the scope of
the present paper, a few orienting remarks are nonetheless in
order.

2.1 Sketch of a unitary analysis

The two uses of passive morphology in Dutch are contrasted below:

    4.   Subjectful "true passive

        De huizen werden verwoest
        the houses became destroyed
        "The houses were destroyed."

    5.   Subjectless "pseudo-passive"

        Er werd gefloten
        there became whistled
        "There was whistling/People whistled/Someone
           whistled."

The pseudo-passive, 5, differs from the true passive, 4, in two ways. First, it does not contain a grammatical subject interpreted as a "logical object." Second, it refers only to human activities. While the houses in 4 could have been destroyed by people, animals, or natural forces, sentence 5 cannot be used to describe the whistling of birds, teakettles, or the wind.

Whereas most traditional grammarians assume that the "two passives" are separate linguistic objects and, hence, that the absolute identity of passive morphology in each is a synchronic accident, Kirsner (1974 and 1975) explicitly considers the hypothesis that they are merely two distinct exploitations of a single unit. Specifically, it is proposed that in both its uses, passive morphology (worden + past participle) is one linguistic sign signaling the single, relatively abstract meaning high participant not focussed, which may be roughly paraphrased as "the logical subject is not the grammatical subject." Clearly, if one is to account for "both passives" with a single meaning, one cannot claim that this meaning is "the grammatical subject is logical object," for the pseudo-passive contains no grammatical subject at all. Rather, one must look at what both true and pseudo-passive have in common. Since in neither is the agent-like entity foregrounded as grammatical subject, it is reasonable to claim that this is, in fact, what passive morphology itself asserts.

Let us now examine the meaning high participant not focussed in more detail. By participant is meant an entity which is centrally involved in the event named by the verb, an entity which participates in the event rather than simply being the scene or circumstance of it. By high participant is meant one which ranks comparatively high on a scale of relative agentivity or potency, more technically a scale of relative contribution to the bringing about of the event named by the verb (cf. Cohen 1972, Diver 1974:24-30, Zubin 1972:23-38). Although high participant may, under various conditions, communicate such notions as "causer," "agent," "instrument," it is a relative meaning and not (as the elements in Filmore 1968) a fixed chunk of absolute semantic substance.

By focussed is meant "foregrounded, in the center of attention." The term is intended to refer specifically to the semantic contribution of the verb ending in what is commonly called "agreement" (5). Traditionally, of course, the verb is said to redundantly "agree" in person and number with the grammatical subject. Yet there are clear instances in Dutch where the number signaled by the verb overrides that

ROBERT S. KIRSNER

on the noun and thus makes its own contribution to the interpretation of the sentence. Consequently, it is assumed here
that one of the participants in the event is semantically
most central or prominent and that the finite verb provides
further information about this prominent participant. With
the exception of so-called "dummy" subjects, which undoubtedly have their own functional explanation, the grammatical
subject refers to that participant which attention has been
most focussed on or directed to (6).

Considering the various components together, we now see
that the meaning high participant not focussed makes the following claim: there is indeed a high participant involved in
the event, a relatively greater contributor to the occurrence
named by the verb, but that participant is not focussed, not
in the center of attention, not foregrounded as grammatical
subject.

2.2   Relative and absolute backgrounding

In Kirsner (1974 and 1975), inferential mechanisms are
proposed accounting for the restriction of the pseudo-passive
to human actions, i.e., for the fact that, in the absence of
a grammatical subject, the meaning high participant not focussed is taken as referring only to people. While we cannot
explore these mechanisms here, it is essential for our understanding of the pseudo-passive to consider one component of
the argument: the demonstration that the pseudo-passive backgrounds the high, "agent-like" participant more strongly than
the true passive.

A true passive such as 4 De huizen werden verwoest "The
houses were destroyed" asserts that there is an additional,
focussed participant--houses--besides the high, non-focussed
one. It is referred to directly, with the noun-phrase de huizen. Consequently, even though passive morphology claims that
the high participant is non-focussed, i.e., backgrounded, we
would argue that it is so only with respect to the particular
focussed participant in the sentence at hand. The backgrounding, in other words, is only relative; it reflects only the
difference in topicality between high and non-high contribu-
tors. Since the focussed participant is there, referred to
with a particular subject noun-phrase de huizen, it necessarily serves as a basis of comparison, a specific standard for
what is not focussed. Consequently, one can infer that the
high participant is less foregrounded than the non-high one,
which is subject, but little more. We are then roughly in
the position of someone confronted with the sentence Compared
to Bill, Tom is not tall. One knows that Tom is shorter than

390

Bill but does not know that Tom is short absolutely. The denial of height, like the denial of focus in a true passive, is only relative.

Consider now the pseudo-passive 5, Er werd gefloten "There was whistling." Here, just as in the true passive, the morphology asserts high participant not focussed. But the high participant is the only entity mentioned; there is no subject, no focussed participant. Consequently, since the high participant is claimed to be not focussed, the resultant backgrounding is absolute, not relative, for it can reflect only on the high participant itself. In terms of the previous analogy, use of the pseudo-passive is comparable to assertion of the sentence Tom is not tall, period. Since no particular standard is mentioned, the denial of height is absolute, i.e., without qualification.

The claim that the pseudo-passive backgrounds or "defocusses" the high participant more strongly than the true passive permits the analyst to make several quantitative predictions about actual language use. As a test of the above argument, we now present three such predictions, together with the relevant data.

The first prediction concerns the ratio of full passives--where the "agent" is mentioned in a prepositional phrase--to so-called "agentless" passives. Given that, in both the true and the pseudo forms, passive morphology signals the meaning high participant not focussed, one would expect that explicit mention of the same non-focussed participant in a prepositional phrase in the same passive sentence would be incoherent with the non-focussing and would therefore tend to be avoided. In other words, since it is inconsistent both to background the high participant with the meaning not focussed and to highlight it by direct mention, one would expect the ratio of full to agentless passives to be small both in the true and in the pseudo forms. However, since the pseudo-passive backgrounds the high participant more strongly than the true passive, we would also expect a difference in the ratios. The stronger the denial of focus to the high participant, the less consistent it should be to specifically refer to it. Accordingly, the pseudo-passive should be even less hospitable to agentive door-phrases than the true passive. We therefore predict that while agentive door-phrases will be relatively infrequent in both true and pseudo-passives, they will be even less frequent in the pseudo-passive than in the true passive.

Table 1 summarizes counts made on seven corpora--over a thousand pages of text. The distributions are as predicted. In the entire sample of 318 true and pseudo-passive sentences,

TABLE 1

Frequency of Full Passives, with Agentive Door-Phrase,
As A Function of Passive Type (7)

Corpus[a]	Type of Passive	N Full	N Agentless
1	pseudo	0	9
	true	8	31
2	pseudo	0	11
	true	10	64
3	pseudo	1	12
	true	15	66
4	pseudo	0	7
	true	5	35
5	pseudo data only	0	9
6	pseudo data only	0	33
7	pseudo data only	1	1
Totals	pseudo	2 (2%)	82 (98%)
	true	38 (16%)	196 (84%)
	both	40 (13%)	278 (87%)

[a] 1 = Behouden huis, in Hermans (1966b); 2 = Jong (1962); 3 =
Haasse (1968); 4 = Reve (1970); 5 = Vestdijk (1950); 6 =
Hermans (1967); 7 = Jongeman, in Hermans (1966a).

only 13% contained door-phrases. The percentage of full true
passives was eight times greater than that of full pseudo-
passives. A chi-square test indicates that the probability
of the observed distribution occurring by chance is less than
0.005.

The second prediction is a direct extension of the
first and concerns the influence of the type of subject noun-
phrase on the occurrence of full (agented) true passives. If,
in the true passive, the backgrounded high participant can
only be less focussed than the given focussed participant,
any change in the foregrounding of the latter should induce a
corresponding shift in the backgrounding of the former. If
the referent of the subject could be--on some absolute scale--
very much focussed, very much foregrounded, then the non-
focussed high contributor would be backgrounded only to a
small degree. If, on the other hand, the focussed participant
itself was already removed from the center of attention, the
non-focussed "agent" would be even more so. In other words,
by increasing the de facto degree of foregrounding on the
referent of the subject, one would decrease the degree to

which focus was denied to the non-focussed "agent." Given that such denial disfavors the occurrence of agentive door-phrases, one would then also increase the relative frequency of full true passives. Consequently, if we could somehow measure the degree of foregrounding of the focussed participant, we would expect to find a direct positive correlation between it and the occurrence of agentive door-phrases.

Since what we are interested in is the extent to which the focussed participant is already in the center of attention, a suitable metric would be the anaphoricity of the subject noun-phrase (cf. Cole 1974:669). Pronominal subjects (not actually naming their referents) are more anaphoric (i.e., their use suggests a more uniquely specified, fore-grounded referent) than full noun-phrases, which can always count as new information (cf. Chafe 1974:114, Kraak 1970:50). Definite full noun-phrases are in turn more anaphoric than indefinite noun-phrases, and er-introduced subjects (in ex-plicitly "presentative" sentences) are the least anaphoric of all (8). Accordingly, we rephrase our prediction as follows: examination of actual language use should reveal a direct, positive relationship between the degree of anaphoricity of the subject noun-phrase of true passives and the relative frequency of the full (agented) form.

We may also make an additional, third prediction. The crucial difference between the "two passives" lies in the presence of a grammatical subject referring to a focussed participant. If one now ranks subject noun-phrases on an anaphoricity scale, one is setting up--within the true pas-sive category--a differentiation entirely analogous to the original one between true and pseudo-forms. A true passive with a highly anaphoric pronominal subject, referring to a most foregrounded focussed participant, is, as it were, a true passive par excellence. It is the "best example" of what a true passive is, for in it the difference between true and pseudo forms is maximized. A true passive with an inde-finite subject, on the other hand, is much more like the sub-jectless pseudo-passive. Though it contains a subject noun-phrase, that subject claims that its referent is not partic-ularly foregrounded, not "focus-worthy." We might expect, then, that if we plotted the relative frequency of full true passives as a function of subject anaphoricity, the sentences with the least anaphoric subject, in addition to having the lowest percentage of door-phrases, would also have a percent-age closest of all to that in the subjectless pseudo-passive.

Table 2 summarizes the data. It may be observed that there is indeed a direct, positive correlation between the anaphoricity of the subject noun-phrase and the percentage of

TABLE 2

Frequency of Full True Passives As A Function of The
Anaphoricity of The Subject NP, with Comparison
to Pseudo-Passives

Corpus[a]	Passive	Ps[b]	A[c]	B[d]	C[e]	D[f]	(E)[g]
1	full	0	0	0	3	4	(1)
	agentless	9	4	5	8	7	(7)
2	full	0	0	1	5	4	(0)
	agentless	11	7	5	38	8	(6)
3	full	1	0	1	4	9	(1)
	agentless	12	7	7	21	18	(13)
4	full	0	0	1	1	2	(1)
	agentless	7	6	3	12	11	(3)
Total	full	1	0	3	13	19	(3)
	agentless	39	24	20	79	44	(29)
% Full Passives:		2	⓪[h]	13	14	30	(9)

[a]1 = Behouden huis, in Hermans (1966b); 2 = Jong (1962); 3 =
Haasse (1968); 4 = Reve (1970); 5 = Vestdijk (1950); 6 =
Hermans (1967); 7 = Jongeman, in Hermans (1966a).

[b]Ps = pseudo-passives.

[c]A = true passives with er-introduced indefinite subjects.

[d]B = true passives with plain indefinites.

[e]C = true passives with definite full NPs.

[f]D = true passives with pronominal subjects.

[g](E) = other subjects (e.g., relative pronouns) not ranked on
ABCD scale.

[h]Circled percentage is most similar to that in Ps.

full passives (9). Furthermore, true passives with the er-
introduced indefinite subjects (least anaphoric) exhibit a
percentage of agentive door-phrases closest to that in the
pseudo-passives, which, of course, contain no subjects at all.
     This last observation is very interesting. To pick an
analogy from Freshman Mathematics, it appears that we may indeed regard the subjectless pseudo-passive as a kind of "semantic limit" one would reach if he could continuously decrease the focus on the referent of the subject noun-phrase
of a true passive. By continuously backgrounding the focussed

participant, one necessarily also continuously backgrounds the non-focussed high contributor. The ultimate end-point of such a process is the absolute removal of the high contributor from the center of attention, something least compatible with its mention in a door-phrase. This is, in fact, what we claim is achieved in the pseudo-passive, where there is no subject and the high participant is non-focussed or backgrounded all by itself. The trend shown in the data of Table 2 may be seen more clearly in Figure 1.

Percentage of Full   (Note: abbreviations same as in
  Passives (with   Table 2; N = total number of pas-
  door-phrase)   sives in each sample.)

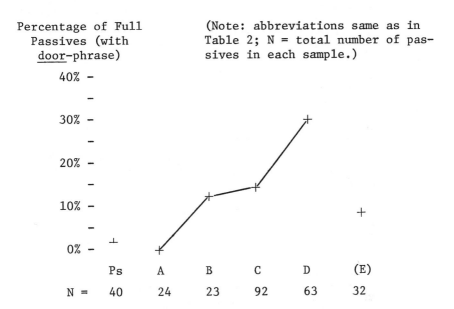

Figure 1. Percentage of full true passives as a function of the anaphoricity of the subject NP, with comparison to subjectless pseudo-passives.

3.   Pseudo-Passive Versus Active:
      Consequences of Backgrounding

Having argued that the pseudo-passive denies focus to the high participant more strongly than the true passive, we now turn to its use by speakers in communicating messages. We shall examine various properties and exploitations of the pseudo-passive and shall demonstrate that, in spite of their diversity, each follows directly from the strong backgrounding of the agent (10) which we have proposed.

3.1   Agentless pseudo-passives

Perhaps the most obvious exploitation of the meaning
<u>high</u> <u>participant</u> <u>not</u> <u>focussed</u> occurs in agentless pseudo-
passives, especially in reference to events where the action
itself is most important and where the identity of the high
participant is either irrelevant or unknown (11).

6.   Ik begon te zien, dat <u>er</u> <u>niet</u> <u>geleefd</u> <u>werd</u> in de
        onwezenlijke buitenbuurthuisjes...<u>er</u> <u>werd</u> <u>geleefd</u>
        in de kantoren, de fabrieken, de ziekenhuizen, de
        café's...   (Nijhoff 1966:22)

        I began to see that <u>life</u> <u>did</u> <u>not</u> <u>go</u> <u>on</u> [literal-
        ly: "there was not living"] in the unreal little
        houses on the edges of the city...<u>life</u> <u>went</u> <u>on</u>
        [lit: "there was living"] in the offices, the
        factories, the hospitals, the cafes...

7.   Terwijl hij het kaartje greep. zijn hoofd voor-
        over, kon hij toch vaaglijk waarnemen dat er
        iemand heen en weer liep voor het raam. Hij
        sloeg zijn ogen op, maar zag niemand. Toch wist
        hij zeker dat <u>er</u> <u>heen</u> <u>en</u> <u>weer</u> <u>gelopen</u> <u>was</u>, het
        was niet iemand geweest die stilgestaan had om
        te kijken, niet iemand die in <u>een</u> richting
        [author's emphasis] was voorbijgelopen.
                                             (Hermans 1967:48)

        As he grasped the card, with his head bent down,
        he could feel vaguely that someone was walking to
        and fro outside, in front of the window. He
        glanced up, but saw nobody. Nevertheless, he
        knew for certain that <u>someone</u> <u>or</u> <u>something</u> <u>had</u>
        <u>been</u> <u>walking</u> <u>to</u> <u>and</u> <u>fro</u> [lit: "that there had
        been walking back and forth"], it had not been
        anyone who had stopped to look, not anyone who
        had passed going in <u>one</u> [author's emphasis] di-
        rection.   (Hermans 1962:41)

Note that in 7 the pseudo-passive clause <u>dat</u> <u>er</u> <u>heen</u> <u>en</u> <u>weer</u>
<u>gelopen</u> <u>was</u> "that there had been walking back and forth" con-
trasts directly with a preceding presentative clause <u>dat</u> <u>er</u>
<u>iemand</u> <u>heen</u> <u>en</u> <u>weer</u> <u>liep</u> <u>voor</u> <u>het</u> <u>raam</u> "that there walked
someone back and forth in front of the window." Whereas the
presentative clause explicitly introduces an <u>iemand</u>, a "someone," onto the scene (whose identity then becomes an issue),
the agentless pseudo-passive, asserting <u>high</u> <u>participant</u> <u>not</u>
<u>focussed</u>, centers attention on the walking itself, particu-
larly on the <u>kind</u> of walking that was involved.

In addition to referring to events with unknown or "ir-relevant" participants, the agentless pseudo-passive may also be used when the agent is, in fact, fully identified. Clear-ly, in such situations the assertion of high participant not focussed constitutes a "demotion": an active removal from fo-cus rather than a simple denial of focus. It is one thing to assert that the agent is backgrounded when one neither knows nor cares who the agent is; it is something else to make this same claim--and to thereby center attention on the action a-lone--when the agent has already been identified and could easily be referred to directly, with the subject noun-phrase of an appropriate active sentence. One may expect, then, that this "demotional" use of the pseudo-passive will have a certain stylistic impact. Consider the following narrative of events immediately following a domestic indiscretion:

8.   Terwijl mijm moeder verkondigde, dat men de man
      in ieder geval gelegenheid moest geven zich te
      verweren, haalde mijn vader onder verveeld ge-
      zucht papier en een envelop uit de muurkast. Er
      werd geschreven, mijn moeder scheen moeite te
      hebben haar ernst te bewaren, het meisje was uit-
      gehuild, en vertelde het verhaal opnieuw...
                                    (Vestdijk 1950:62)

      While my mother was declaring that in any case we
      would have to give the man a chance to explain
      himself, my father walked over to the cupboard in
      the corner to get a sheet of note paper and an
      envelope. My father sat writing [lit: "there was
      writing"], my mother seemed to be having some
      difficulty in keeping a straight face. The maid
      had finished crying and started telling her sto-
      ry all over again...   (Vestdijk 1965:69)

Informants indicate that the use of the pseudo-passive here, instead of, e.g. Hij schreef "He wrote," removes the father from the center of attention. The narrator's camera dollies backwards, away from the father, to encompass the whole scene (12).

From time to time in the Dutch linguistic literature, it has been proposed that agentless pseudo-passives are se-mantically equivalent to active sentences containing the in-definite subjects iemand "someone" and men "one" (cf. Hertog 1972 [1903]:54, Kraak-Klooster 1968:185). It will be obvious that the present use of the pseudo-passive to refer to events with known agents immediately refutes this claim. Consider in addition the following example of a pseudo-passive with

"imperative force"; informants find the suggested active alternatives utterly ludicrous (13):

    9.a.   En nu, Jantije, wordt er geslapen! [mother to
         and now, Johnny, there is sleeping! child]
         "And now, Johnny, go to sleep!"

      b. *En nu, Jantje, slaapt er iemand!
         and now, Johnny, sleeps there someone!
         "And now, Johnny, someone is sleeping!"

      c. *En nu, Jantje, slaapt men!
         and now, Johnny, sleeps one!
         "And now, Johnny, one sleeps/is sleeping."

Since the agentless pseudo-passive does not mention any particular, specific high contributor and thus says nothing a-
bout one's status as either identified or unidentified, it is
less inappropriate for an imperative message, less inconsistent with the inference that the known addressee is intended
as the agent of sleeping, than are either of the explicitly
indefinite subjects (14). For arguments that the pseudo-
passive is, in fact, never equivalent to active sentences
with men or iemand, even when the agent is unknown, see Pollmann (1970:37-39) and Es and Caspel (1973:38). Note also our
discussion of 7 above.

3.2 Full pseudo-passives

    Undoubtedly the most interesting exploitations of the
meaning high participant not focussed occur in full pseudo-
passives, explicitly mentioning the backgrounded agent in a
door-phrase. Since here there is always the possibility of
"paraphrase" with a formally corresponding active sentence,
the issue of contrast immediately arises. How, for example,
will the message communicated with 10.a below, where the referent of de studenten is backgrounded, differ from the message communicated with 10.b, where it is in the very center
of attention, both as subject and topic?

    10.a.   Er wordt door de studenten gestaakt.
          there becomes by the students struck
          "There is striking/a strike by the students."

      b. De studenten staken.
         "The students are striking."

It appears that there are two distinct--and seemingly contra-
dictory--strategies for the use of full pseudo-passives (15).
As we shall see, however, both may profitably be viewed as

ways of resolving the "conflict" (cf. Table 1 in Section 2.2, above) between, on the one hand, the claim of passive morphology that the high contributor is backgrounded and, on the other, the explicit mention of it in a door-phrase.

3.2.1 The direct exploitation of backgrounding

The first and more transparent use of the full pseudo-passive is in describing events globally. Here, although the high participant is indeed mentioned, it is non-focussed, peripheral, and does not become the topic of the sentence or clause in which it appears. Consistent with the lack of emphasis upon its referent, the agentive door-phrase is unstressed and typically occurs "shielded" from sentence-initial position by the weak deictic er, as in 10.a, above.

Empirical evidence for the claim that, in this first use, full pseudo-passives do indeed describe events globally --i.e., that, consistent with backgrounding, the sentence in question is not a predication about the agent--is provided by a wide variety of data. Consider first relative clauses. As is well-known, the head-noun of a relative clause is, in some sense, its topic or theme, the entity about which the clause contributes further information (cf. Schachter 1973). Where the content of the clause is inconsistent with such an interpretation of its head-noun, i.e., where the clause in effect "denies" that its antecedent is its theme, incoherency results (cf. Kuno, this volume). Compare now a pseudo-passive relative clause such as 11.a below with an active relative clause such as 11.b:

11.a. door wie er gelachen was
        "by whom there had been laughing"

   b. die gelachen had
        "who had laughed"

Given that the meaning high participant not focussed backgrounds the agent, then even though that agent is referred to explicitly with the relative pronoun wie in 11.a, it should be less in the center of attention--and hence less likely to be taken as topic--than the referent of the relative pronoun die in 11.b (16). Consequently, we expect the active relative clause to be more coherent than the pseudo-passive one. This is exactly what is observed:

12.a. De man die gelachen had, werd buiten westen
        geslagen.
        "The man who had laughed was knocked uncon-
        scious."

b. *De man door wie er gelachen was, werd buiten
   westen geslagen.
   "The man by whom there had been laughing was
   knocked unconscious."

A second piece of evidence that the high participant,
though mentioned, is not in the center of attention is that
the object of the door-phrase is less likely than the subject of the formally corresponding active sentence to be
taken as co-referential with a highly anaphoric nominal (17).
Beginning with the most anaphoric noun phrase, zero (cf.
Cole 1974:669), we note that although 13.a below is fine,
13.b is incoherent:

13.a. De vrouwen$_i$ lachten en [$\emptyset_i$] huilden.

   "The women laughed and cried."

b. *Er werd door de vrouwen$_i$ gelachen en [$\emptyset_i$]
   huilden.
   "There was laughing by the women and cried."

The incoherency of 13.b correlates with the fact that while
an unstressed personal pronoun—less anaphoric than zero—is
easily interpreted as co-referential with a subject, pointing to a focussed participant, it is less so with the door-
phrase, specifying a non-focussed agent. Compare:

14.a. De vrouwen$_i$ lachten en ze$_i$ huilden.

   "The women laughed and they cried."

b. ?Er werd door de vrouwen$_i$ gelachen en ze$_i$
   huilden. (18)
   "There was laughing by the women and they
   cried."

The unstressed pronoun ze "they" is more easily taken as co-
referential with de vrouwen in 14.a than in 14.b. Note further 15.a below, where a co-referential interpretation is
preferred, and 15.b, where it is not (19).

15.a. Toen de dief haar néerstak, schréeuwde de
   vrouw.
   "When the thief stabbed her, the woman
   screamed."

b. Toen de dief haar néerstak, werd er door de
   vrouw geschréeuwd.
   "When the thief stabbed her, there was screaming by the woman."

A third kind of evidence that the high participant, though mentioned, is not in the center of attention is the incoherence of full pseudo-passives in descriptions of events where the agent would normally be prominent. We consider here three classes of examples. A first case in point is statements of causal relationship between actions, i.e., when one participant does something in direct response to the action of some other participant. Here we may reasonably argue that if both agents are explicitly mentioned, both are in some sense in focus and naturally contrast with each other. Consequently, if the two events are described in order of occurrence and in parallel ways, with each agent a focussed participant, then the message of contrast will be heightened and the interpretation of "direct response" will be reinforced. If, on the other hand, the two events are described asymmetrically, with one agent foregrounded as subject but the other not, the contrast will be de-emphasized and the causality also. For example, an English sentence such as Ford pardoned Nixon and Ter Horst resigned, with parallel structure, seems to many informants to communicate a cause-and-effect relationship more clearly than Ford pardoned Nixon and there was Ter Horst's resignation, which seems to merely list separate events. It will, then, support our claim of backgrounding to observe that full pseudo-passives do not effectively communicate messages of "direct response." Informants indicate that, though the second clause of a compound sentence may indeed contain a full pseudo-passive, the connection between the two events will seem looser and more incidental than when both clauses are active. Consider:

16.a. De koningin draaide zich om en de soldaten
      salueerden.
      "The queen turned around and the soldiers
      saluted."

b. De koningin draaide zich om en er werd door de
      soldaten gesalueerd.
      "The queen turned around and there was saluting
      by the soldiers."

Confronted with this pair, several informants have commented that the saluting is depicted as farther away--both locatively and temporally--and that there is less of a connection between it and the queen's action in the pseudo-passive version. In 16.a the soldiers are close to the queen and salute immediately as she turns around; in 16.b they are at some distance and salute only after a pause.
      Consider also 17:

17.a. De psycholoog liet de bel gaan en het kind
       schreeuwde.
       "The psychologist rang the bell and the child
       screamed."

  b. De psycholoog liet de bel gaan en er werd door
       het kind geschreeuwd.
       "The psychologist rang the bell and there was
       screaming by the child."

Informants testify that in 17.b the child's screaming seems
to be more peripheral and is not caused by the ringing of the
bell.

A second case in which participants responsible for actions would be expected to be in the center of attention and
where a full pseudo-passive would consequently be less appropriate is in vivid narrative. Consider the following:

18.   De gordijnen waren nog dicht. Voorzichtig liep
        ik naar de deur. Op dat moment brak het
        raam. Een vrouw gilde. Zes politieagenten
        liepen de trap op.
       "The curtains were still closed. Cautiously I
        walked to the door. At that moment the
        window broke. A woman screamed. Six po-
        licemen came up the stairs."

Informants indicate that while the active sentence Een vrouw
gilde could be replaced in context by the presentative sentence Er gilde een vróuw "There screamed a woman," the pseudo-
passive Er werd door een vrouw gegíld "There was screaming by
a woman" would be totally incoherent.

A third case where the agent or high contributor is
likely to be in the center of attention, one closely related
to the preceeding, is when the action is perceived directly--
hence, when its description is intended as an eyewitness report rather than a mere statement of fact. It would appear
that when an action is seen or heard, there is a "natural interest" in the participant responsible for it. Indeed, particularly in the case of visual perception, it is often difficult to perceive the action without also perceiving its agent.
Consequently, it is entirely consistent with the claim that
full pseudo-passives background the high participant that
they are not normally interpreted as referring to direct observations. Informants indicate, for example, that compared
with the presentative sentence 19.a, below, which could describe something happening right in front of the speaker, the
pseudo-passive 19.b points only to some future event, or
rather, one less localized around the moment of speaking:

19.a. Er treden drie zangeressen op.
       there perform three [woman] singers
       "Three singers are performing."

   b. Er wordt door drie zangeressen opgetreden.
       there is by   three singers   performing
       "There is performing/a performance by three
          singers."

If one forces the issue by prefacing each sentence with a
command to look, the pseudo-passive becomes incoherent (20).

20.a. Kijk eens! Er treden drie zangeressen op!
       "Just look! Three singers are performing!"

   b. *Kijk eens! Er wordt door drie zangeressen
          opgetreden!
       "Just look! There is a performance by three
          singers!"

A parallel example dealing with auditory perception is given
in 21:

21.a. Luister eens! Wim vloekt!
       "Just listen! Bill is cursing!"

   b. *Luister eens! Er wordt door Wim gevloekt!
       "Just listen! There is cursing by Bill!"

Yet additional evidence is provided by the observation that
full pseudo-passives do not normally occur in sensory verb
complements, where the event described is directly perceived
in the manner specified by the verb. Compare:

22.a. Nurejev danste.
       "Nureyev danced."

   b. Er werd door Nurejev gedánst.
       "There was dancing by Nureyev."

   c. Ik keek toe hoe Nurejev danste.
       "I watched Nureyev dance."

   d. *Ik keek toe hoe er door Nurejev gedánst werd.
       "I watched there being dancing by Nureyev."

The incoherence of pseudo-passives in describing events which
are directly perceived thus constitutes the third case in our
third type of evidence for the claim that agent is indeed
backgrounded.

     A fourth type of evidence that full pseudo-passives
background the high participant they mention (and, hence,
that this participant is not topic or theme of the clause) is
the sense of "aloofness" they communicate. A particularly

telling example occurs in an interview with the mayor of
Rotterdam. In response to the observation that he has been
under attack by various political factions, the mayor responds (21):

23.   Er wordt door die kritische groeperingen
            ontzaglijk overdreven...
      "There is awful exaggerating by those critical
      groups."

Informants indicate that this pseudo-passive sentence, backgrounding the critical groups, is a more general, much more
neutral, detached, and mild statement than the corresponding
active, which has the feel of an accusation:

24.   Die kritische groeperingen overdrijven
            ontzaglijk.
      "Those critical groups exaggerate awfully."

The reason for the neutrality of 23 is obvious. In criticisms
and accusations, it is natural that the speaker should center
attention on the party he holds responsible for the undesired
event. Consequently, one would expect the agent to be foregrounded as subject rather than backgrounded in a door-phrase.
Since the mayor's response does not foreground the critical
groups, it is taken not as a criticism or attack but only as
a rather abstract characterization of what is happening.

     A fifth piece of evidence that full pseudo-passives
background the agent is the interpretation they lend to modal
verbs. Even when the modal communicates a so-called "root"
message (i.e., "obligation" or "permission" rather than "possibility" or "probability"), use of the pseudo-passive favors
the interpretation that the modal refers not to the high participant itself but to the event as a whole. Accordingly,
whereas the active sentence 25.a, below, may be taken as a
statement about the characteristics of the boys (i.e., each
has the capacity to swim), the pseudo-passive 25.b is taken
as a statement about the event: the boys "can" swim, not because of their own abilities but because circumstances permit
it, e.g., because the pool is big enough:

25.a. Alle jongens kunnen zwemmen.
       "All the boys can swim."

   b. Er kan door alle jongens gezwommen worden.
       "There can be swimming by all the boys."

     A sixth and final piece of evidence that this first use
of full pseudo-passives backgrounds the agent is provided by
data on the kinds of door-phrases which occur. We remarked
earlier that it was consistent with the backgrounding that

the noun-phrase referring to the high participant should be unstressed. Nevertheless, we have demonstrated that this unstressed agent--not focussed--is less topical than the unstressed subject of corresponding active sentence (21a). Even unstressed, the agentive door-phrase always counts to some extent as new information--a parenthetical specifying of the high participant, filling out the global description of the action provided by passive morphology. We therefore expect an asymmetry between the class of noun-phrases occurring as subject and the class of noun-phrases occurring in the agentive door-phrase. Noun-phrases whose referents are "naturally" topical and which do not normally refer to new information--e.g., personal pronouns (22)--should be incoherent in the unstressed door-phrase, though acceptable as unstressed subjects. This is, in fact, exactly what we find:

26.a. De vrouw gilde
       "The woman screamed."

   b. Ik gilde
       "I screamed."

   c. Er werd door de vrouw gegild.
       "There was screaming by the woman."

   d. *Er werd door mij gegild.
       "There was screaming by me."

The relative incoherence of 26.d results from the conflict between (i) the claim of passive morphology that the agent is backgrounded and (ii) the claim of the first person pronoun that its referent is so much in the center of attention that it no longer needs to be named. The unacceptability of the highly topical pronoun thus corroborates other evidence that the agent-phrase in full pseudo-passives is not topic.

3.2.2 The indirect exploitation of backgrounding

      The second--and initially paradoxical--exploitation of the full pseudo-passive is not to background the high participant, as before, but rather to emphasize it contrastively. We shall first describe this use and then analyze the semantic mechanisms which underlie it.

      Consistent with the emphasis on the agent communicated here, we find that the door-phrase is stressed and that it often occurs sentence-initially--i.e., "unshielded" by er, in a position of prominence, as in 27.a:

27.a. Door de studenten wordt gestaakt.
       "By the students (there) is striking."

b. Er wordt door de studénten gestaakt.
    "There is striking by the students."

Compare the unstressed agent in 28, illustrating the exploitation discussed in Section 3.2.1 above:

28.   Er wordt door de studenten gestáakt.
      "There is striking by the students."

Because contrastive items do count as new information, albeit of a peculiar sort (23), stressed personal pronouns, interpreted contrastively, are more acceptable in the door-phrase than unstressed ones proved to be in Section 3.2.1. Sentences such as 29.b and 29.c below are felt to be normal, although somewhat formal or bookish compared to the active sentence 29.a:

29.a. Wij speelden die avond niet.
       "We didn't play that evening."

b.   Door óns werd die avond niet gespeeld. (24)
     "By us (there) was that evening no playing."

c.   Er werd door óns die avond niet gespeeld.
     "There was by us that evening no playing."

The reason for the bookishness will be taken up shortly, after discussion of the mechanism of emphasis.

In contrast to the first use of the full pseudo-passive, which is transparently a direct exploitation of the meaning signaled by the morphology, the second use is best characterized as indirect. Indeed, at first glance it seems utterly "illogical" that the meaning high participant not focussed could be an essential ingredient in emphasizing the very participant it claims to background. We shall see, however, that paradox is the heart of the emphatic mechanism.

Consider first of all the contradiction. The meaning high participant not focussed defines, as it were, a "normal strategy" for manipulating the pseudo-passive in which the non-focussed agent—being backgrounded—goes unmentioned (cf. Table 1 in Section 2.2, above). Now in the first use, with the agent unstressed, it is still possible to interpret the presence of the door-phrase as in accordance with the claim of backgrounding. The door-phrase specifies the high participant, but is taken as parenthetical information. In the second use, however, with the door-phrase under full sentence accent and typically preposed, no such "parenthetical" interpretation is possible. The agent is clearly being highlighted, in spite of and indeed "flouting" the claim of backgrounding. What, then, is going on? In particular, what is passive morphology contributing to the message of emphatic contrast?

406

It seems reasonable to claim that what we have here is, in effect, a denial of the possibility of a denial. Though the speaker explicitly raises the <u>possibility</u> of the unimportance of the agent's identity (by signaling <u>high participant not focussed</u>), he specifies the agent and calls attention to it. He thus underscores its very <u>relevance</u> by forcefully <u>denying</u> its <u>irrelevance</u>, much in the way that a double negative (e.g., <u>John did not fail to laugh</u>) draws particular attention to the positive event (cf. <u>John laughed</u>). We would claim, then, that the "paradoxical" role of the meaning <u>high participant not focussed</u> is that it provides a kind of negative semantic "base line" for the emphasis which is achieved (25).

Now it should not be assumed that the stressing and fronting of the <u>door</u>-phrase fully overrides the backgrounding claimed by passive morphology. We noted above that while attention is certainly drawn to the agent, informants still feel that the pseudo-passives are formal and bookish compared to active "paraphrases" with stressed subjects. The reason is that, just as in the earlier exploitation (cf. Section 3.2.1) the claim <u>high participant not focussed</u> is still there and still communicates a somewhat detached, unspontaneous view of the event (26). Compare further, in addition to 29 above, the very first question put to a Dutch soccer star in a newspaper interview (27):

> 30. Je praat véel in het veld. <u>Moet er door álle spelers gepraat worden</u> (is het opdracht?), of moet er één zijn die het spel dirigeert?
>
> "You talk a lot on the field. <u>Must there by all players be talking</u> (is it an order?) or must there be one [player] who directs the game?"

Informants interviewed preferred the original sentence, in context, to the active <u>Moeten álle spelers praten</u>...? "Must all players talk...?" which, as we might predict from the discussion in Section 3.2.1, seemed less neutral and less concerned with the circumstances of play (28).

We conclude discussion of the second use with a brief comment on the reasons for the <u>contrastive</u> interpretation of the emphasized agent. Since it is clear that definite noun phrases, referring to old information, would necessarily be taken as contrastive if stressed, we restrict ourselves to indefinites. Consider now the pseudo-passive sentence 31 below and the presentative active sentence 32:

31. Er werd door een vróuw gegild.
     "There was screaming by a woman."

32. Er gilde een vróuw.
     "There screamed a woman."

There are perhaps three reasons why the stressed noun-phrase een vrouw, even though it is indefinite, is interpreted contrastively in 31 rather than as fully new information, as in 32. First of all, whereas the role in the event of the indefinite subject of 32 is not overtly indicated by the verb morphology and must be determined from lexical meanings alone, the door-phrase in 31 clearly refers to a high participant--a "natural topic" (29). Since agent-like entities tend to be in the center of attention, the claim that een vrouw refers to one suggests that, even though it is stressed and not topical here, the purpose of mentioning it is not to simply "present it" on the narrative scene. The indefinite subject of 32, on the other hand, unspecified for role, has no prior claim to topic status.

Second, whereas the verb in 32 claims through "agreement" that the subject refers to a focussed participant, een vrouw in 31, in a prepositional phrase, is non-focussed. Now a focussed participant--an entity which is in the center of attention as a participant--has more of a claim to being topic of discourse than a non-focussed participant. Because the subject of 32 is focussed (30), detopicalization of it with the weak deictic er is, in a sense, contradictory and is possible only when--as is the case here--the referent is not strongly foregrounded, e.g., if the noun-phrase in question is indefinite. In full pseudo-passives, in contrast, because the non-subject agent is less potentially topical to begin with, there are fewer restrictions on items appearing in the door-phrase. The topicality of even anaphoric items is nearly overridden by the claim that they are not focussed, and, hence, the tolerance for them is much greater. As we have seen in Section 3.2.1, only the most topical items—unstressed pronouns--are excluded. What this means is that even if the same noun-phrase can occur in both pseudo-passive and presentative sentences, it is less explicitly new information in the former than in the latter. Given that both kinds of sentences exist and that the speaker has a choice between them, it is reasonable that the pseudo-passive would tend to be specialized for non-presentative messages.

Third, and most importantly, use of the meaning high participant not focussed implies, as outlined above, that the stressed agent is being mentioned where it otherwise would be omitted altogether. This implication is clearly consonant

408

with a contrastive message--namely that the speaker is "bothering" to specify the high participant (something extra) precisely because there has been confusion about its identity. It is less appropriate, however, in communicating a purely presentative message. If the function of 32 is to introduce a totally fresh participant onto the scene, then mentioning that participant is essential to the task, not "something extra," and it would be a distraction to hint with passive morphology, as in 31, that specifying it would normally be irrelevant. Hence, although een vrouw falls under sentence accent in both 31 and 32 and although it could (at least theoretically) be taken as new information in both, the meaning signaled by passive morphology suggests that it refers to a kind of new information whose mention could have been unnecessary. The door is thus opened to the inference that stressed een vróuw in 31 is really old information which has somehow been ignored or forgotten.

4.   Summary and Conclusion

We have hypothesized that both the true and the pseudo-passive in Dutch are exploitations of a single linguistic sign signaling the meaning high participant not focussed and have presented quantitative evidence to support the claim that the pseudo-passive backgrounds the high participant more strongly than the true passive. We have also examined numerous exploitations of the pseudo-passive and have demonstrated in detail how each nuance communicated and each observed incoherency follows directly from the intense backgrounding of the agent we have proposed. Finally, in our examination we have found it useful to contrast full pseudo-passive sentences with intransitive presentative ones. Unlike the detopicalized subjects of the latter which, unspecified for role, are ultimately interpreted as non-agents and as totally new information, the door-phrase of the former refers explicitly to a high participant--a "natural topic"--which, not foregrounded as subject, is not taken as topic either. We have shown that, as a consequence of its backgrounding, the door-phrase is interpreted not as fully new information but as "something extra": either a parenthetical or a contrastive specification of an agent whose presence on the scene is already signaled by the passive morphology itself.

We conclude by pointing out the general implications of this study. Kirsner (1972 and 1973) demonstrated a "natural link" in Dutch between contribution, participant focus, and topicality: if a focussed participant refers to the most agent-like entity in the event named by the verb, then it is

necessarily topic. Hence, if one claims, as in active presentative sentences, that the participant is focussed but not
topic, then it cannot be agent-like.

Here we have explored a second facet of the topicality
of agentive subjects. If an agent-like focussed participant
is necessarily topic, then the only way that a participant
can be not topic but still agent-like is if it is not focussed (31). It is this second possibility which is explicitly
acknowledged in the meaning <u>high</u> <u>participant</u> <u>not</u> <u>focussed</u>.
It is, then, not an accident that Dutch should invest in such
a meaning, for the assertion that the agent is not <u>subject</u>
constitutes a <u>necessary</u> condition for communicating that it
is not <u>topic</u> of the discourse as a whole. In the Dutch subjectless pseudo-passive we have been able to explore the communicative consequences of such a non-topicalization of the
agent in indeed their purest form.

Notes

1. I would like to thank Wally Chafe and especially Erica C. García for helpful comments on the analysis presented here and also Carina Bast, Dr. A. Bonebakker, Prof. S. Bonebakker, Dorthea Farrar, Gabriella Hurwitz, and Suzanne Hoogeveen for many detailed discussions of the Dutch data. Further acknowledgments for valuable observations are due: Tine Eekman, Prof. Thomas Eekman, Boudewijn Klep, Prof. J.G. Kooij, Prof. J. Smit, Prof. E.M. Uhlenbeck and Ineke Verwayen. This research was supported in part by Grant 2964 from the Academic Senate of the University of California at Los Angeles.

2. For the term, cf. Hetzron (1971) and also Wallin (1936):388. Perhaps the phrase "weakly presentative" would better describe the actual use of such sentences in that they are far less emphatic than their apparent English analogues with there. For detailed discussion, see Kirsner (1972 and 1973).

3. Compare now Hawkinson-Hyman (1974:161). For additional Dutch data on the topicality of agents, cf. Nieuwborg (1973:283).

4. Were one to consider the agentive prepositional phrase as "topic" here, one could not account for the fact that it can never contain the most "topical" noun-phrase of all--an unstressed personal pronoun. In addition, when preposed, as in 3.c, the door-phrase is clearly contrastive. Cf. Kuno (1972b), where a distinction is made between "theme" (roughly "topic") and "contrasted element." See further Section 3, below, for discussion.

5. The term focussed, used here in reference to the semantic contribution of the finite-verb ending, refers only to participants in events. It should therefore not be confused with the term discourse focus used in Kirsner (1973) to characterize sentence-initial ("topic") position. The crucial distinction is as follows: Verb "agreement" in Dutch singles out one participant (of the participants mentioned in the sentence) to be the focussed participant with respect to the event. Initial ("topic") position, on the other hand, is reserved for whatever is in the center of attention in the discourse, whether a participant or not. One would, of course, expect that the focussed participant (the traditional "grammatical subject") would tend in the long run to be in discourse focus (the traditional "topic"), but it need not be in every single case. In other words, though the focussed participant might be in the center of attention relative to the other participants mentioned in the particular sentence

411

in question, it need not always be in the absolute center of attention in the discourse as a whole.

6. Cf. Givón (this volume). On so-called "dummy" subjects, a notion with which we disagree, see Kirsner (1972), chapter 3, especially p. 380. We would argue, for example, that it is the meaning or er, within its own system of spatio-temporal deixis, opposed to hier "here" and daar "there," which allows it to be used as an apparently non-referential "dummy." Space precludes further discussion of this important issue here.

7. The reason for the far greater text frequency of true passives over pseudo-passives (in both full and agentless forms) is discussed in Kirsner (1975).

8. That er-introduced indefinites are even less anaphoric than plain indefinites is shown by the fact that they are more coherent as antecedents of the less anaphoric pronouns and less coherent as antecedents of the most anaphoric pronoun, namely zero (cf. Cole 1974:669). If one ranks pronouns on an anaphoricity scale, it is apparent that zero is more anaphoric than unstressed personal pronouns which, in turn, are more anaphoric than demonstratives (typically stressed). Informants asked to evaluate sentences containing zero, the personal pronoun ze "she," and the demonstrative die "that one" reported the following: The sentence Een meisje$_i$ kwam binnen en [$\emptyset_i$] ging zitten "A girl came in and sat down" was better than Een meisje$_i$ kwam binnen en ze$_i$ ging zitten "There came a girl in and she sat down," but Er kwam een meisje$_i$ binnen en ze$_i$ ging zitten "There came a girl in and she sat down" was better than Er kwam een meisje$_i$ binnen en [$\emptyset_i$] ging zitten "There came a girl in and sat down." Furthermore, although die was third choice, on the average, in both cases, more informants gave a higher rank to Er kwam een meisje$_i$ binnen en die$_i$ ging zitten "There came a girl in and she sat down" than to Een meisje$_i$ kwam binnen en die$_i$ ging zitten "A girl came in and she sat down." Since the referent of the er-introduced subject was more coherently referred to with the less anaphoric pronouns ze and die and the referent of the "plain" subject was more coherently referred to with zero, we conclude that use of er, in explicitly "presentative" sentences, characterizes the referent of the indefinite noun-phrase as even "less" given than would otherwise be the case.

9. If one groups together the two categories of definite subjects (C,D) and also the two categories of indefinite subjects (A,B), one obtains the following: Full passives with definite subjects: 32/155 = 21%. Full passives with indefinite subjects: 3/47 = 6%. A chi-square test indicates that

the probability of this distribution occurring by chance is less than 0.05.

10. Since the traditional notion "agent" corresponds about 90% of the time to what is communicated by "human high participant" in pseudo-passives, we now may use this term, without quotes, as a convenient (if technically inaccurate) synonym.

11. Except where noted, all emphasis in quotations is mine, RSK.

12. For the camera analogy, cf. Fillmore (1974:v-19).

13. Note that 9.b and 9.c are ludicrous only as imperatives, not as statements of fact.

14. For an amusing discussion of the "Gricean" difficulties which arise from the use of the pseudo-passive to avoid the choice between formal U "you" and informal jij "thou," see Hoekstra (1962).

15. The original observation of two strategies is found in a single sentence of Es (1970:219). It should be pointed out, however, that he discusses neither their contradictory character nor the semantic-pragmatic mechanisms involved.

16. With respect to the claim that the referent of die is more focussed or foregrounded than that of wie, we note here that die occurs elsewhere in Dutch grammar as a demonstrative (actually "picking out" its referent) while wie occurs as an interrogative and indefinite (i.e., failing to pick out a referent).

17. Cf. the discussion of the second prediction in Section 2.2 above.

18. The question mark refers only to the co-referential interpretation of ze and de vrouwen.

19. Henceforth, an acute accent will mark stress where indication is necessary.

20. One informant did say that 20.b could be used in pointing to a poster announcing the three singers' performance, but this is clearly not direct observation of the event.

21. "Burgemeester Thomassen: 'Ik blijf vechten voor Rotterdam'." Elseviers Magazine 27, nr. 40, 2 oktober 1971, p. 67.

21a. The case of presentative active sentences, with stressed, non-topical subjects, is taken up in Section 3.2.2 below.

22. On the topicality of personal pronouns, especially those referring to participants in the speech act, see Givón (this volume) and Hyman & Zimmer (this volume).

23.   For some discussion of the problem, cf. Kuno
(1972:272) and Chafe (1974:118-119).
24.   Example from Es (1970:219).
25.   Lest it be thought that I am engaging in slight of
hand here, it should be noted that analogous "propagandistic"
or "emphatic" uses of contradictions occur quite often in
language.   Observe, for example, that the English modal auxiliaries, typically indicating uncertainty about events, may
be used to refer to events whose occurrence is, in fact, certain.   The message resulting from this pitting of the uncertainty of the modal against the certainty of the event is a
synthesis of the two: the event takes place (i.e., its occurrence is certain) in spite of initial "baseline" uncertainty,
and is therefore taken as "surprising."   A case in point is
the modal should.   A sentence like She should be living in
Texas is clearly less certain about her actual living there
than She is living in Texas.   In a presupposed that-clause,
however, where her living there is taken as a fact, should
communicates "surprise."   Compare It is strange that she
should be living in Texas with It is strange that she is living in Texas.   As Jespersen (1964:288) observes, whereas the
indicative states a fact, should "lays more stress on the
strangeness."   We would claim, then, that the use of uncertain should in a presupposed clause to refer to an actuality
is analogous to the exploitation of high participant not focussed where the agent is being emphasized.   Both are examples of the coherent use of contradictions for "propagandistic" effects.
26.   This follows directly from our "Saussurian" claim
that passive morphology in Dutch is the signal of a meaning,
cf. Kirsner (1974) and Reid (1974).   For the meaning signaled
by passive morphology to even be subject to indirect exploitation, it must "be there" to begin with, even though its
contribution to messages in this case will be, as already
stated, indirect, i.e., less obvious.
27.   Interview with Piet Keizer, by N. Scheepmaker,
Vrij Nederland, 1 november 1969.
28.   One informant, a psychotherapist, claimed that the
pseudo-passive question exemplified a less personally involved, more objective interviewing technique.
29.   Compare 32 with Er brak een raam "There broke a
window," where the meanings of noun and verb suggest that the
grammatical subject raam is not agentive.   On the topicality
of high participants, cf. Section 1 and the referents cited
there.
30.   Statements such as "the subject is focussed," or
"een vrouw is non-focussed" are intended merely as convenient

abbreviations for "the subject refers to a focussed participant," or "een vrouw refers to a non-focussed participant."
    31. Informally, if (Agent P & Focussed P) ⊃ Topic P,
then NOT (Topic P) ⊃ NOT (Agent P) OR NOT (Focussed P). In
presentative active sentences, we have NOT (Topic P) & Focussed P, hence NOT (Agent P), where P means "participant."
The pseudo-passive asserts Agent P & NOT (Focussed P), which
is the logical consequence of Agent P & NOT (Topic P).

SUBJECT, THEME, AND THE SPEAKER'S EMPATHY--A
REEXAMINATION OF RELATIVIZATION PHENOMENA

by

Susumu Kuno*

*Research represented in this paper has been supported in part
by the National Science Foundation's grant to Harvard University (Grant No. SOC-7412366). I am greatly indebted to Linda
Shumaker, who has acted as my main native informant, and who
has given me numerous invaluable comments on earlier versions
of this paper. I am also greatly indebted to Etsuko Kaburaki,
whose joint work with me on empathy is outlined in Section 3
of this paper. I have received many valuable comments from
the participants of the Symposium on Subject and Topic, University of California, Santa Barbara, California, March 8-9,
1975, at which I presented the paper.

1.   Theme and Relativization

In Kuno (1973, Chapters 20, 21), I enumerated various
characteristics that Japanese thematic sentences and relative
clause constructions share, and hypothesized that Japanese
relative clauses are derived not by deleting an ordinary NP,
but by deleting the theme of the embedded clauses. Namely, I
proposed that 1-1a and 1-2a, for example, are derived not
from the intermediate structures 1-1b and 1-2b, but from 1-1c
and 1-2c:

1-1a. [Hanako ga yonda] hon
                  read   book
        "the book that Hanako read"

1-1b. [Hanako ga sono hon o yonda] hon
                  the book   read   book

1-1c. [[sono hon wa]$_{Theme}$ Hanako ga yonda] hon
          the book   read   book

1-2a. [sinda noni, dare-mo kanasimanakatta] hito
        died although anyone saddened-was-not person
        "the person who (lit.) although (he) died, no one was
        saddened"

1-2b. [sono hito ga sinda noni, dare—mo kanasimanakatta] hito
        the person died although anyone saddened-was-not person

1-2c. [[sono hito wa]$_{Theme}$ sinda noni, dare-mo kanasimanakatta]
        hito

I further argued that 1-3a, for example, is ungrammatical
because the underlying thematic sentence 1-3b is ungrammatical:

1-3a. *[kono mondai o tokenakatta node, boku ga toita] hito
          this problem could-not-solve since I   solved person
        "the person who (lit.) since (he) could not solve
        this problem, I did"

1-3b. *[Sono hito wa]$_{Theme}$ kono mondai o tokenakatta node,
          the person   this problem could-not-solve

        boku ga toita.
        since I solved

        "Speaking of that person, since he could not solve
        the problem, I did."

Regardless of whether the particular syntactic analysis proposed above turns out to be correct or not, the basic underlying hypothesis of the proposal will remain indisputable:

1-4. <u>The Thematic Constraint on Relative Clauses</u>: A relative clause must be <u>a statement about</u> its head noun.

The above is such a natural and matter-of-fact constraint
that it might appear that it hardly deserves special emphasis.
However, in the literature for linguistic analysis of relative clauses, with the notable exception of Gundel (1974a, b),
there is an almost complete lack of realization that 1-4
holds (1). Take, for example, Ross' Coordinate Structure
Constraint:

1-5. <u>The Coordinate Structure Constraint</u>: In a coordinate
structure, (a) no conjunct may be moved, (b) nor may
any element contained in a conjunct be moved out of
that conjunct. (Ross 1967:158-196) (2)

Ross gives examples of the following sort as evidence for the
above constraint:

1-6a. *The lute which Henry plays and sings madrigals is
warped.

1-6b. *The nurse who polished her trombone and the plumber
computed my tax was a blonde.

I claim that the ungrammaticality of these sentences is due
primarily to violation of the Thematic Constraint on Relative
Clauses, and not to violation of the Coordinate Structure
Constraint. Observe the following sentences:

1-7a. Henry plays the lute and sings madrigals.

1-7b. The nurse polished her trombone and the plumber computed my tax.

It is not possible to regard <u>the lute</u> of 1-7a as representing
the theme of the entire sentence: the sentence might be a
statement about the lute and madrigals, but not just about
the lute. Similarly, 1-7b is a statement about the nurse and
the plumber, and not a statement about the nurse alone.
    Now, compare 1-6 with the following:

1-8a. ?The guitar that Mary bought and Jane paid for its
carrying case was very expensive. (3)

1-8b. This is the kind of organ that Mary bought and thereby angered her husband.

Judgment on grammaticality of these sentences varies, but
there is no question that they are better than 1-6, and some
speakers accept them as perfectly grammatical. Note that the
embedded clauses, before relativization, can be said to be
statements about the guitar and the organ:

1-9a. Mary bought a guitar and Jane paid for its carrying case.

1-9b. Mary bought an organ and thereby angered her husband.

The reason that 1-9a, for example, can be regarded as a statement about a guitar is because the second conjunct Jane paid for its carrying case also says something about the guitar. The following examples from Ross further illustrate the point under discussion.

1-10a. I went to the store and bought some whisky.

1-10b. Here's the whisky which I went to the store and bought.

1-11a. I went to the store and Mike bought some whisky.

1-11b. *Here's the whisky which I went to the store and Mike bought.

1-12a. Tony has a Fiat and yearns for a tall nurse.

1-12b. *The tall nurse who Tony has a Fiat and yearns for is cruel to him.

1-13a. I went to the movies and didn't pick up the shirts.

1-13b. *The shirts which I went to the movies and didn't pick up will cost us a lot of money. (Ross' judgment)

1-14a. Aunt Hattie wants you to be nice and kiss your granny.

1-14b. This is the old lady that Aunt Hattie wants you to be nice and kiss.

1-10b and 1-14b involve violation of the Coordinate Structure Constraint: therefore, they should be ungrammatical, which they are not. Ross conjectured that these sentences did not contain coordinate structures at the time when Relativization applied, but were converted into coordinate structures later, or that they never contained coordinate structures at all.

The Thematic Constraint on Relative Clauses explains naturally the grammaticality of 1-10b, 1-14b, and the ungrammaticality of 1-11b, 1-12b and 1-13b. 1-10a can be regarded as a statement about whisky because the first conjunct I went to the store can be interpreted very easily as an action taken for the purpose of buying whisky. Hence, the grammaticality of 1-10b. On the other hand, in 1-11a, the speaker's action is apparently unrelated to whisky, and therefore, it is not possible to interpret the sentence as a statement about whisky (4). Hence, the ungrammaticality of 1-11b.

1-12b is ungrammatical clearly because 1-12a is not a statement about a tall nurse. Finally, the judgment on the degree of grammaticality for 1-13b varies greatly. The sentence is grammatical to the extent that the first conjunct of 1-13a, I went to the movies, could be taken as saying something about the shirts. Namely, the sentence is grammatical to those who can easily interpret I went to the movies as representing the cause or reason why I didn't pick up the shirts, and is ungrammatical to those who cannot, with intermediate degrees of grammaticality for many speakers.

It is generally believed that if-clauses form islands:

1-15. *The person who I will go to see Mary if I can't see is Jane.

But, observe the following sentence, which is grammatical for many speakers:

1-16. ?The person who I would kill myself if I couldn't marry is Jane.

The above contrast is clearly due to the fact that 1-17a cannot be taken as a statement about Jane, while 1-17b can:

1-17a. I will go to see Mary if I cannot see Jane.

1-17b. I would kill myself if I couldn't marry Jane.

The following example shows that relativization leaving a pronominal copy behind is constrained by 1-4:

1-18a. ?The man who everyone was overjoyed because he resigned from his office was greatly missed when his replacement took office.

1-18b. *The man who I solved the problem because he couldn't solve it got angry with me.

The complex NP relativization that leaves behind a pronominal copy behaves the same way as adverbial clause relativization. Observe the following sentences:

1-19a. ?This is the book which the publisher that promised to publish it has gone bankrupt.

1-19b. *This is the book which the publisher that published it has purchased McGraw Hill.

1-19a is grammatical because the matrix sentence of the relative clause (i.e., the publisher...has gone bankrupt) says something about the book (namely, the publisher can no longer publish the book). On the other hand, 1-19b is ungrammatical because the publisher...purchased McGraw Hill does not seem to be a statement about the book.

422

Now, let us return to relativization that does not leave
a pronominal copy behind. Ross' Complex NP Constraint predicts that the following sentences will be ungrammatical (5).
However, 1-20a is acceptable to some speakers, and for all
speakers, it is considerably better than 1-20c.

1-20a. This is the child who there is nobody who is willing
to accept.

1-20b. ?This is the child who I know a family which is willing to adopt.

1-20c. *This is the child who John married a girl who dislikes.

In the above sentences, what the main clauses of the relative constructions (i.e., there is nobody, I know a family,
and John married a girl) say about the head nouns varies.
Note that the degree of ungrammaticality of these sentences
parallels semantic richness of the relative clause string up
to the head noun of the complex NP. Namely, the more transparent the semantic content of the main clause is, the easier it is to relativize from a complex NP (6). This phenomenon is the direct reflection of the fact that it is easy to
interpret this child in 1-21a as the theme of the sentence,
while it is impossible to interpret it as the theme in 1-21c:

1-21a. There is nobody who is willing to adopt this child.

1-21b. I know a family which is willing to adopt this child.

1-21c. John married a girl who dislikes this child.

Similarly, compare the following sentences, which are due to
McCawley (1974) (the grammaticality judgment is McCawley's):

1-22a. ?Violence is something that I've never met an Englishman who condones.

1-22b. ?Violence is something that Snead is the only Englishman who condones.

1-22c. *Violence is something that Snead is an Englishman
who condones.

1-22d. Then you look at what happens in languages that you
know and languages that you have a friend who knows.
(Charles Ferguson, lecture at University of Chicago,
May 1971)

The degree of grammaticality of these sentences parallels the
degree of grammaticality of the following thematic sentences:

423

1-23a. Speaking of violence, I've never met an Englishman who condones it.

1-23b. Speaking of violence, Snéad is the only Englishman who condones it.

1-23c. ??Speaking of violence, Snĕad is an Englishman who condones it.

1-23d. Speaking of these languages, I have a friend who knows them.

The contrast between 1-23b and 1-23c requires explanation. In the former, <u>Snead</u> is the focus, not the theme, of the comment part of the sentence. Therefore, it is easy to interpret the whole comment part to be a statement about violence. On the other hand, in 1-23c, <u>Snead</u> is not the focus, but the theme. But this contradicts what the beginning of the sentence implies: namely, the forecast that it is going to be about violence. This contradiction makes 1-23c ungrammatical.

The contrast between the near grammaticality of 1-20a, 1-22a, 1-22d and the lower acceptability of 1-20b, 1-20c also requires special mention. The matrix clauses of the relative constructions in the former, namely, <u>there is nobody</u>, <u>I've never met an Englishman</u>, and <u>you have a friend</u> all represent the existence or absence of certain objects. The first is a pure existential sentence. The second two have as their subjects <u>I</u> and <u>you</u>, the most presupposed pronouns. The predicates of these three clauses give generic statements, and they do not refer to any specific actions. Compare the above with the following:

1-24a. *Violence is something that I met an Englishman who condones yesterday.

1-24b. *Violence is something that Jane married an Englishman who condones.

1-24c. *Violence is something that Jane is scheduled to meet an Englishman who condones. cf. Violence is something that Jane is hoping to meet an Englishman who condones.

1-24d. *Then you look at what happens in languages that you know and languages that you married a girl who knows.

The matrix clauses of the relative constructions in these sentences are no longer of the pure existential sentence type, and are not semantically transparent any more.

The above discussions point to the basically semantic nature of the phenomena that Ross tried to account for by the Complex NP Constraint. It seems that the phenomena can be reduced to the question of how easy or how difficult it is to interpret an NP within a complex NP as the theme of the entire sentence. The more transparent in meaning the main clause of the relative construction, the easier it is to interpret an NP in the complex NP as the theme of the entire sentence. The degree of transparency is determined by factors such as the degree to which the subject can be presupposed (I, you, people, etc.), the degree of genericness of the predicate (existential statements versus statements referring to specific actions, etc.). The contrast that I have observed in 1-19 through 1-23 makes it clear that it would be futile to attempt to account for the phenomena by assigning different constituent structures to complex NPs that behave differently with respect to Relativization (7).

The behavior of the so-called reduced relative clauses is also very revealing. Ross (1967:124) noted that expressions such as a girl jealous of x, a girl behind x, and a girl working with x do not allow Relativization and other movement transformations to apply to x, but that expressions such as a statement about x and a picture of x do.

1-25a. *This is the man that Mary knows a girl jealous of.

1-25b. *This is the man that Mary knows a girl behind.

1-25c. *This is the man that Mary knows a girl working with.

1-26a. This is the man that I read a statement about.

1-26b. This is the man that I bought a picture of.

It is clear why 1-26a, 1-26b are grammatical: it is very easy to interpret this man as the theme in the following sentences:

1-27a. I read a statement about this man.

1-27b. I bought a picture of this man.

On the other hand, it is totally impossible to interpret this man of sentence 1-28, which underlies the relative clause of 1-25b, as the theme:

1-28. Mary knows a girl behind this man.

This is due to the fact that behind this man describes the accidental physical location of the girl under discussion. Note the marginal nature of the following sentences:

1-29a. ??Speaking of that man, Phineas knows a girl behind him.

1-29b. ??Speaking of that man, I don't know anyone behind him. (8)

SUSUMU KUNO

Incidentally, in case <u>behind x</u> is used not for accidental physical location, but rather for ranking, it is much easier to regard <u>x</u> as the theme:

1-30a. Speaking of this boy, I know of nobody behind him in the exam scores.

1-30b. ?This is the boy who I know of nobody behind in the exam scores.

The near grammaticality of 1-30b makes a marked contrast with the ungrammaticality of 1-25b.

Now, let us examine 1-25a and 1-25c. The low acceptability of these sentences seems to be due to the fact that it is not easy to interpret <u>this man</u> in the underlying sentences as theme:

1-31a. Mary knows a girl jealous of this man.

1-31b. Mary knows a girl working with this man.

However, if the main clauses are semantically more transparent, much better sentences result:

1-32a. ?Here is the man who there is nobody jealous of.

1-32b. ?Here is the man who there is nobody that is jealous of.

1-33a. Here is the man who there is nobody working with.

1-33b. ?Here is the man who I know everyone working with.

Similarly, observe the following sentences:

1-34a. I bought a book about Marilyn Monroe.

1-34b. I wrote a book about Marilyn Monroe.

1-35a. I lost a book about Marilyn Monroe.

1-35b. I left home a book about Marilyn Monroe.

It is easy to interpret <u>Marilyn Monroe</u> as the theme of 1-34a and 1-34b, but it is next to impossible to interpret the same phrase as the theme of 1-35. This is because one buys or writes books for content, while one does not lose or leave books home for content (9). Now, observe that the above contrast is directly reflected in the degree of acceptability of the following sentences:

1-36a. This is the actress that I bought a book about.

1-36b. This is the actress that I wrote a book about.

1-37a. ?*This is the actress that I lost a book about.

426

1-37b. *This is the actress that I left home a book about.

The observations given in this section point to the basically semantic nature of the Coordinate Structure Constraint, the Complex NP Constraint, and the Island Constraint on Adverbial Clauses. As long as these constraints are stated purely in syntactic terms, their near language universal nature is unexplained. Once it is realized that their syntactic characterizations derive from deeper semantic constraints on themehood, explanations for their near-universal nature automatically follow. There is now urgent need to reexamine all syntactic constraints proposed thus far that have near language universality to see if they are really syntactic constraints or are instead semantic constraints that have superficial and "almost" consistent syntactic realizations (10).

2. Subject and Relativization

Keenan and Comrie (1972) have proposed the following hierarchy for the accessibility of noun phrases for relativization:

2-1.   (i) Subject $>$ Dir Obj $>$ Indir Obj $>$ Obj of Prep
        $>$ Possess NP $>$ Obj of Comparative Part

    (ii) If $X > Y$ and Y dominates Z, then $X > Z$.

I suspect that the above hierarchy for relativization is in fact a hierarchy for accessibility to thematic interpretation of noun phrases. Namely, the subject is the easiest to relativize because it is easiest to interpret the noun phrase in subject position as the theme of the sentence. It is most difficult to relativize the object of a comparative particle because it is most difficult to interpret it as the theme of the sentence. I suspect that languages that do not allow relativization from, say, the Obj-of-Preposition position and below, are languages that do not allow noun phrases in these positions to be interpreted as themes.

In this section, I will first show that in English, it is the thematic subject, and not the focus subject, that is relativized. Next, I will examine relativization in the Obj-of-Comparative-Part position, and in the by-agentive position.

Observe, first, the following sentence:

2-2.   John is the one that I've been talking about.

The sentence is ambiguous between the thematic and focus interpretation of John:

2-3a.   John (Focus) is the ŏne that I've been talking about.

2-3b.   Jŏhn (Theme) is the óne that I've been talking about.

427

Now, note that while 2-4b is grammatical, 2-4a is marginal:

2-4a. ??The person who is the ŏne that I've been talking about is here.

2-4b. The person who is the óne that I've been talking about is here.

I claim that 2-4a is of dubious degree of grammaticality because the focus subject has been relativized.

Secondly, observe the following sentences:

2-5a. John and only John killed Mary. (Focus)

2-5b. John and only John deserves the award. (Theme or Focus)

2-5b is ambiguous between the thematic and focus interpretations of John, but 2-5a is unambiguous: John in this sentence can receive only the focus interpretation. This can be seen by using the so-called Left Topic Dislocation:

2-6a. *John, he and only he killed Mary.

2-6b. John, he and only he deserves the award.

Now, observe the following contrast:

2-7a. *The man who and only who killed Mary was left out from the list of suspects.

2-7b. (?)The man who and only who deserves the award has been left out from the list of nominees.

The ungrammaticality of 2-7a seems due also to the fact that the focus subject of the relative clause has been relativized in violation of the requirement that only themes can be relativized.

Thirdly, observe the following presentational sentences:

2-8a. There came John, tagging along after Mary.

2-8b. Then out of the bushes jumped John.

2-8a and 2-8b are sentences that present new events that the speaker has observed. As such, they are themeless sentences (11). Note that the subject of these sentences cannot be relativized:

2-9a. *The man who there came, tagging along Mary was John.

2-9b. *The man who out of the bushes jumped was John.

It is not the case that presentational sentences reject relativization in all cases: note the grammaticality of 2-10a:

2-10a. John ran into the house out of which came a strange sound.

2-10b. *John ignored the strange sound which out of the house came.

Note that the grammaticality of 2-10a shows that the ungrammaticality of 2-9 cannot be explained away by assuming that the transformation that produces presentational sentences is post-cyclical. The ungrammaticality of 2-10b cannot be attributed to the fact that the word order of the presentational sentence has been destroyed because 2-11b and 2-11c, which preserve the presentational sentence word order, are also ungrammatical:

2-11a. Out of the printer's came the first copy of the book.

2-11b. *The book which out of the printer's came the first copy of looked elegant and attractive.

2-11c. *The book of which out of the printer's came the first copy looked elegant and attractive.

The above observations show that relativization from the subject position requires that the subject be the theme of the relative clause. Now, let us examine the relativizability of the object of the comparative particle, which is lowest in the Keenan-Comrie hierarchy. Keenan and Comrie assume that English allows relativization from this position, but it is in fact difficult to find perfectly grammatical sentences of this pattern:

2-12a. This is the subject that I like better than linguistics.

2-12b. ??This is the subject that I like linguistics better than.

2-13a. Jane, who Tom hit harder than (he hit) Mary, didn't even cry.

2-13b. *Jane, who Tom hit Mary harder than, screamed.

2-14a. Jane, who was brighter than Mary, called her a fool.

2-14b. ?Jane, who Mary was brighter than, called her a fool.

The grammaticality or ungrammaticality of the "b" sentences above seems related to the fact that it is difficult to interpret the following sentences as statements about the underlined NPs:

2-15a. I like linguistics better than <u>this subject</u>.

2-15b. Tom hit Mary harder than (he hit) <u>Jane</u>.

2-15c. Mary is brighter than <u>this girl</u>.

Sentences of the pattern of 2-12, -13, -14 are most acceptable when the object of comparison is indefinite:

2-16a. This is the subject that I like nothing better than.

2-16b. (?)Jane, who Tom has never hit anybody harder than, didn't even cry.

2-16c. I know a girl who nobody is brighter than.

The reason that 2-16a, 2-16b, 2-16c are much more acceptable than 2-12b, 2-13, 2-14b seems obvious: since <u>nothing</u> and <u>nobody</u> in the matrix clause of the relative construction do not qualify as theme of the underlying relative clause, the object of <u>than</u> has a much better chance of being interpreted as such.

     Let us now turn to the relativizability of the by-passive agentive, which is in the Obj-of-Prep category in the Keenan-Comrie hierarchy. It is generally taken for granted that English can relativize the by-passive agentive. However, many sentences involving relativization of this sort are of dubious acceptability:

2-17a. (?)This is the boy by whom Mary was hit.

2-17b. *The boy by whom Mary was hit kicked Jane.

2-17c. ?John talked to the boy by whom Mary was hit.

This fact is undoubtedly related to the fact that it is difficult, although not impossible, to interpret the by-passive agentive as the theme of a passive sentence. Sentences that involve relativization of by-passive agentives are best when the subjects are indefinite:

2-18a. ?Here is the man by whom Mary has been wronged.

2-18b. Here is the man by whom many innocent people have been wronged.

2-19a. ?This is the department by which John Smith was trained.

2-19b. This is the department of linguistics by which many prominent linguists have been trained.

The fact that the by-passive agentive does not easily qualify for themehood is in part due to the fact that it ordinarily represents new information that is not predictable from preceding discourse, and that the subject, especially when it is anaphoric, is taken to be the theme of the passive sentence. Note the following contrast:

2-20a. ?Speaking of this man, Mary has been wronged by him.

2-20b. Speaking of this man, many innocent people have been wronged by him.

2-21a. ?Speaking of this department of linguistics, John Smith was trained by them.

2-21b. Speaking of this department of linguistics, many prominent linguists have been trained by them.

In English, it is easiest to interpret the subject as the theme of the sentence. However, direct object, indirect object, object of preposition and possessive NP can also serve as theme carriers. This seems to be why it is possible to relativize constituents in these positions in English. I conjecture that languages that do not allow relativization of, say, indirect object (where ambiguity is not the controlling factor) are languages that do not allow noun phrases in indirect object position to receive the thematic interpretation.

3. The Speaker's Empathy and Relativization

There is yet another factor that interacts with relativization: namely, the speaker's attitude toward the participants of the event that he is describing. I use the term "empathy" to characterize the speaker's identification, in varying degrees, with a participant in an event. For example, observe the following sentences:

3-1a. John hit Mary.

3-1b. John hit his wife.

3-1c. Mary's husband hit her.

Assume that John's wife's name is Mary. In describing the event in which John hit Mary, the speaker can use any of the above three sentences (and the passive version of 3-1a and 3-1c). 3-1b is a statement in which the speaker describes the event from John's side, and 3-1c from Mary's side. This can be seen from the fact that in 3-1b the speaker refers to Mary as John's wife (an expression which is John-centered), while in 3-1c, he refers to John as Mary's husband (an expression which is Mary-centered). I say that in 3-1b, the speaker is expressing his "empathy" with John, while in 3-1c, he is expressing his empathy with Mary. On the other hand, in 3-1a, the speaker is taking a more neutral position, and is describing the event rather objectively.

Recent research by Kaburaki and Kuno shows that the following principles control the interaction between empathy and syntax. Details are given in Kuno and Kaburaki (1975). I list here only a few examples that each principle is intended to describe:

3-2.   The Ban on Conflicting Empathy Foci: A single sentence cannot contain two or more conflicting foci of the speaker's empathy.

3-3.   *Then, Mary$_i$'s husband$_j$ hit his$_j$ wife$_i$. (12)

In the subject position of 3-3, the speaker has shown his empathy with Mary by referring to her husband as Mary's husband (and not as, say, John). On the other hand, in the object position, the speaker has expressed his empathy with John by referring to Mary as his wife (and not as Mary). Thus, the sentence contains two conflicting foci of the speaker's empathy, and hence, the low acceptability of the sentence.

3-4.   The Surface Structure Empathy Hierarchy: It is easiest for the speaker to empathize with the referent of the subject; it is next easiest for him to empathize with the referent of the object... It is most difficult for him to empathize with the referent of the by-passive agentive.

Subject $\geq$ Object   ... $\geq$ By-Agentive

3-5a.   John talked to Bill about his wife. (John's or Bill's)

3-5b.   John talked to Bill about his beloved wife. (primarily John's, and weakly, Bill's)

3-5c.   Bill was talked to by John about his beloved wife. (Bill's)

3-6a.   John talked to Bill about himself. (primarily John, and weakly, Bill)

3-6b.   Bill was talked to by John about himself. (Bill)

3-7a.   John hit his wife.

3-7b.   ??John's wife was hit by him.

Expressions such as beloved (to x) that represent subjective feeling require that the speaker's empathy be placed on x. The fact that 3-5b primarily means "...about John's wife" shows that it is easier for the speaker to empathize with the referent of the subject than with the referent of the object. The fact that 3-5c cannot mean "...about John's wife" shows that it is next to impossible for the speaker to empathize with the referent of the by-agentive at the exclusion of the referent of the derived passive subject. The fact that the reflexive pronoun behaves in the same way as beloved does, as shown in 3-6, suggests that reflexive pronouns with nonsubjects as antecedents can be used only when the speaker empathizes with their referents. The fact that 3-7b is ungrammatical seems to be due to violation of both 3-4 and 3-2. Namely, the speaker, by referring to John's wife as John's wife (and not as, say, Mary) has shown that he is empathizing with John. On the other hand, by applying Passivization and thereby placing John's wife at the top position and John at the bottom position of the Empathy Hierarchy, the speaker has shown that he is empathizing with John's wife at the exclusion of John. Thus, the sentence contains two conflicting empathy foci, and hence, the unacceptability of the sentence.

3-8. The Speech-Act Participant Empathy Hierarchy: It is easiest for the speaker to empathize with himself (i.e., to express his own point of view); it is next easiest for him to express his empathy with the hearer; it is most difficult for him to empathize with the third party, at the exclusion of the hearer or himself.

Speaker $\geq$ Hearer $\geq$ Third Person

3-9a. (?)John talked to Mary about herself.

3-9b. ?You didn't talk to Mary about herself, did you.

3-9c. ?(?)I talked to Mary about herself.

3-10. ??John was hit by me.

For some speakers, 3-9b, 3-9c are not as good as 3-9a. This seems to be due to the following reason. As I have mentioned concerning 3-6, reflexive pronouns with nonsubjects as antecedents require that the speaker be empathizing with their referents. Thus, 3-9a is a statement in which the speaker is empathizing with Mary instead of John. 3-9b and 3-9c are marginal for some people because the speaker is empathizing with Mary at the exclusion of the hearer or the speaker himself, which is against the common discourse principle, shown in 3-8, of empathizing first with oneself or with the hearer. Similarly, 3-10 is of dubious degree of grammaticality because the speaker is saying that he is not empathizing with himself (i.e., he is not expressing his own point of view). It is for this reason that passive sentences of the pattern of 3-10 can be used only in technical writing or in journalistic reporting style, in which the speaker is allowed to take a detached view of himself.

3-11. The Topic Empathy Hierarchy: It is easier for the
speaker to empathize with an object (e.g., person)
that he has been talking about than with an object
that he has just introduced into discourse for the
first time:

Discourse-anaphoric > Discourse-nonanaphoric

3-12a. John encountered an eight-foot-tall girl on the
street.

3-12b. ??An eight-foot-tall girl encountered John on the
street.

The pattern x encountered y requires that the speaker's empathy be placed on the referent of x: this is because the
speaker could have said y encountered x if he were empathizing with the referent of y. The low degree of grammaticality
of 3-12b shows that it is difficult to empathize with the
referent of an indefinite NP at the exclusion of an anaphoric
NP.

The concept of "theme" and the concept of "empathy" are
closely interrelated, but it is necessary to distinguish the
two. Observe the following sentences:

3-13a. John married a 20-year-old girl.

3-13b. ??A 20-year-old girl married John.

3-14a. John married his present wife in 1960.

3-14b. ??John's present wife married him in 1960.

Marry is another verb which requires that the speaker's empathy be placed on the subject, and not on the object. 3-13b
is strange out of context because an indefinite noun is in
the subject position, and the referent of this noun receives
the speaker's empathy, at the exclusion of the anaphoric John,
thus violating the Topic Empathy Hierarchy. Similarly, 3-14b
is strange out of context because marry requires the speaker's
empathy to be placed on John's wife, while the speaker, by
referring to John's wife as John's wife and to John as John,
is expressing his empathy with John, thus violating the Ban
on Conflicting Empathy Foci.

On the other hand, the object of marry can readily be
the theme of a sentence, as can be seen in the following examples:

3-15a. Speaking of Mary, John finally married her last
month.

3-15b. The girl that John married happened to be a dope-
addict.

3-15a is a sentence about Mary (i.e., with <u>Mary</u> as the theme) in which the speaker is describing the event from John's side.

<u>Receive from</u> also requires that the speaker's empathy be placed on the referent of the subject. Observe the following sentences:

3-16a. I received a package from Mary.

3-16b. ?Tom received a package from me.

3-16c. I gave/sent Tom a package.

3-16c is strange out of context because the speaker is expressing his own point of view by talking about himself, while <u>received from</u> forces his empathy to be placed on the referent of <u>Tom</u>, the subject of the sentence. This results in a violation of the Speech-Act Participant Empathy Hierarchy and hence, in a violation of the Ban on Conflicting Empathy Foci. Now, note that the following sentence is rather difficult to process:

3-17. ??John received back from Mary the package that she had received from him two days before.

The embedded clause says that Mary received the package from John. This is a statement in which the speaker expresses his empathy with Mary at the exclusion of John. On the other hand, the matrix sentence says that John received the package from Mary. This is a statement in which the speaker expresses his empathy with John at the exclusion of Mary. The situation that holds here is shown below:

3-18. Main Clause: John > Mary (the speaker is empathizing with John, and not Mary)

Embedded Clause: Mary > John

The above conflict between the speaker's empathy focus in the embedded clause and in the main clause is what makes 3-17 difficult to process. Note that 3-19a and 3-19b are perfectly grammatical:

3-19a. John received back from Mary the package that he had sent to her two days before.

3-19b. John sent back to Mary the package that she had sent to him two days before.

Note that <u>send</u> does not require that the speaker's empathy be placed on the subject, as can be seen in the following examples:

3-20a. John sent me a package.

3-20b. John's wife sent him a package.

Similarly, observe the following sentence:

3-21. John received from Mary the package that she had received from Jane.

The speaker's empathy towards the participants of the two events is as shown below:

3-22. Main Clause: John > Mary

        Embedded Clause: Mary > Jane

3-21 seems to be grammatical because 3-22 does not involve irreconcilable conflict.

Now, observe the following sentence:

3-23. ??John comforted the girl who had been hit by him.

It seems that the sentence is ungrammatical because it violates the Ban on Conflicting Empathy Foci: the relative clause is a description from the girl's side, and not from John's side. On the other hand, the main clause is most readily interpretable as a statement from John's side (due to the Surface Structure Empathy Hierarchy). Hence, the ungrammaticality of the sentence. Similarly, observe the following sentence:

3-24. ??The girl who John had hit was comforted by him.

The sentence involves the same kind of conflict in the speaker's empathy foci.

One might be tempted to hypothesize, as Ross (1970:233) did, that sentences that contain two coreferential NPs one of which is in the by-passive agentive position are ungrammatical (14). However, the following examples show that such a hypothesis would not work:

3-25a. Mary received from John the book that was written by him.

3-25b. ?Mary heard from John about a book that was written by him.

3-25c. The girl who had been raped by John came to like him.

Receive from and hear from are verbs that require that the speaker's empathy be placed on the subject. Thus, John of 3-25a and 3-25b cannot receive the speaker's empathy. The relative clauses of these two sentences have John in the by-passive agentive position, which is the position that cannot receive the speaker's empathy. Thus, both the main clause

436

and the embedded clause of these two sentences say that the speaker is not describing the event from John's side, and therefore, no conflict results. Similarly, in 3-25c, the speaker is expressing his empathy with the girl, and his lack of empathy with John, by placing <u>John</u> in the by-passive agentive position. The matrix clause of the same sentence can be easily interpreted as a statement from the girl's side. Hence, the complete grammaticality of the sentence, in spite of the violation of Ross' constraint (15).

Similarly, observe the following sentences:

3-26a. John received a letter from a girl who he had met at the station five days before.

3-26b. ??John received a letter from a girl who had met him at the station five days before.

3-27a. ?The girl who married John heard from him that his brother was a spy.

3-27b. ?*The girl who John married heard from him that his brother was a spy.

The main clause of 3-26b is a statement in which the speaker is expressing his empathy with John (because of <u>receive from</u>), while the embedded clause is a statement from the girl's side if <u>met</u> is to be taken as meaning "encountered." Hence, the marginality of the sentence. Similarly, the main clause of 3-27b is a statement from the girl's side (because of <u>hear from</u>), while the embedded clause is a statement from John's side (because of <u>marry</u>). This conflict in the speaker's empathy seems to be what is responsible for the low degree of grammaticality of the sentence.

Note that Ross' constraint, which is based on the presence of a by-passive agentive, is powerless in distinguishing between 3-27a and 3-27b in the above sentences. The empathy perspective, on the other hand, explains both Ross' cases and the above sentences, as well as cases of apparent violation of Ross' constraint, as shown in 3-25.

4. Conclusion

In this paper, I have shown the importance of a functional approach to the analysis of relativization phenomena in English. Starting with the basic semantic principle that a relative clause must be a statement about the head noun, I have shown that Ross' constraints on relativization, which are stated in purely syntactic terms, are probably derivatives of constraints on what qualifies as a theme. I have also shown that the speaker's attitude toward the participants in

437

the event or state described in the relative clause, and his attitude toward the event or state described in the matrix clause, are important factors that determine the degree of grammaticality of sentences involving relative clause constructions.

Much (in fact, too much) has been done in search of syntactic phenomena that, I believe, are basically controlled by nonsyntactic factors. By taking a purely syntactic approach, one can achieve a certain degree of success in one's analysis if semantic factors have consistent syntactic realizations with respect to concepts such as subject, object, etc., or with respect to command and precedence relationships and relative heights in constituent structures. However, such an attempt fails crucially where the underlying semantic factors do not show one-to-one correspondence with syntactic factors. It is time to reexamine every major "syntactic" process and every major "syntactic" constraint from a functional point of view, to find semantic explanations for its existence in case the syntactic characterization holds, and to find a deeper and more accurate semantic generalization in case the syntactic facts are simply superficial and "almost correct" syntactic manifestations of nonsyntactic factors.

Appendix

The following table gives the result of native informant checks of some of the crucial sentences used in this paper. Column II represents the judgment of a linguistically sophisticated native speakers of English. According to these judgments, I have marked the sentences as they appear in the text. Column III represents the judgments of ten linguistically native speakers.

I	II	III		
		No. of People Responding in		
	Grammaticality	Each Category		
Sentence No.	Marking	√	?	*
1-6a,b	*	0	0	10
1-8a	?	0	4	6
1-8b	√	2	3	5
1-10b	√	3	3	4
1-11b	*	0	2	8
1-12b	*	1	0	9
1-13b	*	1	1	8
1-14b	√	6	2	2
1-15	*	0	2	8
1-16	?	3	2	5
1-18a	?	2	3	5
1-18b	*	1	1	8
1-20a	√	3	6	1
1-20b	?	1	4	5
1-20c	*	0	1	9
1-22a	?	5	2	3
1-22b	?	4	2	4
1-22c	*	0	2	8
1-22d	√	6	2	2
1-23a	√	8	2	0
1-23b,d	√	9	1	0
1-23c	??	6	3	1

1–24a,b	*	0	0	10
1–24c	*	0	3	7
1–25a	*	1	1	8
1–25b,c	*	1	2	7
1–26a	√	9	1	0
1–26b	√	10	0	0
1–29a,b	??	5	4	1
1–33a	√	7	3	0
1–33b	?	3	6	1
1–36a,b	√	10	0	0
1–37a	*?	3	1	6
1–37b	*	1	1	8
2–4a	??	3	4	3
2–4b	√	6	3	1
2–7a	*	1	3	6
2–7b	(?)	5	4	1
2–9b	*	0	3	7
2–11b	*	0	3	7
2–11c	*	1	2	7
2–14a	√	9	1	0
2–14b	?	5	3	2
2–18a	?	6	3	1
2–18b	√	9	1	0
2–19a	?	6	3	1
2–19b	√	10	0	0
3–7a	√	10	0	0
3–7b	??	7	3	0
3–9a	(?)	7	1	2
3–9b	?	4	5	1
3–9c	?(?)	5	3	2
3–12a	√	10	0	0
3–12b	??	6	0	4

3-13b	??	7	2	1
3-14b	??	8	2	0
3-16a,c	√	10	0	0
3-16b	?	4	6	0
3-17	??	5	4	1
3-19a	√	7	3	1
3-19b	√	10	0	0
3-23	??	3	5	2
3-24	??	6	2	2
3-25a	√	7	1	2
3-25b	?	5	3	2
3-25c	√	10	0	0
3-27a	?	5	4	1
3-27b	*?	3	3	4

Notes

1. Gundel argues that Left Dislocation (e.g., <u>Tom</u>, I like, but <u>Bill</u>, I don't) and Right Dislocation (e.g., It's so phony, <u>that ridiculous smile of his</u>), as they interact with Ross' Coordinate Structure Constraint (see below), are subject to the following constraint, which captures the same idea as 1-4:

   (i) A noun phrase, x, that is adjoined to a sentence, S, must be semantically relevant to any sentence, S', that is immediately dominated by S; i.e., S' must be a meaningful predication about x.

She further suggests that Relativization, as it interacts with the Coordinate Structure Constraint, is subject to (i).

2. Grosu (1973) has shown convincingly that it is necessary to distinguish between a and b : a is inviolatable, but b is not. In what follows, I will concern myself only with the question of when b can be violated.

3. The grammaticality marking of the crucial sentences in this paper is based primarily on the intuition of a linguistically sophisticated native speaker of English. I give in the Appendix responses of ten linguistically naive native speakers on some of the crucial sentences. I am indebted to Barbara Hecht for carrying out the native check for these sentences.

4. Note that (i), although marginal, is considerably better than 1-11b if Mike is taken to be a member of the group of people referred to by <u>we</u>:

   (i) ??Here is the whisky that we went to the store and Mike bought.

In this interpretation, the first conjunct represents an action that is related to the one represented by the second conjunct.

5. <u>Ross' Complex NP Constraint</u>: No element contained in a sentence dominated by a noun phrase with a lexical head noun may be moved out of that noun phrase by a transformation.

6. Erteschik (1972) has shown that in Danish, extractability from embedded clauses is controlled not by Ross' Complex NP Constraint, but by semantic factors such as the following:

   (i) the more semantically complex the matrix verb is, the more difficult it is to extract a constituent from the complement clause;

   (ii) the more unique or presupposed the complement is, the more difficult it is to extract a constituent from the complement clause.

She also contrasts the following three English sentences (the

grammaticality judgments are hers):
(iii) a. *This is the kind of weather that <u>there are</u> many people who like.
b. **This is the kind of weather that <u>I know</u> many people who like.
c. ***This is the kind of weather that <u>he made fun of</u> many people who like.

It seems that what controls both the facts observed by Erteschik and the facts regarding coordinate structures and adverbial clauses that I have discussed before is the Thematic Constraint on Relative Clauses.

7. For example, McCawley (1974) has proposed four different constituent structures for relative clauses.

8. 1-29a and 1-29b are not as unacceptable as I would like to have them. This seems to be due to the fact the pattern <u>Speaking of x</u> can be used not only for confirming the themehood of x, but also for establishing an incidental bridge between the preceding discourse and the subsequent one. In this usage, the expression means something like "Talk of x reminds me of...", and the relationship between x and the main part of the sentence can be very remote indeed. It seems that the pattern <u>As for x</u>, which does not have this latter usage, produces more clearcut judgment on these sentences:
(i) a. *As for that man, Phineas knows a girl behind him.
b. *As for that man, I don't know anyone behind him.

9. This observation is due to Michael Bierman (1972).

10. In this section, I have discussed a functional reanalysis of island constraints only as they apply to Relativization. Since island constraints also apply to focus transformations (Yiddish Movement, Wh-Q Movement, and It-Clefting), it is necessary to generalize the Thematic Constraint for Relative Clauses to cover these cases as well. It seems that syntactically marked focus also requires that the rest of the sentence be a meaningful predication about it.

The difference between theme and focus, then, seems to lie in the different types of judgment that thematic and focus sentences involve. A thematic sentence represents a recognition of what the rest of the sentence is a predication about, and the affirmation or denial of that predication. On the other hand, a sentence with a syntactically marked focus involves recognition of a presupposed predication, and acceptance or rejection of the focus as a value for the variable in the predication. See Kuroda (1972) for differences in the types of judgments that thematic and nonthematic sentences involve.

11. See Kuno (1972b) for details.

12. The following discourse is acceptable:

(i) a. Speaker A: Who hit his wife?

    b. Speaker B: Mary$_i$'s husband$_j$ hit his$_j$ wife$_i$.

Namely, (i-b) can be used in the context in which hitting one's own wife has been talked about. The presence of <u>then</u> at the beginning of 3-3 is intended to rule out this kind of context from consideration.

    13. I am indebted to Etsuko Kaburaki (personal communication 1974) for this observation.

    14. Ross' constraint reads as follows: "If a deep structure subject NP and some other NP in the same deep structure are coreferential, then the former NP may not become a passive agent."

    15. Similarly, observe the following contrast:

(i) a. The girl who married John was told by him that her brother was a spy.

    b. ??The girl who John married was told by him that her brother was a spy.

FROM TOPIC TO SUBJECT IN INDO-EUROPEAN

by

W.P. Lehmann

In recent linguistic work it has been made clear that
the essential constituent of the sentence is the verb, often
a verb with an object. That is to say, the syntactic element
generally referred to as subject is secondary. This conclusion has been supported by various observations.

Among the most weighty evidence in favor of the primacy
of the object-verb constituent in sentences is the relationship of other central syntactic constructions to the verb,
and to the verb-object construction. Two such verbally or
object-verbally related constructions are adpositions, which
parallel the object-verb relationship in any given language,
and comparisons of inequality, which likewise parallel the
object-verb relationship.

Moreover, modifiers of nouns and of verbs are so placed
that they do not disrupt the object-verb or verb-object relationship. Nominal modifiers, such as relative constructions,
descriptive adjectives and genitives, are placed on the side
of the object opposite the verb; in OV languages these constructions are placed before nouns, in VO languages after
them. In addition, verbal modifiers, like sentence interrogatives, negatives, reflexive markers and so on, are placed
on the side of the verb opposite the object in consistent VO
and OV languages (Lehmann 1973). Accordingly, many of the
fundamental syntactic constructions in language agree in
their pattern of arrangement with that of the object-verb
construction. It is difficult to escape the conclusion that
the object-verb construction is the fundamental syntactic
pattern in a language.

On the other hand, the subject plays a disruptive role
when it is involved in such fundamental constructions, interfering with the optimum arrangement. If all languages were
constructed consistently in accordance with the basic principle to which I have referred, any specific language would be
either OV or VO. The various constructions mentioned could
then be arranged without interfering with one another. In an
OV language the interrogative and negative markers would be
aligned after the verb, and nominal modifiers before the object or other nouns. In an optimum VO language the alignment
would be reversed, but again there would be no interference.
When, however, a subject is added to the two principal constituents of the sentence construction, major interference
may result.

The interference occasioned by the introduction of a
subject is least in an OV language since such languages then
have an SOV order. To be sure, nominal modifiers with objects
bring about a break between the subject and object, particularly if the second of these two nominal elements is accom-

panied by a lengthy relative construction. But such a break
is minor. The interference is not nearly as disruptive as it
may be when a subject is introduced in a VO language, particularly when the subject precedes the verb, that is, in SVO
languages. In SVO languages the placement of nominal modifiers introduces complexities by requiring material modifying
noun subjects to stand between the subject and the verb. Even
more consequential, verbal modifiers must be adjusted with
reference to the subject.

A few of the complexities may be sketched to illustrate
the kinds of interference with the basic sequence. Interrogative markers must be so designed in an SVO language that the
subject as well as the verb is taken into consideration.
Similarly, negative markers. Accordingly the conflated constructions result which provide such fascination in analysis.
Among such conflated interrogatives are those in English with
wh-. Moreover, negatives too come to be conflated, as with
indefinites and adverbs. But some of the greatest problems
arise because such verbal qualifiers as reflexives and reci-
procals must be adjusted to nominal subjects as well as to
the central verbal element. In meeting these requirements,
reflexive pronouns and other kinds of reflexive markers are
introduced in SVO languages. Similar problems are caused by
the development of auxiliaries, to represent such qualifiers
as necessitative, volitional and causative. The awkward patterns used to represent such syntactic features in SVO languages need only be recalled to support the view that from a
typological point of reference the subject is a secondary element in the sentence.

A query may be interpolated here then on the very presence of SVO languages in human societies. If they are typologically cumbersome, why are they tolerated? This query is
particularly notable when one considers that the languages
which have been extended in use beyond their basic group of
speakers, that is, the languages of civilization, are SVO:
English, Russian, Chinese, Spanish, French, and among others,
Arabic, as it is used for communication among the various
peoples in the Middle East. The answer to this query is based
on perceptual and sociological criteria rather than typological, and accordingly it will not be pursued at length here.
It may merely be noted that verbs, as the distinctive elements
in sentences containing subjects, are so placed that subjects
and objects are carefully demarcated. SVO languages then are
perceptually simple, though typologically complex. And unfortunately the SVO structure of the major languages of western civilization has led to an erroneous emphasis on the role
of the subject in language.

In dealing with the problem of subject typologically, we must keep in mind awkward problems in terminology. For, in accordance with an important paper by Li and Thompson (1974c), many languages are more precisely characterized as topic-prominent rather than as subject-prominent. Further, in topic-prominent languages, the sentence may be viewed as consisting of a topic and comment rather than a subject and predicate in the narrow sense. But as I indicate below, a topic-comment language can develop into a subject-predicate language. Accordingly the term "subject" may be used in a broad sense, as well as in the sense indicated by Li and Thompson.

In its broader sense a subject may have various functions. Halliday, citing Sweet, distinguishes four such functions (1970:164; see also Jespersen 1924:145-154):

"The subject, in its traditional sense, is thus a complex of four distinct functions, three in the structure of the clause...: 1. actor ('logical subject'): ideational; 2. modal subject ('grammatical subject'): interpersonal; 3. theme ('psychological subject$_1$'): textual; together with a fourth function which is in the structure of the 'information unit': 4. given ('psychological subject$_2$'): textual."

When we examine Halliday's examples, which illustrate these different functions, we find that those elements which he views as expressing the "theme" are comparable to those which Li and Thompson identify as supporting the analysis of topics in Putonghua, as in their example (1974c:5):

Zhuōzi-shang fang le yi-tiáo miànbāo
table-on place aspect a-classifier bread
"A loaf of bread was sitting on the table."

This sentence, given with their translation, is cited by Li and Thompson to demonstrate that the first element is a topic. If a translation comparable to those of Halliday's were given, the English equivalent might be proposed as:

"On the table a loaf of bread was sitting."

A loaf of bread would then be the grammatical subject, in Halliday's terminology, and On the table the psychological subject or theme, as it is in Chinese.

If we consider the four functions which Halliday cites as frequently expressed by the subject in English sentences and the sentences of other languages similar in patterning, a subject-prominent language can be identified as one in which these four functions are normally indicated by the subject, as in the sentence (Halliday 1970:159):

My mother gave me these beads.

In languages which are not subject-prominent, on the other hand, the function of grammatical subject may not be expressed overtly, and the psychological subject or theme is more notable in the sentence. If there were a syntactic change, leading to the requirement that a grammatical subject be expressed in a matrix sentence, the item often expressed as topic would be the subject. A topic-prominent language would in this way develop into a subject-prominent language. In this paper I propose that such a development took place in Indo-European. I will sketch briefly some implications of such a development for our understanding of the Indo-European languages and of language in general.

My primary concern will be with early stages of Indo-European. For by the time of the classical periods of such dialects as Greek and Latin, the subject was prominent. Indeed, as I have pointed out elsewhere (Lehmann 1974a, 1974b), the subject was so prominent in the classical periods that infinitive clauses could develop. Thus from earlier constructions like:

He promised: "I will go."

there was a development to constructions like:

He promised he would go.

and subsequently:

He promised to go.

By its prominence the subject dominated not only the verb of the matrix sentence but also that of the subordinate sentences and clauses. In this way characteristic syntactic processes arose in the Indo-European languages, such as the sequence of tenses notable in the earlier stages of these languages and the types of complementation involving nonfinite verb forms. By examining the syntactic patterning at various stages in dialects like Greek, we can document such changes in the extent of domination by subjects. But such documentation does not demonstrate that earlier stages of the language were topic-prominent. For such demonstration we will have to rely especially on examination of texts in early Vedic and Hittite. In carrying out such examination I note particularly the criteria which Li and Thompson have discussed as characteristic of topic-prominent languages (1974; see also E.L. Keenan, Definition of Subject, this volume).

My examples of Vedic Sanskrit I take from a hymn to Rudra, Book II, Hymn 33 of the Rigveda (see Macdonell 1917: 56-67).

450

Examining this poem for the properties Li and Thompson
have identified as distinctive for subject-prominent languages, we note first that its 60 lines contain only one subject
occupying initial position, that is, the topic position
(stanza 12, 1.1). Typical clause patterns may be illustrated
by citing the first stanza:

```
á    te,  pitar   Marutām,   sumnám  etu;
hither thy oh-father of-Maruts grace  it-should-come

má   naḥ súryasya  samdṛ́śo   yuyothāḥ
do-not us  sun's    from-view you-should-separate

adhí no vīró árvati  kṣameta
toward us hero to-horse may-he-be-merciful

prá jāyemahi,   Rudra,  prajábhiḥ
ahead we-will-  oh-Rudra with-children
    generate-
    (for our own
     benefit)
```

"May thy grace come hither, oh father of Maruts,
Do not deprive us of the sight of the sun.
May the hero be merciful to us, to our horses,
    [OR on horseback]
May we be prolific, oh Rudra, with children."

Leaving aside the first two properties identified by Li
and Thompson for topic-prominent languages, since these are
semantic and accordingly manipulable in accordance with the
reader's interpretation of an ancient poetic text, we may
examine these and other Vedic lines for the third property,
that is: "the topic does not have a selectional relation with
any verb." This property is in keeping with Meillet's observation that the choice of cases is determined by their function in Proto-Indo-European, not by the verb (1937:358): "Le
cas auquel sont mis les compléments de dépend pas du verbe,
mais seulement du sens à exprimer." Meillet gives examples
from Greek. Examples can readily be cited from Vedic, as in
this Rudra poem. In line four of this stanza, prájahiḥ is
instrumental, not because of any grammatical relationship
with the verb jāyemahi but because of the sense of the passage. The Rigveda provides ample evidence to support
Meillet's conclusion that one word does not govern another in
Proto-Indo-European (359): "il n'y aurant pas en indo-
européen de 'rection' du'un mot par un autre, comme il y en a
en latin par example." Indo-European accordingly fits well
the property of lack of selectional relationship between topic and verb that Li and Thompson have identified for a topic-

prominent language.

    In accordance with this property, Li and Thompson point to a characteristic construction of Chinese, known as the "double subject." In this construction two nouns accompany a verb, as in their example:

> Tā tóu téng.
> he head ache
> "He with regard to his head aches = He has a headache."

This construction has a parallel in Vedic, in the so-called "double accusative," where one of the accusatives specifies the other (Macdonell 1916:303-304):

> RV 1.161.13
> śvánam bastó bodhayitáram abhravīt
> dog   buck   wakener   he-said
> "The he-goat said the dog was the wakener."

In these patterns the additional accusative must be interpreted by its sense in the passage, rather than as a grammatical accompaniment in any construction. While many of the examples may be viewed as oppositional, the relationship may be as loose as that in Chinese, as in:

> mariṣyántam céd yájamānam mányeta
> about-to-die ptc. sacrificer if-he-thinks
> "If he thinks the sacrificer (is) going to die."
> (Macdonell 1916:304)

As in the Chinese example, the additional accusative specifies the other rather than standing in a government relationship to the verb.

    As a further property, Li and Thompson cite the role of the verb as determining a subject, but not a topic. If, as is general in language, certainly SVO and SOV languages, the topic is placed early in the clause, this Rigvedic stanza and others in the poem illustrate the topic-prominent characteristics of the Rigveda. In the first line, the god addressed, Rudra, is the topic, though not the subject. In the second and third lines, the worshippers are topics, though Rudra is subject. The topics in these three lines are only loosely connected to the predicate. In the fourth line, the beneficent powers of the storm-god for promoting fertility are topicalized in the verb. This stanza is by no means atypical; topicalization in general may affect a variety of elements in the early Indo-European materials, and only subsequently is the grammatical subject more commonly so affected.

A further property, agreement of subject and predicate, becomes increasingly regular in the Indo-European dialects. Since like the other dialects Vedic is developing towards a subject-prominent structure, when a subject is found expressed overtly in a sentence, its nominative form typically shows agreement with the predicate.

As a final property, Li and Thompson cite the prominent role of the subject, but not the topic, in reflexivization. In Vedic, and early Indo-European generally, reflexivization was indicated by forms of the verb, the so-called middle. When a syntactic pattern came to develop to indicate reflexivization as the middle was losing its reflexive force, one of the patterns was the use of the adjective philós in Gree, priyás in Sanskrit; both are generally glossed "dear." These adjectives did not always refer to the subject, as in the following line:

RV 1.154.5

táD asya priyám abhí pátho aśyam
that of-his "dear" toward path I-wish-to-reach

Macdonell translates the line: "I would attain to that dear domain of his." But as he and other interpreters state, this domain is heaven, Visnu's own or proper domain. The adjective priyá is accordingly an indicator of reflexive relationship between the genitive asya and pátho, rather than between the subject "I" and pátho. Thus priyá here, in not referring to the subject of the verb, illustrates the loose relationship of reflexivization which is characteristic of topic-prominent languages.

Other characteristics pointed out by Li and Thompson for topic-prominent languages also are true of Proto-Indo European. Among these is the lack of a passive.

Moreover, sentences may have no expressed topic. In Proto-Indo-European and many of the early dialects, subjectless and topicless sentences are used for natural phenomena, like "rain, snow" and the like, and also for personal feelings.

Topic-prominent languages also lack dummy subjects, like "it, there." These too develop late in the Indo-European dialects. They are not even found in such a late dialect as Latin, as in expressions like pluit "(it) is raining" and paenitet "(it) is grievous."

In further support of the statements made here, for which evidence is given by citations from Vedic, Hittite texts could also be cited. Rather than list such patterns, I refer to Carol Justus's paper (Justus, this volume). There she illuminates further the use of ku-constructions as signals of topic hierarchy. Accordingly the recognition that topic-prominent languages must be distinguished from subject-prominent languages clarifies further one of the difficult problems of early Indo-European syntax, while supporting the view that Proto-Indo-European in its earlier stages was a topic-prominent language.

Yet in the course of three millennia, from such a topic-prominent language, subject-prominent languages have developed. Subjects are expected for most sentences in Classical Latin and Greek, as well as Classical Sanskrit, and certainly in late dialects like Germanic. The subjects are first introduced as amplifications of the person markers in the verb. The subject itself then becomes more prominent, eventually reducing the importance of the verbal person marker, which then may be lost, as for the most part in the modern Germanic dialects.

It would be instructive to determine the mechanism by which such a change was introduced, both for our understanding of Indo-European and of other language families. Yet since the modifications which led to the shift in Indo-European are prehistoric, Indo-Europeanists will have to look to other language families for support of the hypotheses they construct to account for events which they have to interpret without a continuous series of texts.

We may assume that an important step towards the prominence of subjects in Indo-European is the introduction of personal endings on verbs. Since this process was carried out in early Proto-Indo-European, we can only hypothesize about the basis for it. In an earlier, unpublished paper I have proposed that the so-called person markers were originally introduced to indicate congruence. This hypothesis is supported by the greater number of endings in the third person than in the first and second, among other evidence. Moreover, an alternate theory, that the personal endings are in origin suffixed pronouns encounters problems in the data concerned (Lehmann 1974a:201). Yet whatever their origin, personal endings must be assumed for early Proto-Indo-European, though their distribution was defective; only later was a full set developed in the plural, as well as in the dual.

Expression of person through personal endings presumably would lead to a syntactic system in which subjects are prominent, or even mandatory, as in the Indo-European dialects. But we know very little about the functioning of such markers in a language, in contrast with the expression of person through other devices. Jespersen, in his discussion of "person" (1924:214-215), deals with the relationship between this category and local adverbs, such as here and there. He also

cites a monograph of 1893 in which person marked with pronominal elements is derived from local markers, calling this
"an interesting view." But he refrains from further comment,
in accordance with his practice "in this volume [to] keep
aloof from speculations about primitive grammar and the origin of grammatical elements" (215). Subsequent linguistic
treatments of person, as by Kurylowicz (1964:148-170) and
Benveniste (1971:195-204, 217-230), are primarily concerned
with explicating the relationships in languages which contain
personal endings, notably the Indo-European. If we wish to
learn something more general about the functioning of personal
endings in language, we will have to go outside the Indo-
European area. Turkish with its personal endings in an OV
language, and Japanese, with person indicated by other devices, might be examined as classical examples.

Comparing these two languages for the presence of topics
or subjects, one notes that subjects are far more prominent
in Turkish than in Japanese. In addition, Turkish clauses
with third person verbs generally have the subject in first
position. Moreover, Turkish has no device like the Japanese
wa construction which permits the use of topics; if an item
is to be topicalized in Turkish, it is placed initially. To
be sure, subjects are not required for first and second person verb forms, much as in early Greek and Latin. Yet, subjects are relatively prominent in Turkish, much more so than
in Japanese. I would like to suggest that this characteristic of Turkish is in keeping with the presence of personal
endings in the verb. Further, that the use of subjects is
less prominent in Turkish than in the Indo-European dialects,
even when they maintained many OV patterns, because the development of personal endings in the Turkish verb system is
much more recent (Deny 1952:329).

Other languages should be examined regarding such a hypothesis; but the materials in the Indo-European languages show
a steady increase in the use of subjects. Even in the Classical Greek histories, subjects are more frequent than in the
earliest texts; in the Hellenistic period, and in Latin, subjects are even more frequent, until eventually as in the
modern dialects they are mandatory, whether as regular subjects or dummy subjects. The modern Indo-European dialects
then are standard examples of subject-prominent languages.

Although I have suggested that the presence of personal
endings in verb forms was influential in the development of
the Indo-European languages to subject-prominent languages,
this was a mechanism for the development, not the motivating
force. If we wish to seek further for this, we might note
the parallelism between the development from topic-prominence

to subject-prominence and that from an OV structure to a VO
structure in the Indo-European languages. Moreover, the
characteristic topic-prominent languages cited by Li and
Thompson are OV, or they have been influenced by OV languages,
or like Chinese they are developing towards an OV structure.
In their impressive paper, Li and Thompson have suggested that
"one of the characteristics according to which a general linguistic typology can be established is subject-prominence vs.
topic-prominence" (1974c:31). I suggest that this characteristic be related to the more fundamental typological characteristic having to do with the position of the object with
reference to its verb.

I have also been concerned with pointing out that this
characteristic like other typological characteristics may
change. We have ample documentation for such syntactic change
in Indo-European languages, and also earlier discussion concerning it, as in Dover's book on Greek Word Order. I cite
this book primarily to provide corroboration for the views
expressed here, though the corroborative data are presented
in a totally different way and require considerable interpretation for those not in the British Classical tradition.
Dover states that word order in early Greek was determined by
"logical principles." Two elements were central in sentences,
N and C. N corresponds to topic or theme; C to rheme. Eventually in Dover's view these two elements were less prominent
than subject and verb; subject essentially replaced N as
Greek developed towards "an increasing dominance by syntactical patterns of order" (1960:68).

This treatment of Greek syntax provides support for the
views presented above. In accordance with them the Indo-
European languages developed from topic-prominent languages
to subject-prominent languages. The development may well be
related to other syntactic changes, notably from an OV structure to a VO structure. The prominence of subjects in any
given language may then provide further evidence for understanding that language. And subject-prominence may be another feature yielding insights into the characteristics which
make up the central fabric of languages.

SUBJECT AND TOPIC: A NEW TYPOLOGY OF LANGUAGE*

by

Charles N. Li
Sandra A. Thompson

*This paper is an amalgamation of three earlier papers and
renders them obsolete: (1) "Chinese as a Topic-Prominent Language," prepared and circulated for the 7th International
Conference on Sino-Tibetan Languages and Linguistics, October,
1974; (2) "Subject and Topic: A New Typology of Language,"
presented at the LSA Annual Meeting, New York, December, 1974;
(3) "Evidence Against Topicalization in Topic-Prominent Languages," circulated prior to the Symposium on Subject and
Topic. We are grateful to the participants of the Symposium
and to James H-Y Tai for their valuable comments and to Dr.
Edward Hope, who responded from Bangkok to our inquiries about
a number of Lisu constructions. During the preparation of
this paper, Charles N. Li was supported by a fellowship from
the American Council of Learned Societies.

I. Introduction. Since the emergence of descriptive
linguistics, linguists have disagreed among themselves over
the question of the extent to which languages could be expected to differ from one another. The present paper is an
attempt to lay the foundation for a typology based on the
grammatical relations subject-predicate and topic-comment.
The notion of subject has long been considered a basic grammatical relation in the sentential structure of a language.
However, the evidence we have gathered from certain languages
suggests that in these languages the basic constructions
manifest a topic-comment relation rather than a subject-predicate relation. This evidence shows not only that the
notion of topic may be as basic as that of subject in grammatical descriptions, but also that languages may differ in
their strategies in construction sentences according to the
prominence of the notions of topic and subject. According to
our study, there are four basic types of languages: (i) languages that are subject-prominent (a term introduced by E.L.
Keenan); (ii) languages that are topic-prominent; (iii) languages that are both subject-prominent and topic-prominent;
(iv) languages that are neither subject-prominent nor topic-
prominent. In subject-prominent (Sp) languages, the structure of sentences favors a description in which the grammatical relation subject-predicate plays a major role; in topic-
prominent (Tp) languages, the basic structure of sentences
favors a description in which the grammatical relation topic-
comment plays a major role. In type (iii) languages, there
are two equally important distinct sentence constructions,
the subject-predicate construction and the topic-comment construction; in type (iv) languages, the subject and the topic
have merged and are no longer distinguishable in all sentence
types. In order to clarify the subject-predicate construction and the topic-comment construction, we may use two types
of English sentences as examples:

1 John   hit Mary.
   Subject   Predicate

2 As for education, John prefers Bertrand Russell's ideas.
         Topic   Comment

In Sp languages, the basic sentence structure is similar to
1, whereas in Tp languages, the basic sentence structure is
similar to 2. However, this is not to say that in Tp languages, one cannot identify subjects, or that Sp languages do
not have topics. In fact, all the languages we have investigated have the topic-comment construction, and although not
all languages have the subject-predicate construction, there
appear to be ways of identifying subjects in most Tp langua-

ges. Our typological claim will simply be that some languages can be more insightfully described by taking the concept
of topic to be basic, while others can be more insightfully
described by taking the notion of subject as basic. This is
due to the fact that many structural phenomena of a language
can be explained on the basis of whether the basic structure
of its sentences is analyzed as subject-predicate or topic-
comment.

According to a number of criteria which we will outline
below, and a small sample of languages which we have investigated, the following typological table may be established:

Subject-Prominent Languages	Topic-Prominent Languages
Indo-European	Chinese
Niger-Congo	Lahu (Lolo-Burmese)
Finno-Ugric	Lisu (Lolo-Burmese)
Simitic	.
Dyirbal (Australian)	.
Indonesian	.
Malagasy	.
.	
.	
.	

Subject-Prominent and Topic-Prominent Languages	Neither Subject-Prominent nor Topic-Prominent Languages
Japanese	Tagalog
Korean	Illocano
.	.
.	.
.	.

It is obvious that the above table touches on only a
very small number of languages in the world. This is partly
due to the fact that in order to establish topic-prominence,
a careful investigation of the syntactic structures of a
language is necessary. Since the tradition in linguistic
studies emphasizes the subject as the basic, universal grammatical relation, grammarians tend to assume that sentences
of a language are naturally structured in terms of subject,
object, and verb. In general, it is not considered that the
basic structure of a sentence could be described in terms of
topic and comment (1). There are exceptions. For example,
Schachter and Otanes (1972) stated that the Tagalog basic

sentence structure should not be described in terms of the
notion subject. Another example is E. Hope (1974) who has
described a remarkable Tp language, Lisu, a Lolo-Burmese
language. But in general, it is often difficult to determine
the typology of a language in terms of subject-prominence and
topic-prominence on the basis of reference grammars since
many such grammars are biased toward the subject-predicate
analysis. Modern generative linguistics does not represent
any advance in this particular area. The assumption remains
that the basic sentence structure should be universally described in terms of subject, object, and verb. Our goal in
this paper is, therefore, a modest one: we wish to establish
the value and the validity of a typology based on the notions
of subject-prominence and topic-prominence. We will proceed
as follows. First, we will outline the differences between
subjects and topics in terms of a number of properties which
they do not share; then we will discuss some of the characteristics of Tp languages. We will then show that the topic-
comment structure in Tp languages is indeed a basic sentence
type, and finally we will explain the implications of the
typology for the study of universal grammar.

    II. Subject vs. Topic. (a) Definite. According to
Chafe (this volume), a definite noun phrase is one for which
    "I think you already know and can identify
    the particular referent I have in mind."
One of the primary characteristics of topics, then, is that
they must be definite (2) (see Chafe, this volume, for further remarks on definiteness).

    According to this characterization of definiteness,
proper and generic NPs are also understood as definite. The
conditions regarding the speaker's assessment of the hearer's
knowledge under which a proper noun can be appropriately
used are the same as those under which a definite common
noun phrase can be used. A generic noun phrase is definite
because its referent is the class of items named by the noun
phrase, which the hearer can be assumed to know about if he
knows the meaning of that noun phrase (3).

    A subject, on the other hand, need not be definite. For
example, the subjects of 3 and 4 are indefinite:

3 A couple of people have arrived.

4 A piece of pie is on the table.

    (b) Selectional relations. An important property of the
topic is that it need not have a selectional relation with
any verb in a sentence; that is, it need not be an argument
of a predicative constituent. This property of topic is

particularly noticeable among the topic-prominent languages
since the topic-comment construction in such languages, as we
will try to show, represents the basic sentence type. Consider sentences 5, 6, 7, and 8, all of which represent common
sentence types in their respective languages. The underlined
constituent in each sentence is the topic.

5 <u>hɛ   chi tê pê</u>ʔ   ɔ dàʔ jâ   (Lahu)
   field this one classifier rice very good
   "This field (topic), the rice is very good."

6 <u>hɔ   ɔ</u> na-qhɔ̂ yɨ̀ ve   yɔ̀   (Lahu)
   elephant   topic nose long prt. declarative
          marker   marker
   "Elephants (topic), noses are long."

7 <u>Neì-chang   huǒ</u> xìngkui   xiāofang-duì laí
   that-classifier fire fortunate fire-brigade come

   de   kuài   (Mandarin)
   adv. particle quick
   "That fire (topic), fortunately the fire-brigade came
   quickly."

8 <u>Neì-xie shùmu</u> shù-shēn   dà   (Mandarin)
   those   tree   tree-trunk big
   "Those trees (topic), the trunks are big."

The topics in these sentences, 5 "this field," 6 "elephants,"
7 "that fire," 8 "those trees," have no selectional relation
with the verbs. Similarly, in Japanese, the topic marked by
the particle <u>wa</u>, and in Korean, the topic marked by the particle <u>(n)ɨn</u> need not be selectionally related to the verb of
the sentence, as shown in 9 and 10:

9 <u>siban-ɨn</u>   hakkjo - ga   manso   (Korean)
   now - topic   school - subject many
      marker   marker
   "The present time (topic), there are many schools."

10 <u>Gakkoo - wa</u>   buku - ga   isogasi-kat-ta (Japanese)
   school - topic I - subject   busy - past tense
      marker   marker
   "School (topic), I was busy."

The subject, on the other hand, always has a selectional
relation with some predicate in the sentence. It is true
that the surface subject of some sentences may not be selectionally related to the main surface verb. For example,
classical transformational analyses (e.g., Chomsky 1965;
Rosenbaum 1967; Postal 1971; Postal and Ross 1971) recognize
the surface subject, "John," in the following sentences to be

selectionally unrelated to the main predicates, "be easy" and "appear."

11 John is easy to please.

12 John appears to be angry.

This fact, however, does not contradict our claim that the subject of a sentence is always selectionally related to some predicate in the sentence. In the surface structure, the subject might not be adjacent to the predicate to which it is selectionally related, and it might even have assumed a new grammatical relationship with a verb to which it is not selectionally related. But the fact remains that a selectional relation must exist between the subject of a sentence and some verb in that sentence (4), whereas no such relationship need exist between topic and verb (5).

(c) Verb determines "Subject" but not "Topic." A correlate of the fact that a subject is selectionally related to the verb is the fact that, with certain qualifications, it is possible to predict what the subject of any given verb will be (6). Thus, in English, if a verb occurs with an agent as well as other noun phrases, the agent will become the subject unless a "special" construction is resorted to, such as the passive. (This way of stating the fact about subjectivalization is due to Fillmore, 1968:37.) If the verb is intransitive, either the patient or the actor, depending on whether the verb is a stative verb or an action verb, will be the subject. If the verb is causative, the causer will be the subject. These facts represent some of the language-independent generalizations about how the subject is determined by the verb. There is no doubt that not all verbs in a language can be classified with respect to subjectivization on a language-independent basis. For example, in English, the verb "enjoy" will take the experiencer but not the accusative as the subject, whereas the verb "please" will have the accusative noun phrase but not the experiencer as the subject. But the fact remains that given a verb, the subject is predictable.

The topic, on the other hand, is not determined by the verb; topic selection is independent of the verb. Discourse may play a role in the selection of the topic, but within the constraints of the discourse, the speaker still has considerable freedom in choosing a topic noun phrase regardless of what the verb is. This characteristic of the topic is clearly demonstrated by our earlier examples, 5-8, with topic-comment structure.

(d) Functional role. The functional role of the topic is constant across sentences; as Chafe (this volume) suggests:

> "What the topics appear to do is limit the
> applicability of the main predication to a
> certain restricted domain. . . . The topic
> sets a spatial, temporal, or individual
> framework within which the main predication
> holds."

Clearly, this function of specifying the domain within which
the predication holds is related to the structure of the
discourse in which the sentence is found. The topic is the
"center of attention"; it announces the theme of the discourse. This is why the topic must be definite (see section
II(a) above). The functional role of the topic as setting
the framework within which the predication holds precludes
the possibility of an indefinite topic. A feel for the
bizarreness of such a topic can be gained from considering
the impossibility of interpreting the following English sentence:

13 *A dog, I gave some food to $\left\{\begin{array}{l}\emptyset \\ \text{it} \\ \text{one}\end{array}\right\}$ yesterday.

Looking at the functional role of the subject, on the
other hand, reveals two facts. First, some NPs which can be
clearly identified as subjects do not play any semantic role
in the sentence at all; that is, in many subject-prominent
languages, sentences may occur with "empty" or "dummy" subjects (see section III(c) below). Second, in case the subject NP is not empty, the functional role of the subject can
be defined within the confines of a sentence as opposed to a
discourse. According to Michael Noonan (personal communication), the subject can be characterized as providing the orientation or the point of view of the action, experience,
state, etc., denoted by the verb. This difference in the
functional roles between the subject and the topic explains
the fact that the subject is always an argument of the verb,
while the topic need not be (see section II(b) above). The
explanation runs as follows: if we are to view the action,
experience, state, etc., denoted by the verb from the point
of view of an entity (or orient the description towards that
entity), the entity must be involved in the action, experience or state, etc., and must therefore be an argument of the
verb. Thus we see that the distinct functions of the topic
and the subject turn out to explain the differences between
them in definiteness and selectional relations.

(e) Verb-agreement. It is well known that the verb in
many languages shows obligatory agreement with the subject of
a sentence. Topic-predicate agreement, however, is very
rare, and we know of no language in which it is widespread or

464

obligatory. The reason for this is quite straightforward: topics, as we have seen, are much more independent of their comments than are subjects of their verbs. Evidence of this independence can be found in the fact, discussed in section II(a) and II(c), that the topic need not have any selectional relationship to any verb and that the topic is not determined by the verb of the sentence. Given this independence, it is to be expected that a constituent in the comment is not normally marked to agree with some grammatical property of the topic. Morphological agreement, then, where some <u>inherent</u> properties of the subject noun are represented by verbal affixes, is a common kind of surface coding for subjects (see E.L. Keenan, <u>Definition of Subject</u>, this volume) (7).

(f) Sentence-initial position. Although the surface coding of the topic may involve sentence position as well as morphological markers, it is worth noting that the surface coding of the topic in all the languages we have examined always involve the sentence-initial position. In Lisu, Japanese, and Korean, the topic is obligatorily codified by morpheme markers. In Lahu, the topic is optionally codified by morpheme markers. But regardless of the morpheme markers, the topic in these languages must remain in sentence-initial position. Subject, on the other hand, is not confined to the sentence-initial position. In Malagasy and Chumash, for example, the subject occurs in sentence-final position, while Arabic and Jacaltec, for example, are VSO. The reason that the topic but not the subject must be in sentence-initial position may be understood in terms of discourse strategies. Since speech involves serialization of the information to be communicated, it makes sense that the topic, which represents the discourse theme, should be introduced first. The subject, being a more sentence-oriented notion, need not receive any priority in the serialization process.

(g) Grammatical processes. The subject but not the topic plays a prominent role in such processes as reflexivization, passivization, Equi-NP deletion, verb serialization, and imperativization (see E.L. Keenan, <u>Definition of Subject</u>, this volume). Thus the reflexive pronoun generally marks a co-referential relation with the subject of the sentence; passivization may be viewed, at least in part, as a process promoting the patient to the subjecthood; in Equi-NP deletion, the deleted constituent in the complement is generally the subject; verb serialization, which is found in the Niger-Congo languages and the Sino-Tibetan languages, involves the concatenation of a series of verb phrases with one identical subject; the deleted second person morpheme in an imperative sentence is always the subject. The reason that the topic is

not involved in such grammatical processes is partially due
to the fact that the topic, as we have shown earlier, is syntactically independent of the rest of the sentence. Reflexivization, passivization, Equi-NP deletion, verb serialization,
etc., are concerned with the internal syntactic structure of
sentences. Since the topic is syntactically independent in
the sentence, it is not surprising that it does not play a
role in the statement of these processes.

To sum up this section on the differences between the
subject and the topic, we note that seven criteria have been
established. These criteria are not intended to constitute a
definition of either notion, but are rather designed to serve
as guidelines for distinguishing the topic from the subject.
We may single out three basic factors underlying these criteria: discourse strategy, noun-verb relations, and grammatical processes. The subject has a minimal discourse function
in contrast with the topic.   Hence, the topic but not
necessarily the subject is discourse-dependent, serves as the
center of attention of the sentence, and must be definite.
As for noun-verb relations and grammatical processes, it is
the subject rather than the topic that figures prominently.
Thus, subject is normally determined by the verb, and is
selectionally related to the verb; and the subject often
obligatorily controls verb agreement. These properties of
the subject are not shared by the topic. In conclusion, the
topic is a discourse notion, whereas the subject is to a
greater extent a sentence-internal notion. The former can be
understood best in terms of the discourse and extra-sentential
considerations; the latter in terms of its functions within
the sentence structure.

III. Characteristics of Topic-Prominent Languages.
Having examined a number of properties of topics as opposed
to subjects, let us now turn to a discussion of some of the
grammatical implications of topic-prominence and subject-
prominence.

(a) Surface coding. In Tp languages, there will be a
surface coding for the topic, but not necessarily for the
subject. For example, in Mandarin, the topic is always in
initial position; in Lisu and Lahu, the topic is coded by a
morphological marker. In none of these languages is there
any surface coding for subject, though, as we have pointed
out, the subject notion can be identified as playing a role
in certain grammatical processes. In Japanese and Korean,
which are both Tp and Sp, there is a morpheme marking the
topic (wa and (n)ɨn, respectively) as well as one marking the
subject (ga and ka, respectively).

(b) The passive construction. The passive construction is common among Sp languages. Among Tp languages, on the other hand, passivization either does not occur at all (e.g., Lahu, Lisu), or appears as a marginal construction, rarely used in speech (e.g., Mandarin), or carries a special meaning (e.g., the "adversity" passive in Japanese) (8). The relative insignificance of the passive in Tp languages can be explained as follows: in Sp languages, the notion of subject is such a basic one that if a noun other than the one which a given verb designates as its subject becomes the subject, the verb must be marked to signal this "non-normal" subject choice. Fillmore states this requirement as follows for the verb "give" in English:

> "The 'normal' choice of subject for sentences
> containing an A(gent). . . is the A. The
> verb <u>give</u> also allows either O(bject) or
> D(ative) to appear as subject as long as this
> 'non-normal' choice is 'registered' in the V.
> This 'registering' of a 'non-normal' subject
> takes place via the association of the feature
> [+ passive] with the V." (Fillmore, 1968:37)

In Tp languages, it is the topic, not the subject, that plays a more significant role in sentence construction. Any noun phrase can be the topic of a sentence without registering anything on the verb. It is, therefore, natural that the passive construction is not as widespread in Tp languages as it is in Sp languages.

(c) "Dummy" subjects. "Dummy" or "empty" subjects, such as the English <u>it</u> and <u>there</u>, the German <u>es</u>, the French <u>il</u> and <u>ce</u>, may be found in an Sp language but not in a Tp language. This is because in an Sp language a subject may be needed whether or not it plays a semantic role. Examples from English include:

14 <u>It</u> is raining.

15 <u>It</u> is hot in here.

16 <u>It</u> is possible that the war will end.

17 <u>There</u> is a cat in the garden.

In a Tp language, as we have emphasized, where the notion of subject does not play a prominent role, there is no need for "dummy" subjects. In cases where no subject is called for, the sentence in a Tp language can simply do without a subject. For example, the Mandarin sentences corresponding to 15-17 are respectively 18-20.

18 Zhèr   hěn   rè   (Mandarin)
    here   very hot
    "It is hot in here."

19 Kěnéng   zhè - chang   zhànzhen jìu - yào
    possible   this - class. war   will soon

        jiēsu   le   (Mandarin)
        end   aspect
    "It is possible that this war will soon end."

20 Yǒu   yì - tiáo   maō   zài huāyuán-li (Mandarin)
    exist   one - class. cat   at   garden -in
    "There is a cat in the garden."

(d) "Double subject." Tp languages are famous for
their pervasive so-called "double subject" constructions. A
number of examples have already occurred in our exposition.
Here are four more, each from a different language:

21 Sakana wa   tai   ga   oisii   (Japanese)
    fish   top. red snapper subj. delicious
    "Fish (topic), red snapper is delicious."

22 Pihengki - nɨn   747 - ka   khɨ - ta   (Korean)
    airplane - top.   - subj. big - stative
    "Airplanes (topic), the 747 is big."

23 Nèike shù   yèzi   dà   (Mandarin)
    that   tree   leaves big
    "That tree (topic), the leaves are big."

24 hɔ   ɔ   na - qhɔ̂   yɨ   ve   yɔ̀   (Lahu)
    elephant   top. nose   long prt. declar.
    "Elephants (topic), noses are long."

Such sentences are, of course, the clearest cases of
topic-comment structures. First, the topic and the subject
both occur and can thus be distinguished easily. Second, the
topic has no selectional relationship with the verb. Third,
no argument can be given that these sentences could be derived by any kind of "movement" rule from some other sentence
type. Fourth, all Tp languages have sentences of this type,
while no pure Sp languages do, as far as we know.

It has been suggested (Teng 1974) for Mandarin and by
Park (1973) for Korean that these sentences involve a "sentential predicate." That is, a Mandarin sentence such as

25 Tā   tóu   téng
    he   head   ache
    "He has a head-ache."

is analyzed by Teng (1974) as having the following structure:

468

26

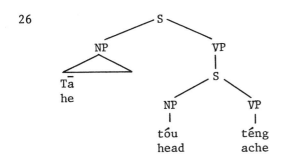

(p. 461, Figure 2)

While we agree with the spirit of this approach, we feel that his analysis makes sense only if languages with "double sub-ject" constructions are seen as Tp. This is because in an Sp language, a <u>predicate</u> cannot be a sentence. If it were a sentence, it would leave the subject grammatically "stranded," as it were, with nothing to be the subject of. Viewing such constructions as composed of a topic and a comment, however, involves no anomaly since sentential <u>comments</u> are quite na-tural, given the grammatical independence of the topic from the rest of the sentence (9).

The pervasiveness of the "double subject" construction, then, is a significant feature of Tp languages (10). In sec-tion IV(d), we will consider the basicness of "double sub-ject" sentences in more detail.

(e) Controlling co-reference. In a Tp language, the topic, and not the subject, typically controls co-referential constituent deletion (11). Some examples from Mandarin in-clude:

27 Nèike shù   yèzi   dà,   suǒyi wǒ bu   xǐhuān ___.
   that   tree leaves big   so   I   not like
   "That tree (topic), the leaves are big, so I don't
   like <u>it</u>."

The deleted object in the second clause can only be under-stood to refer to the topic "that tree," and not to the sub-ject "leaves."

28 Nèi kuài tián dàozi zhǎngde hěn dà,
   that piece land rice grow   very big

   suǒyi _____ hěn zhǐqián.
   so   very valuable

   "That piece of land (topic), rice grows very big, so
   <u>it</u> (the land) is very valuable."

Similarly, the deleted constituent in 28 refers to the topic "that piece of land," and not to the subject "rice."

Sentence 29 illustrates a case in which the subject "fire brigade" cannot control the deletion in the second clause, and the topic "that fire" is incompatible with that clause, so it is incoherent:

29 Nèi   chang   huǒ   xiāofángduì láide zǎo,
    that classifier fire fire brigade came   early

    (*)suǒyi _____ hěn lèi
    so   very tired

"That fire (topic), the fire brigade came early, so they're very tired."

The point we are making is that in a Tp language, the topic takes precedence over the subject in controlling co-reference (12).

(f) V-final languages. Tp languages tend to be verb-final languages, as has been pointed out by Hsieh Hsin-I and W.P. Lehmann (personal communication). Japanese, Korean, Lisu, and Lahu are mature and indisputable verb-final langua-ges, and Chinese, as we have argued elsewhere (see Li and Thompson 1974a and 1974b) is in the process of becoming one. In the final section, we will suggest a possible explanation for this fact.

(g) Constraints on topic constituent. In certain Sp languages, the topic-comment type of sentence is highly con-strained in terms of what can serve as the topic constitu-ent. Indonesian, for instance, only allows the surface sub-ject constituent and the genitive of the surface subject con-stituent to be the topic (13). Consider sentence 30, a simple subject-predicate construction in Indonesian,

30 Ibu   anak itu   membeli sepatu   (Indonesian)
    mother child that buy   shoe
"That child's mother bought shoes."

where the subject is ibu anak itu "that child's mother." The entire subject may be the topic:

31 Ibu   anak itu , dia membeli sepatu (Indonesian)
    mother child that , she buy   shoe
"That child's mother, she bought shoes."

The genitive of the subject, anak itu "that child," may also be the topic:

32 Anak   itu , ibu - nja   membeli sepatu (Indonesian)
    child that , mother - poss. buy   shoe
                        suffix
"That child, his mother bought shoes."

470

However, if the object noun phrase, <u>sepatu</u> "shoe," of sentence 30 is the topic, the sentence is ungrammatical:

```
33  *Sepatu itu  , ibu      anak   itu     membeli (Indonesian)
     shoe   that , mother   child  that     buy
```

In topic-prominent languages, on the other hand, there are no constraints on what may be the topic.

(h) Basicness of topic-comment sentences. Perhaps the most striking difference between a Tp language and a non-Tp language is the extent to which the topic-comment sentence can be considered to be part of the repertoire of basic sentence types in the former but not in the latter. In the next section we will provide evidence for the basicness of topic-comment sentences in Tp languages.

To summarize this section, we have brought out a number of distinguishing characteristics of Tp languages. In these languages, topics are coded in the surface structure and they tend to control co-referentiality; the topic-oriented "double subject" construction is a basic sentence type, while such subject-oriented constructions as the passive and "dummy" subject sentences are rare or non-existent.

IV. On the Basicness of Topic-Comment Sentences in Tp Languages. Our aim in this section will be to show that topic-comment structures in Tp languages cannot be viewed as being derived from any other sentence type.

We would like to make it quite clear that we are not arguing against any particular formulation according to which such a derivational relationship might be established; rather we are arguing against the desirability in principle of viewing topic-comment sentences as derivative, marginal, marked, or otherwise unusual sentence types in these languages. That is, we are not saying that some generative apparatus could not be imagined which would "handle" the cases we are about to present. Our claim is that the data which these Tp languages present are most <u>naturally</u> accounted for by taking the topic-comment sentences to be basic and not derived.

(a) On the notion "basic sentence," E.L. Keenan (<u>Definition of Subject</u>, this volume), in discussing the definition of "subject," offers a definition of "basic" sentence:

> "i) a sentence A is <u>more basic</u> than a sentence B if, and only if, the syntactic form and the meaning of B are understood as a function of those of A. (E.g., the form of B is some modification [possibly addition to] that of A, and the meaning of B is some modification of that of A.)

"ii) a sentence is a <u>basic sentence</u> in L if and
only if no other sentence of L is more basic
than it."

According to both of these criteria, topic-comment sentences
in Tp languages are basic. There are no sentences more basic
than they in terms of which their meaning or form can be specified.

(b) Lisu. The clearest data supporting this claim can
be found in Lisu, a Tp language described in Hope (1974). Our
data will be taken from this work and his response to our
inquiry about a number of Lisu constructions while he was
doing field work in Thailand. In Lisu, as we will endeavor
to show, even the grammatical relations Agent and Patient
cannot be identified. Thus, there is no way to identify the
notion of subject. It is clear, then, that in Lisu, there is
simply no subject-predicate sentence form from which the
topic-comment sentences could be said to be derived.

(1) Grammatical relations. The sentence word order in
Lisu is verb-final. If there is more than one noun phrase
preceding a verb, then the sentence is normally ambiguous as
to which noun phrase represents the agent or the actor and
which noun phrase represents the patient. The structure of a
simple declarative sentence with a transitive verb will only
indicate which noun phrase is the topic but not which noun
phrase is the agent. Sentences 34 and 35 are typical simple
declarative sentences in Lisu.

34 làthyu   nya   ánà   khù - a
    people topic dog bite - declarative
           marker   marker

    "People (topic) {they bite dogs."
                    {dogs bite them."

35 ánà   nya   làthyu   khù - a
    dog topic people bite - declarative
        marker   marker

    "Dogs (topic) {they bite people."
                  {people bite them."

Sentences 34 and 35 are equally ambiguous as far as agency is
concerned. Both sentences may mean either <u>people bite dogs</u>
or <u>dogs bite people</u>. The two sentences are different only in
terms of the topic. In 34, <u>làthyu</u> "people" is the topic,
whereas in 35 <u>ánà</u> "dog" is the topic. One may wonder if a
language such as Lisu, which completely neglects the codification of agency or subjecthood would give rise to communication problems. Of course, there are sentences which are

ambiguous, such as 36:

36 làma   nya   ánà   kyù - a
    tiger   topic   dog   bite - declarative
            marker   marker

"Tigers (topic), {they bite dogs."
                 {dogs bite them."

The fact is, however, that this total disregard for agency or
subjecthood in the structure of the language does not impair
its communicative function, as much as might be expected.
First of all, the context, whether linguistic or extra-lin-
guistic, provides a great number of semantic cues. Secondly,
semantic properties such as humanness and animacy play a significant role in disambiguating sentences which may be otherwise ambiguous because of the lack of any indication of
agency or subjecthood. In terms of pragmatics, one may safely
assume that when one hears either 34 or 35, the intended meaning would be dogs bite people, since people are normally not
expected to bite other creatures. Thus, although 34 and 35
are theoretically ambiguous, they do not present a communication problem in most circumstances. But the structure of the
Lisu verb system also serves to minimize the potential ambiguity. For example, let us contrast the Lisu verb thywu
"burn" with the English verb burn. Although both verbs share
a great deal in meaning, there is a significant semantic difference between them. The Lisu verb thywu implies that what
is being burnt must be inanimate. The English verb burn does
not have such a selectional restriction. Thus, the Lisu sentence 37, whose English translation is acceptable, is ungrammatical:

37 *làthyu   gu   nya   ánà   thywu - a
    person   that   topic   dog   burn - declarative
                     marker   marker
    "That person burned the dog."

Instead, a causative construction would have to be used to
express this proposition.

Consider another Lisu verb sye "kill." Although it
shares most of the meaning of the English verb kill, it has
very different selectional properties. The Lisu verb sye
obligatorily co-occurs with the noun yi-pə "an end," but need
not occur with a patient noun which is selectionally required
by the English verb, kill. Sentence 38 illustrates the usage
of sye "kill."

38 ása   nya   yí-pɔ́   syɛ̀ - a
    asa   topic end   kill - declarative
        marker   marker
    "Asa killed and an end resulted."

To further demonstrate that Agent and Patient are not
systematically distinct in the grammar of Lisu, and hence,
that there is no possibility of identifying the subject in
Lisu sentences, we would like to cite some additional data.

39 làthyu   nya   áyà   ami   khwa - a   mu - a
    people   topic buffalo field   hoe - decl.   see - decl.
          marker   marker   marker

                    ⎧ they saw the buffaloes hoeing
    "The people (topic), ⎨   the field."
                    ⎩ the buffaloes saw them hoeing
                         the field."

40 áyà   nya   làthyu   ami   khwa - a   mu - a
    buffalo   topic people   field   hoe - decl.   see - decl.
            marker   marker   marker

                       ⎧ they saw the people hoeing
    "The buffaloes (topic), ⎨   the field."
                       ⎩ the people saw them hoeing
                            the field."

41 ami   nya   áyà   làthyu   khwa - a   mu - a
    field   topic buffalo people   hoe - decl.   see - decl.
          marker   marker   marker

                    ⎧ the buffaloes saw the people
    "The field (topic), ⎨   hoeing it."
                    ⎩ the people saw the buffaloes
                         hoeing it."

42 ánà   nya   làma   dzà   hí - a
    dog   topic tiger   eat   difficult - decl.
        marker   marker

                    ⎧ they are difficult for tigers to eat."
    "Dogs (topic), ⎨ tigers are difficult for them to eat."

43 làma   nya   ánà   dzà   hí - a
    tiger   topic dog   eat   difficult - decl.
        marker   marker

                     ⎧ they are difficult for dogs to eat."
    "Tigers (topic), ⎨ dogs are difficult for them to eat."

44 ánà   nya   làma   dzà   nĭsy̆ɨ - a
    dog   topic   tiger   eat   want - decl.
           marker   marker

    "Dogs (topic), {tigers want to eat them."
                   {they want to eat tigers."

45 làma   nya   ánà   dzà   nĭsy̆ɨ - a
    tiger   topic   dog   eat   want - decl.
            marker   marker

    "Tigers (topic), {dogs want to eat them."
                     {they want to eat dogs."

These Lisu sentences clearly show that neither word order nor morphology allows a grammatical distinction to be made between nouns in different relationships with the verb, and that there is, therefore, no identifiable subject in the sentence structure of this language.

(2) Reflexive. In the Thailand dialect of Lisu, the reflexive consists of a construction which is either of the form repeating the co-referential NP meaning literally NP's body or of the form meaning his body where a pronoun is being used.

46 làma   nya   làma kudwè   khù - a
    tiger   topic   tiger body   bite   decl.
            marker   marker
    "The tiger (topic), he bit his body."

47 làma   nya   yí kudwè   khù - a
    tiger   topic   he body   bite   decl.
            marker   marker
    "The tiger (topic), he bit his body (i.e., himself)."

48 làma kudwè   nya   làma   khù - a
    tiger body   topic   tiger bite   decl.
                  marker   marker
    "His body (topic), the tiger bit it."

49 yí kudwè   nya   làma   kyù - a
    he body   topic   tiger bite   decl.
                  marker   marker
    "His body (topic), the tiger bit it."

(3) Co-ordination. The coordination marker in Lisu is ce. If several topic noun phrases are conjoined, ce is used to replace one or all of the topic markers nya.

475

51 làthyu   <u>ce</u>   làma   nya   ánà khù - <u>a</u>
   people co-ord tiger topic dog bite   decl.
                      marker   marker

"People and tigers (topic), {they bite dogs."
                             {dogs bite them."

52 làthyu nya   làma   <u>ce</u>   ánà khù - <u>a</u>
   people topic tiger co-ord dog bite   decl.
   marker   marker

  a. "People and tigers (topic), {they bite dogs."
                                 {dogs bite them."

  b. "People (topic), {they bite dogs and tigers."
                         {dogs and tigers bite them."

Again the above examples indicate that co-ordination does not
involve any notion of subject. The two readings of 52 do
indicate that co-ordination in Lisu follows the general constraint that the conjoined constituents should be semantically and syntactically parallel. (See Schachter 1974.)
Hence, although 51 is ambiguous as far as the agent of biting
is concerned, the conjoined NPs, <u>làthyu</u> "people" and <u>làma</u>
"tiger" must have the same semantic role with respect to the
action of biting. Sentence 52 is four-way ambiguous. However, the (a) readings are related to a surface structure in
which <u>làthyu</u> "people" and <u>làma</u> "tiger" are conjoined topics
and in which the co-ordination marker <u>ce</u> has replaced the
topic marker <u>nya</u>, of the second topic, <u>làma</u> "tiger." The (b)
readings, on the other hand, have a surface structure in which
only the NP, <u>làthyu</u> "people," is the topic, and the co-ordination marker <u>ce</u> conjoins the other two NPs, <u>làma</u> "tiger" and
<u>ánà</u> "dog," which are not topics. These examples show that
the notion of subject does not play any role in the structure
of compound sentences in Lisu.

    The Lisu examples presented above demonstrate that the
syntactic relation of a noun phrase to the verb in a sentence
is indeterminate, and that the notion of subject is quite
irrelevant in the description of the sentences of this language. The only relevant notion in the syntactic structure
of Lisu sentences is the topic, which is always marked by the
morpheme <u>nya</u> and occupies the sentence initial position.

    It might be suggested that Lisu is actually closer to
being a subject-prominent language than we have made it out
to be. Recall that, as mentioned in footnote 2, <u>nya</u> does
appear as a marker in sentences containing no presupposed
noun phrases such as:

```
53  swu   nya   átha̋   də̀  -  a
    one   topic forge  knife - decl.
          marker             marker
    "Someone is forging a knife."
```

Recall also that the rule governing the appearance of <u>nya</u> in
such sentences is that it goes with the agent if there is one,
with the dative if there is no agent, with the object if
there is no dative, and with the instrumental if there is no
dative. Now we might say that this function of <u>nya</u> is a
subject-marking function since some noun phrase is being
singled out not according to its case role, but according to
a hierarchy that is typically invoked for subject-prominent
languages.

In support of our claim that Lisu is essentially a
topic-prominent language, however, we want to point out that
this apparently subject-oriented <u>nya</u>-marking mechanism is
restricted to sentences involving no presupposed noun phrases, which are extremely rare in actual language use. Even
a superficial study of discourse shows that communication
typically involves some noun phrase whose referent is assumed
by the speaker to be known to the hearer. Since this subject-
marking function of <u>nya</u> occurs only in this relatively rare
sentence type, and since the notion of subject seems to play
no other role in the grammar of Lisu, then, we claim that the
basic sentence structure is topic-comment, with no candidates
for any source from which it can be said to be derived.

(c) Mandarin. We are not the first to suggest that
Mandarin Chinese is a Tp language. Hong (1956), Householder
and Cheng (1967), Tai (1973), Huang (1973), and Alleton
(1973) mention the idea, and Chao (1968:67-104) discusses the
Topic-Comment concept at some length. It is important to
note that, although he uses the terms subject and predicate
throughout, we can interpret these terms as topic and comment.
That this is his intention can be seen from the following remark:

> "The grammatical meaning of subject and predi-
> cate in a Chinese sentence is topic and comment,
> rather than actor and action." (p. 69)

What we are interested in, of course, is the <u>distinction</u> between topic and subject and its implications for the establishment of a linguistic typology.

Now, unlike Lisu, Mandarin does have structures that
could be called subject-predicate sentences. For example,

```
53  Wǒde   dìdi    xǐhuan chī  píngguǒ
    my     brother like   eat  apple
    "My brother likes to eat apples."
```

In this example, the word order parallels that of its English translation. From examples of this type, one could conclude that Mandarin is, like English, a Sp language with the subject in initial position. In addition, although we are describing Mandarin as Tp, as indicated earlier, the notion of subject clearly plays a role in certain sentence structures. For example, the serial verb construction must be described as a sequence of predicates sharing the same subject:

54 Zhāng-sān mǎi le piào jìnqu
   Zhang-san buy asp. ticket go in

"Zhang-san bought a ticket {and went in."
                            {to go in."

Serial verb sentences, as we described them in Li and Thompson (1973), may generally be interpreted as expressing either purpose or actions which are consecutive, simultaneous, or alternating. We can show that the notion of subject must be referred to in an account of this construction by giving an example in which the noun shared by the two predicates is an agent of one and an experiencer of the other. That is, serial verb sentences cannot be described by simply referring to the agent of the two predicates:

55 Wǒ huā le gián xiǎngshòu
   I spend aspect money enjoy

"I spent money {and had a good time."
               {to have a good time."

Furthermore, 56–59 illustrate that the subject may control reflexivization.

56 John xǐhuàn tā - zìji
        like he - self
   "John likes himself."

57 John dǎ tā - zìji
        hit he - self
   "John hit himself."

58 John shì tā - zìji de péngyǒu
        is he - self genitive friend
   "John is his own friend."

59 *John, wǒ xǐhuān ta - zìji
         I like he self
   *"John (topic) I like himself."

Sentence 59 shows that when the sentence contains a topic which can be distinguished from what one might want to call the subject, this topic does not control reflexivization.

478

Thus, the grammar of Mandarin must refer to the subject to describe the process of reflexivization (see E.L. Keenan, Definition of Subject, this volume). However, even for Mandarin, the evidence against considering topic-comment sentences to be derived from sentences of a subject-predicate form is very strong. Thus many normal topic-comment sentences whose topics have no selectional relationship with the verb in the comment have no subject-predicate sources. Following are some examples of this type.

60 Huáng - sè   de   tǔ-dì dàfen zuì héshi
   yellow - color relative soil manure most suitable
                  clause
                  marker
   "The yellow soil (topic), manure is most suitable."

61 Nèi - zuo   fángzi xìngkui qù - nián
   that - classifier house fortunate last - year

   mei xià xuě
   not snow

   "That house (topic), fortunately it didn't snow last year."

62 Dòngwu wǒ zǔzhang bǎo - shǒu   zhèngce
   animal I advocate conservation policy
   "Animals (topic), I advocate a conservation policy."

63 Zèi - jian   shìqing nǐ bù néng guang
   this - classifier matter you not can only

   máfan yī-ge rén
   bother one person

   "This matter (topic), you can't just bother one person."

The pervasiveness of sentences of this type provides very clear evidence against a process of topicalization.

In addition, the subject is not systematically codified in the surface structure of Mandarin sentences. There is simply no noun phrase in Mandarin sentences which has what E.L. Keenan has termed "subject properties" (Definition of Subject, this volume). This means that a noun phrase which one might want to defend as a subject is impossible to identify as such. As a case in point, let us look briefly at a certain construction which we think provides a clear illustration of the difference between Sp and Tp languages. We can call this construction the "pseudo-passive." Here are two examples:

64 Zhèi - jian   xīnwen guǎngbò   le
   This - classifier news broadcast aspect
   "This news (topic), it has been broadcast."

65 Neì - běn   shū yijīng chūbǎn le
   That - classifier book already publish aspect
   "That book (topic), it has already been published."

Because the initial noun is in an object case relationship
with the verb (see Fillmore 1968), one might try to claim
that such sentences are actually passives.

A similar sentence type exists in Bahasa Indonesia, as
described by S. Chung (this volume). She shows that a sentence which is superficially an object topicalization is
actually a passive because the fronted object noun can be
shown to be functioning as a subject. A demonstration of
this sort cannot be given for sentences such as 64 and 65 in
Mandarin because, except as noted above, there seem to be no
processes which refer to subject and no surface clues by
which a subject could be identified (14).

(d) The "double subject" construction. The "double
subject" sentences, as we have suggested (see above, Section
III(d)), are prototypical topic-comment sentences. They are
widespread in Chinese, Japanese, Korean, Lisu, and Lahu. If
we can show that such sentences are not derived, then we will
have given very strong support for our case. Precisely the
same arguments against deriving the "double subject" sentences from any other sentence type hold for all the Tp languages we have examined.

The only source which has, to our knowledge, ever been
suggested for the "double subject" sentence is a subject-
predicate type of sentence in which there is a genitive relationship expressed between NP_1 and NP_2. Thus, for Korean, we
could say that 66 was related to 67:

66 John - ɨn   məli - ka   aphɨ - ta
        topic   head subj. sick stative
   "John has a headache."

67 John - ɨi   məli - ka   aphɨ - ta
        gen.   head subj. sick stative
   "John's head aches."

Or, for Mandarin, we could say that 68 should be derived from
69:

68 Xiàng   bízi cháng
   elephant nose long
   "Elephants have long noses."

69 Xiàng   de   bízi   cháng
   elephant gen. nose   long
   "Elephants' noses are long."

However, as pointed out in Yang (1972) and Teng (1974), there
are many "double subject" sentences in which there are no
genitive or partitive relationships between the two initial
noun phrases. Examples include:

70 TV - in Zenith - ka tintin - ha - ta   (Korean)
                         strong   stative
   "The TV (topic), Zenith is durable."

71 Tāmen   shéi   dōu   bu   lái   (Mandarin)
   they   anyone all   not come
   "They (topic), none of them are coming."

Thus, a genitive relationship only exists for a subset of
"double subject" sentences. There is no gain, then in viewing such sentences as being derived from subject-predicate
sentences with genitive phrases as subjects.

Even in those cases in which a genitive relationship
between the two noun phrases can be maintained, though nothing
would be gained by postulating a derivation of "double subject" sentences from genitive subject sentences. This is because a "re-interpretation" would have to be claimed to have
occurred in order to account for the fact that, in Mandarin
at least, these two sentence types control co-referential
noun phrase deletion differently. Compare 72 and 73:

72 Nèike shù   de   yèzi   tài   dà,   suóyi wǒ   bu
   that   tree 's   leaves too   big   so   I   not

      xǐhuān _____
      like

   "That tree's leaves are too big, so I don't like them."

73 Nèike shù   yèzi   tài   dà,   suóyi wǒ   bu
   that   tree leaves too   big   so   I   not

      xǐhuān _____
      like

   "That tree (topic), the leaves are too big, so I don't
   like it."

In 72 the controller of the interpretation of the deleted
constituent in the second clause is the subject "that tree's
leaves," while in 73 the controller is the topic "that tree."
Deriving 73 from 72 thus does not appear to be indicated.
Teng (1974) presents a number of other arguments against such
a derivation.

(e) Distribution. We hope to have shown that there is no reason to view topic-comment sentences in Tp languages as "marked" or otherwise special. However, it has been suggested to us that perhaps such sentences are more restricted in their distribution than other sentence types, in particular that they may not occur as freely in restrictive relative clauses and non-asserted complements (15). But in fact, this is not the case. We present the following examples from Mandarin which show that clauses which must be analyzed as topic-comment structures can be embedded as restrictive relative clauses and as non-asserted complements. First, a relative clause structure:

74 Wǒ bu   xǐhuān nèi   zhǒng yǐ jīn   sānshi
    I   not like   that kind   one catty 30

    kuài - qián   de   dòuzi
    dollars   rel. beans
                  marker

"I don't like that kind of beans that costs 30 dollars a catty."

The source sentence for the underlined relative clause is:

75 Nèi zhǒng dòuzi yǐ   jīn   sānshi kuài - qián
    that kind   beans one catty 30   dollars
"That kind of beans (topic) one catty is 30 dollars."

which clearly cannot be analyzed as a subject-predicate construction. Here is another relative clause example:

76 Nèi - kē   yèzi hěn dà   de   shù
    that - classifier leaves very big rel. marker tree

    feichang gāo
    unusual tall
"That tree with big leaves is exceptionally tall."

Once again, the sentence underlying the underlined relative clause could not be claimed to be a subject-predicate construction:

77 Nèi - kē   shù   yèzi   hěn dà
    that - classifier tree leaves very big
"That tree (topic) the leaves are very big."

We can also easily show that topic-comment sentences can be embedded as presupposed complements. Here is one example:

78 Wǒ fǎndui tāmen shéi dōu bu lái
   I   oppose they   anyone all   not   come
   "I oppose the fact that none of them are coming."

The underlined complement, once again, can only be a topic-comment clause.

What examples 74-78 show, then, is that it is not the case that topic-comment sentences in a Tp language are necessarily restricted to asserted clauses. Thus, the argument that such sentences are more "marked" because of this more limited distribution can be seen to have no empirical basis.

What we have tried to do in this section is to argue that the topic function, which is highly marked and set off from the rest of the sentence in Sp languages, has in Tp languages been integrated into the basic syntax of the sentence. The topic notion must be reckoned with in constructing an adequate grammatical description of these languages, and topic-comment sentences must be counted among the basic sentence types provided by the language.

V. The Typology and Some Diachronic Implications. We have presented evidence in favor of a typological distinction between languages in which the notion of topic plays a prominent role as opposed to those in which the notion of subject plays a prominent role. As with all typological distinctions, of course, it is clear that we are speaking of a continuum. Thus, Lisu, as we have seen, is more Tp than Mandarin. Philippine languages, as suggested by Schachter (this volume) seem to be neither highly Sp nor highly Tp, while Japanese and Korean could be described as both Sp and Tp. Malagasy, as described by E.L. Keenan (Malagasy, this volume), seems to be less Sp than English does. These facts can be schematically represented as follows:

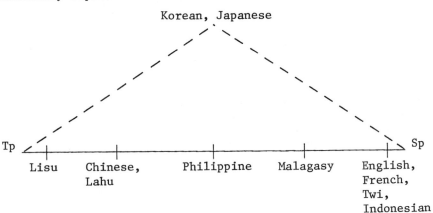

On the basis of synchronic as well as diachronic phenomena, it seems clear that subject and topic are not unrelated notions. Subjects are essentially grammaticalized
topics; in the process of being integrated into the case
frame of the verb (at which point we call them subjects),
topics become somewhat impure, and certain of their topic
properties are weakened, but their topic-ness is still recog-
nizable (16). That is why many of the topic properties are
shared by subjects in a number of languages. For example,
some Sp languages do not allow indefinite subjects.

What we are proposing here is that the universal notion
of topic may be manifested in different ways across languages.
In some languages, such as Lisu and Mandarin, the topic properties are coded in a topic constituent, and topic-comment
sentences figure among the basic sentence structures of these
languages. In other languages, such as Malagasy (see E.L.
Keenan, Malagasy, this volume), some topic properties are
carried by the subject, the constituent which is grammatically closely related to the verb and which plays a major role
in the description of a number of grammatical processes. In
such languages, to express unambiguously the topic as the
discourse theme involves a separate proposition whose only
function is topic establishment. In English, for example, we
might do it this way:

79   {Remember}
      {You know} Tom? Well, he fell off his bike yesterday.

Interestingly, this strategy is very commonly used by English-
speaking children (see E.O. Keenan and B.B. Schieffelin, this
volume) and by users of American Sign Language (see L. Friedman, this volume). In topic-prominent languages, on the
other hand, topic-establishment is built into the syntactic
structure of the sentence. The differences between the two
types of languages can have profound structural implications,
as we have tried to show.

On the basis of the cross-linguistic evidence we have
presented, we suggest the diachronic schema shown on the next
page.

To return to the question raised earlier as to why the
Tp languages are overwhelmingly verb-final, we offer the following speculation: in propelling a language from stage (C)
through stage (D) and then to stage (A), the sentence type
that plays a major role is the "double subject" type of sentence. The more such sentences are used in the language, the
closer the language comes to stage (A), since these are topic-
comment structures par excellence. Now note that the "double
subject" constructions are always of the form:

Tp

(A)   topic notion integrated
      into basic sentence struc-
      ture; topic and subject
      distinct

                                      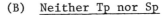

(D)   Both Tp and Sp   (B)   Neither Tp nor Sp

      topic sentences become   topic becomes more clo-
      less marked, more   sely integrated into case
      basic   frame of verb

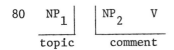

      Sp

(D)   topic has become inte-
      grated into case frame of
      verb as a subject; subject
      and topic often indistinct,
      subjects having some non-
      topic properties; sentences
      with clear topics are
      highly marked

---

80   NP$_1$ | | NP$_2$ V
     topic   comment

which is precisely the typical sentence structure of a verb-
final language. This sentence type becomes pervasive as the
relationship between NP$_1$ and NP$_2$ becomes less and less constrained.

     In conclusion, we hope to have pointed to a new arena
to observe the enactment of a familiar drama: a synchronic
typology is shown to be simply a slice of a diachronic cycle
in which different languages are caught at various stages.
In our search for linguistic universals, we are reminded that
a typology is really a description of strategies for accomplishing the same communicative goals.

485

Notes

1. Thus Dixon (1972) makes the strong claim that "Each natural language is either strictly nominative-accusative, or strictly nominative-ergative in syntax (p. 129)." Clearly, our proposal involves a rejection of Dixon's claim, since we have found languages in which no "nominative" can be identified at all.

2. There is an apparent exception in Lisu; the nya morpheme which is the topic marker appears also in sentences involving no presuppositions at all, such as

(i) swu   nya   àthà   dɘ   - a
     one   topic   knife   forge - decl.
           marker   marker
     "Someone is forging a knife."

In such sentences, nya is automatically added to the Agent if there is one, to the Dative if there is no agent, to the Object if there is no Dative, or to the Instrumental if there is no Object. Nya appears to function in two quite distinct ways, then, depending on whether or not the sentence contains any presupposed noun phrases. Hope (1974) refers to this distinction with his terms "primary" and "secondary" topicalization.

3. Kuno (1972b:270) makes a similar point, using the term "theme" for what we are calling Topic: "The theme must be either anaphoric (i.e., previously mentioned) or generic, ..." The term "theme," incidentally, though used by Kuno in much the same way as we are using "topic," is not used by Prague school linguists in the same way. Firbas, for example, who has perhaps written more on the notions of "theme" and "rheme" than anyone else, considers the "theme" to be the element which may be inferred from the context and which contributes the least to the development of the communication (Firbas 1966). Crucial to his development of this notion is the fact that every sentence can be said to have a theme. However, not every sentence has a topic.

4. So-called "dummy subjects" are only apparent exceptions, since they have no semantic content, and cannot therefore be included in a generalization concerning the semantic relationship between nouns and verbs.

5. We are not claiming, of course, that the topic has nothing to do with the comment. We do not expect to find a language in which the following type of sentence occurs:

(i) *My mother (topic), Harry can't stand chocolate mousse.

However, we do not believe the oddness of a sentence like (i) to be a grammatical problem, but rather a pragmatic one. The point which we will continue to emphasize in the text is that the relationship between a subject and its verb is much more grammatically constrained than that between a topic and the comment. An explanation for this difference in terms of the functional role of topic and subject is offered in Section II(d) below.

6. We are grateful to Paul Schachter for calling this fact to our attention. See also E.L. Keenan (Definition of Subject, this volume).

7. Talmy Givón (this volume) takes a different position. According to him, all agreement is topic-agreement, where "agreement" includes resumptive subject pronouns, as in

(i) My mother she just came in.

While we are convinced by the evidence supporting Givón's claim that agreement arises diachronically from resumptive pronouns, we do take issue with the claim that agreement morphemes and subject pronouns are indistinguishable synchronically. We know of no evidence against the hypothesis that by the time the pronoun has become a bound agreement morpheme the noun with which it agrees is no longer simply a topic but is integrated into the grammatical system as a subject. Evidence is, however, difficult to find, since none of the topic-prominent languages that we have investigated have well-developed anaphoric pronoun systems.

8. We are grateful to Irwin Howard for calling to our attention the correlation between topic-prominence and special passives. For some discussion, see Howard (1969) and Kuno (1973). There is, however, some evidence that both Mandarin and Japanese are moving away from passives expressing only adverse effects, which may be due to the influence of English translations (G. Bedell, personal communication; see also Howard, 1969).

9. There are more serious objections to certain details of Teng's analysis. For example, Teng's sentential predicate is claimed to be a VP. But, as has been pointed out by Charles Tang and Marie-Claude Paris, the "sentential predicate" only obeys the tests for VP-hood (which exploit the pre-VP position of modals and certain adverbs) if it is a lexicalized unit of some kind. Thus the "sentential predicate" tóu téng "head ache" in 25 behaves like a VP, but yèzi dà "leaves big" in 23 does not:

(i) Tā yòu tóu téng le
   he again head ache aspect
   "He has a head-ache again."

(ii) *Nèi - kē   shù   yòu   yèzi   dà   le
       that - class. tree again leaves big aspect
       "That tree again has big leaves."

For more discussion of "double-subject" sentences, see Li and Thompson (in preparation).

10. We are aware that subject markers (ga and ka) sometimes occur with the topics in "double subject" constructions in Japanese and Korean respectively. It appears that subject markers can appear with topics in certain discourse situations, but we do not at present understand this phenomenon well enough to be more precise.

11. An exception may be the deletion of a first-person pronoun on identity with a non-topic first person pronoun in a preceding clause. Thus, some speakers of Mandarin accept the following sentence, where the deleted constituent is understood to refer to the subject "I," and not to the topic "this character":

(i) Zhèige   zì   wǒ bu   renshi ,   suǒyi _____
     this   character I   not recognize so

            bu   kàn   zhèiběn xiǎoshuō
            not   read this   novel

     "This character, I don't recognize, so (I) won't read this novel."

12. It is appropriate here to point out that there is no inconsistency between (1) using topic-predicate incompatibility as evidence in arguing that topics control deletion and (2) pointing out that topics are independent of predicated (see Section II(b) and II(c)). Topics may be independent of predicated in terms of grammatical processes and selectional relations if there is also a subject in the clause, but in a clause in which there is no subject distinct from the topic, as in the second clauses of 27–29, then of course subject and topic properties cannot be distinguished. The point is that the NP which is understood as filling the blanks in 27–29 is the topic of the first clause and not its subject. (We are grateful to Greg Lee and Fu Yi-Chin for their comments on this point.)

13. Following Soemarmo's (1970) analysis of Indonesian, we consider the topic-comment structure to be the one that involves the "left dislocation" of a constituent. Those sentences that contain an initial noun phrase marked by the postposition jang are analyzed as having the focus presupposition structure rather than the topic-comment structure. For example, the sentence

```
Anak    itu    jang    membeli    sepatu
child   Art.           buy        shoe
"It was the child who bought shoes."
```

has a focus <u>anak itu</u> marked by <u>jang</u> and a presupposition:
"someone bought shoes."

14. Of course, one could try to suggest that sentences
such as 64 and 65 are derived from sentences with the object
in final position by a rule of object preposing. It is
important to note, however, that object preposing generally
does not entail agent-deletion, which one would have to postulate to account for sentences such as 64 and 65. In addition, no such rule can be invoked to account for examples
such as 60-63, which do not differ from the "pseudo-passive"
in any way, except that the topic in the "pseudo-passive" has
a selectional relationship with the verb.

15. See Hooper and Thompson (1973) for a discussion of
this notion.

16. This formulation was suggested to us by Wallace
Chafe (personal communication). For a discussion of case
frames, see Fillmore (1968).

THE SUBJECT IN PHILIPPINE LANGUAGES: TOPIC, ACTOR,
ACTOR-TOPIC, OR NONE OF THE ABOVE?

by

Paul Schachter

0   Introduction

The status of subject and object as linguistic universals is commonly taken for granted. For example, the familiar
typological classification of languages as SVO, SOV, etc.,
presupposes the universal occurrence of S's and O's, and this
assumption is also implicit in such recent claims about linguistic universals as Keenan and Comrie's (1972) accessibility
hierarchy and the set of claims embodied in David Perlmutter
and Paul Postal's theory of relational grammar (1). The
assumption in question, however, is less than obviously correct in the case of the languages of the Philippines. Students of Philippine languages, at any rate, have shown a dis-
quieting indecisiveness or diffidence with regard to which,
if any, of the sentence constituents that occur in these languages are appropriately identified as subjects and objects.
Thus a recent paper (McKaughan 1973) is largely devoted to a
retraction of its author's earlier usage of the term subject
in his writings on Philippine languages in favor of a different usage for this term. And many grammatical descriptions
of Philippine languages manage to avoid the subject-object
terminology altogether.

The present paper is centrally concerned with the question of whether or not there are identifiable subjects in the
sentences of Philippine languages (and only indirectly concerned with the question of whether or not there are identifiable objects). As background for a consideration of this
question, Section 1 of the paper presents a sketch of the
characteristic sentence structures found in Philippine language. This is followed by a presentation of arguments for
and against the subjecthood of three different classes of
sentence constituents: the topic (Sections 2 and 3), the
actor (Sections 4 and 5) and the actor-topic (Sections 6 and
7). In Section 8, the conclusion is drawn that these three
different constituent classes in fact share the properties
commonly associated with subjects, and that this division of
labor follows from the characteristics of the constituent
classes in question. This section also briefly considers the
implications of the facts of Philippine languages for the
status of subject as a linguistic universal.

1   Characteristic Sentence Structures

This sketch of the characteristic sentence structure of
Philippine languages makes use of examples from Tagalog, but
the languages of the Philippines are sufficiently similar
that examples from any one language can safely be taken as
paradigmatic. (Certain differences among the languages will,

however, be mentioned from time to time, both in the course of this sketch and in subsequent sections.) The sketch will be limited to what may be called <u>simple narrative sentences</u>. (Brief descriptions of two other types of simple sentences, <u>verbless sentences</u> and <u>existential sentences</u>, are given in Sections 2 and 3 respectively.)

The simple narrative sentence of Tagalog consists of a verb followed by a string of (one or more) noun phrases, one of which is marked as what Philippinists commonly call the <u>topic</u>. Formally, the topic is marked either by the use of a topic pronoun form or by a prenominal topic marker. Notionally, the topic is always interpreted as definite. (For further discussion of the semantics of the topic, see below.)

Any non-topic noun phrases that occur in the sentence are marked for case--again, either by the use of a distinctive pronoun form or by a prenominal marker. Unlike topics, case-marked noun phrases may in general be interpreted as either definite or indefinite. The cases do, however, have some semantic labels such as actor, goal, direction, beneficiary, etc. (These labels are not necessarily to be taken at face value; in particular, see the discussion of the actor later in this section.) There is also a case-marking affix on the verb, which indicates the case role of the topic noun phrase. Thus there are <u>actor-topic verbs</u>, <u>goal-topic verbs</u>, <u>direction-topic verbs</u>, and <u>beneficiary-topic verbs</u> (among others), and the topics that occur with these verbs may be called the <u>actor-topic</u>, the <u>goal-topic</u>, etc. Each case role is represented only once per simple sentence, so if there is an actor-topic, there is no other actor phrase in the sentence; if there is a goal-topic, there is no other goal phrase, and so on.

Let us look now at some examples. (In the glosses that accompany these and subsequent examples, the following abbreviations are used: AT, GT, DT, and BT preceding the glosses of verbs indicate that the verbs are marked as, respectively, actor-topic, goal-topic, direction-topic, and beneficiary-topic, and A, G, D, B, and T preceding the glosses of nouns and pronouns indicate that the (pro)nouns are marked as, respectively, actor, goal, direction, beneficiary, and topic.)

1   a. <u>Mag</u>-salis   <u>ang babae</u> ng bigas sa sako
        AT- will-take-out   T-woman   G-rice   D-sack

           para sa bata.
           B-child

          "The woman will take some rice out of a/the sack for a/the child."

b. Aalis<u>in</u>   ng babae <u>ang bigas</u> sa sako
   GT-will-take-out A-woman   T-rice   D-sack

      para sa bata.
      B-child

   "A/The woman will take the rice out of a/the sack
   for a/the child."

c. Aalis<u>an</u>   ng babae ng bigas <u>ang sako</u>
   DT-will-take-out A-woman   G-rice   D-sack

      para sa bata.
      B-child

   "A/The woman will take some rice out of the sack
   for a/the child."

d. <u>Ipag</u>-salis   ng babae ng bigas sa sako
   BT-will take out   A-woman   G-rice   D-sack

      <u>ang bata</u>.
      T-child

   "A/The woman will take some rice out of a/the
   sack for the child."

The four sentences of 1 all express the same event, but differ from one another in the choice of topic. The topic marker for common nouns is <u>ang</u>, and the topic phrase of each sentence is underlined. Also underlined is the verbal affix that indicates the case role of the topic. Thus <u>mag</u>- in la is an actor-topic affix, -<u>in</u> in lb a goal-topic affix, -<u>an</u> in lc a direction-topic affix, and <u>ipag</u>- in ld a beneficiary-topic affix (2). In the English equivalents of these sentences, the topic must always be marked as definite. Thus la requires a translation with "the woman," lb with "the rice," etc. The non-topic noun phrases, on the other hand, may or must be translated as <u>in</u>definite (3). As the examples show, the non-topic case markers that occur with common nouns are <u>ng</u> (pronounced [naŋ]) for both actor and goal, <u>sa</u> for direction, and <u>para sa</u> for beneficiary.

It should be pointed out that, except for the initial position of the verb, the ordering of the constituents in the examples of 1 is arbitrary. That is, any ordering of the actor, goal, direction, and beneficiary phrases is permissible, and the topic may occur in any order in relation to the non-topic phrases. Indeed, there does not even seem (surprisingly enough) to be any clearly <u>preferred</u> ordering of postverb constituents in Tagalog. (But, as will be pointed out in Section 4, there are some other Philippine languages for which this is not the case.)

Before concluding this sketch, I would like to say something more about the semantics of the topic and the actor, since the labels topic and actor, though fairly well established in the usage of Philippinists, may be somewhat misleading to those unfamiliar with Philippine languages, and since the topic and the actor (and their intersection, the actor-topic) are the candidates for subjecthood that will be considered in subsequent sections.

According to Li and Thompson (this volume), the term topic, as generally used by non-Philippinists, designates a sentence constituent that has the following semantic properties: 1) the topic is always "definite"; 2) the topic functions as the "center of attention" established by the discourse context. In the usage of Philippinists, however, it is only the first of these properties that is consistently associated with the constituent that is identified as the topic. That this constituent need not represent the center of attention is evident from examples like 2 and 3, in which the discourse context overtly directs attention to a referent which is subsequently represented by a non-topic nominal:

2   Kung tungkol kay Maria, hinuhugasan   niya
     if   about   Maria   GT-is-washing A-she

        ang mga pinggan.
        T-dishes

     "As for Maria, she is washing the dishes."

3   Speaker A: Nasaan si Maria?
               where T-Maria
               "Where's Maria?"

     Speaker B: Hinuhugasan   niya   ang mga pinggan.
               GT-is-washing A-she   T-dishes
               "She's washing the dishes."

In these examples the center of attention established by the discourse context (the preceding "as for" expression in 2, the preceding question in 3) is clearly Maria, but the pronoun that refers to Maria is the non-topic actor pronoun niya and the sentence topic is ang mga pinggan "the dishes."

While the constituent identified as the topic need not represent the center of attention, this constituent does always have a "definite" referent, and expresses, as Diller (1970, p. 128) puts it, "information assumed by the speaker to be shared by the hearer." It is for this reason that the English equivalents of topics are always definite noun phrases, such as common nouns preceded by the, proper nouns, or personal pronouns. (In fact, at least one Philippinist,

Wolfenden (1971), prefers to use the label <u>definite noun phrase</u>, rather than the label <u>topic</u>, in referring to the constituent in question.) Putting it somewhat differently, we can say that the referentiality of the topic is always presupposed. Unfortunately, however, although the presupposition of referentiality is a necessary condition for topicality, it is not a sufficient one, since there may also be non-topic noun phrases with presupposed referentiality, such as the pronouns in 2 and 3 or all of the underlined expressions in 4:

4   Dadalhin   <u>ni Rosa</u> ang pera <u>kay Juan</u>
    GT-will-take-to A-Rosa   T-money   D-Juan

    <u>para sa iyo</u>.
    B-you

    "Rosa will take the money to Juan for you."

When a sentence contains more than one noun phrase whose referentiality is presupposed, it is not always clear why one of these noun phrases, rather than another, is chosen as topic (4). Under such circumstances, it seems that there is often a good deal of leeway with regard to the choice of topic, even in a fixed discourse context, but this is a matter that requires further investigation.

To turn now to the semantic properties associated with the actor phrase, the label <u>actor</u> should not be taken as equivalent to <u>agent</u>, at least if <u>agent</u> is associated with some such role as "the typically animate perceived instigator of the action" (c.f. Fillmore, 1968:24). That this interpretation would be inappropriate should be clear from examples 5-7. (In each of these examples the expression representing the actor is underlined. The examples are presented in pairs, with the actor as topic, and an actor-topic verb, in the first member of each pair, and the actor as non-topic, and a goal-topic or direction-topic verb, in the second member of each pair.)

5   a. Nagtiis   <u>ang babae</u> ng kahirapan.
        AT-endured T-woman   G-hardship
        "The woman endured some hardship."

    b. Tiniis   <u>ng babae</u> ang kahirapan
        GT-endured A-woman   T-hardship
        "A/The woman endured the hardship."

6   a. Tumanggap   <u>ang estudyante</u> ng liham.
        AT-received T-student   G-letter
        "The student received a letter."

    b.   Tinanggap   ng estudyante ang liham.
         GT-received   A-student   T-letter
         "A/The student received the letter."

7   a.   Lumapit   ang ulap sa araw.
         AT-approach T-cloud   D-sun
         "The cloud approached the sun."

    b.   Linapitan   ng ulap ang araw.
         DT-approach A-cloud T-sun
         "A/The cloud approached the sun."

The examples of 5 and 6 show that an animate actor is not
necessarily the "instigator" of the action, and the examples
of 7 show that the actor need not even be animate.

While I know of no really satisfactory generalization
about the semantic characteristics associated with the actor
(and perhaps none is possible, given the dependency of the
interpretation of the actor's role on the interpretation of
the verb), I find that the following characterization (taken
from Benton 1971:167) will, if interpreted charitably enough,
cover most cases: "the entity to which the action of the verb
is attributed." (The requisite charitable interpretation
allows "action" to serve as a cover term for actions, happen-
ings, and conditions in general.) I also find Benton's term
attribute of action more tenable than the term actor, but I
shall continue to use the latter on the basis of its being
shorter, better established, and innocuous enough once its
inadequacies have been explained.

One generalization that can be made about the actor is
that it is translated quite regularly by the active surface
subject in English. But this cannot be taken as a semantic
generalization unless one is willing to claim, and able to
substantiate the claim, that some valid semantic characterization of the class of English active subjects is possible.
While this claim is not, to my knowledge, one that has been
seriously investigated, it may in fact be worth considering,
and I shall return to it briefly in subsequent sections.

With the above inconclusive discussion of the semantics
of the topic and the actor as background, let us turn now to
consider the extent to which the properties of each might
warrant its being identified as a subject.

2   The Topic as Subject: Arguments For

A prima facie case can be made for considering the
topic in Philippine language equivalent to the subject in
some other languages on the basis of distribution. Indeed,
if one makes the rather common assumption that logically

complete declarative sentences must contain a subject and a predicate, then the topic is the only plausible candidate for subjecthood, since there are fundamental sentence types whose only constituents are a predicate verb, noun, or adjective and a topic nominal. Consider, for example, the following sentences. (Unless otherwise indicated, examples are from Tagalog.)

8 Magtatrabaho   ang lalaki.
   AT-will-work   T-man
   "The man will work."

9 Papawisan   ang lalaki.
   GT/DT-will-sweat T-man
   "The man will sweat."

10 Abogado   ang lalaki.
    lawyer   T-man
    "The man is a lawyer."

11 Matalino   ang lalaki.
    intelligent T-man
    "The man is intelligent."

Sentences 8 and 9 consist of an intransitive verb plus a topic noun phrase (5). Sentences 10 and 11 are verbless, or equational, sentences, consisting respectively of a predicate nominal plus a topic and a predicate adjective plus a topic. Thus if one assumes that complete sentences in general contain subjects, there is no choice but to say that the topic nominal is the subject in cases like 8 through 11.

Two other arguments in favor of identifying the topic as the subject may be formulated on the basis of certain recent claims about linguistic universals. First, Keenan and Comrie (1972) have proposed that constraints on the types of sentence constituents that a language allows to be relativized must reflect the universal accessibility hierarchy (example 12) (where ">" means "greater than or equal to in accessibility" with regard to relative clause formation):

12 Subj. $\geq$ DO $\geq$ IO $\geq$ OPrep. $\geq$ Poss-NP $\geq$ O-Comp.-Particle

What this hierarchy claims is that, if a language allows direct objects (DO) to be relativized, it must also allow subjects to be relativized, if it allows indirect objects (IO) to be relativized, it must also allow direct objects to be relativized, etc. (The remaining abbreviations in 12 stand for prepositional object, possessive noun phrase, and object of comparative particle.) Since the implicational relations in 12 are unidirectional, it follows that if a language allows only one constituent type to be relativized, that constituent type must be the subject.

Now in Philippine languages it is clear that only topics can be relativized. Relative clauses in these languages
have the form of sentences with deleted topics, and the missing topic of the relative clause is always understood as being co-referential with the head of the relative construction.
For example, compare the sentences of 13 with the grammatical
relative constructions of 14 and the ungrammatical strings of
15. (In the glosses of 14 and 15, Li stands for the "linker"
-ng that introduces relative clauses.)

13 a. Bumasa   ang lalaki ng diyaryo.
         AT-read   T-man   G-newspaper
         "The man read a newspaper."

    b. Binasa   ng lalaki ang diyaryo.
         GT-read   A-man   T-newspaper
         "A/The man read the newspaper."

14 a. Matalino   ang lalaking bumasa   ng diyaryo.
         intelligent T-man-Li   AT-read   G-Newspaper
         "The man who read a newspaper is intelligent."

    b. Interesante ang diyaryong binasa   ng lalaki.
         interesting T-newspaper-Li GT-read   A-man
         "The newspaper that the man read is interesting."

15 a. *Interesante ang diyaryong bumasa   ang lalaki
          interesting T-newspaper-Li AT-read   T-man

    b. *Matalino   ang lalaking binasa   ang diyaryo
          intelligent T-man-Li   GT-read   T-newspaper

Given the sentence 13a, in which there is an actor-topic verb
and a non-topic goal, it is possible to relativize the actor-
topic but not the goal (compare 14a and 15a). On the other
hand, given the sentence 13b, in which there is a goal-topic
verb and a non-topic actor, it is possible to relativize the
goal-topic but not the actor. Since only the constituents
that Philippinists identify as topics are accessible to relativization, it follows from Keenan and Comrie's claims with
regard to the accessibility hierarchy that these constituents
must be subjects.

The second recent claim that favors the identification
of topics as subjects is one made within the framework of
Perlmutter and Postal's theory of relational grammar. According to Bell (1974), relational grammar claims that only
"terms of grammatical relations"--i.e., subjects, objects,
and indirect objects--may "launch floating quantifiers,"
where a "floating quantifier" is one which has been permitted
"to leave its NP, as in 'The men were all surprised' from

'All the men were surprised'." In Tagalog, the quantifier
lahat "all" usually occurs within a noun phrase, but some
speakers also use a construction in which lahat follows the
sentence-initial verb (c.f. Schachter and Otanes 1972:147-
148 for details). In the latter case lahat is always understood as referring to the sentence topic, as in the following
examples. (The nouns in the examples are preceded by the
pluralizing particle mga ([mana]) glossed as "pl.")

16 a. Sumusulat lahat ang mga bata ng mga liham.
        AT-write   all   T-Pl-child   G-Pl-letter
        "All the children are writing letters."

    b. Sinusulat lahat ng mga bata ang mga liham.
        GT-write   all   A-Pl-child   T-Pl-letter
        "The/Some children write all the letters."

In 16a lahat can only be understood as referring to the
actor-topic, in 16b to the goal-topic. Thus, if it is in
fact the case that only "terms" may launch floating quantifiers, then the topics of the sentences of 16 are terms, and
the simplest account of this fact is provided by identifying
the topic as the subject.

A final argument for identifying the topic as the subject may be built on certain facts having to do with grammatical agreement in Kapampangan. Kapampangan is unusual among
Philippine languages in requiring that predicate verbs must
in some cases be followed by particles that agree in person
and number with specified co-occurring noun phrases. The
rule is that, subject to certain conditions that need not
concern us here (6), in actor-topic sentences there is a
single particle agreeing with the topic, while in non-actor-
topic sentences there are two particles, one agreeing with
the topic, the other with the actor. The examples of 17,
taken from Richards (1971), illustrate this rule. (In the
glosses accompanying these examples, TAP stands for topic
agreement particle and AAP for actor agreement particle. In
17a the TAP is marked as third-person-singular. In 17b the
AAP and the TAP are marked as third-person-singular and third-
person-plural respectively. As the glosses and translations
of the noun phrases show, number is obligatorily indicated in
Kapampangan topic and actor phrases, but not in Kapampangan
goal phrases.)

17 a. Menakit ya   ng anak ing lalaki
        AT-saw   TAP G-child T-Sg-man
        "The man saw a child/some children."

b. Ikit   na   la   ning lalaki   ding anak
    GT-saw   AAP   TAP   A-Sg-man   T-Pl-child
    "A/The man saw the children."

Now it is clear that, in many languages that have both
well-defined subjects and grammatical agreement, it is the
subject noun phrase with which the predicate regularly agrees.
This being the case, it seems reasonable to suggest (and has
in fact been suggested--e.g., by Li and Thompson 1974c) that
the control of agreement may be useful as a criterion for
distinguishing subjects from other noun phrases. And given
that in Kapampangan, if there is any agreement at all there
must be agreement with the topic, one might reasonably argue
that the Kapampangan agreement data favor an identification
of the topic as the subject. (But see Section 4 for another
--equally reasonable--interpretation of these data.)

3   The Topic as Subject: Arguments Against

    The first argument of the preceding section was based
on the assumption that all logically complete declarative
sentences have subjects. Given this assumption, and given
the fact that there are sentence types in Philippine languages
in which the only available candidate for subjecthood is the
topic, one must conclude that the topic should be identified
as the subject, at least in some cases. The assumption on
which this argument is based, however, is open to challenge;
for there is at least one sentence type that occurs in
Philippine language that does not appear to contain any candidate for the role of subject. The sentence type in question is the existential sentence, some examples of which are
given below. (In the glosses of these examples, E is the
gloss for the existence marker <u>may</u>.)

  18 May aksidente (Kagabi).
      E-accident   last-night
      "There was an accident (last night)."

  19 May liham   (para sa iyo).
      E-letter   B-you
      "There's a letter (for you)."

  20 May   dumarating.
      E-AT-is-coming
      "There's someone coming."

Existential sentences appear to consist minimally of an existence marker and a predicate. They do not contain a topic
nominal, and indeed need not contain any nominal at all (c.f.
20). They thus show that the assumption underlying the first

argument of the preceding section is incorrect, and weaken
whatever force this argument may have had.

There are also some arguments that can be offered
against the claim that the topic should be identified as the
subject. To start with perhaps the weakest of these, it was
noted in Section 1 that the topic nominal is always definite:
i.e., that its referent is always presupposed. Is this, one
may ask, a reasonable kind of semantic restriction to be imposed on a subject? Certainly one finds no such restriction
on the subject in English or other familiar languages, and
the existence of this restriction in the case of the Philippine topic might thus be considered evidence against the
hypothesis that the latter is properly identified as a subject.

E.L. Keenan (Definition of Subject, this volume) has
suggested, however, that, while subjects need not always be
definite, they tend universally to be more regularly referential than objects or other nominals. If this suggestion is
correct, it would not be too surprising to find that some
languages had regularized the universal tendency and imposed
a requirement that subjects must be maximally referential:
i.e., definite. Thus the obligatory definiteness of the
topic is not necessarily very disturbing to one who advocates
identifying the topic as the subject.

Much more disturbing, it seems to me, is the fact that
the topic does not play the role that one might expect the
subject to play in certain grammatical processes: notably,
reflexivization and coreferential complement subject deletion
(to borrow Postal's 1970 term). To begin with the case of
reflexivization, in all languages that I know of where the
identity of the subject is not in doubt, the subject of a
simple sentence may control reflexivization but may not itself be reflexivized. (In some languages, such as Swedish,
moreover, only the subject may control reflexivization.) It
is therefore puzzling, if one believes that topics in Philippine languages are subjects, to discover sentences like 21
and 22:

21 Sinaktan ng babae ang kaniyang sarili.
    DT-hurt   A-woman   T-her-self
    "A/The woman hurt herself."

22 Iniisip   nila   ang kanilang sarili.
    DT-think-about A-they   T-their-self
    "They think about themselves."

(Reflexives in Tagalog are formed with a possessive pronoun
and the nominal sarili "self.") In the above examples it is
clearly the topic that has been reflexivized, the reflexivi-

zation being controlled by the non-topic actor. There are,
to be sure, cases in which the topic does appear to control
reflexivization, such as 23, which is a paraphrase of 22.

23 Nag-iisip   sila   sa kanilang sarili.
   AT-think-about T-they D-their-self
   "They think about themselves."

The operant generalization, however, is that it is the actor
that controls reflexivization, whether or not the actor is
also the topic. And in any case examples like 21 and 22 show
that topics do not function as one expects subjects to function with regard to reflexivization.

Just the same point can be made with regard to coreferential complement subject deletion. This is the process said
to be involved in the derivation of an English sentence like
I want to leave from an underlying structure more like I want
ₛ[I leave]. As the name of the process indicates, the process is thought to involve the deletion of the subject of a
complement clause. Now consider in this connection the following Tagalog sentences:

24 a. Nag-atubili   siyang   hiramin   ang pera
      AT-hesitated T-he-Li GT-borrow T-money

      sa bangko.
      D-bank

   "He hesitated to borrow the money from a/the bank."

   b. Nag-atubili   siyang   hiraman   ng pera
      AT-hesitated T-he-Li DT-borrow G-money

      ang bangko.
      T-bank

   "He hesitated to borrow money from the bank."

   c. Nag-atubili   siyang   humiram   ng pera
      AT-hesitated T-he-Li AT-borrow G-money

      sa bangko.
      D-bank

   "He hesitated to borrow money from a/the bank."

While the complement clauses contained in these sentences can
reasonably be analyzed as involving deletion (see Section 4),
it is certainly not the topic that is regularly deleted.
Thus the complement clauses of 24a and 24b, which contain
goal-topic and direction-topic verbs, do not delete the topic,
and it is only in 24c, where the complement clause contains
an actor-topic verb, that the topic is deleted. Once again

then, we find that topics do not function as we expect subjects to function with respect to an important grammatical
process, and so we are led to look elsewhere in our quest
for the subject in Philippine language.

4   The Actor as Subject: Arguments For

The last two arguments of Section 3, although they were
presented as arguments against identifying the topic as the
subject, can also be considered to be arguments for identifying the actor as the subject. (I am now using the term actor
to refer both to non-topic nominals in the actor case and to
topic nominals occurring with actor-topic verbs.) That is,
it is the actor, rather than the topic, that manifests the
properties usually associated with subjects in regard to the
processes of reflexivization and coreferential complement
subject deletion (also known as equi-noun-phrase deletion).
As examples 21 through 23 show, the actor, whether or not it
is also the topic, may control reflexivization. On the other
hand, the actor may never itself be reflexivized--again,
regardless of whether or not it is the topic. Thus the following are ungrammatical (cf. 22 and 23 respectively):

25 a. *Iniisip   sila   ng kanilang sarili.
        DT-think about   T-they   A-their-self

    b. *Nag-iisip   sa kanila ang kanilang sarili.
        AT-think-about   D-they   T-their-self

Both in controlling reflexivization and in not itself being
subject to reflexivization, the actor manifests subject-like
properties.

Similarly, it is always the actor that is absent in
structures analyzable as involving equi-noun-phrase deletion.
If we compare the complement clauses of 24 with their sentential counterparts in 26, we see that in each case the clause
may be formed by deleting the actor phrase from the sentence
(whether or not the actor is also the topic) and changing
the finite verb form to a non-finite form:

26 a. Hiniram   niya ang pera sa bangko
        GT-borrowed   A-he T-money   D-bank
        "He borrowed the money from a/the bank."

    b. Hiniraman   niya ng pera ang bangko.
        DT-borrowed   A-he G-money T-bank
        "He borrowed money from the bank."

    c. Humiram   siya ng pera sa bangko.
        AT-borrowed   T-he G-money D-bank
        "He borrowed money from a/the bank"

So if it is the case that equi-noun-phrase deletion involves
deletion of a coreferential complement subject (as it consistently does in languages with easily-identified subjects),
then we must conclude that the actor should be identified as
the subject in Philippine languages.

A number of additional arguments can be given in support
of this conclusion. Consider first the way in which the actor
functions in imperative sentences. E.L. Keenan (Definition
of Subject, this volume) has suggested that in general "the
addressee of second person imperatives can be expressed by a
subject." In Philippine languages, it is clear that the addressee phrase, when present, is always expressed by an actor
(which may or may not also be the topic), as in the following
Tagalog examples:

27 a. Magbigay ka   sa kaniya ng kape
      AT-give   T-you D-him   G-coffee
      "Give him some coffee."

   b. Bigyan   mo   siya   ng kape
      DT-give   A-you T-him   G-coffee
      "Give him some coffee."

   c. Ibigay   mo   sa kaniya ang kape
      GT-give   A-you D-him   T-coffee
      "Give him the coffee."

Thus Keenan's generalization holds for Philippine languages
only if the actor is identified as the subject.

Moreover, the identification of the actor as the subject is also required in order for another generalization
that has been made about imperatives to hold for Philippine
languages. The generalization in question is one reportedly
proposed by Kenneth Hale (7), to the effect that, where an
imperative lacks an overtly indicated subject, a second-
person subject is understood. Consider in the light of this
generalization the following examples of imperative sentences
in Cebuano and Waray. (Tagalog does not provide relevant
examples in this case. The Cebuano example (28) is taken
from Bell 1974, the Waray example (29), from Diller 1970.)

28 Ibalik   ang libro kanako
   GT-give-back T-book   D-me
   "Give me back the book."

29 Paglutu hit panihapun
   AT-cook G-supper
   "Cook supper."

These sentences lack an overt expression of the actor, and a
second person actor is understood. Thus, if Hale's generali-

zation is to apply to them, the understood second-person actor must be the subject.

It can also be argued that the Kapampangan agreement data cited in Section 2 favor the identification of the actor as the subject as much as they favor the identification of the topic as the subject. As was noted in Section 2, actor-topic sentences in Kapampangan have a single particle agreeing with the topic, while non-actor-topic sentences have two particles, one agreeing with the topic, the other with the actor (cf. examples 17a-b). One might thus make the generalization that there is always agreement with the actor (whether or not the actor is also the topic) just as easily as the generalization that there is always agreement with the topic (whether or not the topic is also the actor). So if the control of agreement is a useful criterion for distinguishing subjects from other noun phrases, actor phrases are as subject-like as topic phrases in this respect.

Another subject-like property of actor phrases is relevance to word order. As was mentioned in Section 1, the ordering of noun phrases after the initial verb is extremely free in Tagalog, but this is not true of certain other Philippine languages. For example, in Pangasinan (cf. Benton 1971), the normal order of constituents in sentences that consist of a verb, an actor, and a goal is verb-actor-goal, regardless of whether the actor or the goal is the topic. Now it is usually assumed that the ordering of major sentence constituents is statable in terms of the categories verb, subject, and object. This assumption can be maintained if the actor in a language like Pangasinan is identified as the subject (and the goal as the object--in which case the languages are classifiable as VSO languages). If, however, the actor is not the subject, then we must claim--somewhat uncomfortably, I should think--that word order in Philippine languages is simply not comparable with word order in other languages.

A final argument in favor of identifying the actor as the subject may be built upon the fact, noted in Section 1, that the actor is quite regularly translated by the surface subject of an active sentence in English (8). Even if one does not know how to explain this fact, it seems extremely unlikely that such a regular correspondence should be accidental. But, of course, one would like to be able to explain the fact, and it seems to me at least possible that an explanation is to be found in a semantic property that is shared by the actor in Philippine languages and the active surface subject in English. As was previously noted, one Philippinist claims that the actor expresses "the entity to which the action of the verb is attributed," and this claim, if inter-

preted liberally, seems fairly tenable. Could it be that
there is some sense in which active surface subjects in English (and in languages in general) also express "the entity
to which the action of the verb is attributed"? Although I
think that this is a hypothesis that may be worth pursuing,
I have not in fact pursued it. In any case, it seems to me
that the fact that actors are translated by subjects--whatever
the explanation for this may be--argues for their being subjects.

5   The Actor as Subject: Arguments Against

One reason for questioning the identification of the
actor as the subject might be the fact that formally the actor is not one constituent type but two: the non-topic actor
(which is identified by means of a distinctive case marker or
pronoun form) and the actor-topic (which is identified by
means of a distinctive affix on the verb). In other languages, subjects usually appear to constitute a formally homo-
geneous set (9), and the lack of formal homogeneity in the
set of actors might be considered to weigh against the actor's
being analyzed as the subject.

In addition to this rather weak argument, there are two
stronger ones. First, if, as commonly assumed, logically complete declarative sentences must contain a subject and a predicate (cf. Sections 2 and 3), then the actor cannot in
general be the subject. This is because there are many logically complete declarative sentences, belonging to several
different sentence types, that do not contain actors--at
least if we interpret the term actor, as we have been, as
referring either to a non-topic nominal in the actor case or
to the topic of an actor-topic verb. The following Tagalog
sentences, repeated from earlier sections, illustrate this
point.

9   Papawisan   ang lalaki
    GT/DT-will-sweat   T-man
    "The man will sweat."

10 Abogado   ang lalaki
    lawyer   T-man
    "The man is a lawyer."

11 Matalino   ang lalaki
    intelligent   T-man
    "The man is intelligent."

18 May aksidente   (kagabi)
    E-accident   (last-night)
    "There was an accident (last night)."

20 May dumarating.
    F-AT-is-coming
    "There's someone coming."

I know of no evidence to suggest that these sentences contain
actors, either overtly or at some abstract level of analysis.
It therefore seems to be the case either that the actor is
not the subject (or at least not the only subject) in Philippine languages or that these languages must have more than
the usual share of subjectless sentences.

A second serious problem is that the actor fails to
show certain syntactic properties that have been claimed to
be universal properties of the subject. I refer here to the
syntactic properties cited in Section 2 as evidence for considering the topic to be the subject: relativizability and
the ability to "launch floating quantifiers." While actor-
topics are certainly relativizable and able to launch floating quantifiers, these properties appear to depend upon the
status of actor-topics as topics rather than their status as
actors. Evidence for this is that non-topic actors lack the
properties in question, never undergoing relativization and
never launching floating quantifiers.

Thus if these properties are indeed properties associated with subjects, actors--or at least non-topic actors--
cannot be subjects. It seems clear, then, that in spite of
the fair number of subject-like properties associated with the
actor, the identification of the actor as the subject remains
problematical.

6   The Actor-Topic as Primary Subject: Arguments For

In a generative grammar it is both possible and usual
to derive some surface subjects--which may be called primary
subjects--directly from underlying subjects and other surface
subjects by means of transformations. In this section I present a few pieces of evidence that may favor an analysis in
which actor-topics in Philippine languages are generated as
primary subjects, while non-actor topics are derived transformationally. (According to this analysis, simple actor-
topic sentences in Philippine languages would thus have essentially the same status as active sentences in the standard
generative account of English, while non-actor-topic sentences
would have essentially the same status as English passives.)

The evidence in question has to do with the fact that
certain distinctions that can be made in actor-topic sentences
cannot be made in sentences of other types. For example, Bell
(1974) reports that in Cebuano certain verbal aspects are normally distinguished only in actor-topic sentences. A similar

claim can be made for Tagalog, where verbs in general are
inflectable for three aspects (perfective, imperfective,
contemplated) but actor-topic verbs are also inflectable for
a fourth aspect, the recent-perfective (cf. Schachter and
Otanes 1972:371-375). It is also the case that only actor-
topic verbs in Tagalog may be marked (optionally) for agreement with a plural topic, as in 30, and that there are certain
derived-verb formations, such as the "social-verb" formation
in 31, that are found only with actor-topics:

30 Nag(sipag)luto sila   ng pagkain
    AT-(Pl)-cooked   T-they   G-supper
    "They cooked some food."

31 Nakikikain   siya ng hapunan   sa Nanay
    AT-is-eating-with T-he G-supper   D-mother
    "He is eating supper with Mother."

It seems reasonable to suggest that, if some particular
structure is derivationally primary, that structure may be
elaborated in certain ways in which other structures are not
elaborated. If this suggestion is correct, then the facts
just cited may argue for the primacy of the actor-topic sentence type, and hence for an analysis in which the actor-
topic is generated as a primary subject.

Such an analysis, moreover, can rather easily be made
to accommodate some of the facts cited in previous sections.
For example, suppose that, under this analysis, topics in
general are regarded as surface subjects--some primary,
others transformationally derived. Then some of the subject-
like properties of topics that were mentioned in Section 2--
e.g., unique accessibility to relativization--may quite
plausibly be accounted for as properties associated with surface subjects. Similarly, some of the subject-like properties
of actors mentioned in Section 4 may be accounted for as properties associated with underlying subjects. For example,
the preferred word order in Pangasinin (actor precedes goal,
regardless of topicalization) can be treated as an ordering
of the underlying subject (the actor) and the underlying
object (the goal). Thus an analysis in which actors are regarded as underlying subjects and topics as surface subjects,
and in which the surface subjects are divided into two sub-
classes, primary (actor-topic) and derived (non-actor-topic),
appears to have some merit.

7   The Actor-Topic as Primary Subject: Arguments Against

On the other hand, there are at least three arguments
that can be offered against this analysis.

First, sentences in which there is no overt or recoverable actor--e.g., sentences like 9-11, cited in Section 2 and repeated in Section 5--constitute something of a problem for an analysis that treats the actor-topic as the primary subject (though it is a less severe problem than these sentences constitute for an analysis that treats the actor as the subject simpliciter). At the very least, in order to be able to account for such sentences, one would have to modify the claim that the actor-topic is the primary subject to a more modest claim that the actor-topic is the primary subject in sentences whose predicates are transitive verbs.

Second, there are in Tagalog (and, I believe, in other Philippine languages) a good many actor-topic transitive verbs that are distributionally more restricted than their goal-topic counterparts (10). While the goal-topic forms of these verbs may occur as predicates of simple narrative sentences, the actor-topic verbs may not, and are found only in relative clauses and certain nominalizations. (The nominalizations in question appear to be analyzable as headless relative clauses.)

The following examples illustrate these distributional properties:

32 a. Tinakot   ng lalaki ang bata
     GT-frightened A-man   T-child
     "A/The man frightened the child."

  b. *Tumakot   ang lalaki ng bata
     AT-frightened T-man   G-child

33 a. Nasaan ang lalaking tumakot   ng bata?
     where   T-man-Li   AT-frightened G-child
     "Where is the man who frightened a child?"

  b. Nasaan ang tumakot   ng bata?
     where   T-AT-frightened G-child
     "Where is the one who frightened a child?"

As these examples show, the goal-topic verb tinakot occurs as the predicate of a simple narrative sentence (cf. 32a), but the actor-topic verb tumakot fails to occur in such a sentence (cf. 32b), although it may occur in a relative clause (example 33a) of a nominalization (example 33b).

How could this distribution be accounted for in an analysis in which the actor-topic is generated as a primary subject and the goal-topic as a derived subject? Presumably the verbs in question would have to be marked with a lexical feature that would have the effect of requiring them to undergo the goal-topic transformation in just the right cases-- i.e., in main clauses but not necessarily in relative clauses, etc. While such a lexical marking is no doubt possible, it is unappealing, requiring as it does, an otherwise unneeded formal device of considerable power (11). On the other hand, if goal-topic sentences are not necessarily derived from underlying actor-topic sentences, all that is needed to account for the distribution reflected in examples like 32–33 is a contextual feature on certain actor-topic verbs, constraining their insertion to the appropriate contexts.

The third argument against the analysis under consideration, which I owe to Bell (1974), presupposes the correctness of certain syntactic universals that have been proposed within the framework of relational grammar. In this theoretical framework, as was mentioned in Section 2, certain grammatical properties are associated uniquely with so-called terms of grammatical relations: i.e., subjects, objects, and indirect objects. Moreover, the following Relational Annihilation Law is said to hold universally:

34 Relational Annihilation Law: If an NP_i assumes a grammatical relation j previously borne by NP_j, then NP_j ceases to bear any grammatical relation; it becomes a <u>chômeur</u> (French for "unemployed person").

According to the Relational Annihilation Law, then, if an underlying subject is transformationally replaced by a derived subject, the original subject, having become a <u>chômeur</u>, will no longer have those properties that are associated uniquely with terms (12).

Now included among the syntactic properties that are said to be unique to terms are control over reflexivization and control over equi-noun phrase deletion (coreferential complement subject deletion). In Philippine languages, as we have already seen, control over reflexivization is vested in the actor, whether or not the actor is also the topic: cf. examples 22 and 23, repeated below:

22 Iniisip   nila   ang kanilang sarili
   DT-think-about A-they   T-their-selves
   "They think about themselves."

23 Nag-iisip   sila   sa kanilang sarili
   AT-think-about T-they   T-their-selves
   "They think about themselves."

It is also the case that the actor, whether or not it is also the topic, may control equi-noun phrase deletion, as the following examples show:

35 a. Nagbalak   siyang   mangisda
        AT-planned   T-he-Li   AT-go-fishing
        "He planned to go fishing."

    b. Binalak   niyang   mangisda
        GT-planned   A-he-Li   AT-go-fishing
        "He planned to go fishing."

But according to the analysis under consideration, in which the actor is the underlying subject and the topic the surface subject, a non-topic actor must be a subject whose original role has been assumed by another noun phrase. Thus, according to the Relational Annihilation Law, 34, the non-topic actor should be a _chômeur_, and should not be able to control reflexivization, as it does in 22, or equi-noun phrase deletion, as it does in 35b. Therefore, if the Relational Annihilation Law is valid (and it appears to have a certain amount of cross-linguistic support), the analysis under consideration must be wrong: the actor-topic cannot be a primary subject because the non-topic actor is clearly not a _chômeur_.

8   Conclusion

Where does all of this leave us, then, in our quest for the subject in Philippine languages? We have seen that, while the topic and the actor each have certain syntactic properties that are frequently associated with subjects in other langua-ges, they each lack some such properties as well. We have also seen that, while there are certain subject-like proper-ties that are unique to actor-topics, an analysis that regards actor-topics as primary subjects, with actors in general cor-responding to underlying subjects and topics in general to surface subjects, is probably untenable.

The obvious conclusion, it seems to me, is that there is in fact no single syntactic category in Philippine langua-ges that corresponds to the category identified as the subject in other languages. Rather, there is a division of subject-like properties between the category we have been calling the topic and the category we have been calling the actor, with a few subject-like properties reserved for the intersection of the topic and the actor, the actor-topic. While this con-clusion is certainly somewhat surprising, it need not neces-sarily be regarded as alarming. It may be the case, as a matter of fact, that Philippine languages have a unique con-tribution to make to our understanding of the nature of sub-jects in general.

What the Philippine evidence suggests is that there are two basically quite different kinds of syntactic properties that are ordinarily associated with subjects. Since in most languages these two different kinds of properties are associated with a single syntactic category, linguists have generally not been led to sort the properties out. In Philippine languages, however, the properties are conveniently sorted out by the grammatical systems themselves, so that one is given a clearer view than usual of the basis for the properties, and the properties are seen to make a kind of sense one might not otherwise have attributed to them.

The Philippine evidence points to a distinction between what may be called <u>reference-related properties</u> and <u>role-related properties</u> of subjects. The reference-related properties are those which, in Philippine languages, are associated with the topic. As was explained in Section 1, the topic is always definite, having a "given," or pre-established, referent. And the definiteness of the topic seems to provide a plausible basis for at least some of the syntactic properties that are associated with it. For example, as we have seen (cf. Section 2), only topics can be relativized. Now since the referent of a relativized nominal is necessarily "given"--that is, necessarily identical with the referent of the head of the relative construction--it seems very reasonable to choose for relativization the syntactic category that is regularly associated with a pre-established referent. One might thus suggest that the reason why (or, at any rate, <u>one</u> reason why), in languages with well-defined subjects, the subject turns out to be the most easily relativized category (cf. Keenan and Comrie 1972) is that the subject is the category most often used for expressing a pre-established referent in such languages.

The role-related properties of subjects are those which, in Philippine languages, are associated with the actor. The actor represents "the entity to which the action is attributed" (cf. Section 1), and this semantic property seems to underlie at least some of the syntactic properties of actors. For example, as we have seen (cf. Section 4), only actors are deleted under equi-noun-phrase deletion, an example being 24a, repeated below:

```
24  a.  Nag-atubili    siyang    hiramin     ang pera
        AT-hesitated   T-he-Li   GT-borrow   T-money

            sa bangko
            D-bank
```

"He hesitated to borrow money from the bank."

(Cf. 26a, also repeated below.)

26 a. Hiniram   niya ang pera sa bangko
        GT-borrowed A-he T-money   D-bank
        "He borrowed money from the bank."

It seems clear that in sentences involving equi-noun-phrase
deletion, the action expressed in the complement construction
is always overtly attributed to a nominal in the <u>matrix</u> sentence. It therefore makes sense to exclude from the complement itself the nominal that would, if present, be interpreted in this same way--i.e., the actor. Thus one might suggest that the reason why, in languages with well-defined subjects, it is the subject that is omitted in cases of equi-
noun-phrase deletion, is that the subject is the category
used for expressing the actor, the entity to which the action
is attributed.

   In addition to properties of subjects that are clearly
reference-related (such as relativizability) and properties
that are clearly role-related (such as deletability under
equi-noun-phrase deletion), there also appear to be properties
that may be <u>either</u> reference-related <u>or</u> role-related. According to the Philippine evidence, at least, the governing of
agreement is such a property. Thus in Kapampangan there is
agreement both with the topic and with the actor (cf. Sections
2 and 4), while in Tagalog, agreement requires a convergence
of the topic and the actor in the form of the actor-topic (cf.
Section 6). Such a convergence, it seems to me, may also
underlie subject-predicate agreement in languages with well-
defined subjects.

   Apart from providing insight into the syntactic properties associated with subjects in other languages, Philippine
languages may have another type of important contribution to
make to general linguistic theory. For if the conclusion
that I have reached, to the effect that the sentences of
Philippine languages do not have subjects, is in fact correct,
then obviously it cannot be the case that <u>subject</u> represents
a linguistic universal. Rather, it represents a common, but
non-universal, clustering of properties which need not in
principle be assigned to a single constituent type. Now the
universality of subjects has not only been commonly taken for
granted; it has also, as was mentioned at the beginning of
this paper, been presupposed in the postulation of various
other putative linguistic universals. It seems to me that
these postulated universals may all need to be re-examined in
the light of the Philippine evidence.

PAUL SCHACHTER

Notes

1. My main source of information about relational
grammar has been an unpublished paper by Bell (1974), which
presents a very clear, though not necessarily authoritative,
summary of the theory.
2. The Tagalog verb-case-marking system is more complex than that of many other Philippine languages, in that
Tagalog has (and these other languages do not have) a number
of different, lexically-determined verbal affixes for indicating actor-topic, goal-topic, etc. Thus, while some Tagalog
verbs take mag- to indicate the actor topic, others take different affixes, such as -um- or mang-, for this purpose.
There is also considerable lexically-determined variation in
Tagalog with regard to the case interpretation of specific
affixes. Thus, -an is a direction-topic affix with some verbs
but a goal-topic affix with others. For further details, see
Schachter and Otanes 1972:284-355.
3. Specifically, the non-topic actor, direction and
beneficiary may be indefinite while the non-topic goal must
be indefinite. Definite non-topic goals do, however, occur
in Tagalog in certain more complex structures--cf. Schachter
and Otanes 1972:382-383.   And in some other Philippine lan-
guages--e.g., Waray (cf. Diller 1970) and Bicol (Talmy Givón,
personal communication)--definite non-topic goals may occur
in simple sentences as well.
4. In the case of 4 itself, however, it is clear why
the goal--rather than the actor, direction, or beneficiary--
has been chosen as topic. As was explained in Note 3, a non-
topic goal in a simple Tagalog sentence necessarily has an
indefinite referent, while a non-topic actor, direction, or
beneficiary may have either a definite or an indefinite referent. Thus a simple sentence with a non-topic goal can never
be used when the referent of the goal phrase is in fact definite, or presupposed. Under such circumstances, the speaker
has no choice but to make the goal the topic, as in 4. If
any other topic were chosen in 4, the sentence would necessarily mean "Rosa will take some money to Juan for you"
rather than "Rosa will take the money to Juan for you."
5. Like transitive verbs, intransitive verbs are
formed with affixes that indicate the case role of the topic.
Thus magtatrabaho in 8 contains the actor-topic affix mag-,
while papawisan in 9 contains the direction-topic or goal-
topic affix -an. In the latter case, it is not in fact clear
whether the verb should be classified as direction-topic or
goal-topic. This is a problem that could not arise with a
transitive verb formed with -an, even though -an occurs with

516

both direction-topic and goal-topic transitive verbs. For
with a transitive verb formed with -an, one could get independent evidence about the case role of the topic nominal:
namely, the case marker that the nominal in question took
when the case-marking affix on the verb was changed, making
some other nominal in the sentence the topic. For intransitive verbs, no such independent evidence is available, since
there is no other nominal in the sentence that can be made
the topic, and thus there is no possibility of changing the
case-marking affix on the verb. Nevertheless, it seems clear
that, since -an indicates direction-topic and goal-topic for
transitive verbs, it should be associated with these functions
for intransitive verbs as well. (I have gone into this matter
at what may seem inordinate length because Bell (1974) implies
that in Cebuano all intransitive verbs may be regarded as
actor-topic. It seems to me that examples like 9 strongly
suggest that this is not the case in Tagalog.)

6. For details, see Richards 1971:193-196.

7. My source for this is Bell 1974.

8. The converse of this does not hold, however, since
there are various active sentences in English whose translation equivalents in Philippine languages apparently do not
contain actors: e.g., certain narrative sentences with intransitive predicates, such as 9 above, as well as all equational
and existential sentences.

9. However, ergative languages, in which subjects of
transitive and intransitive verbs are formally distinct,
obviously fail to conform to this generalization.

10. The Tagalog verbs that show the distributional restrictions in question appear to fall into three semantic
classes: 1) verbs that require animate objects, with meanings
like "frighten," "surprise," "starve," and "kill"; 2) verbs
that denote ways of fragmenting or disintegrating an object,
with meanings like "break," "grind," "pulverize," and "burn";
3) the verbs meaning "remember" and "forget." For details,
cf. Schachter and Otanes 1972:296, 299-300.

11. Note that even the powerful device of "positive
absolute exception" features proposed in Lakoff (1970) would
be inadequate to account for the facts of 32-33, since the
positive exception feature in question would have to be conditional rather than absolute.

12. I believe that the Relational Annihilation Law
stated in 34 may be an early version, which has since been
revised, and that in the revised version a term whose original function has been assumed by another NP may be "demoted"
instead of becoming a chômeur. Since terms are hierarchi-
cally ranked, with the subject having the highest rank, a

"demoted" subject could conceivably become either a direct or an indirect object. It seems clear, however, that this additional possibility is irrelevant to the cases in Philippine languages that are about to be discussed. That is, there is no basis for analyzing a non-topic actor as an underlying subject that has been relegated to the role originally assigned to a direct or indirect object. In the first place, a non-topic actor may easily occur in a sentence in which the presumed underlying direct and indirect objects are both still intact; e.g.,

(i)   Ipinansusulat   niya   ng liham   sa kanila
      IT-is-writing   A-he   G-letter   D-them

      ang makinilya
      T-typewriter

"He is writing a letter to them on the typewriter."

(In (i), ipinansusulat is an instrument-topic (IT) verb; i.e., a verb that selects as topic the noun phrase expressing the instrument used to perform the action.) And secondly, the surface case-marking of a non-topic actor is not identical to that of either a non-topic goal (the presumed underlying direct object) or a non-topic directional phrase (the presumed underlying indirect object).

ON THE UNIVERSALITY OF SUBJECT: THE ILOCANO CASE*

by

Arthur Schwartz

*I wish to thank S. Grant, D. Moran, and J. Watters for allow-
ing me to incorporate some of their own work on Ilocano. Our
informant was Norberta Tagatac from Bantay, Ilocos Sur.

0.   Assumptions and Thesis

I am going to assume, for the purposes of this paper, that the validity of the notion "surface grammatical subject" (hereafter, "subject") for at least certain languages is uncontroversial. It is relatively immaterial whether the actualization involves person agreement with the finite verb (as in Telegu and Hebrew), a case-marking particle (as in Japanese and Maranao), position (as in Sre and Indonesian), or some combination of these. What does matter is the recognition of a semantic-syntactic convergence across languages, in which—over a considerable range of different predicates— the same argument is chosen as the subject for each predicate. To illustrate, for predicates like see, burn, and build, the argument that is the perceiver, the remote agent of the burning, or that which is the creator should turn out to be subject. For a predicate like want/desire/like, the argument may be thought of as an experiencer. But generally, that argument (the Agent-Perceiver-Experiencer, let us say) is animal, if not human; animate, if not animal; motile, if not animate (e.g., fire, wind, water). And, I will further assume that where there is an option in the language allowing for that argument in subject function to be displaced, that other construction (whether "impersonal" or "passive") is the marked one. Thus, not only are ergative constructions in accusative languages marked, but true ergative systems— like Dyirbal—are the most marked of all.

In pursuing the claim that subject is universal, i.e., obligatory for every system, I find few language-types that offer a real challenge to the hypothesis. Ergative systems are indeed one kind of problem, since their subject (in transitive expressions) departs most blatantly from that semantic-syntactic convergence alluded to in the first paragraph, and since a good many are mixed—morphologically one thing, but syntactically another (Anderson, this volume; Dixon 1972:128-9). So-called topic-prominent languages like Lisu (cf. Li and Thompson, this volume) are another difficulty, since subject is apparently all but effaced by the dominating presence of the topic—that is to say, there seems to be little or no need to refer to anything like subject in accounting for the structure of the system. A third major counter-example occurs in the Philippine group comprising Tagalog, Ilocano, Kapampangan and others (cf. Schachter, this volume), where the natural convergence of subject with that argument that Activates/Perceives/Experiences what the predicate asserts is treated rather cavalierly. Subject (if it occurs at all in this language-type) ranges over types of arguments that would normally find prominent expression in

other languages only through complex constructions like the
cleft or pseudo-cleft. My interest in Ilocano is in establishing the fact that subject does occur here (and so--by a
reasonable projection--in the rest of the Philippine group
as well), to estimate the degree of markedness, and to understand the value of departing from the unmarked condition.

1. Preliminaries: the Ilocano Sentence

Ilocano is a predicate-first language, the type that
Greenberg (1966) designated as VSO (taking "S" as that nominal in an Agent/Perceiver/Experiencer relation to the predicate, and "O" in an analogously "semantic" sense). And like
a number of other Philippine languages, it uses verb-morpho-
logy as a major device in expressing the cast of any one
particular assertion. That is, with a root like <u>kabil</u>
"hit," several affixes can be attached (most being mutually
exclusive) which will shift the slant of the predication.
Thus--

(i) <u>ag-kabil</u> <u>ti lalaki</u> <u>ti babai</u>
      hit   boy   girl

(ii) <u>kabil-en</u> <u>ti lalaki</u> <u>ti babai</u>
       hit   boy   girl

(iii) <u>k-um-abil</u> <u>ti lalaki</u> <u>ti babai</u>
        hit   boy   girl

(iv) <u>maka-kabil</u> <u>ti lalaki</u> <u>ti babai</u>
        hit   boy   girl

In (i-iv), the boy does the hitting, and the girl gets hit.
But each affix "focusses" the proposition a little differently. Some affixes contribute a distinct meaning, in addition to focussing on a certain nominal: for example, <u>maka-</u>
is necessarily Agent/Perceiver/Experiencer (APE) in focus
but also means "can, is able to." Thus, sentence (iv)
translates as "the boy is able to hit a girl." Another prefix, <u>ma-</u>, is also abilitative, but focusses on the Patient:

(v) <u>ma-kabil</u> <u>ti babai</u> <u>iti lalaki</u>
      hit   girl   boy

Sentence (v) means "the girl can be hit (is hittable) by a
boy."

Among the various reflexes engendered by these verb
affixes and the way they focus a proposition, there is one--
the distribution of definiteness over the arguments--which
is particularly subtle. For the most part, I will not be
glossing <u>ti</u> and <u>iti</u> since it will either be clear from the

discussion where the definiteness is located or its location
will be irrelevant to the matter(s) being discussed. Only
in the final section, Section 9, is something made of a
definite-indefinite opposition.

2.   Definiteness and Referentiality

There is by now a substantial body of evidence pointing
to an association of definiteness and referentiality with
subject, to the extent that we can view this correlation as
the unmarked instance (Hetzron 1970; E.L. Keenan, <u>Definition
of Subject</u>, this volume; Li & Thompson, 1975). This universal can be variously paraphrased--for example, that while
some arguments in a simplex sentence may be required to be
indefinite and/or non-referential, the subject cannot; or
that, if any one argument in a proposition is obligatorily
definite, that argument must be the subject; etc. In Ilocano, the so-called focussed nominal is always definite, as
can be seen by the behavior of proper nouns and personal pronouns:

(A)   <u>maka-bisito</u> <u>ni Pedro</u> <u>iti babai</u>
      can   kiss   Pedro   woman
      "Pedro can kiss a woman"

      *<u>maka-bisito</u> <u>iti babai</u> <u>ni Pedro</u>
      can   kiss   woman   Pedro
      "a woman can kiss Pedro"

(B)   <u>maka-bisito</u> <u>iti babai</u>
      can   kiss   woman
      "he can kiss a woman"

      *<u>maka-bisito</u> <u>iti babai</u> <u>isuna</u>
      can   kiss   woman   he
      "a woman can kiss him"

Such sentences show that <u>maka-</u> is an APE-focussing affix,
and that only a definite APE is acceptable with such an
orientation. Sentences like

(A)   <u>bisito-en</u> <u>ti babai</u> <u>ni Pedro</u>
      kiss   woman   Pedro
      "the woman kisses Pedro"

      *<u>bisito-en</u> <u>iti babai</u> <u>ni Pedro</u>
      kiss   woman   Pedro
      "a woman kisses Pedro"

```
    *bisito-en  ni Pedro  iti babai
     kiss          Pedro     woman
     "Pedro kisses a woman"
```

(B) bisito-en ni Pedro isuna
     kiss   Pedro   she
     "Pedro kisses her"

```
    *bisito-en  ni Pedro
     kiss          Pedro
     "Pedro kissed someone"
```

show that -en is a Patient focus, and that the nominal in
that focus must be definite. (We note, in passing, that with
APE in focus, the Patient is obligatorily indefinite: *maka-
bisito ni Pedro ni Maria "Pedro can kiss Maria" vs. bisito-
en ni Pedro ni Maria "Pedro kisses Maria." This constraint
holds also for all embedded clauses but the relative.)

We extend this generalization by observing the behavior
of Beneficiary nominals, in and out of focus:

(i) i-pauit-ko   dagiti kankanta
     Pat send I plur   songs

     ka-dagiti dua nga agbasbasa
       to   two   students

     "I (will) send the songs to two students"

(ii) pauit-ak   dagiti dua nga agbasbasa
     /pauit-an-ko/
     send Ben I plural two   students

     ti kankanta
        songs

     "I (will) send songs to the two students"
    *"I (will) send songs to two students"

In (ii), the Beneficiary nominal is in focus, and is obligatorily definite; but in (i) it is not in focus (kankanta is
in focus there), and so need not be.

It will perhaps have been noticed that in almost all the
sentences cited thus far the APE has been definite, whether
in focus or not. This constraint certainly holds when APE is
in first position. But, when neither in first position nor
in focus, then that nominal can be indefinite (in fact, must
be): e.g.,

     ma-kagat ti pusa iti aso
     can bite   cat   dog
     "the cat can be bitten by {*the / a} dog"

Except for existential propositions (<u>adda NP</u>.... "there is/
are...."), the construct "first position"--in the sense of
immediately post-predicate--may carry with it a condition of
definiteness; if so, this must be characterized for a "base"
order of constituents, since there are sentences like

> <u>maka-bisito</u> <u>ti lalaki</u> <u>ni Maria</u>
> can kiss   boy   Maria
> "Maria can kiss a boy"

in which an indefinite nominal appears in first position.
But this form is fairly certainly a variant of

> <u>maka-bisito</u> <u>ni Maria</u> <u>ti lalaki</u>
> can kiss   Maria   boy
> "Maria can kiss a boy"

which exhibits the usual sequence. One of the reasons for
relating the two forms is the fact that <u>ti lalaki</u> in these
constructions can also appear as <u>iti lalaki</u>, with the meaning "a boy." But <u>iti N</u>, in general, can not occupy "first
position." At any rate, the point is that the APE nominal
need not, even in atomic sentences, be definite. But the
Focus nominal is always obligatorily definite, regardless of
position.

3.   Reflexivization as a Subject-Property

Anaphoric pronominal reference is, generally, a phenomenon whose constraints can be stated in terms of two param-
eters--that of "subordination," and that of "(temporal)
linearity" (cf. for example, Langacker 1969). Reflexivization, in many languages, is one kind of anaphora whose domain is the simplex sentence; and consequently, "subordination" is irrelevant to it. (I am thinking of the <u>eius</u>/<u>suus</u>
"his/his own" distinction in Latin, for example.) Since
most of the work done on reflexivization in this sense
(i.e., excluding "emphatic reflexives" like <u>himself</u> in <u>he</u>
<u>admits it himself</u>) has drawn its data from SVO, SOV, and VSO
systems in which "S" in fact was subject, it has rather
tacitly been assumed that the subject in some way is a governing factor in reflexive formation. However, as Chapin
(1970:369-70) demonstrated for Samoan, the relevant parameter is really that of precedence:

> <u>sa</u> <u>sogi</u> <u>e Ioane</u> <u>ia lava</u>
> past cut   by John   him
> "John cut himself"

*sa sogi   e ia lava   Ioane
past cut   by him   John
"John cut himself"

sa sogi   Ioane   e ia lava
past cut   John   by him
"John cut himself"

*sa sogi   ia lava   e Ioane
past cut   him   by John
"John cut himself"

where e "by" marks the APE nominal, and the Patient nominal is unmarked (except for pronouns, when o appears). Thus, the two acceptable Samoan forms are, schematically--

Verb   Agent   Patient
$$\begin{bmatrix} \text{Pro} \\ \text{Reflex} \end{bmatrix}$$

Verb   Patient   Agent
$$\begin{bmatrix} \text{Pro} \\ \text{Reflex} \end{bmatrix}$$

and forms in which the pronoun (in fact, any pronoun) precedes its antecedent are unacceptable. Even in a subject-oriented system like English (cf. Lehmann 1974b), reflexivization is not subject-controlled:

if you $\begin{bmatrix} \text{add} \\ \text{subtract} \\ \text{multiply} \end{bmatrix}$ any number $\begin{bmatrix} \text{to} \\ \text{from} \\ \text{by} \end{bmatrix}$ itself,

the result is....

but is rather a matter of precedence:

*if you $\begin{bmatrix} \text{add} \\ \text{subtract} \\ \text{multiply} \end{bmatrix}$ itself $\begin{bmatrix} \text{to} \\ \text{from} \\ \text{by} \end{bmatrix}$ any number,

the result is....

Of course, "backwards pronominalization" is possible when the pronoun is in some sense "lower" than the co-referent NP following: cf. he left the room and John smiled (where he and John cannot be co-referential) alongside when he left the room, John smiled (where he and John can be). In Samoan, where the relevant nominals are sister constituents--

```
         S
       / | \
      V  NP  NP
```

526

simple temporal precedence determines the direction of pronominalization. But in Malagasy, where the base order
allows for a Verb-Phrase constituent (cf. Schwartz 1972;
E.L. Keenan, Definition of Subject, this volume), the pronoun can be introduced before its (subject) antecedent:

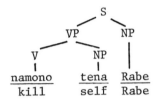

In Ilocano, in the simplex transitive sentence, the
Patient must be indefinite when the APE is in focus:

> ag-kabil ti lalaki ti babai
> APE hit   boy   girl
> "the boy hits {$_{*the}^{a}$} girl"

And, given that personal pronouns (such as reflexives) are
definite, the reflexive pronoun cannot appear in APE-
focussed propositions--

> *ag-kabil ti lalaki ti bagi na
> APE hit   boy   body his
> "the boy hits himself"

> *k-um-abil ti lalaki ti bagi na
> APE hit   boy   body his
> "the boy hits himself"

but only under Patient-focus:

> kabil-en ti lalaki ti bagi na
> hit PAT   boy   body his
> "the boy hits himself"

Moreover, whatever the focus, the direction of pronominalization (as in Samoan) cannot be reversed:

> *ag-kabil ti bagi na ti lalaki
> APE hit   body his   boy
> "the boy hits himself"

> *kabil-en ti bagi na ti lalaki
> hit PAT   body his   boy
> "the boy hits himself"

even with the obligatory definiteness carried by "first position" allowing for the reflexive pronoun. Ilocano, unlike
Malagasy, has no VP-constituent--and thus, the subject can-

not be introduced "subordinately" in anticipation of the antecedent. The implication of all this for general principles of co-referentiality is that "command" must be refined somewhat. But, in any case, Ilocano--like English and Samoan--appears to use the reflexive form as an expression of anaphoric disambiguation rather than one of subject-control and reflexive transitivity.

4. Relative Clause Formation

The relative clause in Ilocano is of that type in which the head nominal surfaces and, as expected for a predicate-first system, requires that the clause follow the head. An invariant particle nga, quite analogous to English that in subordination generally, initiates the clause and forms a constituent with it, serving as a nominalization marker. Also typical of such relative clause formation is the fact that the "lower" co-referential noun does not surface at all; so that the overall feel of the construction is again like that of the English N that S (with the S "deformed" by deletion) except for the verb standing in clause-initial position.

Recent studies of relativization in general have established fairly solidly three properties of the co-referential nominal in the embedded clause: (i) that it is definitized and pronominalized (Kuroda 1968); (ii) that its function within the clause places it within a universal "accessibility hierarchy" (Keenan & Comrie 1972), which takes on further bounds of a language-specific sort; and (iii) that it has a particular semantic salience within its clause (Kuno, this volume), perhaps akin to "focus" in the sense of Chomsky (1970).

All the evidence in Ilocano points conclusively to the fact that the embedded co-referential nominal would be the focus of its clause, were it to surface. That is, if we have unembedded forms like

(a) ag-kabil TI LALAKI ti babai
    APE hit   boy   girl
    "the boy hits a girl"

(b) kabil-en ti lalaki TI BABAI
    hit PAT   boy   girl
    "the boy hits the girl"

(c) i-pauit-ko BAGITI KANKANTA ka-dagiti babbai
    send I   songs   to   girls
    "I send songs to the girls"

(where the focus in each sentence has been capitalized), we find relative clauses of the form--

    (aa) <u>ti lalaki</u> <u>nga ag-kabil ti babai</u>
            boy   that hit   girl
        "the boy that hits a girl"

    (bb) <u>ti babai</u> <u>nga kabil-en ti lalaki</u>
            girl   that hit   boy
        "the girl that the boy hits"

    (cc) <u>ti kankanta</u> <u>nga i-pauit-ko ka-dagiti babbai</u>
           songs   that send I   girls
        "the songs that I send to the girls"

and no other:

    (aaa) *<u>ti babai</u> <u>nga ag-kabil ti lalaki</u>
             girl   that hit   boy
        "the girl that the boy hits"

    (bbb) *<u>ti lalaki</u> <u>nga kabil-en ti babai</u>
            boy   that hit   girl
        "the boy that hits the girl"

    (ccc) *<u>dagiti babbai</u> <u>nga i-pauit-ko ti kankanta</u>
            girls   that send I   songs
        "the girls that I send the songs"

It is the unequivocal fact that no other nominal but the focus can serve as the co-referential counterpart to the matrix noun that establishes focus as subject in Ilocano; for, according to the "accessibility hierarchy," if a system allows only one function within a clause to be relativized, that function will be the subject. English (and other Germanic languages) substantiate this universal constraint in the participial relative, i.e., the type <u>anyone [throwing cans and bottles] will be evicted</u>. For example, given the clause <u>the boys throw stones at the dog</u>, one can form only a subject-relative:

    the boys [∅ throw-ing stones at the dog] ran away

    *the stones [the boys throw-ing ∅ at the dog] hit
      the car

    *the dog [the boys throw-ing stones at ∅] went mad

The Ilocano focus is obligatorily definite, as was seen in Section 2. But recall that the APE nominal in first position is also obligatorily definite. All the more striking, therefore, is the fact that the semantics of APE in and of itself do not suffice to bring it to relativizability--as

the ungrammaticality of (bbb) above indicates. The behavior
of reflexivization is particularly instructive, in this respect. Suppose a form like bisito-en ti babai ti bagi-na
"the woman kisses herself," where -en shows that ti bagi-na
"herself" is the Patient nominal in focus. What relative
form might one anticipate for "the woman who kisses herself"?
If definiteness and co-referentiality (and even first position) were the sole desiderata, the following derivation
would be reasonable: ti babai [nga [bisito-en ti babai ti
bagi-na]] → ti babai nga bisito-en ti bagi-na. But the predicted outcome is totally unacceptable. It is precisely the
requirement that the co-referential nominal be in focus that
rules out this possibility.

The only form allowed for "the woman who kisses herself" is ti babai nga manang-bisito ti bagi-na, which contains a putative well-formed clause *manang-bisito ti babai
ti bagi-na in APE-focus. But the latter is a non-existent
construction: it does not observe the condition that the
Patient in an APE-focussed proposition be indefinite. This
condition, it should be noted, holds for all clauses but the
relative:

> nang-kabil ti babai ti lalaki
>   hit   girl   boy
> "the girl hit {*the / a} boy"

> ti babai ti nang-kabil ti lalaki
> girl   hit   boy
> "it's the girl who hit {*the / a} boy"

> ammo-m nga nang-kabil ti babai ti lalaki
> know you   hit   girl   boy
> "you know that the girl hit {*the / a} boy"

It is the relaxation of this constraint on the indefiniteness of the Patient in APE-focus clauses that permits a relativizable form of the reflexive. Apparently, the cost of
nga manang-bisito ti bagi-na--with no counterpart elsewhere
in the system--is a language-specific concern and tolerable,
compared to nga bisito-en ti bagina--which does have a proper correspondent, but which violates the universal primacy
of the subject-relative.

5.   Ti-Nominalization and Focus

Complement clauses in Ilocano take two forms--among

other properties, one is marked by a clause-initial <u>ti</u>
(roughly, a "definite article"), the other by clause-initial
<u>nga</u> (corresponding, more or less, to English <u>that</u>). The
<u>nga</u>-type seems to me to have a more general distribution and
to be less constrained in its internal structure, vis-a-vis
the basic shape of the atomic proposition. But the two appear to be equivalent as nominalized propositions, in the
sense that they "compare": with <u>palalo</u> "hard" as predicate,
we can have

<u>na-pal-palalo</u>	<u>nga kinagat ti aso ti pusa</u>	<u>ngem</u>
harder	bit dog cat	than

<u>ti pinang-kagat-na ti tulang</u>
biting   it   bone

"the dog bit the cat harder than it bit the bone"

in which <u>pinang-kagat</u> is the past tense (-<u>in</u>- as past tense
marker) of a nominalization like "biting," whether act or
manner. And the difference in degree of noun-ness is probably like (or less than) that of finite and non-finite
clauses in an English comparative, e.g., <u>it is more impor-</u>
<u>tant [just to have delegates there] than [that they outnum-</u>
<u>ber the major slate]</u>.

    <u>Ti</u>-clauses function in cleft-like constructions, in a
way that suggests the subject WH-clause of the English
pseudo-cleft:

<u>lalaki</u> <u>ti ag-taray</u>
boy   APE run
"(the one) who runs is a boy"

<u>ti lalaki</u> <u>ti ag-taray</u>
boy   APE run
"(the one) who runs is the boy"

with <u>(ti) lalaki</u> functioning as predicate. This cleft-
construction supplies the basic form of WH-questions like

<u>anya</u> <u>ti kinagat ti aso?</u>
what   bit   dog
"what did the dog bite?"

<u>anya</u> <u>ti nang-kagat ti pusa?</u>
what   bit   cat
"what bit the cat?"

<u>sadino</u> <u>ti pag-taray-an ti lalaki?</u>
where   run   boy
"where does the boy run?"

531

sinu   ti in-ayat ti lalaki?
who   love   boy
"who did the boy love?"

I cite these forms to establish the fact that the ti-clause
is a focus-oriented nominalization, so that a form like ti
ag-taray can be glossed as "the one who runs" or "the run-
ner" since it has an APE focus; ti kinagat ti aso can be
glossed as "that which the dog bit" or "the thing bitten by
the dog" since it is Patient-focussed; ti pag-taray-an as
"the running-place" since it has a locative focus. The nga-
clause does not have such an orientation, is always "propositional" in sense, and shows the internal completeness of
unembedded atomic sentences.

The unmarked character of nga-clauses is also indicated
by the fact that all "propositional" verbs admit nga-
complements while ti-clause complements are not always possible. For example, the verbs mavat and kayat "want" show
the following distribution:

(i)   mayat-ak   nga mapan
      want I   go
      "I want to go"

(ii) *mayat-ak   ti mapan
      want I   go
      "I want to go" (in fact, no interpretation
                          possible)

(iii) kayat-ko   ti mapan
      want I   go
      "I want to go"

(iv) kayat-ko   nga mapan
      want I   go
      "I want someone to go"

A number of properties manifested by these sentences are of
interest to us: first, note the "unspecified APE" of (iv).
We must posit such a free deletion not only because of native speaker intuition for this particular proposition, but
because of a general process of ti-formation which we will
come to shortly. Second, note that in (i) the deletion of
the NP in the nga-clause obtains on two conditions: (a) co-
referentiality with the APE of the matrix; and (b) its being
in focus.

What we are concerned with, of course, is a contrast
between ti mapan and nga mapan. Forms (iii) and (iv) give
us that contrast; and what distinguishes kayat from mayat
(both from the root ayat "desire") is that the former is

Patient-focussed while the latter is APE-focussed. (Hence, the difference in pronominal forms: -ko the non-focussed clitic, -ak the focussed. We will return to the signifi- cance of this morphological opposition later.) It is rea- sonable to infer from just these facts that a third condi- tion is necessary in order to account for ti-complement clauses: i.e., that the clause itself be in focus.

But there is one more constraint needed, as the follow- ing facts show:

(v) kinayat ti lalaki nga kabil-en ti babai
     wanted   boy   hit PAT ti girl
     "the boy wanted to be hit by the girl"

(vi) kinayat ti lalaki ti ma-kabil iti babai
     wanted   boy   PAT hit   girl
     "the boy wanted to be hit by a girl"

In both (v) and (vi), the NP deleted in the embedded clause is co-referential with matrix lalaki, as well as being the focus of the clause. The clause itself, given that kayat is the Patient-focus form of ayat, is in focus. Then what distinguishes (v) from (vi) is simply the sequential posi- tion of the deleted nominal: in (vi), it follows the predi- cate ma-kabil immediately; in (v), it does not follow its predicate immediately. Compare the unembedded forms

(v') kabil-en ti babai ti lalaki
      hit PAT   girl   boy
      "the boy is hit by the girl"

(vi') ma-kabil ti lalaki iti babai
      PAT hit   boy   girl
      "the boy is hit by a girl"

We should also note the form

(vii) kinayat ti lalaki ti ma-kabil
      wanted   boy   PAT hit

which can only mean "the boy wanted to be hit" and shows "unspecified agent" (not necessarily in focus) deletion. With these various conditions, we are forced to predict that

(viii) kinayat ti lalaki nga ma-kabil ti babai
       wanted   boy   PAT hit   girl

can only mean "the boy wanted the girl to be hit" because (a) ma- indicates Patient-focus; (b) ti babai indicates definiteness; and (c) nga indicates that deletion, if it occurs, is not on a condition of co-referentiality. Thus, the inference is that ti babai is the focus of the embedded clause, and that the APE nominal is that "unspecified agent" which can be freely deleted.

Further confirmation of these various constraints is found in a full accounting of such constructions as

(ix) narigat   nga i-lako ti balay
      difficult   PAT sell   house
      "it is difficult to sell the house"

(x)   narigat   ti ag-lako iti balay
      difficult   APE sell   house
      "it is difficult to sell a house"

(xi) narigat kanya-k   ti ag-lako iti balay
      difficult for I   APE sell   house
      "it is difficult for me to sell a house"

The contrast between (ix) and (x) is explicable if we assume an "unspecified agent": roughly--

(ix') narigat   (FOR ONE)   i-lako (THAT ONE) ti balay
       difficult   PAT sell   house

(x')   narigat   (FOR ONE)   ag-lako (THAT ONE) iti balay
       difficult   APE sell   house

Some sanction for these reconstructions is supplied by (xi), which--given all we understand of ti-complementation at this point--should derive from:

(xi') narigat   kanya-ko   ag-lako (SIAK) iti balay
       difficult for I   APE sell   I   house

and which, because we have all conditions met (i.e., focus of siak, co-referentiality with matrix -ko, first position after lako, as well as the clause itself in focus), assumes the ti-nominalization. (x') similarly satisfies all conditions, and so reduces to (x) with the free deletion of FOR ONE. (ix') cannot surface with a ti-complement because the co-referential NP of the embedded clause is not in focus: i- is a Patient prefix, and ti balay is definite, clear indications that THAT ONE, while in first position and co-referential with matrix ONE, is not in focus.

I have gone to some length in accounting for ti-complementation in order to support the claim that focus in Ilocano corresponds to subject in other systems--in that when certain conditions are met (essentially, co-referentiality with a matrix argument, and subject-function within the embedded clause), a reduction of the embedded proposition is allowed. This process might be called "infinitiva-lization" in more familiar languages. Further language-specific constraints (e.g., in Ilocano, that the complement

clause itself be in subject-relation to the matrix predicate)
are not to the point, but do lend support to the central
function of focus in Ilocano--that is to say, that while it
may not correspond in all respects to what passes for subject in other systems, it does function equivalently in
several significant ways, and is by no means a marginal
grammatical relation.

6. "Promotion" to Subject

In the previous section, we saw that one of the conditions for reduction to <u>ti</u>-nominalization was that the focussed co-referential NP in the embedded clause be in "first
position," i.e., follow its predicate immediately. Earlier,
in the section on Definiteness and Referentiality, moreover,
we noted that first position bears with it obligatory definiteness, even when not in focus: for example--

  (i)   <u>bisito-en</u> <u>ti babai</u> <u>ti lalaki</u>
        kiss PAT   girl   boy
        "${the \atop *a}$} girl kisses the boy"

Finally, first position also carries with it an APE relation
to the predicate. Thus, in both of the following sentences--

  (ii) <u>bisito-en</u> <u>ti babai</u> <u>TI LALAKI</u>
        kiss PAT   girl   boy

  (iii) <u>ag-bisito</u> <u>TI BABAI</u> <u>(i)ti lalaki</u>
        APE kiss   girl   boy

regardless of the focus (indicated by capitalization), the
girl does the kissing, and the boy gets kissed. This base
position of APE is supported by the order of pronominal clitics: <u>in-ayat-kami</u> means "we were loved," but <u>in-ayat-da-</u>
<u>kami</u> can only mean "they loved us," not "we loved them."
All of these observations point to first position as
the natural locus of the subject--where indeed the APE nominal is normally situated. As it turns out, any nominal in
focus is "promoted" toward that slot. In some cases, the
non-focus APE prompts that position (and in those instances,
it must be definite), so that focus must take second place.
Certainly, when APE is not definite, it gives way to the
obligatorily definite focus:

  (iv) <u>ma-bisito</u> <u>TI BABAI</u> <u>(i)ti lalaki</u>
        PAT kiss   girl   boy
        "the girl can be kissed by a boy"

When in focus, the Beneficiary--like the Patient--will move
as far forward as it can:

(v) <u>i-pauit-ko</u> <u>dagiti kankanta</u>
PAT send I   songs

<u>ka-dagiti dua nga agbasbasa</u>
to   two   students

"I send the songs to (the) two students"

(vi) <u>pauit-ak</u> <u>dagiti dua nga agbasbasa</u> <u>ti kankanta</u>
send I   two   students   songs
"I send the two students songs"

and, in certain causative constructions, will even take over
first position:

(vii) <u>pa-bado-an</u> <u>ti balasang</u> <u>(i)ti kamiseta</u>
CAUS wear BEN   lady   shirt

<u>kenni Maria</u>
Maria

"Maria dresses the lady in a shirt"

Thus, the focus is oriented toward the beginning of
the sentence and, barring a definite APE, will usually take
first position. One very reasonable explanation for this
drift forward invokes the same principle as that which accounts for the natural association of definiteness with the
subject: that known material is usually rehearsed and abbre-
viated (e.g., pronominalized) as a bridge with what has gone
before, while new matter which is indefinite is introduced
later.

Note, moreover, that when case-marked nominals (e.g.,
Beneficiary <u>ka-</u>, as in (v) above) are promoted to focus,
whatever preposition or particle there may be must be
dropped: (vi), given its predicate /<u>pauit-an-ko</u>/ in Beneficiary focus, cannot appear with <u>...ka-dagiti...</u>. This
neutralization is what Fillmore (1968) posited for subject-
formation as a general schema.

7.   The Marked Status of Non-APE Focus

There are a number of indications that the unmarked
focus is the APE nominal. First, as was pointed out in the
last section on "Promotion," the focus is announced as early
as possible. Since APE is normally in first position, an
APE-focus satisfies all desiderata. Second, there are more
verbal affixes for APE-focus than for any other:

```
APE--      ag-, -um-, maka-, ma-, mang-
Pat--      -en, i-, ma-
Ben--      -an, i-
Dir--      i-, -an
Instr--    pag-
Loc--      pag- -an
etc.
```

and, furthermore, the number and differentiation of affixes
decreases as the "distance" from the predicate increases.
Thus, Patient-focus is the next most differentiated focus,
Beneficiary next most, and so on. Homonymy increases in the
more distant cases: that is to say, marked categories are
syncretistic.

Third, with APE-focus, no complements are excluded.
But in certain non-APE focus, agency cannot be expressed:
compare Beneficiary focus in the causative--

```
na- pa- kita -an   ti ubing   ti libro
PAST CAUS see  BEN    child       book
"the child was shown the book"
```

```
*na- pa- kita -an   ni Pedro   ti ubing   ti libro
PAST CAUS see  BEN     Pedro      child       book
"Pedro showed the child the book"
```

with, say, Patient-focus:

```
im- pa- kita   ni Pedro   ti libro   ti ubing
PAT CAUS see      Pedro      book       child
PAST
"Pedro showed the child the book"
```

Fourth, with "adjectival" predicates, apparently the only
focus possible is APE since relativization is restricted to
just that nominal: for example, from the base

```
asideg   ti aso   ti pusa
close      dog       cat
"the dog is close to the cat"
*"the cat is close to the dog"
```

we can only form

```
ti aso   nga asideg ti pusa
dog      that close     cat
"the dog that is close to the cat"
```

and not:

```
*ti pusa   nga asideg ti aso
cat        that close    dog
"the cat that the dog is close to"
```

Fifth, and last, the third person singular APE is unmarked in focus, in the sense that it has no pronoun clitic:
e.g., <u>matay-ak</u> "I die," <u>matay-ka</u> "you (sg.) die," as opposed
to <u>matay</u> "he/she/it dies." But it is marked by -<u>na</u> when not
in focus:

<u>bisito-en-na</u>   TI BABAI
kiss   PAT he   girl
"he kisses the girl"

cf. *<u>ag-bisito-na</u>   iti babai
APE kiss   he   girl
"he kisses a girl"

Zero "inflection" for the third person singular is a common
phenomenon, but the parallel I see here is more like that of
present vs. past tense: the present is the unmarked category
for a number of reasons, one being that the third singular
is often uninflected in contrast to non-present forms which
show inflection. So, in Ilocano, the absence of a pronominal clitic for the focussed third singular APE contrasts
with the presence of such a clitic for the non-focussed, as
if to say that APE-focus requires less marking than any
other orientation--which in turn means that more information
can be taken for granted (and not given overt expression) in
this category than in any other.

8. "Topic" in Ilocano

In spite of the evidence presented in sections 2-7, we
might entertain a view of focus in Ilocano as something
other than subject. A plausible alternative is to call it a
topic, which then forces us to some kind of cross-linguistic
characterization. I take the Li & Thompson attempt (this
volume) as one of the more thorough-going efforts to get at
this phenomenon--if indeed it is the same thing across languages. The criterial parameters they advance are (i) definiteness, (ii) selectional restrictions, and (iii) person-
number concord: specifically, (i) that the topic is always
definite (including "generic" definiteness); (ii) that its
semantic range may go beyond that of the "field" of the predicate; and (iii) that it does not participate in morphological concord with that predicate. The following English
sentences illustrate these properties:

(A)   (i)   And <u>Janie,</u> <u>she</u> can't finish a joke right to save
         herself.

    (ii)   As far as <u>developers</u> are concerned, I just don't
         take <u>their</u> promotional tactics seriously.

   (iii)   <u>these people who were standing at the window</u>, we're trying to figure out what <u>they</u> were doing there.

(B)   As for <u>the Center</u>, well, the less said about so-called "think tanks," the better.

The types in (A) show co-referentiality between the topic and some nominal in the sentence: in (i), the pronominal relationship is with the subject of the main verb; in (ii), it is with a genitive to the direct object of the main verb; in (iii), it is with the subject of a subordinate clause. Type B shows that it can participate in more "remote" semantic relationships, like class-member ("think tank"-Center).

   With respect to Ilocano, we ask two questions: (1) does focus meet these criteria?; and (2) if not, does some other nominal (in some other construction)? First of all, the obligatory definitenes of focus is clear, not only with "situational" propositions but with generics as well: e.g.,

     <u>ag-kamat</u> <u>ti aso</u> <u>iti pusa</u>
     APE chase   dog   cat
     "dogs chase cats" or "as for dogs, they chase cats"

Second, the semantic range of arguments that are focussable also supports its interpretation as topic. From an array of complements to a verb like <u>puted</u> "cut," including agentive <u>lalaki</u> "man," patient <u>kawayan</u> "bamboo," beneficiary <u>babai</u> "woman," and instrumental <u>buneng</u> "large knife, bolo"--the following simplex sentences can be formed:

APE-focus:

    <u>nag-puted</u> <u>TI LALAKI</u> <u>ti kawayan</u> <u>iti buneng</u>
    PAST cut   man   bamboo   knife
    APE

       <u>a para ti deyta babai</u>
       for   that woman

    "the man cut bamboo for that woman with a knife"

PAT-focus:

    <u>pinuted</u> <u>ti lalaki</u> <u>TI KAWAYAN</u> <u>iti buneng</u>
    cut   man   bamboo   knife

       <u>a para ti deyta babai</u>
       for   that woman

    "the man cut the bamboo with a knife for that woman"

BEN-focus:

<u>puted-an</u> <u>ti lalaki</u> <u>TI BABAI</u> <u>iti kawayan</u>
cut   man   woman   bamboo

       <u>iti buneng</u>
       knife

"the man cuts the woman bamboo with a knife"

INSTR-focus:

<u>pag-puted</u> <u>ti lalaki</u> <u>TI BUNENG</u> <u>iti kawayan</u>
cut   man   knife   bamboo

    <u>a para ti deyta babai</u>
    for   that woman

"the man uses the knife to cut bamboo for that
    woman"

There is no way, however, that genitives can be focussed.
And genitives, as is well known, commonly occur as topics.

The third property--absence of verbal concord, in the
sense of person-number agreement--is somewhat unclear in
Ilocano. Pronominal clitics occur, but for the most part,
they do not co-occur with free nouns or pronouns. Only in
the case of homophonous -na and -da do we find such a copying: e.g.,

    <u>in-avat-na-k</u>
    PAT love he me
         you
    "he loved me" or "you (sg.) loved me"

    <u>in-ayat-na-k</u> <u>ti lalaki</u>
    PAT love he me   man
    "the man loved me" (only interpretation)

It may be that in -na (and -da) we see the beginnings of an
agreement system. It is, at the moment, an option: cf. <u>in-</u>
<u>ayat-ak ti lalaki</u> "the man loved me" in which the clitic -na
does not appear. We might take the position that even at
this stage--the point at which cliticization (phonological
incorporation into the verbal "word") has taken place--con-
cord obtains. If so, then focus in Ilocano fails the third
requirement, and thus appears an unlikely candidate for the
topic construction.

As a matter of fact, a topic construction--distinct
from focus--does occur in Ilocano. So, from the untopical-
ized (but focussed) sentence

```
na-buung   [ ti baso  [deyta babai  [nga ammo-m]]]
PAST break   NP glass   that  woman   S    know you
"the glass of that woman that you know broke"
```

we can form a topicalized version like

```
[deyta babai  [nga ammo-m]] ket
 that  woman   S    know you
```

```
[  na-buung  ti baso-na]
   S    break       glass her
   PAST
"that woman that you know, her glass broke"
```

As far as I can determine, such topicalization is narrowly
constrained in Ilocano, both syntactically and semantically.
For example, the co-referentiality cannot be extended into
a subordinate clause:

```
*deyta babai  ket  ammo-m    nga na-buung-na ti baso
 that  woman       know you   PAST break she  glass
"that woman, you know that she broke the glass"
```

And yet, as is obvious from the genitival relation (in "that
woman you know, her glass broke"), this nominal function
cannot be related to focus, as we understand it. Neither is
it a version of the cleft:

```
sika   ti nang-surat ti babai
you       PAST write     woman
"it is you who wrote to a woman"
```

```
cf. *sika  ket  ti nang-surat ti babai
     you        PAST write     woman
"it is you who wrote to a woman"
```

Besides, the cleft construction allows indefinites, like
lalaki ti nang-surat ti babai "it is a boy who wrote to a
woman," while the ket-form does not. In fact, one of the
strongest reasons for suspecting that topic in Ilocano is
expressed in this form is the obligatory definiteness of the
S-initial nominal.

We are led to the following considerations: if topic in
Ilocano is realized in terms of the ket-construction, and
focus is not subject, then focus must be posited as another
major grammatical category in general linguistic theory. It
cannot be identified with focus, in the usual sense: for example, the question

```
anya   ti kinnan-mo idi kalman
what      ate   you  yesterday
"what did you eat yesterday?"
```

can be answered with

> nangan-ak ti mansanas idi kalman
> ate   I   apple   yesterday
> "I ate an apple yesterday"

where ti mansanas is indefinite and not in focus--but it is
the "focal" response to anya "what" from a presuppositional
point of view. Since Ilocano focus shares several critical
properties with what would otherwise be called subject, I
think it is preferable to take it as such, not only to force
a stronger stand on its universality (i.e., that it is required, not just available), but to push toward a better understanding of why there is such a fundamental requirement
in the first place.

9.   Summary

I have offered the following as a demonstration that
focus in Ilocano is subject:
- (1) its obligatory definiteness and referentiality
- (2) its being the sole relativizable nominal
- (3) its function in complement-clause reduction (ti-
        nominalization)
- (4) its placement early in the utterance (so-called old
        information)
- (5) its natural (= unmarked) affiliation with APE

In the last section, we considered whether focus could be
topic, and found that it was not--at least on one view of
topic. Perhaps the most obvious but most easily overlooked
property of focus (and subject as well, should it prove distinct) is that there is only one such per simplex sentence--
unlike topics which, in some languages like Lisu, can have
several co-referential relationships (Hope 1974)--

> ása nya alĕ lǽ nva phwu gɔ̀ -a
> Asa TOP Ale to TOP money give DEC
> "Asa gave Ale some money"
> (where both Asa and to Ale are presupposed and
> topicalized, and a rough English equivalent might
> be "as for Asa and Ale, (he) gave (him) money")

Occasionally in Ilocano there seems to occur a construction in which either or both of certain nominals can be
taken as focus:

> (i)   i-suru ti balasang ti ubing ti kanta
>   CAUS learn   lady   child   song
>   "the lady teaches the child the song"

and alongside this form, we find two relative clauses:

(ii)   <u>ti ubing nga</u>   <u>i-suru ti balasang ti kanta</u>
      child that CAUS learn lady   song
    "the child that the lady teaches the song"

(iii) <u>ti kanta nga</u>   <u>i-suru ti balasang ti ubing</u>
      song   that CAUS learn lady   child
    "the song that the lady teaches the child"

which suggests that, in (i), either <u>ubing</u> "child" or <u>kanta</u>
"song"--both definite--are relativizable. If this were the
case, such constructions would be damaging indeed to the
view of focus as subject. But there is a subtle difference
between (ii) and (iii): the former does not allow <u>kanta</u> to
be indefinite--

(iia) <u>ti ubing nga</u>   <u>i-suru ti balasang *iti kanta</u>
      child that CAUS learn lady   child
    "the song that the lady teaches a child"

If what we have been claiming about focus is correct, then
(ii) and (iii) correspond to distinct constructions. (ii)
does correspond to (i), where <u>ubing</u> as expected is in focus
and relativizable. (Note "second position" for <u>ubing</u>, which
is as far forward as focus can go with APE definite.) And
(i), as expected, does not allow <u>kanta</u> to be indefinite.
(iii), on the other hand, corresponds to

(iv)   <u>i-suru ti balasang ti kanta</u> $\{{iti \atop ti}\}$ <u>ubing</u>
    CAUS LEARN lady   song   child
    "the lady teaches the song to $\{{a \atop the}\}$ child"

where, as expected, <u>kanta</u> is in focus (and second position)
and <u>ubing</u> may be definite or indefinite. Thus, all the evidence supports the claim that there is only one focus to a
simplex sentence--which is to say, there is only one subject
to a predicate.

SUBJECT PROPERTIES IN THE NORTH RUSSIAN PASSIVE

by

Alan Timberlake

1. In this paper I will consider the problem of identifying the subject in passive constructions in North Russian
dialects, relying on E.L. Keenan's discussion (<u>Definition of
Subject</u>, this volume) of the subject as a complex of properties. I will suggest that the distribution of subject properties is unusual. The underlying object of the passive has
fewer subject properties than might be expected for the
derived subject of a passive. Conversely, and more striking-
ly, the underlying subject of the passive has more subject
properties than might be expected for the agent of a passive.
The North Russian constructions therefore illustrate a type
of passive in which promotion of the underlying object and
demotion of the underlying subject are not complete. In addition, I will suggest a motivated reason why the underlying
subject of the North Russian passive should act like a subject (1).

The passive constructions are found in the area north
of a line which extends from the 56th parallel in the western
central dialects to the 60th parallel in the northeastern
dialects (Kuz'mina and Nemčenko 1971:map 1); the area includes,
for example, Pskov, Novgorod, Leningrad, and Archangel, but
not Moscow. The data used here comes from published studies
of the syntax of these dialects, notably the recent monograph by Kuz'mina and Nemčenko (1971; hereafter KN) (2).
These studies rely for the most part on a general dialect
survey conducted in the 1940s which included only a few questions on syntax; the data is therefore sketchy, and is cited
in these studies without context, and without reference to
other syntactic features of a given dialect (KN 5). Although
there are in fact some significant differences in the area
considered--particularly between the western central and the
northeast areas--subject properties seem to be consistent
throughout the whole area; accordingly, I will cite examples
without specific geographical information and refer to the
whole area simply as North Russian (NR). I will discuss the
NR constructions by contrasting them with the passive in
Contemporary Standard Russian (CSR).

2. Before discussing subject properties, I will give
an outline of the general properties of the CSR passive and
the NR passive.

The CSR passive has the following properties: (a) It
is formed only from verbs which are transitive; further, it
is limited to transitive verbs which imply that the object
will be affected as a consequence of the action. Thus,
verbs of emotion and perception (<u>počuvstvovat'</u> "feel,"
<u>uvidet'</u> "catch sight of," <u>poprosit'</u> "request"), verbs involv-

ing motion (<u>minovat'</u> "pass by"), semelfactives (<u>liznut'</u> "lick once"), and verbs involving superficial contact (<u>uronit'</u> "drop, let slip") ordinarily do not form passives in CSR (Bondarko and Bulanin 1967:159).

(b) The underlying subject is in the nominative and (c) it is the grammatical subject, in the sense that it produces agreement for gender, number, and person in the predicate (3).

1 Prestupnik zaderžan (policiej)
   criminal   arrested instr.
   nom.m.sg. part.m.sg.
   "the criminal has been arrested (by the police)"

Thus, in 1 the underlying object <u>prestupnik</u> is in the nominative, and the passive participle is masculine singular, in agreement with the noun. (d) As in 1, the underlying subject may be expressed as an adverbial constituent in the instrumental, although it is usually omitted; it is omitted when the underlying subject is understood to be indefinite or clear from the context, or when no specific agent is understood (4).

In addition, it may be noted that (e) the CSR participial passive is formed only from perfective verbs (implying that the action is bounded, or completed) (5); a distinct passive construction for imperfective verbs (implying that the action is not bounded, hence durative, generic, repetitive, or attempted) is expressed by means of reflexive verbs. I will not consider the so-called reflexive passive here. Finally, (f) the participial passive construction is intransitive and typically stative (Baláž 1959, Isačenko 1968:451, Krasil'nikova 1973:186-90). It may describe a state resulting from a preceding action, as in 1 (where the criminal has been arrested and is presumably still in custody), or a state which is not conceived of as resulting from an action, as in 2:

2 Ja ubežden
   I convinced
     part.m.sg.
   "I am convinced"

Only occasionally does the passive seem to describe an action:

3 Vrač Konstantin Andreevič Radionov v tjaželom

     sostojanii byl snjat s poezda
               aux. part.
               m.sg. m.sg.
   "Dr. K.A.R. was taken from the train in serious condition" (Baláž 1959:74)

Even here the passive can be interpreted statively, as focussing on the condition in which the doctor was taken from the
train, rather than on the action itself.

3. The NR passive constructions have the following
properties: (a) They are freely formed from intransitive as
well as from transitive verbs:

4 U menja uže vstato bylo
  me   stood aux.
      part. n.sg.
      n.sg.
 "by me there's already been getting up"
 ("I have already gotten up") (KN 99)

5 Mnogo begano v kolxoze
 much run
    part.n.sg.
 "there's been a lot of running down on the kolkhoz"
 (KN 98)

6 S molodyx god vezde žito
  young years   lived
        part.n.sg.
 "there's been living everywhere since youth" (KN 101)

7 Posmotreli po polju -- vsjudu xoženo -- bol'šie i
 looked   field   walked big
          part.n.sg.

   malen'kie sledy
   small   tracks

 "They looked around the field -- there'd been walking
 everywhere -- there were large and small tracks"
 (KN 101)

In 4-7 the passive participles are all formed from intransitive verbs; the participles, and the auxiliary in 4, are all
neuter singular, the form used in impersonal sentences in
Russian (sentences lacking a grammatical subject).
 In some of these dialects the construction is even
formed from reflexive verbs:

8 Bylo zapisanos' v školu-to u menja
 aux. registered   me
 n.sg. part.n.sg.
 "there was signing myself up at school by me" (KN 99)

9 U menja vyspanos'-to teper'
   me   slept out
           part.n.sg.
"there's been sleeping myself out by me now" (KN 100)

Here again the auxiliary in 8 and the participles in 8-9 are neuter singular, since there is no subject to agree with. Reflexive verbs in Russian are not necessarily syntactically equivalent to the combination of a transitive verb plus reflexive direct object; corresponding to <u>vyspat'sja</u> "sleep oneself out" there is no *<u>vyspat' sebja</u>. It is true, however, that reflexive verbs cannot take an accusative direct object, so that they are formally specified as intransitive (6). Since the passive constructions can be formed from intransitive verbs, as in 4-7, and even from reflexive verbs, as in 8-9, it is clear that there is no constraint on transitivity in the NR passive.

(b,c) When the verb is in fact transitive, there are three ways to express the underlying object. First, it may be expressed in the accusative, where it is obviously not the grammatical subject and there is no agreement in the predicate.

10 U menja bylo   telenka zarezano
    me   aux.   calf   slaughtered
            n.sg. acc.   part.n.sg.
"by me there's been slaughtered a calf" (KN 38)

In 10 the underlying object remains in the object case (accusative); both the auxiliary and the participle are neuter singular, indicating there is no grammatical subject (7). Compare:

11 Ee muža ubito   na vojne
    man   killed   war
    acc.   part.n.sg.
"there was killed her husband during the war" (KN 37)

As a second possibility, the object may be expressed in the nominative, but without producing agreement in the predicate:

12 Pereexano   bylo   doroga tut
    crossed   aux.   road
    part.n.sg. n.sg. nom.f.sg.
"there's been crossing over the road there" (KN 36)

In 12 the underlying object is a feminine noun, expressed in the nominative; the auxiliary and the participle, however, are both neuter singular, not in agreement with the noun. Compare:

550

13 U lisicy uneseno kuročka
    fox   carried chicken
           part.n.sg. nom.f.sg.
    "by the fox was carried off a chicken" (KN 27)

As a third possibility, the object may be expressed in the
nominative with agreement in the predicate:

14 U rybaka byl   sxvačen medvežij jazyk
          aux.   caught bear's tongue
          m.sg. part.m.sg.   nom.m.sg.
    "by the fisherman was caught a bear's tongue" (KN 24)

In 14 both the auxiliary and the participle agree with the
nominative noun. Compare:

15 Šapka-to u parnja v okno brošena
    hat   guy   window thrown
    nom.f.sg.   part.f.sg.
    "the hat was thrown out the window by the fellow"
    (KN 24)

I will discuss the relationship of these three variants of
passives formed from transitives in Section 4.
    (d) In the NR constructions the underlying subject is
expressed by a prepositional phrase, u plus the genitive, as
in 4, 8-10, 13-15 above; this expression of the agent in NR
is restricted to animate nouns. The u + genitive phrase is
used in CSR and NR in the predicate expression of possession
(Mrázek and Brym 1962, Isačenko 1974):

16 U   menja mašina
    prep. me   car
          gen.   nom.
    "I have a car"

It can also be used with the passive participle to express
the benefactor or possessor of the results of an action:

17 U menja postroen dom
              built   house
    "I have/had a house built"

Sentence 17 is formally parallel to the NR sentences given
above, but has a narrower semantic range. In CSR 17 means
that the speaker is in possession of a house which has been
built, regardless of who did the building (Mrázek and Brym
1962:111, Krasil'nikova 1973:188). In NR 17 can have this
meaning, but it can also mean simply that the speaker did the
building himself, regardless of whether he is in possession
of the results. That is, u + genitive with the passive participle designates the benefactor-possessor in CSR, but desig-

nates both the benefactor-possessor and the agent in NR (8).

The difference between the use of u + genitive in CSR and NR can be illustrated by two tests. First, sentences like 17 are anomalous in CSR when there is no tangible result which could be possessed (Mrázek and Brym 1962:111):

18 *U menja vse s"edeno
    ("I have it all eaten up")

But since u + genitive can designate the agent in NR, such sentences are possible in NR:

19 U ètogo muzika ikony i propity
        man   drunk up
    "by this man the icons have even been drunk up"
    ("by this man the icons have even been squandered
    through drinking")   (KN 22)

Second, it is possible to expand a sentence like 17 in CSR with the real agent expressed in the instrumental:

20 U menja dom postroen sosedjami
    "I had a house built by my neighbors"

This would be impossible in NR. Conversely, it is possible to expand a sentence like 17 in NR with a second u + genitive phrase, so that one represents the benefactor-possessor (here u menja) and the other the agent (u kur):

21 U menja tri jajca svezix bylo tol'ko polozeno u kur
        eggs   aux.   laid
                          n.sg.
    "I just had three fresh eggs laid by the hens"
    (Matveenko 1961:125)

This would be impossible in CSR. It is the u + genitive phrase as an expression of the agent which shows a number of subject properties in NR.

(e) The NR constructions are freely formed from imperfective verbs, as in 5-7 above. (f) Semantically, the NR constructions are similar to the CSR passive in having a stative meaning, but there may be some subtle differences among the different subtypes in NR. The transitive type with nominative-with-agreement can describe a state which does not necessarily result from an action, whereas the other types--intransitive, or transitive with object in the accusative or nominative-without-agreement--seem to describe only a state which results directly from a preceding action. These subtypes therefore have a clear perfect meaning, and are often identified as possessive perfects (Kuznecov 1949, Maslov 1949).

The properties of the CSR passive and the NR passive constructions are summarized in Fig. 1.

	CSR	NR
transitivity	transitive	transitive intransitive
object case, agreement	nominative-with-agreement	accusative nominative-without-agreement nominative-with-agreement
agent case	instrumental	u + genitive
aspect	perfective	perfective imperfective

Fig. 1

4. Case, agreement. As noted above, the underlying object of the CSR passive is necessarily nominative and is necessarily the grammatical subject, in that it causes agreement in the predicate. In the NR constructions, on the other hand, there are three possibilities for expressing the underlying object: accusative, nominative-without-agreement, and nominative-with-agreement (9). One might ask what the relationship of the three subtypes is: they could be low-level variants of a single passive construction, or they could represent several distinct types of passives. The evidence favors the first interpretation.

Consider first the subtypes of accusative and nominative-without-agreement. There is at least historical evidence that the choice between these two subtypes was governed by the type of noun phrase involved: the accusative subtype was used for pronouns and masculine animate nouns while the nominative-without-agreement subtype was used for other nouns (KN 36, 54). This (historical) distribution of case according to animacy suggests that the two subtypes do not represent distinct constructions (10).

Consider next the nominative-with-agreement subtype. It might be supposed that it directly continues the CSR passive, since in both the underlying object is in the nominative and causes agreement; in this way it might represent a construction distinct from the other two. However, the nominative-with-agreement subtype in NR shares all these characteristics of the two other NR subtypes; some of these characteristics are impossible for the CSR passive. Thus, the nominative-with-agreement construction in NR has the agent expressed by u + genitive, not by the instrumental (see 14-15 above). Moreover, it may be formed from imperfective verbs, even prefixed derived imperfectives:

22 Rubaxa   vsja   vyšivana
    shirt   all   embroidered
    nom.f.sg.   part.f.sg.
    "the shirt is all embroidered" (KN 53)

Further, in the distribution of subject properties the nominative-with-agreement subtype does not differ significantly from the other two subtypes, except obviously in case and agreement of the underlying object.

    It seems, then, that the nominative-with-agreement construction in NR is not a separate passive construction, but one variant of the NR passive. It is interesting that adverbial specifications of time and distance can be expressed in the nominative and cause agreement in the predicate, as in:

23 U menja odna zima   xožena
           winter   walked
           nom.f.sg. part.f.sg.
    "by me one winter was walked (to school)" (KN 26)

Ordinarily, adverbial specifications are unlikely candidates for promotion to subject status; the fact that they can become subjects in these constructions suggests that the promotion of underlying object to subject is a low-level and inessential part of the basic NR passive construction.

    In a canonical passive like the CSR passive, the underlying object is promoted to subject status, and behaves like a subject with respect to all subsequent rules; correlatively, the underlying subject is demoted and ceases to behave as a subject (Perlmutter and Postal, forthcoming). In the NR passive constructions, however, the underlying object does not necessarily acquire even the typical subject properties of nominative case and agreement, the properties which are universally the easiest for promoted objects to acquire (E.L. Keenan, Definition of Subject, this volume). Since the underlying object in the NR passive is only optionally promoted, it is perhaps not surprising that the underlying subject of the NR passive is not fully demoted, but retains a number of subject properties. Let us consider these subject properties, beginning with equi and a second deletion process.

    5. Deletion. In CSR equi operates in a straightforward fashion to produce infinitival embeddings. Only the

subject of an embedded clause can be deleted. The controller
for equi can be the matrix subject (obescat' "promise"), an
accusative object (poprosit' "request"), or a dative object
(prikazat' "order"), depending on the semantics of the matrix
verb (Brecht 1972). Only subject-controlled equi (including
purpose clauses) is of interest here.

Consider a verb like zabyt' "forget," which can occur
with a nominal object or a sentential object (and allows
subject-controlled equi):

24 Kto-to zabyl očki
    "someone forgot his glasses"

25 My zabyli zakryt' okno
    "we forgot to close the window"

With a nominal object this verb regularly allows a passive
(sentence 26), but with an infinitival object the passive is
impossible (sentence 27) (Lönngren 1970:29):

26 Očki zabyty kem-to
    "the glasses have been forgotten by someone"

27 *Zakryt' okno zabyto (nami)
    ("it has been forgotten to close the window (by us")

There are several possible ways to describe a sentence
like 27. One could suggest that equi is impossible when the
matrix verb is passive, or that infinitival objects cannot be
promoted by the passive. These possible suggestions are con-
tradicted for Russian by verbs with dative-controlled equi,
for which the passive is normal:

28 Prikazali rabočim sdelat' remont
    "they ordered the workers to make the repair"

29 Rabočim prikazano sdelat' remont
    "it's been ordered to the workers to make the repair"

A more plausible explanation for 27 is that the displaced underlying subject of the passive in CSR is a peripheral constituent, and as such is not capable of serving as
the controller for equi. This explanation could be phrased
in various ways; I will state it simply as follows: however
passive and equi apply, the controller for equi must end up
as a grammatical, not a peripheral, constituent (11).

In contrast to CSR, NR regularly allows equi to be controlled by the passive agent. Examples of this are well-
attested, and cover a wide range of verbs. It is found with
transitive verbs:

30 Ne dumano   pit' moloka
        thought   drink milk
        part.n.sg. inf.
    "it's not been thought to drink any milk" (KN 200)

With intransitive nonreflexive verbs:

31 U ej v Leningrad postupat' uexano
                        enroll   gone
                        inf.   part.n.sg.
    "by her there was going off to Leningrad to enroll"
    (KN 200)

32 U babki naverno ujdeno   kosit'
        grandma   gone   mow
                        part.n.sg. inf.
    "by grandmother there was probably going out to mow"
    (Matveenko 1961:123)

And even with intransitive reflexive verbs:

33 U nego bylo vzjatos' skosit' gectar
        him   aux.   taken   mow
              n.sg. part.   inf.
              n.sg.
    "by him was undertaken to mow the hectare" (KN 99)

Thus, it is normal in NR to embed an infinitive under a
passive even when the underlying subject of the passive--the
controller for equi--has been displaced. This means that the
underlying subject in NR is not a peripheral constituent; it
continues to behave like a subject in its control of equi (12).

The second deletion process involves deletion in embedded clauses with passive participles which function as adverbial modifiers to verbs expressing states:

34 Smotrit, a tam ego obe lošadi privjazany k derevu
                                horses tied
                                        part.pl.

        stojat
        stand
        3pl.

    "he looks, and there both his horses stand tied to a
    tree" (KN 250)

In 34 the matrix sentence consists of the subject lošadi and
the stative verb stojat; the participle describes the state
in which the subject stands, "having been tied up." Compare:

35 Takie kuči-to byvajut u ix navoločeno
  piles occur   dragged
  nom.pl. 3pl.   part.n.sg.
  "such piles are found dragged together by them (ants)"
  (KN 250)

Here the structure of the sentence is basically the same,
except that an overt agent (u ix) is expressed with the embedded passive participle, suggesting that it does represent a
reduced sentence.

  The derivation of such constructions is not clear, but
two points may be made. First, there is presumably a deletion
of a noun phrase in the embedded sentence, which is constrained
to be identical to the subject of the matrix verb. Second,
the deletion presumably takes place after the embedded sentence has undergone the passive; otherwise, there would be no
way to ensure that the passive would apply after the deletion
had already taken place. Formally, it seems that the passive
applies on the lower cycle, and the embedding (with deletion)
takes place on the upper cycle.

  Now consider 36:

36 U Šurki bylo vcera prijdeno namazanos'
     aux.   arrived   slicked up
     n.sg.   part.n.sg. part.n.sg.
  "by Shurka there was arriving yesterday all slicked up"
  (KN 250)

In 36 the matrix verb is passive, so that the deletion is
controlled by the displaced underlying subject. For this
rule, then, there is evidence comparable to the evidence for
equi: the underlying subject of the passive can be the controller for deletion; it is therefore not a peripheral constituent.

  The conditions on the target of deletion in this construction are also interesting. In 34-35 above the deleted
noun phrase was the underlying object of the passive participle. But consider 37:

37 Oni živut ne zapisanos'
  they live   registered
    3pl.   part.n.sg.
  "they live together, not having registered themselves"
  (KN 8)

In 37 the deleted noun phrase is the underlying subject of
the (reflexive) passive participle. Given the argument
above, deletion can occur only after the passive has applied
on the lower cycle, so deletion must have operated on a string
like the following:

557

38 [U nix ne zapisanos']
    gen.   part.n.sg.

That is, the target for deletion can be the displaced underlying subject of a passive. This formation is regular for
intransitive reflexive verbs; compare 36 above or 39:

39 Ja uže spliju uže okutanos'
    I   sleep   wrapped up
                        part.n.sg.
    "I am already sleeping, having already wrapped myself
    up" (KN 250)

In both deletion processes examined in this section,
the underlying subject of the passive can control deletion.
This suggests that the underlying subject retains some subject properties even after it has been displaced; it does not
behave as a peripheral constituent. Further, for the second
deletion process, the underlying subject (of reflexive verbs)
is still accessible to deletion. This is another indication
that the underlying subject of the passive is a grammatical
constituent (13).

6. Reflexivization. Control of reflexivization can be
identified as a property of subjects in Russian (Perlmutter
and Postal, forthcoming; E.L. Keenan, Definition of Subject,
this volume). Here I will present arguments about the reflexive possessive pronominal adjective svoj "one's own," since
I have no data about the reflexive pronoun sebja "oneself" in
NR. In the control of svoj-reflexivization there is a significant difference between the CSR and the NR passive constructions. There are two subcases to consider.
    First, in CSR the underlying object (derived subject)
can regularly control svoj-reflexivization in the displaced
underlying subject (Klenin 1974):

40 Otec   zabyt   svoimi det'mi
    father forgotten   children
    nom.   part.m.sg.   instr.
    m.sg.
    "the father has been forgotten by his own children"

This seems to be impossible in the NR passive; thus, there
are no cases like the following:

41 *U svoix detej otec zabyt
                    nom. part.m.sg.
                    m.sg.
    ("by his own children the father has been forgotten")

```
42  *U svoix detej otec   zabyto
              nom.   part.
              m.sg.  n.sg.

43  *U svoix detej otca zabyto
              acc. part.n.sg.
```

Conversely, in CSR the displaced underlying subject cannot control <u>svoj</u>-reflexivization in the underlying object (derived subject) (Klenin 1974). There are no sentences like 44 in CSR:

```
44  *Svoj otec zabyt det'mi
    ("their own father has been forgotten by the
    chidren")
```

This pattern is regular in NR passives; it is attested for all three subtypes of the NR transitive passive. With object case (here genitive instead of accusative):

```
45  Odežki   svoej svezeno
    clothes        brought
    gen.           part.n.sg.
    "there's been bringing together some of my clothes"
    (KN 64)
```

With nominative and no agreement:

```
46  U Šurki privedeno   svoja staraja nevesta
            brought                     bride
            part.n.sg.                  nom.f.sg.
    "by Shurka was brought around his own old bride"
    (KN 35)
```

With nominative and partial agreement (a historically transitional type):

```
47  A u menja svoj rebenok byl   vzjato v Slancy
                  child    aux.  taken
             nom.      m.sg. part.
                            n.sg.
    "by me my own son was taken to Slancy"   (KN 36)
```

And finally, with nominative and agreement:

```
48  U nego svoja izba   postavlena
                 hut    built
            nom.   part.
            f.sg.  f.sg.
    "by him his own hut has been built"   (KN 23)
```

If control of <u>svoj</u>-reflexivization is symbolized by an arrow, the contrast between CSR and NR is given by 49:

49   CSR   NR
        agent → object   *   √
        object → agent   √   *

Thus, with respect to svoj-reflexivization, CSR and NR have
diametrically opposed behavior: in CSR the underlying object
(derived subject) is the natural controller, while in NR the
underlying subject is the natural controller. This shows
that the underlying subject of the NR passive, although it is
displaced to u + genitive, continues to behave like a subject.
Conversely, the underlying object does not behave like a subject with respect to svoj-reflexivization, even when it has
the subject properties of case and agreement (see 46-48).

        7. Topic properties. It can be assumed that, other
things being equal, the grammatical subject is the unmarked
topic. Information about topic structure in NR is sketchy,
but there are four indications of topic properties which
could be mentioned.
        First, word order generally reflects the degree of
topicality in Russian. In the CSR passive the normal word
order is OV(S), suggesting that the agent phrase is usually
not the topic. In the NR constructions formed from intransitive verbs, the usual order is SV; in constructions formed
from transitive verbs, the most common order is SOV, with OSV
a close second (Petrova 1968:123). These facts suggest that
the agent phrase of the NR passive is regularly the topic;
certainly it is the topic more than the agent phrase of the
CSR passive.
        Second, although subject pronouns are normally used in
Russian, they can be omitted when the subject is already
given by a major constituent in the discourse; I will refer
to the omission of the subject pronoun under discourse conditions as strong pronominalization. It is difficult to define
the types of major constituents which can control strong pronominalization, but there is apparently a hierarchy of sub-
ject/object/oblique (Peškovskij 1956:399-400), with animacy
and definiteness probably also relevant (see the topicality
hierarchies in Givón, this volume). In any case, the underlying subject of a passive in CSR cannot control strong pronominalization; compare:

50 Esli by ty   vzjal udočku, to nalovil by ryby
           you   took pole   caught
           nom.   m.sg.   m.sg.
           m.sg.
    "if you had taken a fishing pole, (you) would've
    caught a lot of fish"

51 *Esli by udočka byla vzjata toboj, to nalovil by ryby
("if a fishing pole had been taken by you, (you)
would've caught a lot of fish")

In NR, on the other hand, the underlying subject of a passive
can control strong pronominalization:

52 Vot udočka u tebja byla by vzjata, vot by nalovil togda
"had a fishing pole been taken by you, (you) would've
caught a lot" (KN 25)

53 Započivano u nej: nabegalas'
                       her   ran out
                       f.sg. f.sg.
"there's been resting by her: (she) ran herself out"
(KN 100)

54 U ego   vybežano na bereg, da napilsja vody, da v les
   him   run   shore   drank   water
   m.sg.   m.sg.

       i ušel
"by him there was running out onto the bank, (he) had
his fill of water, and (he) went off into the woods"
(Šapiro 1953:143)

The fact that the agent phrase can control strong pronominalization in NR suggests that it has topic and, indirectly, subject properties.
    Third, it is common in Russian discourse and folk liter-
ature to construct parallel clauses with contrasts between
constituents which are more or less parallel in function
(Jakobson 1966). In CSR it would be impossible to put the
agent phrase of the passive in parallelism with a grammatical
subject, but in NR it is possible:

55 Žili dva brata. U onnovo bylo ženjanos', a drugoj byl
   live   brothers one   married   other

       xolostoj
       bachelor
"there lived two brothers. By one there'd been getting
married, but the other was a bachelor" (Sokolov and
Sokolov 1915:113)

56 U menja zabyto, a Stepanida pomnit
   me   forgotten   remembers
"by me it's been forgotten, but Stepanida remembers"
(Maslov 1949:94)

Here the agent phrase is put in parallel construction and explicitly contrasted with a following grammatical subject in

the nominative: 55 u onnovo vs. drugoj, 56 u menja vs. Stepanida. In parallel discourse, then, the NR u + genitive agent
phrase can be equivalent to a grammatical subject.

Fourth, there is a construction of strong topicalization, commonly used in responses to questions, in which the
topicalized constituent is expressed in the nominative at the
left of the sentence, which follows after an intonation
break. If the topicalized constituent is the subject, no
pronoun copy need be left behind:

57 a. Petju ne videli?

    b. Petja? Ne prixodil ešče
       nom.   arrived
       m.sg.   m.sg.

    a. "have you seen Petja?"
    b. "Petja? (he) still hasn't come"
      (Zemskaja 1973b:262)

If the topicalized constituent is not a subject, a pronominal
copy is left behind:

58 Petja? Ego poslali v magazin
   "Petja? They sent him to the store"

In CSR this construction is marginal for the instrumental
agent of a passive; to the extent that it is possible, it requires that a pronominal copy be left behind. In NR, however,
the agent of a passive may regularly be strongly topicalized,
without a pronominal copy. Thus, 60 is related to 59 by
strong topicalization:

59 U nego armiju ne otsluženo
       army   served
       acc.   part.n.sg.
  "by him there hasn't been serving out his army term"

60 A on -- esce armiju ne otsluženo
   nom.
  "as for him -- there hasn't been serving out his army
  term" (KN 38)

The underlying subject of the NR passive behaves like a subject in strong topicalization.

These four tests of subjecthood, in terms of topic and
discourse properties, all show that the displaced underlying
subject of the passive in NR behaves naturally as a topic,
and is equivalent to a grammatical subject in topic properties; it does not behave as a peripheral constituent (14).

8. The NR type of passive, where the agent phrase has strong subject properties, seems to be diachronically stable; the use of u + genitive for the agent has been maintained for over three hundred years (Petrova 1968:119, Filin 1971:284). Nevertheless, the strong subject properties of the agent phrase allow for the possibility of its diachronic reanalysis as a grammatical subject. Two types of reanalysis are attested, each with an intermediate transitional stage (data from Filin 1948, Matveenko 1961).

First, it is possible to interpret the agent phrase of the passive as a grammatical subject and express it like other grammatical subjects. Transitionally, the agent is expressed in the nominative without agreement in the predicate:

```
61  Any     fsi f kolxos uexano
    they                 gone
    nom.pl.              part.n.sg.
    "they've all gone off to the kolkhoz"
```

As a subsequent development, agreement is introduced:

```
62  Sestra   v vojnu vyexana byla  k nam
    sister   war     come    aux.
    nom.f.sg.        part.   f.sg.
                     f.sg.
    "sister had come out to us during the war"
```

When 62 develops, the underlying subject is a true grammatical subject; the verb form becomes simply a perfect tense form, and is no longer a passive (15).

Second, it is possible to interpret the agent phrase of the passive as the subject and express other subjects in the same way; thus, u + genitive comes to be used with ordinary finite verbs. Transitionally, this occurs without agreement:

```
63  U kogo  pogiblo  v èto vremja?
    who     perished      time
    m.sg.   n.sg.
    "who perished during that time?"
```

As a subsequent stage of development, agreement is occasionally introduced:

```
64  Segodnja u menja i xleba ne vzjala
    today      me      bread    took
               f.sg.            f.sg.
    "today I didn't take any bread"
```

It is not clear whether the use of u + genitive ever develops systematically for all types of finite verbs.

Both types of reanalysis are only sporadically attested
(the first type is more common), and it is impossible to specify these developments geographically. Still, the two types
of reanalysis show that the agent phrase is like a subject,
since it is possible to reinterpret it diachronically as a
grammatical subject.

9. In the NR passive we have observed an unusual distribution of subject properties between the underlying object
and the underlying subject. The underlying object can acquire
the subject properties of case and agreement, but these properties are optional. For some other subject properties, the
evidence is not clear, since objects--as grammatical consti-
tuents⊚-can control equi and can behave as the topic (see fn.
12-14). But for the control of svoj-reflexivization, the
evidence is clear: the underlying object does not behave as a
subject, even when it is nominative and produces agreement.
On the other hand, the displaced underlying subject has a
number of subject properties, summarized in Fig. 2.

---

deletion	control of equi
	control of deletion in adverbial passive
	target for deletion in adverbial passive
reflexivization	control of svoj-reflexivization
topic	word order
	control of strong pronominalization
	parallelism with subjects in discourse
	strong topicalization

Fig. 2

The fact that the underlying object can optionally acquire the coding properties of case and agreement without
necessarily acquiring other subject properties (control of
reflexivization) is in accord with the promotional hierarchy
proposed by E.L. Keenan (Definition of Subject, this volume).
What is more striking is the fact that the underlying subject
has many subject properties: it loses the coding properties
of case and agreement, but retains the subject properties
listed in Fig. 2. This fact suggests three conclusions.
First, the promotional hierarchy can also be viewed in
reverse as a demotion hierarchy, so that demoted subjects
will first lose case and agreement, and only if they lose
these properties will they also lose other subject properties.

Second, it is apparently possible to have partial or incomplete demotion of subjects. Third--given that the promotion of the underlying object is at best an optional and low-level phenomenon in the NR passive--it is apparently possible to have a demotion of subjects which is not the direct result of the promotion of objects. In this case, it is true, it is only a partial demotion.

10. Before concluding, there is one further point to be considered. It is tempting to see a connection between the degree of promotion of the underlying object and the degree of demotion of the underlying subject in the Russian passive constructions. In CSR promotion of the object is complete and obligatory, demotion of the subject is complete and obligatory. In NR promotion of the object is optional and incomplete, demotion of the subject is only partial (16). There probably is some correlation between demotion and promotion, but it does not seem to be as clearcut as the contrast between CSR and NR might suggest. For example, there is an impersonal passive construction in Ukrainian in which the underlying object is not promoted--it stays in the accusative, where it is obviously not the grammatical subject--yet the underlying subject is fully demoted to a peripheral status, expressed (if at all) by the instrumental (Shevelov 1963:139-46).

There is, however, another way of looking at the degree of demotion undergone by the underlying subject in CSR as opposed to NR. In CSR the underlying subject is displaced to an instrumental phrase; instrumental phrases by nature are highly peripheral constituents, which do not participate in any major syntactic rules in Russian. In NR, however, the underlying subject is displaced to the u + genitive phrase; in its other functions, u + genitive behaves as a grammatical constituent which participates in many syntactic rules. I suggest that a demoted subject takes on the properties of the constituent type to which it is demoted, just as a promoted object takes on the properties of a subject.

In order for this suggestion to be interesting, it is important to show that the u + genitive phrase which arises through demotion of the underlying subject of the passive does in fact behave like the u + genitive phrase which occurs in other functions. (Here we should limit our attention to the use of u + genitive in predicate possessive sentences and exclude the strictly locative use; cf. Isačenko 1974:45-46, Mrázek and Brym 1962.) I will give some evidence which shows that the agentive u and the possessive u have similar syntactic properties.

First, deletion. It is difficult to give evidence
about control of deletion, since <u>u</u> + genitive possessive
phrases do not ordinarily occur in equi contexts. But consider the following:

65 Mne   nekodga boltat'
    me   no time gossip
    dat.   inf.
    "there's no time for me to gossip"

The structure of 65 is problematic, but it seems that the
dative pronoun <u>mne</u> is a constituent of the matrix sentence,
and that it controls equi in the infinitive. A slightly awkward variant of 65 may be formed with <u>u</u> + genitive:

66 U menja nekogda boltat'
    "I have no time for gossip"

If 65 and hence 66 involve equi, 66 seems to be a case where
possessive <u>u</u> + genitive controls equi.

Second, reflexivization. It is well known that <u>svoj</u>
can modify the subject of possessive sentence and refer back
to the <u>u</u> + genitive constituent:

67 U menja svoja mašina
                 car
    "I have my own car"

Third, topic properties. In predicate possessive sentences the unmarked word order is as in 67, with the <u>u</u> +
genitive phrase first (Isačenko 1974:46). This correlates
with the unmarked word order in NR passives.

Fourth, animacy. In the literature on the NR passive
it is repeatedly mentioned that the <u>u</u> + genitive phrase is
limited to animate nouns, primarily human at that (Filin
1948:44, Maslov 1949:96, Matveenko 1961:123, Petrova 1968:
121). Occasional examples have been recorded for inanimate
nouns, but these always seem to involve transferred animacy,
as for example <u>u traktora</u> "by the tractor." Similarly, the
use of <u>u</u> + genitive in predicate possessive sentences is limited almost exclusively to animates (Mrázek and Brym 1962:111,
Isačenko 1974:46, 54):

68 *U knigi interestnyj sjužet
       book   plot
    ("the book has an interesting plot")

These four similarities suggest that the <u>u</u> + genitive
agent phrase and the <u>u</u> + genitive possessive phrase are by
and large equivalent in their syntactic behavior. It seems,

then, that a demoted subject takes on the properties of the constituent type to which it is demoted.

11.   In summary, this paper has tried to establish two points. First, the underlying subject in the NR passive constructions behaves like a subject with respect to all rules except case and agreement (similarly, and less surprisingly, the underlying object has few subject properties).   Second, the underlying subject of the NR passive behaves like a subject because it is identified with the u + genitive possessive phrase, which generally in Russian behaves like a subject.

Notes

1. In the following the passive and other syntactic relationships are assumed to be transformational rules; further, the concept of subject property is defined in terms of transformations. It is clear, however, that the concept of subject property (and the subject-like behavior of the agent phrase in the NR passive) must be accounted for regardless of whether the passive and other rules are expressed as transformations or as paradigmatic relationships between different sentence types.

2. See also Filin (1948), Maslov (1949), Kuznecov (1949), Matveenko (1961), and Petrova (1968).

3. There are two classes of exceptions to this statement. First, the underlying object can be in the genitive (and not produce agreement) when the sentence is negated:

(i)   Dokumentov ne obnaruženo
        gen.   part.n.sg.
        "there were no documents found"

This is simply the genitive of negation applied to the subject of an intransitive existential sentence. Second, the underlying object does not have to be expressed:

(ii)   Zdes' nakureno
              part.n.sg.
        "it's been smoked up here"

In these cases the verb must be semantically transitive (cf. nakurit' komnatu "smoke up a room"). To account for such sentences one could say that if the underlying object is expressed as a constituent, it must be in the nominative and produce agreement in the predicate.

4. In fact, the use of the instrumental to express the agent is virtually nonexistent in spoken Russian (Krasil' nikova 1973:187).

5. Historically, the participle could be formed from unprefixed imperfective verbs. This type of formation has become unproductive and is disappearing from the literary language (Isačenko 1968:343, 450), although some imperfective participles remain lexicalized as adjectives.

6. Fortunatov (1899), Peškovskij (1956:289). This constraint is evidently in the process of being eliminated, as shown by Butorin (1966).

7. The impersonal passives (sentences 10–11) are superficially similar to the following sentence type, in which there is an accusative object, no grammatical subject, and a neuter singular verb form:

(i)   Vsju rož ubilo gradom
          rye killed hail
          acc. n.sg. instr.
          "all the rye was killed by the hail"

Despite certain similarities, (i) has a number of properties which make it distinct from the impersonal passive: (a) the underlying object can only be in the accusative, never in the nominative (with or without agreement); (b) the verb is finite, not participial; (c) this construction is typically accompanied by an instrumental complement expressing the natural or meteorological force which produced the action, but it can never be used with a human or animate agent (Šapiro 1953:137); (d) this construction is not localized to any particular dialect area of Russian.

     8. It follows that it is not always possible in NR to assign exclusively either the benefactive-possessive or agentive meaning to a given u + genitive phrase.

     9. There is yet another possibility. The underlying object is expressed in the nominative, but the participle invariantly has the masculine singular form:

(i)   U nix byl   postavlen   konjušnja
          aux. built   stable
          m.sg. part.m.sg. nom.f.sg.
          "by them a stable got built" (KN 79)

This construction, which is found in a compact area in the western central dialects, apparently represents a later reanalysis of the subtypes discussed here (KN 88). I will discuss this reanalysis in another place.

     10. This distribution of case is reminiscent of the distribution of case in the nominative object with infinitive construction (Timberlake 1974), and suggests a possible historical connection (KN 46–47), which I will discuss elsewhere.

     11. According to Perlmutter and Postal (forthcoming), only terms (subject, object, indirect object) can control equi.

     12. Underlying objects can control equi in active sentences like (i) and can continue to control equi in their passives (ii):

(i)   Sosedej   poprosili pomoč' stroit' dom
          neighbors asked   help build house
          acc.   3pl.   inf. inf. acc.
          "they asked the neighbors to help build the house"

(ii)   Poprošeno sosedi bylo pomoč' dom stroit'
       part.n.sg. nom.   aux.
       "the neighbors were asked to help build the house"
       (KN 95)

Since both subjects and object can control equi, equi does
not provide a test for determining the extent to which underlying objects are promoted to subject in the NR passive.
    13.   The fact that the underlying object is deleted in
34-35 seems to suggest that it was promoted to subject before
deletion. On the other hand, the participle does not necessarily agree with the underlying object, as in 35, so the
situation is unclear. In any case, the conditions on deletion are in part semantic, since it is only participants
which are affected by the event (underlying objects, underlying subjects of reflexive verbs) which can undergo deletion
in this construction.
    14.   It is more difficult to determine the subject status
of the underlying object by using topic properties, since objects of active sentences can easily be topics anyhow. In
these NR passive constructions there seems to be a partial
correlation between case and agreement and topic properties:
the nominative-with-agreement type seems to behave as the
topic more readily than the nominative-without-agreement or
the accusative types.
    15.   The reanalysis is actualized earlier for intransi-
tives than transitives; if the change is in fact only carried
through for intransitives, it would amount to the creation of
an ergative case paradigm in the new perfect.
    16.   It is striking that the NR passive constructions
are so different from the passive of CSR and the central and
southern dialects. In addition to differences in promotion
and demotion, they differ in constraints on aspect and transitivity (cf. Fig. 1). Since they both developed from a common source (the Old Russian passive), the complementary properties of these two types of passives suggests that this is
a syntactic example of bifurcation: opposite choices in the
historical development from a single source (Andersen 1974).
    Babby and Brecht (1975:347-8) suggest that the CSR and
the NR passives represent different combinations of the same
basic syntactic process (presumably promotion and demotion).
While this may be true, it is not clear that the two types of
passives "are derived in essentially the same way," or that
it is appropriate to use NR data in arguments about the syntactic status of the passive in CSR.

REFERENCES

Aissen, Judith. 1974. The syntax of causative constructions. Unpublished Ph.D. dissertation, Harvard University.

Aissen, Judith. 1975. Presentational-there insertion: a cyclic root transformation. To appear in CLS XI.

Allen, W.S. 1956. Structure and system in the Abaza verbal complex. In transactions of the Philological Society (1956). 127-176.

Alleton, Viviane. 1973. Grammaire du Chinois. Paris: Presses Universitaires de France.

Andersen, H. 1974. Towards a typology of change: bifurcating changes and binary relations. Historical linguistics, 2, ed. by J. Anderson and C. Jones, 17-60.

Anderson, J.M. and Charles Jones. Eds. 1974. Historical linguistics, 1 & 2. Amsterdam: North Holland Publishing Company.

Anderson, Stephen R. 1971. On the Role of Deep Structure in Semantic Interpretation. Foundations of Language 7:387-396.

Anderson, Stephen R. (forthcoming). Ergativity and Linguistic Structure. Cambridge, Mass: MIT Press.

Andrews, A. 1973. Agreement and deletion. CLS IX, ed. by C. Corum, T. Smith-Stark, and A. Weiser, 23-33. Chicago: Chicago Linguistic Society.

Atkinson, Martin. 1974. Prerequisites for reference. B.A.A.L. seminar, University of Newcastle-upon-Tyne, England.

Babby, L. and R. Brecht. 1975. The syntax of voice in Russian. Lg.51.342-67.

Bach, Emmon. 1971. Questions. Linguistic inquiry 2.153-66.

Bach, Emmon. 1974. Syntactic theory. New York: Holt, Rinehart and Winston.

Bach, Emmon and Robert T. Harms. 1968. Universals in linguistic theory. New York: Holt, Rinehart and Winston.

Balǎž, Gerhard. 1959. Časový význam predikačne použitých tvarov príčasti minulých trpných v ruštine. Československá rusistika 4.65-75.

Bates, Elizabeth. 1974. Language and context: studies in the acquisition of pragmatics. Unpublished Ph.D. dissertation, University of Chicago.

Bell, Sarah. 1974. Some notes on Cebuano and relational grammar. Unpublished paper.

Bellugi, U. and S. Fischer. 1972. A comparison sign language and spoken language: rate and grammatical mechanisms. Cognition: international journal of cognitive psychology 1.173-200.

Benton, Richard. 1971. Pangasinan reference grammar. Honolulu: University of Hawaii Press.

Benveniste, Emile. 1971. Problems in general linguistics. Trans. by Mary E. Meek. Coral Gables: University of Miami Press.

Berman, A. 1974. Adjectives and adjective complement constructions in English. Report no. NSF-29, Formal linguistics. Cambridge, Mass.: Harvard University.

Bierman, M. 1972. The left branch condition reconsidered. MS. Harvard University.

Bloom, Lois. 1973. One word at a time. The Hague: Mouton.

Boas, Franz and Ella Deloria. 1939. Dakota grammar. Memoirs of the National Academy of Sciences, vol. 23, no. 2.

Bokamba, E.G. 1971. Specificity and definiteness in Dzamba. Studies in African linguistics 2. 3.217-38.

Bolinger, Dwight L. 1961. Contrastive accent and contrastive stress. Lg.37.83-96.

Bondarko, A.B. and L.L. Bulanin. 1967. Russkij glagol. Leningrad: Prosvescenie.

Boyes, P. 1972. Visual processing and the structure of sign language. MS. University of California, Berkeley.

Brecht, R. 1972. Problems of deixis and hypotaxis: towards a theory of complementation. Unpublished Ph.D. dissertation, Harvard University.

Brown, Roger. 1958. How shall a thing be called? Psychological review 65.14-21.

Brugmann, Karl. 1916. Vergleichende Laut-, Stammbildungs- und Flexionslehre nebst Lehre vom Gebrauch der Wortformen der indogermanischen Sprachen. 2. Bearbeitung. 2. Band, 3. Teil. Strassburg.

Butorin, D.I. 1966. Ob osobyx slučajax vinitel'nogo prjamogo ob"ekta v sovremennom russkom literaturnom jazyke. Normy osvremennogo russkogo literaturnogo slovoupotreblenija, ed. by G.A. Kačevskaja and K.S. Gorbačevič, 125-36. Moscow-Leningrad: Nauka.

Capell, Arthur. 1969. A survey of New Guinea languages. Sydney, Australia: Sydney University Press.

Capell, Arthur. 1971. Arosi grammar. Pacific linguistics, Series B, No. 20. The Australian National University.

Carroll, John B. 1958. Process and content in psycholinguistics. In Current trends in the description and analysis of behavior, ed. by R. Glaser. Pittsburgh: University of Pittsburgh Press.

Carruba, Onofrio. 1964. Hethitish -(a)šta, -pa, und die anderen "Ortsbezugspartikeln". Orientalia N.S. 33.405-436.

Carruba, Onofrio. 1969. Die Chronologie der hethitischen Texte und die hethitischen Geschichte der Grossreichzeit. Deutsche Orientalistentage (Vortrage), Würzburg, 1968. ZDMG Supp.I.226-49.

Catford, Ian C. 1975. Ergativity in Caucasian Languages. Talk given at UCLA, March, 1975.

Chafe, Wallace L. 1970. Meaning and the structure of language. Chicago: University of Chicago Press.

Chafe, Wallace L. 1972. Discourse structure and human knowledge. In Language comprehension and the acquisition of knowledge, ed. by Roy O. Freedle and John B. Carroll. Washington: V.H. Winston.

Chafe, Wallace L. 1974. Language and consciousness. Lg.50. 111-33.

Chafe, Wallace L. (in press). Creativity in verbalization and its implications for the nature of stored knowledge. In Discourse production and comprehension, ed. by Roy O. Freedle. Hillsdale, N.J.: Lawrence Erlbaum Assoc.

Chao, Y.R. 1968. A grammar of modern spoken Chinese. Berkeley and Los Angeles: University of California Press.

Chapin, Paul. 1970. Samoan pronominalization. Language 46.366-78.

Chatelain, Heli. 1964 [1888]. Gramatica elementar do Kimbundu. Ridgewood, N.J.: Gregg Press.

Chomsky, Noam. 1965. Aspects of the theory of syntax. Cambridge, Mass.: MIT Press.

Chomsky, Noam. 1970. Deep structure, surface structure, and semantic interpretation. Studies in general and Oriental linguistics, ed. by R. Jakobson and S. Kawamoto, 52-91. Tokyo: TEC Corporation for Language Research.

Chung, Sandy. 1976. An object-creating rule in Bahasa Indonesia. To appear in Linguistic inquiry 7.

Churchward, C. Maxwell. 1953. Tongan grammar. London: Oxford University Press.

Clark, Herbert H. 1973. Comprehension and the given-new contract. Paper presented at the Conference on the Role of Grammar in Interdisciplinary Linguistic Research, University of Bielefeld, Bielefeld, Germany, Dec. 11, 1973.

Clark, Herbert H. and Susan E. Haviland. (in press). Comprehension and the given-new contract. In Discourse production and comprehension, ed. by Roy O. Freedle. Hillsdale, N.J.: Lawrence Erlbaum Assoc.

Cohen, D. 1972. On inferring participant roles in Biblical Aramaic. MS. Columbia University.

Cole, P. 1974. Indefiniteness and anaphoricity. Lg.50.665-74.

Comrie, Bernard. 1974. Causatives and universal grammar. Transactions of the Philological Society.

Cornelius, Friedrich. 1973. Geschichte der Hethiter. Darmstadt: Wissenschaftliche Buchgesellschaft.

Corsaro, William. 1974. Sociolinguistic patterns in adult-child interaction. MS. Indiana University, Bloomington.

Craig, Colette. 1975. Jacaltec syntax: a study of complex sentences. Unpublished Ph.D. dissertation, Harvard University.

Craig, Colette. (forthcoming). Disambiguation and hierarchies in Jacaltec. Papers in Mayan linguistics, ed. by Marlys McClaran. Los Angeles: UCLA American Indian Culture Center.

Creider, Chet. 1974. Thematization in Luo. MS. University of Western Ontario, London, Ontario.

Cromack, Robert. 1968. Language systems and discourse structure in Cashinawa. Hartford studies in linguistics 23, vol. 1. Hartford seminary dissertation, Hartford, Connecticut.

Culicover, Peter and Kenneth Wexler. 1974. The Invariance Principle and Universals of Grammar. Social Sciences working papers, W.55, School of Social Sciences, University of California, Irvine.

Danoesoegondo, P. 1971. Basa Indonesia for beginners, book 2. Sydney: Sydney University Press.

DeMatteo, A. 1975. Visual imagery and its representation in the American Sign language. MS. University of California, Berkeley.

Delbrück, Berthold. 1900. Bergleichende Syntax der indogermanischen Sprachen. III. Strassburg.

Deny, J. 1952. Langues turques, langues mongoles et langues toungouzes. In Les langues du monde, ed. by A. Meillet and M. Cohen, 319-30. Paris: Champion.

DeRijk, Rudolph. 1966. Redefining the Ergative. Unpublished paper, MIT.

Dillard, L. 1972. Black English: its history and usage in the United States. New York: Vintage Press.

Diller, Timothy. 1970. Case grammar and its application to Waray, a Philippine language. Unpublished Ph.D. dissertation, UCLA.

Diver, W. 1974. Substance and value in linguistic analysis. Semiotext[e] 1.11-30.

Dixon, R.M.W. 1972. The Dyirbal language of North Queensland. Cambridge: Cambridge University Press.

Donellan, K. 1966. Reference and definite descriptions. In Philosophic review LXXV No. 3, 281-304.

Dover, K.J. 1960. Greek word order. Cambridge: Cambridge University Press.

Dumezil, Georges. 1967. Documents anatoliens sur les langues et les traditions du Daucase V: Etudes abkhaz. Paris: Maisonneuve.

Dyen, I. 1964. Beginning Indonesian, lessons 1-24. Washington, D.C.: U.S. Department of Health, Education and

Welfare, Office of Education (Language Development Program, NDEA).

Echols, J. and H. Shadily. 1963. An Indonesian-English dictionary, 2nd ed. Ithaca: Cornell University Press.

Edge, V. and L. Herrmann. 1975. Reversible, non-multidirectional verbs in American Sign language. MS. University of California, Berkeley.

Emonds, J. 1970. Root and structure-preserving transformations. Unpublished Ph.D. dissertation, MIT.

Erteschik, N. 1972. On the nature of island constraints. Paper presented at the 47th Annual Meeting of the LSA, Atlanta, Ga., Dec. 27-9, 1972.

Es, G.A. van. 1970. Plaats en functie van de passieve constructie in het syntactisch systeem van het Nederlands. Tijdschrift voor Nederlandse Taal- en Letterkunde.86. 127-56, 213-33.

Es, G.A. van and P.P.J. van Caspel. 1973. Bijzondere toepassingen van de grondstructuren: de passieve constructie II. Publicaties van het Archief voor de Nederlandse Syntaxis. Reeks I, nr. 24. Rijksuniversiteit te Groningen.

Filin, F.P. 1948. Zametki o zapisjax materialov po sintaksisu. Bjulleten' dialektologiceskogo sektora instituta russkogo jazyka 4(1968). 23-60.

Filin, F.P. 1971. K istorii oborota s stradatel'nymi pricastijami na -n- i -t-. Problemy istorii i dialektologii slavjanskix jazykov. Sbornik statej k 70- letiju clena-korrespondenta AN SSSR V. I. Borkovskogo, 276-84. Moscow: Nauka.

Fillmore, Charles. 1968. The case for case. Universals in linguistic theory, ed. by E. Bach and R. Harms, 1-90. New York: Holt, Rinehart and Winston.

Fillmore, Charles. 1974. Pragmatics and the description of discourse. Berkeley studies in syntax and semantics 1, ed. by C. Fillmore, G. Lakoff, and R. Lakoff. University of California, Berkeley.

Fillmore, C.J. 1975. Against checklist theories of semantics. To appear in Berkeley linguistics society 1.

Firbas, Jan. 1966a. Non-thematic subjects in contemporary English. Travaux linguistique de Prague 2.239-56.

Firbas, Jan. 1966. On defining the theme in functional sentence analysis. Travaux linguistiques de Prague 1.267-80.

Fischer, Susan. 1973. Sign language and linguistic universals. To appear in the proceedings of the Franco-German Conference on French Transformational Grammar. Berlin: Athaenium.

Fischer, Susan. 1975. Influences on word order change in American Sign language. In Word order and word order change, ed. by C.N. Li, 1-25.

Fortunatov, F.F. 1899. O zalogax russkogo glagola. Izv. ORJAS IAN 4.1153-58.

Frantz, D. 1971. Toward a generative grammar of Blackfoot. Publication of the Summer Institute of Linguistics.

Friedman, Lynn A. 1973. Space, time, and person reference in the American Sign Language. To appear in Lg.51.3.

Friedman, Lynn A. 1974a. On the physical manifestation of stress in the American Sign language. MS. University of California, Berkeley.

Friedman, Lynn A. 1974b. A comparative analysis of oral and visual language phonology. MS. University of California, Berkeley.

Friedman, Lynn A. 1975. Phonological processes in the American Sign language. To appear in Berkeley linguistic society 1.

Friedman, Lynn A. (forthcoming). Phonology of a soundless language: phonological structure of the American Sign language.

Friedman, Lynn A. and R. Battison. 1973. Phonological structures in the American Sign language. National Endowment for the Humanities grant report AY-8218-73-136.

Friedrich, Johannes. 1960a. Hethitisches Elementarbuch, 1. Teil. Kurzegefasste Grammatik. Heidelberg: Winter.

Friedrich, Johannes. 1960b. Hethitisches Keilschrift-Lesebuch. Teil II. Schrifttafel und Erläuterungen. Heidelberg: Winter.

Friedrich, Johannes. 1959. Die hethitischen Gesetze. Leiden: Brill.

Friedrich, Johannes. 1952-66. Hethitisches Wörterbuch. Heidelberg: Winter.

Friedrich, Johannes and Annelies Kammenhuber. 1973. Materialen zu einem hethitischen Thesaurus. Heidelberg: Winter.

Frishberg, N. 1974. Arbitrariness and iconicity: historical change in American Sign language. To appear in Lg.

Fulas, H. 1974. A pseudo-object construction in Amharic. Proc. IV Congresso Internazionale di Studi Etiopici. Rome: Academia Nazionale dei Lincei.

Fuller, Michael. 1971. French verbs of perception and causation: a case grammar. Ph.D. dissertation, University of Washington.

Garfinkel, Harold. 1967. Studies in ethno-methodology. Englewood Cliffs, N.J.: Prentice-Hall.

Garvey, Catherine. 1975. Contingent queries. MS. Johns Hopkins University.

Gelb, I.J. 1963. A study of writing, 2nd ed. Chicago: University of Chicago Press.

George, L. 1974. Ergativity and relational grammar. In Papers from the 5th Meeting of the New England Linguistic Society.

Gildersleeve, B.L. and G. Lodge. 1913. Latin grammar. 3rd ed. London: MacMillan and Co.

Givón, Talmy. 1971. Historical syntax and synchronic morphology: an archaeologist's field trip. Papers from the 7th Regional Meeting, Chicago Linguistic Society.

Givón, Talmy. 1974a. Serial verbs and syntactic change: Niger-Congo. In Word order and word order change, ed. by C.N. Li, 47-112.

Givón, Talmy. 1974b. Syntactic change in Lake-Bantu: a rejoinder. Studies in African linguistics 5.1.117-39.

Givón, Talmy. 1975a. Toward a discourse definition of syntax. MS. UCLA.

Givón, Talmy. 1975b (in press). Universal grammar, lexical structure and translatability. In Anthology on the theory of translation, ed. by M. Guenthner-Reutter and F. Guenthner. Cambridge: Cambridge University Press.

Givón, Talmy. 1975c. Negation in language: pragmatics, function, ontology. MS. UCLA Colloquim, Jan. 1975.

Goetze, Albrecht. 1925. Hattušiliš. Der Bericht über seine Thronbesteigung nebst den Paralleltexten. Mitteilungen der Vorderasiatisch- Ägyptischen Gesellschaft, 29. Hethitische Texte, Heft I.

Goetze, Albrecht. 1933. Uber die Partikeln -za, -kan, und -san der hethitischen Satzverbindung. Archiv Orientalni 5.1-38.

Goetze, Albrecht. 1955. Ritual for the erection of a new palace. Ancient near-eastern texts relating to the Old Testament, ed. by J.B. Pritchard, 357-8. Princeton: Princeton University Press.

Goetze, Albrecht. 1957. Kleinasien. Kulturgeschichte des alten Orients. München: Beck.

Goetze, Albrecht and Holger Pedersen. 1934. Mursilis Sprachlähmung. Copenhagen: Munksgaard.

Goffman, Erving. 1963. Behavior in public places. New York: Free Press.

Gougenheim, Georges. 1929. Etude sur les periphrases verbales de la langue Francaise. Paris: Belles Lettres.

Green, Georgia. 1971. A study in pre-lexical syntax: the interface of syntax and semantics. Unpublished Ph.D. dissertation, University of Chicago.

Green, Georgia. 1974. The function of form and the form of function. Papers from the Tenth Meeting of the Chicago

Linguistic Society, ed. by M. Lagaly, R. Fox, and A. Bruck, 186-97. Chicago: Chicago Linguistic Society.

Greenberg, Joseph. 1966 (1963). Some universals of grammar with particular reference to the order of meaningful elements. In Universals of language, ed. by J.H. Greenberg, 73-113. Cambridge, Mass.: MIT Press.

Greenfield, Patricia Marks and Joshua H. Smith. 1976. Communication and the beginnings of language: the development of semantic structure. New York: Academic Press.

Grice, H.P. 1975. Logic and conversation. In Syntax and semantics, vol. 3, ed. by Peter Cobe and Jerry L. Morgan. New York: Academic Press.

Gross, Maurice. "L'Ordre de Quelques Transformations en Malgache". ms.

Grosu, A. 1973. On the non-unitary nature of the coordinate structure constraint. Linguistic inquiry 4.1.88-92.

Gruber, Jeffrey. 1967a. Topicalization in child language. Foundations of language 3.37-65.

Gruber, Jeffrey. 1967b. Functions of the lexicon in formal descriptive grammars. Santa Monica: Systems Development Corporation.

Gundel, J.M. 1974a. The role of topic and comment in linguistic theory. Ph.D. dissertation, University of Texas, Austin.

Gundel, J.M. 1974b. Left dislocation and the role of topic-comment structure in linguistic theory. Presented at the 49th Annual Meeting of the Linguistic Society of America, Dec. 27-30, 1974, New York.

Güterbock, Hans G. 1974. Appendix: Hittite parallels. Journal of Near Eastern Studies 33.323-327.

Haasse, H. 1968. De meermin. Amsterdam: Querido.

Hahn, Adelaide. 1946. The origin of the relative kwi- kwo-. Lg.22.68-85.

Hahn, Adelaide. 1949. The non-restrictive relative in Hittite. Lg.25.346-74.

Haile, G. 1970. The suffix pronoun in Amharic. In Papers in African linguistics, ed. by C.W. Kim and H. Stahlke. Edmonton: Linguistic Research.

Hale, Kenneth. 1967. Preliminary remarks on Walbiri grammar. Manuscript, MIT Linguistics Department.

Hale, Kenneth. 1968. Review of P.W. Hohepa, Profile-generative grammar of Maori. In Journal of the Polynesian Society, 77:83-99.

Halliday, Michael A.D. 1967. Notes on transitivity and theme in English: II. Journal of linguistics 3.199-244.

Halliday, Michael A.K. 1970. Language structure and language function. In New horizons in linguistics, ed. by John

Lyons. New York: Penguin Books.

Hardy, Robert S. 1941. The old Hittite kingdom: a political history. American journal of semitic languages and literature 58.177-216.

Haupt, P. 1878. The oldest Semitic verb. Journal of the Royal Asiatic Society of Great Britain and Ireland 10.244-51.

Haviland, Susan E. and Herbert H. Clark. 1974. What's new? Acquiring new information as a process in comprehension. Journal of verbal learning and verbal behavior 13.512-21.

Hawkinson, A. and L. Hyman. 1975. Hierarchies of natural topic in Shona. Studies in African linguistics 5.147-70.

Held, Warren H., Jr. 1957. The Hittite relative sentence. Lg.Diss.55. Baltimore: Waverly Press.

Hermann, Eduard. 1893-4. Gab es im indogermanischen nebensätze? Kuhns Zeitschrift für vergleichende Sprachforschung 33.481-535.

Hermans, W.F. 1962. The dark room of Damocles. Trans. by R. Edwards. London: Heinemann.

Hermans, W.F. 1966a. Een landingspoging op Newfoundland. Amsterdam: Van Oorschot.

Hermans, W.F. 1966b. Paranoia. Amsterdam: Van Oorschot.

Hermans, W.F. 1967. De donkere kamer van Damocles. Amsterdam: Van Oorschot.

Hertog, C. den. 1972 [1903]. Nederlandse spraakkunst I, ed. by H. Hulshof. Amsterdam: W. Versluys.

Hess, H. 1968. The syntactic structure of Mesquital-Otomi. The Hague: Mouton.

Hetzron, Robert. 1970. Nonverbal sentences and degrees of definiteness in Hungarian. Lg.46.899-927.

Hetzron, Robert. 1971. Presentative function and presentative movement. Studies in African linguistics. Supplement 2.79-105.

Hetzron, Robert. 1973. Review of L'edification de la langue Hongroise, by A. Sauvageot. Journal of linguistics, 345-9.

Hinds, J. 1974. On the status of the VP node in Japanese. Indiana University Linguistics Club. Bloomington, Indiana.

Hoekstra, T. 1962. Is er al geschoren? De nieuwe taalgids 62.46.

Hoffman, J.B. and Anton Szantyr. 1965. Lateinische Syntax und Stilistik. München: Beck.

Hoffner, Harry A., Jr. 1969. On the use of Hittite -za in nominal sentences. Journal of Near Eastern studies 28.225-30.

Hong, Xin-heng. 1956. Hànyǔ yǔfǎ wèntí yánjiù (Studies of the problems of Chinese syntax). Shanghai, China: Xīn Zhi-shi chūbǎnshì.

Hooper, J. and S. Thompson. 1973. On the applicability of root transformations. Linguistic inquiry 4.465-97.

Hope, Edward. 1974. The deep syntax of Lisu sentences. Ph.D. dissertation, Australian National University, Pacific Linguistics, Series B, No. 34.

Hornby, Peter A. 1971. Surface structure and the topic-comment distinction: a developmental study. Child development 42.1975-88.

Hornby, Peter A. 1972. The psychological subject and predicate. Cognitive psychology 3.632-42.

Hornby, Peter A., Wilbur A. Hass, and Carol F. Feldman. 1970. A developmental analysis of the 'psychological' subject and predicate of the sentence. Language and speech 13. 182-93.

Horton, A.E. 1949. A grammar of Luvale. Johannesburg, South Africa: Witwatersrand University Press.

Householder, Fred W. and Robert L. Cheng. 1967. Universe-scope relations in Chinese and Japanese. Unpublished Manuscript, University of York.

Howard, Irwin. 1969. A semantic-syntactic analysis of the Japanese passive. The journal newsletter of the association of teachers of Japanese. 6:40-46.

Huang, Shuan Fan. 1973. Movement in Mandarin syntax. Bulletin of the College of Liberal Arts. National Taiwan University, No. 22.

Hudson, Grover. 1974. Amharic preposition embedding and relative clause history. Paper presented at the Conference on Word Order and Word Order Change, University of California, Santa Barbara, Jan. 1974.

Huisman, R.D. 1973. Angaataha verb morphology. In Linguistics, Vol. 110:43-54.

Huttenlocher, Janellen. 1974. Origins of language comprehension. In Theories in cognitive psychology, ed. by R.L. Solso. Hillsdale, N.J.: Lawrence Erlbaum Assoc.

Hyde, V. 1971. An introduction to the Luiseño language. Malki Museum Press.

Hyman, Larry M. 1974. On the change from SOV to SVO: evidence from Niger-Congo. In Word order and word order change, ed. by C.N. Li, 113-47. Austin: University of Texas Press.

Hyman, Larry M. and Karl E. Zimmer. 1974. Remarks on French causatives. MS.

Imparati, Fiorello and C. Saporeti. 1965. L'autobiografia di Hattusili I. Studi Classici i Orientali 14.40-76.

Isacenko, A.V. 1968. Die russische Sprache der Gegenwart, 1: Formenlehre. Halle: VEB Max Niemeyer.

Isacenko, A.V. 1974. On have and be languages: a typological sketch. Slavic forum. Essays in linguistics and literature, ed. by M. Flier, 43–77. The Hague and Paris: Mouton.

Jacobsen, W.H. 1967. Switch-reference in Hokan-Coahurltecan. In studies in southwestern ethnolinguistics. Dell Hymes (ed.). The Hague: Mouton.

Jakobson, Roman. 1966. Grammatical parallelism and its Russian facet. Lg.42.399–429.

James, Carlton T. 1972. Theme and imagery in the recall of active and passive sentences. Journal of verbal learning and verbal behavior 11.205–11.

Jespersen, Otto. 1924. The philosophy of grammar. London: Allen and Unwin.

Jespersen, Otto. 1961. A modern English grammar on historical principles, part VII, syntax. London: Allen and Unwin.

Jespersen, Otto. 1964. Essentials of English grammar. Birmingham: University of Alabama Press.

Jespersen, Otto. 1969. Analytic syntax. New York: Holt, Rinehart and Winston.

Johnson, David. 1974a. On the role of grammatical relations in linguistic theory. In Papers from the 10th regional meeting of the Chicago Linguistic Society.

Johnson, David. 1974b. Toward a theory of relationally based grammar. Ph.D. dissertation, University of Chicago.

Johnson, David. 1974c. Prepaper on relational constraints on grammar. Unpublished manuscript. Mathematical Sciences Department, T.J. Watson Research Center, IBM, Yorktown Heights, N.Y.

Johnson-Laird, P.N. 1968a. The interpretation of the passive voice. Quarterly journal of experimental psychology 20.69–73.

Johnson-Laird, P.N. 1968b. The choice of the passive voice in a communicative task. British journal of psychology 59.7–15.

Jong, L. de. 1962. De overval. Amsterdam: Querido.

Josephson, Folke. 1972. The function of the sentence particles in Old and Middle Hittite. Acta Universitatis Upsaliensis. Studia Indoeuropaea Upsaliensia, 2. Uppsala.

Kammenhuber, Annelies. 1969. Die Sprachtufen des Hethitischen. Kuhns Zeitschrift für vergleichende Sprachforschung 83. 256–89.

Kammenhuber, Annelies. 1969a. Hethitisch, Palaisch, Luwisch und Hieroglyphenluwisch. Handbuch der Orientalistik. 1. Abteilung, 2. Band, 1. und 2. Abschnitt, 2. Lieferung. Leiden: Brill.

Kammenhuber, Annelies. 1971a. Texte der Hethiter. Heidelberg: Winter.

Kammenhuber, Annelies. 1971b. Das Verhältnis von Schriftduktus zu Sprachstufe im Hethitischen. Münchener Studium zur Aprachwissenschaft 29.75-109.

Karttunen, Lauri. 1968. What makes definite noun phrases definite? Report P-3871. Santa Monica: Rand Corporation.

Kayne, Richard S. 1969. The transformational cycle in French syntax. Ph.D. dissertation, MIT.

Keenan, Edward L. 1970. Two kinds of presupposition in natural language. In Studies in linguistic semantics. C.J. Fillmore and D.T. Langendoen, eds. Holt, Rinehart and Winston.

Keenan, Edward L. 1972. Relative Clause Formation in Malagasy. Chicago Witch Hunt, ed. by Paul M. Peranteau, Judith N. Levi & Gloria C. Phares, 169-189. Chicago Linguistic Society.

Keenan, Edward L. 1972a. On semantically based grammar. Linguistic inquiry, III.4:413-461.

Keenan, Edward L. 1974. The functional principles. In Papers from the 10th regional meeting of the Chicago Linguistic Society.

Keenan, Edward L. 1975a. The logical diversity of natural languages. Paper presented to the Conference on the origins and evolution of language and speech. To appear in the Annals of the New York Academy of Sciences.

Keenan, Edward L. 1975b. Some Universals of Passive in Relational Grammar. In Papers from the XIth Regional Meeting of the Chicago Linguistic Society.

Keenan, Edward L. and Bernard Comrie. 1972. Noun phrase accessibility and universal grammar. Paper presented at the 47th Annual Meeting of the LSA, Atlanta, Ga., Dec. 27-9, 1972.

Keenan, Edward L. and Robert D. Hull. 1973. The logical presuppositions of questions and answers. In Prasupositionen in der Linguistik und der Philosophie, ed. by Franck and Petöfi. Athënaum.

Keenan, Elinor O. 1974. Conversation and Oratory in Vakinankaratra Madagascar. Ph.D. dissertation, University of Pennsylvania.

Keenan, Elinor Ochs. 1974a. Conversational competence in children. Journal of child language 1:2.

Keenan, Elinor Ochs. 1974b. Again and again: the pragmatics
of imitation in child language. Paper presented to the
Annual Meeting of the American Anthropological Association, Mexico City, Nov. 1974.

Keenan, Elinor Ochs and Bambi B. Schieffelin. 1975. Discontinuous discourse. Paper presented at the American Anthropological Meeting, San Francisco.

Keenan, Elinor Ochs, Bambi B. Schieffelin, and Martha Platt.
(forthcoming). Questions in a discourse context.

Keenan, Elinor Ochs. 1975a. Making it last: repetition in
children's discourse. In Papers of the Berkeley Linguistic Society, University of California, Berkeley.

Keenan, Elinor Ochs. 1975b. Evolving discourse: the next
step. Paper presented at the Stanford Child Language
Conference, 1975.

Keenan, Elinor Ochs and Ewan Klein. 1975. Coherency in
children's discourse. Journal of psycholinguistic research.

Kimenyi, A. 1975. Topicalization and discourse structure in
KinyaRwanda. MS. UCLA.

Kimenyi, A. and W. Wilkins. 1974. Strategies of constructing
definite description: some evidence from Rwanda. MS.
UCLA.

King, R. 1967. Functional load and sound change. Lg.43.831-
52.

Kintsch, Walter. 1974. Representation of meaning in memory.
Hillsdale, N.J.: Lawrence Erlbaum Assoc.

Kiparsky, Paul. 1969. Explanations in phonology. In Goals
of linguistic theory, ed. by S. Peters. Englewood
Cliffs, N.J.: Prentice-Hall.

Kirsner, Robert S. 1972. On deixis and degree of differen-
tation in Modern Standard Dutch. Ph.D. dissertation,
Columbia University.

Kirsner, Robert S. 1973. Natural focus and agentive interpretation: on the semantics of Dutch expletive er. Papers
from the 3rd California Linguistics Conference. Stanford
occasional papers in linguistics 3.101-13.

Kirsner, Robert S. 1974. On pragmatic inference and communicative strategies: the problem of the Dutch 'pseudo-
passive'. Paper presented at the LSA Winter Meeting,
New York.

Kirsner, Robert S. 1975. Dutch secret agents and their problems: on the mechanism of the restriction of the Dutch
'pseudo-passive' to human actions. Lecture to Berkeley
Linguistics Group.

Klenin, E. 1974. Russian reflexive pronouns and the semantic
roles of noun phrases in sentences. Unpublished Ph.D.
dissertation, Princeton University.

Klima, Edward. 1969 [1964]. Relatedness between grammatical systems. Modern studies in English, ed. by David Reibel and Sanford Schane, 227-46. Englewood Cliffs, N.J.: Prentice-Hall.

Kraak, A. 1970. Zinsaccent en syntaxis. Studia Neerlandica 4.41-62.

Kraak, A. and W. Klooster. 1968. Syntaxis. Culemborg: Stam-Kemperman.

Krasil'nikova, E.V. 1973. Morfologija. In Russkaja razgovornaja reč', ed. by E.A. Zemskaja, 151-216. Moscow: Nauka.

Kunene, Sr. Euphrasia. 1975. Zulu pronouns and discourse structure. MS. UCLA.

Kuno, Susumu. 1972a. Pronominalization, reflexivization, and direct discourse. Linguistic inquiry 3.2.161-95.

Kuno, Susumu. 1972b. Functional sentence perspective: a case study from Japanese and English. Linguistic inquiry 3. 269-320.

Kuno, Susumu. 1973. The structure of the Japanese language. Cambridge, Mass.: MIT Press.

Kuno, Susumu. 1974. Super Equi-NP deletion is a pseudo-transformation. NELS V, 29-44. Cambridge, Mass.: North Eastern Linguistic Society.

Kuno, S. and J. Robinson. 1972. Multiple Wh questions. Linguistic inquiry 3.463-87.

Kuno, S. and E. Kaburaki. 1975. Empathy and syntax. In Formal linguistics, Report no. NSF-30. Department of Linguistics, Harvard University.

Kuroda, S.-Y. 1968. English relativization and certain related problems. Lg.44.244-66.

Kuroda, S.-Y. 1972. The categorical and the thetic judgment: evidence from Japanese syntax. Foundations of language 9.153-85.

Kurylowicz, Jerzy. 1964. The inflectional categories of Indo-European. Heidelberg: Winter.

Kuznecov, P.S. 1949. K voprosu o skazuemostnom upotreblenii pričastij i deepričastij v russkix govorax. Materialy i issledovanija po russkoj dialektologii, 3, 59-83. Moscow-Leningrad: AN SSSR.

Kwee, J. 1965. Teach yourself Indonesian. London: The English Universities Press.

Lakoff, George. 1965. On the nature of syntactic irregularity. Report no. NSF-16, Mathematical linguistics and automatic translation. Cambridge, Mass.: Harvard University.

Lakoff, George. 1970. Irregularity in syntax. New York: Holt, Rinehart and Winston.

Langacker, Ronald W. 1969. On pronominalization and the
chain of command. In Modern studies in English, ed. by
D. Reibel and S. Schane, 160-86. Englewood Cliffs, N.J.:
Prentice-Hall.

Langacker, Ronald W. and Pamela Munro. 1975 (in press). Passives and their meaning. To appear in Lg.

Laroche, Emmanuel. 1971. Catalogue des textes hittites.
Etudes et commentaires 75. Paris: Klincksieck.

Lasnik, H. and R. Fiengo. 1974. Complement object deletion.
Linguistic inquiry. V.4:535-573.

Lawler, J. 1975. On coming to terms in Achenese: the function of verbal disagreement. In Functionalism. Chicago
Linguistic Society Publication.

Lehmann, Winfred P. 1972a. Contemporary linguistics and
Indo-European studies. Publications of the Modern Language Association 87.976-93.

Lehmann, Winfred P. 1972b. The comparative method as applied
to the syntactic component of language. Canadian journal
of linguistics 17.167-74.

Lehmann, Winfred P. 1973. A structural principle of language
and its implications. Lg.49.47-66.

Lehmann, Winfred P. 1974a. Proto-Indo-European syntax.
Austin: University of Texas Press.

Li, Charles N. Ed. 1975. Word order and word order change.
Austin: University of Texas Press.

Li, Charles N. and Sandra A. Thompson. 1973. Serial verb
constructions in Mandarin Chinese: subordination or co-
ordination? In You take the high node and I'll take the
low node. Chicago Linguistic Society.

Li, Charles N. and Sandra A. Thompson. 1974a. Historical
change of word order: a case study in Chinese and its
implications. In Anderson and Jones (1974), 199-217.

Li, Charles N. and Sandra A. Thompson. 1974b. An explanation
of word order change SVO→SOV. Foundations of language
12.201-14.

Li, Charles N. and Sandra A. Thompson. 1974c. Chinese as a
topic-prominent language. Paper presented at the 7th
International Conference on Sino-Tibetan Language and
Linguistics, Atlanta, Ga.

Li, Charles N. and Sandra A. Thompson. 1974d. Subject and
topic: a new typology of language. Paper presented at
the Winter Meeting of the LSA.

Li, Charles N. and Sandra A. Thompson. 1975. The semantic
function of word order: a case study in Mandarin. In
Word order and word order change, ed. by C.N. Li, 163-95.

Li, Charles N. and Sandra A. Thompson. (in preparation). On
"double subject" constructions.

Limber, J. 1973. The genesis of complex sentences. In Cognitive development and the acquisition of language, ed. by T. Moore. New York: Academic Press.

Lofstedt, Einar. 1933. Syntactica. II: Syntaktisch-stilistische Gesichtspunkte und Probleme. Lund: Gleerup.

Lofstedt, Einar. 1970 [1911]. Philologisches Kommentar zur Pereginatio Aetheriae. Darmstadt: Wissenschaftliche Buchgesellschaft.

Lomtatidze, K. 1975. Class lectures on Abkahaz, Tbilisi; reported in personal communication by Alice Harris.

Lönngren, Lennart. 1970. Upotreblenie kratkoj formy stradatel'nogo pričastija prosedsego vremeni v sovremennom russkom jazyke. (Acta Universitatis Upsalensis. Studia Slavica upsaliensia, 81).

Lyons, J. 1971. Introduction to theoretical linguistics. Cambridge: Cambridge University Press.

MacDonald R. and S. Dardjowidjojo. 1967. A student's reference grammar of modern formal Indonesian. Washington, D.C.: Georgetown University Press.

Macdonell, Arthur A. 1916. A Vedic grammar for students. Oxford: Clarendon.

Macdonell, Arthur A. 1951 [1917]. A Vedic reader for students. London: Oxford University Press.

MacWhinney, Brian. 1975. Psycholinguistic approach to pragmatic focusing. MS. University of Denver.

Mandel, M. 1975. Something similar: iconicity and conventionality in American Sign language. MS. University of California, Berkeley.

Mardirussian, Galust. 1975. Noun Incorporation in Universal Grammar. In Papers from the 11th Chicago Linguistic Society Meeting.

Maratsos, M. 1974. Preschool children's use of definite and indefinite articles. Child development 45.446-55.

Martinet, Andre. 1958. La construction ergative et les structures élémentaires de l'énoncé. Journal de psychologie normale et pathologique. 55(3):377-392.

Maslov, Ju.S. 1949. K voprosu o proisxozdenii possessivnogo perfekta. Uč. zap. LGU 97.76-104.

Matisoff, James A. 1973. The grammar of Lahu. Los Angeles, Berkeley: University of California Press.

Matveenko, V.A. 1961. Nekotorye osobennosti struktury stradatel'no-bezličnogo oborota v russkix govorax. Materialy i issledovanija po russkoj dialektologii (novaja serija), 2, 103-39.

McCawley, James D. 1974. Toward a coherent account of relative (and relative-like) clauses. Presented at the Harvard Linguistic Circle Colloquium, Cambridge, Mass., Nov. 1974.

McCawley, Noriko A. 1972. On the Treatment of Japanese Passives. In CLS-VIII. pp. 259-269.

McKaughan, Howard. 1973. Subject versus topic. Parangal Kay Cecilio Lopez, ed. by A. Gonzales. Linguistic Society of the Philippines.

Meillet, Antoine. 1937. Introduction à l'étude comparative des langues indo-europeennes, 8th ed. Paris: Hachette.

Mirikitani, L. 1972. Kapampangan syntax. Oceanic linguistics publication, No. 10.

Moravcsik, Edith. 1974. Object-verb agreement. Working papers in language universals 15.25-140. Stanford University.

Mowrer, O. Hobart. 1954. The psychologist looks at language. In Readings in the psychology of language, ed. by L.A. Jakobovits and M.S. Miron. Englewood Cliffs, N.J.: Prentice-Hall.

Mrázek, R. and J. Brym. 1962. Sémantika a funkce ruského genitivu s předložkou 'u'. Sborník prací filosofické fakulty brnénské university A-10.99-118.

Mulhausler, P. 1973. Reduplication and repetition in New Guinea Pidgin. MS.

Munro, Pamela. 1974. Topics in Mojave syntax. Ph.D. dissertation, University of California, San Diego.

Munro, Pamela. 1974a. Imperatives, passives and perfectives in Chemhueri. Paper presented at the American Anthropological Association Meeting, Mexico City, Mexico.

Nakau, Minoru. 1973. Sentential complementation in Japanese. Tokyo: Kaitakusha.

Neu, Erich. 1968. Das hethitische Mediopassiv und seine indogermanischen Grundlagen. Studien zu den Boghazköi-texten 6. Wiesbaden: Harrassowitz.

Neu, Erich. 1970. Ein althethitisches Gewitter-ritual. Studien zu den Boghazköi-texten 12. Wiesbaden: Harrassowitz.

Neu, Erich. 1974. Der Anitta-text. Studien zu den Boghazköi-texten 18. Wiesbaden: Harrassowitz.

Nieuwborg, E. 1973. De plaatsing van het substantivisch onderwerp in reflexieve constructies. Leuvense Bijdragen 62.273-83.

Nijhoff, M. 1966. Lees maar, er staat niet wat er staat. Den Haag: Bert Bakker/Daamen.

Olson, David R. and Nikola Filby. 1972. On the comprehension of active and passive sentences. Cognitive psychology 3.361-81.

Otero, C. 1967. The syntax of mismo. Actes du Xe Congres International des Linguistes. Bucarest: Editions de l'Academie de la RSR (1970).

Otero, C. 1969. El otro 'se'. Actas del XI Congreso Internacional de Linguistica y Filologia Romancia 1965. Madrid: CSIC.

Otero, C. 1974. Grammar's definition vs. speaker's judgment: from the psychology to the sociology of language. MS. UCLA.

Otten, Heinrich. 1964. Schrift, Sprache und Literatur der Hethititer. Neuere Hethiterforschung, ed. by George Walser. Wiesbaden: Steiner.

Otten, Heinrich, ed. 1965. Studien zu den Boghazköi-texten. Wiesbaden: Harrassowitz.

Otten, Heinrich. 1973. Ein althethitische Erzahlung um die Stadt Zalpa. Studien zu den Boghazköi-texten 17. Wiesbaden: Harrassowitz.

Otten, Heinrich and Vladmir Souček. 1969. Ein althethitisches Ritual für das Königspaar. Studien zu den Boghazköi-texten 8. Wiesbaden: Harrassowitz.

Park, Byzing-Soo. 1973. Multiple subject constructions in Korean. Linguistics 100:63-76.

Peet, W. 1975. The nominative shift in Hawaii Creole pronominalization. Paper presented to the International Conference on Pidgins and Creoles, Honolulu, Jan. 1975.

Perfetti, Charles A. and Susan R. Goldman. 1974. Thematization and sentence retrieval. Journal of verbal learning and verbal behavior 13.70-9.

Perlmutter, D. and P. Postal. 1974. Linguistic Institute Lectures. University of Massachusetts, Amherst, Mass.

Perlmutter, D. and P. Postal. (forthcoming). Relational grammar.

Peškovskij, A.M. 1956. Russkij sintaksis v naučnom osveščenii. 7th ed. Moscow: Min. prosveščenija.

Petrova, Z.M. 1968. Posessivnyj perfekt v pskovskix govorax. Pskovskie govory, 2, 118-26. Pskov: Min. Prosveščenija RSFSR.

Philips, Sue. 1974. The invisible culture. Unpublished Ph.D. dissertation, University of Pennsylvania, Philadelphia.

Piaget, J. 1926. Language and thought of the child. London: Routledge and Kegan Paul.

Pinkham, Jessie. 1974. Passive and faire-par causative construction in French. Senior essay, Harvard University.

Pokorny, Julius. 1959. Indogermanisches etymologisches Wörterbuch. 1. Band. München: Francke.

Pollmann, T. 1970. Passieve zinnen en het geimpliceerd logisch subject. Studia Neerlandica 2.34-50.

Postal, Paul. 1970. On coreferential complement subject deletion. Linguistic inquiry 1.439-500.

Postal, Paul. 1971. Cross-over phenomena. New York: Holt, Rinehart and Winston.

Postal, Paul and J.R. Ross. 1971. Tough movement si, tough deletion no! Linguistic inquiry 2.544-6.

Rajemisa-Raolison, Régis. 1966. Grammaire malgache, 5ème édition. Fianarantsoa, Madagascar.

Raman, Carol Justus. 1973. The Old Hittite relative construction. Ph.D. dissertation, University of Texas, Austin.

Raman, Carol Justus. 1972. The Hittite relative construction. Paper presented at the Winter Meeting of the LSA.

Ramstedt, G.J. 1968. A Korean grammar. Anthropological publications. Oosterhout N.B., the Netherlands.

Reid, W. 1974. The Saussurian sign as a control in linguistic analysis. Semiotext[e] 1.31-53.

Reiner, Erica. 1951. Un aspect de la proposition relative accadienne. Revue d'Assyriologie 45.25-9.

Reve, G.K. van het. 1970. De ondergang van de familie Boslowitz. Amsterdam: Van Oorschot.

Richards, Charles. 1971. A case grammar of Pampangan. Unpublished Ph.D. dissertation, UCLA.

Rosenbaum, Peter. 1967. The grammar of English predicate complement construction. MS.

Ross, J.R. 1967. Constraints on variables in syntax. Ph.D. dissertation, MIT.

Ross, John R. 1971. Primacy. Paper read at Winter LSA Meeting, St. Louis, Mo.

Sacks, Harvey. 1968. Lecture notes. Sociology department, University of California, Irvine.

Ross, J.R. 1970. On declarative sentences. In Readings in English transformational grammar, ed. by A.J. Jacobs and P.S. Rosenbaum, 222-77. Lexington, Maxx.: Ginn and Co.

Sankoff, Gillian and Penelope Brown. 1975. On the origins of syntax in discourse: a case study of Tok Pisin relatives. MS. Université de Montreal, University of California, Berkeley.

Sapiro, A.B. 1953. Očerki po sintaksisu russkix narodnyx govorov. Stroenie predloženie. Moscow: AN SSSR.

Sacks, Harvey and Emmanuel Schegloff. 1974. Two preferences in the organization of reference to persons in conversation and their interaction. In Ethnomethodology: labelling theory and deviant behavior, ed. by N.H. Avison and R.J. Wilson. London: Routledge and Kegan Paul.

Sandmann, Manfred. 1954. Subject and predicate: a contribution to the theory of syntax. Edinburgh: Edinburgh University Press.

Schachter, Paul. 1973. Focus and relativization. Language 49.19-46.

Schachter, Paul. 1974. Constraints on co-ordination. Indiana University Linguistics Club.

Schachter, Paul. 1974a. A non-transformational account of serial verbs. In Studies in African Linguistics, Supplement 5.

Schachter, Paul and Fe Otanes. 1972. A Tagalog reference grammar. Los Angeles, Berkeley: University of California Press.

Schegloff, Emmanuel and Harvey Sacks. 1973. Opening up closings. Semiotica 8.4.289-327.

Schieffelin, Bambi B. 1975a. Looking and talking: developmental study of gaze direction and language acquisition. MS. Columbia University.

Schieffelin, Bambi B. 1975b. Communicative functions of pointing: a developmental study. MS. Columbia University.

Schuchardt, Hugo. 1896. Über den passiven Charakter des Transitivs in den Kaukasischen Sprachen. Sitzungsberichte der Akademie der Wissenschaften, Wien, Philologisch-historischen Klasse. 133:1-90.

Schwartz, Arthur. 1972. The VP-constituent of SVO languages. In Syntax and semantics, vol. 1, ed. by J. Kimball, 213-35. New York: Academic Press.

Schwartz, Benjamin. 1947. A Hittite ritual text (KUB 29.1 = 170/c). Orientalia 16.23-55.

Schwyzer, Eduard and A. Debrunner. 1966 [1949]. Griechische Grammatik. Syntax und syntaktische Stilistik. München: Beck.

Schwyzer, Eduard and A. Debrunner. 1968 [1938]. Griechische Grammatik. Allgemeiner Teil. Lautlehre. Wortbildung. Flexion. München: Beck.

Scollon, Ronald. 1973. A real early stage: an unzippered condensation of a dissertation on child language. Working papers in linguistics 5.6. Honolulu: University of Hawaii.

Sgall, P., E. Hajičová and E. Benešová. 1973. Topic, focus, and generative semantics. Kronberg-Tanus: Scriptor Verlag.

Shevelov, G. 1963. The syntax of modern literary Ukranian. The simple sentence. The Hague: Mouton.

Soemarmo. 1970. Subject-predicate, focus-presupposition, and topic-comment in Bahasa Indonesia and Javanese. Unpublished Ph.D. dissertation, UCLA.

Sohn, K.-M. 1973. Relative clause formation in Micronesian languages. Working papers in linguistics 5.8.93-124. Honolulu: University of Hawaii.

Sokolov, B. and Ju. Sokolov. 1915. Skazki i pesni belozerskogo kraja. St. Petersburg: ORJaS IAN.

Stern, Daniel N. 1974. Mother and infant at play: the dyadic interaction involving facial, vocal, and gaze behaviors. In The effect of the infant on the caregiver, vol. 1, 187-213. The origin of behavior series, ed. by M. Lewis and L. Rosenblum. New York: Wiley.

Sturtevant, E.H. 1930. Relatives in Indo-European and Hittite. Lg. monograph 7.141-9.

Szemerenyi, Oswald. 1970. Einführung in die vergleichende Sprachwissenschaft. Darmstadt: Wissenschaftliche Buchgesellschaft.

Tai, James H-Y. 1973. A note on the ba-construction. Paper presented at the 6th International Conference on Sino-Tibetan Language and Linguistics, San Diego, California.

Tannenbaum, Percy H. and Frederick Williams. 1968. Generation of active and passive sentences as a function of subject or object focus. Journal of verbal learning and verbal behavior 7.246-52.

Tchekoff, Claudie. 1972. Une langue a construction ergative: l'avar. La Linguistique 8(2):103-115.

Teng, Shou-hsin. 1974. Double nominatives in Chinese. Language 50.3.455-73.

Thompson, H. 1975. The nature of subordination in the American Sign language. MS. University of California, Berkeley.

Thurstone, Thelma G. 1956. The test of memory mental abilities. Personnel and Guidance Journal, 35.

Timberlake, Alan. 1974. The nominative object in North Russian. Slavic transformational syntax, ed. by R. Brecht and C. Chvany, 219-43. Michigan Slavic materials 10. Ann Arbor: University of Michigan.

Traugott, Elizabeth. 1974. Spatial expressions of tense and temporal sequencing: a contribution to the study of semantic fields. MS. Stanford University.

Trithart, Lee. 1975. Relational Grammar and Chichewa Subjectivization Rules. In Papers from the 11th Chicago Linguistic Society Meeting.

Tucker, A.N. and J. Tompo Ole Mpaayei. 1955. A Maasai grammar. Publications of the African Institute of Leydon, No. 11. London: Longmans, Green and Co.

Tyson, A. 1974. Pleonastic pronouns in Black English. MS. University of Southern California.

Unal, Ahmet and A. Kammenhuber. 1974. Das althethitische Loserakel KBo XVIII 151. Kuhns Zeitschrift fur vergleichende Sprachforschung.

Valdman, A. 1975. A Pidgin origin for Creole French? Paper presented at the International Conference on Pidgins and Creoles, Honolulu, Jan. 1975.

Van Dijk, Teun, A. 1972. Some aspects of text grammars. The Hague: Mouton.

Vennemann, Theo. 1968. On the use of paradigmatic information in a competence rule of modern German phonology. Paper presented at the Summer Meeting of the LSA.

Vennemann, Theo. (in press). Topics, sentence accent, ellipsis: a proposal for their formal treatment. In Formal semantics in natural language, ed. by Edward L. Keenan. Cambridge, Mass.: Cambridge University Press.

Vestdijk, S. 1950. De koperen tuin. Den Haag: Nijgh and Van Ditmar.

Vestdijk, S. 1965. The garden where the grass band played. Trans. by A. Brotherton. London: Heinemann.

Wallin, I. 1936. Om det grammatiska subjektet: en semologisk och morfologisk studie. Uppsala: Appelbergs Boktryckeri-aktiebolaget.

Watkins, Calvert. 1964. Preliminaries to the reconstruction of Indo-European sentence structure. In Proceedings of the Ninth International, ed. by Horace G. Lunt, 1035-45. Janua Linguarum, Series Maior. The Hague: Mouton.

Watkins, Calvert. 1963. Preliminaries to a historical and comparative analysis of the syntax of the Old Irish verb. Celtica 6.1-49.

Wolfenden, Elmer. 1971. Hiligaynon reference grammar. Honolulu: University of Hawaii Press.

Yang, In-seok. 1972. Korean syntax. Soeul: Paek Hap Sa.

Zemskaja, E.A., ed. 1973a. Russkaja razgovornaja rec'. Moscow: Nauka.

Zemskaja, E.A. 1973b. Nabljudenija nad sintagmatikoj razgovornoj reci. In Russkaja razgovornaja rec', ed. by E.A. Zemskaja, 225-66. Moscow: Nauka.

Zubin, D. 1972. The German case system: exploitation of the dative-accusative opposition for comment. MS. Columbia University.

Zubin, D. 1974. Experimental validation of a linguistic analysis. Paper presented at the Summer Meeting of the LSA.

A 6
B 7
C 8
D 9
E 0
F 1
G 2
H 3
I 4
J 5